W9-AQI-937

Stephen L. Pevar is a senior staff counsel of the American Civil Liberties Union and has served on the ACLU's national legal staff since 1976. From 1971 through 1974, he was a legal services attorney on the Rosebud Sioux Indian Reservation in South Dakota. From 1983 through 1999, in addition to his ACLU position, he was an adjunct professor at the University of Denver School of Law, where he taught federal Indian law. He has litigated a number of Indian rights cases and has lectured extensively on the subject. Pevar graduated from Princeton University in 1968 and from the University of Virginia School of Law in 1971. He lives in Connecticut with his wife, Laurel, and their two children, Lianna and Elena.

Saginaw Chippewa Tribal College
2274 Enterprise Drive
Mt. Pleasant, MI 48858

WITHDRAWN

AN AMERICAN CIVIL LIBERTIES UNION HANDBOOK

THE RIGHTS OF
INDIANS
AND TRIBES

The Authoritative ACLU Guide to
Indian and Tribal Rights

Third Edition

§

Stephen L. Pevar

General Editor of the Handbook Series
Eve Cary

NEW YORK UNIVERSITY PRESS
New York and London

NEW YORK UNIVERSITY PRESS
New York and London
www.nyupress.org

© 2004 by the American Civil Liberties Union
All right reserved. Third edition 2004

Library of Congress Cataloging-in-Publication Data
Pevar, Stephen L.
The rights of Indians and tribes:
the authoritative ACLU guide to Indian and tribal rights /
Stephen L. Pevar.—3rd ed.   p. cm.—
(An American Civil Liberties Union handbook)
Includes index.
1. Indians of North America—Civil rights.
2. Indians of North America—Legal status, laws, etc.
I. Title.   II. Series
KF8210.C5 P48   2002
342.73'0872—dc21
ISBN 0–8147–6718–4 (pbk. : alk. paper)   2002018890

New York University Press books are printed on acid-free paper,
and their binding materials are chosen for strength and durability.

Manufactured in the United States of America

p 10 9 8 7

To Laurel, Lianna, and Elena

CONTENTS

Appendixes

Introduction to the ACLU Handbook Series

Eve Cary, General Editor

This book is one of a series published in cooperation with the American Civil Liberties Union (ACLU), which are designed to inform individuals about their rights in particular areas of law. A guiding principle of the ACLU is that an informed citizenry is the best guarantee that the government will respect individual civil liberties. These publications carry the hope that individuals informed of their rights will be encouraged to exercise them. In this way, rights are given life. If rights are rarely used, however, they may be forgotten and violations may become routine.

In order to understand and exercise individual rights, it is important to know something about how our legal system works. The basic document that sets up our legal system is the United States Constitution. The Constitution explains how we elect the government of the United States and provides the government with the specific powers it needs to run the country. These include the power to pass laws that are "necessary and proper" for carrying out the other powers. The government does not have the authority to do anything that the Constitution does not permit it to do. Therefore, a better question to ask than "Do I have the right to do this?" is "Does the government have the right to stop me from doing this?"

Although the government may not deny a citizen the right to do something unless the Constitution gives it the power to do so, the framers of the Constitution thought certain rights are so critical they should be specifically guaranteed. Therefore, the framers added ten amendments, known as the Bill of Rights, that are among the most important rights the government may never deny to its citizens. Four of the amendments that make up the Bill of Rights are particularly important for individuals seeking to understand their rights in relation to the government.

The First Amendment contains two important statements. The first is that "Congress shall make no law . . . abridging freedom of speech, or of the press; or the right of the people peaceably to assemble, and to petition the government for a redress of grievances." This means that a person cannot be forbidden from or punished for expressing opinions out loud or in print, either individually or with a group of people, as long as he or she does it at a reasonable time and in a reasonable place and manner.

The second statement of the First Amendment is that "Congress shall make no law respecting an establishment of religion, or prohibiting the free exercise thereof." This means that the government may neither prohibit nor encourage the practice of a particular religion; indeed, government may not encourage the practice of religion at all. In short, religion is none of the government's business.

The Fourth Amendment says, "The right of the people to be secure in their persons, houses, papers, and effects, against unreasonable searches and seizures, shall not be violated, and no Warrants shall issue, but upon probable cause, supported by Oath or affirmation, and particularly describing the place to be searched, and the persons or things to be seized." This means that the police may neither search a person nor anything he or she is carrying, nor may they make an arrest, unless they have a very good reason for believing that the person has committed a crime. Moreover, they may not search a house or other private place without a warrant signed by a judge who has decided it is reasonable to believe that the person involved has committed a crime. (Note that the police have more leeway in searching automobiles.)

The Fifth Amendment says, "No person shall . . . be deprived of life, liberty, or property without due process of law." This means that the government may not punish individuals without giving them a fair chance to defend themselves.

In addition to the rights guaranteed by the Bill of Rights, the Fourteenth Amendment says, "No State shall deprive any person of life, liberty or property without due process of law; nor deny to any person within its jurisdiction the equal protection of the laws." This amendment means that, just as the federal government may not punish individuals without giving them a fair chance to defend themselves, the government of a state may not do so either. Moreover, all laws must apply equally to all citizens who are in the same situation as one another. For example, the government may not pass a law saying that people of one race or sex or religion are allowed to do something that people of another race or sex or religion are not allowed to do. (It may, however, pass laws that apply to children but not to adults, since children are not always in the same situation as adults. For example, laws requiring children but not adults to go to school are constitutional, as are laws prohibiting children from buying alcohol and cigarettes.)

Before going any further, it is important to understand two things. First, when we talk about "the government" in this book, we mean not only elected officials but also the people who are hired to work for the government, such as police officers and public school principals. All of these people must obey the Constitution when they are performing their jobs.

Second, the Constitution applies *only* to the people who work for the government. It does not apply to private people. This means, for example, that while the principal of a public school may not make students say prayers in class because that would violate the First Amendment guarantee of freedom of religion, students in parochial or other private schools may be required to pray.

In addition to the United States Constitution, each state also has its own constitution. Many of the provisions of these state constitutions are the same as those in the United States Constitution, but they apply only to the actions of state officials. Thus, a public school principal in New York is prohibited from holding religious services in school, not just by the federal Constitution but also by the New York State Constitution. While a state may not deny its citizens rights guaranteed by the United States Constitution, it may, and often does, provide more rights. For example, while the Supreme Court has held that the death penalty does not violate the federal constitution, the Massachusetts Supreme Court has held that it does violate the Massachusetts Constitution.

Although federal and state constitutions do not oversee the actions of private individuals, limitations on personal behavior do exist. Both Congress and all of the state legislatures pass laws that apply to private people. The laws enacted by Congress are for the entire country. Those passed by the state legislatures are just for the people of that state. Thus, for example, people in New York may have more or fewer or different rights and obligations than do the people in Louisiana. In fact, in Louisiana anyone over the age of eighteen can buy alcohol, while in other states the legal drinking age is twenty-one.

Just as we have separate federal and state governments, we also have separate systems of federal courts and state courts. The job of the federal courts is to interpret laws passed by Congress; the job of the state courts is to interpret laws passed by their own state legislatures. Both courts have the power to interpret the United States Constitution. State courts may, in addition, interpret their own state constitutions.

In this book, you will read about lawsuits that individuals have brought in both federal and state courts asking the courts to declare that certain actions by state officials are illegal or unconstitutional. In the federal system, these suits are filed in a district court, which is a trial court that decides cases in a particular district. The district court hears the evidence and reaches a decision. The losing party may then appeal to one of the thirteen circuit courts of appeals, which hear appeals from several districts. The loser in the Circuit court may ask the Supreme Court of the United States to decide the case. Because the Supreme Court agrees to hear only a small fraction of the cases that litigants wish to bring before it, as a practical matter, the circuit court is usually the court of last resort. Each state also has its own court system. All are a little different from one another, but each works in basically the same way as the federal court system, beginning with a trial court, which hears evidence, followed by two levels of appellate courts.

In such a complicated system, it is inevitable that courts may disagree about how to interpret a particular law. When this occurs, the answer to the question "What are my rights?" may be "It depends where you live." Moreover, the law may change; in some areas of law, it is changing very rapidly. An effort has been made in this book to indicate areas of the law in which movement is taking place, but it is not always possible to predict precisely when this will happen or what the changes will be.

If you believe that your rights have been violated, you should of course, seek legal assistance. The ACLU affiliate office in your state may be able to guide you to the available legal resources. If you consult a lawyer, take this book with you as he or she may not be familiar with the law applicable to your particular situation. You should be aware, however, that litigation is usually expensive, takes a long time, and carries with it no guarantee of success. Fortunately, litigation is not always necessary to vindicate legal rights. On occasion, government officials themselves are not aware of their legal obligations to respect the rights of individuals and may change their practices or policies when confronted by an individual who is well informed about the law. We hope that this book will help provide the basic information about the legal principles applicable to this area of law and will, as well, suggest arguments that you might make on your own behalf to secure your rights.

This introduction is being written in the aftermath of the terrorist attacks on the World Trade Center and on the Pentagon. It is precisely at times of national stress like these that civil liberties come under attack. It is therefore crucial in such times that Americans rededicate themselves to protecting the precious liberties that our Constitution and laws guarantee us. This book is part of that effort.

The principle purpose of this handbook, as well as the others in this series, is to inform individuals of their legal rights. The authors from time to time suggest what the law should be, but their personal views are not necessarily those of the ACLU. For the ACLU's position on the issues discussed in this handbook, the reader should write to Public Education Department, ACLU, 125 Broad Street, 18th Floor, New York, NY 10004-2400 or access <http://aclu.org/>.

PREFACE

This book is the product of a promise that I made to my clients and my friends on the Rosebud Sioux Indian Reservation in the early 1970s, as we struggled to understand what rights Indians and tribes have under federal law. The first edition of this book was published in 1983.

The reader should know at the outset that this book addresses what the law *is*—the hundreds of treaties, statutes, and court decisions that comprise the complex web known as federal Indian law—and *not what the law or public policy ought to be.* It does not raise, much less attempt to answer, such questions as the following: What is in the best interests of Indian tribes? Should we maintain the reservation system? Should the federal government continue to provide financial assistance to Indian tribes? These questions are weighty, and a fair discussion of them would require enormous effort and another book. I have made a conscious decision to leave them to others to discuss. Of course, learning what the law is— which this book explains—can help people decide what the law and public policy ought to be.

Federal Indian law is unique, encompassing concepts and rules that are often unexpected and bewildering to those unfamiliar with it. Indians and tribes have difficulty defending their rights—and as a result, have lost some of them—due to the complexity of federal Indian law. By seeking to explain the confusing principles that comprise this body of law, this book hopes to assist Indians and tribes exercise and defend their rights and help others understand and appreciate the difficulties Indians and tribes face in their struggle for justice.

I would like to thank the people whose encouragement and support were so instrumental to the completion of this book. This includes my immediate family (Laurel, Lianna, and Elena); my two brothers (Peter and Jeff); and my extended family (Margaret Hoskins, Bonnie Hoskins, Jim Llamas, Melissa and David Schreff, Jill and Keith Levine, and Cindy Pevar). I also wish to acknowledge some wonderful friends from whom I have drawn inspiration over the years: Barbara Barton, Larry Nault, Mike

Butyn, Mark Perkell, Sandy and Laurel Rosenberg, Marshall and Debbie Matz, King Golden, Nancy Stone, Josh Stein, Philip Tegeler, Anne Goldstein, Stephen Metcalf, Michael Livingston, Arlynna Howell Livingston, Julian and Diane Spirer, Mark and Nancy Cornell, Jeanne Kaufmann, and Steve Robinson. Last but not least, I wish to acknowledge my colleagues within the ACLU, whose tireless work on behalf of civil liberties is truly remarkable.

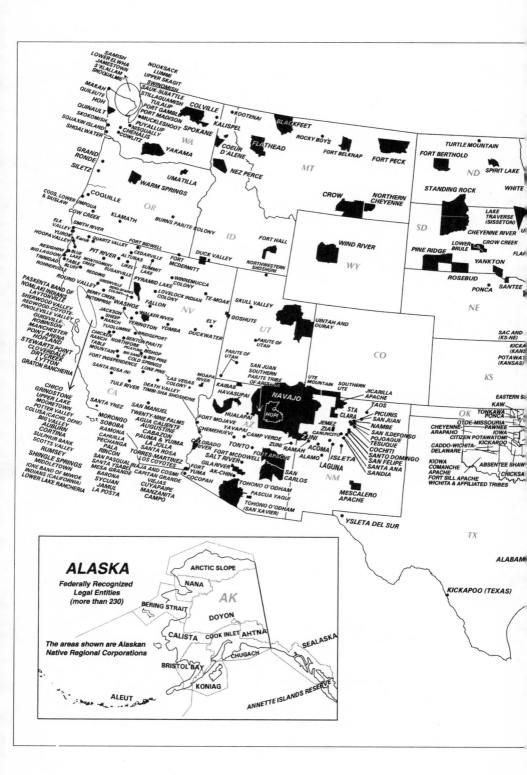

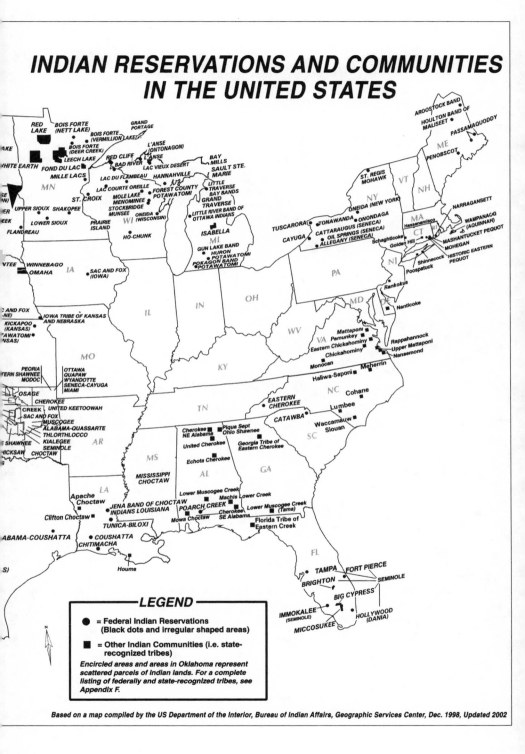

INDIAN RESERVATIONS AND COMMUNITIES IN THE UNITED STATES

RED LAKE
BOIS FORTE (NETT LAKE)
GRAND PORTAGE
BOIS FORTE (VERMILLION LAKE)
L'ANSE (ONTONAGON)
BOIS FORTE (DEER CREEK)
LEECH LAKE
RED CLIFF
L'ANSE
BAY MILLS
SAULT STE. MARIE
WHITE EARTH
FOND DU LAC
BAD RIVER
LAC VIEUX DESERT
MILLE LACS
LAC DU FLAMBEAU
HANNAHVILLE
BAY BANDS
LAC COURTE OREILLE
FOREST COUNTY POTAWATOMI
LITTLE TRAVERSE
ST. CROIX
MOLE LAKE
MENOMINEE
STOCKBRIDGE
MUNSEE
GRAND TRAVERSE
UPPER SIOUX
SHAKOPEE
PRAIRIE ISLAND
ONEIDA (WISCONSIN)
LITTLE RIVER BAND OF OTTAWA INDIANS
LOWER SIOUX
WI
ISABELLA
MI
FLANDREAU
HO-CHUNK
GUN LAKE BAND
HURON POTAWATOMI
POKAGON BAND POTAWATOMI

AROOSTOCK BAND
HOULTON BAND OF MALISEET
PASSAMAQUODDY
ME
PENOBSCOT
ST. REGIS MOHAWK
VT
NH
NARRAGANSETT
NY
ONEIDA (NEW YORK)
MA
WAMPANOAG (AQUINNAH)
TUSCARORA
TONAWANDA
ONONDAGA
Hassanemisco
CT
RI
MASHANTUCKET PEQUOT
CAYUGA
CATTARAUGUS (SENECA)
OIL SPRINGS (SENECA)
ALLEGANY (SENECA)
Schaghticoke
Golden Hill
MOHEGAN
NJ
Shinnecock
HISTORIC EASTERN PEQUOT
Poospatuck

WINNEBAGO
OMAHA
IA
SAC AND FOX (IOWA)
Rankokus
MD
DE
Nanticoke

IOWA TRIBE OF KANSAS AND NEBRASKA
IL
IN
OH
KICKAPOO (KANSAS)
TAWATOMI
WV
Mattaponi
Pamunkey
VA
Eastern Chickahominy
Rappahannock
Upper Mattaponi
Nansemond
Chickahominy
MO
KY
Monocan
Meherrin
Haliwa-Saponi

PEORIA
ERN SHAWNEE
MODOC
OTTAWA
QUAPAW
WYANDOTTE
SENECA-CAYUGA
MIAMI
NC
Cohane
OSAGE
CHEROKEE
EASTERN CHEROKEE
Lumbee
CREEK
UNITED KEETOOWAH
CATAWBA
Waccamauw
Siouan
SAC AND FOX
MUSCOGEE
ALABAMA-QUASSARTE
THLORTHLOCCO
KIALEGEE
SEMINOLE
CHOCTAW
TN
Cherokee NE Alabama
Piqua Sept Ohio Shawnee
United Cherokee
Georgia Tribe of Eastern Cherokee
SC
HICKAW
AR
Echota Cherokee
MISSISSIPPI CHOCTAW
AL
GA

Apache Choctaw
JENA BAND OF CHOCTAW INDIANS LOUISIANA
Lower Muscogee Creek
Machis Lower Creek
POARCH CREEK
Lower Muscogee Creek (Tama)
Clifton Choctaw
LA
Cherokee SE Alabama
Mowa Choctaw
Florida Tribe of Eastern Creek
TUNICA-BILOXI
ABAMA-COUSHATTA
COUSHATTA
CHITIMACHA
FL
Houma

TAMPA
FORT PIERCE
BRIGHTON
SEMINOLE
BIG CYPRESS
IMMOKALEE (SEMINOLE)
HOLLYWOOD (DANIA)
MICCOSUKEE

LEGEND

● = Federal Indian Reservations (Black dots and irregular shaped areas)

■ = Other Indian Communities (i.e. state-recognized tribes)

Encircled areas and areas in Oklahoma represent scattered parcels of Indian lands. For a complete listing of federally and state-recognized tribes, see Appendix F.

Based on a map compiled by the US Department of the Interior, Bureau of Indian Affairs, Geographic Services Center, Dec. 1998, Updated 2002

THE RIGHTS OF
INDIANS AND TRIBES

1

A History of Federal Indian Policy

pproximately five hundred nations were prospering in what is now the United States when Europeans first arrived in North America. They lived in communities spread all across the land. Each nation possessed its own government, culture, and language, and the peoples of these nations shared a deep religious faith centered in the sanctity of nature.[1]

Most of these people lived along the coasts, the major rivers, and the Great Lakes, as they do today. Their societies were complex and specialized. There were Indian* political leaders, religious leaders, doctors, artisans, architects, sculptors, mathematicians, food gatherers, and poets. Each nation lived off its land: agricultural tribes developed irrigation systems, while tribes dependent on fish and game developed ways to catch, store, and preserve their food. Some tribes were nomadic, following the seasonal migrations of fish and game. Other tribes built villages and towns, some constructing housing complexes complete with gardens and courtyards. Nearly a thousand years ago, the Anasazi Indians in the Southwest built a housing complex so large, it was not until 1882 that a larger one was constructed in New York City. Commercial networks spanned the continent, and nations traded food, clothing, and crafts.

---

* Considerable thought was given to using *Native American* rather than *Indian* in this book. *Indian* was chosen for three reasons. First, although many Indians use the terms *Indian* and *Native American* interchangeably, there seems to be a preference for the word *Indian*. Second, most Indian organizations and groups, including the National Congress of American Indians and the American Indian Movement, use *Indian* in their titles. Last, virtually all federal Indian laws, such as the Indian Reorganization Act, and federal agencies, such as the Bureau of Indian Affairs, use *Indian*.

1

When the Europeans arrived, most Indian tribes openly welcomed, assisted, and traded with them, allowing the foreigners to live in their territory. Sadly for the Indians, they underestimated the Europeans and were too trusting. As Professor Sharon O'Brien writes, "What leaders of Indian nations did not understand, often until it was too late, was the way the Europeans viewed Indians. They were not white or Christian. They were savages—wild and brutish—in the minds of many."[2] Europeans maintained their friendship with the Indians only when it served their interests, and as soon as they grew strong enough to overpower the Indians, they took advantage of it.

The balance of power in North America shifted away from the Indians in the late eighteenth century, around the time of the American Revolutionary War. During that century, the population of the British colonies "doubled every twenty-five years and increased 400 percent between 1700 and 1750. The population of North Carolina shot from 45,000 in 1750 to 275,000 in 1775"; by 1775, as many as 50,000 whites had already moved west of the Appalachian mountains.[3] After the colonists defeated the British, there was no stopping them in their quest for land. Indians tried desperately to hold onto their homelands, but the tide of migration was against them. "The new nation, born of a bloody revolution and committed to expansion, could not tolerate America as Indian country. Increasingly, Americans viewed the future as one without Indians."[4]

War and disease reduced the Indian population from more than a million people at the time of Columbus to about three hundred thousand in 1900, but since then, their number has grown at a faster pace than has that of whites. According to the 2000 census, the American Indian and Alaska Native population is 2.47 million (0.9 percent of the country's total population), increasing 17.9 percent in the last decade, while the country's overall growth rate is 10.7 percent.[5]

Indians live throughout the United States. The states with the highest Indian populations are California, Oklahoma, Arizona, New Mexico, and Washington, in that order.[6] Most Indians live west of the Mississippi River, but 25 percent live in the Northeast, and more than eighty thousand live in North Carolina, which has the sixth-largest Indian population of any state. Nearly half the Indian population lives on or near Indian reservations.[7] Some 315 Indian reservations exist in the United States covering more than 55 million acres of land (about 2 percent of the country's land mass). Reservations range in size from the 15.4-million-acre Navajo reservation (nearly as large as West Virginia) to some that are less than 100 acres.

There are more than 560 federally recognized[8] Indian tribes (sometimes also referred to as nations, bands, villages, pueblos, rancherias, and communities, depending on the tribe's preference) in the United States; 226 of these are located in Alaska. The rest are located in thirty-four other states.

As a group, Indians are the most disadvantaged people in our society. They have the lowest life expectancy, living only two-thirds as long as whites.[9] Indians also suffer from an unemployment rate of nearly 45 percent, about ten times the national average;[10] the unemployment rate on the reservation of the Oglala Sioux in South Dakota is more than 70 percent.[11] Nearly one-third of Indian households live below the poverty level, a number twice as high as the white population, and on some reservations, the poverty rate approaches 65 percent.[12] Many Indian households lack basic necessities that other Americans take for granted, such as running water and electricity.[13] Eighty-one percent of homes on the Navajo reservation do not have telephone service, and half the Navajo homes are heated by wood.[14] Indians fall well below the national average in quality of housing and education. More than a third of Indian homes are in substandard condition,[15] and half the adult Indian population lacks a high school diploma, with only 9 percent earning undergraduate or professional degrees, compared with 20 percent for the nation as a whole.[16] "The red man continues to be the most poverty stricken and economically deprived segment of our population, a people whose plight dwarfs the situation of any other Americans, even those in the worst big city ghettos."[17]

During the past ten years, nearly two hundred tribes have built gambling casinos on their reservations. Some are highly profitable, and on those reservations, economic conditions have improved. For the majority of reservation Indians, however, similar improvements are unlikely to occur anytime soon because of overall health, housing, and unemployment problems; alcoholism; lack of economic opportunities; and persistent racial discrimination. Many Indian reservations are located far from industrial centers and have no valuable natural resources that can be exploited; those tribes remain dependent on government support for their economic survival.

People often ask why so many Indians choose to continue living on reservations. The answer is complex, but much of it has to do with the determination of Indians to preserve their land, government, culture, religion, and traditions. While most groups migrated to this country in order to assimilate into it, Indian tribes have resisted assimilation and fought for their autonomy and independence.[18]

An overarching problem that reservation Indians face today is the confusing pattern of federal laws that regulate so many of their activities. No other ethnic or cultural group is so heavily regulated. The goal of this book is to help clarify federal Indian law—the federal laws, regulations, court decisions, and policies that influence and regulate so much of Indian life—so that Indians and tribes can better understand it and use it to their benefit.

Federal Indian law can be understood more easily if it is placed in historical perspective.[19] Even here, though, generalizations are dangerous, and substantial dispute exists regarding the interpretation of historical events. Some commentators liken the federal-Indian relationship to a pendulum that has shifted back and forth between attempts to annihilate tribes during certain periods of time and attempts to support tribal self-government and autonomy at other times.[20] Other commentators believe, as one recently asserted, that "American policy toward the Indians has always revolved around the same central theme: how can 'we,' the superior, enlightened, Christian people, help/destroy 'them,' the inferior, uncivilized, pagan people; in such a way as to eliminate . . . Indian people as members of distinct societies."[21]

Still, whether one sees a common theme or shifting attitudes, the fact remains that federal policies toward Indians have changed often and abruptly since the Revolutionary War, producing both immediate and long-term effects. A brief summary of these policy changes will help place the current status of Indian law in its context.

1492–1787: TRIBAL INDEPENDENCE

North America was "discovered" by Columbus in 1492. (It is fair to ask whether, had the Cherokees sailed a ship to Spain in 1492, historians would credit them with having discovered Europe.) Columbus mistakenly thought that he had landed in the East Indies, and the native peoples became known as "Indians." A century later, people from England, France, Spain, and Holland began settling in the New World. Treaties and agreements were made exchanging European goods for Indian land and assistance. These early settlements could not have survived without the active support and assistance of the Indians.

As European settlements expanded and multiplied, fights erupted among them over land. Invariably, each settlement attempted to enlist the support of neighboring Indian tribes. The best way to gain their support was by promising to respect tribal land rights and offering them European goods. The so-called French and Indian War (or Seven Years' War) that ended in 1763 pitted the British against the French for the control of the Northeast and much of Canada. The Iroquois Confederacy,[22] the most powerful group of Indians in the region, sided with the British in that conflict. Had the Iroquois chosen differently, people in the United States might speak French today.[23]

Shortly after the victory, the English king, appreciative of the tribes' allegiance, issued a proclamation designed to sharply limit the taking of additional Indian land by the colonists. The colonists, however, largely ignored it, frequently invading Indian territory and stealing land. Relations between Indians and settlers became increasingly strained and violent.

When the Revolutionary War erupted between the colonists and the British, few tribes were drawn initially into the fray. "Most Indian people seem to have regarded it as a family quarrel in which they had no business meddling,"[24] and remaining neutral seemed the prudent course. But the Americans were aware that many tribes sympathized with the British, with whom they had been trading and whose king had promised to protect their lands. Fearing that the tribes would ultimately support the British, the colonists developed a strategy "to carry the war into Indian country, destroy Indian villages, and burn Indian crops" so as to discourage or prevent Indians from giving assistance to the British.[25] These preemptive strikes caused most of the eastern tribes to openly support and aid the British, although others, including the Oneidas and Tuscaroras in New York and the Mohegans and Pequots in Connecticut, sided with their American neighbors.[26] Much of the war was fought on Indian land: Indian towns were burned; Indian homes and crops were plundered and destroyed; and Indian people were killed. For example, roughly half of the Pequots who joined the American forces did not return home.[27] "The

American Revolution was a disaster for most Indian Americans, and the turmoil it generated in Indian country continued long after 1783."[28]

1787–1828: Agreements Between Equals

The official position of the U.S. government following the Revolutionary War was to regard Indian tribes as having equal status with foreign nations, and efforts were made to maintain good relations with them. As the U.S. Supreme Court noted in 1832, "The early journals of Congress exhibit the most anxious desire to conciliate the Indian nations. . . . The most strenuous exertions were made to procure those supplies on which Indian friendships were supposed to depend; and everything which might excite hostility was avoided."[29] The United States, weakened after years of war with England, needed to avoid further hostilities. "The Indian nations were militarily powerful and still a threat to the young United States."[30]

Indian tribes were concerned about protecting their sovereignty and their land, and Congress quickly passed laws to assure them that they had nothing to fear from the United States in those regards. For instance, the Northwest Ordinance of 1787 declared: "The utmost good faith shall always be observed towards Indians; their land and property shall never be taken from them without their consent."[31] In 1790, Congress prohibited whites from obtaining Indian lands except with the consent of the federal government, restricted whites from trading with Indians except in compliance with strict federal standards, and authorized the prosecution of whites who committed crimes against Indians.[32] In 1793, Congress prohibited non-Indians from settling on Indian lands, prohibited federal employees from trading with Indians, and exempted Indians from complying with state trade regulations.[33] No laws were passed limiting the ability of Indians to govern themselves; Congress continued to respect tribal sovereignty.

Few of these laws were actively enforced, however, particularly those that might discourage settlers from moving west. "A flood of backcountry settlers invaded Indian country. . . . With the Peace of Paris [which ended the Revolutionary War in 1783] under their belts, Americans now set about taking over Indian lands as the spoils of victory."[34] The federal government usually overlooked the illegal taking of Indian land by settlers. "The government meant to restrain and govern the advance of the whites, not to prevent it forever."[35]

1828–1887: Relocation of the Indians

The federal government's attitude towards Indians changed abruptly in 1828 when Andrew Jackson became President of the United States. Under Jackson's administration, what previously had been an unspoken policy now became a publicly stated goal: removal of the eastern Indian tribes to the West. This removal policy became "the dominant federal Indian policy of the nineteenth century."[36]

The rapid increase in the population of the United States and the desire for more land created enormous pressure to move westward into Indian territories and also to relocate the eastern tribes, so as to make their lands available for white settlement. The United States was now stronger, both economically and militarily, and it no longer needed to avoid hostility with the Indians. In 1830, Congress passed the Indian Removal Act,[37] which authorized the President to "negotiate" with eastern tribes for their relocation west of the Mississippi River. Between 1832 and 1843, most eastern tribes were removed to the West, or forced to live on smaller reservations in the East. (The "Trail of Tears," in which fifteen thousand Indians died during their forced march to the Oklahoma Indian Territory, is discussed in chapter 15.) In their treaties with the United States, many eastern tribes were promised that their new homes in Arkansas, Kansas, Iowa, Illinois, Missouri, or Wisconsin would be theirs permanently. The United States broke almost every one of these treaties, often within a few years after they were signed, and some tribes moved several times to "permanent" homes farther west.

The discovery of gold in California in 1848 and in the Black Hills of South Dakota in 1874 brought tens of thousands of settlers to the West and increased the desire for Indian land. The U.S. Cavalry went along with them, not to enforce the treaties under which tribes were guaranteed permanent homes but to protect the non-Indian trespassers. Weakened by military campaigns, western tribes one by one were forced to accept reservation life. "Hence, by the 1870s, the government had successfully placed Native Americans in a state of coerced dependency" on the federal government.[38]

Also during this period, particular emphasis was placed on "educating" and "civilizing" Indian youth. By 1887, more than two hundred schools had been established under federal supervision, with an enrollment of over fourteen thousand Indian children, many of whom were forcibly removed from their families. The authoritarian rule of these schools is notorious: children were severely punished if they spoke their native language or practiced their traditions; they were forbidden from wearing native clothing or engaging in their religious practices; and they were allowed almost no contact with their families on the reservation.[39]

Congress passed several laws during the mid-nineteenth century designed to increase federal control over Indians and promote their assimilation into white society. Congress authorized federal courts to prosecute Indians who committed certain crimes on the reservation[40] and placed federal agents on Indian reservations to supervise tribal activities more closely.

A century after Congress passed the Northwest Ordinance in 1787—which acknowledged the independence of Indian tribes—a new law was passed reflecting how their status had depreciated in the eyes of the federal government since that time. In 1871, Congress passed a law that prohibited federal officials from making any additional treaties with Indian tribes.[41] The passage of this statute had both symbolic and practical effect. Symbolically, its passage meant that Congress no longer considered tribes as independent nations capable of signing a treaty; as a practical matter, it meant that Congress could limit tribal powers and take Indian land anytime it wanted to, simply by passing a law to that effect, a power that Congress immediately began exercising.

1887–1934: ALLOTMENT AND ASSIMILATION

Federal Indian policy between 1887 and 1934 was shaped by two forces. The first was a desire to take additional land from the Indians for settlement by whites. The second was a belief shared by many non-Indian social reformers that the best way to help Indians overcome their poverty was by encouraging them to assimilate into white society. Although their motives differed, both groups joined in compelling Congress in 1887 into passing the General Allotment Act (GAA),[42] also known as the Dawes Act. The ultimate objectives of the GAA "were simple and clear cut: to extinguish tribal sovereignty, erase reservation boundaries, and force the assimilation of Indians into the society at large."[43]

To accomplish these goals, the GAA authorized the President (who, in turn, delegated this power to the Secretary of the Interior) to divide communally held tribal lands into separate parcels ("allotments"). Each tribal member was assigned an allotment and, after a twenty-five-year "trust" period, was to be issued a deed to it. All remaining tribal land (the "surplus" land) was then to be sold to non-Indian farmers and ranchers. Congress hoped that by allowing non-Indians to live on the reservation, the goals of the settlers and those of the humanitarian social reformers could both be satisfied: land would become available for non-Indian settlement, and Indian poverty would be eliminated once Indians emulated the work habits of their new neighbors.

The first goal was accomplished—land was freed for non-Indian settlement—but the second goal failed miserably. Rather than assist Indians overcome poverty, the GAA drove them further into it. Most Indians fiercely resisted assimilation and did not want to abandon their communal society to become farmers and ranchers. Besides, not only were many allotments unsuitable for small-scale agriculture but few Indians possessed the capital to buy the equipment, cattle, or seeds to initiate these ventures. Thousands of impoverished Indians sold their allotments to white settlers or lost their land in foreclosures when they were unable to pay state real estate taxes. Of the nearly 150 million acres of land that tribes owned in 1887, less than 50 million acres remained in 1934 when the GAA was repealed. The Yankton Sioux in South Dakota, for example, held nearly 500,000 acres of land prior to the GAA. Today, primarily as a consequence of the GAA, only 36,000 acres remain under their control.[44]

In 1924, Congress passed a law conferring U.S. citizenship on all Indians born in the United States who had not yet become citizens through treaties or statutes.[45] Obtaining citizenship, however, did little to improve the many economic and political problems that Indians faced.

1934–1953: INDIAN REORGANIZATION

In the early 1930s, federal Indian policy abruptly changed again, and a more humane approach was adopted. A number of factors precipitated this shift. For one thing, the onset of the Great Depression all but eliminated the desire and the financial ability of non-Indians to purchase additional Indian land. Also, the Brookings Institute issued in 1928 what became known as the Meriam Report,[46] a provocative and influential study that chronicled the severe and hopeless conditions faced by Indians, including extreme poverty, devastating epidemics, inadequate food, and inadequate education, that occurred as a result of the federal government's previous policies. Mounting public criticism and a growing sentiment to restore tribal independence encouraged President Franklin D. Roosevelt to change radically the policies of previous administrations.[47]

Roosevelt appointed John Collier as Commissioner of Indian Affairs in 1933. Collier, who had long criticized the federal government's Indian policies, declared in 1934: "No interference with Indian religious life or expression will hereafter be tolerated. The cultural history of Indians is in all respects to be considered equal to that of any non-Indian group."[48]

In June 1934, at Collier's urging, Congress passed the Indian Reorganization Act (IRA),[49] also known as the Wheeler-Howard Act. The express purpose of the IRA was "to rehabilitate the Indian's economic life and to give him a chance to develop the initiative destroyed by a century of oppression and paternalism."[50]

The IRA, discussed further in chapter 6, was "the first federal Indian policy in over 100 years that did not have the explicit purpose of undermining the status of the Indian nations."[51] The IRA sought to rejuvenate tribal government. For one thing, it protected the tribe's remaining land base by prohibiting the further allotment of tribal land.[52] It also authorized the Secretary of the Interior to add lands to existing reservations, to create new reservations for tribes that had lost all their land, and to restore to tribal ownership any land declared "surplus" under the GAA and not yet sold to non-Indians.[53] In addition, Indian tribes were encouraged to adopt their own constitutions, to become federally chartered corporations, and to assert their powers of self-government. The IRA also established a $20 million revolving credit fund from which loans could be made to incorporated tribes.[54]

Moreover, the IRA sought to increase Indian influence in the management of federal Indian programs by requiring that Indians be given a preference in employment within the Bureau of Indian Affairs (BIA), the agency that administers most of those programs.[55] Today, thanks to the IRA, more than 85 percent of BIA employees are Indians.

The IRA has been criticized as paternalistic, because tribes were not consulted in its development, and also as insufficient, because tribes remained subject to substantial federal control; but regardless of its shortcomings, it was a giant step in the right direction. Between 1934 and 1953, Indian landholdings increased by over two million acres; federal funds were spent to improve reservation roads, homes, health facilities, community schools, and irrigation systems; and tribal governments experienced a revitalization after a century of oppression.

1953–1968: Termination

The benevolent attitude reflected in the IRA was short-lived. In 1949, the Hoover Commission issued a report recommending the "complete integration" of Indians into white society. It asserted that assimilation was in the Indians' best interests and would also save money for the federal government by ending federal Indian programs.[56] When President Dwight D. Eisenhower entered the White House in 1953, the federal government abandoned the goals of the IRA. The government's new policy, drawing upon the recommendations of the Hoover Commission, was called *termination:* termination of the tribe's trust relationship[57] with the United States and, as a consequence, its loss of federal benefits and support services and the destruction of its government and reservation.[58] Heralded as the policy that would set the Indians free,[59] termination brought Indian tribes to the brink of total disaster.

In 1953, Congress adopted House Concurrent Resolution No. 108, which declared that federal benefits and services to Indian tribes should be ended "as rapidly as possible."[60] In the decade that followed, Congress terminated its trust relationship with 109 tribes. Each tribe was ordered to cease exercising governmental powers and to disperse all land and property to tribal members. Their reservations were then eliminated, and the state acquired full jurisdiction over this land and the people who resided there.

In an effort to reduce federal obligations to Indians even further, Congress passed Public Law 83-280,[61] generally known as P.L. 280. This law gave six states (Alaska, California, Minnesota, Nebraska, Oregon, and Wisconsin) criminal jurisdiction over Indian reservations, allowing them to enter the reservation to arrest Indians and prosecute them in state courts.

State governments have long resented the presence of Indian reservations within their borders, pockets of land over which they have so little control. Termination gave the states the control they wanted. Moreover, by terminating some of the more successful tribes, Congress sent a message to all tribes that political or commercial success could result in a sudden withdrawal of federal services and the elimination of the reservation. This warning continues to worry tribes today, decades after the end of the termination era. "The risk of total destruction of the Indian community is too great to treat lightly."[62]

Another program developed during this period and aimed at assimilating Indians was "relocation." Created in 1956, the relocation program offered job training and housing assistance to Indians who would leave the reservation for urban areas.[63] Some thirty-five thousand Indians entered the program during the next decade, nearly a third of whom returned home, often after discovering that promises of jobs and decent housing were illusory.[64]

1968–THE PRESENT: TRIBAL SELF-DETERMINATION

In 1968, President Lyndon Johnson declared: "We must affirm the rights of the first Americans to remain Indians while exercising their rights as Americans. We must affirm their rights to freedom of choice and self-determination."[65]

Federal Indian policy thus shifted its course once again. The federal government's termination policies were now viewed as destructive and inhumane and were repudiated. President Richard Nixon, who had been Vice President during the termination era, denounced the termination policy in 1970, stating: "This, then, must be the goal of any new national policy toward the Indian people: to strengthen the Indian sense of autonomy without threatening his sense of community."[66] In 1983, President Ronald Reagan similarly endorsed tribal self-determination: "This administration intends to restore tribal governments to their rightful place among governments of this nation and to enable tribal governments, along with State and local governments, to resume control over their own affairs."[67]

Since the late 1960s, Congress for the most part has promoted tribal sovereignty and autonomy while at the same time recognizing and honoring its obligations to safeguard and enhance the welfare of Indian people.[68] For example, in 1968 Congress prohibited states from acquiring any additional authority over Indian reservations under P.L. 280 without the consent of the affected tribe,[69] and many tribes terminated during the termination era have been restored to federal status.[70] An Indian Business Development Fund was created by Congress to stimulate Indian business and employment.[71] Two loan funds, the Indian Financing Act[72] and the Native American Programs Act,[73] were created to help develop Indian commercial opportunities and resources. The Indian Self-Determination and Education Assistance Act of 1975,[74] a particularly important law, requires federal agencies to allow tribes to administer various federal Indian programs on the reservation. Many tribes have used this opportunity to run their own health, law enforcement, education, and social services programs, giving them more control over their lives. The Indian Child Welfare Act of 1978,[75] discussed in chapter 17, gives Indian tribes and Indian families substantial protection from the removal of Indian children from their families by state agencies and state courts. The Indian Mineral Development Act of 1982[76] authorizes tribes to enter into joint-venture agreements with mineral developers to maximize the value of tribal mineral resources. The Indian Tribal Government Tax Status Act of 1982[77] extends to Indian tribes many of the tax advantages enjoyed by the states, such as the ability to issue tax exempt bonds to finance government programs. The Indian Gaming Regulatory Act of 1988,[78] discussed in chapter 16, confirms the authority of Indian tribes to engage in gaming to raise revenue and promote economic development. The Indian Health Care Improvement Act[79] provides for greater Indian control of reservation health care. In 2002, the No Child Left Behind Act[80] became law, imposing greater accountability for student progress and academic achievement on government agencies, and the law expressly includes Indian and Native Alaska children as beneficiaries.

In addition to these legislative efforts by Congress, in 1994, President Bill Clinton issued an executive order that requires all federal agencies to conduct their business with tribes on a "government-to-government" basis, respectful of tribal sovereignty.[81] In 2000, President Clinton issued an executive order that reaffirms "the right of Indian tribes to self-government" and requires federal agencies to work closely with tribal governments to protect "tribal trust resources, and Indian tribal treaty and other rights."[82]

THE FUTURE

In light of the radical and sudden changes that have occurred in the past, the future of federal-Indian relations is impossible to predict. Today's era of self-determination can become tomorrow's era of termination.

In recent decades, Indian tribes have increasingly asserted their treaty and statutory rights, often causing a backlash in the process. Indeed, bills were introduced in Congress in 1995 that, if passed, would have gutted some Indian programs and ended others, undermining Indian tribes to such an extent that the person in charge of the BIA, Assistant Secretary of Indian Affairs Ada Deer (a member of the Menominee Tribe), accused Congress of returning to a termination mentality. In a newspaper editorial written while Congress was debating these laws, Assistant Secretary Deer called the bills unethical and immoral, stating, "This country's first Americans deserve better treatment. They deserve honesty, candor and respect. The United States, at the very least, should keep its promises."[83] The bills were defeated.

In 2001, Gail Norton, appointed as Secretary of the Interior by President George W. Bush, told tribal leaders: "I take very seriously my responsibility as trustee for Indian lands, trust moneys, and federal obligations to the tribes under treaties and laws."[84] However, only time will tell whether the President and Congress—and the nation—will support and promote tribal sovereignty in the years ahead or will once again actively seek to destroy tribal self-government and autonomy and take Indian land.

NOTES

1. *See* Sharon O'Brien, *American Indian Tribal Governments* (Norman: Univ. of Oklahoma Press, 1989) at 14–15.

2. A. Josephy Jr., *500 Nations* (New York: Alfred A. Knopf, 1994) at 156.

3. Colin G. Calloway, *The American Revolution in Indian Country* (Cambridge: Cambridge Univ. Press, 1995) at 19.

4. *Id.* at xv.

5. "Census Bureau: Native Populations to Double," *Indian Country Today* (Nov. 11, 2000) at B1. *See also* "Jobs Cited as Indians' Top Need," *Denver Rocky Mountain News* (July 8, 1999) at 7A (citing Census Bureau and Bureau of Indian Affairs reports).

6. *See* "Census Bureau," note 5 above.

7. David H. Getches et al., *Federal Indian Law.* 4th ed. (St. Paul: West Publishing Co., 1998) at 14.

8. The process of obtaining federal recognition is discussed in chapter 15, sec. F.

9. Getches, note 7 above, at 16.

10. *See* National Congress of American Indians, "An Introduction to Indian Nations in the United States," (Washington, D.C.: National Congress of American Indians, undated) at 5; Getches, note 7 above, at 15.

11. Statement of Oglala Lakota Nation President Harold Salway, quoted in "Salway Says Oglala Vision Can Tap into Initiatives," *Indian Country Today* (July 19, 1999) at A2.

12. *See* "Census Bureau" and "Jobs Cited," note 5 above. *See also* "An American Indian Protagonism," *Indian Country Today* editorial (Sept. 27, 2000) at A4; Getches, note 7 above, at 15.

13. *See* Getches, note 7 above, at 16.

14. "Clinton Unveils Plan to Close Digital Divide on Reservations," *Denver Rocky Mountain News* (Apr. 18, 2000) at 44A. *See also* D. Bambi Kraus, "Wealth, Success and Poverty in Indian Country," *Poverty and Race (May/June 2001)* at 4.

15. Getches, note 7 above, at 16.

16. Getches, note 7 above, at 19.

17. R. Strickland, "Genocide-at-Law: An Historic and Contemporary View of the Native American Experience," 34 *U. Kan. L. Rev.* 713, 716 (1986). *See also* Getches, note 7 above, at 15–18.

18. *See* D'Arcy McNickle, *They Came Here First* (New York: Harper and Row, Perennial Library, 1975) at 283; Getches, note 7 above, at 26–30.

19. For additional information on the history of federal Indian policy, *see* Francis Prucha, *The Great Father: The United States Government and the American Indians* (Lincoln: Univ. of Nebraska Press, 1984); S. Lyman Tyler, *A History of Indian Policy* (Washington, D.C.: Government Printing Office, 1973), and the extensive bibliography listed at 281–309; Josephy Jr., note 2 above.

20. This view is discussed in Robert N. Clinton et al., *American Indian Law.* 3d ed. (Charlottesville: Michie Co., 1991) at vi–vii; Emma R. Gross, *Contemporary Federal Policy Toward American Indians* (New York: Greenwood Press, 1989) at 11–12.

21. Robert B. Porter, "A Proposal to the *Hanodaganyas* to Decolonize Federal Indian Control Law," 31 *Univ. of Mich. J. of L. Reform* 899, 921 (1998).

22. The composition and influence of the Iroquois Confederacy is discussed in ch. 15, sec. E.

23. *See* C. Colden, *History of the Five Indian Nations* (Ithaca, N.Y.: Cornell Univ. Press, 1958).

24. Calloway, note 3 above, at 28.

25. *Id.* at 47, 65.

26. *Id.* at 34.

27. *Id.*

28. *Id.* at 291. *See also id.* at 26–64.

29. *Worcester v. Georgia,* 31 U.S. 515, 549 (1832).

30. Porter, note 21 above, at 922.

31. Act of Aug. 7, 1789, 1 Stat. 50.

32. 1 Stat. 137, codified as 25 U.S.C. Secs. 68 and 177.

33. 1 Stat. 329.

34. Calloway, note 3 above, at 280, 281.

35. Francis Prucha, *American Indian Policy in the Formative Years* (Cambridge: Harvard Univ. Press, 1962) at 187. *See also* Tyler, note 19 above, at 48–51.

36. Vine Deloria Jr., *American Indian Policy in the Twentieth Century* (Norman: Univ. of Oklahoma Press, 1985) at 242.

37. 14 Stat. 411.

38. *Cobell v. Babbitt*, 91 F. Supp.2d 1, 7 (D.D.C. 1999), *aff'd in relevant part*, 240 F.3d 1081 (D.C. Cir. 2001). *See U.S. v. Kagama*, 118 U.S. 375, 384–85 (1886); *U.S. v. Sandoval*, 231 U.S. 28 (1913).

39. Tyler, note 19 above, at 88; Strickland, note 17 above, at 729.

40. *See* 18 U.S.C. Secs. 1152 (first enacted in 1834) and 1153 (first enacted in 1883). These laws are discussed in ch. 8.

41. 16 Stat. 544, 566 codified as 25 U.S.C. Sec. 71.

42. 24 Stat. 388, as amended, 25 U.S.C. Secs. 331–58.

43. *County of Yakima v. Confederated Tribes and Bands of Yakima Indian Nation*, 502 U.S. 251, 254 (1992). For an extended discussion of the General Allotment Act, *see* Tyler, note 19 above, at 95–104; D. Otis, *The Dawes Act and the Allotment of Indian Lands* (Norman: Univ. of Oklahoma Press, 1973). *See also Cass County, Minnesota v. Leech Lake Band of Chippewa Indians*, 524 U.S. 103 (1998).

44. *South Dakota v. Yankton Sioux Tribe*, 522 U.S. 329, 356 (1998).

45. 43 Stat. 984, codified at 8 U.S.C. Sec. 1401(a)(2). Many Indians prior to 1924 had become citizens through treaties or statutes.

46. *See* Lewis Meriam et. al, eds., "The Problem of Indian Administration" (Institute for Government Research, 1928). *See generally*, Getches, note 7 above, at 193–94.

47. *See* Tyler, note 19 above, at 112–22.

48. Commissioner of Indian Affairs, *Annual Report* (1934) at 90.

49. 48 Stat. 984, codified as 25 U.S.C. Secs. 461 *et seq.*

50. H.R. Rep. No. 1804, 73d Cong., 2d Sess., at 6 (1934). *See also* 25 U.S.C. Sec. 450. *See Morton v. Mancari*, 417 U.S. 535, 542 (1974).

51. Porter, note 21 above, at 933.

52. 25 U.S.C. Sec. 461. *See Cass County*, note 43 above, 524 U.S. at 108. ("In 1934, federal Indian policy shifted dramatically when Congress enacted the Indian Reorganization Act, which ended the practice of making federal allotments to individual Indians.")

53. 25 U.S.C. Secs. 465, 463.

54. 25 U.S.C. Sec. 470.

55. 25 U.S.C. Sec. 472.

56. *See* Commission on Organization of the Executive Branch of the Government, *Indian Affairs: A Report to Congress* (1949).

57. The source and scope of the federal government's trust relationship with Indian tribes is discussed in ch. 3.

58. Termination is discussed in ch. 5, sec. B. *See also* Tyler, note 19 above, at 168–81.

59. *See* Getches, note 7 above, at 204–5.

60. H.R. Cong. Res. 108, 83d Cong. (1953).

61. 67 Stat. 488, codified as 18 U.S.C. Sec. 1162, 28 U.S.C. Sec. 1360. P.L. 280 is discussed at length in ch. 7.

62. Vine Deloria Jr., *Custer Died for Your Sins* (New York: Avon Books, 1969) at 138.

63. Pub. L. No. 959 (1956).

64. *See* O'Brien, note 1 above, at 86.

65. Presidential Documents, Weekly Compilation of, 1968, vol. 4, no. 10 (Washington, D.C.: Government Printing Office, 1968).

66. Message from the President of the United States, 1970, "Recommendations for Indian Policy" H.R. Doc. No. 91-363, 91st Cong., 2d Sess. (July 8, 1970), *reprinted in* Francis Prucha, ed., *Documents of United States Indian Policy.* 2d ed. (Lincoln: Univ. of Nebraska Press, 1990) at 256–58.

67. Statement on Indian Policy, 19 Weekly Comp. Pres. Doc. 98 (Jan. 24, 1983).

68. These obligations—both their source and scope—are discussed in ch. 3.

69. 25 U.S.C. Sec. 1322. This change reflects a "dramatic shift in national policy toward Indians" by preventing states from unilaterally acquiring criminal jurisdiction in Indian country under Public Law 83-280. *Rosebud Sioux Tribe v. South Dakota,* 900 F.2d 1164, 1174 (8th Cir. 1990), *cert. denied,* 500 U.S. 915 (1991).

70. *See, e.g.,* Menominee Restoration Act of Dec. 22, 1973, codified at 25 U.S.C. Sec. 903; Confederated Tribes of Coos, Lower Umpqua & Siuslaw Indians Restoration Act of October 17, 1984, codified at 25 U.S.C. Sec. 714 *et seq.*

71. 25 U.S.C. Secs. 1521 *et seq.*

72. 25 U.S.C. Secs. 1451 *et seq.*

73. 42 U.S.C. Secs. 2991 *et seq.*

74. Pub. L. No. 93-638, codified as 25 U.S.C. Secs. 450f *et seq.* and in scattered sections of 5, 25, 42, and 50 U.S.C.

75. 25 U.S.C. Secs. 1901–63 (1978).

76. 25 U.S.C. Secs. 2101–8.

77. Pub. L. No. 97-473, 96 Stat. 2607, codified as amended in scattered sections of 26 U.S.C.

78. 25 U.S.C. Secs. 2701–21.

79. 25 U.S.C. Secs. 1613–82.

80. Pub. L. No. 107-110, 115 Stat. 1425 (Jan. 8, 2002).

81. "Government-to-Government Relations with Native American Tribal Governments," Presidential Memorandum of Apr. 24, 1994, 59 Fed. Reg. 22951 (1994).

82. "Consultation and Coordination with Indian Tribal Governments," Presidential Memorandum of Nov. 6, 2000, Exec. Order No. 13084 (2000).

83. Ada Deer, "Congress Doesn't Say It, but Termination Is the Real Goal," *Indian Country Today,* (Sept. 28, 1995,) at A5.

84. Quoted in "Norton Speaks to Tribes and Indian Affairs Committee," *Indian Country Today* (Mar. 7, 2001) at A1.

11

Definitions: *Indian, Indian Tribe, Indian Country,* and *Indian Title*

A. *INDIAN*

Who is an Indian?

There is no single definition of the term *Indian*. Determining who is an Indian can be difficult, even controversial. For example, people who have one-eighth Indian blood and seven-eighths Caucasian blood may call themselves Indians, but other people might disagree with that characterization.

The term *Indian* can be defined in either an ethnological (racial) or in a legal sense.[1] Indians are a distinct race of people, as are Caucasians, Negroes, and Mongoloids. However, neither in an ethnological nor legal sense is there a universally accepted method of determining who is an Indian.

Each government—tribal, state, and federal—determines who is an Indian for purposes of that government's laws and programs. This can result in someone being an Indian under tribal law but not under federal law,[2] under federal but not tribal law,[3] under tribal but not state law,[4] and so forth.[5]

Congress has created many programs for Indians, using varying definitions of the word *Indian*. For some programs, anyone of Indian descent is eligible to participate; for other programs, the applicant must have a minimum blood quantum (often one-fourth Indian blood); and still other programs allow all members of federally recognized Indian tribes to qualify, regardless of how these tribes have defined the term.[6] As a result of these different standards, the same person may qualify as an Indian for one program but not for another.[7] The Census Bureau takes a simple approach to these problems by listing every person on the census as an Indian who claims to be one.

Congress has created some programs for Indians without defining the term. When that occurs, the federal agencies implementing those laws determine who is eligible. Some of these agencies have been accused of being too stringent in their definitions,[8] resulting in court challenges. In those situations, the courts generally use a two-part test to determine who is an Indian. First, the person must have some Indian blood, some identifiable Indian ancestry. Second, the Indian community must recognize this person as an Indian.[9]

Each Indian tribe has eligibility requirements for membership. Many tribes require that a person have at least one-fourth tribal blood to be enrolled, but others require less; to become enrolled in some tribes, the applicant need only be descended from someone listed on the tribe's membership roll.

Indian tribes have the authority to determine who is an Indian for tribal purposes but not for state or federal purposes. Thus, when the federal government distributes federal money to, or creates programs for, tribal members, it determines who is eligible, and it can ignore the tribe's membership list and adopt a different standard.[10] To be considered an Indian for federal purposes, an individual must have some Indian blood; consequently, a non-Indian adopted into an Indian tribe cannot be considered an Indian under federal law.[11]

Are the Native people of Alaska, including the Eskimos and Aleuts, considered Indians?

The Native people of Alaska are comprised of three groups: Eskimos, Aleuts, and American Indians. Eskimos and Aleuts are ethnologically distinct from, but related to, the American Indian. Eskimos and Aleuts constitute the majority of Alaska's Native population.

When Congress enacts Indian legislation, it usually states that the law applies also to Eskimos and Aleuts, except in those rare situations in which Congress decides to exclude them. There are a number of laws, however, that apply only to Alaska Natives, the most important of which are discussed in chapter 15, section C.

**Can an Indian be a citizen of both the United States and an
Indian tribe?**

Yes. In 1924, Congress extended U.S. citizenship to all Indians born
in the United States.[12] Many Indians had become citizens before this time
by treaty or federal statute. In 1905, the Supreme Court held that Indians
who had been granted U.S. citizenship could not participate in federal
Indian programs, which were intended, the Court said, for noncitizens.[13]
Eleven years later, the Court reversed that decision.[14] It is now settled that
an Indian can be both a citizen of the United States and a member of an
Indian tribe and have all the benefits and obligations that arise out of that
dual status.

B. *INDIAN TRIBE*

What constitutes an Indian tribe?

As with the term *Indian,* the term *Indian tribe,* both ethnologically
and legally, has more than one definition. A group of Indians can call itself
a tribe and be recognized as such by other tribes. However, to qualify for
the many benefits that Congress has made available to federally recognized
tribes, the group must satisfy the seven requirements for federal recognition established by the Department of the Interior. (These requirements
are discussed in chapter 15, section F. The group seeking recognition must
show, for instance, that it has continuously occupied a particular geographic territory and that its government has maintained authority over
its members.) Some 560 Indian tribes and Native tribal organizations are
federally recognized.

Federal recognition by the Interior Department guarantees that an Indian tribe will qualify to participate in virtually all federal Indian programs. However, a denial of federal recognition does not necessarily disqualify a tribe from all of these programs. Tribal members, for instance,
can still enforce a treaty that their ancestors made with the United States
even though the federal government refuses to recognize the continued
existence of the tribe.[15] Similarly, tribes not officially recognized by the
Department of the Interior may participate in federal programs that Congress has not limited to federally recognized tribes.[16]

Tribes may be defined by their political, rather than their ethnological,
identity. On occasion, the federal government has placed ethnologically
distinct tribes on the same reservation, and these tribes have taken on a

single political identity.[17] An example is the Fort Belknap Indian Community in Montana, which is one tribe politically but is composed of two ethnological tribes, the Gros Ventre and Assiniboine.[18] Also, single ethnological tribes that were divided and placed on different reservations have obtained separate political identities. Various bands of Sioux, Chippewa, and Shoshone were placed on separate reservations and are now treated as different tribes politically.

Is an Indian nation different from an Indian tribe?

The terms *nation, tribe, and band* have been used interchangeably in Indian treaties and statutes. The term *nation* usually refers to a government independent from any other government, possessing the power of absolute dominion over its territory and people.

Some tribal governments prefer to call themselves nations rather than tribes, often reflecting the belief that the United States has no right to exercise any power or authority over them. This subject is further discussed in chapter 5.

C. INDIAN COUNTRY

Broadly speaking, *Indian country* is all the land under the supervision of the U.S. government that has been set aside primarily for the use of Indians. This includes all land *within* an Indian reservation and all land *outside* a reservation that has been placed under federal superintendence and designated primarily for Indian use.

As a general rule, state laws do not apply to Indians in Indian country; tribal and federal laws apply instead. If someone says, "The crime took place in Indian country," this indicates that the state has no jurisdiction to prosecute the crime. Thus, determining the status of the land in question is one of the first inquiries that must be undertaken in determining which government can exercise its authority.[19]

"Indian country" is defined in a federal criminal statute. This law, Title 18, U.S. Code, Sec. 1151 (18 U.S.C. § 1151), states:

"Indian country" . . . means (a) all land within the limits of any Indian reservation under the jurisdiction of the United States government, notwithstanding the issuance of any patent, and including rights-of-way running through the reservation, (b) all dependent Indian communities within the borders of the United

States whether within the original or subsequently acquired territory thereof, and whether within or without the limits of a state, and (c) all Indian allotments, the Indian titles to which have not been extinguished, including rights-of-way running through the same.

Courts have applied the same definition of *Indian country* to civil cases. Thus, just as most crimes by Indians in Indian country are governed by tribal and federal law, not state law, so are most civil matters involving Indians, such as divorce, inheritance, taxation, child custody, and contract disputes.[20] Deciding whether a territory is Indian country is an issue of law rather than an issue of fact; therefore, a judge makes this determination, not a jury.[21]

Section 1151 identifies three territories as being Indian country. Under subsection (a) of 1151, Indian country includes *all* land within the boundaries of an Indian reservation, including land owned by a non-Indian.[22] Rights-of-way through an Indian reservation, such as railroad tracks, utility power lines, and state and federal highways, remain a part of Indian country.[23] Once a reservation is created for Indians by the federal government, all the land within it becomes Indian country even if no official proclamation says so;[24] even if years go by before the tribe defends its property interests;[25] and even if the land is owned by the tribe in fee (that is, it is not federally owned trust land).[26]

Under subsection (b) of 1151, Indian country includes "all dependent Indian communities" within the United States.[27] Thus, land located *outside* a reservation is Indian country if it has been set aside by the federal government for the use, occupancy, or benefit of Indians and the land is under the superintendence of the federal government.[28] The Pueblos of New Mexico, whose lands are owned by the tribes themselves but are under federal supervision, is an example.[29] Other examples include tribal housing projects,[30] federal and tribal schools for Indian children,[31] and tribal government buildings[32] when located on federal trust land. Should a tribe purchase land outside the reservation, it normally will not be considered to qualify as Indian country[33] unless the tribe succeeds in having the land converted by the Secretary of the Interior into trust status.[34]

Who actually uses the land is not a factor in determining whether it is a dependent Indian community under subsection (b). The only two factors are whether the federal government intended to set the area apart primarily for Indians and whether the federal government substantially supervises its use.[35] This principle was made clear by the Supreme Court in a 1998 case that held that the territory set aside by Congress for the Native peoples of Alaska was not a dependent Indian community, despite the fact that the land is used primarily by Alaska Natives and is exempt by federal law from state real estate taxation. The Court held in the 1998 case that these lands satisfied neither the "intended primarily for Indian use" nor the "federal supervision" tests because the federal law creating this territory allows the Native peoples to sell the land to non-Indians at any time, and Congress did not place the land under comprehensive supervision by the federal government.[36] In reaching this decision, the Court used a different definition of "dependent Indian community" than the ones lower federal courts had been using, thus casting some doubt on these earlier cases.[37]

Subsection (c) of 1151 includes as Indian country all *trust* and all *restricted* allotments of land located outside an Indian reservation.[38] (Both trust and restricted allotments are parcels of land that have been assigned by the federal government to an individual Indian and cannot be sold or leased without the consent of the federal government. The difference is that a trust allotment is owned by the federal government, whereas a restricted allotment is owned by the Indian.) Hundreds of these individual allotments exist today, often as the result of Congress's having eliminated the reservation in which these allotments once existed. These allotments remain Indian country.[39]

To summarize, all land within an Indian reservation is Indian country, even land owned by a non-Indian. In addition, dependent Indian communities are considered Indian country, and so are trust and restricted Indian allotments outside a reservation.

Are non-Indians permitted to live in Indian country?

Yes. Many non-Indians live in Indian country. (As explained in chapter 1, the federal government sold millions of acres of reservation land to non-Indians in the years between 1887 and 1934.) On some reservations, most land is owned by non-Indians, yet by virtue of subsection (a) of 1151, the entire reservation remains Indian country.

What is an *Indian reservation?*

An *Indian reservation* is land that has been set aside by the federal government for the use, possession, and benefit of an Indian tribe or group of Indians. Most reservations were created by some formal means, such as a treaty, a statute passed by Congress, or an executive order issued by the President. Some were created by implication, as when Congress took action that implied ownership of certain land by a particular tribe.[40]

The terms *Indian reservation* and *Indian country* are often used interchangeably, but they are not the same. Indian country is a larger concept because it includes not only all Indian reservations but also dependent Indian communities and trust and restricted allotments located outside a reservation.

D. *Indian Title*

What is Indian title?

Not long after the United States gained its independence from Great Britain, the Supreme Court was asked to determine who owned the land still occupied by the Indians: the Indians or the U.S. government. The Court decided this question in *Johnson v. McIntosh* (1823).[41] The specific issue in that case was whether a non-Indian who purchased land from an Indian tribe had obtained valid title. The Supreme Court held that the non-Indian had not acquired valid title because the land was not the tribe's to sell. The U.S. government had become the owner of all the land within the United States by virtue of the "discovery" of the North American continent by its European ancestors and the "conquest" of its inhabitants. It did not matter to the Court that Europeans had not discovered North America—on which there already existed over five hundred independent nations—and certainly had not conquered all the Indians living there. The Court's decision was a pragmatic and popular one.[42] A ruling that the Indians "actually owned their own land would have up-ended the entire American land tenure system and might have bankrupted the new nation's already weakened treasury if compensation had to be paid for the illegal takings [of Indian land] accomplished to date."[43]

The Court went on to hold, though, that as the original inhabitants of the United States, Indian tribes have a right to continue to occupy and use their aboriginal lands. The federal government could extinguish this interest at its pleasure, but until it did so, the Indians had the right to remain on their original territory. This possessory interest has been called *Indian right of occupancy, Indian title,* and *aboriginal title.* As explained in *Johnson v. McIntosh* and in later cases, the principles of Indian title are the following: (1) The federal government acquired ownership of all the land within the United States by discovery and conquest; (2) Indians retain a perpetual right to remain on their ancestral lands until such time as Congress decides to take this land for another purpose; (3) Indian title is a possessory and not a property interest (that is, Indians have a right to possess their ancestral land but not to own it unless Congress gives them ownership rights); and (4) Indian title may not be sold by the Indians without authorization from the federal government.[44]

In order to prove Indian title, the tribe must show by historical evidence that the land in question was part of its ancestral lands and was occupied and controlled exclusively by it.[45] (A tribe can permit other tribes to share its land without losing aboriginal title, but lands continuously wandered over by adverse tribes cannot be claimed by any of these tribes as aboriginal lands.)[46] A tribe need not show that the federal government recognized its right of occupancy through a treaty, statute, or other formal act but only that they lived on certain lands continuously and the federal government has never taken any formal action to terminate the tribe's right of occupancy.[47]

Indian title is a sacred and valuable property interest.[48] It is a right that only the federal government can extinguish, and a cancellation of Indian title "cannot be lightly implied in view of the avowed solicitude of the Federal Government for the welfare" of Indians.[49] Some formal act showing an intention to terminate Indian title is required, such as an order from Congress removing a tribe from its territory so that the land could be used for another purpose.[50] When Congress accepts a new state into the Union, that state must honor and respect any Indian title that exists within its borders.[51] However, when a tribe abandons its homelands, such as when it agrees to relocate to a new reservation, it loses its Indian title.[52]

The tribe's interest in continued occupancy is so important that the tribe is entitled to bring a court action to eject trespassers;[53] the federal government has an obligation to help the tribe eject trespassers;[54] and a court must recognize a tribe's Indian title unless it is clear that Congress intended to abolish the tribe's interest.[55] For example, even if the United States sells ancestral tribal land to a railroad, the railroad takes that land subject to aboriginal Indian title unless Congress clearly indicates otherwise.[56] Indian title includes the right not only to occupy the property but also to use its natural resources, such as water and timber, and to hunt and fish on the property.[57] Likewise, when Congress extinguishes Indian title, the tribe loses its interests in the land as well as its right to use the natural resources found on or within the land.[58]

Indian title is an important protection. In several recent cases, federal courts have upheld a tribe's Indian title even though the present-day non-Indian "owners" of these lands could trace their own "titles" back 150 years during which time Indians did not occupy the territory.[59] The fact is, unless aboriginal title has been extinguished by Congress, any grant or conveyance of the property, whether by the Indian tribe, the United States, a state, or any other party, is subject to the tribe's superior right of occupancy. Several cases involving Indian title are presently being litigated in New York, and are discussed in chapter 15, section E.

When the federal government extinguishes Indian title, must it compensate the tribe for the value of its occupancy rights?

As just explained, every tribe has the right to occupy its ancestral lands until Congress decides otherwise, a right known as Indian title. However, there are two kinds of Indian title: *recognized* and *unrecognized*. Recognized title carries a legal right that the other does not—the right to compensation if it is terminated by Congress.

Indian title becomes "recognized" when Congress has taken some formal action, whether by treaty, statute, or agreement, that exhibits a clear intention to confer upon the tribe a right to permanent occupancy. Once that occurs, any subsequent removal of this protected interest by the federal government must be compensated under the Just Compensation Clause of the Fifth Amendment to the U.S. Constitution.[60] For example, a tribe is entitled to be compensated if it has a treaty guarantee of permanent and exclusive occupancy and the United States then places a second tribe on the reservation.[61] On the other hand, when Congress has not "specifically recognized" a right to permanent ownership, Indian title "may be extinguished by the government without compensation."[62]

The Supreme Court has been criticized for holding that Indian title is not protected by the Fifth Amendment unless it has been officially recognized.[63] In enacting the Alaska Native Claims Settlement Act of 1971, Congress decided to compensate Alaska Natives for all claims based upon Indian title, whether recognized or not,[64] but most other tribes have not been so fortunate.[65]

May individual Indians claim Indian title to land?

Yes. Individual Indians who can show that their lineal descendants held and exclusively occupied, as individuals, a particular tract of land from time immemorial and that this title has never been extinguished by Congress have a continued possessory interest (Indian title) in that land.[66]

May the courts reverse a congressional decision to extinguish Indian title?

No. The extinguishment of Indian title by Congress is not subject to review by the courts, the Supreme Court has held.[67] The power of Congress in this regard is supreme, and neither the manner nor the time of extinguishment may be challenged. A court may only determine whether the Indian title being extinguished is recognized title for which compensation must be paid. However, only Congress may extinguish Indian title. Indian title may not be extinguished even by a President or a federal agency.[68]

NOTES

1. *See* Felix Cohen, *Handbook of Federal Indian Law* (Charlottesville: Michie Co., 1982) at 19–24.

2. *Nofire v. U.S.,* 164 U.S. 657 (1897).

3. *Halbert v. U.S.,* 283 U.S. 753 (1931). Congress determines who is an Indian for federal purposes, not the tribe. *See Simmons v. Eagle Seelatsee,* 244 F. Supp. 808, 813–15 (E. D. Wash. 1965), *aff'd per curiam,* 384 U.S. 209 (1966).

4. *See Montana ex rel. Poll, Lindlief and Juneau v. Montana Ninth Judicial Dist. Court,* 851 P.2d 405 (Mont. 1993).

5. *See State v. Sebastian,* 701 A.2d 13 (Conn. 1997) (holding that someone can be an Indian under tribal law but not under state or federal law for purposes of criminal jurisdiction).

6. *See, e.g.,* 25 U.S.C. Sec. 479. In *LaPier v. McCormick,* 986 F.2d 303 (Mont. 1993), the court held that an Indian whose tribe was terminated by the federal government is not an "Indian" for purposes of determining criminal jurisdiction. The concept of federal recognition is discussed in ch. 15, sec. F.

7. *See Schmasow v. Native American Center,* 978 P.2d 304 (Mont. 1999) (finding that an Indian from a terminated tribe qualified for an employment preference as an Indian but not for certain other benefits as an Indian).

8. *See, e.g., Malone v. Bureau of Indian Affairs,* 38 F.3d 433 (9th Cir. 1994), and *Zarr*

v. Barlow, 800 F.2d 1484 (9th Cir. 1986) (invalidating an agency regulation that too narrowly restricted eligibility for Indian education benefits).

9. *U.S. v. Keys,* 103 F.3d 758, 761 (9th Cir. 1996); *U.S. v. Dodge,* 538 F.2d 770, 776 (8th Cir. 1976), *cert. denied,* 429 U.S. 1099 (1977).

10. *Martinez v. Southern Ute Tribe,* 249 F.2d 915, 920 (10th Cir. 1957); *Ordinance 59 Ass'n v. U.S. Dept. of Interior Secretary,* 163 F.3d 1150, 1160 (10th Cir. 1998). Congress has allowed Indians who are not members of federally recognized tribes to qualify for Indian health care benefits. *See* 25 U.S.C. Sec. 1603(c).

11. *U.S. v. Rogers,* 45 U.S. 567 (1846); *Montana ex rel. Poll,* note 4 above; *State v. Attebery,* 519 P.2d 53 (Ariz. 1974).

12. 42 Stat. 253, codified as 8 U.S.C. Sec. 1401(a)(2).

13. *In re Heff,* 197 U.S. 488 (1905).

14. *U.S. v. Nice,* 241 U.S. 591 (1916).

15. *Greene v. Babbitt,* 64 F.3d 1266, 1270 (9th Cir. 1995); *U.S. v. Washington,* 384 F. Supp. 312, 406 (W. D. Wash. 1974), *aff'd,* 520 F.2d 676 (9th Cir. 1975), *cert. denied,* 423 U.S. 1086 (1976).

16. *Golden Hill Paugussett Tribe of Indians v. Weicker,* 39 F.3d 51, 57–59 (2d Cir. 1994); *Cook Inlet Native Ass'n v. Bowen,* 810 F.2d 1471 (9th Cir. 1987); *Joint Tribal Council of Passamaquoddy Tribe v. Morton,* 528 F.2d 370 (1st Cir. 1975); *Schmasow,* note 7 above; *State v. Dana,* 404 A.2d 551 (Maine 1979), *cert. denied,* 444 U.S. 1098 (1980).

17. When this occurs, a member of one tribe can acquire certain rights in the other tribe that otherwise would not have been available. *See Williams v. Clark,* 742 F.2d 549 (9th Cir. 1984), *cert. denied sub nom. Elvrum v. Williams,* 471 U.S. 1015 (1985).

18. *See Cherokee Nation of Oklahoma v. Babbitt,* 117 F.3d 1489 (D.C. Cir. 1997) (holding that the Delaware Tribe, though ethnologically distinct, was merged by Congress with the Cherokee Nation of Oklahoma as one tribe politically).

19. *Alaska v. Native Village of Venetie Tribal Government,* 522 U.S. 520, 527 n.1 (1998); *South Dakota v. Yankton Sioux Tribe,* 522 U.S. 329, 333 (1998); *Indian Country, U.S.A., Inc. v. Oklahoma Tax Comm'n,* 829 F.2d 967, 973 (10th Cir. 1987), *cert. denied sub nom. Oklahoma Tax Comm'n v. Muscogee (Creek) Nation,* 487 U.S. 1218 (1988).

20. *See* cases cited in note 19 above. Criminal jurisdiction in Indian country is discussed in ch. 8 and civil jurisdiction in ch. 9.

21. *U.S. v. Cook,* 922 F.2d 1026, 1031 (2d. Cir.), *cert. denied,* 500 U.S. 941 (1991); *U.S. v. Levesque,* 681 F.2d 75, 78 (1st Cir.), *cert. denied,* 459 U.S. 1089 (1982); *U.S. v. Sohappy,* 770 F.2d 816 (9th Cir. 1985), *cert. denied,* 477 U.S. 906 (1986); *State v. Payne,* 892 P.2d 1032, 1033 (Utah 1995).

22. 18 U.S.C. Sec. 1151(a). *See Seymour v. Superintendent,* 368 U.S. 351 (1962); *U.S. v. John,* 437 U.S. 634 (1978).

23. 18 U.S.C. Sec. 1151(c). *See Gourneau v. Smith,* 207 N.W.2d 256 (N.D. 1973). However, as discussed in ch. 9, there are situations in which the state, not the tribe, has jurisdiction to regulate activities on rights-of-way within the reservation.

24. *U.S. v. John,* 437 U.S. 634 (1978); *Langley v. Ryder,* 778 F.2d 1092, 1094–95 (5th Cir. 1985).

25. *Indian Country, U.S.A.,* note 19 above.

26. *Id.*

27. 18 U.S.C. Sec. 1151(b).

28. *See Native Village of Venetie,* note 19 above; *U.S. v. Sandoval,* 231 U.S. 28 (1913); *U.S. v. McGowan,* 302 U.S. 535 (1938).

29. *Sandoval,* note 28 above; *State v. Warner,* 379 P.2d 66 (N.M. 1963).

30. *U.S. v. South Dakota,* 665 F.2d 837 (8th Cir. 1981), *cert. denied,* 459 U.S. 823 (1983); *U.S. v. Martine,* 442 F.2d.1022 (10th Cir. 1971).

31. *C.M.G. v. Oklahoma,* 594 P.2d 798 (Okla. Ct. App.), *cert. denied,* 444 U.S. 992 (1979).

32. *U.S. v. Roberts, 185 F.3d 1125 (10th Cir. 1999), cert. denied,* 120 S.Ct.1960 (2000).

33. *See Blunk v. Arizona Dept. of Transportation,* 177 F.3d 879, 883–84 (9th Cir. 1998); *Narragansett Indian Tribe v. Narragansett Electric Co.,* 89 F.3d 908 (1st Cir. 1996); *Buzzard v. Oklahoma Tax Comm'n,* 992 F.2d 1073 (10th Cir.), *cert. denied,* 510 U.S. 994 (1993).

34. *Roberts,* note 32 above.

35. *U.S. v. South Dakota,* note 30 above; *Martine,* note 30 above; *Levesque,* note 21 above.

36. *Native Village of Venetie,* note 19 above.

37. *See, e.g., Pittsburgh and Midway Coal Mining Co. v. Watchman,* 52 F.3d 1531, 1545 (10th Cir. 1995), using a four-part test that considered, among other things, who lived in the area. The test used by the Supreme Court in *Venetie* is entirely a land-based inquiry.

38. 18 U.S.C. Sec. 1151(c). *See U.S. v. Ramsey,* 271 U.S. 467 (1926); *Beardslee v. U.S.,* 387 F.2d 280 (8th Cir. 1967).

39. *DeCoteau v. District County Court,* 420 U.S. 425, 427, 429 (1975); *Oklahoma Tax Comm'n v. Citizen Band Potawatomi Indian Tribe,* 498 U.S. 505 (1991); *Ahboah v. Housing Authority of Kiowa Tribe,* 660 P.2d 625 (Okla. 1983); *Ramsey,* note 38 above.

40. *Minnesota v. Hitchcock,* 185 U.S. 373, 390 (1902); *Sac and Fox Tribe of Mississippi,* 596 F.2d 145 (8th Cir. 1978), *cert. denied,* 439 U.S. 955 (1978).

41. 21 U.S. 543 (1823).

42. *See* J. Y. Henderson, "Unraveling the Riddle of Aboriginal Title," 5 *Am. Indian L. Rev.* 75 (1977).

43. Robert B. Porter, "A Proposal to the *Hanodaganyas* to Decolonize Federal Indian Control Law," 31 *Univ. of Mich. J. of Law Reform* 899, 921 (1998) (footnotes omitted).

44. *See U.S. v. Santa Fe Pacific R.R. Co.,* 314 U.S. 339 (1941); *Tee-Hit-Ton Indians v. U.S.,* 348 U.S. 272 (1955); *Oneida Indian Nation v. County of Oneida,* 414 U.S. 661 (1974); *Alabama–Coushatta Tribe of Texas v. U.S.,* 2000 WL 1013532 (Fed. Cl. 2000). For a critical review of the doctrine of discovery and conquest and Indian title, *see* Henderson, note 42 above.

45. *Santa Fe,* note 44 above. *See also Six Nations v. U.S.,* 173 Ct. Cl. 899, 911 (1965); *Sac and Fox Tribe of Indians of Oklahoma v. U.S.,* 315 F.2d 896, 903 (Ct. Cl. 1963).

46. *Santa Fe,* note 44 above, 314 U.S. at 345.*See Alabama-Coushatta Tribe,* note 44 above, 2000 WL at *12–14, and *Strong v. U.S.,* 518 F.2d 556, 561 (Ct. Cl.), *cert. denied,*

423 U.S. 1015 (1975) (discussing the situations in which exclusive possession is not necessary in order to prove Indian title).

47. *See Oneida Indian Nation,* note 44 above, 414 U.S. at 669; *Santa Fe,* note 44 above, 314 U.S. at 347; *Alabama-Coushatta Tribe,* note 44 above, 2000 WL at *12–14.

48. *Santa Fe,* note 44 above, 314 U.S. at 345; *Alabama-Coushatta Tribe,* note 44 above, 2000 WL at *10.

49. *Santa Fe,* note 44 above, 314 U.S. at 354.

50. *U.S. v. Gemmill,* 535 F.2d 1145, 1148–49 (9th Cir.), *cert. denied,* 429 U.S. 982 (1976). *See also Confederated Tribes of Chehalis Indian Reservation v. State of Washington,* 96 F.3d 334, 341–42 (9th Cir. 1996), *cert. denied,* 520 U.S. 1168 (1997) (finding that an Executive Order opening the tribe's aboriginal lands to settlement by whites was sufficient to extinguish the tribe's aboriginal title). *See generally Alabama-Coushatta Tribe,* note 44 above.

51. *Alabama-Coushatta Tribe,* note 44 above, 2000 WL at *40–41; *Lipan Apache Tribe v. U.S.,* 180 Ct. Cl. 487, 498–99 (1967).

52. *Santa Fe,* note 44 above, 314 U.S. at 357–58; *Menominee Indian Tribe v. Thompson,* 161 F.3d 449, 462 (7th Cir. 1998), *cert. denied,* 526 U.S. 1066 (1999).

53. *Oneida Indian Nation,* note 44 above.

54. *Santa Fe,* note 44 above; *Tee-Hit-Ton,* note 44 above.

55. *Santa Fe,* note 44 above.

56. *Id. See also Lac Courte Oreilles Band of Lake Superior Chippewa Indians v. Voight,* 700 F.2d 341 (7th Cir.), *cert. denied,* 464 U.S. 805 (1983).

57. *See U.S. v. Adair,* 723 F.2d 1394, 1413–14 (9th Cir. 1983), *cert. denied,* 467 U.S. 1252 (1984), and cases cited therein.

58. *Confederated Tribes of Chehalis,* note 50 above, 96 F.3d at 341; *Western Shoshone Nat'l Council v. Molini,* 9511 F.2d 200, 202–3 (9th Cir. 1991), *cert. denied,* 506 U.S. 822 (1992).

59. *Catawba Indian Tribe v. South Carolina,* 865 F.2d 1444 (4th Cir.), *cert. denied,* 491 U.S. 906 (1989).

60. *Tee-Hit-Ton,* note 44 above; *Shoshone Tribe of Indians v. U.S.,* 299 U.S. 476 (1937); *Karuk Tribe of California v. Ammon,* 209 F.3d 1366, 1373 (Fed. Cir. 2000), *cert. denied,* 121 S.Ct. 1402 (2001). However, once the tribe has been paid, Indian title is extinguished. *U.S. v. Dann,* 873 F.2d 1189, 1194 (9th Cir.), *cert. denied,* 493 U.S. 890 (1989).

61. *Shoshone Tribe,* note 60 above. *See also Santa Fe,* note 44 above. Proof that the U.S. failed to honor its obligations under the Indian Nonintercourse Act, 25 U.S.C. Sec. 177, to protect a tribe's land from loss can also be sufficient to entitle a tribe to compensation. *See Alabama-Coushatta Tribe,* note 44 above.

62. *Tee-Hit-Ton,* note 44 above, 348 U.S. at 289. *See also Karuk Tribe,* note 60 above, 209 F.3d at 1380; *Inupiat Community of the Arctic Slope v. U.S.,* 680 F.2d 122 (Ct. Cl.), *cert. denied,* 459 U.S. 969 (1982).

63. *See, e.g.,* Felix Cohen, *The Legal Conscience. Selected Papers of Felix S. Cohen.* Ed. Lucy K. Cohen. (New Haven: Yale Univ. Press, 1960) at 264–67; Henderson, note 42

above. *See also Shoshone Indians v. U.S.,* 324 U.S. 335, 359 (1945) (Douglas, J., dissenting).

64. 42 U.S.C. Secs. 1601 *et seq.* For a further discussion of this act, see ch. 15, sec. B.

65. *See, e.g., Shoshone Indians,* note 63 above; *Tee-Hit-Ton,* note 44 above.

66. *U.S. v. Dann,* note 60 above; *U.S. v. Dann,* 470 U.S. 39, 50 (1985).

67. *Santa Fe,* note 44 above.

68. *Id.; U.S. v. Dann,* note 60 above, 873 F.2d at 1195 n.5.

III

The Trust Responsibility

What is *the doctrine of trust responsibility?*

A principle that "has long dominated the government's dealings with Indians," the Supreme Court noted in 1983, is "the undisputed existence of a general trust relationship between the United States and the Indian people."[1] This relationship is one of the most significant and motivating concepts in federal Indian law.

The Supreme Court first recognized the existence of a federal-Indian trust relationship in its early cases interpreting Indian treaties.[2] Between 1787 and 1871, the United States entered into nearly four hundred treaties with Indian tribes. During those years, "the native nations were still relatively powerful and autonomous," and although the United States might have been able to overpower them in warfare, victory would have been very costly.[3] In an effort to avoid those costs, the United States frequently entered into peace treaties with Indian tribes. In these treaties, the United States obtained the land it wanted from the tribes, and in return, the United States set aside other reservation lands for those tribes and guaranteed that the federal government would respect "the sovereignty of the tribes, . . . would 'protect' the tribes, . . . [and would] provide food, clothing, and services to the tribes."[4]

The Supreme Court has held that treaties of this nature create a special relationship between Indian tribes and the federal government—a unique bond—that obligates the government to keep its end of the bargain, now that the tribes have kept theirs. The promises made in exchange for millions of acres of tribal land impose on the federal government "moral obligations of the highest responsibility and trust."[5] This principle—that the government has a duty to keep its word and fulfill its promises—is known as *the doctrine of trust responsibility.*[6]

32

What does the doctrine of trust responsibility require of federal officials?

In the nearly two centuries since the doctrine of trust responsibility was first recognized by the Supreme Court, the courts, as well as Congress and the executive branch of government, have had numerous occasions to describe the scope of the trust doctrine. During most of the nineteenth century, the trust doctrine was viewed as a source of federal power *over* Indians. For example, the doctrine was cited as a justification for the passage of laws aimed at assimilating Indians into non-Indian society.[7]

Such a "negative" interpretation of the trust doctrine—in which it becomes a sword against Indians rather than a shield for them—was repudiated decades ago. The trust doctrine is viewed today as a source of federal responsibility *to* Indians, creating two sets of commitments, one broad and the other more narrow. Broadly, the trust doctrine requires the federal government to support and encourage tribal self-government and economic prosperity, duties that stem from the government's treaty guarantees to "protect" Indian tribes and respect their sovereignty.[8] In 1977, a Senate report expressed this obligation as follows:

The purpose behind the trust doctrine is and always has been to ensure the survival and welfare of Indian tribes and people. This includes an obligation to provide those services required to protect and enhance Indian lands, resources, and self-government, and also includes those economic and social programs which are necessary to raise the standard of living and social well-being of the Indian people to a level comparable to the non-Indian society.[9]

Under this broad approach, the federal government's trust duty "is owed to all Indian tribes,"[10] including those that did not enter into treaties with the United States.[11] The trust doctrine "transcends specific treaty promises and embodies a clear duty to protect the native land base and the ability of tribes to continue their ways of life."[12]

The second duty under the trust doctrine arises from the fact that Congress, primarily through legislation, has placed most tribal land and other property under the control of federal agencies, depriving tribes of the ability to manage these resources on their own. As explained in chapter 5, virtually everything a tribe might wish to do with its land and other property must be approved by the federal government, which actively supervises most tribal resources. Courts have recognized that when Congress delegates to federal officials the power to control or manage tribal resources, their actions with respect to those resources must then "be judged by the most exacting fiduciary standards."[13] A trustee-beneficiary relationship is created under the law, similar to the relationship between a guardian and a ward.[14] As a result, the federal government, as the guardian of tribal resources, must remain loyal to its Indian beneficiaries, using utmost skill both to preserve the property entrusted to its care and make it productive.[15] As the Supreme Court noted in 1993, "[T]he law is well established that the Government in its dealings with Indian tribal property acts in a fiduciary capacity."[16]

Although there exists a general trust relationship between the federal government and Indian tribes, it is often difficult to identify any precise tasks the government must undertake in order to fulfill its responsibilities. This difficulty is illustrated by two Supreme Court cases, one decided in 1980, *United States v. Mitchell (Mitchell I)*[17] and the other in 1983, *United States v. Mitchell (Mitchell II).*[18]

The plaintiffs in *Mitchell I* were the Quinault Indian Tribe, as well as tribal members who owned individual parcels of trust land on the reservation. They sued the United States in the Court of Claims to recover damages for the government's alleged mismanagement of timber resources located on their lands. Recovery was sought under the General Allotment Act (GAA)[19] and under various other statutes that imposed on the Department of the Interior a duty to supervise and control the growth and harvesting of timber on Indian lands. The Court of Claims held that the plaintiffs were entitled to damages under the GAA. But the GAA contains no instructions to federal officials on how they must manage tribal timber, and the Supreme Court held that although the GAA created a "general" or "bare" trust relationship between the federal government and the tribe, it imposed no enforceable duties regarding these resources. The Court therefore remanded the case to the Court of Claims to consider whether the plaintiffs' other statutory claims might lead to a different result.

On remand, the Court of Claims again ruled in favor of the plaintiffs but relied this time upon federal statutes and regulations that give federal officials control and supervision over virtually every aspect of tribal timber production, including its harvesting and sale. Given that these laws and regulations require federal officials to perform specific duties in managing

Indian timber resources, the Supreme Court said, they create an enforceable trust obligation to manage them in the beneficiary's best interests. "Where the Federal Government takes on or has control or supervision over tribal monies or properties," the Court explained, "[a] fiduciary relationship normally exists with respect to such monies or properties," unless Congress has provided otherwise.[20] As a result, the plaintiffs were entitled to recover damages from the federal government for the violation of these trust duties.

Thus, the more specific is the obligation, the higher the duty of care.[21] *Mitchell II* "clearly establishes the existence of a fiduciary relationship when statutes and regulations give the Federal Government a pervasive role in management of Indian properties."[22] Federal officials instructed by Congress to manage, control, or supervise tribal resources are duty-bound by the trust doctrine (1) to *consult* with the tribe in determining how best to use those resources,[23] (2) to carefully analyze all relevant information regarding how to manage them,[24] (3) to make their decisions based on the tribe's best interests,[25] and (4) to maintain and provide to the tribe an accurate accounting of all transactions regarding these resources.[26]

How can a statute create a trust responsibility?

It is easier to see how a treaty, as opposed to a statute, can create a trust responsibility. In a treaty, the tribe has exchanged land for promises; therefore, the tribe has a right to have those promises fulfilled. No similar exchange is apparent when Congress enacts a statute. Yet, as *Mitchell II* illustrates, a statute can create trust duties.

This is true for two reasons. First, statutes often are the vehicles by which Congress creates the programs and services necessary to fulfill its treaty promises. Indeed, as explained in the next chapter, given that Congress ended all treaty making with Indian tribes in 1871, legislation is now the primary means by which Congress can satisfy its treaty commitments. The Supreme Court recently noted that "Congress may fulfill its treaty obligations and its responsibilities to the Indian tribes by enacting legislation dedicated to their circumstances and needs."[27]

Second, as discussed earlier, Congress has delegated to federal agencies the power to administer and supervise most Indian resources. Courts have recognized, as the Supreme Court did in *Mitchell II,* that these delegations of authority create a fiduciary duty to manage the resources wisely and in the tribe's best interests, just as the tribe would manage them.[28]

Does the United States have a trust relationship with every Indian tribe?

A broad interpretation of the federal government's trust responsibility would recognize a trust relationship with every Indian tribe. However, the Department of the Interior, which administers most of the federal government's Indian programs, believes that only those tribes officially "recognized" by the Department have a trust relationship with the United States, entitling them to participate in the Department's programs.[29] (The process by which tribes can obtain federal recognition is explained in chapter 15, section F.)

The Supreme Court has yet to determine the extent to which the trust doctrine applies to "nonrecognized" tribes. Several lower federal courts, however, have rejected the Interior Department's position and have held that a nonrecognized tribe may have at least a limited trust relationship with the federal government. For example, courts have held that members of nonrecognized tribes may enforce treaties signed between their tribes and the United States even though the Interior Department does not recognize the continued existence of those tribes.[30] Courts have also held that members of nonrecognized tribes may participate in programs that Congress has not restricted to members of recognized tribes.[31]

Does the trust doctrine apply to individual Indians?

Under a broad interpretation of the trust doctrine, the federal government would owe trust duties to all tribal members, both on and off the reservation. In certain situations, courts have recognized the existence of such a duty,[32] but for the most part, off-reservation Indians have only been allowed to participate in those few federal programs that Congress has expressly made available to them.[33] In 1977, a Senate commission expressed the opinion that the federal government's trust responsibility extends to off-reservation Indians, and it criticized the government for withholding most Indian programs from them.[34] Of course, statutes specifically requiring federal officials to provide services to off-reservation Indians create a trust obligation to do so.[35]

Does the trust responsibility extend to off-reservation activities that affect reservation Indians?

Yes. For example, activities by federal agencies undertaken off the reservation that would diminish on-reservation water supplies[36] or would pollute the reservation[37] have been held to violate the trust doctrine.

May Congress terminate a trust relationship?

Yes. Congress may terminate its trust relationship with an Indian tribe at any time, with or without the tribe's consent.[38] During the "termination era," discussed in chapter 1, Congress terminated its trust relationships with 109 tribes. In each case, it accomplished this by passing a law that prohibited the tribe from exercising governmental powers, required the tribe to distribute all of its property and assets to tribal members or to a state-chartered corporation, eliminated the reservation, and declared that the tribe's trust relationship with the United States had ended.[39]

However, a trust relationship can only be terminated by an express and clear act of Congress.[40] Termination will not be implied, and federal officials must perform their trust duties until directed otherwise by Congress.[41] Even the tribe may not terminate the relationship,[42] nor may a state terminate the tribe's trust relationship with the federal government. The federal government's trust obligations do not diminish if a state decides to provide services to an Indian tribe and the tribe decides to accept those services.[43]

In what ways can a tribe benefit from having a trust relationship with the United States?

Tribes that have a trust relationship with the United States are automatically eligible to participate in numerous federal programs, such as loan, housing, health-care, employment, education, and land development programs. Many of the more than 560 tribes and tribal groups officially recognized by the Department of the Interior would suffer severe economic hardship without this assistance.

Does the trust relationship ever operate to a tribe's detriment?

Yes. There is a constant clash between the federal government's trust responsibilities and the tribe's interest in self-government. The federal government has severely injured tribes in the name of protecting them,[44] and many tribes would rid themselves of the "strings" attached to federal assistance if they could afford to do so.

A significant part of the problem is the paternalistic attitude that the Bureau of Indian Affairs (BIA) has long maintained. As a Senate report stated in 1977:

The Bureau of Indian Affairs . . . has used the trust doctrine as a means to develop a paternalistic control over the day to day affairs of Indian tribes and individuals. Federal-Indian trust law, as expressed by both Congress and the courts, calls for Federal protection, not Federal domination. . . . The relationship should be thought of not only in the terms of a moral and legal duty, but also as a partnership agreement to insure that Indian tribes have available to them the tools and resources to survive as distinct political and cultural groups.[45]

Federal agencies have been reluctant to allow Indians to exercise greater control over their lives and property and are notorious for mismanaging Indian resources. In other words, not only have federal agencies maintained a tight grip on Indian resources but they have mismanaged them as well. As one federal appellate court recently stated, it is "clear that the federal government has failed time and again to discharge its fiduciary duties" to Indians.[46] Court cases have found, for example, that the Indian Health Service had ignored a duty to provide adequate health care consistent with federal law;[47] that the Secretary of the Interior had tried to evade duties to an Indian tribe required by the Indian Gaming Regulatory Act;[48] and that the Secretary had violated trust duties by assisting a coal company during the company's negotiations with an Indian tribe, deliberately misleading the tribe and acting in "direct contravention" of his statutory obligations.[49] A court also criticized the Secretary for claiming that the Department of the Interior had no duty to assist Indians obtain a public education, a claim the court called "simply incredible."[50]

In the most highly publicized case involving violations of trust duties in recent years, a lawsuit filed in 1996 alleged that more than $2 *billion* was missing from bank accounts managed by government officials for some three hundred thousand tribal members. The Secretary of the Interior admitted during the trial that serious errors in judgment had been made and that his department had not honored its trust obligations. The judge presiding over the case found that the federal defendants had even attempted to "cover-up [their] misconduct."[51] Ultimately, the court found a "century-long reign of mismanagement" and violations of the law, and it ordered massive reforms.[52]

This is not to say that federal agencies always act improperly regarding tribal interests; in fact, federal agencies and their many dedicated employees assist tribes every day in countless ways. Federal agencies have even been sued by non-Indian groups that have accused them of unfairly *protecting* tribal interests. For example, the Army Corps of Engineers was sued when it refused to allow a non-Indian company to construct a fish farm in a manner that the Corps said would interfere with an Indian tribe's treaty right to fish at that location.[53] The National Park Service was sued by non-Indians for having requested that the public voluntarily refrain from climbing Devil's Tower (located on Park Service lands in Wyoming) during the weeks that local Indian tribes conduct traditional religious ceremonies at that site.[54] The Secretary of Commerce was sued by a group of non-Indians for restricting their access to certain ocean fisheries that were necessary, the Secretary said, to protect Indian treaty fishing rights.[55] In all three cases, the courts upheld the agency actions.

Overall, however, the United States "has been notoriously unfaithful in observing its commitments to the Indian tribes."[56] Even the Secretary of the Interior admitted in 2002 "a need for significant improvement in trust management" of Indian resources.[57] Ultimately, of course, the fault lies with Congress. Congress has the responsibility to honor and fulfill this nation's treaty commitments and to ensure that the Department of the Interior is doing its job properly. Yet Congress has broken nearly all of its Indian treaties and has terminated Indian tribes. Congress has a trust responsibility to enhance the social and economic well-being of Indian people, but Indians continue to be the most disadvantaged and impoverished group in our society, as explained in chapter 1.

The Supreme Court has recognized that Congress cannot always remain loyal to Indians to the exclusion of other interests; in some situations, the government's loyalties are divided. For example, Congress must allocate scarce water resources to federal reclamation projects and military bases as well as to Indian reservations.[58] However, few federal interests are as old and well established as the federal government's trust responsibility to Indians. Unless a compelling government interest requires otherwise, Congress should honor the treaty commitments it made to Indian tribes.

In May 2001, Secretary of the Interior Gail Norton expressed a strong commitment to honor the Department of the Interior's trust responsibilities when she stated: "I believe that bringing the Department's trust practices into the twenty-first century and living up to the fiduciary responsibilities we owe Indian tribes and trust beneficiaries are critical missions of the Department."[59] A few months later, however, Norton announced a plan to transfer all Indian trust-related responsibilities to a new agency that would be created outside the BIA called the Bureau of Indian Trust Assets Management (BITAM).

Norton's plan was immediately and universally criticized within Indian country.[60] Critics charged that BITAM would "gut" the BIA—duplicating rather than streamlining the chain of command, thereby making it more difficult for tribes to enforce their rights—and would compete with the BIA for congressional funding. Although agreeing that the BIA must be radically improved, critics claimed that Norton's plan would do more harm than good. A number of tribes and tribal groups offered alternative plans.[61]

Particularly aggravating to tribes was the fact that no one within the BIA had consulted with tribal leaders while developing the BITAM proposal. In 1994 and again in 2000, President Bill Clinton issued two executive orders[62] that require all officials within the executive branch of government to consult with Indian tribes prior to and in conjunction with any administrative activity that would directly impact them. These orders were not repealed by Clinton's successor, George W. Bush, who took office in January 2001, and therefore should have been followed by Norton. Indeed, due to the government's trust responsibilities to Indian tribes, a federal agency normally must consult with its constituent tribes, and these recent executive orders merely codified and helped further explain existing obligations.[63] Consultation, of course, requires more than the giving of an ultimatum and more than just a discussion. It requires that the agency inform the tribe of all the facts, give the tribe sufficient time to consider the situation in the fashion most appropriate to the tribe, and then accept the tribe's solution unless compelling reasons require otherwise. Perhaps nothing else is more important to the future of federal-tribal relations than the development of meaningful consultation. As one commentator has stated, "successful consultations between tribal liaisons and federal decision makers—far beyond the halls of Congress—can contribute to the creation of more enlightened, better constructed, and more effective federal policies, projects, and regulations," greatly assisting both tribes and the federal government achieve their goals.[64] Norton set a bad precedent early in the Bush administration when she issued the BITAM plan—a plan that would impact every tribe in the country—without consulting with tribal leaders. Ultimately, Norton withdrew her initial plan, to the great relief of tribes, and is currently considering tribal proposals.

Can the federal government's trust responsibilities be enforced by the courts if it is being violated?

It depends on whether the trust responsibility is being violated by Congress or by a federal agency. As explained in chapter 5, Congress has plenary power to regulate Indian affairs, and courts cannot order Congress to undertake any actions on behalf of Indians or tribes. With respect to Congress, then, the trust responsibility is a moral and ethical rather than a legally enforceable duty.[65] In fact, if Congress decides to terminate an Indian program—or even terminate an Indian tribe—a federal court has no authority to prevent it.[66] Indians thus must rely on the good faith of Congress to keep the promises it made more than a century ago in exchange for Indian land.

However, Indians and tribes *can* compel federal officials to perform the duties Congress has delegated to them because Congress has the authority to modify a trust relationship, but administrative agencies do not. Federal officials must faithfully execute their trust duties, and courts are required to carefully scrutinize their actions.[67] Even when a statute allows federal officials to make choices and exercise discretion, such as deciding when to lease tribal land and at what price, these agencies have an "overriding duty . . . to deal fairly with Indians,"[68] and their actions are judged by the "stricter standards" that apply to a fiduciary.[69] Indians have successfully used the trust doctrine, for example, to prevent federal officials from selling tribal land;[70] from diverting water from their reservations;[71] from denying them access to their property;[72] from mismanaging their timber, oil, and other natural resources;[73] from failing to maintain in a reasonable state of repair trust land used by the government;[74] and from failing to properly manage and distribute funds held by the government for Indians and tribes.[75] Indians have obtained money damages for injuries caused by agency mismanagement.[76] Chapter 18 explains how to file a lawsuit against federal officials who are violating their trust obligations.

The doctrine of trust responsibility also plays an important role in *interpreting* federal statutes and treaties, many of which contain vague and ambiguous provisions. As a result of the trust doctrine, an unclear term in a treaty or statute must be interpreted in the manner most helpful to the tribe. Given the trust doctrine, courts must always assume that Congress intends to assist rather than injure a tribe, and interpreting laws and treaties in favor of the tribe is consistent with that assumption. As one court recently stated, as a result of "the unique trust relationship between the federal government and Native Americans," if an ambiguity in a statute or treaty "can reasonably be construed as the Tribe would have it construed, it must be construed that way."[77] Thus, federal officials, as a result of the trust doctrine, should interpret their responsibilities to Indians broadly and assist them to the maximum extent allowable under the treaties and statutes they are implementing.

NOTES

1. *U.S. v. Mitchell,* 463 U.S. 206, 225 (1983). *See also Cobell v. Norton,* 240 F.3d 1081, 1098 (D.C. Cir. 2001) ("the government has longstanding and substantial trust obligations to Indians"); Felix Cohen, *Handbook of Federal Indian Law* (Charlottesville: Michie Co., 1982) at 221 (stating that the trust doctrine is "one of the primary cornerstones of Indian law").

2. *Cherokee Nation v. Georgia,* 30 U.S. 1 (1831); *Worcester v. Georgia,* 31 U.S. 515 (1832).

3. M. C. Woods, "Indian Land and the Promise of Native Sovereignty: The Trust Doctrine Revisited," *Utah L. Rev.* 1471, 1496–97 (1994).

4. *Id.* at 1497 (footnotes omitted).

5. *Seminole Nation v. U.S.,* 316 U.S. 286, 296–97 (1942). *See also U.S. v. Mitchell,* 463 U.S. 206, 225 (1983); *Morton v. Mancari,* 417 U.S. 535, 551–52 (1974); *U.S. v. Mason,* 412 U.S. 391, 397 (1973).

6. For a further discussion of the trust doctrine, *see* Woods, note 3 above; Reid Chambers, "Judicial Enforcement of the Federal Trust Responsibility to Indians," 27 *Stan. L. Rev.* 1213 (1975); Nancy Carter, "Race and Power Politics as Aspects of Federal Guardianship over American Indians: Land Related Cases, 1887–1924," 4 *Am. Indian L. Rev.* 197 (1976); A. Skibine, "Gaming on Indian Reservations: Defining The Trustee's Duty in the Wake of *Seminole Tribe v. Florida,*" 29 *Ariz. St. L. J.* 121, 142–69 (1997).

7. *See U.S. v. Kagama,* 118 U.S. 375 (1886).

8. *See Jicarilla Apache Tribe v. Supron Energy Corp.,* 782 F.2d 855 (10th Cir. 1986) *(en banc), adopting in relevant part* 728 F.2d 1555, 1567 (10th Cir. 1984) (dissenting opinion), *modified,* 793 F.2d 1171, *cert. denied,* 479 U.S. 970 (1986); *McNabb for McNabb v. Heckler,* 628 F. Supp. 544 (D. Mont. 1986), *aff'd,* 829 F.2d 789 (9th Cir. 1987); *Manchester Band of Pomo Indians, Inc. v. U.S.,* 363 F. Supp. 1238 (N.D. Cal. 1973); *Pyramid Lake Paiute Tribe of Indians v. Morton,* 354 F. Supp. 252 (D.D.C. 1972), *rev'd on other grounds,* 499 F.2d 1095 (D.C. Cir. 1974); *White v. Califano,* 581 F.2d 697 (8th Cir. 1978). *See also* American Indian Policy Review Commission, *Final Report* (Washington, D.C.: Government Printing Office, 1977) at 128–30.

9. American Indian Policy Review Commission, note 8 above, at 130.

10. *Lincoln v. Vigil,* 508 U.S. 182, 195 (1993), quoting with approval *Hoopa Valley Tribe v. Christie,* 812 F.2d 1097, 1102 (9th Cir. 1986).

11. *See U.S. v. Sandoval,* 231 U.S. 28, 48 (1913) (recognizing that a trust relationship exists with the Pueblos of New Mexico, despite the fact that no treaties were signed with any of the Pueblos).

12. Woods, note 3 above, at 1506.

13. *Seminole Nation,* note 5 above, 316 U.S. at 296–97.

14. *See Cherokee Nation v. Georgia,* 30 U.S. 1, 16–17 (1832).

15. *See Mitchell* and *Cobell v. Norton,* note 1 above, and cases cited in note 8 above.

16. *Lincoln v. Vigil,* note 10 above, 508 U.S. at 194 (internal quotation omitted).

17. 445 U.S. 535 (1980).

18. 463 U.S. 206 (1983).

19. 25 U.S.C. Secs. 331 *et seq.*

20. *Mitchell,* note 1 above, 463 U.S. at 225 (internal quotation omitted).

21. *See Navajo Nation v. U.S.,* 263 F.3d 1325, 1328–29 (Fed. Cir. 2001), *cert. granted,* 122 S.Ct. 2326 (2002); *McNabb for McNabb v. Bowen,* 829 F.2d 787, 792 (9th Cir. 1987). Thus, statutes that create no specific duties create no enforceable trust obligations. *See Mitchell v. U.S.,* 445 U.S. 535 (1980); *Lincoln v. Vigil,* note 10 above.

22. *Cheyenne-Arapaho Tribes of Oklahoma v. U.S.,* 966 F.2d 583, 589 (10th Cir. 1992), *cert. denied,* 507 U.S. 1003 (1993). *See also Cobell v. Norton,* note 1 above, 240 F.3d at 1088; *Brown v. U.S.,* 86 F.3d 1554, 1559–63 (Fed. Cir. 1996); *Assiniboine and Sioux Tribes of Fort Peck Indian Reservation v. Board of Oil and Gas Conservation of State of Montana,* 792 F.2d 782 (9th Cir. 1986); *Jicarilla Apache,* note 8 above, 728 F.2d at 1563–73. *See also Pelt v. Utah,* 104 F.3d 1534 (10th Cir. 1996) (holding that a federal statute delegating authority to state officials over Indian property creates trust duties that can be enforced against those officials).

23. *See, e.g., Klamath Tribes v. U.S.,* 1996 WL 924509 at *8 (D. Or. 1996). For a discussion of what constitutes meaningful consultation, and the importance of it, *see* notes 62–64 below and accompanying text.

24. *Woods Petroleum Corp. v. Dept. of Interior,* 47 F.3d 1032, 1038–41 (10th Cir.) *(en banc), cert. denied,* 516 U.S. 808 (1995); *Cheyenne-Arapahoe Tribes,* note 22 above.

25. *See* cases cited in notes 21 and 22 above and *Jicarilla Apache,* note 8 above.

26. *Cobell v. Norton,* note 1 above, 240 F.3d at 1103–5; *Yankton Sioux Tribe v. U.S.,* 623 F.2d 159 (Ct. Cl. 1980); *Jicarilla Apache,* note 8 above.

27. *Rice v. Cayetano,* 120 S.Ct. 1044, 1058 (2000).

28. *See* cases cited in notes 21 and 22 above and *Loudner v. U.S.,* 108 F.3d 896, 900–901 (8th Cir. 1997). *See also Miller v. Anadarko Area Director,* IBIA 93–126-A (July 6, 1994) *reprinted in* 22 Indian L. Rep. 7003, 7005 (1995) (holding that a statute authorizing the Secretary of the Interior to distribute funds to Indians creates a trust duty to distribute them properly).

29. The subject of recognition is discussed in ch. 15, sec. F.

30. *U.S. v. Washington,* 384 F. Supp. 312 (W.D. Wash. 1974), *aff'd,* 520 F.2d 676 (9th Cir. 1975), *cert. denied,* 423 U.S. 1086 (1976).

31. *See Joint Council of the Passamaquoddy Tribe v. Morton,* 528 F.2d 370 (1st Cir. 1975) (holding that nonrecognized tribes enjoy protection under the Indian Nonintercourse Act, 25 U.S.C. Sec. 177); *Alabama-Coushatta Tribe of Texas v. U.S.,* 2000 WL 1013532 at *46–47 (Fed. Cl. 2000) (same); *Gibson v. Babbitt,* 72 F. Supp.2d 1356, 1360 (S.D. Fla. 1999) (recognizing that Congress has provided certain health care benefits to members of nonrecognized Indian tribes).

32. *See Morton v. Ruiz,* 415 U.S. 199, 237–38 (1974); *U.S. v. Holliday,* 70 U.S. 407 (1865); *Loudner,* note 28 above; *Pelt,* note 22 above; *McNabb,* note 21 above.

33. *But see Morton v. Ruiz,* note 32 above (holding that the BIA could not unilaterally deny welfare benefits to off-reservation Indians without following its formal rule-making procedures and giving Indians an opportunity to comment on the proposed rule).

34. American Indian Policy Review Commission, note 8 above, at 131–32.

35. *Loudner,* note 28 above; *Pelt,* note 22 above; *Malone v. BIA,* 38 F.3d 433, 438 (9th Cir. 1994); *St. Paul Intertribal Housing Bd. v. Reynolds,* 564 F. Supp. 1408 (D. Minn. 1983); *Eric v. Secretary of U.S. Dept. of Housing and Urban Development,* 464 F. Supp. 44 (D. Alaska 1978).

36. *Pyramid Lake,* note 8 above.

37. *Nance v. Environmental Protection Agency,* 645 F.2d 701 (9th Cir. 1981), *cert. denied,* 454 U.S. 1081 (1981).

38. *Menominee Tribe of Indians v. U.S.,* 391 U.S. 404 (1968).

39. *See, e.g.,* 25 U.S.C. Secs. 564, 677, 691. The subject of termination is also discussed in ch. 5, sec. B.

40. *Menominee Tribe,* note 38 above; *Heckman v. U.S.,* 224 U.S. 413 (1912); *U.S. v. Nice,* 241 U.S. 591 (1916).

41. *Passamaquoddy Tribe,* note 31 above.

42. *Kennerly v. District Court of 9th Judicial Dist. of Montana,* 400 U.S. 423 (1971); *Passamaquoddy Tribe,* note 31 above.

43. *See* cases cited in note 42 above.

44. This topic has received considerable attention. *See, e.g.,* Vine Deloria Jr., *Custer Died for Your Sins* (New York: Avon Books, 1969); E. S. Cahn, ed., *Our Brother's Keeper: The Indian in White America* (New York: World Publishing, 1969); American Indian Policy Review Commission, note 8 above, at 121–38; Robert B. Porter, "A Proposal to the *Hanodaganyas* to Decolonize Federal Indian Control Law," 31 *Univ. of Mich. J. of Law Reform* 899 (1998).

45. American Indian Policy Review Commission, note 8 above, at 106, 127. *See also* authorities cited in note 44 above.

46. *Cobell v. Norton,* note 1 above, 240 F.3d 1081, 1086 (D.C. Cir. 2001).

47. *See McNabb,* note 21 above.

48. *Pueblo of Sandia v. Babbitt,* 47 F. Supp.2d 49 (D.D.C. 1999).

49. *Navajo Nation,* note 21 above, 263 F.3d at 1332.

50. *Meyers by and through Meyers v. Board of Educ. of San Juan Sch. Dist.,* 905 F. Supp. 1544, 1562 (D. Utah 1995).

51. *Cobell v. Babbitt,* 37 F. Supp.2d 6, 13 (D.D.C. 1999).

52. *Cobell v. Babbitt,* 91 F. Supp.2d 1, 53 (D.D.C. 1999), *aff'd in relevant part,* 240 F.3d 1081 (D.C. Cir. 2001).

53. *Northwest Sea Farms, Inc. v. U.S. Army Corps of Engineers,* 931 F. Supp. 1515 (W.D. Wash. 1996).

54. *Bear Lodge Multiple Use Ass'n. v. Babbitt,* 175 F.3d 814 (10th Cir. 1999), *cert. denied,* 120 S.Ct. 1530 (2000).

55. *Parravano v. Masten,* 70 F.3d 539 (9th Cir. 1995), *cert denied,* 518 U.S. 1016 (1996).

56. American Indian Policy Review Commission, note 8 above, at 130. *See also U.S. v. Ahtanum Irrig. Dist.,* 236 F.2d 321, 328 (9th Cir. 1956), *cert. denied,* 352 U.S. 988 (1957), and cases cited in notes 8 and 22 above.

57. Gale Norton, "American Indian Trust Reform: The Challenge to Consensus," *reprinted in Indian Country Today* (Feb. 27, 2002 at A5.)

58. *Nevada v. U.S.*, 463 U.S. 110 (1983).

59. Statement of Gail Norton made May 20, 2001, quoted in *Indian Country Today* (July 18, 2001) at A1.

60. *See* "Tribes Prepare Alternative Trust Plan," *Indian Country Today* (Jan. 23, 2002) at A1, A2 (noting that "the tribes in unison [were] against the plan."); Forrest Gerard, "An Alternative Trust Plan For Interior," *reprinted in Indian Country Today* (Dec. 19, 2001) at A5; Gregg Bourland, "Position Paper on Trust Reform," *reprinted in Indian County Today* (Jan. 23, 2002) at A5.

61. *See* sources cited in note 60 above.

62. *See* ch. 1, notes 81 and 82 and accompanying text.

63. *See Pueblo of Sandia v. U.S.*, 50 F.3d 856, 862 (10th Dir. 1995); *Oglala Sioux Tribe of Indians v. Andrus*, 603 F.2d 707, 720 (8th Cir. 1979); *Klamath Tribes*, note 23 above; *Lower Brule Sioux Tribe v. Deer*, 911 F. Supp. 395 (D.S.D. 1995); *Mescalero Apache Tribe v. Rhoades*, 804 F. Supp. 251, 262 (D.N.M. 1992).

64. Derek Haskew, "Federal Consultation with Indian Tribes: The Foundation of Enlightened Policy Decisions, or Another Badge of Shame?" 24 *Am. Ind. L. Rev.* 21, 23 (1999/2000).

65. *See, e.g., Tee-Hit-Ton Indians v. U.S.*, 348 U.S. 272 (1955); *Mitchell*, note 1 above; Woods, note 3 above, at 512–13.

66. *Lone Wolf v. Hitchcock*, 187 U.S. 553 (1903); *Menominee Tribe*, note 38 above; *Yankton Sioux Tribe v. U.S. Dept. of Health & Human Services*, 869 F. Supp. 760, 766 (D.S.D. 1994).

67. *See* cases cited in notes 8 and 22 above; *Lane v. Pueblo of Santa Rosa*, 249 U.S. 110 (1919); *Cramer v. U.S.*, 261 U.S. 219 (1923); *U.S. v. Creek Nation*, 295 U.S. 103 (1935); *Seminole Nation*, note 5 above.

68. *Morton v. Ruiz*, 415 U.S. 199, 236 (1974).

69. *Cobell v. Norton*, note 1 above, 240 F.3d at 1099 (internal citation omitted).

70. *Lane*, note 67 above; *Cramer*, note 67 above.

71. *Pyramid Lake*, note 8 above.

72. *Creek Nation*, note 67 above.

73. *See Mitchell*, note 1 above; *Navajo Nation*, note 21 above; *Jicarilla Apache*, note 8 above; *Pyramid Lake*, note 8 above; *Klamath Tribes*, note 23 above.

74. *White Mountain Apache Tribe v. U.S.*, 249 F.3d 1364 (Fed. Cir. 2001), *cert. granted*, 122 S.Ct. 1604 (2002).

75. *See Loudner*, note 28 above; *Cobell v. Norton*, note 1 above; *Manchester Band*, note 8 above.

76. *Mitchell*, note 1 above; *Navajo Nation*, note 21 above; *Jicarilla Apache*, note 8 above; *Manchester Band*, note 8 above.

77. *Ramah Navajo Chapter v. Lujan*, 112 F.3d 1455, 1462 (10th Cir. 1997), quoting *Muscogee (Creek) Nation v. Hodel*, 851 F.2d 1439, 1445 (D.C. Cir. 1988), *cert. denied*, 488 U.S. 1010 (1989). *See also Oneida County, N.Y. v. Oneida Indian Nation of New York State*, 470 U.S. 226, 247 (1985); *U.S. v. Washington*, 157 F.3d 630, 643 (9th Cir. 1998), *cert. denied*, 526 U.S. 1060 (1999); *McNabb*, note 21 above, 829 F.2d at 793–94.

IV

Indian Treaties

What is a treaty? Who can sign a treaty on behalf of the United States?

A treaty is a contract between nations. The U.S. Constitution authorizes the President, with the consent of two-thirds of the Senate, to enter into a treaty on behalf of the United States.[1]
The Constitution declares that treaties are "the supreme law of the land."[2] Treaties therefore are superior to state constitutions and state laws and are equal in authority to laws passed by Congress.[3] A treaty can be made on any subject, but it may not deprive a citizen of a right guaranteed by the Constitution; the Constitution is always superior to any law or treaty.[4] The United States has signed hundreds of treaties with foreign countries on subjects such as trade and commerce, fishing on the high seas, international travel, rules of war, and the use of nuclear energy.

How many Indian tribes have treaties with the United States?

Nearly four hundred treaties were signed between Indian tribes and the United States; most tribes have at least one treaty with the federal government.[5] Until 1871, treaties were the accepted method by which the United States conducted its formal relations with Indian tribes. (As explained below, Congress passed a law in 1871 prohibiting the federal government from entering into any additional treaties with Indian tribes.)

What do the Indian treaties say?

The United States began making treaties with Indian tribes soon after the Declaration of Independence was signed in 1776, even before it had won the Revolutionary War in 1783. In 1778, for instance, a treaty was signed with the Delawares in the Ohio valley in an effort to secure the tribe's neutrality and obtain a right of passage across its lands.[6]

The vast majority of Indian treaties signed after 1783 had the same theme: the tribe relinquished land to the United States, and the tribe received a set of promises in exchange. As explained in chapter 3, until the late nineteenth century, Indian tribes were still a military threat, and the United States entered into treaties with tribes in an effort to avoid costly warfare over land. These treaties "expressly recognized the sovereignty of the tribes," and many "contained express assurances that the federal government would 'protect' the tribes. While individual treaties differed from tribe to tribe, . . . nearly all promised a permanent homeland, and many . . . contained federal promises to provide food, clothing, and services to the tribes."[7] In exchange for peace, then, the United States promised in most of its Indian treaties to create a federally protected reservation for the tribe, to respect the tribe's sovereignty, and to provide for the well-being of tribal members.

These treaties usually assured the Indians that they would not be forced to move from their new reservation. In 1854, Sen. Sam Houston described the perpetual nature of these land assignments in the following terms: "As long as water flows, or grass grows upon the earth, or the sun rises to show your pathway, or you kindle your camp fires, so long shall you be protected by this Government, and never again be removed from your present habitations."[8] The 1858 treaty between the United States and the Yankton Sioux Tribe of South Dakota, for example, promised that the federal government would protect the tribe's "quiet and peaceful possession" of its new reservation and that "no white person" would "be permitted to reside or make any settlement upon any part" of the reservation without the tribe's consent.[9] Only rarely has the United States lived up to these types of promises, and those given the Yankton Sioux were broken soon after the treaty was signed.[10]

Is an Indian treaty a grant of rights to a tribe?

As just mentioned, Indian treaties were designed to take land from a tribe in exchange for a set of promises. Little effort was made in any of these treaties to list the rights that each tribe was presumed to retain, such as its inherent right to hunt, fish, and use the water on its territory.

Thus, an Indian treaty should be viewed, the Supreme Court has explained, "not [as] a grant of rights to the Indians, but a grant of rights from them."[11] Tribes therefore have many rights, in addition to those listed in treaties. In fact, any right that a sovereign nation would normally possess that is not expressly extinguished by a treaty (or by a subsequent federal statute) is generally "reserved" to the tribe.[12] This is a fundamental principle of Indian law known as the *reserved rights doctrine*. For example, a tribe retains the right to fish on its reservation even if that right is not conferred in its treaty; the treaty's silence on the subject means that this inherent right was unaffected by the treaty.[13]

Did Indian tribes enter into treaties voluntarily?

Before the War of 1812, most treaties between the United States and Indian tribes were negotiated between relative equals.[14] In 1812, the United States again went to war against England, both to secure the Americans' right to engage in commerce on the high seas without British intervention and to obtain British landholdings in the Mississippi valley and in the Great Lakes. As they did during the American Revolutionary War, a number of tribes sided with the British (including the Shawnees, under the leadership of Tecumseh) because the British had promised to protect tribal lands from American encroachment. American forces defeated the combined British and Indian forces (and Tecumseh was killed in one of the battles).

The American victory in the War of 1812 removed the last major threat of European intervention in U.S. internal affairs. The federal government, which had grown stronger over the years, could now focus its military power on the Indians, and Indian treaties after the War of 1812 were rarely voluntary.[15]

The Creeks, Choctaws, Chickasaws, and Cherokees, located in the southeastern part of the country, suffered some of the first losses. In a series of treaties between 1816 and 1835, all four tribes were compelled to relinquish most of their ancestral homelands in exchange for land in Indian Territory (now the state of Oklahoma) and were forcibly relocated there.

In the decades that followed, tens of thousands of white settlers and prospectors moved westward, and the U.S. Cavalry went along to protect them. One by one, the tribes were forced to sign treaties and were placed on reservations, often hundreds of miles from their original homelands.[16]

Does the United States still enter into treaties with Indian tribes?

No. In 1871, Congress passed a law (Title 25, United States Code, Section 71, often written as 25 U.S.C. § 71) that prohibited the federal government from entering into additional treaties with Indian tribes. Since then, Congress has regulated Indian affairs through legislation.

Section 71 was passed largely because the House of Representatives disliked its exclusion from Indian policy making. Under the Constitution, treaties are made by the President and the Senate, whereas a federal law must be passed by both houses of Congress, the Senate and the House of Representatives. The House pressured the Senate into passing this law so that it could have a hand in formulating Indian policy.[17]

The passage of section 71 had severe consequences for Indian tribes. It was now easy for Congress to take tribal land, given that the passage of a law, unlike the creation of a treaty, does not require the tribe's consent. Numerous laws were passed during the next several decades that removed land the federal government had promised in earlier treaties would belong to the tribes forever.

Did section 71 repeal the earlier Indian treaties? If not, are all of these treaties valid today?

Section 71 states that "no obligation of any treaty . . . shall be hereby invalidated or impaired." Thus, section 71 did not affect any existing Indian treaty.

This does not mean that every Indian treaty is still valid today. In fact, most Indian treaties have been abrogated, that is, broken or breached, by Congress. In *Lone Wolf v. Hitchcock* (1903),[18] the Supreme Court held that an Indian treaty has the same dignity as a federal law but no greater dignity, and in the same way that one federal law can amend or repeal an earlier one, a federal law can amend or repeal an earlier treaty. Congress has abrogated many Indian treaties in this fashion.[19]

The *Lone Wolf* decision has been extensively criticized on the grounds that it dishonors the word of the United States and permits Congress to break promises made to people who have already fulfilled their end of the bargain.[20] It is as if federal officials are now telling Indian tribes: "We've given the matter some more thought, and we've decided not to give you the rest of what we owe you." As former Supreme Court Justice Hugo Black stated in criticizing Indian treaty abrogation: "Great nations, like great men, should keep their word."[21]

Yet the Supreme Court has consistently held that "Congress has the power to abrogate Indians' treaty rights."[22] In a 1977 case, for example, the Court reviewed a treaty in which Congress promised never to diminish the size of a tribe's reservation without the tribe's consent. Not long after the treaty was signed, Congress passed a law reducing the size of the reservation. The Supreme Court upheld the power of Congress to abrogate the treaty and take the land.[23]

The Fifth Amendment to the Constitution provides that Congress may not deprive anyone of "private property . . . without just compensation." Indian treaty rights are a form of private property protected by the Just Compensation Clause, the Supreme Court has held. Therefore, although Congress may abrogate an Indian treaty, it must adequately compensate a tribe for the value of any rights or property that are lost.[24]

Money often provides little "compensation" to people who have lost their homes and sacred lands. In a 1980 case, the Supreme Court awarded the Sioux more than $100 million in compensation for the loss of the Black Hills, their sacred lands, which had been guaranteed to them in a treaty.[25] A number of Sioux then filed a lawsuit seeking to have Congress keep the money and instead return the land, but the court held that the judicial branch of government (the courts) cannot prevent the legislative branch (Congress) from taking Indian land.[26] Most Sioux have refused to accept the compensation that was awarded, and their money sits unclaimed in a federal bank.

How are Indian treaties interpreted when a dispute arises as to their meaning?

Many disputes have arisen over the terms and provisions of Indian treaties, often involving valuable interests in land, water, minerals, and hunting and fishing rights.[27] The Supreme Court has developed three rules that govern the interpretation of Indian treaties, called the "canons of treaty construction." First, ambiguities in treaties must be resolved in favor of the Indians.[28] Second, these treaties must be interpreted as the Indians would have understood them.[29] Finally, Indian treaties must be construed liberally in favor of the Indians.[30] As the Supreme Court recently noted, "[W]e interpret Indian treaties to give effect to the terms as the Indians themselves would have understand them," interpreting them "liberally in favor of the Indians."[31]

These canons benefit the treaty tribe, as the Supreme Court intended they would, to help compensate for the fact that tribes were at a significant disadvantage in the treaty-making process. Treaties were negotiated and written in English. The Indians could never be certain what they were signing and were dependent on government agents to translate for them. Also, most treaties were signed under the threat of force and were inherently unfair. Finally, as explained in chapter 3, a treaty creates a trust relationship between the tribe and the United States, a relationship that requires the federal government to enhance, not injure, tribal interests.[32] Consequently, Indians should receive the benefit of the doubt when questions arise regarding how a treaty should be interpreted. As the Supreme Court explained in a 1989 case interpreting several Indian treaties:

Accordingly, it is the intention of the parties, and not solely that of the superior side, that must control any attempt to interpret the treaties. When Indians are involved, the Court has long given special meaning to this rule. It has held that the United States, as the party with presumptively superior negotiating skills and superior knowledge of the language in which the treaty is recorded, has a responsibility to avoid taking advantage of the other side. The treaty must therefore be construed, not according to the technical meaning of its words to learned lawyers, but in the sense in which they would naturally be understood by the Indians.[33]

These canons have been extremely important to Indians, resulting in favorable court decisions in scores of cases. Recently, for example, the Supreme Court held that an 1837 treaty conferred on the tribe a right to hunt and fish on land outside the reservation because that is probably the way the tribe had interpreted it at the time.[34] Similarly, courts have held that (1) a treaty that gave tribes a right to fish "in common with citizens of the territory" conferred not just an equal opportunity to catch fish but reserved to the tribes a right to capture up to 50 percent of the available resource;[35] (2) a treaty that created a reservation for a tribe to be held "as Indian lands are held," reserved to the tribe enough water to make the reservation productive, even though the treaty said nothing about water rights;[36] (3) a treaty that intended to change a nomadic tribe into an agrarian one entitled the tribe to a sufficient amount of water to raise cattle on the reservation, even though the treaty said nothing about such a right;[37] (4) a treaty that granted Indians the right to fish in a lake adjoining their reservation was interpreted to reserve to them the right to moor their boats on a shoreline now owned by a municipality, even though no language in the treaty expressly conferred that right;[38] and (5) a treaty that granted a tribe "the right, in common with citizens of the United States, to travel upon all public highways," conferred a right to haul tribal timber on state roads without paying state licensing fees, even though the treaty did not expressly confer that tax immunity.[39]

These same canons also apply to the interpretation of federal statutes regarding Indians, and thus they have broad application.[40] As the Supreme Court has stated, "[S]tatutes are to be construed liberally in favor of the Indians, with ambiguous provisions interpreted to their benefit."[41]

What standards are used to determine whether Congress has abrogated a treaty?

Although the Supreme Court held in *Lone Wolf* that Congress may abrogate an Indian treaty at any time, other decisions of the Court have sought to limit the reach of that decision. The Supreme Court has recognized that Indian treaty rights, although capable of being abrogated by Congress, "are too fundamental to be easily cast aside."[42] Thus, a court must not deem a treaty to have been abrogated unless Congress has made its intention to do so "clear and plain."[43] Treaty abrogation may not be inferred.[44]

In 1973, the Supreme Court held that a treaty can be deemed to have been abrogated by a federal law if the law's "surrounding circumstances and legislative history" indicated a congressional intent to abrogate the treaty, even if the law contains no express statement of abrogation.[45] This is known as the *implied abrogation* standard,[46] but even here the evidence must show that Congress actually considered the effect the law would have on the treaty and deliberately chose to abrogate it.[47]

May an administrative agency abrogate an Indian treaty?

No. A federal agency may not abrogate an Indian treaty without specific congressional authorization.[48] For example, the Army Corps of Engineers has the general authority to build dams for flood control, but it may not build a dam on land reserved to an Indian tribe without the express consent of Congress.[49]

May a state abrogate an Indian treaty?

No. A state may not abrogate Indian treaty rights.[50] Even if the treaty was made before the state entered the Union, that state must honor the treaty unless Congress decrees otherwise.[51]

How can treaty rights be enforced?

Indian treaties have the same force and effect as federal statutes. A violation of an Indian treaty is a violation of federal law.

Indians and tribes are entitled to enforce their treaty rights. If state or federal officials are violating these rights, a lawsuit can be filed in federal court to halt the violation.[52] Treaty rights can also be raised as a defense in a state[53] or federal[54] criminal prosecution, and if the treaty protects the activity for which the defendant is being prosecuted, the charges must be dismissed. For example, if state game officials arrest someone for hunting or fishing out of season, that person is not guilty of the charges if he or she was exercising a treaty right at the time in question.[55] Chapter 18 explains how to file a lawsuit to protect treaty rights.

Indian treaties belong not just to Indians; they belong to everyone in the United States. Perhaps some of these treaties seem "unfair" to non-Indians under today's standards, just as many of these treaties seemed unfair to Indians at the time they were written. But regardless of how they seemed then or seem now, the citizens of this country have a legal, moral, and ethical duty to enforce these treaties. Indians paid dearly for their treaty rights, and the federal government should keep its end of the bargain. Some people, calling these treaties "ancient documents," argue that it is time to ignore them. On the contrary, these documents deserve the same continuing respect as the venerable Declaration of Independence and U.S. Constitution. As one court observed in enforcing a century-old treaty, "[T]he mere passage of time has not eroded, and cannot erode, the rights guaranteed by solemn treaties that both sides pledged on their honor to uphold."[56]

NOTES

1. U.S. Const., art. II, sec. 2, cl. 2.
2. U.S. Const. art. VI, sec. 2, provides:

This Constitution, and the laws of the United States which shall be made in Pursuance thereof; and all Treaties made, or which shall be made, under the Authority of the United States, shall be the Supreme Law of the Land; and the Judges in every State shall be bound thereby, any Thing in the Constitution or Laws of any State to the Contrary notwithstanding.

3. *See Worcester v. Georgia,* 31 U.S. 515 (1832); *U.S. v. Forty-Three Gallons of Whiskey,* 93 U.S. 188 (1876).

4. *Asakura v. City of Seattle,* 265 U.S. 332 (1924).

5. For a comprehensive discussion of Indian treaties, *see* Felix Cohen, *Handbook of Federal Indian Law* (Charlottesville: Michie Co., 1982) at 33–67.

6. Colin G. Calloway, *The American Revolution in Indian Country* (Cambridge: Cambridge Univ. Press, 1995) at 37.

7. M. C. Woods, "Indian Land and the Promise of Native Sovereignty: The Trust Doctrine Revisited," 1994 *Utah L. Rev.* 1471, 1497 (footnotes omitted).

8. *Cong. Globe,* 33d Cong., 1st Sess., App. 202 (1854).

9. Arts. IV, X, 11 Stat. 744, 747.

10. *See South Dakota v. Bourland,* 508 U.S. 679 (1993).

11. *U.S. v. Winans,* 198 U.S. 371 (1905).

12. *Menominee Tribe v. U.S.,* 391 U.S. 404 (1968); *U.S. v. Dion,* 476 U.S. 734, 739 (1986); *Swim v. Bergland,* 696 F.2d 712 (9th Cir. 1983).

13. *See Winans,* note 11 above.

14. *Worcester,* note 3 above, 31 U.S. at 548.

15. *See generally* C. Wilkinson and J. Volkman, "Judicial Review of Indian Treaty Abrogation: 'As Long as Water Flows, or Grass Grows upon the Earth'—How Long a Time Is That?" 63 *Cal. L. Rev.* 601, 608–10 (1975).

16. *See, e.g., Choctaw Nation v. Oklahoma,* 397 U.S. 620, 630–31 (1970). *See also* Wilkinson and Volkman, note 15 above, at 608–11.

17. *See Antoine v. Washington,* 420 U.S. 194, 202 (1975).

18. 187 U.S. 553 (1903).

19. *See Hagen v. Utah,* 510 U.S. 399, 404 (1994).

20. *See* Vine Deloria Jr., *Custer Died for Your Sins* (New York: Avon Books, 1969) at 35–59; S. Steiner, *The New Indians* (New York: Dell Publishing Co., 1968) at 160–74. *See also* Wilkinson and Volkman, note 15 above, at 604.

21. *Federal Power Commission v. Tuscarora Indian Nation,* 362 U.S. 99, 142 (1960) (Black, J., dissenting).

22. *South Dakota v. Bourland,* 508 U.S. 679, 687 (1993). *See also Hagen,* note 19 above; *Rosebud Sioux Tribe v. Kneip,* 430 U.S. 584 (1977), and cases cited therein.

23. *Rosebud Sioux Tribe,* note 22 above.

24. *Shoshone Tribe v. U.S.,* 299 U.S. 476, 497 (1937); *Menominee Tribe v. U.S.,* 391 U.S. 404, 413 (1968). *See also Menominee Indian Tribe v. Thompson,* 161 F.3d 449, 457 (7th Cir. 1998), *cert. denied,* 526 U.S. 1066 (1999).

25. *U.S. v. Sioux Nation of Indians,* 448 U.S. 371 (1980).

26. *Sioux Tribe of Indians v. U.S.,* 862 F.2d 275 (8th Cir.), *cert. denied,* 490 U.S. 1075 (1989).

27. *See, e.g.,* cases cited in note 22 above (land rights); *Menominee Tribe,* note 12 above (hunting and fishing rights); *Winters v. U.S.,* 207 U.S. 564 (1908) (water rights).

28. *Carpenter v. Shaw,* 280 U.S. 363, 367 (1930); *DeCoteau v. District County Court for 10th Judicial District,* 420 U.S. 425, 447 (1975); *Bryan v. Itasca County, Minnesota,* 426 U.S. 373, 392 (1976).

29. *Jones v. Meehan,* 175 U.S. 1, 10 (1899); *U.S. v. Shoshone Tribe,* 304 U.S. 111, 116 (1938); *Choctaw Nation v. Oklahoma,* 397 U.S. 620, 631 (1970).

30. *Tulee v. Washington,* 315 U.S. 681, 684–85 (1942); *Washington v. Washington State Commercial Passenger Fishing Vessel Ass'n,* 443 U.S. 658, 690 (1979); *Oneida County, N.Y. v. Oneida Indian Nation of New York State,* 470 U.S. 226, 247 (1985).

31. *Minnesota v. Mille Lacs Band of Chippewa Indians,* 526 U.S. 172, 196, 194 n.5 (1999), respectively.

32. This subject is discussed in ch. 3.

33. *Passenger Fishing Vessel Ass'n,* note 30 above, 443 U.S. at 675–76, *citing Jones,* note 29 above, 175 U.S. at 10. *See also U.S. v. Washington,* 157 F.3d 630, 643 (9th Cir.), *cert. denied,* 526 U.S. 1060 (1999).

34. *Mille Lacs Band,* note 31 above. *See generally* Wilkinson and Volkman, note 15 above. *See also* cases cited in note 27 above.

35. *See Passenger Fishing Vessel Ass'n,* note 30 above, and cases cited therein. Indian fishing rights are discussed in ch. 11.

36. *Winters,* note 27 above. *See also Menominee Tribe,* note 12 above, 391 U.S. at 406.

37. *Swim,* note 12 above. *See also U.S. v. Adair,* 723 F.2d 1394 (9th Cir. 1983), *cert. denied,* 467 U.S. 1252 (1984).

38. *Grand Traverse Band of Ottawa and Chippewa Indians v. Director, Michigan Dept. of Natural Resources,* 141 F.3d 635 (6th Cir.), *cert. denied,* 525 U.S. 1040 (1998).

39. *Cree v. Flores,* 157 F.3d 762 (9th Cir. 1998).

40. *See Montana v. Blackfeet Tribe,* 471 U.S. 759, 766 (1985); *Oneida County, N.Y.,* note 30 above, 470 U.S. at 247; *Ramah Navajo Chapter v. Lujan,* 112 F.3d 1455, 1461–62 (10th Cir. 1997); *Confederated Tribes of Chehalis Indian Reservation v. Washington,* 96 F.3d 334, 342 (9th Cir. 1996), *cert. denied,* 520 U.S. 1168 (1997).

41. *Montana v. Blackfeet Tribe,* 471 U.S. 759, 766 (1985). *See also Connecticut v. U.S. Dept. of the Interior,* 228 F.3d 82, 92 (2d Cir. 2000), *cert. denied,* 121 S.Ct. 1732 (2001).

42. *U.S. v. Dion,* 476 U.S. 734, 739 (1986).

43. *U.S. v. Santa Fe Pacific R.R. Co.,* 314 U.S. 339, 353 (1941).

44. *Mille Lacs Band,* note 31 above, 526 U.S. at 202; *Passenger Fishing Vessel Ass'n,* note 30 above, 443 U.S. at 690; *Menominee Tribe,* note 12 above, 391 U.S. at 412–13. *See also U.S. v. Winnebago Tribe of Nebraska,* 542 F.2d 1002 (8th Cir. 1976).

45. *Mattz v. Arnett,* 412 U.S. 481, 505 (1973).

46. *See South Dakota v. Bourland,* 508 U.S. 679 (1993); *Rosebud Sioux Tribe,* note 22 above; *DeCoteau,* note 28 above. *But see Solem v. Bartlett,* 465 U.S. 463 (1984); *Oregon Dept. of Fish and Wildlife v. Klamath Indian Tribe,* 473 U.S. 753, 754 (1985).

47. *U.S. v. Dion,* 476 U.S. 734, 738–40 (1986). *See also Bourland,* note 46 above, 508 U.S. at 693; *Mille Lacs Band,* note 31 above, 526 U.S. at 202–3; *Oyler v. Allenbrand,* 23 F.3d 292 (10th Cir.), *cert. denied,* 513 U.S. 909 (1994).

48. *Menominee Tribe,* note 12 above; *Oneida Indian Nation v. Oneida County,* 414 U.S. 661, 670 (1974).

49. *Winnebago Tribe,* note 44 above. *See also U.S. v. Eberhardt,* 789 F.2d 1354, 1361 (9th Cir. 1986); *Phillips Petroleum Co. v. U.S. Environmental Protection Agency,* 803 F.2d 545, 556 (10th Cir. 1986); *Donovan v. Coeur d'Alene Tribal Farm,* 751 F.2d 1113, 1116 (9th Cir. 1985).

50. *Winters,* note 27 above; *Arizona v. California,* 373 U.S. 546 (1963).

51. *Winters,* note 27 above; *Antoine,* note 17 above. *See also Mille Lacs Band,* note 31 above, 526 U.S. at 203–8.

52. *See Puyallup Tribe, Inc. v. Dept. of Game of State of Washington,* 433 U.S. 165 (1977); *Winnebago Tribe,* note 44 above.

53. *Mattz,* note 45 above; *Cree v. Flores,* 157 F.3d 762 (9th Cir. 1998).

54. *U.S. v. Cutler,* 37 F. Supp. 724 (D. Idaho 1941); *U.S. v. White,* 508 F.2d 453 (8th Cir. 1974). *See also Dion,* note 42 above.

55. *Antoine,* note 17 above; *Puyallup Tribe,* note 52 above.

56. *U.S. v. Washington,* 384 F. Supp. 312, 406 (W.D. Wash. 1974), *affirmed,* 520 F.2d 676 (9th Cir. 1975), *cert. denied,* 423 U.S. 1086 (1976).

V

Federal Power over Indian Affairs

W hen the American Revolutionary War erupted in 1775, most Indian tribes remained neutral, refusing to get involved in what seemed like an internal, family dispute. Many Indians, though, distrusted the American colonists (who often stole tribal land to expand their settlements) and favored the British (who generally honored their agreements with tribes, and whose king had issued a proclamation in 1763 that sought to prohibit the forceful taking of Indian land by the colonists).[1]

Knowing that tribes tended to sympathize with the British, and fearful that the Indians would support and feed British soldiers, the colonists began destroying Indian crops and villages.[2] These preemptive strikes had the effect of pushing neutral tribes into the British camp. By the end of the war, "most Indian peoples came around to siding with the British,"[3] although several tribes with whom the Americans had developed close ties (such as the Oneidas, Tuscaroras, Mohegans, and Pequots), supported the colonists, and many members of these tribes died alongside their American allies.[4]

The American Revolutionary War resulted in "a total war in Indian country" and was disastrous for Indian tribes.[5] Hundreds of Indians were killed; Indian homes and crops lay in ruins; tribal economies had collapsed; and tribal towns and villages were choked with refugees.[6] Many tribes or parts of tribes had fled west, creating a "domino effect" all the way to the Pacific, as each tribe in turn pushed other tribes westward, often leading to armed conflict among them.[7]

Not long after the Revolutionary War ended, the newly formed federal government claimed to own all the land in the United States, as a "spoil" of war.[8] Indians, of course, disagreed, but by the end of the nineteenth century, virtually every Indian tribe in the country had been placed on a reservation after either "consenting" to relinquish land to the federal government or being forced to do so.

Federal Indian policy, many people claim, has been driven from its inception "by greed, avarice, and the pursuit of manifest destiny"[9] and has been "ultimately genocidal in both practice and intent."[10] Some critics believe that the United States has no legitimate right to regulate tribal governments and assert that it should halt all further attempts to do so.[11] Despite these claims, all three branches of the federal government— legislative, executive, and judicial—have consistently upheld the government's power over Indians and its authority to regulate their property and affairs.[12] Given this unbroken history, the federal government probably will never permit Indian tribes to regain their complete autonomy, although it has moved further in that direction in recent years, as discussed in chapter 1.

A. THE SOURCE AND SCOPE OF FEDERAL POWER OVER INDIANS

What is the source of federal power over Indians?

The ultimate source of the federal government's power over Indians is its military strength. The U.S. Constitution provides the legal rationale for implementing that power. Article I, section 8, clause 3 (the Commerce Clause) provides that "Congress shall have the Power . . . to regulate Commerce with foreign Nations, and among the several States, and with the Indian Tribes." Article II, section 2, clause 2 (the Treaty Clause) gives the President and the Senate the power to make treaties on behalf of the United States, including treaties with Indian tribes. The Supreme Court held in 1832 that these two constitutional provisions, the Commerce and the Treaty Clauses, provide Congress with "all that is required" for complete control over Indians and tribes.[13] Given that Congress abolished treaty making with tribes in 1871, as explained in the previous chapter, the Treaty Clause is no longer cited as a source of federal control over Indians, and the Supreme Court now relies entirely on the Commerce Clause.[14]

In addition to the Treaty and Commerce Clauses, older Supreme Court decisions cited two other sources of federal power over Indians. The first is a rule of international law that states, "[D]iscovery and conquest [gives] the conquerors sovereignty over and ownership of the lands thus obtained."[15] In 1823, the Supreme Court held that by virtue of the "discovery" of North America by the Europeans and the "conquest" of its inhabitants, the federal government (as the Europeans' successor) was entitled to enforce its laws over all persons and property within the United States.[16]

The doctrine of trust responsibility (discussed in chapter 3) also was cited in early Supreme Court cases as a source of federal power over Indians. Many Indian treaties guarantee that the federal government will "protect" the treaty tribes. This promise, the Court held, gave the federal government not only the duty to protect them but also the power.[17] It has been many years since the Court has cited the Treaty Clause, the discovery doctrine, or the doctrine of trust responsibility as a source of federal power over Indians; only the Commerce Clause is cited today.

Each of these justifications for federal control over Indian affairs can be disputed. First, Europeans did not "discover" this continent, on which more than five hundred nations already lived. Second, the Constitution permits Congress to regulate commerce and to enter into treaties *with* tribes; nothing in the Commerce and Treaty Clauses expressly confers upon Congress any power *over* tribes. Finally, the trust doctrine requires the United States to honor the promises it made to Indian tribes in treaties, in which the tribes relinquished their homelands to the federal government; no tribe surrendered its right of self-government in any treaty. Thus, depending on one's perspective, the justifications given for federal control over Indians and tribes are either convincing or absurd. The federal government, however, continues to maintain its authority over Indian tribes, and its courts continue to uphold its asserted legal right to do so.

What is the scope of federal power over Indian affairs?

Congress has *plenary power*—full and complete power—over all Indian tribes, their governments, their members, and their property.[18] As the Supreme Court recently stated: "Congress possesses plenary power over Indian affairs, including the power to modify or eliminate tribal rights," and Congress can assist or destroy an Indian tribe as it sees fit.[19]

Are there any limits on the power of Congress over Indian affairs?

The Supreme Court has recognized that the "power of Congress over

Indian affairs may be of a plenary nature; but it is not absolute."[20] The two most important constitutional limitations on congressional power over tribal affairs are the Due Process and the Just Compensation Clauses, both contained in the Fifth Amendment.[21] However, few federal Indian laws have been invalidated under these provisions.

The Due Process Clause provides that no person may be deprived of life, liberty, or property without due process of law. This clause thus prohibits Congress from enacting any law that is arbitrary, unreasonable, or invidiously discriminatory, including laws that discriminate on the basis of race.[22] Indians and tribes have challenged many federal laws under the Due Process Clause. However, for reasons explained below, they have lost virtually all of these cases.

The Just Compensation Clause prohibits the federal government from taking private property without paying fair and adequate compensation. As explained in the last chapter, rights and interests given Indians in a treaty or statute are a form of private property protected by the Just Compensation Clause; therefore, any taking of them by the federal government must be compensated. Courts have required that fair compensation be paid for the loss of Indian hunting and fishing rights,[23] for the taking of land belonging to an Indian[24] or a tribe,[25] and for the loss of an Indian's tax immunity.[26] This limitation on congressional power does not prevent Congress from taking the property or interest; it only requires that compensation be paid for any seizure that occurs.

Another limitation on Congress, at least in theory, is the doctrine of trust responsibility, which obligates the federal government to remain loyal to Indians and tribes, to act in their best interests, and to fulfill the promises made to them in treaties.[27] But the trust doctrine is not *legally* enforceable against Congress; for reasons explained in chapter 3, a court, for example, may not order Congress to honor a treaty commitment or prevent Congress from taking Indian land. Indian tribes can only hope that Congress has the moral and ethical integrity to honor the commitments and fulfill the promises it made to them decades ago in exchange for Indian land, an integrity that in many instances has fallen short.

Given that the Constitution prohibits race discrimination, why is Congress allowed to treat Indians and non-Indians differently?

Over the years, Congress has passed hundreds of laws that treat Indians differently from non-Indians—sometimes to the benefit of Indians, other times to their detriment. Federal laws, for example, provide Indians with certain housing, financial, medical, and educational benefits that non-Indians are not eligible to receive, while other laws place unique restrictions on Indians and tribes regarding the sale and use of their land and other property.

Given that the Due Process Clause prohibits race discrimination, it is fair to ask why Congress can differentiate in this fashion. The answer, according to the Supreme Court, lies in the fact that these laws are not to be viewed as racial legislation. In the first place, the Constitution expressly authorizes Congress to regulate commerce with Indian tribes; thus, there is a constitutional basis for enacting laws unique to Indians. Moreover, there are important historical and political reasons for treating Indians differently: they were the early inhabitants of this territory. Thus, as the Supreme Court has stated, "classifications expressly singling out Indian tribes as subjects of legislation are expressly provided for in the Constitution and supported by the ensuing history of the federal government's relations with Indians."[28]

The Supreme Court's decision in *Morton v. Mancari* (1974)[29] applies this principle. At issue in that case was a federal law (the Indian Preference Act of 1934, 25 U.S.C. § 472) that requires that members of federally recognized Indian tribes receive hiring preferences for job vacancies within the Bureau of Indian Affairs (BIA). Non-Indians challenged this employment preference under the Due Process Clause, contending that it constituted impermissible race discrimination. In a unanimous decision, the Court upheld the Preference Act. The Constitution gives Congress the power to treat Indians "as a separate people," the Court said.[30] The Preference Act was politically, not racially, motivated: Congress wanted to give Indians greater control within the BIA, the agency that administers most of the federal government's Indian programs. This was a reasonable, and therefore permissible, exercise of Congress's plenary power over Indians.[31]

Therefore, each federal Indian law must be examined in its historical, political, and cultural context to determine if it constitutes race discrimination. Congress is permitted to give Indians special rights and benefits if doing so is a reasonable exercise of Congress's plenary powers over Indians.[32] Likewise, Congress may impose unique restrictions or disadvantages on Indians if reasonably related to a legitimate federal interest.[33] Indeed, it appears that not a single federal Indian law has ever been invalidated on the grounds that it constitutes race discrimination.

Does Congress have the authority to discriminate among groups of Indians?

Yes. Laws that discriminate among groups of Indians are reviewed by courts under the same "rational basis" test as laws that discriminate between Indians and non-Indians. Using that test, courts have allowed Congress to distribute funds only to tribal members possessing a certain degree of tribal blood[34] and to give property to one Indian tribe that otherwise would have gone to another.[35] Congressional discretion is extremely broad. Any legislation that can be "tied rationally to the fulfillment of Congress's unique obligation toward the Indians" is a valid exercise of congressional authority.[36]

B. IMPLEMENTATION OF FEDERAL POWER

Congress has virtually unlimited authority to regulate Indians and tribes, as just explained. The rest of this chapter examines the ways in which Congress has implemented that power through administration of Indian affairs; regulation of tribal governments; termination; regulation of tribal membership; regulation of Indian land, tribal assets, and individual property; regulation of trade and liquor; and exercise of criminal jurisdiction.

1. Administration of Indian Affairs

Only Congress has the authority to formulate the federal government's Indian policies, but it obviously cannot administer these policies on a day-to-day basis. Congress has delegated this task to various federal agencies, which have enormous control over many aspects of tribal life.

What powers have been delegated by Congress to federal agencies regarding the administration of Indian policy?

The Constitution divides the federal government into three separate branches: legislative, judicial, and executive. The legislative branch (Congress) makes the law. The judicial branch (the courts) interprets the law. The executive branch (whose chief officer is the President) administers the law. Federal administrative agencies, such as those administering Indian programs, are part of the executive branch of government. These agencies are created by Congress but staffed with people appointed by the President or persons acting under the President's command.

The first agency Congress created to administer Indian policy, the Office of Indian Affairs, was established in 1824 and placed within the now-defunct War Department. In 1849, Congress transferred this agency to the newly created Department of the Interior, where it remains today, although in 1947 the Office of Indian Affairs was renamed the Bureau of Indian Affairs.

The highest official in the Department of the Interior is the Secretary of the Interior, and the highest official in the BIA is the Assistant Secretary of Indian Affairs. Both are appointed by the President but must be confirmed by the Senate. The BIA employs some ten thousand people, more than 85 percent of whom are Indian (as a result of the Indian Preference Act discussed earlier).

The Department of the Interior administers the majority of the federal government's Indian programs, mostly through the BIA. For example, the Department regulates the sale and lease of Indian land, operates social welfare programs on reservations, controls the use of water on irrigated Indian lands, regulates and approves Indian wills, operates Indian schools, purchases land for Indians and tribes, and regulates federal law enforcement on reservations.[37] The Departments of Health and Human Services, Housing, and Agriculture also administer Indian programs, including various health care, housing, and food programs for Indians.

Congress creates federal Indian policy and then decides which agency will implement it. That agency must faithfully perform its duties; it may not act beyond the powers conferred by Congress or ignore the duties delegated to it.[38]

What powers have been delegated by Congress to the President?

A law passed by Congress in 1834 gives the President the general power to "prescribe such regulations as he may think fit for carrying into effect the various provisions of any act relating to Indian affairs."[39] But currently, the President has no specific powers regarding Indians. Congress has delegated enormous authority to the Secretary of the Interior (as discussed later in this chapter), who is appointed by the President, but Congress has given no specific authority to the President.

During the nineteenth century, several Presidents created Indian reservations without congressional consent, but Congress passed a law in 1919 prohibiting the creation of any more of these "Executive Order" reservations.[40] As part of the General Allotment Act of 1887 (GAA), Congress authorized the President to assign parcels of tribal land to tribal members and to sell the remaining ("surplus") tribal land to non-Indians,[41] but Congress eliminated that power in 1934.[42]

As chief executive, a President can exert tremendous influence in Indian affairs, but few Presidents within the past century have taken advantage of that opportunity and instead have largely ignored Indians and tribes. When President Clinton visited an Indian reservation in 1999, he was the first President to do so in more than fifty years.

Can Congress delegate authority to Indian tribes?

Yes. Congress can delegate powers to Indian tribes, just as it can to federal agencies.[43] In 1953, for example, Congress authorized tribes to regulate the sale of liquor within the reservation, thereby allowing tribes to license all persons who sell liquor on the reservation and even ban its sale entirely.[44]

The single most important law delegating authority to Indian tribes is the Indian Self-Determination and Education Assistance Act of 1975 (ISDEA), also known as the Indian Self-Determination Act (ISDA).[45] The ISDA authorizes Indian tribes to submit "self-determination" contracts to the federal agencies that operate certain Indian programs. (These contracts are called "638" contracts because the statute that created the ISDA was Public Law 93-638.) The agency must approve a contract unless it issues written findings that explain why the contract fails to meet ISDA standards, and any such denial can be appealed by the tribe to a federal court.[46] If the contract is approved, the agency must transfer to the tribe all funds given by Congress to that agency for the operation of the program, and the tribe then administers the program subject only to the agency's general oversight. As a result of the ISDA, Indian tribes now operate schools, health clinics, social welfare programs, water treatment facilities, and law enforcement activities formerly operated entirely by federal agencies, making ISDA one of the most significant laws promoting Indian self-governance ever passed by Congress.[47] For example, Indian tribes and tribal agencies currently have more than three hundred ISDA contracts with the Indian Health Service, an agency within the Department of Health and Human Services, regarding the provision of reservation medical care.

Have federal officials done a good job in their administration of Indian affairs?

Federal officials have done a poor job administering the nation's Indian policies, as discussed in chapter 3, and some of the most vocal critics have been these officials themselves. In 1979, the person in charge of the BIA described the bureau as "a public administration disaster" that must make "radical changes" in the way it treats Indians and administers Indian programs,[48] and his successor described the bureau in similar terms in 1987.[49] In 1999, Assistant Secretary of Indian Affairs Kevin Gover acknowledged that the BIA had "a lousy reputation, much of it deserved."[50] "The federal government, through the very agency I now head," Gover said, "sought to make tribal governments weak, and the Indian people weaker still."[51]

As a federal court recently noted, it is "clear that the federal government has failed time and again to discharge its fiduciary duties" to Indians.[52] Federal agencies administering the government's Indian programs have been found to be inefficient, patronizing, insensitive, and antagonistic to tribal autonomy.[53] They have undermined tribal self-government and mismanaged tribal resources.[54] In 1999, for instance, BIA officials admitted being unable to account for nearly $2 *billion* in money belonging to Indians and tribes that had been entrusted to their care.[55]

As the branch of government in charge of Indian policy, Congress is ultimately responsible for these failures. Many things need to be fixed, including eliminating the patronizing attitude of the BIA.[56] Inadequate funding by Congress is another major part of the problem. Due to substantial cutbacks in funding since 1980, "Congress has disabled the [BIA] to the point where it cannot operate properly," Assistant Secretary Gover stated in 1999.[57] Although Congress substantially increased its expenditures for Indian programs in 2000, the federal government, Gover admitted, was still "far, far short" of meeting its obligations to Indian people.[58]

2. Regulation of Tribal Governments

Another way in which Congress regulates Indian affairs is by regulating tribal governments. The most comprehensive federal law regulating tribal powers is the Indian Civil Rights Act of 1968 (ICRA), discussed in chapter 14, which prohibits any tribal action that would violate the civil rights listed in the act. The ICRA also limits the punishments that tribal courts may impose on persons convicted of a crime to one year in tribal jail and a $5,000 fine.

Congress also has passed laws, discussed in chapter 7, that limit tribal powers to regulate the activities of non-Indians on land they own within the reservation. In addition, Congress has restricted a few tribes, such as the Osage Tribe in Oklahoma, regarding the forms of government they may adopt.[59]

For the most part, though, Congress has allowed tribes to regulate their internal affairs free from federal control. Those tribes that organized themselves under the Indian Reorganization Act of 1934 (IRA), as explained in chapter 1, were required by the Secretary of the Interior to include in their constitutions a provision stating that the Secretary had to approve all tribal ordinances before they could become effective.[60] However, the Secretary announced several years ago that tribes could amend their constitutions and remove the requirement of secretarial oversight.[61]

Congress has passed several laws in recent years that have given even its critics "some reason to be optimistic that the federal government is committed to reestablishing a true government-to-government relationship with the Indian nations."[62] The ISDA, discussed above, is one of these laws, and others are listed in chapter 1. In addition to these congressional actions, two executive orders issued by President Clinton, one in 1994 and the other in 2000, require all federal agencies to operate within a government-to-government relationship with federally recognized tribes and to consult and cooperate with tribes on agency activities that affect them.[63] Thus, the legislative and executive branches of government have taken steps in recent years to support tribal self-government and autonomy.

What role may federal officials play in choosing tribal leaders?

Usually, federal officials play no role, but there are two narrow situations in which Congress has allowed them to intervene in the process of choosing tribal leaders. First, Congress has determined that tribes organized under the IRA may amend their constitutions (under which they elect their leaders) only by following an election process supervised by the Secretary of the Interior.[64] This law, though, requires the Secretary to approve constitutional amendments endorsed by the tribe unless the amendments violate federal law or the election process was flawed.

Second, there have been times in which members of an Indian tribe have been unable to agree on which person or group had won the election. When that situation has occurred, the Secretary of the Interior has sometimes chosen on a temporary basis which person or persons will be considered the tribe's legitimate government, so that the United States and the tribe can continue to engage in government-to-government relations until the tribe can resolve the conflict under tribal law.[65] Federal courts have upheld these interventions in extreme cases, holding that federal law, and particularly the IRA, charge the Secretary "with supervising [tribal] elections and ensuring their fundamental integrity."[66] One federal court also has held that tribal members who conspire to deprive other members of their right to vote in a tribal election or who attempt to rig its outcome can be prosecuted under federal anti-conspiracy laws and that federal officials have a duty to prosecute these offenders.[67]

For good reason, federal officials rarely intervene in tribal election disputes. Few things are of such fundamental importance to a tribe as choosing its political leaders and its own form of government, and federal officials normally should leave these decisions to the tribe.[68] When the Secretary intervenes in such disputes, an effort must be made to avoid unnecessary interference with a tribe's right of self-government.[69]

3. Termination

Congress has also exerted its authority over Indian affairs by terminating tribal governments. Congress can do nothing worse to an Indian tribe; termination, as many people view it, is equivalent to genocide.[70]

What is termination?

Termination is the process by which Congress ends the federal government's trust relationship with an Indian tribe, thereby disqualifying the tribe for the many federal services that Congress has made available only to federally recognized tribes. (These benefits are discussed in chapter 15, section F.)

Between 1954 and 1966, Congress terminated 109 tribes, most of them in Oregon and California. In each case, Congress passed a law directing the Secretary of the Interior to distribute all the tribe's property to tribal members or to a tribal corporation, if the tribe chose to incorporate itself under state law. Once the tribe's property was distributed, the reservation was eliminated, and the Secretary placed a notice in the Federal Register that the tribe was terminated. At that point, the trust relationship ended, and tribal members became fully subject to state law.[71]

Nothing causes tribes and their members to lose more rights than termination. This act is the ultimate weapon of Congress and the ultimate fear of tribes. Despite its drastic effect, the Supreme Court has held that Congress has the power under the Commerce Clause to terminate an Indian tribe.[72]

Why did the federal government terminate Indian tribes?

A number of explanations were offered for the government's termination policy. Some proponents claimed that termination was in the best interest of the Indians. Termination, they said, would help Indians integrate into "American" society and, by doing so, reduce Indian poverty.[73] But many Indians believe that Congress did not design termination to help them but rather to help non-Indians obtain Indian land and to save money for the federal government by eliminating the government's treaty promises and trust responsibilities.[74]

Has Congress halted its termination policy?

Yes, at least for now. Congress last terminated a tribe in 1966, and since then, it has even restored to federal status several of the terminated tribes.[75] In 1970, President Nixon explained why the federal government had abandoned its termination policy. The federal government, Nixon said, entered into many agreements with Indian tribes in which the government "has made specific commitments to the Indian people [often in exchange for] vast tracts of land," commitments that create a "special relationship between Indians and the Federal Government." These agreements "carry immense moral and legal force," and terminating that relationship and reneging on the commitments made to the Indians "would be no more appropriate than to terminate the citizenship rights of any other American."[76]

Many non-Indians continue to advocate for the termination of Indian tribes. To prevent that from occurring, Indians must constantly make an effort to educate the public and Congress on why this nation should honor its treaty commitments and foster tribal sovereignty.

**Have the courts established any protective rules
regarding termination?**

Due to the harm caused by termination, courts have created protective
rules governing its application. The Supreme Court has held that although
a court cannot prevent Congress from terminating a tribe, a court must
refuse to recognize that a termination has occurred in the absence of a
"clear and unequivocal" act of Congress.[77] In addition, the Supreme Court
has held that vested rights survive termination unless Congress expressly
extinguishes them. In *Menominee Tribe v. United States* (1968),[78] the
Court held that even though the Menominee Reservation had been terminated, tribal members could continue to exercise their treaty right to hunt
and fish on the land that had been their reservation because the Menominee Termination Act had not expressly extinguished that right. (Congress
has since restored the Menominee Tribe to federal status, and it is once
again a federally recognized tribe.)

Finally, courts have held that termination must comply with the Just
Compensation and Due Process Clauses of the Constitution.[79] Therefore,
Congress must provide monetary compensation for any land or other
vested interests that are lost through termination.[80] In addition, if federal
officials fail to comply with all of the requirements of a termination law,
a federal court may "unterminate" the tribe.[81]

4. Regulation of Tribal Membership

**Who controls tribal membership: the tribe or the
federal government?**

Actually, both do. Indian tribes determine tribal membership for tribal
purposes (such as deciding who is eligible to enroll in the tribe),[82] and the
federal government determines tribal membership for federal purposes
(such as deciding which tribal members qualify for federal education
scholarships).[83] As with all other aspects of tribal affairs, Congress can
limit tribes in their own enrollment policies, but Congress rarely has done
so. This subject is discussed more fully in chapter 2, section A.

5. Regulation of Indian Land

The forceful taking of tribal land, and the extensive regulation of what
remains, says a great deal about Congress's Indian policies. Indians have

relatively little land left—roughly 55 million acres, about 2 percent of the United States—and it is heavily regulated by Congress. Congress justifies its pervasive regulation of Indian land on the grounds that tribes and reservation Indians are not yet ready to manage their property.[84] Most tribal land is in trust status, owned by the United States.

During the nineteenth century, many tribes at first were placed on fairly large reservations, but as time went on and non-Indians wanted additional Indian land, Congress either diminished the size of these reservations or abolished them and moved the tribes to smaller reserves. The General Allotment Act of 1887, discussed in chapter 1, employed yet another method for acquiring Indian land: the federal government sold "surplus" land *within* Indian reservations to non-Indians. The GAA also authorized federal officials to allot parcels of the tribe's land to tribal members, and hundreds of these Indian allottees were subsequently given deeds to their allotments, giving them full ownership rights and rendering the land subject to state real estate taxation. Many of these allottees subsequently sold their land to non-Indians or lost their land through foreclosures when they did not pay state taxes.

What is *Indian trust land?* In what ways does the federal government regulate the sale of Indian trust land?

There are two broad categories of land owned by Indians and tribes: *trust* and *nontrust.* Trust land is owned by the federal government but set aside for the exclusive use of an Indian or a tribe, the "beneficial owner." Nontrust land (also called *fee, fee patent,* or *deeded land*) is owned outright by an Indian or tribe; Indians and tribes can own land, both on and off the reservation, just as anyone else can.

There are advantages and disadvantages in having land in trust status. The main advantage is that trust land, being federally owned, is immune from state tax and zoning laws and most other forms of state regulatory jurisdiction, and crimes that occur on trust land involving Indians are not subject to state prosecution.[85] The main disadvantage is that trust land may not be sold or used by its beneficial owner without the federal government's consent. However, most Indians and tribes who have trust land usually opt to keep it in trust status, believing that the advantages outweigh the disadvantages.

Under the GAA, hundreds of Indians were compelled to accept deeds to their allotments and soon lost their land through tax foreclosures or by selling the land to non-Indians. In 1934, as part of the IRA, Congress prohibited the federal government from issuing any more of these "forced" deeds. Today, Indians who have inherited these remaining trust allotments will not be issued a deed unless they request one.[86]

An Indian allottee who wishes to obtain a deed to a trust allotment must prove that he or she "is competent and capable of managing his or her affairs."[87] Once the applicant proves competency, the Secretary of the Interior must issue the deed.[88] Determinations of competency are left by law to the Secretary's sound discretion, and courts generally do not overrule the Secretary's decision.[89]

When an Indian allottee requests the issuance of a deed and indicates on the application an intention to sell the land once the deed is issued, the Secretary usually offers the tribe the right to purchase the land at market price.[90] If the tribe declines, the Secretary must issue a deed to a qualified Indian allottee even if the tribe requests that the application be denied.[91] Federal law also permits Indians to sell their trust land through an installment contract, subject to secretarial approval, with the purchaser paying a portion of the price at periodic intervals.[92]

Congress does not regulate the sale of nontrust land owned by an individual Indian, and Indians who own fee land may sell it at anytime to anyone. Fee land owned by a tribe, however, is restricted. The Indian Nonintercourse Act (a version of which was first passed in 1790) prohibits tribes from selling any interest in land unless the sale is approved by the federal government.[93] Any sale of tribal land without the government's consent is void.[94]

How does the federal government regulate the leasing of trust land?

Indian trust land may be leased only in accordance with the laws passed by Congress and the regulations established by the Secretary of the Interior. Any noncomplying lease is invalid.[95] A separate federal statute governs each kind of trust lease, including farming and grazing leases; mining leases; oil and gas exploration leases; and leases for public, religious, educational, recreational, residential, or business purposes.[96] The Secretary has issued extensive regulations governing the terms and conditions of these various leases, and each type of lease has its own requirements.[97] For instance, a lease for grazing purposes may not exceed a term of ten years, whereas a lease for residential purposes may be made for twenty-five years.

The Secretary usually approves a tribe's request to lease its land unless there is evidence of mistake, fraud, or undue influence in the terms of the lease.[98] A lease of Indian trust land is subject to cancellation by the Secretary if later found to violate federal law or if its terms and conditions are not being met.[99] In such cases, the parties to the lease are entitled to a hearing before the cancellation takes effect, and the Secretary's decision can be reviewed by a court.[100] Indians and tribes who believe that the Secretary has violated federal law or trust duties in negotiating a lease can seek judicial review.[101]

Does the federal government regulate the inheritance of Indian land?

Congress has decided not to regulate the inheritance of nontrust land. Therefore, tribal law controls the inheritance of this property if it is located within the reservation, and state law controls if it is located outside the reservation.

On the other hand, as the owner of trust land, Congress regulates its inheritance, and the Supreme Court has upheld its authority to do so.[102] For instance, Congress has determined that (1) if an Indian dies without a will, the Indian's trust land will be inherited according to state law rather than tribal law; (2) if an Indian dies with a will, any assignment of trust land made in the will is invalid unless it previously had been approved by the Secretary of the Interior; and (3) if an Indian dies without a will and without legal heirs, the Indian's trust land will go (escheat) to the tribe.[103]

Congress has directed the Secretary of the Interior to administer federal laws governing the inheritance of trust land, and the Secretary has issued extensive regulations on the subject.[104] A decision by the Secretary regarding the inheritance of trust property can be reviewed by a court to ensure that it is not arbitrary and capricious or otherwise contrary to federal law.[105]

As with every other area of Indian law, Congress does not have absolute authority over Indian inheritance. In 1987, the Supreme Court reviewed a federal statute that prevented Indians from inheriting fractions of trust land worth less than $100 a year in annual lease income; instead, the statute gave those real estate interests to the tribe. The Court held that the statute constituted a taking of property without just compensation in violation of the Just Compensation Clause of the U.S. Constitution.[106] In 1997, the Supreme Court also held unconstitutional Congress's second attempt to have these fractionated interests escheat to the tribe because

this statute, too, failed to pay adequate compensation to the Indian beneficiaries.[107]

**Are there other ways in which Congress regulates trust land, besides
its sale, lease, and inheritance?**

Yes. Besides controlling the sale, lease, and inheritance of trust land,
the federal government also controls easements and rights-of-way on trust
land, such as railways, highways, power lines, and oil and gas pipelines, all
of which must be approved by the Secretary of the Interior.[108] (In most
circumstances, a right-of-way across tribal land also requires the tribe's
approval.)[109] The Secretary also manages the forestry on and irrigation of
trust land.[110] In addition, by federal statute (25 U.S.C. § 81), no contract
or agreement may be made with Indian tribes "relative to their lands"
unless it is approved by the Secretary of the Interior. Under this statute,
for instance, a contract between an Indian tribe and a non-Indian company to construct a gambling casino on tribal trust land requires federal
approval.[111] In addition, any Indian who wishes to mortgage a trust allotment (which is permitted in certain situations even though the federal
government owns the land) must obtain prior secretarial approval.[112]

Can Indians and tribes acquire additional trust land?

Yes. Indians and tribes can acquire additional trust land by two methods, but both require secretarial action. First, the Secretary can use federal
funds (when Congress makes them available) to purchase privately owned
land and convert it to trust land for an Indian or tribe.[113] This authority
is discretionary, and the Secretary cannot be forced to purchase land even
when funds are available.[114] Some years, Congress has appropriated no
money for this purpose.[115]

Second, an Indian or tribe can purchase deeded land (on or off the
reservation) and request that the Secretary convert it to, or exchange it for,
trust land.[116] The statute authorizing these trust acquisitions does not limit
eligibility to federally recognized tribes.[117]

Considerable controversy has erupted over some of these trust acquisitions and conversions, especially when the tribes applying for them have
announced plans to use the property for a gambling casino. State and local
officials have voiced strong opposition to some of these plans due to the
radical changes a casino would cause to the surrounding non-Indian community and because trust land cannot be taxed by the state, thus reducing

the state's revenue. During the past several years, in Connecticut for instance, the state government as well as the counties surrounding the Mashantucket Pequot Reservation have strenuously opposed the tribe's application to convert to trust status 186 acres of land the tribe had purchased adjacent to its reservation, land that would enable the tribe to increase the size of its casino, already the world's largest. In a recent decision, a federal court of appeals upheld the right of the Secretary to convert the land to trust status.[118]

Some states have taken the position that the Secretary should employ a "needs" test and reject applications from tribes that are already financially stable and do not need more land. Until 2001, the Secretary's regulations did not require applicants to show that they are "needy" or "landless" to qualify, but in that year Assistant Secretary of Indian Affairs Neal McCaleb, appointed to that post by newly elected George W. Bush, withdrew the existing regulations and announced that a "needs" test might be created and that the Secretary might also begin to consider whether the surrounding community opposed the designation.[119] These suggested changes are strongly opposed by Indian tribes, which believe that states and towns should have no say in whether land is returned to Indian tribes and that the federal government should do whatever it can to restore land to tribes.

In 1995, a federal court of appeals ruled that the law authorizing the Secretary to accept trust conversions was unconstitutional,[120] thereby casting doubt on the status of thousands of acres of land that has already been converted to trust status under this program. However, the Supreme Court vacated the decision on technical grounds without ruling on the merits of the issue,[121] and the Secretary continues to convert land to trust status.[122]

Can Congress diminish the size of or abolish an Indian reservation?

Yes. Congress has diminished the size of many reservations and abolished many others and has used four methods in doing so. First, Congress has sometimes abolished entire reservations and either created a new reservation for the tribe elsewhere or, as it did during the termination era to 109 tribes, simply eliminated the reservation. Second, Congress has removed Indians from a portion of their reservation and eliminated all the trust land in that portion, declaring it "restored to the public domain."[123] Third, in a variation on the second method, Congress has restored to the public domain a portion of the reservation but allowed any trust allotments located within the restored area to remain in trust status. This extinguished the tribe's control over the area except for the remaining trust allotments, which are still considered "Indian country." (*Indian country* is defined in chapter 2.) Fourth, Congress has "opened" reservations to settlement by non-Indians, allowing them to purchase unoccupied ("surplus") land *within* the reservations. The GAA, discussed earlier, is a prime example of this method. (The first three methods changed the exterior boundaries of the reservation, but this last method did not.)

In some situations, it has been difficult to tell whether a law passed by Congress was designed to diminish the boundaries of a reservation or just open the reservation to non-Indian settlement. The Supreme Court has held that if a reasonable doubt exists as to what Congress intended, it will be presumed that Congress did not diminish the reservation.[124] In certain cases, though, a majority of the Court has held that a diminishment had occurred even though the dissenting Justices found no clear intent on the part of Congress to diminish it.[125]

Are there any limitations on the federal government's control over Indian land?

The major limitation is the Just Compensation Clause, but as explained earlier, it does not stop Congress from taking Indian land; it only guarantees that Congress will pay compensation for any land that is taken.[126] Compensation must be paid not only for the land but also for everything of value found on or within the land, such as timber and minerals and fish and game, and the government must pay interest from the day the land was taken until the compensation is paid.[127]

6. Regulation of Tribal Assets

What control does Congress have over tribal assets?

The power of Congress to regulate tribal assets—including land, money, and other property—is "one of the most fundamental expressions, if not the major expression, of the constitutional power of Congress over Indian affairs."[128] As with the other exercises of congressional power discussed above, federal power over tribal assets is plenary.[129] This power is so extensive that Congress can order a tribe to distribute all of its assets and to disband as a government—a power that Congress exercised with disastrous results during the termination era.

Federal statutes give the Secretary of the Interior authority to administer certain tribal assets, including tribal land, as already explained. The Secretary also has the authority to take tribal funds and use them to pay for Indian education, road construction, hospitals, medical supplies, and tribal insurance.[130] The Secretary has no independent authority to manage tribal assets and may only do what Congress has authorized, and federal officials must properly manage the property placed under their control.[131]

7. Regulation of Individual Property

Does Congress regulate the individual property of Indians?
Congress regulates some property; other property, it does not. As is the case with other citizens, Indians can own private property, including land, cattle, automobiles, and the like. Congress does not regulate *private* property owned by Indians any differently than private property owned by non-Indians.

However, Congress does regulate individual Indian *trust* property. Many Indians were issued allotments of trust land under the GAA, and hundreds of these trust allotments still exist today.[132] This trust land, which is owned by the United States, is regulated by the federal government, as described earlier in this chapter.

When Indians lease their trust lands, the lease funds are paid to the Secretary of the Interior, who must then deposit them into the beneficiary's Individual Indian Money (IIM) account, also controlled by the federal government. Considerable controversy surrounds these IIM accounts. A federal court recently found that federal officials have so badly mismanaged these accounts that Indians may have lost as much as two billion dollars that should have been deposited in them.[133]

8. Regulation of Trade and Liquor

Does Congress have the power to regulate trade with Indians?
Yes. The Commerce Clause of the Constitution gives Congress the express power to regulate commerce with the Indian tribes. The Supreme Court has described this power as being "plenary"—full and complete.[134]

There is almost no aspect of Indian trade that is not regulated by the federal government. As early as 1790, Congress passed a comprehensive law to regulate trade and commerce with the Indian tribes, and most of its provisions are still in effect.[135] This law requires all persons except Indians "of the full blood" who trade on an Indian reservation to obtain a federal license and obey restrictions on the goods and services being offered and the manner of their sale. Violators are subject to a fine and forfeiture of their goods.[136]

Congress has delegated to the Assistant Secretary of Indian Rights (the person in charge of the BIA) the authority to regulate Indian trade.[137] Only the Assistant Secretary (or a designee) may issue a trader's license, and no license may be issued unless the applicant proves that he or she is "a proper person to engage in such trade."[138] The Assistant Secretary has enacted regulations describing in detail how trade with Indians must be conducted and the goods and services that can be sold.[139]

Any individual who discovers that someone is violating these laws and regulations may file a lawsuit against that person in the name of the United States.[140] If the court finds a violation, the trader's goods must be confiscated by the federal government and sold, and the person filing the suit is entitled to half the proceeds.[141] If federal officials ignore their duty to regulate reservation trade, a court can order them to enforce the law.[142]

Congress has decided that federal employees who work directly with Indians and tribes may not trade with them except on behalf of the United States.[143] This law ensures that these persons cannot profit personally from their employment relationship with Indians.

Does the government's power to regulate trade include the power to regulate liquor?

Yes, and Congress has made extensive use of this power.[144] In 1892, Congress passed a law prohibiting all sales of liquor to Indians, both on and off the reservation. The law was later amended to prohibit only sales of liquor to Indians on or near Indian reservations and later amended again to prohibit only on-reservation sales. Under the current law, each tribe decides for itself what types of liquor regulations to establish, and tribes have the authority to issue their own liquor licenses,[145] to refuse to issue a liquor license to non-Indians,[146] and to ban entirely the sale of liquor on the reservation (as a few tribes have done).

9. Exercise of Criminal Jurisdiction

Indian tribes had their own systems of criminal justice long before Europeans arrived on this continent, and each tribe decided for itself what behavior would be prohibited and what punishment would be imposed for misconduct. Until 1885, the federal government did not interfere with tribal systems for punishing crimes committed by one reservation Indian against another.

In 1885, Congress passed the Major Crimes Act,[147] which authorized federal officials to prosecute Indians who committed certain crimes on the reservation. The act was passed in response to a highly publicized trial that occurred in the Dakota Territory in 1883. An Indian by the name of Crow Dog was arrested and prosecuted by federal officials for murdering a Chief of the Brule Sioux, Spotted Tail. Crow Dog appealed his conviction to the Supreme Court, arguing that federal officials had no right to prosecute him for something that occurred on an Indian reservation between two Indians. The Supreme Court agreed with Crow Dog and ordered his release.[148]

Congress quickly responded. Believing that Indians would become "civilized a great deal sooner"[149] if they were subjected to certain federal criminal laws, Congress passed the Major Crimes Act, which authorized the federal government to prosecute the following seven crimes when committed by an Indian in Indian country against any other person: murder, manslaughter, rape, assault with intent to kill, arson, burglary, and larceny. Since then, more crimes have been added to the list.[150] Chapter 8 further explains the federal government's criminal jurisdiction in Indian country.

Notes

1. *See* Colin G. Calloway, *The American Revolution in Indian Country* (Cambridge: Cambridge Univ. Press, 1998) at 22–47.

2. *Id.* at 46–64.

3. *Id.* at 65.

4. *Id.* at 32–34.

5. *Id.* at 46.

6. *Id.* at 290–91.

7. *Id.* at 61, 288.

8. *Id.* at 273–93. *See Johnson v. McIntosh*, 21 U.S. 543 (1823) (holding that the federal government owned all the land in the United States based on the concept of "discovery and conquest").

9. Robert B. Porter, "A Proposal to the *Hanodaganyas* to Decolonize Federal Indian Control Law," 31 *U. Mich. Journal of Law Reform* 899, 939 (1998).

10. Robert A. Williams Jr., "The Algebra of Federal Indian Law: The Hard Trail of Decolonizing and Americanizing the White Man's Indian Jurisprudence," *Wis. L. Rev.* 219, 265 (1986); *see also* Porter, note 9 above.

11. *See* Porter, note 9 above; Robert N. Clinton, "Redressing the Legacy of Conquest: A Vision Quest for a Decolonized Federal Indian Law," 46 *Ark. L. Rev.* 77 (1993); Williams, note 10 above; Emma R. Gross, *Contemporary Federal Policy Toward American Indians* (New York: Greenwood Press, 1989); Nell Jessup Newton, "Federal Power over Indians: Its Sources, Scope, and Limitations," 132 *U. Pa. L. Rev.* 195, 199 (1984); Francis Prucha, *The Great Father* (Lincoln: Univ. of Nebraska Press, 1984); Vine Deloria Jr., *Behind the Trail of Broken Treaties* (New York: Delacorte, 1974); Alvin Josephy, *Red Power* (New York: McGraw-Hill, 1971).

12. *Worcester v. Georgia*, 31 U.S. 515 (1832); *Menominee Tribe v. U.S.*, 391 U.S. 404 (1968); *Antoine v. Washington*, 420 U.S. 194 (1975).

13. *Worcester*, note 12 above, 31 U.S. at 559.

14. *See County of Yakima v. Confederated Tribes of Yakima Indian Nation*, 502 U.S. 251, 257 (1994); *Morton v. Mancari*, 417 U.S. 535, 551–52 (1974). *See also U.S. v. Lomayaoma*, 86 F.3d 142, 146 (9th Cir.), *cert. denied*, 519 U.S. 909 (1996).

15. *Tee-Hit-Ton Indians v. U.S.*, 348 U.S. 272, 279 (1955).

16. *Johnson v. McIntosh*, 21 U.S. 542 (1823).

17. *U.S. v. Kagama*, 118 U.S. 375, 382–83 (1886).

18. *U.S. v. Sandoval*, 231 U.S. 28 (1913); *Mancari*, note 14 above.

19. *South Dakota v. Yankton Sioux Tribe*, 522 U.S. 329, 343 (1998). *See also Santa Clara Pueblo v. Martinez*, 436 U.S. 49, 56 (1978).

20. *Delaware Tribal Business Committee v. Weeks*, 430 U.S. 73, 84 (1977), citing *U.S. v. Tillamooks*, 329 U.S. 40, 54 (1946).

21. The Fifth Amendment provides: "No person shall be . . . deprived of life, liberty, or property, without due process of law; nor shall private property be taken for public use, without just compensation."

22. *Bolling v. Sharpe*, 347 U.S. 497 (1954); *U.S. v. Antelope*, 430 U.S. 641 (1977); *Hodel v. Irving*, 481 U.S. 704 (1987).

23. *Menominee Tribe*, note 12 above.

24. *Babbitt v. Youpee*, 519 U.S. 234 (1997); *Hodel v. Irving*, 481 U.S. 704 (1987); *Antoine v. U.S.*, 710 F.2d 477 (8th Cir. 1983).

25. *Shoshone Tribe of Indians v. U.S.*, 299 U.S. 476 (1937); *U.S. v. Sioux Nation of Indians*, 448 U.S. 371 (1980). The amount of compensation that must be paid is the value of the land at the time it was taken, plus interest. *U.S. v. Creek Nation*, 295 U.S. 183 (1935).

26. *Choate v. Trapp*, 224 U.S. 665 (1911). *But see Tiger v. Western Investment Co.*, 221 U.S. 286 (1911).

27. The scope of the government's trust responsibility is discussed in ch. 3.

28. *Antelope*, note 22 above, 420 U.S. at 645. *See also Rice v. Cayetano*, 120 S.Ct. 1044, 1058 (2000); *Washington v. Confederated Bands and Tribes of the Yakima Indian Nation*, 439 U.S. 463, 500–501 (1979).

29. 417 U.S. 535 (1974).

30. *Id.* at 553 n.24.

31. *See also Preston v. Heckler,* 734 F.2d 1359 (9th Cir. 1984).

32. *See, e.g., Washington v. Washington Commercial Passenger Fishing Vessel Ass'n,* 443 U.S. 658 (1979) (fishing); *Winters v. U.S.,* 207 U.S. 564 (1908) (water); *Alaska Chap., Assoc. General Contractors v. Pierce,* 694 F.2d 1162 (9th Cir. 1982) (commercial).

33. *Antelope,* note 22 above.

34. *Tiger,* note 26 above; *Simmons v. Eagle Seelatsee,* 244 F. Supp. 808 (E.D. Wash. 1965), *aff'd mem.,* 384 U.S. 209 (1966); *Weeks,* note 20 above. When Congress terminated the Ute Indian Tribe, it distributed property based upon blood quantum of tribal members. *See Ute Distribution Corp. v. Ute Indian Tribe,* 149 F.3d 1260 (10th Cir. 1998).

35. *Northern Cheyenne Tribe v. Hollowbreast,* 425 U.S. 649 (1976).

36. *Mancari,* note 14 above, 417 U.S. at 555. *See also Yakima Indian Nation,* note 14 above.

37. *See respectively,* 25 U.S.C. Secs. 391–415(d), 13, 381, 371–80, 271–304(b), 463–65, 174–202.

38. *U.S. v. George,* 228 U.S. 14 (1913); *Morton v. Ruiz,* 415 U.S. 199 (1974); *Northern Arapaho Tribe v. Hodel,* 808 F.2d 741, 748 (10th Cir. 1987); *U.S. v. Winnebago Tribe of Nebraska,* 542 F.2d 1002 (8th Cir. 1976).

39. 25 U.S.C. Sec. 9.

40. Act of June 30, 1919, sec. 27, 41 Stat. 3, 34.

41. 25 U.S.C. Sec. 331.

42. 25 U.S.C. Sec. 461.

43. *See U.S. v. Mazurie,* 419 U.S. 544 (1975); *Bugenig v. Hoopa Valley Tribe,* 266 F.3d 1201, 1210 (9th Cir. 2001) *(en banc), cert. denied,* 122 S.Ct. 1296 (2002).

44. 18 U.S.C. Sec. 1611. *See id.* This subject is discussed in ch. 6, sec. B(9).

45. Pub. L. No. 93-638, 88 Stat. 2203, codified as 25 U.S.C. Sec. 450 *et seq.*

46. The provision allowing for court review under the ISDA is Sec. 450(f)(a)(2).

47. The ISDA has been given a broad and liberal interpretation by the courts. *See, e.g., Ramah Navajo Chapter v. Lujan,* 112 F.3d 1455 (10th Cir. 1997); *Ramah Navajo School Board v. Babbitt,* 87 F.3d 1338 (D.C. Cir. 1996); *Ramah Navajo School Board v. New Mexico Taxation and Rev. Dept.,* 977 P.2d 1021 (N.M. App. 1999). For a discussion of the ISDA, including the 1988 amendments, *see* T. Johnson and J. Hamilton, "Self-Governance for Indian Tribes: From Paternalism to Empowerment," 27 *Conn. L. Rev.* 1251 (1995).

48. Statement of Forrest Gerard Before the National Congress of American Indians, Washington, D.C., Jan. 18, 1979.

49. Statement of Ross Swimmer quoted in "Blunt BIA Director Runs into Bureaucratic Wall," *Arizona Republic* (Oct. 4, 1987) at 9–11.

50. Quoted in "Looking out for Indians," *Princeton Alumni Weekly* (Oct. 20, 1999) at 39.

51. Quoted in "Conquering Fear: Kevin Gover Delivers Passionate Address," *Indian Country Today* (Oct. 18, 1999) at A1.

52. *Cobell v. Norton,* 240 F.3d 1081, 1086 (D.C. Cir. 2001).

53. *See* Special Comm. on Investigations of the Select Comm. on Indian Affairs, "Final Report and Legislative Recommendations," S.Rep. No. 101-216, at 49–56 (1989). *See also* the sources cited in note 11 above and E. Cahn, ed., *Our Brother's Keeper: The Indian in White America* (New York: World Publishing, 1969).

54. .*See Cobell,* note 52 above; *City of Tacoma, Washington v. Andrus,* 457 F. Supp. 342 (D.D.C. 1978); *McClanahan v. Hodel,* 14 Indian L. Rep. 3113 (D.N.M. 1987).

55. *See Cobell,* note 52 above.

56. This subject is discussed in ch. 3. *See also* Porter, note 9 above, at 952; W. Ron Allen, "Gover's BIA Legacy: Lessons for the Next Administration," *Indian Country Today* (Sept. 13, 2000) at A5.

57. Quoted in "BIA: Can It Be Fixed?" *American Indian Report* (Oct. 1999) at 10.

58. Quoted in "A Most Disgraceful Act of Under-Investment," *Indian Country Today* (Mar. 1, 2000) at A1.

59. *See Fletcher v. U.S.,* 116 F.3d 1315 (10th Cir. 1997) (describing the manner in which Congress has prescribed the form of government for the Osage Tribe). *See also Cherokee Nation of Oklahoma v. Babbitt,* 117 F.3d 1489 (D.C. Cir. 1997) (holding that Congress had eliminated the political existence of the Delaware Tribe and merged it with the Cherokee Tribe).

60. *See Kerr-McGee Corp. v. U.S.,* 471 U.S. 195, 198 (1985).

61. *See id.; Fort McDermitt Paiute Shoshone Tribe v. Acting Phoenix Area Director,* 17 IBIA 144, 147 (16 Indian L. Rep. 7047) (1989).

62. Porter, note 9 above, at 986.

63. *See* "Government-to-Government Relations with Native American Tribal Governments," Presidential Memorandum of Apr. 24, 1994, 59 Fed. Reg. 22951 (1994), and "Consultation and Coordination with Indian Tribal Governments," Presidential Memorandum of Nov. 6, 2000, Exec. Order No. 13084 (2000). These executive orders require that considerable efforts be undertaken by federal agencies when dealing with tribal interests. *See* Derek Haskew, "Federal Consultation with Indian Tribes: The Foundation of Enlightened Policy Decisions, or Another Badge of Shame?" 24 *Am. Ind. L. Rev.* 21 (1999/2000). Federal agencies that have failed to consult with Indian tribes in an adequate manner have had their actions reversed by courts for that neglect. *See Klamath Tribes v. U.S.,* 1996 WL 924509 (D. Or. 1996).

64. 25 U.S.C. Sec. 476. *See Thomas v. U.S.,* 189 F.3d 662 (7th Cir. 1999), *cert. denied,* 121 S.Ct. 33 (2000).

65. *See Shenandoah v. U.S. Dept. of the Interior,* 159 F.3d 708, 710 (2d Cir. 1998) (noting that BIA had temporarily recognized a person as interim tribal chairperson). This subject is discussed in more detail in ch. 6, sec. B(1). The various competing and complex issues in these instances are discussed in *Shenandoah, id.,* at 712–13; *Goodface v. Grassrope,* 708 F.2d 335, 338–39 (8th Cir. 1983); *Frease v. Sacramento Area Director, BIA,* 17 IBIA 241 (16 Indian L. Rep. 7093) (1989); *Crooks v. Area Director,* 14 IBIA 181 (13 Indian L. Rep. 7038) (1986).

66. *Shakopee Mdewakanton Sioux (Dakota) Community v. Babbitt,* 107 F.3d 667, 670 (8th Cir. 1997). *See also U.S. v. Wadena,* 152 F.3d 831, 847 (8th Cir. 1997), *cert. denied,* 526 U.S. 1059 (1999) (holding that the Secretary "has a direct responsibility as a trustee to protect the civil rights" of voters in tribal elections). Federal courts, however, may not get involved in resolving tribal election disputes that are purely intratribal, not involving federal officials. *See U.S. Bancorp v. Ike,* 171 F. Supp.2d 1122, 1125 (D. Nev. 2001).

67. *Wadena,* note 66 above, 152 F.3d at 844–47.

68. *See* Timothy Joranko and Mark Van Norman, "Indian Self-Determination at Bay:

Secretarial Authority to Disapprove Tribal Constitutional Amendments," 29 *Gonz. L. Rev.*
81 (1993/94). *See also King v. Norton,* 160 F. Supp.2d 755 (E.D. Mich. 2001).

69. *See Wheeler v. Dept. of Interior,* 811 F.2d 549, 552 (10th Cir. 1987); *Ransom v.
Babbitt,* 69 F. Supp.2d 141 (D.D.C. 1999); *Harjo v. Kleppe,* 420 F. Supp. 1110, 1144–46
(D.D.C. 1976), *aff'd,* 581 F.2d 949 (D.C. Cir. 1978); *Brady v. Acting Phoenix Area Director,* 30 IBIA 294 (25 Indian L. Rep. 7051) (1998); *See also Thomas v. U.S.,* 141 F. Supp.2d
1185 (W.D. Wis. 2001) (holding that the Secretary may not interfere with tribal elections
beyond the authority granted by Congress).

70. *See, e.g.,* R. Strickland, "Genocide-at-Law: An Historic and Contemporary View
of the Native American Experience," 34 *U. Kan. L. Rev.* 713 (1986); M. A. Jaimes, ed.
The State of Native America: Genocide, Colonization, and Resistance (Boston: South End
Press, 1992).

71. *See, e.g.,* Menominee Termination Act, 25 U.S.C. Secs. 985 *et seq.;* Klamath Termination Act, 25 U.S.C. Secs. 564 *et seq. See* discussion, *South Carolina v. Catawba Indian
Tribe,* 476 U.S. 498 (1986).

72. *Menominee Tribe,* note 12 above.

73. *See* American Indian Policy Review Commission, *Final Report* (Washington,
D.C.: Government Printing Office, 1977) at 447–53; Felix Cohen, *Handbook of Federal
Indian Law* (Charlottesville: Michie Co., 1982) at 170–80, 811–13; Robert N. Clinton,
et al., *American Indian Law.* 3d ed. (Charlottesville: Michie Co., 1991) at 155–58. *See also
Ute Distribution Corp.,* note 34 above, 149 F.3d at 1261.

74. *See* Vine Deloria Jr., *Custer Died for Your Sins* (New York: Avon Books, 1969) at
60, 81; Porter, note 9 above, at 933–36; Prucha, note 11 above, at 1046–59.

75. *See, e.g.,* 25 U.S.C. Sec. 903 (Menominee Tribe); 25 U.S.C. Secs. 861–61c
(Wyandotte, Peoria, and Ottawa Tribes); 25 U.S.C. Sec. 761 (Paiute Tribe).

76. President Nixon's Message to Congress, July 8, 1970, 6 Pres. Doc. 894, *reprinted
in* 116 Cong. Rec. S23258–23262 (July 8, 1970).

77. *U.S. v. Nice,* 241 U.S. 591, 599 (1916).

78. 391 U.S. 404 (1968).

79. These constitutional provisions are quoted in note 21 above.

80. *Cherokee Nation v. So. Kansas R.R. Co.,* 135 U.S. 641 (1890); *Klamath and Modoc
Tribes v. U.S.,* 436 F.2d 1008 (Ct. Cl. 1971).

81. *Smith v. U.S.,* 515 F. Supp. 56 (N.D. Cal. 1978); *Duncan v. Andrus,* 517 F. Supp.
1 (N.D. Cal. 1977); *Hardwick v. U.S.,* No. C-79-1710SW (N.D. Cal. 1979).

82. *Santa Clara Pueblo v. Martinez,* 436 U.S. 49 (1978); *Ordinance 59 Ass'n v. U.S.
Dept. of the Interior Secretary,* 163 F.3d 1150 (10th Cir. 1998). *See also* 43 C.F.R. Sec.
4.330(b) (Interior Board of Indian Appeals shall not adjudicate tribal enrollment disputes).

83. *Cherokee Nation v. Hitchcock,* 187 U.S. 294 (1902); *Eagle Seelatsee,* note 34 above;
Tiger, note 26 above; *Ruff v. Hodel,* 770 F.2d 839 (9th Cir. 1985).

84. *See* Cohen, note 73 above, at 508–9. *See also* K. Kickingbird and K. Ducheneaux,
One Hundred Million Acres (New York: Macmillan, 1973).

85. The subject of state criminal and civil jurisdiction on Indian trust land is discussed in chaps. 8 and 9, respectively.

86. 25 U.S.C. Sec. 349. The application process is set forth in 25 C.F.R. Part 152
(1990).

87. 25 U.S.C. Sec. 349.

88. *Oglala Sioux Tribe v. Hallett,* 708 F.2d 326 (8th Cir. 1983); *Oglala Sioux Tribe v. Commissioner of Indian Affairs,* IBIA 79-11-A (6 Indian L. Rep. I-30) (1979).

89. 25 U.S.C. Sec. 349.

90. 25 C.F.R. 152.27.

91. *See* cases cited in note 88 above.

92. *See Stuart v. U.S.,* 109 F.3d 1380 (9th Cir. 1997).

93. 25 U.S.C. Sec. 177.

94. *Sandoval,* note 18 above; *County of Oneida, N.Y. v. Oneida Indian Nation of New York State,* 470 U.S. 226 (1985); *Joint Tribal Council of the Passamaquoddy Tribe v. Morton,* 528 F.2d 370 (1st Cir. 1975). *But see Lummi Indian Tribe v. Whatcom County, Washington,* 5 F.3d 1355 (9th Cir. 1993), *cert. denied,* 512 U.S. 1228 (1994) (holding that an Indian tribe that purchases fee land from a private owner can later sell it without the federal government's consent).

95. *Bunch v. Cole,* 263 U.S. 250 (1923); *Lawrence v. U.S.,* 381 F.2d 989 (9th Cir. 1967).

96. 25 U.S.C. Secs. 393, 396, 398 (and 212.1), and 415 respectively.

97. 25 C.F.R. Part 162.

98. *See* Memorandum of the Solicitor, Interior Department, May 22, 1937.

99. *Bunch,* note 95 above; *U.S. v. So. Pacific Transp. Co.,* 543 F.2d 676 (9th Cir. 1976).

100. *Woods Petroleum v. Dept. of Interior,* 47 F.3d 1032 (10th Cir. 1995) *(en banc); Danks v. Fields,* 696 F.2d 572 (8th Cir. 1982); *Pence v. Kleppe,* 529 F.2d 135 (9th Cir. 1976); *Coomes v. Atkinson,* 414 F. Supp. 975 (D.S.D. 1976). *But see Lummi Indian Tribe,* note 94 above (holding that no hearing was necessary in that case).

101. *See Woods Petroleum,* note 100 above; *Kenai Oil and Gas, Inc. v. Dept. of Interior,* 671 F.2d 383 (10th Cir. 1982).

102. *U.S. v. Bowling,* 256 U.S. 484 (1921); *Blanset v. Cardin,* 256 U.S. 319 (1921).

103. 25 U.S.C. Secs. 348, 373, and 373(a), respectively. *See Cultee v. U.S.,* 713 F.2d 1455 (9th Cir. 1983), *cert. denied,* 466 U.S. 950 (1984).

104. 43 C.F.R. Subpart D, secs. 4.200 *et seq.*

105. *See Tooahneppah (Goombi) v. Hickel,* 397 U.S. 598 (1970); *Kicking Woman v. Hodel,* 878 F.2d 1203 (10th Cir. 1989). *See also Dull Knife v. Morton,* 394 F. Supp. 1299 (D.S.D. 1974) (the Secretary must probate Indian estates within a reasonable time).

106. *Hodel v. Irving,* 481 U.S. 704 (1987).

107. *Babbitt v. Youpee,* 519 U.S. 234 (1997).

108. 25 U.S.C. Secs. 311–18.

109. 25 U.S.C. Sec. 324. *See Blackfeet Indian Tribe v. Montana Power Co.,* 838 F.2d 1055 (9th Cir.), *cert. denied,* 488 U.S. 828 (1988); *McClanahan v. Hodel,* 14 Indian L. Rep. 3113 (D.N.M. 1987).

110. 25 U.S.C. Secs. 466 and 381, respectively.

111. *Barona Group of Capitan Grande Band of Mission Indians v. American Management & Amusement, Inc.,* 840 F.2d 1394, 1404 (9th Cir. 1987); *Wisconsin Winnebago Bus. Comm. v. Koberstein,* 762 F.2d 613, 619 (7th Cir. 1985). One court has held that Sec. 81 does not apply to contracts relating to tribal fee lands but only to tribal trust lands. *Penobscot Indian Nation v. Key Bank of Maine,* 112 F.3d 538 (1st Cir. 1997).

112. 25 U.S.C. Sec. 483a. *See Northwest So. Dak. PCA v. Smith*, 784 F.2d 323 (8th Cir. 1986); *Federal Land Bank of Wichita v. Burris* 790 P.2d 534 (Okla. 1990).

113. *See* 25 U.S.C. Sec. 463e (consolidating land within the reservation) and 25 U.S.C. Sec. 465 (acquiring land within or outside of an existing reservation). *See Stevens v. Comm'r*, 452 F.2d 741 (9th Cir. 1971).

114. *McAlpine v. U.S.*, 112 F.3d 1429 (10th Cir. 1997), *cert. denied*, 522 U.S. 984 (1997).

115. In 1989, the Secretary claimed that he had no money at all for these purchases. *See Confederated Tribes of the Coos, Lower Umqua and Siuslaw Indians v. U.S.*, 16 Indian L. Rep. 3087 (D. Or. 1989).

116. 25 U.S.C. Sec. 465. *See Chase v. McMasters*, 573 F.2d 1011 (8th Cir. 1978). The procedures governing the Secretary's exercise of discretion in this regard are set forth in 25 C.F.R. Part 151. *See generally* Mary Jane Sheppard, "Taking Land into Trust," 44 *S.D. L. Rev.* 681 (1999).

117. 25 U.S.C. Sec. 465. *See Pit River Home and Agricultural Coop. Ass'n v. U.S.*, 30 F.3d 1088, 1096 (9th Cir. 1994).

118. *Connecticut v. Babbitt*, 228 F.3d 82, 94 (2d Cir. 2000), *cert. denied*, 121 S.Ct. 1732 (2001).

119. The regulations governing land acquisition are set out in 25 C.F.R. Part 151. The courts have held that the Secretary must follow these regulations. *See Citizen Band Potawatomi Indian Tribe v. Collier*, 142 F.3d 1325 (10th Cir. 1998); *City of Tacoma*, note 54 above; *Florida v. U.S. Dept. of the Interior*, 768 F.2d 1248 (11th Cir. 1985), *cert. denied*, 475 U.S. 1011 (1986). For a comment on the Bush Administration's proposed changes to these regulations, *see* "Interior's Land into Trust Quandry," *Indian Country Today* (editorial) (Sept. 5, 2001) at A4; "Which Way on Land into Trust," *Indian Country Today* (editorial) (Dec. 5, 2001) at A4.

120. *South Dakota v. U.S. Dept. of the Interior*, 69 F.3d 878 (8th Cir. 1995).

121. *U.S. Dept. of the Interior v. South Dakota*, 519 U.S. 919 (1996).

122. Courts continue to uphold the authority of the Secretary to make trust conversions under Sec. 465. *See Connecticut v. Babbitt*, note 118 above; *U.S. v. Roberts*, 185 F.3d 1125 (10th Cir. 1999), *cert. denied*, 120 S.Ct. 1960 (2000). The Interior Board of Indian Appeals, the agency that reviews decisions of the Secretary, also upholds this authority. *See May v. Acting Phoenix Area Director*, IBIA 97-151-A, 97-161-A (Jan. 28, 1999), *reprinted in* 26 Indian L. Rep. 7077 (1999).

123. *See, e.g.*, 17 Stat. 633 (1873), restoring a portion of a reservation to the public domain. *See also Russ v. Wilkins*, 624 F.2d 914 (9th Cir. 1980).

124. *See South Dakota v. Yankton Sioux Tribe*, 522 U.S. 329 (1998); *Hagen v. Utah*, 510 U.S. 399 (1994); *Solem v. Bartlett*, 465 U.S. 463 (1984); *Mattz v. Arnett*, 412 U.S. 481 (1973).

125. *See, e.g., Rosebud Sioux Tribe v. Kneip*, 430 U.S. 584 (1976).

126. *Escondido Mutual Water Co. v. La Jolla Band of Mission Indians*, 466 U.S. 765 (1984).

127. *Sioux Nation*, note 25 above; *U.S. v. Shoshone Tribe*, 304 U.S. 111 (1938); *Menominee Tribe*, note 12 above.

128. *Weeks,* note 20 above, 430 U.S. at 86 (citation omitted).

129. *Id. See also Sizemore v. Brady,* 235 U.S. 441 (1914); *Hollowbreast,* note 35 above.

130. 25 U.S.C. Secs. 123 and 123a.

131. As discussed in ch. 18, lawsuits can be filed against federal officials who violate the duties delegated to them by Congress.

132. This subject is discussed in more detail in ch. 1.

133. *See Cobell,* note 52 above.

134. *Worcester,* note 12 above.

135. 1 Stat. 137, now codified as 25 U.S.C. Secs. 177, 261–64.

136. 25 U.S.C. Sec. 264. *Cf. Rockbridge v. Lincoln,* 449 F.2d 567 (9th Cir. 1971).

137. 25 U.S.C. Sec. 261.

138. 25 U.S.C. Sec. 262.

139. 25 C.F.R. Part 140.

140. 25 U.S.C. Sec. 264.

141. 25 U.S.C. Sec. 201. *See, e.g., U.S. ex rel. Hornell v. One 1976 Chevrolet Station Wagon,* 585 F.2d 978 (10th Cir. 1978).

142. *Rockbridge,* note 136 above; *Rosebud Sioux Tribe v. U.S.,* 714 F. Supp. 1546 (D.S.D. 1989).

143. 25 U.S.C. Sec. 68. *See, e.g., Moffer v. Watt,* 690 F.2d 1037 (D.C. Cir. 1982).

144. *See U.S. v. Forty-Three Gallons of Whiskey,* 93 U.S. 188 (1876); *Perrin v. U.S.,* 232 U.S. 478 (1914).

145. 18 U.S.C. Sec. 1161.

146. *U.S. v. Mazurie,* 419 U.S. 544 (1975).

147. Now codified as 18 U.S.C. Sec. 1153. The Major Crimes Act is reproduced in appendix D.

148. *Ex parte Crow Dog,* 109 U.S. 556 (1883).

149. 16 Cong. Rec. 936 (1865) (remarks of Rep. Cutcheon), cited in *Keeble v. U.S.,* 412 U.S. 205, 211–12 (1973).

150. *See* note 147 above.

VI

Tribal Self-Government

I ndian tribes were self-governing nations centuries before Europeans arrived on this continent, and they still exercise the powers of a sovereign government. Indian tribes, the Supreme Court has recognized, "exercise inherent sovereign authority over their members and territories."[1]

The Supreme Court discussed the inherent right of tribal sovereignty in 1832 in *Worcester v. Georgia.*[2] The issue in *Worcester* was whether the state of Georgia could impose its laws on the Cherokee Indian Reservation, located within the state. In holding that Georgia could not extend its laws within the reservation, the Court stated:

Indian nations [are] distinct political communities, having territorial boundaries, within which their authority is exclusive, and having a right to all the lands within those boundaries, which is not only acknowledged, but guaranteed by the United States. . . . Indian nations had always been considered as distinct, independent political communities, retaining their original rights, as the undisputed possessors of the soil from time immemorial. . . . The Cherokee nation, then, is a distinct community, occupying its own territory, with boundaries accurately described, in which the laws of Georgia can have no force, and the citizens of Georgia, have no right to enter, but with the assent of the Cherokees themselves, or in conformity with treaties, and with the acts of Congress.[3]

The *Worcester* doctrine of inherent tribal sovereignty has undergone some modification over the years, but its basic premises remain the same. Indian tribes have the *inherent* right of self-determination and self-government. Congress has the authority to limit or abolish these powers, but the powers that tribes possess are not delegations of authority from the United States or from any other government; rather, tribes possess them as a consequence of their historic status as independent nations.

A. The Source and Limits of Tribal Power

What is the source of tribal power?

The source of an Indian tribe's power is its people. Indian tribes and their members have the inherent right to govern themselves, a right they have possessed "from time immemorial."[4] As a federal appellate court stated in 2002: "Indian tribes are neither states, nor part of the federal government, nor subdivisions of either. Rather, they are sovereign political entities possessed of sovereign authority not derived from the United States, which they predate. [Indian tribes are] qualified to exercise powers of self-government . . . by reason of their original tribal sovereignty."[5]

What are the limits of tribal power?

The Supreme Court has consistently held that although Indian tribes have inherent sovereign powers, "Congress has plenary authority to limit, modify or eliminate the powers of local self-government which the tribes otherwise possess."[6] This is a principle of law that is ultimately based, as explained in the previous chapter, on military power. The federal government has the physical power to limit the activities of Indian tribes and to abolish their governments. Over the years, Congress has abolished many tribal governments and has limited the authority of the rest. The exercise of this power has been extensively criticized on both legal and moral grounds.[7]

Indian tribes have two types of limitations on their governmental powers: *express* and *implied.* Congress has expressly prohibited tribes from exercising certain powers, such as selling tribal land without the federal government's permission[8] and incarcerating someone in tribal jail for more than a year for any one offense.[9] These express limitations are discussed in chapter 5. In addition to the express limits on tribal power, "Indian tribes have lost many of the attributes of sovereignty" by implication, the Supreme Court has held, due to their "dependent status," that is, by virtue of their "incorporation into the United States."[10] For instance, Indian tribes may no longer declare war on a foreign government or exercise certain powers over non-Indians (as discussed later in this chapter); they have impliedly lost those powers due to their subordinate position as "conquered" nations under the control of the federal government.[11] However, those powers not expressly removed by Congress or lost by implication are retained (reserved) by the tribe. (This principle, known as the *reserved rights doctrine,* is discussed in chapter 4.)

Indian tribes occupy a unique position in U.S. society. The Supreme Court has described them as "quasi-sovereign" and "semi-independent,"[12] possessing "attributes of sovereignty over both their members and their territory."[13] Thus, tribal powers are inherent, but they can be, and have been, limited expressly and by implication.

The recent assertion of hunting, fishing, and water rights by certain tribes, as well as the financial success of some tribes that have gaming casinos, has prompted many non-Indians to urge Congress to dilute tribal rights even further. Whether Congress will bow to this pressure remains to be seen. For the past several decades, as explained in chapter 1, Congress has acted on the premise that it is in the best interests of Indian tribes and the United States to promote tribal self-government and enhance tribal economic opportunities.

Are tribal powers limited by the U.S. Constitution?

No. The Supreme Court held more than a century ago that the U.S. Constitution does not limit the exercise of tribal authority.[14] There is nothing in the Constitution that requires Indian tribes to conform their powers of self-government to its provisions. Tribal governments thus may enact laws that would violate the U.S. Constitution if those same laws had been enacted by the federal or state governments.[15]

B. The Scope of Tribal Powers

Tribal governments have the same powers as the federal and state governments to regulate their internal affairs, with a few notable exceptions. The remainder of this chapter examines the nine most important areas of tribal authority: (1) the right to form a government; (2) the right to determine tribal membership; (3) the right to regulate tribal land; (4) the right to regulate individually owned land; (5) the right to tax; (6) the right to maintain law and order; (7) the right to regulate the conduct of nonmembers; (8) the right to regulate domestic relations; and (9) the right to engage in and regulate commerce and trade.

1. The Right to Form a Government

Does an Indian tribe have the right to form a government?

Yes. The right to form a government is the first element of sovereignty; thus, Indian tribes have the right to form their own governments.[16] Long before Europeans arrived on this continent, each tribe had a government. In fact, "one school of thought even maintains that Indian influence was so pervasive among the founding fathers' generation that the League of the Iroquois [a confederacy of Indian tribes in the northeast] provided a model for the framing of the United States Constitution."[17]

The right to form a government includes the right to establish the qualifications for tribal office, to determine how tribal officials are chosen, and to define their powers. A tribe can require that candidates for tribal office be enrolled in the tribe and speak the tribe's language,[18] and the tribe can disqualify for office persons with felony convictions or those who engaged in misconduct during a prior term in office.[19] Each tribe also has the power to determine who may vote in tribal elections.[20] As with all other tribal powers, a tribe's ability to form and operate a government is subject to the plenary authority of Congress,[21] but Congress has rarely interfered with this aspect of tribal sovereignty.[22]

What types of governments do Indian tribes have?

Tribal governments vary considerably, and wide differences exist from one tribe to the next regarding the structure of government, court systems, election procedures, membership requirements, and the rights afforded tribal members. Most tribes elect their leaders, but a few tribes are theocracies (in which religious leaders control the government), and others determine their leaders by heredity. Some tribes have a centralized government, while others are decentralized; the Hopi Tribe in Arizona, for example, is a union of nine self-governing villages, with each village deciding for itself how it shall be organized.[23] The Saint Regis Mohawk Tribe in New York is governed by three chiefs, chosen in staggered elections for three-year terms.[24]

The nature of tribal government was dramatically altered by the Indian Reorganization Act of 1934 (IRA)[25] and by similar laws passed in 1936 applicable to tribes in Alaska and Oklahoma.[26] As explained in chapter 1, the IRA was intended to put an end to the destructive policies of the General Allotment Act of 1887 (GAA) and help tribes revitalize their governments. Many traditional tribal governments were ill-equipped to manage the types of affairs associated with modern reservation life, such as the need to collect taxes, borrow money, enter into business contracts, operate federally funded programs, and manage tribal and private property; the IRA was enacted with the goal of assisting tribes in each of those areas.

Immediately following passage of the IRA, the Secretary of the Interior drafted a model constitution containing the provisions that the Secretary believed would assist tribes initiate and operate an effective government. The model was circulated to Indian tribes, and federal agents went to many reservations to promote its adoption. As required by the IRA, elections were held on each reservation to determine whether the tribe wished to restructure its government pursuant to the act. The IRA was accepted by 181 tribes and rejected by 77.

The IRA allowed each tribe, with the approval of the Secretary of the Interior, to draft a constitution giving the tribe specific governmental powers. The Secretary was directed by the act to approve constitutions that created a tribal council possessing the authority to employ legal counsel; negotiate contracts with federal, state, and local governments; and prevent the disposition of tribal property without the tribe's permission.[27] The Secretary encouraged tribes, in addition, to give their councils the power to borrow money and pledge tribal property as security for loans; to levy and collect taxes and impose licenses; to establish a tribal court system and enact a criminal code; to remove from the reservation nonmembers whose presence was injurious to the tribe; and to create subordinate tribal organizations for economic, educational, or other purposes. To induce tribes to accept restructuring under the IRA, Congress created a loan program under which millions of dollars of federal funds could be loaned to tribes that adopted IRA constitutions.[28]

In order to qualify as an IRA tribe, however, the tribe's constitution had to be approved by the Secretary of the Interior,[29] and the Secretary required each tribe to include a provision in its constitution that subjected every tribal ordinance to secretarial approval before it could become effective.[30] This requirement prompted many tribes to reject the IRA. Although ineligible for IRA loans, non-IRA tribes were more autonomous because neither their constitutions nor their ordinances had to be submitted to the Secretary for approval. (As noted in chapter 5, section B(2), the Secretary has since notified IRA tribes that they may amend their constitutions and eliminate the requirement of secretarial approval of their ordinances, and many tribes have done so.)[31]

The IRA helped rejuvenate tribes both politically and economically, and it certainly was a vast improvement over the assimilationist policies it replaced. However, the IRA was enacted with little input from tribes, and those tribes that adopted IRA constitutions had to follow a model that created a government acceptable to non-Indian leaders in Washington. For many tribes, the IRA has resulted "in the concentration of power [in the hands of a few people] that had not previously existed"[32] and in the adoption of a government that often ignores "the unique governing traditions and structures of the Indian nation."[33]

Today, many tribal governments have the same three branches as the federal and state governments: legislative (the tribal council), executive (the chairperson), and judicial (the tribal courts). However, even the tribes that organized under the IRA were not required to have this "separation of powers," and quite a few opted not to create an executive or judicial branch of government.[34]

Are tribal elections subject to federal review?

In most situations, tribal elections are not subject to review. "The right to conduct an election without federal interference is essential to the exercise of the [tribe's] right to self-government."[35] Unless Congress has consented to intervention by federal officials, which has rarely been given, tribes determine for themselves such matters as who may vote in tribal elections, who may run for tribal office, and how tribal elections will be administered.[36]

There are only two situations in which federal officials have exerted some control over tribal elections. Both were discussed in chapter 5, section B(2), and are briefly summarized here. First, when disputes have arisen within a tribe as to which person or group won the tribal election, federal officials have sometimes recognized a temporary government until such time as the tribe can resolve the dispute under tribal law. This enables the federal government to carry out its government-to-government relations with the tribe until the tribe resolves the controversy.[37]

Second, by federal statute, IRA tribes may amend their constitutions only with the consent of the Secretary of the Interior. This secretarial power, however, is limited. The Secretary may reject the tribe's proposal only when, in essence, adoption of it would result in a violation of federal law; in other words, its adoption would result in authorizing the tribe to do something it is forbidden by federal law from doing.[38]

How well have Indian tribes adapted to their new governmental systems?

Many tribes now have a government radically different from their traditional form of government, and their leaders govern under a different set of rules. Some Indians have learned how to use these new systems to their personal advantage, governing in a discriminatory and tyrannical manner. These (often rapid) changes in tribal government have produced "a peculiar kind of conflict that is not easily resolved."[39] Deep factionalism has developed on some reservations between "traditionalists" and "moderns," as well as along economic, religious, and political lines. "In recent years American Indian protests against their own tribal officials have seemingly become commonplace."[40] On some reservations, there is a "crippling division and distrust of tribal government."[41]

This does not necessarily mean, of course, that federal officials should intervene. As with other nations, Indian tribes have the right to experiment with different structures, policies, and laws and to fashion through trial and error the government that best suits their needs. After all, as first written, the U.S. Constitution legalized slavery and denied women the right to vote, and it took great struggles to change these policies. Tribal governments should be afforded similar latitude to make adjustments.[42]

2. The Right to Determine Tribal Membership

Does a tribe have the right to determine who qualifies for membership?

Yes. Indian tribes have the inherent authority to determine who can join the tribe. If tribes lost this power, they could not control their future. As the Supreme Court has noted, "A tribe's right to define its own membership for tribal purposes has long been recognized as central to its existence as an independent political community."[43]

Tribal authority to determine membership includes the power to take membership away from (disenroll) a person.[44] It also includes the right to adopt persons into the tribe and determine which benefits of membership they will have.[45]

What restrictions has Congress placed on tribal membership?

The Supreme Court has held that Congress has the authority to limit tribal sovereignty over membership determinations,[46] but that unless Congress acts, each tribe enjoys the exclusive right to determine tribal membership for tribal purposes.[47] Few tribes have been limited by Congress in their enrollment decisions.

Federal courts are not permitted to resolve disputes arising out of tribal enrollment policies unless expressly authorized by Congress,[48] and Congress has given courts no general powers in this regard. As one federal court recently stated in dismissing a lawsuit filed by persons who claimed they had been unjustly denied enrollment by tribal officials: a tribe's ability to determine its membership "lies at the very core of tribal self-determination; indeed, there is perhaps no greater intrusion upon tribal sovereignty than for a federal court to interfere with a sovereign tribe's membership determinations."[49] Other federal courts have dismissed similar complaints regarding tribal enrollment determinations, recognizing that Indians tribes have the inherent right to determine their membership.[50]

In addition to being barred from federal court, most challenges to tribal enrollment decisions may not be brought in tribal court, either. As explained in chapter 18, a tribal court may only hear those cases that the tribe's legislature has authorized it to hear. Many tribal legislatures have not authorized their courts to hear lawsuits filed against the tribe or its officials, including suits challenging enrollment decisions.[51] In those instances, persons who believe their rights have been violated have no judicial remedy. Also, no remedy is available through the Department of the Interior's grievance process, administered by the Interior Board of Indian Appeals. An Interior Department regulation precludes the board from adjudicating tribal enrollment disputes unless expressly authorized to do so by Congress or by the Secretary or Assistant Secretary of the Interior, and the board has not been granted any general reviewing authority regarding tribal enrollment determinations.[52]

What are the qualifications for tribal membership?

Tribes usually base eligibility for membership on lineal descent from a tribal member, often requiring that the applicant possess a minimum fraction (quantum) of tribal blood. The most common blood quantum requirement is one-fourth. Some tribes require as little as one-thirty-second degree of tribal blood or only evidence of lineage to someone whose name appears on the tribe's original membership roll, created when the tribe became federally recognized. The Constitution of the Mohegan Tribe of Indians in Connecticut requires proof only of lineal descent from someone whose name appears on the 1996 tribal role, the year the tribe finally obtained its federal recognition. (The process of federal recognition, as well as the Mohegan Tribe and its battle for federal recognition, is discussed in chapter 15, sections F and A, respectively.) In contrast, the Constitution of the White Mountain Apache Tribe in Arizona requires applicants for membership to be at least one-half Indian and at least one-quarter White Mountain Apache.

The increase in mixed marriages has caused many tribes to reduce the tribe's blood quantum for membership. As a result, many people are now eligible for membership who were ineligible previously. In recent years, partly as a result of liberalized membership criteria and partly as a result of the financial benefits of belonging to a tribe that operates a successful gambling casino, some tribes have experienced an increased interest in tribal enrollment. The Sault Ste. Marie Tribe of Chippewa Indians, which has a successful casino and reduced its blood quantum for membership, saw its enrollment surge from thirteen hundred members in 1975 to twenty-two thousand in 1995.[53]

Tribes often have qualifications for membership apart from blood quantum. Some tribes require residence on the reservation for a certain length of time or residence at the time of application. Several tribes in New Mexico are patrilineal, allowing only offspring of male tribal members to enroll (and thus denying membership to a person whose father has no tribal blood even if the mother is a full-blooded member).[54] The Oneida Nation of New York has a matrilineal system, and persons qualify for membership only if they have at least one-quarter tribal blood from their maternal side.[55]

May a person become a member of two Indian tribes?

Indians whose parents are members of two tribes may qualify for membership in both. Many tribes, though, will not allow persons to join who already are enrolled in another tribe unless they agree to withdraw their membership from the first tribe upon their admission into the second.

3. The Right to Regulate Tribal Land

Land on Indian reservations can be divided into three categories: (1) land owned by the federal government for the benefit of the tribe or a tribal member (*trust* land), (2) land owned privately by the tribe or a member (*fee* or *deeded* land), and (3) fee land owned by nonmembers. The first category of land—Indian trust land—is discussed in this section, and the other two categories are discussed later in this chapter.

Does an Indian tribe have the right to regulate its property?

In *Merrion v. Jicarilla Apache Tribe* (1982),[56] the Supreme Court reconfirmed the principle that Indian tribes, as "a fundamental attribute of [their] sovereignty," have the right to regulate reservation land "unless divested of it by federal law or necessary implication of their dependent status."[57] In *Merrion*, the Court upheld the right of an Indian tribe to tax the value of oil and gas removed from tribal trust lands by a non-Indian company operating under a contract with the tribe. The power to tax activities occurring on tribal land, the Court explained, is derived from the tribe's greater right "to tribal self-government and territorial management."[58]

Indian tribes have the inherent right to regulate hunting and fishing on tribal land;[59] to eject trespassers from tribal land;[60] to tax Indians and non-Indians who use tribal land for farming, grazing, or other purposes under contracts with the tribe or with tribal members;[61] to regulate commercial activities on tribal land;[62] to take private land for tribal use provided that adequate compensation is paid to the owner (the power of eminent domain);[63] and to require non-Indians who wish to engage in commerce with the tribe and its members to purchase a tribal business license.[64]

Merrion dealt with tribal taxation of non-Indians on *Indian trust* land, but the broad language used by the Court in deciding the case (quoted above) suggested that a tribe had a similarly expansive right of "territorial management" to tax non-Indians on *non-Indian* land within the reservation. (As explained in chapter 1, as a result of the GAA, non-Indians own millions of acres of land on Indian reservations.) However, that notion was repudiated by the Supreme Court in *Atkinson Trading Co., Inc. v. Shirley* (2001).[65] The Court held in *Atkinson*, as discussed more fully in section 7 of this chapter, that Indian tribes normally may not exercise any power over nonmembers on non-Indian land. In fact, as also explained in section 7, the Supreme Court in *Nevada v. Hicks* (2001)[66] even curtailed certain tribal powers over nonmembers on *Indian* land.

Tribal authority over *Indians* on Indian land is virtually absolute. However, as a result of recent Supreme Court decisions, tribal authority over *non-Indians* is limited, even when they engage in activities on Indian lands.

In what ways has Congress expressly restricted the right of tribes to regulate their property?

Congress has restricted the ability of Indian tribes to sell their own fee land by requiring federal consent to any such sale. Greater restrictions have been placed on the tribe's ability to sell, use, or lease trust land (which is owned by the federal government). These limits, discussed in chapter 5, section B(5), have been extensively criticized due to the manner and extent to which they encroach on tribal self-determination.[67] However, as a result of the doctrine of trust responsibility (discussed in chapter 3), tribal trust land—although controlled and regulated by the federal government—must be administered by federal officials in the tribe's best interests and in accordance with tribal wishes. Thus, in most instances, the "determination of the use of its own land is peculiarly the province of the tribe involved."[68]

In addition to the restrictions listed above, a few laws limit tribal powers to engage in certain activities on the reservation, such as the Indian Gaming Regulatory Act of 1988 (discussed in chapter 16), which restricts tribal authority to engage in gambling on the reservation. Other laws confirm or enhance tribal powers, such as the Clean Water Act (discussed in chapter 12), which authorizes Indian tribes to regulate the quality of water flowing to the reservation.[69]

What kinds of property can tribes own?

Indian tribes can own the same kinds of property non-Indians can own, both real and personal. Real property consists of land and items attached to or found within the land, such as buildings, timber, and minerals. Personal property consists of all other kinds of property, such as cattle, bank accounts, automobiles, furniture, clothing, and other movable property.

In addition, Indian tribes can have two property interests in land that non-Indians do not have: *trust* land and *Indian title* land. Tribal trust land is land that has been set aside for the exclusive use and benefit of a tribe but is owned by the United States. The tribe may use, lease, mortgage, or sell the tribe's interests in this land only if the federal government consents.[70]

Indian title land is land that has always been a part of a tribe's ancestral homesite. A tribe has the right to continue living on this land until Congress removes its right to do so. This right of continued occupancy is known as Indian title, and is discussed in chapter 2, section D.

How have Indian tribes obtained their interests in land?

There are six ways in which Indian tribes have obtained interests in land: treaty, federal statute, executive action, purchase, action of a foreign nation, and aboriginal possession. As explained in chapter 4, Congress passed a law in 1871 that prohibited the federal government from entering into any additional treaties with Indian tribes, but prior to then, treaties were the usual means of negotiation between the United States and tribal governments. Most tribes have signed at least one treaty with the federal government in which they acquired vested rights to reservation lands. Since 1871, Congress has regulated Indian affairs through legislation, and some of these statutes created—while others reduced or eliminated— Indian reservations.

Some tribes obtained their reservations by an executive order, that is, through a decree issued by the President of the United States. These "Executive Order" reservations are as valid as those created by Congress through treaties or statutes.[71] In 1919, Congress passed a law prohibiting the President from creating any additional Indian reservations, and only Congress can create a reservation today.[72]

The Secretary of the Interior is authorized by Congress to purchase land for tribes using federal funds appropriated for that purpose;[73] some reservations have been created, and many have been expanded, through these purchases. The Secretary is also authorized by federal law to convert into trust status land that a tribe has purchased on its own, whether located on[74] or off[75] the reservation. This authority—and the controversy the exercise of it has spawned—is discussed in chapter 5, section B(5).

Before the United States became a nation, many Indian tribes received land grants from the foreign countries occupying North America, including Spain, Mexico, France, and Great Britain, and some of these interests were later ratified by the United States.[76] The Pueblos of New Mexico hold the most significant of these grants, which they received from Spain and Mexico, as discussed in chapter 15, section B.

Lastly, Indian tribes have an interest in land known as *Indian title* a possessory interest that allows them to live on their ancestral lands until such time as Congress decides to terminate the tribe's right of continued occupancy. This interest is discussed in chapter 2, section D.

What are the advantages and disadvantages of having tribal land in trust status?

The greatest disadvantage of having tribal land in trust status is that the tribe lacks full control over it. Everything a tribe may want to do with trust property—sell, lease, mortgage, or develop it—requires federal approval, a constant source of aggravation to many tribes.[77]

The advantages, however, outweigh the disadvantages in most instances. Because it is owned by the federal government, trust land is immune from state tax and zoning laws,[78] and it may not be seized under the state's power of eminent domain[79] or lost through adverse possession.[80] In addition, trust land normally qualifies as Indian country, and the state therefore lacks general criminal and civil jurisdiction over Indian activities occurring on trust land.[81] These advantages are so great that when a tribe purchases private land, it usually asks the Secretary of the Interior to transfer it into trust status, a conversion authorized by federal law.[82]

If a tribe sells or leases tribal land in violation of federal restrictions, is the transfer valid?

No. Any transfer of tribal land—whether trust or non-trust—in violation of federal law is invalid and may be rescinded at any time by the United States,[83] by the tribe,[84] or by any tribal member whose rights are affected.[85]

The critical law in this area is the Indian Nonintercourse Act (INA),[86] first passed by Congress in 1790, which requires the federal government to approve the transfer of all interests in tribal land. Without that approval, the transfer is void and the agreement can be rescinded at any time. In one case, an interest in tribal land that a railroad purchased a century earlier was rescinded because Congress had not consented to the transfer.[87]

The INA was intended to give the federal government control over the sale of Indian land and to protect tribes from unscrupulous land-grabbers.[88] The INA has received considerable attention in recent years because portions of Maine, Massachusetts, Connecticut, Rhode Island, and New York apparently were removed from Indian tribes without the federal government's consent, thus casting doubt on the legality of these transfers.[89] In 1980, Congress appropriated $81.5 million to settle lawsuits brought by tribes in Maine seeking to recover nearly two-thirds of the state's land mass, which allegedly had been taken in violation of the INA. This amount included funds for the purchase of 305,000 acres of land for the tribes.[90]

What is communal property?

Few Indian tribes believed in individual ownership of land. Any land controlled by the tribe belonged to the entire community, and each member had the same right to use it as any other member. This concept of land ownership, known as communal property, was a guiding principle of Indian life: land could not be privately owned, which meant that members of the community had to work together to harvest or gather what they could from it. Anglo-American values, on the other hand, tend to glorify private property and individual wealth.

During the late nineteenth century, Congress devised a plan that it hoped would result in the assimilation of Indians into Anglo-American society. Congress realized that assimilation could succeed only if Indian communal property was destroyed and Indians learned to live and think like "Americans." The GAA (passed in 1887), discussed in chapter 1, was the vehicle by which Congress sought to achieve this goal. Under the GAA, tribal communal lands were divided into parcels (allotments) and assigned to tribal members for their individual ownership, and the tribe's "surplus" land was then sold to non-Indians. Congress repealed the GAA in 1934, but by then, two-thirds of all communal lands had passed from tribal ownership.[91] The concept of communal property remains intact on many reservations where tribal lands still exist, but the presence of so many individually owned parcels of land within the reservation has undermined the concept of communal property, a change many Indians deeply regret.

4. The Right to Regulate Individually Owned Land

Does the tribe have the right to regulate privately owned property within the reservation?

Every government places restrictions on the use of private property in order to protect the safety and welfare of its citizens and resources. Indian tribes retain the inherent right to exercise this power unless Congress has limited that right or tribes have lost it by implication, due to their dependent status.[92]

Courts have upheld the inherent right of Indian tribes to zone land, including land owned by a non-Indian when a significant tribal interest is being threatened by the manner in which the non-Indian is using the land;[93] to determine who may inherit private property belonging to a deceased tribal member;[94] to take private land for a public use (the power of eminent domain);[95] and to tax and impose health, safety, and employment regulations on businesses within the reservation, including in certain circumstances (as discussed below) businesses owned by non-Indians and located on non-Indian land within the reservation.[96]

Over the years, Congress has given non-Indians the right to own land on Indian reservations. Non-Indians acquired these rights primarily through the GAA, which, as previously mentioned, opened many Indian reservations to settlement by non-Indians. Today, in fact, the majority of Indian reservations are "checkerboarded," with parcels of land owned by non-Indians scattered throughout the reservation. (On some reservations, more land is owned by non-Indians than by Indians.)

In addition to giving non-Indians the right to own reservation land, Congress has also given non-Indians various rights-of-way over tribal land, such as rights-of-way to railroads (for the purpose of laying tracks), to utilities (for the purpose of running transmission lines), and to states (for the purpose of building highways), although since 1948, a right-of-way over tribal land requires the consent of the tribe.[97]

The Supreme Court has held that when a non-Indian acquires a federal right to own or use land on an Indian reservation, the tribe may no longer "assert a landowner's right to occupy and exclude" that interest holder from that land,[98] unless the statute or agreement under which the interest in land was conveyed expressly reserves this power to the tribe. As a consequence of losing the greater right to occupy and exclude, the Court has held, the tribe necessarily loses the lesser right to regulate activities occurring on that land. (The Supreme Court decisions establishing this principle are discussed in section 7 of this chapter.) It is important to emphasize, though, that even with respect to land owned by or leased to a nonmember, the tribe *always* retains the sovereign right, the Supreme Court has recognized, to prohibit any activity on that land that imperils the "political integrity, the economic security, or the health or welfare of the tribe."[99]

5. The Right to Tax

Do Indian tribes have the right to levy and collect taxes?

Yes. For most governments, Indian and non-Indian alike, taxation provides the best and most reliable means of raising the revenue needed to manage their affairs and provide services to their citizens. The Supreme Court has recognized that Indian tribes possess the right to tax as part of their inherent sovereign powers: "The power to tax is an essential attribute of Indian sovereignty because it is a necessary instrument of self-government and territorial management. This power . . . derives from the tribe's general authority, as sovereign, to control economic activity within its jurisdiction."[100]

The right of a tribe to tax its own members has never been seriously questioned. On the other hand, tribal taxation of non-Indians has been vigorously challenged. In 1904, the Supreme Court upheld the right of a tribe to impose a personal property tax on the value of cattle owned by a non-Indian that were grazing on reservation land he leased from the tribe.[101] In *Merrion v. Jicarilla Apache Tribe* (1982),[102] the Supreme Court upheld the right of a tribe to tax oil and gas extracted by a non-Indian company on tribal trust land under a lease with the tribe. Courts have also upheld a tribe's right to collect a business license tax from a non-Indian engaged in trade on the reservation[103] and to tax non-Indians on the value of their leasehold interests in tribal lands.[104]

In 2001, the Supreme Court addressed for the first time the question of whether Indian tribes may tax non-Indians *on non-Indian fee land* (land owned privately by a non-Indian) within the reservation. As discussed more fully in chapter 10, the Court held in *Atkinson Trading Co., Inc. v. Shirley*[105] that as a general rule, "Indian tribes lack civil authority over nonmembers on non-Indian fee land," including the right to tax them.[106] A tribe may tax a non-Indian on non-Indian land, the Court said, in two limited circumstances: when the non-Indian has entered into a consensual relationship with the tribe, such as a business venture, or when the conduct of the non-Indian imperils a significant tribal interest.[107]

In short, Indian tribes possess an inherent right to tax, and this right is vast regarding the taxation of tribal members. However, while Indians have the right to tax non-Indians, as *Merrion* recognizes, this right is limited to the two circumstances described in *Atkinson.*

6. The Right to Maintain Law and Order

Does an Indian tribe have the right to maintain law and order and to criminally prosecute tribal members?

Yes. Indian tribes, like other nations, have the inherent right to make their own laws governing their internal affairs and enforce them, in both criminal and civil contexts, so as to maintain law and order. This includes the power to maintain a police force, establish tribal courts and jails, and punish tribal members who violate tribal law.[108] As the Supreme Court stated in 1978, a tribe's "right of internal self-government includes the right to prescribe laws applicable to tribe members and to enforce those laws by criminal sanctions.[109] Similarly, a tribe has the inherent right to resolve civil disputes between tribal members, such as those arising out of contracts, torts, and child custody matters, and to establish court systems for resolving civil disputes.[110]

Does a tribe have the right to criminally prosecute non-Indians?

No. In *Oliphant v. Suquamish Indian Tribe* (1978),[111] the Supreme Court held that non-Indians who violate tribal law are immune from prosecution in tribal court unless Congress has expressly conferred that power on the tribe (and Congress has not given any tribe this power, it appears). The reasoning given by the Court for this ruling, as well as the difficulties this lack of authority is causing Indian tribes, is discussed in chapter 8.

Does a tribe have the right to prosecute nonmember Indians?

Yes. Indians on a reservation who do not belong to that reservation's tribe (*nonmember* Indians) are subject to the tribe's criminal jurisdiction to the same extent as tribal members. In *Duro v. Reina* (1990),[112] the Supreme Court held that a tribe may not prosecute nonmember Indians, but in response to *Duro,* Congress passed a law affirming the authority of Indian tribes to exercise criminal jurisdiction over nonmember Indians.[113]

What restrictions has Congress placed on tribal law enforcement?

As in all other areas of tribal power, Congress may limit tribal authority over law enforcement,[114] and Congress has done so in several respects. The most far-reaching limitations are contained in the Indian Civil Rights Act of 1968,[115] discussed in chapter 14. This law limits the penalties that tribal courts can impose in criminal cases to one year of imprisonment and a $5,000 fine. In addition, it requires that tribal courts extend almost all of the rights to criminal defendants who appear in their courts that the U.S. Constitution imposes on the state and federal courts in their prosecution of criminal defendants.

As explained in chapter 8, Congress has given state officials in some states and federal officials in the remaining states the authority to prosecute Indians who commit certain crimes in Indian country. The tribes, however, retain the right to prosecute these Indians for the same or related offenses.[116]

What types of court systems do tribes have?

Indian tribes had their own systems for maintaining law and order centuries before Europeans arrived in North America. These differed greatly from European systems. Tribes handled misbehavior primarily through public scorn, the loss of tribal privileges, or the payment of restitution to an injured party rather than by imprisonment. Banishment was usually reserved as the extreme punishment, although on occasion a serious offense might be avenged by the injured party's family.[117]

By the late nineteenth century, as explained more fully in chapter 1, federal officials had embarked on a mission to disrupt and destroy tribal governments and to assimilate Indians into Anglo-American society. As part of this effort, the federal government sought to impose "white man's law" on Indian reservations. This included the creation of a Court of Indian Offenses on most reservations. These courts were often administered by the tribes but were always under the control of federal agents. The rules and procedures governing these courts were issued by the Secretary of the Interior and were published in the Code of Federal Regulations (CFR). The courts, which became known as *CFR courts,* tended to be informal, combining Indian custom with western law. Their main function was to provide Indians with a way to prosecute crimes and resolve disputes in a manner acceptable to federal officials.

When Congress passed the Indian Reorganization Act of 1934,[118] it authorized Indian tribes to establish their own courts and enact law and order codes, subject to the approval of the Secretary of the Interior. The courts created in this fashion are known as "tribal courts." Most non-IRA tribes have created similar courts that are today also called "tribal courts." The vast majority of tribes now have tribal courts, although about twenty-five still have CFR courts,[119] and another thirty have "traditional" courts, which rely primarily on the tribe's traditional methods of resolving disputes and enforcing tribal law.[120]

Tribes are free to fashion their own court systems, except to the extent demanded by the Indian Civil Rights Act of 1968,[121] as discussed in chapter 14. Tribal courts vary considerably as a result of many factors, including differences in the size of tribes, their wealth and other resources, the importance of traditions, and the needs of the community.[122] Tribal courts are quickly learning to apply a set of laws and procedures unknown to them until fairly recently. Except for some of the Pueblo tribes in New Mexico which rely heavily on traditional procedures, "tradition plays a small part in modern-day Indian courts."[123] Many tribes have multilevel, sophisticated judicial systems, with traffic courts, criminal courts, and trial and appellate courts. The courts of the Navajo Nation process over forty-five thousand cases a year and publish decisions in an official reporter.

Each tribe sets its own eligibility requirements for judges, which vary from tribe to tribe. Some tribes require that judges be tribal members, and some require that they be state-licensed attorneys. Some tribes elect their judges, but on most reservations, they are appointed by the tribal council. Each tribe also determines who may appear as an attorney or counselor in tribal court,[124] and some tribes, such as the Navajo Nation, have their own bar examinations.

Few tribes have the means to adequately fund their court systems, and Congress has not provided sufficient funding for this purpose. In 1991, after conducting a series of hearings on the subject, the U.S. Commission on Civil Rights issued a report criticizing "the failure of the United States Government to provide proper funding for the operation of tribal judicial systems."[125] The report noted that insufficient funding has led to backlogs in deciding cases, deteriorating courtrooms, an inability to train court staff, and inadequate salaries to judges and other court officials, all of which undermine the judicial system and prevent its proper functioning. The report recommended that Congress provide financial assistance aimed at upgrading tribal court systems.[126]

Must a tribe have an appellate court?

No. Many tribes have an appellate court, but there is nothing that requires a tribe to create one. On some reservations, the tribal council serves as the appellate court. Some tribes have joined together to create an intertribal appellate court. In Nevada, the Intertribal Court of Appeals was created by more than twenty tribes to hear appeals arising from the tribal courts on those reservations.

7. The Right to Regulate the Conduct of Nonmembers

Do Indian tribes have the right to regulate the conduct of nonmembers on the reservation?

Every nation has the inherent power to determine who may enter its territory and under what conditions they may remain, and Indian tribes are no exception. "A tribe's power to exclude nonmembers entirely or to condition their presence on the reservation is . . . well established."[127]

As with all other tribal powers, however, a tribe's authority to exclude nonmembers can be limited by Congress or lost by implication due to their "dependent" status under federal authority.[128] Congress has passed laws that limit the ability of tribes to exclude nonmembers in a variety of situations. The law at issue in *Montana v. United States* (1981)[129] authorized non-Indians to purchase land on Indian reservations; the law at issue in *South Dakota v. Bourland* (1993)[130] authorized non-Indians to enter an Indian reservation and make recreational use of a lake that was formed when the federal government constructed a dam within the reservation; the law at issue in *Strate v. A-1 Contractors* (1997)[131] conferred upon the state of North Dakota a right-of-way to construct a public highway on tribal trust land; in *Atkinson Trading Co., Inc. v. Shirley* (2001),[132] a non-Indian hotel owner had his privately owned land encircled by an Indian reservation when Congress increased the size of the reservation, but he continued to own the land. In each case, the Supreme Court held that the setting aside of reservation lands for ownership by, or use of, nonmembers had the effect of restricting the tribe's right to regulate activities by nonmembers on those lands. For instance, the Court explained in *Bourland* that by opening tribal lands to the public at large for recreational purposes, Congress thereby "eliminated the Tribe's power to exclude non-Indians from these lands, and with that the incidental regulatory jurisdiction formerly enjoyed by the Tribe" to control hunting and fishing by non-Indians on that property.[133]

The Supreme Court based these decisions on the general rule that because of their "incorporation" into the United States and their "dependent" status under federal law, Indian tribes have necessarily lost many of their original powers.[134] One power they have lost is the general authority to regulate the activities of non-Indians; the principle is now well established, the Court said, that a tribe's sovereign powers "do not extend to the activities of nonmembers of the tribe," unless Congress has expressly conferred those powers.[135]

There are two important exceptions—known as the "*Montana* exceptions"—to this rule, however, and they are discussed in chapter 9. To briefly summarize them, unless Congress has conferred a greater right upon the tribe, an Indian tribe may regulate the conduct of non-Indians on non-Indian land when (but only when) (1) the non-Indian has entered into a consensual relationship with Indians or the tribe, such as a joint business venture,[136] or (2) the non-Indian is engaging in an activity that imperils the tribe's political integrity, economic security, or health and welfare.[137] The burden is on the tribe to show that one of these two exceptions exists; otherwise, the tribe may not regulate non-Indian activity on non-Indian land unless Congress has delegated that power to them.

The Supreme Court's decision in *Nevada v. Hicks* (2001),[138] reflects the extent to which the Court recently stripped tribes of many of the powers they were presumed to possess to regulate the activities of non-Indians on the reservation. Floyd Hicks, a member of the Fallon Paiute–Shoshone Tribe of Western Nevada, sued state game wardens who had entered his home located on Indian trust land on the reservation and conducted what he alleged was an illegal search and seizure. His lawsuit, filed in tribal court, sought damages against these state officers for the violation of his tribal and federal rights. Every court to consider the question, both tribal and federal, agreed that Hicks had a right to proceed with his lawsuit in tribal court, until the case reached the Supreme Court.

The Supreme Court reversed these lower court decisions. The Court applied a principle it had never applied in a case involving tribal authority over non-Indians on *Indian* land. The Court held that the issue presented in *Hicks* must be examined from the general principle that "[w]here nonmembers are concerned, the exercise of tribal power beyond what is necessary to protect tribal self-government or to control internal relations is inconsistent with the dependent status of the tribes, and so cannot survive without express congressional delegation."[139] According to the Court, the fact that the activity occurred on Indian trust land was simply one of many factors to consider.[140] The Court applied the two "*Montana* exceptions" to the facts presented in *Hicks* and concluded that the tribe and its courts could not exercise jurisdiction over the state game wardens. Neither *Montana* exception was satisfied: the game wardens did not have a business or other type of consensual relationship with the tribe, and depriving the tribal court of power to determine the legality of their behavior (and thus requiring Hicks to file his lawsuit in a state or federal court instead) would not imperil a significant tribal interest.[141]

It is now clear that tribal authority over non-Indians, even with respect to activities occurring on Indian trust land, is narrow. However, Indian tribes continue to have a "safety net" and may regulate non-Indian activities when necessary to protect the survival of a substantial tribal interest.

8. The Right to Regulate Domestic Relations

Does a tribe have the right to regulate the domestic relations of its members?

Domestic relations include marriage, divorce, adoptions, and similar matters relating to home and family life. Regulation of domestic relations is an integral aspect of sovereignty. The Supreme Court has confirmed that "unless limited by treaty or statute, a tribe has the power . . . to regulate domestic relations among tribe members."[142]

Congress has the ability to limit these tribal powers, but unless it does, a tribe possesses not only the inherent but also the exclusive right to regulate the domestic relations of its members within the reservation. *Fisher v. District Court*,[143] decided by the Supreme Court in 1976, illustrates this principle. In that case, a reservation Indian couple had been given foster custody of an Indian child by a tribal court. Wanting to adopt the child, the couple filed an adoption petition, not in tribal court but in state court. The child's mother opposed the petition, but the state court granted the adoption. The Supreme Court reversed. The tribe had a vital interest in this matter because all parties to the adoption—the child, the mother, and the foster parents—were reservation Indians, and the tribe had authorized its own courts to hear these types of cases. Therefore, the Court said, the tribe's authority over this proceeding was exclusive, and the state lacked jurisdiction to intervene. It would seriously interfere with tribal self-government if states were allowed "to subject a dispute arising on the reservation among reservation Indians to a forum other than the one they have established for themselves."[144] The Indian Child Welfare Act of 1978, discussed in chapter 17, supports the inherent right of Indian tribes to determine the custody of their children.

Do Indian tribes still rely on Indian custom to determine the validity of marriages, divorces, and adoptions?

Indian custom remains important on most reservations, particularly in the area of domestic relations. The central role of the family, the respect given to elders, the assistance that extended family members give to raising the children of relatives, and the overall importance of kinship have unique significance in Indian life.[145]

Many Indian customs have changed over the years, influenced by the very different non-Indian culture that surrounds it. Some tribes now require their members to comply with state law concerning marriage, divorce, and adoption, although many tribes issue their own marriage licenses and their tribal courts issue divorce and adoption decrees.[146] A few tribes have passed laws forbidding marriage, divorce, or adoption by Indian custom.[147]

If Indians are married off the reservation under state law, can they be divorced in a tribal court?

Yes. Any court can divorce couples who were married elsewhere, provided that the legislature has given the court this power. People married in Colorado can obtain a divorce in Nevada if they meet Nevada's requirements for divorce. Similarly, Indians married under state law can be divorced in a tribal court if they meet the tribe's requirements, and they can also be divorced according to tribal custom, provided that the tribe recognizes the continued validity of such divorces.[148]

9. The Right to Engage in and Regulate Commerce and Trade

Do Indian tribes have the right to engage in commerce and trade?

Certainly. An Indian tribe has the inherent right to engage in business activities in the tribe's own name[149] and to create and license corporations distinct from the tribe.[150] Many tribes own their own businesses, including craft industries; mining, fishing, and gambling operations; ski resorts, motels, restaurants, supermarkets, and gas stations.

Congress has passed a number of laws to assist tribes in their economic development. Tribes that incorporated themselves under the IRA can receive federal loans for business purposes.[151] The Buy-Indian Act[152] requires the Bureau of Indian Affairs (BIA) to employ Indian labor and purchase Indian products in fulfilling BIA contracts, whenever practicable. The Indian Mineral Development Act of 1982[153] provides federal assistance to Indian tribes in developing and marketing mineral resources. The Indian Gaming Regulatory Act of 1988,[154] discussed in chapter 16, establishes a comprehensive system for regulating gaming on Indian lands.

Many Indian reservations are located far from urban and industrial centers, have few marketable minerals or other natural resources, and are not located near transportation hubs or major highways. Thus they often find it difficult to attract industry, resulting in severe unemployment and poverty on the reservation. The federal government should make a strenuous effort to improve economic conditions on these reservations, for example, by providing tax incentives to businesses willing to locate on an Indian reservation. Providing economic assistance to tribes that have been placed by the federal government on isolated and barren territories would seem appropriate and necessary until they become financially self-sufficient.[155]

Do Indian tribes have the right to regulate the commerce and trade that non-Indians conduct on the reservation?

As explained in section 7, Indian tribes have the inherent right to regulate activities on the reservation, but this right can be—and has been—limited by Congress, and by the necessary implication of the "dependent" status of Indian tribes under federal law. As a result, Indian tribes may regulate commerce and trade by nonmembers in certain circumstances but not in others, depending on the presence or absence of various factors.

As explained earlier, the Supreme Court held in *Merrion* in 1982 that an Indian tribe could tax the oil and gas produced on reservation trust land by a non-Indian company. The factors that tipped the scales in the tribe's favor included the fact that the company had entered into a business contract with the tribe, and the mineral production was being done on trust land. In contrast, the Supreme Court held in *Atkinson* in 2001 that an Indian tribe could not impose a hotel occupancy tax on the guests who stayed at a hotel owned by a non-Indian on non-Indian land within the reservation. The factors that tipped the scales against the tribe included the fact that the guests had no business contract or other consensual relationship with the tribe, and the activity being taxed was occurring on privately owned property.

True, the factors were more favorable to the tribe in *Merrion* than in *Atkinson,* but the tribe in *Atkinson* lost that case primarily because the Supreme Court's recent cases have created a more difficult test than a tribe previously had to satisfy in order to exercise jurisdiction over nonmembers. In *Merrion,* for example, the Court used expansive language in describing the overall scope of tribal powers, stating, for instance, that each Indian tribe has the "general authority, as sovereign, to control economic activity within its jurisdiction."[156] Nineteen years later in *Atkinson,* the Court retreated from all language of that nature, admitting that "parts of the *Merrion* opinion" suggest a "broader scope" of tribal authority than the Court now would attribute to an Indian tribe.[157] Rather than issue broad pronouncements as to inherent tribal sovereignty, as it did in *Merrion*, the *Atkinson* Court emphasized instead the "general rule that Indian tribes lack civil authority over nonmembers on non-Indian fee land."[158] And in *Hicks*, decided a few weeks after *Atkinson*, the Court extended that "general rule" so as to prevent a tribe from regulating the activities on nonmembers on *Indian trust* lands. It is still possible for tribes to satisfy the modern test used by the Court (and described in section 7 of this chapter), but it will take compelling facts to do so. It remains the case, however, that Indian tribes continue to have broad authority to regulate commercial activity involving tribal members on the reservation, even if non-Indians also are involved. In a recent case, for instance, a federal appellate court upheld a tribe's right to require non-Indian businesses on the reservation that employed tribal members to comply with the tribe's "right-to-work" law that prohibited them from requiring their employees to join a labor union.[159] The court held that the tribal law was "clearly an exercise of sovereign authority over economic transactions on the reservation."[160]

At the same time that the Supreme Court has been eroding tribal authority,[161] Congress for the most part has supported and encouraged tribes to engage in and regulate business activities on the reservation. For example, Congress specifically exempted Indian tribes from compliance with the Civil Rights Act of 1964 (Title VII),[162] thus allowing tribal corporations to give tribal members a preference in hiring and promotion.[163] The purpose of this exemption "was to promote the ability of sovereign Indian tribes to control their own economic enterprises."[164] Congress also has exempted Indian tribes from compliance with the Americans with Disabilities Act (ADA).[165] The Age Discrimination in Employment Act (ADEA),[166] although not expressly exempting tribes, has been interpreted by the courts to be inapplicable to tribal government activity, including commercial activity.[167]

A federal law expressly authorizes Indian tribes to regulate the sale and use of alcoholic beverages in Indian country,[168] including (with certain exceptions) on land owned by non-Indians.[169] Under this statute, violations of tribal liquor ordinances can constitute violations of federal law and are subject in that instance to federal prosecution.

Congress has given federal officials several responsibilities regarding reservation commerce, including the duty to require every person other than a full-blooded Indian to obtain a federal license to trade on the reservation.[170] These regulatory powers generally do not limit tribal powers but impose federal regulations in addition to the tribe's regulations. Tribes are not allowed to pass a law that conflicts with federal law, but they are not prevented from regulating the same activity. For example, people who trade on an Indian reservation can be required to purchase both a federal and tribal trader's license.

10. Other Rights of Indian Tribes

Indian tribes have numerous rights in addition to those discussed in this chapter, and these are addressed elsewhere in this book. For instance, chapter 4 discusses Indian treaty rights. Tribal rights under the doctrine of trust responsibility are discussed in chapter 3. Chapter 11 addresses hunting, fishing, trapping, and gathering rights, and chapter 12 discusses water rights. Last, but not least, the right of tribes to file lawsuits to protect their rights is discussed in chapter 18.

NOTES

1. *Oklahoma Tax Commission v. Citizen Band Potawatomi Indian Tribe,* 498 U.S. 505, 509 (1991), citing *Cherokee Nation v. Georgia,* 8 L.Ed. 25 (1831). *See also U.S. v. Wheeler,* 435 U.S. 313, 323 (1978); *Merrion v. Jicarilla Apache Tribe,* 455 U.S. 103 (1982).
   2. 1 U.S. 515 (1832).
   3. *Worcester v. Georgia,* 31 U.S. 515, 557, 558, 560 (1832). *See County of Yakima v. Confederated Tribes and Bands of Yakima Indian Nation,* 502 U.S. 251, 257 (1992) (discussing *Worcester*).
   4. *Worcester,* note 3 above, 31 U.S. at 558. *See also Wheeler,* note 1 above, 435 U.S. at 328; *Santa Clara Pueblo v. Martinez,* 436 U.S. 49, 55 (1978); *McClanahan v. Arizona Tax Comm'n,* 411 U.S. 164, 168–73 (1973).
   5. *National Labor Relations Board v. Pueblo of San Juan,* 276 F.3d 1186, 1192 (10th Cir. 2002) *(en banc)* (footnotes and citations omitted).
   6. *Santa Clara Pueblo,* note 4 above, 436 U.S. at 56. *See also McClanahan,* note 4 above; *National Farmers Union Ins. Cos. v. Crow Tribe of Indians,* 471 U.S. 845, 851 and n.10 (1985).
   7. *See* ch. 5, notes 9–11, and accompanying text.
   8. 25 U.S.C. Sec. 177.
   9. 25 U.S.C. Sec. 1302(7).
   10. *Atkinson Trading Co., Inc. v. Shirley,* 121 S.Ct. 1825, 1830 (2001). *See also Nevada v. Hicks,* 121 S.Ct. 2304 (2001); *Wheeler,* note 1 above, 435 U.S. at 326.
   11. *Worcester,* note 3 above, 31 U.S. at 559. *See also Atkinson,* note 10 above, 121

S.Ct. at 1830; *Washington v. Confederated Tribes of the Colville Indian Reservation,* 447 U.S. 134, 152–54 (1980).

12. *U.S. v. Kagama,* 118 U.S. 375, 381 (1886).

13. *U.S. v. Mazurie,* 419 U.S. 544, 557 (1975). *See also Atkinson,* note 10 above, 121 S.Ct. at 1835.

14. *Talton v. Mayes,* 163 U.S. 379 (1896).

15. *Santa Clara Pueblo,* note 4 above; *Native American Church v. Navajo Tribal Council,* 272 F.2d 131 (10th Cir. 1959).

16. *Santa Clara Pueblo,* note 4 above, 436 U.S. at 56; *Pueblo of Santa Clara Rosa v. Fall,* 273 U.S. 315 (1927).

17. Colin G. Calloway, *The American Revolution in Indian Country* (Cambridge: Cambridge Univ. Press, 1998) at 298. *See also* Felix Cohen, *Handbook of Federal Indian Law* 128 (Washington: U.S. Govt. Printing Office, 1941).

18. *See respectively Shortbull v. Looking Elk,* 677 F.2d 645 (8th Cir.), *cert. denied,* 459 U.S. 907 (1982), and *Day v. Hopi Election Board,* 16 Indian L. Rep. 6057 (Hopi Tr. Ct. 1988).

19. *See respectively Means v. Oglala Sioux Tribal Council,* 11 Indian L. Rep. 6013 (Og. Sx. Tr. Ct. 1984), and *Runs After v. U.S.,* 766 F.2d 347 (8th Cir. 1985).

20. *Wounded Head v. Tribal Council of Oglala Sioux Tribe,* 507 F.2d 1079 (8th Cir. 1975).

21. *See Santa Clara Pueblo,* note 4 above, 436 U.S. at 56.

22. One tribe whose form of government has been subjected to considerable federal control is the Osage Tribe. *See Fletcher v. U.S.,* 116 F.3d 1315, 1327 (10th Cir. 1997) (noting that "Congress has prescribed the form of tribal government for the Osage Tribe").

23. *See Kavena v. Hopi Indian Tribal Court,* 16 Indian L. Rep. 6063 (Hopi Tr. App. Ct. 1989).

24. *See Ransom v. Babbitt,* 69 F. Supp.2d 141 (D.D.C. 1999).

25. 25 U.S.C. Secs. 461 *et seq.*

26. *See* Alaska Native Reorganization Act, 49 Stat. 1250, and the Oklahoma Indian Welfare Act, 49 Stat. 1967.

27. 25 U.S.C. Sec. 476.

28. 25 U.S.C. Sec. 477.

29. 25 U.S.C. sec. 476. *See Merrion,* note 1 above.

30. *See Kerr-McGee Corp. v. Navajo Tribe,* 471 U.S. 195 (1985). This subject is discussed in ch. 5, sec. B(2).

31. The Secretary of the Interior has on occasion not approved a tribal law under the authority granted by these tribal constitutions. *See, e.g., Cheyenne River Sioux Tribe v. Andrus,* 566 F.2d 1085 (8th Cir. 1977). However, when secretarial review is required by tribal constitution but not by federal law, the Secretary's authority is only as broad as the tribal constitution provides. *See Zinke and Trumbo, Ltd. v. Phoenix Area Director,* IBIA 95–13-A (Jan. 5, 1995), *reprinted in* 22 Indian L. Rep. 7063 (1995).

32. Robert B. Porter, "Strengthening Tribal Sovereignty Through Government Reform: What Are the Issues?" 7 *Kan. J. of Law and Public Policy* 72, 84 (Winter 1997). For a further discussion of the pros and cons of the IRA, *see* L. Tyler, *A History of Indian Policy* (Washington: U.S. Govt. Printing Office, 1973) at 131–36.

33. Robert B. Porter, "Decolonizing Indigenous Governance: Observations on Restoring Greater Faith and Legitimacy in the Government of the Seneca Nation," 8 *Kan. J. of Law and Public Policy* 97, 98 (Winter 1999).

34. For example, the constitution of the White Mountain Apache Tribe in Arizona, an IRA tribe, creates a legislative branch of government but not an executive or a judicial branch.

35. *Wheeler v. Swimmer,* 835 F.2d 259 (10th Cir. 1987).

36. *Wheeler v. U.S. Dept. of Interior,* 811 F.2d 549 (10th Cir. 1987); *Means v. Oglala Sioux Tribal Council,* 11 Indian L. Rep. 3024 (D.S.D. 1984); *Committee to Save Our Constitution v. U.S.,* 11 Indian L. Rep. 3035 (D.S.D. 1984).

37. *Goodface v. Grassrope,* 708 F.2d 335 (8th Cir. 1983); *Milam v. Dept. of the Interior,* 10 Indian L. Rep. 3013 (D.D.C. 1982).

38. The current procedure for constitutional amendment is set out in 25 U.S.C. Secs. 461–479a and its associated regulations, 25 C.F.R. Secs. 81.1–81.24. For a summary of the process, *see Shakopee Mdewakanton Sioux (Dakota) Community v. Babbitt,* 107 F.3d 667 (8th Cir. 1997).

39. Vine Deloria Jr., ed., *American Indian Policy in the Twentieth Century* (Norman: Univ. of Oklahoma Press, 1985) at 11.

40. T. Holm, "The Crisis in Tribal Government," in Deloria, *American,* note 39 above, at 135. *See also* Porter, "Decolonizing," note 33 above.

41. Porter, "Decolonizing," note 33 above, at 109.

42. Robert B. Porter, a member and former Attorney General of the Seneca Nation, has suggested several ways in which tribal governments can improve their structures and enhance their legitimacy. *See* Porter, "Decolonizing," note 33 above.

43. *Santa Clara Pueblo,* note 4 above, 436 U.S. at 72 n.36. *See also Chapoose v. Clark,* 607 F. Supp. 1027 (D. Utah 1985), *aff'd,* 831 F.2d 931 (10th Cir. 1987).

44. *Roff v. Burney,* 168 U.S. 218 (1897). *See Estate of Antoine (Ke Nape) Hill,* IBIA 78–15 (7 Indian L. Rep. 5075) (1980).

45. *Cherokee Intermarriage Cases,* 203 U.S. 76 (1906).

46. *Wallace v. Adams,* 204 U.S. 415, 423 (1907) ("The power of Congress over the matter of citizenship in . . . Indian tribes [is] plenary.") *See also* cases cited in note 6 above.

47. Congress, however, has the exclusive right to determine tribal membership for federal purposes. *See* ch. 2, sec. A. *See also Chapoose,* note 43 above.

48. *Santa Clara Pueblo,* note 4 above; *Anderson v. Las Vegas Tribe of Paiute Indians,* 103 F.3d 137 (9th Cir. 1996), *cert. denied,* 520 U.S. 1169 (1997).

49. *Smith v. Babbitt,* 100 F.3d 556, 559 (8th Cir. 1996), *cert. denied,* 522 U.S. 807 (1997).

50. *See Anderson,* note 48 above; *Ordinance 59 Ass'n v. U.S. Dept. of the Interior Secretary,* 163 F.3d 1150 (10th Cir. 1998); *Apodaca v. Silvas,* 19 F.3d 1015 (5th Cir. 1994). However, when a tribe banished a tribal member from the reservation, a federal court held that the member could challenge the tribe's decision in federal court pursuant to the Indian Civil Rights Act of 1968, 25 U.S.C. Secs. 1301 *et seq. See Poodry v. Tonawanda Band of Seneca Indians,* 85 F.3d 874 (2d Cir. 1996).

51. *See Paul v. Southern Ute Indian Tribe,* 24 Indian L. Rep. 6038 (S.W. Intertr. Ct. App. 1997); *Teasley v. Kootenai Tribe of Idaho,* 25 Indian L. Rep. 6148 (Kootenai Tr. Ct. 1998).

114 *The Rights of Indians and Tribes*

52. 43 C.F.R. Sec. 4.330. *See King v. Portland Area Director, BIA,* No. IBIA 97–138-A (31 IBIA 56, July 9, 1997).

53. "Sault Ste. Marie Chippewa Ease Membership Criteria," *Indian Country Today* (Apr. 9, 1996) at A1.

54. *Id.*

55. "Enrollment Orphans: Does Adoption Help?" *Indian Country Today* (Feb. 25, 1996) at A1, A2.

56. 455 U.S. 130 (1982).

57. *Id.* at 137. *See also Marsh v. Brooks,* 49 U.S. 223 (1850); *Pueblo of Isleta v. Universal Constructors, Inc.,* 570 F.2d 300 (10th Cir. 1978).

58. *Merrion,* note 1 above, 455 U.S. at 137.

59. This subject is discussed in ch. 11.

60. *Marsh,* note 57 above; *Ortiz-Barraza v. U.S.,* 512 F.2d 1176 (9th Cir. 1975). *See also Merrion,* note 1 above.

61. *Morris v. Hitchcock,* 194 U.S. 384 (1904).

62. *Merrion,* note 1 above; *So. Pacific Transp. Co. v. Watt,* 700 F.2d 550 (9th Cir.), *cert. denied,* 464 U.S. 960 (1983); *United Nuclear Corp. v. Clark,* 584 F. Supp. 107 (D.D.C. 1984).

63. *Boardman v. Oklahoma City Housing Auth.,* 445 P.2d 412 (Okla. 1968); *Seneca Constitutional Rights Organization v. George,* 348 F. Supp. 51 (W.D.N.Y. 1972). *Cf.* 25 U.S.C. Sec. 1302(5).

64. *Maxey v. Wright,* 54 S.W. 807 (Ct. App. Ind. T.), *aff'd,* 105 F. 1003 (8th Cir. 1900).

65. 121 S.Ct. 1825 (2001).

66. 121 S.Ct. 2304 (2001).

67. *See, e.g.,* V. Deloria Jr., *Custer Died for Your Sins* (New York: Avon Books, 1969) at 128–47; American Indian Policy Review Commission, *Final Report* (Washington, D.C.: Government Printing Office, 1977) at 128–32, 247–99. This subject is further discussed in ch. 5, sec. B(5).

68. *Hawley Lake Homeowners' Ass'n v. Deputy Ass't Sec'y—Indian Affairs,* 13 IBIA 276 (1985), *reprinted in* 12 Indian L. Rep. 7043, 7049. *See* discussion in ch. 5, sec. B(5).

69. *Wisconsin v. Environmental Protection Agency,* 266 F.3d 741 (7th Cir. 2001). *See also State of Montana v. U.S. Environmental Protection Agency,* 137 F.3d 1135 (9th Cir.), *cert. denied,* 525 U.S. 921 (1998); *City of Albuquerque v. Browner,* 97 F.3d 415 (10th Cir. 1996), *cert. denied,* 522 U.S. 965 (1997).

70. The federal government's control over Indian trust land is discussed in ch. 5, sec. B(5).

71. *Spalding v. Chandler,* 160 U.S. 394 (1896); *Merrion,* note 1 above, 455 U.S. at 133 n.1.

72. Act of June 30, 1919, Sec. 27, 41 Stat. 3, 34. *See also* 25 U.S.C. Sec. 398d.

73. 25 U.S.C. Sec. 465.

74. 25 U.S.C. Sec. 463(e).

75. 25 U.S.C. Sec. 465.

76. *See Mitchell v. U.S.,* 33 U.S. 307 (1835); *Worcester,* note 3 above, 31 U.S. at 545–49.

77. *See* note 67 above and accompanying text.

78. *Santa Rosa Band of Indians v. Kings County,* 532 F.2d 655 (9th Cir. 1975), *cert. denied,* 429 U.S. 1038 (1977).

79. *Minnesota v. U.S.,* 305 U.S. 382 (1939).

80. *Adverse possession* is a doctrine of law that allows a nonowner to acquire a possessory interest in land as a result of that person's long-term and unobstructed use or occupation of it. However, adverse possession does not apply to federal property, and thus it does not apply to trust land. *See Joint Tribal Council of the Passamaquoddy Tribe v. Morton,* 528 F.2d 370 (1st Cir. 1975).

81. *Indian country* is defined in ch. 2, sec. B. The extent to which a state can exercise jurisdiction in Indian country is discussed in ch. 7 (civil jurisdiction) and ch. 8 (criminal jurisdiction).

82. 25 U.S.C. Sec. 463e.

83. *Board of Commissioners v. U.S.,* 308 U.S. 343 (1939); *Bunch v. Cole,* 263 U.S. 250 (1923).

84. *Passamaquoddy Tribe,* note 80 above.

85. *Ewert v. Bluejacket,* 259 U.S. 129 (1922).

86. 25 U.S.C. Sec. 177.

87. *U.S. v. Southern Pacific Transportation Co.,* 543 F.2d 676 (9th Cir. 1976).

88. *See FPC v. Tuscarora Indian Nation,* 362 U.S. 99, 119 (1960).

89. *See, e.g., Passamaquoddy Tribe,* note 80 above; *Mohegan Tribe v. Connecticut,* 638 F.2d 612 (2d Cir. 1981); *Mashpee Tribe v. New Seabury Corp.,* 427 F. Supp. 899 (D. Mass. 1977), *aff'd,* 592 F.2d 575 (1st Cir.), *cert. denied,* 444 U.S. 866 (1979); *Schaghticoke Tribe of Indians v. Kent School Corp.,* 423 F. Supp. 780 (D. Conn. 1976); *Narragansett Tribe of Indians v. Southern Rhode Island Land Development Corp.,* 418 F. Supp. 798 (D.R.I. 1976). The ongoing litigation involving Connecticut and New York tribes is discussed in ch. 15.

90. 25 U.S.C. Secs. 1721–35.

91. This subject is discussed in ch. 1.

92. *Sizemore v. Brady,* 235 U.S. 441 (1914); *Montana v. U.S.,* 450 U.S. 544 (1981); *Merrion,* note 1 above.

93. *Knight v. Shoshone and Arapaho Indian Tribes,* 670 F.2d 900 (10th Cir. 1982). *But see Brendale v. Confederated Tribes and Bands of Yakima Indian Nation,* 492 U.S. 408 (1989) (holding that Indian tribes generally may not zone land in an area of the reservation predominately inhabited by non-Indians, as discussed in more detail in ch. 7).

94. *Jones v. Meehan,* 175 U.S. 1 (1899). *Cf. Wheeler,* note 1 above, 435 U.S. at 322 n.18.

95. *Seneca,* note 63 above.

96. *FMC v. Shoshone-Bannock Tribes,* 905 F.2d 1311 (9th Cir. 1990), *cert. denied,* 499 U.S. 943 (1991); *Cardin v. De La Cruz,* 671 F.2d 363 (9th Cir.), *cert. denied,* 459 U.S. 967 (1982); *Arizona Public Service Co. v. Office of Navajo Labor Relations,* 17 Indian L. Rep. 6105 (Nav. Sup. Ct. 1990).

97. 25 U.S.C. Sec. 324.

98. *Strate v. A-1 Contractors,* 520 U.S. 438, 456 (1997). *See also South Dakota v. Bourland,* 508 U.S. 679, 688 (1993).

99. *See Atkinson,* note 10 above, 121 S.Ct. at 1830; *Montana,* note 92 above, 450

U.S. at 566; *Bourland,* note 98 above, 508 U.S. at 696. *See also Bugenig v. Hoopa Valley Tribe,* 266 F.3d 1201 (9th Cir. 2001), *cert. denied,* 122 S.Ct. 1296 (2002) (holding that Congress can delegate to a tribe the right to regulate non-Indian land on the reservation).

100. *Merrion,* note 1 above, 455 U.S. at 130. *See also Crow Creek Sioux Tribe v. Buum,* 10 Indian L. Rep. 6031 (Intertr. Ct. App. 1983), and *Thompson v. Cheyenne River Sioux Tribe,* 13 Indian L. Rep. 6005 (Chy. R. Sx. Tr. 1986).

101. *Morris v. Hitchcock,* 194 U.S. 384 (1904).

102. 455 U.S. 130 (1982).

103. *Buster v. Wright,* 135 F. 947 (8th Cir. 1905).

104. *Iron Crow v. Oglala Sioux Tribe,* 231 F.2d 89 (8th Cir. 1956).

105. 121 S.Ct. 1825 (2001).

106. *Id.* at 1832.

107. *Id.* at 1830–34.

108. *Wheeler,* note 1 above; *Oliphant v. Suquamish Indian Tribe,* 435 U.S. 191 (1978); *Ortiz-Barraza,* note 60 above.

109. *Wheeler,* note 1 above, 435 U.S. at 322 (citations omitted). *See also U.S. v. Doherty,* 126 F.3d 769, 778 (6th Cir. 1997), *cert. denied,* 524 U.S. 917 (1998); *U.S. v. Antelope,* 430 U.S. 641, 643 n.2 (1977).

110. *See Wheeler,* note 1 above; *Fisher v. District Court,* 424 U.S. 382 (1976); *Williams v. Lee,* 358 U.S. 217 (1959).

111. 435 U.S. 191 (1978).

112. 495 U.S. 676 (1990).

113. Pub. L. No. 101–511, Sec. 8077, 104 Stat. 1856, 1892–93 (1990) and Pub. L. No. 102–137, Sec. 1, 105 Stat. 646 (1991), codified at 25 U.S.C. Sec. 1301(2), (4).

114. *See* cases cited in note 60 above.

115. 25 U.S.C. Secs. 1301 *et seq.*

116. Prosecution of the same person for the same crime by the tribe and the state or by the tribe and the federal government does not constitute double jeopardy. *See Wheeler,* note 1 above.

117. *See Ex parte Crow Dog,* 109 U.S. 556 (1883).

118. 25 U.S.C. Secs. 461 *et seq.*

119. The authority of Congress to delegate to the Secretary of the Interior the power to create CFR courts on Indian reservations has been upheld by the federal courts. *See Tillett v. Lujan,* 931 F.2d 636, 639 (10th Cir. 1991); *Colliflower v. Garland,* 342 F.2d 369 (9th Cir. 1965). The federal regulations governing the CFR courts are found in 25 C.F.R. Sec. 11.

120. For a more detailed look at Indian courts, *see* National American Indian Court Judges Association, *Indian Courts and the Future.* David Getches, ed. (Washington: National American Indian Court Judges Association, 1978); F. Pommersheim, "The Contextual Legitimacy of Adjudication in Tribal Courts," 18 *N.M.L. Rev.* 51 (1988); M. Taylor, "Modern Practice in Tribal Courts," 10 *U. Puget Sound L. Rev.* 231 (1987).

121. *Selam v. Warm Springs Tribal Correctional Facility,* 134 F.3d 948, 954 (9th Cir. 1998); *Smith v. Confederated Tribes of Warm Springs,* 783 F.2d 1409 (9th Cir. 1986), *cert. denied,* 479 U.S. 964 (1987). *See also U.S. v. Jones,* 11 Indian L. Rep. 6010 (Hoop Ct. App. 1984).

122. *See* U.S. Commission on Civil Rights, *The Indian Civil Rights Act* (June 1991) at 32–36.

123. National American Indian Court Judges Association, note 120 above, at 43.

124. *See LaFloe v. Smith,* 12 Indian L. Rep. 6007 (Ft. Peck Ct. App. 1984); *Navajo Nation v. McDonald,* 16 Indian L. Rep. 6085 (Nav. Sup. Ct. 1989).

125. U.S. Commission on Civil Rights, note 122 above, at 72.

126. *Id.* at 71–74.

127. *New Mexico v. Mescalero Apache Tribe,* 426 U.S. 324, 333 (1983). *See also Merrion,* note 1 above, 455 U.S. at 144–45; *Olguin v. Lucero,* 87 F.3d 401 (10th Cir. 1996), *cert. denied,* 519 U.S. 982 (1996); *Hardin v. White Mountain Apache Tribe,* 779 F.2d 476 (9th Cir. 1985).

128. *Montana,* note 92 above; *Bourland,* note 98 above.

129. 450 U.S. 544 (1981).

130. 508 U.S. 679 (1993).

131. 520 U.S. 438 (1997).

132. 121 S.Ct. 1825 (2001).

133. *Bourland,* note 98 above, 508 U.S. at 689.

134. *Atkinson,* note 10 above, 121 S.Ct. at 1830.

135. *Montana,* note 92 above, 450 U.S. at 565; *Bourland,* note 98 above, 508 U.S. at 695 n.15; *Nevada v. Hicks,* note 10 above, 121 S.Ct. at 2309. Congress has conferred powers on Indian tribes on occasion. *See Bugenig,* note 99 above, and note 169 below and accompanying text.

136. *Colville,* note 11 above, 447 U.S. at 152; *Williams v. Lee,* 358 U.S. 217 (1959); *FMC,* note 96 above; *Snow v. Quinault Indian Nation,* 709 F.2d 1319 (9th Cir. 1983), *cert. denied,* 467 U.S. 1214 (1984).

137. *See* note 99 above and accompanying text.

138. 121 S.Ct. 2304 (2001).

139. *Id.* at 2309–10 (internal citation and italics omitted).

140. *Id.* at 2310.

141. *Id.* at 2310.

142. *Wheeler,* note 1 above, 435 U.S. at 324 n.15. *See also Morris v. Sockey,* 170 F.2d 599 (10th Cir. 1948); *Begay v. Miller,* 222 P.2d 624 (Ariz. 1950).

143. 424 U.S. 382 (1976).

144. *Id.* at 387–88.

145. For a discussion of tribal customs in domestic relations matters, *see The World of the American Indian* (Washington: National Geographic Society, 1974).

146. *See Sam v. Moyle,* 27 Indian L. Rep. 6253 (Duckwater Shoshone Tr. Ct. 2000) (granting divorce decree to persons married under tribal custom and determining child support based on state law and tribal law).

147. *See respectively Estate of Matthew Cook,* IBIA 80–28 (1981), *reprinted in* 8 Indian L. Rep. 5052 (1981), and *Navajo Nation v. Murphy,* 15 Indian L. Rep. 6035 (Nav. Sup. Ct. 1988).

148. *Estate of John Ignace,* IBIA No. 76–6 (1976).

149. *Mescalero Apache Tribe v. Jones,* 411 U.S. 145 ((173); *Turner v. U.S.,* 248 U.S. 354 (1919); *White Mountain Apache Tribe v. Shelley,* 480 P.2d 654 (Ariz. 1971).

150. *Namekagon Development Co., Inc. v. Bois Fort Reservation Housing Authority,* 395 F. Supp. 23 (D. Minn. 1974), *aff'd,* 517 F.2d 508 (8th Cir. 1975); *Navajo Tribe v. Bank of New Mexico,* 700 F.2d 1285 (10th Cir. 1983).

151. 25 U.S.C. Secs. 477, 482.

152. 25 U.S.C. Sec. 47.

153. 25 U.S.C. Secs. 2101–8.

154. 25 U.S.C. Secs.2701 *et seq. See U.S. v. Sisseton-Wahpeton Sioux Tribe,* 897 F.2d 358 (8th Cir. 1990); *Lac Du Flambeau Band of Lake Superior Chippewa Indians v. Wisconsin,* 713 F. Supp. 645 (W.D. Wis. 1990).

155. For more information on this subject, *see* D. Vinje, "Cultural Values and Economic Development on Reservation," in Deloria, *American,* note 39 above, at 155–75.

156. *Merrion,* note 1 above, 455 U.S. at 137.

157. *Atkinson,* note 10 above, 121 S.Ct. at 1831–32.

158. *Id.* at 1832.

159. *Pueblo of San Juan,* note 5 above.

160. *Id.* at 1200.

161. For a scholarly and comprehensive discussion of the erosion of tribal powers in recent decisions of the Supreme Court, *see* David Getches, "Beyond Indian Law: The Rehnquist Court's Pursuit of States' Rights, Color-Blind Justice and Mainstream Values," 86 *Minn. L. Rev.* 267 (2001).

162. 42 U.S.C. Sec. 2000 *et seq.*

163. 42 U.S.C. Sec. 2000e(b), 2000e-2(I). *See Pink v. Modoc Indian Health Project, Inc.,* 157 F.3d 1185 (9th Cir. 1999), *cert. denied,* 528 U.S. 877 (1999); *Dille v. Council of Energy Resource Tribes,* 801 F.2d 373 (10th Cir. 1986).

164. *Dille,* note 163 above, 801 F.2d at 375.

165. 42 U.S.C. Secs. 12101 *et seq.;* Sec. 12111(5)(b)(1). *See Florida Paraplegic Assoc. v. Miccosukee Tribe,* 166 F.3d 1126, 1130–34 (11th Cir. 1999); *Giedosh v. Little Wound School Board,* 995 F. Supp. 1052 (D.S.D. 1997).

166. 29 U.S.C. Secs. 621 *et seq.*

167. *Equal Employment Opportunity Comm'n v. Karuk Tribe Housing Auth.,* 260 F.3d 1071 (9th Cir. 2001); *Equal Employment Opportunity Comm'n v. Cherokee Nation,* 871 F.2d 937 (10th Cir. 1989); *Equal Employment Opportunity Comm'n v. Fond Du Lac Heavy Equipment and Constr. Co., Inc.,* 986 F.2d 246 (8th Cir. 1993). *But see Reich v. Mashantucket Sand and Gravel,* 95 F.3d 174 (2d Cir. 1996), and *Donovan v. Coeur d'Alene Tribal Farm,* 751 F.2d 1113, 1116 (9th Cir. 1985) (holding that Occupational Safety and Health Act, 29 U.S.C. Secs. 651 *et seq.,* applies to tribal corporations even though Congress did not expressly make it applicable).

168. 18 U.S.C. Sec. 1161. *See Rice v. Rehner,* 463 U.S. 713, 715 (1983); *Mazurie,* note 13 above; *City of Timber Lake v. Cheyenne River Sioux Tribe,* 10 F.3d 554 (8th Cir. 1993), *cert. denied,* 512 U.S. 1236 (1994).

169. *See Mazurie,* note 13 above; *City of Timber Lake,* note 168 above.

170. 25 U.S.C. Secs. 261–64. The federal government's regulation of Indian trade is discussed in ch. 5, sec. B(8).

VII

State Power over Indian Affairs

ince the earliest days of the United States, state governments have attempted to impose their laws on Indian reservations. Efforts by Georgia in 1832 to regulate reservation activities led to the single most important case in federal Indian law: *Worcester v. Georgia*. The Supreme Court held in *Worcester* that state laws "can have no force" on an Indian reservation without the express consent of Congress.[1]

States normally have the right to regulate all persons and activities within their borders. The U.S. Constitution, however, gives Congress exclusive authority over certain subject areas, and Indian affairs is one of them.[2] Therefore, as a general rule, a state may not enforce its laws on reservation Indians without express congressional consent.[3]

Congress has rarely consented to state jurisdiction over reservation Indians. As the Supreme Court has noted, "[T]he policy of leaving Indians free from state jurisdiction and control is deeply rooted in the Nation's history."[4]

States and tribes have often been at odds with one another. However, they share many of the same governmental and societal concerns, and their economies, natural resources, and the health and welfare of their citizens are often linked. Increasingly, states and tribes are realizing that the closer they work together, the better off they both will be. Many states and tribes have entered into agreements and compacts with each other to regulate the use of water and other natural resources, to coordinate law enforcement activities, to facilitate extradition of criminal suspects, and to regulate certain aspects of reservation gaming. Significantly, the National Conference of State Legislatures (NCSL) and the National Congress of American Indians (NCAI) recently joined together to create the

State-Tribal Relations Project, designed to promote intergovernmental co-operation.[5] It is hoped that the future will see more cooperative efforts similar to these.

A. State Jurisdiction over Reservation Indians

To what extent may the state regulate the activities of reservation Indians?

In *Worcester*, the Supreme Court held that state law could not be enforced in Indian country unless Congress had given its express consent. Since then, the Court has retreated somewhat from this principle,[6] and there are situations in which states may apply their laws in Indian country without congressional consent. As explained later in this chapter, this new analysis has expanded the ability of states to regulate the activities of *non-Indians* on the reservation but not those of Indians. It remains the general rule that reservation Indians may not be regulated by the state unless Congress has given its express consent.[7]

Does Congress need the state's consent in order to give rights to Indians?

No. The U.S. Constitution, as explained in chapter 5, confers plenary power on Congress over Indian affairs. Consequently, state consent is not required in order for Congress to confer rights or protections on Indians and tribes.[8] Even if a federal law was passed or an Indian treaty was signed before the state entered the Union, the state still must obey the law or treaty. For example, any hunting, fishing, or water rights given by the federal government to Indians before a territory became a state, must be honored by the state upon its admission into the Union.[9]

Do *nonmember Indians* enjoy the same immunity from state regulation as tribal members?

A *nonmember Indian* is an Indian who is living on or visiting another tribe's reservation. The Supreme Court has held in a variety of contexts that nonmember Indians do not enjoy the same immunities from state law that tribal members do; for instance, tribal members are exempt from paying state sales taxes when they purchase goods on the reservation, but nonmember Indians do not have that immunity.[10]

B. Congressional Authorization of State Jurisdiction

As just noted, states normally may not enforce their laws in Indian country unless authorized by Congress. States have often pressured Congress for authorization to impose various kinds of laws in Indian country. Although Congress has rarely bowed to this pressure, three federal laws (or groups of laws) have been enacted during the past two hundred years that have significantly increased state jurisdiction in Indian country: the General Allotment Act of 1887, Public Law 83-280 (enacted in 1953), and the termination laws enacted from 1953 through 1966.

1. The General Allotment Act of 1887

In what ways did the General Allotment Act increase state jurisdiction in Indian country?

The General Allotment Act of 1887 (GAA)[11] has been discussed in previous chapters.[12] To summarize, the GAA authorized federal officials to allot to tribal members parcels of the tribe's communally held land and to sell the rest of the tribe's land to non-Indians. The allotments made to tribal members were kept in trust status (that is, the federal government still owned the land) for a period of years, but at the end of that period, many Indians received deeds to their individual allotments and could then sell them. Hundreds of these allotments were subsequently sold to non-Indians. By the time the GAA was repealed in 1934, tribes had lost almost two-thirds of the lands they held in 1887 (a loss of nearly ninety million acres), and tribal government and Indian culture were greatly affected by the presence of so many non-Indians now living on the reservation.

The GAA did not give the states any power over Indians themselves, unlike the next two laws we shall review. It did, however, increase state authority over the *privately owned land* created by the act. First, the GAA authorized the states to tax the value of all the land—the ninety million acres—that had been removed from trust status, whether the land was now owned by a non-Indian, by an Indian, or by the tribe.[13] These taxes have added millions of dollars to state treasuries.

Second, the GAA increased the power of states—and correspondingly decreased the power of tribes—to regulate activities occurring on the land owned by non-Indians within the reservation. As explained in chapter 6, section 7, the Supreme Court held in *Montana v. United States* (1981)[14] that hunting and fishing by non-Indians on their own land within the reservation is governed by state—and not tribal—law, unless the tribe can show either that (1) the non-Indian owner has entered into some type of consensual relationship with the tribe (such as a lease or commercial contract), or (2) the activity of the non-Indian owner threatens a substantial tribal interest. Similarly, the Supreme Court has held that as a result of the GAA, non-Indians who live in an area of the reservation inhabited mostly by non-Indians need only obey state laws regarding how their land can be used (zoning laws), unless the tribe can show that one of the above two "*Montana* exceptions" is present.[15]

In short, the GAA did not give states any power over Indians, but it vastly increased state jurisdiction over those portions of Indian reservations that are owned by non-Indians. Under the *Montana* rule, states, not tribes, may regulate the activities occurring on privately owned land within the reservation (except in the narrow circumstances discussed above) and may tax the value of that land.

2. Public Law 83-280

As discussed in chapter 1, the years between 1953 and 1968 are known as the "termination era" in federal Indian history. During this period, Congress tried to destroy Indian tribes, force Indians to assimilate into Anglo-American society, and reduce the government's assistance to Indians.

Enacted on August 15, 1953, Public Law 83-280[16] (often written as "P.L. 280" or "Pub. L. 280") is a product of the termination era. It was designed primarily to alleviate the lawlessness that pervaded some Indian reservations, caused largely by inadequate tribal law enforcement programs.[17] To reduce reservation crime, though, Congress could have provided funds to improve tribal programs, but instead it enacted P.L. 280, which authorized certain states to arrest and prosecute Indians who commit crimes on reservations. "Without question," the Supreme Court has stated, P.L. 280 reflects "the general assimilationist policy followed by Congress from the early 1950s through the late 1960s."[18]

In what ways did P.L. 280 increase state jurisdiction in Indian country?

P.L. 280 is somewhat complicated. (A copy is reprinted in appendix B.) First, the act provides that five states "shall have jurisdiction over offenses committed by or against Indians" in Indian country "to the same extent that such state" has criminal jurisdiction elsewhere within the state.[19] These five states are known as the *mandatory* states, and they were given full criminal jurisdiction in Indian country: California, Minnesota (except for the Red Lake Reservation), Nebraska, Oregon (except for the Warm Springs Reservation), and Wisconsin (except for the Menominee Reservation). In 1958, Alaska was added by Congress as a sixth mandatory state (except for the Annette Islands).[20]

P.L. 280 authorized the other forty-four states, at their option, to acquire the same jurisdiction the mandatory states had received; they could acquire criminal jurisdiction at any time, simply by passing a law agreeing to exercise that power.[21] These states are known as the *option* states. Only ten option states took steps to assume any jurisdiction under P.L. 280; most states did not want the financial burden of prosecuting reservation crime. The jurisdiction these states opted to accept is discussed below and illustrated in the second list.

With respect to civil jurisdiction, P.L. 280 did little to increase state powers. The portion of P.L. 280 that confers *criminal* jurisdiction authorizes the mandatory states to prosecute reservation Indians "to the same extent" they prosecute non-Indians elsewhere. In contrast, the portion of P.L. 280 that relates to *civil* jurisdiction provides that the mandatory states "shall have jurisdiction over civil causes of action" involving reservation Indians. Although the mandatory states later argued that this language consented to broad civil jurisdiction—including taxing powers—in Indian country, the Supreme Court rejected that argument in *Bryan v. Itasca County, Minnesota* (1976).[22] In a unanimous decision, *Bryan* found nothing in P.L. 280 "remotely resembling an intention [by Congress] to confer general state civil regulatory control over Indian reservations."[23] P.L. 280, the Court said, allows state *courts* to adjudicate civil cases filed by or against individual Indians that arise in Indian country, such as a contract dispute, a tort action, or a divorce proceeding.[24] It does not authorize state *legislatures* to exercise regulatory (legislative) jurisdiction over Indians or tribes.[25] Thus, a state may not tax reservation Indians,[26] zone Indian land,[27] or regulate reservation gambling operations[28] merely because it has acquired jurisdiction under P.L. 280; its civil jurisdiction extends only to resolving reservation disputes in state courts.

P.L. 280 does not divest tribes of any of their powers, give states any authority over tribes, or waive tribal sovereign immunity from suit.[29] (The doctrine of tribal sovereign immunity is discussed in chapter 18.) There-fore, when exercising their P.L. 280 jurisdiction, state courts may not decide cases filed against an Indian tribe unless the tribe has consented to be sued. Moreover, P.L. 280 expressly provides that in exercising the state's adjudicatory powers, the court may not determine the ownership of trust land, interfere with treaty rights, or encumber trust property.[30]

What is "partial" P.L. 280 jurisdiction?

P.L. 280 does not expressly authorize an option state to assume any-thing less than the full criminal jurisdiction that Congress gave to the mandatory states. However, most option states that assumed any jurisdic-tion under P.L. 280, assumed only partial jurisdiction. These states limited their jurisdiction to (1) less than all the Indian reservations in the state, (2) less than all the geographic areas within an Indian reservation, or (3) less than all subject matters of the law. For instance, as the second list below illustrates, Montana only assumed criminal jurisdiction on the Flat-head Indian Reservation, one of several reservations in the state, and Idaho and Washington assumed jurisdiction only with respect to a few crimes. In 1979, the Supreme Court held that it was legal under P.L. 280 for an option state to assume only partial jurisdiction, even though this created a "checkerboard" situation in which some portions of the reservation and not others, and some crimes and not others, were subject to state jurisdic-tion.[31]

Which reservations within the six mandatory states are under P.L. 280 state jurisdiction?

The six mandatory states acquired the following jurisdiction under P.L. 280:[32]

State	Extent of Jurisdiction
Alaska	All Indian country within the state, except the Annette Islands
California	All Indian country within the state
Minnesota	All Indian country within the state, except the Red Lake Reservation
Nebraska	All Indian country within the state

Oregon	All Indian country within the state, except the Warm Springs Reservation
Wisconsin	All Indian country within the state, except the Menominee Reservation

Which reservations within the option states are under P.L. 280 state jurisdiction?

Ten option states sought to acquire jurisdiction under P.L. 280. Only Florida accepted the full jurisdiction given the mandatory states. The other nine sought only partial jurisdiction. The pattern of state jurisdiction within the option states is as follows:

State	*Extent of Jurisdiction*
Arizona	All Indian country within the state, limited to enforcement of the state's air and water pollution control laws.[33]
Florida	All Indian country within the state.[34]
Idaho	All Indian country within the state, limited to the following subject matters: compulsory school attendance; juvenile delinquency and youth rehabilitation; dependent, neglected, and abused children; mental illness; domestic relations; operation of motor vehicles on public roads.[35]
Iowa	Only over the Sac and Fox Indian community in Tama County, limited to certain criminal and civil jurisdiction.[36]
Montana	Limited to jurisdiction over any reservation that gives its consent. In 1965, the Confederated Salish and Kootenai Tribes consented to some state jurisdiction, but in 1993, at the tribe's request, the state returned most of its misdemeanor jurisdiction to the tribe, retaining its felony jurisdiction.[37]
Nevada	Over the Ely Indian Colony, and any other reservation that may subsequently consent.[38]
North Dakota	Limited to civil jurisdiction over any reservation that gives its consent.[39] No tribe has consented.

South Dakota   All Indian country within the state with tribal consent.
                When no tribe consented, the state attempted to pass laws
                conferring jurisdiction on the state, but these laws were
                invalidated by courts, primarily on procedural grounds, and
                the state has no P.L. 280 jurisdiction.[40]

Utah   All Indian country within the state with tribal consent.[41] No
                tribe has consented.

Washington   All fee patent (deeded) land within Indian country.
                Jurisdiction on trust land is limited to the following eight
                subjects unless the tribe requests full jurisdiction: adoptions,
                dependent children, juvenile delinquency, compulsory school
                attendance, public assistance, domestic relations, mental
                illness, and operation of motor vehicles on public roads.
                Several tribes have requested state jurisdiction, including the
                Chehalis, Muckleshoot, Nisqually, Quileute, and Tulalip.[42]

Can the option states still acquire jurisdiction under P.L. 280?

Many Indian tribes strongly opposed P.L. 280 at the time of its passage, objecting to state jurisdiction in Indian country. Afterward, tribes
continued to worry because option states could acquire jurisdiction over
them whenever they wanted. In response to these concerns, Congress
amended P.L. 280 in two significant respects in 1968.[43] First, Congress
placed a tribal consent requirement in the law. An option state can no
longer obtain any P.L. 280 jurisdiction over a tribe unless a majority of the
tribe's members, voting in a special election called for this purpose, gives
its consent.[44]

Second, the 1968 amendments authorize the United States, through
the office of the Secretary of the Interior, to accept a "retrocession" (a
return) of any jurisdiction acquired by a state under P.L. 280.[45] The Secretary is not required to accept a state's offer to retrocede its jurisdiction.
Also, a tribe cannot force a state to retrocede its jurisdiction over the tribe,
nor can it prevent the Secretary from accepting a retrocession.

Have any states retroceded jurisdiction to the United States?

Yes, several have. Nebraska retroceded its jurisdiction over the Omaha
Tribe in 1970 except for traffic violations on public roads. Washington
retroceded its jurisdiction over the Quinault Tribe in 1969 and the Su

quamish Port Madison Tribe in 1972. Minnesota retroceded its jurisdiction over the Bois Forte Indian Reservation in 1973 and the Nett Lake Reservation in 1975. Nevada retroceded jurisdiction over all but one of its tribes (the Ely Indian Colony) in 1975. In 1976, when Congress restored the Menominee Tribe to federal status after terminating the tribe in 1961, Wisconsin retroceded the jurisdiction it had acquired by the termination.[46] In 1981, Oregon retroceded its criminal jurisdiction over the Umatilla Reservation.[47]

When Nebraska retroceded its jurisdiction over the Omaha Tribe, it also offered to retrocede its jurisdiction over the Winnebago Tribe. The Winnebagos opposed the retrocession, and respecting their wishes, the Secretary of the Interior refused to accept Nebraska's offer with respect to the Winnebago Reservation. A federal court later upheld the right of the Secretary to make that choice.[48] In 1986, Nebraska again offered to retrocede criminal jurisdiction on the Winnebago Reservation, the tribe indicated its approval, and the federal government accepted retrocession.

3. Termination Laws

In addition to the GAA and P.L. 280, Congress has used one other means to significantly increase state jurisdiction over Indians. This third method, termination, is the most devastating to Indian interests of the three.

The process of termination and its effects are explained in earlier chapters of this book.[49] Between 1953 and 1966, Congress passed laws that terminated 109 tribes. Each of these laws ended the trust relationship between the United States and the tribe, required the tribe to distribute all of its property to its members, and eliminated the reservation. Tribal members thus became fully subject to state law and so did their lands.

4. Other Congressional Authorizations of State Jurisdiction

Congress has passed several laws that confer some amount of state jurisdiction over particular tribes. Oklahoma and New York have been given some jurisdiction over Indian tribes in those states, as discussed in chapter 15. In 1978, Congress passed a law that resolved a land dispute in Rhode Island concerning territory claimed by the Narragansett Indian Tribe. The law created a reservation for the Narragansetts of approximately eighteen hundred acres of land, and it provided that these lands "shall be subject to the civil and criminal laws and jurisdiction of the State of Rhode Island."[50] In 1980, Congress passed a unique statute regarding the Penobscot Nation and the Passamaquoddy Tribe in Maine. Under this law, both tribes retain exclusive jurisdiction over their "internal tribal matters" such as membership and elections, but in all other respects they have the same rights and are subject to the same state laws as a municipality of Maine.[51] In 1984, Congress passed a law conferring on the state of Colorado "criminal and civil jurisdiction within the boundaries of the town of Ignacio, Colorado . . . within the Southern Ute Indian Reservation, as if such State had assumed jurisdiction pursuant to" P.L. 280.[52]

Congress has also given the states jurisdiction over certain subject matters. For example, Congress has prohibited the introduction of liquor in Indian country except in compliance with state (and tribal) law.[53] As a result of this statute, states can require persons selling liquor on the reservation to purchase a state license and pay state business taxes.[54] Another federal law authorizes the Secretary of the Interior to allow state officials to inspect reservation health conditions and enforce the state's sanitation and quarantine regulations on Indian reservations.[55] In addition, Congress has authorized the states to seize by eminent domain (that is, to take for a public purpose) any federal land allotted to an Indian, provided that the Indian is paid fair compensation for the value of the land.[56] There is also some authority for the view that Congress has authorized the states to regulate public utility services on Indian reservations[57] and to require employers within Indian country, including tribal members who are employers, to comply with workers' compensation laws passed by the states.[58]

Thus, every state may exercise some jurisdiction on Indian reservations, with the mandatory P.L. 280 states being allowed to exercise the most. However, no state has the authority to regulate internal tribal matters, including determinations of membership, tribal elections, and business and social transactions between tribal members. On the whole, Congress has kept tribal governments and tribal members free from state jurisdiction. This is somewhat surprising given the constant pressure that many state officials have placed on Congress to increase state jurisdiction over Indians.

C. STATE JURISDICTION WITHOUT CONGRESSIONAL AUTHORIZATION

As explained at the outset of this chapter, the Supreme Court held in *Worcester* in 1832 that state laws "can have no force" in Indian country without the consent of Congress. *Worcester* thus established an "absolute" rule: if Congress consented, the state could act; without consent, state jurisdiction was absolutely barred, even with respect to the activities of non-Indians on the reservation. However, the Court began eroding *Worcester* fifty years later, holding that even without congressional consent, a state (1) could prosecute non-Indians who commit crimes against other non-Indians on an Indian reservation[59] and (2) could tax the personal property owned by non-Indians on an Indian reservation.[60] Since then, the Court has further diluted *Worcester*, shifting away, as it has admitted, "from the idea of inherent Indian sovereignty as a bar to State jurisdiction";[61] instead, the Court has increasingly elevated the importance of state interests over the interests of the tribe.

The Supreme Court has replaced the *Worcester* rule with a two-part test to determine which state laws may be enforced in Indian country without congressional consent: the *federal preemption* and the *infringement* tests. A state law must pass both tests in order to be valid.[62]

Which state laws violate the federal preemption test?

The Supremacy Clause of the U.S. Constitution declares that in those subject areas assigned by the Constitution to the primary or exclusive authority of Congress, federal law is "the supreme law of the land."[63] As a result, any state law that conflicts with federal law in one of those areas is said to be "preempted" by federal law. Given that the regulation of Indian affairs is an area assigned to the primary control of Congress (as explained earlier), a state law regulating Indian affairs that is inconsistent with federal law violates the federal preemption test.[64]

The federal preemption test is easy to apply when a state law is clearly inconsistent with some federal law or Indian treaty, but it is more difficult to apply when Congress has not expressly prohibited the specific action the state is attempting. In order to determine whether a state law is preempted by federal law in that circumstance, the state's interests in enforcing its law on the reservation are balanced against the federal and tribal interests in preventing state intrusion. The preemption analysis, the Supreme Court has held, requires "a particularized inquiry into the nature of the state, federal and tribal interests at stake . . . to determine whether, in the specific context, the exercise of state authority would violate federal law."[65] The state law must be declared invalid "if it interferes or is incompatible with federal and tribal interests reflected in federal law, unless the

State interests at stake are sufficient to justify the assertion of State authority."[66]

Tribal sovereignty—although lacking some of the force it had under the *Worcester* test—continues to plays an important role in modern preemption analysis. This is because the preemption test balances federal interests against state interests, and the federal government always has a *significant* interest in "encouraging tribal self-sufficiency and economic development."[67] Thus, the federal government's interest in fostering tribal sovereignty provides "an important 'backdrop' against which" state laws affecting Indians and tribes must be examined.[68]

Given the "backdrop" of tribal sovereignty, the more a state law impacts tribal members, the more likely it is to fail the preemption test. As the Supreme Court stated in 1983, it is only in "exceptional circumstances [that] a State may assert jurisdiction over the on-reservation activities of Tribal members."[69] In a 1995 case, the Court acknowledged that a "categorical approach" should be taken in cases involving a state's attempt to tax reservation Indians and tribes: such taxation will always violate the Supremacy Clause unless expressly authorized by Congress.[70] State law is "generally inapplicable" to reservation Indians and tribes, the Court has explained, because the state's interest in regulating their activities is likely to be minimal, whereas the federal and tribal interests in promoting tribal self-government and economic self-sufficiency are likely to be great.[71]

Conversely, state laws that primarily affect nonmembers are more likely to pass the preemption test, given that tribes usually lack a strong interest in protecting nonmembers from the operation of state law.[72] Indeed, as discussed in chapter 9, virtually every law regulating non-Indians on the reservation has been upheld by the courts—including state tax laws—except in those rare situations in which enforcement of the law substantially interfered with a significant tribal interest.

Preemption cases involving Indians and tribes are often difficult to resolve because a wide variety of factors must be considered, including (1) the extent to which the tribe or tribal members are affected by the state's regulation; (2) the extent to which the federal government is already regulating the conduct that the state is seeking to regulate; (3) the nature of the state's interests in enforcing its law on the reservation; and (4) whether the state is providing any benefits or services in exchange for the burdens (usually, state taxes) the state is seeking to impose.

The Supreme Court first employed the preemption test in *Warren*

Trading Post Co. v. Arizona Tax Commission (1965).[73] The issue in that case was whether Arizona could impose its "gross proceeds" tax (a tax on total income) on a non-Indian company that operated a trading and grocery store on the Navajo reservation. In defending the law, the state pointed out that no federal law expressly prohibited the tax, the taxpayer was non-Indian, and it was the same tax that all businesses within the state had to pay. The Court, however, recognized that other factors had to be considered. First, a treaty with the Navajos assured them relative security against state law. Second, the federal government regulates virtually every aspect of trade on Indian reservations, and the state tax, the Court said, would "disturb or disarrange" the comprehensive federal plan.[74] Moreover, the non-Indian trading company would likely raise the price of its goods to offset the tax, and since most of its customers were Indians, they would be the ones paying the tax. Balancing the interests, the Court held that Arizona's tax was preempted by federal law.

The Supreme Court's next preemption case was *McClanahan v. Arizona Tax Commission* (1973).[75] The Court held in *McClanahan* that Arizona could not assess state income taxes on a Navajo Indian who lived and worked on her reservation. Especially in light of the Navajo treaty, the fact that this tax was being applied directly to a tribal member, and given the "backdrop" of tribal sovereignty, the Court found that federal interests outweighed state interests. Reservation employment by tribal members is an activity, the Court held, "totally within the sphere which the relevant treaties and statutes leave for the Federal Government and for the Indians themselves."[76]

The Supreme Court reached a similar conclusion in *White Mountain Apache Tribe v. Bracker* (1980).[77] The White Mountain Apache Tribe of Arizona had contracted with a non-Indian company to cut, haul, and sell tribal timber, with the tribe sharing in the profits. Arizona sought to tax the fuel used by the company to haul the timber on roads built and maintained by the tribe and by the federal government. The state also sought to tax the profits made on the company's sale of the timber. The non-Indian company challenged the state taxes and won. Applying the federal preemption test, the Court noted that the federal government regulated virtually every aspect of tribal timber production; the tribe had a strong interest in keeping its timber production free from state regulation; the value in the item being taxed (the timber) was generated entirely on the reservation; and the state was providing no services in exchange for the money it was trying to collect. Given that the tribal and federal interests far outweighed the state's interests, the Court held that the state tax was preempted by federal law.

In similar fashion, the Supreme Court has ruled that unless Congress has consented, a state (1) may not tax the income made by a non-Indian construction company and paid by a tribe for building a school on the reservation,[78] (2) may not require non-Indians who hunt or fish on tribal land to purchase a state game license and comply with state game laws,[79] and (3) may not enforce state gambling laws on Indian reservations.[80] In all three cases, the Court found that tribal and federal interests outweighed state interests. Using the same analysis, other courts have held that federal law preempts states from regulating the disposal of hazardous waste,[81] the placement of billboards,[82] and the harvesting of timber[83] on tribal land.

The Supreme Court's 1989 decision in *Cotton Petroleum Corp. v. New Mexico*[84] marked a shift in the Court's traditional preemption analysis and gave the interests of the state far more weight than in any previous decision. The issue in *Cotton Petroleum* was whether New Mexico could impose a severance tax on oil and gas produced by a non-Indian company on tribal land. In 1982, the Court had ruled that the tribe could impose its own taxes on this mineral production;[85] the issue here was whether New Mexico could impose a similar ("double") tax.

The Court, voting 6 to 3, upheld the tax, even though it acknowledged that this double taxation might discourage mineral producers from searching for oil and gas on tribal lands, thereby reducing the tribe's income. The Court also acknowledged that New Mexico collects millions of dollars more in revenue from taxing tribal oil and gas than it spends on reservation services and that the federal government extensively regulates oil and gas production on Indian reservations. These factors likely would have led earlier Supreme Courts to invalidate the state tax, but not the current Court, which upheld the tax. There was no proof, the Court said, that the tax would make the tribe's oil and gas unmarketable; a state is not required to spend on the taxpayer as much money as it collects from the taxpayer; and the federal government's regulation of oil and gas was not comprehensive or direct enough to preempt New Mexico's tax. The Justices who dissented in *Cotton Petroleum* wrote that the majority's decision "distorts" the preemption test.[86]

In *Warren Trading Post,* the Supreme Court's first preemption case, the

Court indicated that no state burdens on reservation trade could ever pass the preemption test, given that state laws are not permitted to disturb a comprehensive federal plan, and Congress had adopted a comprehensive plan for regulating reservation trade.[87] In 1994, consistent with the Court's overall reformulation of the preemption test, the Court repudiated this analysis. In *Department of Taxation and Finance of New York v. Milhelm Attea & Bros., Inc.,* the Court held that *Warren Trading Post* had gone too far in suggesting that no state burdens on reservation trade are allowed, and the Court upheld a New York law that compelled off-reservation, non-Indian wholesalers who sold cigarettes to tribal vendors on the reservation to collect the state's cigarette taxes on the amount of cigarettes sold by those vendors to non-Indian customers.[88]

Nothing in *Milhelm Attea* dilutes the importance of the preemption test in safeguarding *Indians and tribes* from state taxation and regulation, and even under the current preemption test, the tax at issue in *Warren Trading Post* would likely still be invalidated today.[89] In both *Warren Trading Post* and *Milhelm Attea,* the taxes at issue were being collected from a non-Indian business, but the critical difference between the two cases is that in *Warren Trading Post* the tax was actually being paid by the Indian customers who bought goods at the trading post, whereas in *Milhelm Attea* the tax was actually being paid by the non-Indian customers who purchased cigarettes from tribal vendors (tribal members were exempt from the tax). The facts of *Milhelm Attea* thus present a stronger case for state taxation than those in *Warren Trading Post,* regardless of which analysis is used.

In summary, the preemption test remains a formidable—if not insurmountable—barrier against state encroachments on the reservation when the intrusion would significantly affect Indians or tribes. On the other hand, when the exercise of state jurisdiction would have little impact on Indians or tribes, it usually will pass the preemption test.

Which state laws violate the infringement test?

In 1959, the Supreme Court held in *Williams v. Lee* that a state may not infringe "on the right of reservation Indians to make their own laws and be ruled by them."[90] This principle has become known as the infringement test. It protects the inherent right of Indian tribes to be self-governing.

In *Williams,* a non-Indian who owned a store on the Navajo Reservation sued a member of the tribe in state court, seeking to collect a business debt. A tribal court was available to hear this case, but the store owner filed suit in state court anyway. The state court ruled in favor of the non-Indian. However, the Supreme Court ruled on appeal that the state court had no right to decide this controversy. The store owner had to use the tribal court because "to allow the exercise of state jurisdiction here would undermine the authority of the tribal courts over Reservation affairs and hence would infringe on the right of the Indians to govern themselves."[91]

The Court reached a similar conclusion in *Fisher v. District Court* (1976).[92] The issue in *Fisher* was whether a state court had jurisdiction in a proceeding in which all parties were reservation Indians to determine whether a foster-care family would be allowed to adopt an Indian child over the objection of the child's natural mother. Applying the infringement test, the Court held that the state court lacked jurisdiction. Permitting a state court to decide the custody of this child "plainly would interfere with the powers of self-government" by subjecting a dispute arising on the reservation among tribal members "to a forum other than the one they have established for themselves."[93]

As *Williams* and *Fisher* illustrate, tribal courts normally have exclusive jurisdiction to decide disputes involving reservation Indians unless Congress has consented to concurrent jurisdiction by the state. When Congress passed P.L. 280 in 1953, it authorized the courts in certain states to resolve disputes involving reservation Indians but, as explained earlier, the majority of states have no such authority.[94]

Is the combination of the preemption and infringement tests equal in scope to the *Worcester* rule?

Not quite. The *Worcester* rule prohibited all state laws from being enforced in Indian country without congressional consent. This absolute bar has been replaced by the federal preemption and infringement tests. The combination of these tests is nearly as formidable as the *Worcester* rule with respect to state laws that significantly affect reservation Indians and tribes. Thus far, in fact, every effort by the states to regulate an activity that primarily involves reservation Indians and tribes has failed either the preemption or infringement tests unless it was authorized by Congress.

The Supreme Court's recent decision in *Nevada v. Hicks* (2001),[95] addressed several questions regarding state and tribal jurisdiction in Indian country. One question was whether state law enforcement officers could legally execute a state court search warrant on a tribal member's home based on an allegation that the tribal member had poached bighorn sheep outside the reservation.

The Court began its analysis in *Hicks* by reaffirming the principle that "state law is generally inapplicable" to on-reservation conduct involving only Indians.[96] However, the Court held that when reservation Indians engage in activities outside the reservation, state officials may later enter the reservation, as they did in this case, and serve them with state judicial process—including search and arrest warrants—regarding those activities.[97] In reaching this conclusion, the Court used some rather expansive language, stating that "State sovereignty does not end at a reservation's border,"[98] and "an Indian reservation is considered part of the territory of the State."[99] Whether the Court will apply that language so as to permit other forms of state jurisdiction in Indian country is impossible to predict, of course. But given the Court's recent trends, as discussed in more detail in chapter 9, it is certainly within the realm of possibility. For now, though, *Hicks* stands only for the proposition that a state may exercise jurisdiction over Indians on the reservation for activities engaged in off the reservation, even searching their reservation homes and arresting them for violations of state law.

Thus, dilution of the *Worcester* rule has had almost no effect on state jurisdiction over *Indians* for activities undertaken *on* the reservation. Dilution of *Worcester* has greatly assisted states, though, in their efforts to regulate (1) *non-Indians* on the reservation, and (2) Indians on the reservation regarding their off-reservation conduct. It is no longer the case that state law "can have no force" on Indian reservations, although it remains true, as the Supreme Court reaffirmed in *Hicks*, that "state law is generally inapplicable" to reservation Indians regarding their on-reservation activities.[100]

D. State Jurisdiction over Off-Reservation Indians

What powers do the states have over off-reservation Indians?

Indians who leave the reservation even briefly become subject to the same state laws as everyone else unless a federal law or treaty grants an immunity. As the Supreme Court stated in 1973, "Absent express federal law to the contrary, Indians going beyond reservation boundaries have generally been held subject to nondiscriminatory State law otherwise applicable to all citizens of the State."[101] Thus, an Indian who commits a crime off the reservation can be prosecuted by the state in the same manner as anyone else who commits that crime.[102] Furthermore, as just explained, the Supreme Court held in *Hicks* that Indians can be subjected to state search and arrest warrants on the reservation for activities they engaged in outside the reservation.

There is, however, an exception to the rule that Indians who leave the reservation become fully subject to state law: when Indians are engaging in a federally protected right outside the reservation, such as a federal treaty right to hunt or fish, state law is generally inapplicable and need not be obeyed.[103] (This subject is discussed more fully in chapter 11.) Similarly, a state may be prohibited from regulating an off-reservation activity when doing so would infringe on tribal sovereignty.[104] To illustrate, when a tribe in the exercise of its inherent sovereign powers enacts a motor vehicle registration law under which tribal members residing on the reservation must obtain a tribal license plate for their personal vehicles, a state may not then arrest and prosecute these persons for failing to have the state's license plate when they drive their vehicles off the reservation.[105] In that type of situation, as one court recently noted, "state law has had to accommodate tribal sovereignty."[106]

NOTES

1. *Worcester v. Georgia,* 31 U.S. 515, 561 (1832).

2. U.S. Const., art. I, sec. 8, cl. 3. The federal government's authority over Indian affairs is the subject of ch. 5.

3. *See Oklahoma Tax Commission v. Chickasaw Nation,* 515 U.S. 450, 458 (1995); *McClanahan v. Arizona State Tax Comm'n,* 411 U.S. 164 (1973); *Bryan v. Itasca County, Minnesota,* 426 U.S. 373 (1976); *Williams v. Lee,* 358 U.S. 217 (1959).

4. *McClanahan,* note 3 above, 411 U.S. at 168, citing *Rice v. Olson,* 324 U.S. 786, 789 (1945).

5. An informative pamphlet entitled *Government to Government* (June 2000) can be obtained from either NCSL (1560 Broadway, Suite 700, Denver, CO 80202) or NCAI (1301 Connecticut Ave., N.W., Suite 200, Washington, D.C. 20036). The cost is $20.

6. *See Strate v. A-1 Contractors,* 520 U.S. 438 (1997); *Dept. of Taxation and Finance of New York v. Milhelm Attea & Bros., Inc.,* 512 U.S. 61 (1994); *Moe v. Salish and Kootenai Tribes,* 425 U.S. 463, 481–83 (1976).

7. *See, e.g., Chickasaw Nation,* note 3 above, 515 U.S. at 458.

8. *Dick v. U.S.*, 208 U.S. 340 (1908); *Winters v. U.S.*, 207 U.S. 564 (1908).

9. *See* cases cited in note 8 above. *See also Puyallup Tribe v. Dept. of Game*, 391 U.S. 392 (1968).

10. *See Arizona Dept. of Rev. v. Blaze Construction Co.*, 526 U.S. 32 (1999); *Washington v. Confederated Tribes of Colville Reservation*, 447 U.S. 134, 160–61 (1980).

11. 25 U.S.C. Secs. 331 *et seq.*

12. *See* ch. 1 and ch. 6, sec. B.

13. *See County of Yakima v. Confederated Tribes and Bands of Yakima Indian Nation*, 502 U.S. 251 (1992) (holding that the state can tax deeded land owned by an Indian on the reservation), and *Cass County, Minnesota v. Leech Lake Band of Chippewa Indians*, 524 U.S. 103 (1998) (holding that the state can tax deeded land owned by an Indian tribe on the reservation).

14. 450 U.S. 544 (1981).

15. *Brendale v. Confederated Tribes and Bands of Yakima Indian Nation*, 492 U.S. 408 (1989).

16. 18 U.S.C. Sec. 1162; 28 U.S.C. Sec. 1360.

17. *See* H.R. Rep. No. 848, 83d Cong., 1st Sess. 1–6 (1953). *See also Bryan*, note 3 above, 426 U.S. at 379; *Three Affiliated Tribes v. Wold Engineering*, 476 U.S. 877 (1986); *Confederated Tribes of Colville Reservation v. Washington*, 938 F.2d 146, 147 (9th Cir. 1991).

18. *Washington v. Confederated Bands and Tribes of Yakima Indian Nation*, 439 U.S. 463, 488 (1979).

19. 18 U.S.C. Sec. 1162(a) (criminal jurisdiction); 28 U.S.C. Sec. 1360(a) (civil jurisdiction).

20. Pub. L. No. 85-615, Sec. 1, 72 Stat. 545. Codified in the provisions cited in note 16 above.

21. Pub. L. No. 83-280, Secs. 6, 7.

22. 426 U.S. 373 (1976).

23. *Bryan*, note 3 above, 426 U.S. at 384.

24. *Id.* at 390.

25. *See id.* at 385–89; *Wold Engineering*, note 17 above; *In re Marriage of Purnel*, 60 Cal. Rptr.2d 667 (Ct. App. 1997) (holding that state court is authorized by P.L. 280 to adjudicate divorce proceedings and order payment of child support). *See generally, Great Western Casinos, Inc. v. Morongo Band of Mission Indians*, 88 Cal. Rptr.2d 828, 842–843 (Ct. App. 1999).

26. *Bryan*, note 3 above.

27. *Santa Rosa Band of Indians v. Kings County*, 532 F.2d 655 (9th Cir. 1975), *cert. denied*, 429 U.S. 1038 (1977).

28. *California v. Cabazon Band of Mission Indians*, 480 U.S. 202, 216 (1987).

29. *Bishop Paiute Tribe v. County of Inyo*, 291 F.3d 549, 557 (9th Cir. 2002), petition for *certiorari* pending; *Houghtaling v. Seminole Tribe of Florida*, 611 So.2d 1235 (Fla. 1993); *Atkinson v. Haldane*, 569 P.2d 151, 152 (Alaska 1977).

30. *See, e.g., Boisclair v. Superior Court*, 51 Cal.3d 1140, 1153–56 (Cal. 1990) (holding that a court in a P.L. 280 state cannot hear any case in which the ownership of trust land might be decided).

138   *The Rights of Indians and Tribes*

31. *Washington v. Confederated Bands and Tribes of Yakima Indian Nation,* note 18 above.

32. *See* 18 U.S.C. Sec. 1162(a) (criminal jurisdiction) and 28 U.S.C. Sec. 1306(a) (civil jurisdiction). Originally, Alaska was denied jurisdiction over the Metlakatla Indian Community but a 1970 amendment to P.L. 280 placed it under the state's criminal jurisdiction.

33. Ariz. Rev. Stat. Ann. Sec. 49-561. Except for this limited jurisdiction, Arizona "may not exercise subject matter jurisdiction over transactions arising on Indian reservations." *Neena v. Moreno,* 647 P.2d 1163, 1164 (Ariz. App. 1982). Some tribes in Arizona contend that the state failed to pass this law in a proper manner under P.L. 280, but no tribe has yet filed suit challenging its validity.

34. Fla. Stat. Ann. Sec. 285.16. *See Houghtaling,* note 29 above (noting statute but granting tribe sovereign immunity from suit); *Serian v. State,* 588 So.2d 251, 252 (Fla. App. 1991).

35. Idaho Code Secs. 67-5101 through 5103. *See State v. Barros,* 957 P.2d 1095 (Idaho 1998).

36. Iowa Code Ann. 1.12 through 1.14. *See Youngbear v. Brewer,* 415 F. Supp. 807 (N.D. Iowa 1976), *aff'd,* 549 F.2d 74 (8th Cir. 1977), for a discussion of the state's criminal jurisdiction, and *State ex rel. Dept. of Human Services v. Whitebreast,* 409 N.W.2d 460 (Iowa 1987) (civil jurisdiction). The limited jurisdiction acquired by Iowa does not include jurisdiction over the Sac and Fox Tribe but only over its members. *See Meier v. Sac and Fox Tribe,* 476 N.W.2d 61 (Iowa 1991).

37. Mont. Rev. Code Ann. Secs. 2-1-301 through 2-1-306. *See State v. Spotted Blanket,* 955 P.2d 1347, 1351 (Mont. 1998); *Liberty v. Jones,* 782 P.2d 369 (Mont. 1989). Those areas not covered by the tribe's consent cannot be adjudicated in state court. *See Balyeat Law, P.C. v. Pettit,* 931 P.2d 50 (Mont. 1998); *Balyeat Law, P.C. v. Pettit,* 967 P.2d 398 (Mont. 1998).

38. Nev. Rev. Stat. Sec. 41.430. *See Snooks v. Ninth Judicial Dist. Court,* 919 P.2d 1064 (Nev. 1996) (holding that state courts have no jurisdiction beyond that conferred by the statute).

39. North Dakota Century Code Chap. 27-19.

40. Although statutes are still on the books, *see* S.D.C.L. 1-1-12 through 1-1-21, which purport to confer P.L. 280 jurisdiction on the state, both state and federal courts have held that these statutes are defective, and that South Dakota acquired no jurisdiction under P.L. 280. *See Rosebud Sioux Tribe v. South Dakota,* 900 F.2d 1164 (8th Cir. 1990), *cert. denied,* 500 U.S. 915 (1991); *State v. Spotted Horse,* 462 N.W.2d 463, 467 (S.D. 1990).

41. Utah Code Ann. 63-36-201 *et seq.*

42. Wash. Rev. Code Secs. 37.12.010 through 150. *See State v. Cooper,* 928 P.2d 406 (Wash. 1996); *In re Estate of Cross,* 891 P.2d 26 (1995); *Cordova v. Holwegner,* 971 P.2d 531 (Wash. App. 1999). Of course, as with the mandatory states, Washington cannot enforce laws that are civil rather than criminal in nature. *See Confederated Tribes of Colville Reservation v. Washington,* 938 F.2d 146 (9th Cir.), *cert. denied,* 503 U.S. 997 (1992).

43. 25 U.S.C. Secs. 1321–26.

44. 25 U.S.C. Secs. 1322, 1326. A state cannot acquire P.L. 280 jurisdiction unless this election procedure is followed. *Kennerly v. District Court*, 400 U.S. 423 (1971).

45. 25 U.S.C. Sec. 1323(a). The President has designated the Secretary of the Interior to accept retrocessions. *See* Exec. Order 11435, Fed. Reg. 17339 (1968).

46. *See Omaha Tribe of Nebraska v. Village of Walthill*, 334 F. Supp. 823, 833-35 (D. Neb. 1971), *aff'd per curiam*, 460 F.2d 1327 (8th Cir. 1972).

47. 46 Fed. Reg. 2195 (1981).

48. *Omaha Tribe*, note 46 above. *See also U.S. v. Brown*, 334 F. Supp. 536 (D. Neb. 1971).

49. *See* ch. 1, and ch. 5, sec. B.

50. 25 U.S.C. Sec. 1701, 1708. For a history of the Narragansett settlement, *see Rhode Island v. Narragansett Indian Tribe*, 19 F.3d 685, 689 (1st Cir. 1994).

51. 25 U.S.C. Secs. 1721–35, the Maine Indian Claims Settlement Act. For a discussion of this act, *see Passamaquoddy Tribe v. Maine*, 75 F.3d 784, 787 (1st Cir. 1996); *Akins v. Penobscot Nation*, 130 F.3d 482 (1st Cir. 1997).

52. Pub. L. 98-290, Sec. 5, 98 Stat. at 202.

53. 18 U.S.C. Sec. 1161.

54. *Rice v. Rehner*, 463 U.S. 713 (1983). *See also Citizen Band Potawatomi Indian Tribe v. Oklahoma Tax Comm'n*, 975 F.2d 1459 (10th Cir. 1992).

55. 25 U.S.C. Sec. 231. *See Northern v. Kings County*, 694 P.2d 40 (Wash. App. 1985).

56. 25 U.S.C. Sec. 357. *See Nebraska Pub. Power Dist. v. 100.95 Acres of Land*, 719 F.2d 956 (8th Cir. 1983); *So. California Edison Co. v. Rice*, 685 F.2d 354 (9th Cir. 1982). The statute is limited to allotted land; tribal land cannot be condemned by the state under Sec. 357. *See U.S. v. City of McAlester*, 604 F.2d 42 (10th Cir. 1977).

57. *See Cheyenne River Sioux Tribe Telephone Authority v. P.U.C.*, 595 N.W.2d 604 (S.D. 1999), relying on 47 U.S.C. Sec. 152(b). *But see Baker Electric Cooperative, Inc. v. Devils Lake Sioux Indian Tribe*, 28 F.3d 1466 (8th Cir. 1994).

58. 40 U.S.C. Sec. 290. *See State ex rel. Industrial Comm'n v. Indian Country Enterprises, Inc.*, 944 P.2d 117 (Idaho 1997).

59. *U.S. v. McBratney*, 104 U.S. 621 (1881).

60. *Utah and No. Ry. v. Fisher*, 116 U.S. 28 (1885).

61. *McClanahan*, note 3 above, 411 U.S. at 172. *See also County of Yakima*, note 13 above, 502 U.S. at 687–88.

62. *White Mountain Apache Tribe v. Bracker*, 448 U.S. 136, 143 1980).

63. U.S. Const. art. VI, sec. 2. *See McClanahan*, note 3 above; *Bracker*, note 62 above.

64. *Bracker*, note 62 above, 448 U.S. at 142; *Warren Trading Post Co. v. Arizona Tax Comm'n*, 380 U.S. 685 (1965).

65. *Bracker*, note 62 above, 448 U.S. at 145 (citations omitted). *See also Milhelm Attea*, note 6 above, 512 U.S. at 73.

66. *New Mexico v. Mescalero Apache Tribe*, 462 U.S. 324, 334 (1983).

67. *California v. Cabazon Band of Mission Indians*, 480 U.S. 202, 216 (1987); *New Mexico v. Mescalero Apache Tribe*, note 66 above, 462 U.S. at 344; *Bracker*, note 62 above, 448 U.S. at 142.

68. *Bracker,* note 62 above, 448 U.S. at 143, citing *McClanahan,* note 3 above, 411 U.S. at 172. *See Prairie Band of Potawatomi Indians v. Pierce,* 253 F.3d 1234, 1253–54 (10th Cir. 2001).

69. *New Mexico v. Mescalero Apache Tribe,* note 66 above, 462 U.S. at 331–32. *See also Nevada v. Hicks,* 121 S.Ct. 2304, 2311 (2001) ("When on-reservation conduct involving only Indians is at issue, state law is generally inapplicable.") (Internal citation omitted.)

70. *Chickasaw Nation,* note 3 above, 515 U.S. at 458.

71. *Bracker,* note 62 above, 448 U.S. at 144. *See also Hicks,* note 69 above, 121 S.Ct. at 2312.

72. *See Washington v. Confederated Tribes of the Colville Indian Reservation,* 447 U.S. 134, 161 (1980). Chapter 9 discusses situations in which states have been permitted to exercise civil jurisdiction over reservation nonmembers.

73. 380 U.S. 685 (1965).

74. *Bracker,* note 62 above, 448 U.S. at 144.

75. 411 U.S. 164 (1973).

76. *McClanahan,* note 3 above, 411 U.S. at 179–80.

77. 448 U.S. 136 (1980).

78. *Ramah Navajo School Board v. Bureau of Revenue,* 458 U.S. 832, 839 (1982).

79. *Mescalero Apache Tribe,* note 66 above.

80. *Cabazon Band,* note 67 above; *Tamiami Partners, Ltd. v. Miccosukee Tribe of Indians of Florida,* 63 F.3d 1030 (11th Cir. 1995). In response to the *Cabazon Band* decision, Congress passed the Indian Gaming Regulatory Act, discussed in ch. 16, which authorizes state regulation of certain gaming on Indian reservations.

81. *Washington Dept. of Ecology v. EPA.,* 752 F.2d 1465 (9th Cir. 1985).

82. *California v. Naegle Outdoor Adv. Co.,* 698 P.2d 150 (Cal. 1985), *cert. denied,* 475 U.S. 1045 (1986).

83. *In re: Blue Lake Forest Products, Inc. v. Hong Kong and Shanghai Banking Corp., Ltd.,* 30 F.3d 1138 (9th Cir. 1994).

84. 490 U.S. 163 (1989).

85. *Merrion v. Jicarilla Apache Tribe,* 455 U.S. 103 (1982).

86. *Cotton Petroleum Corp. v. New Mexico,* 490 U.S. 163, 204 (1989) (Blackmun, Brennan, Marshall, JJ., dissenting).

87. *Warren Trading Post,* note 64 above, 380 U.S. at 690.

88. *See Milhelm Attea,* note 6 above.

89. *See In re: Blue Lake Forest Products, Inc.,* note 83 above.

90. *Williams v. Lee,* 358 U.S. 217, 220 (1958).

91. *Id.* at 223.

92. 424 U.S. 382 (1976).

93. *Fisher v. District Court,* 424 U.S. 382, 387–88 (1976).

94. *See Geiger v. Pierce,* 758 P.2d 279, 281 (Mont. 1988); *Crow Tribe of Indians v. Montana,* 819 F.2d 895, 902–3 (9th Cir. 1987), *aff'd,* 484 U.S. 997 (1988). Chapter 9 discusses this issue in further detail.

95. 121 S.Ct. 2304 (2001).

96. *Id.*

97. *Id.* at 2313.

98. *Id.* at 2311.

99. *Id.*

100. *Id.* at 2311 (internal quotation omitted).

101. *Mescalero Apache Tribe v. Jones*, 411 U.S. 145, 148–49 (1973). *See also Chickasaw Nation*, note 3 above, 515 U.S. at 464.

102. *See Hicks*, note 69 above, 121 S.Ct. at 2312 ; *Ward v. Race Horse*, 163 U.S. 504 (1896), *overruled on other grounds, Minnesota v. Mille Lacs Band of Chippewa Indians*, 526 U.S. 172 (1999).

103. *Antoine v. Washington*, 420 U.S. 194 (1975); *Washington v. Washington State Commercial Passenger Fishing Vessel Ass'n.*, 443 U.S. 658 (1979).

104. *See Prairie Band*, note 68 above; *In re Blue Lake Forest Products, Inc.*, note 83 above, 30 F.3d at 1141; *Red Lake Band of Chippewa Indians v. State*, 248 N.W.2d 722 (Minn. 1976); *Queets Band of Indians v. Washington*, 765 F.2d 1399 (9th Cir. 1985), *vacated as moot*, 783 F.2d 154 (9th Cir. 1986).

105. *See Prairie Band*, note 68 above; *Red Lake Band*, note 104 above; *Queets*, note 104 above.

106. *Prairie Band*, note 68 above, 253 F.3d at 1252.

VIII

Criminal Jurisdiction in Indian Country

What is criminal jurisdiction?

Criminal jurisdiction is the power of a government to establish rules of conduct and to punish those who violate the rules. Normally, a government can exercise its full criminal jurisdiction everywhere within its borders. In theory, then, the tribe, the state, and the federal government can each exercise its full criminal jurisdiction on an Indian reservation. But Indian reservations are an exception to the rule. On no reservation can all three governments exercise their full criminal jurisdiction.

Criminal jurisdiction in Indian country is, as the Supreme Court has noted, "a complex patchwork of federal, state, and tribal law" whose contours are defined in statutes and court decisions issued randomly during the past two centuries.[1] Although this is a confusing area of federal Indian law, five principles created by the Supreme Court and three laws passed by Congress answer most questions regarding criminal jurisdiction in Indian country.

What are the five most important court-created principles regarding the exercise of criminal jurisdiction in Indian country?

The five most important court-created principles regarding the exercise of criminal jurisdiction in Indian country are the following:

1. Congress has final authority to determine which governments may exercise criminal jurisdiction in Indian country, and Congress can expand or limit the jurisdiction that the tribe, the state, and the federal governments possess.[2]

2. An Indian tribe has the inherent right to exercise criminal jurisdiction

142

over tribal members. "An Indian tribe's power to punish tribal offenders is part of its own retained sovereignty."[3]

3. An Indian tribe may not exercise criminal jurisdiction over non-Indians unless Congress has conferred that power on the tribe. The Supreme Court announced this principle in *Oliphant v. Suquamish Indian Tribe* (1978).[4]

4. Neither the state, the Supreme Court held in *Worcester v. Georgia* (1832),[5] nor the federal government, the Supreme Court held in *Ex parte Crow Dog*,[6] may exercise criminal jurisdiction over tribal members for crimes committed on the reservation unless Congress has expressly conferred that power.

5. A state may exercise criminal jurisdiction over non-Indians for crimes committed on the reservation against other non-Indians. The Supreme Court announced this principle in *United States v. McBratney* (1881).[7]

These five principles may be summarized as follows: Congress has the ultimate authority to decide which government may exercise criminal jurisdiction in Indian country. *Unless Congress has determined otherwise,* the tribe may prosecute tribal members but not non-Indians; the state may only prosecute non-Indians who commit crimes against other non-Indians; and the federal government may not prosecute anyone.

What are the three most important statutes regarding criminal jurisdiction in Indian country?

Several laws passed by Congress have altered criminal jurisdiction in Indian country by permitting either the state or the federal government to exercise jurisdiction it would not otherwise have. The three most important laws are Public Law 83-280,[8] the Indian Country Crimes Act (also known as the General Crimes Act and the Federal Enclaves Crimes Act),[9] and the Major Crimes Act.[10] (These laws are reproduced in appendixes B, C, and D of this book, respectively.) As a result of these laws, every Indian reservation is now subject to either state or federal criminal jurisdiction to some extent.

Public Law 83-280: Public Law 83-280 (P.L. 280) was passed by Congress in 1953. As discussed more fully in chapter 7, P.L. 280 required six states (the *mandatory* states) to exercise full criminal jurisdiction in Indian country, with certain Indian reservations within those states being excepted. The other forty-four states (the *option* states) were permitted to accept similar jurisdiction at their option, and a few of these states opted to acquire criminal jurisdiction in Indian country. The lists in chapter 7 show which states possess P.L. 280 jurisdiction.

Within the six mandatory states (California, Oregon, Wisconsin, Minnesota, Alaska, and Nebraska), Indians are subject to the same state criminal laws that apply to everyone else and may be prosecuted in state court for crimes committed in Indian country. Congress has conferred upon a few other states, including New York and Maine, criminal jurisdiction in Indian country similar to the jurisdiction conferred by P.L. 280. The authority received by these other states is discussed later in this chapter.

Those Indian reservations not placed by Congress under state criminal jurisdiction have been placed under federal criminal jurisdiction, primarily as a result of the Indian Country Crimes of 1834 and the Major Crimes Act of 1885. These statutes, though, do not give the federal government the full criminal jurisdiction that P.L. 280 confers on the mandatory states.

Indian Country Crimes Act: The Indian Country Crimes Act of 1834 (ICCA) authorizes the federal government to extend all of its criminal laws into Indian country except with respect to three types of crimes: (1) crimes committed by one Indian against the person or property of another Indian, (2) crimes that by treaty remain under exclusive tribal jurisdiction, and (3) crimes for which the Indian defendant has already been punished under tribal law. These three exceptions were intended by Congress to ensure that tribes retained exclusive control over matters of central importance to tribal government.[11]

Major Crimes Act: The Major Crimes Act (MCA) was passed by Congress in 1885 in response to *Ex parte Crow Dog*,[12] a case decided by the Supreme Court two years earlier. In *Ex parte Crow Dog*, the Court ordered federal officials to release an Indian who had murdered another Indian on an Indian reservation because Congress had not given federal officials the authority to prosecute reservation crimes committed by one Indian against another. (As noted above, the ICCA expressly withheld this jurisdiction from the federal government.) Believing that Indians should be made subject to federal jurisdiction when they commit certain heinous crimes, Congress passed the MCA, which gave the federal government jurisdiction over seven "major" crimes when committed by an Indian against any other person in Indian country, including murder, manslaughter, kidnapping, and rape. The MCA has been amended several times and today covers more than a dozen crimes; among the crimes added since 1885 are robbery, incest, sexual abuse of a minor, and assault with a dangerous weapon.

The lists below illustrate the pattern of criminal jurisdiction in Indian country *in non–P.L. 280 states* (that is, in those states that have not been given criminal jurisdiction in Indian country by Congress). The first list shows the pattern of jurisdiction when the crime committed is covered by the MCA. The second shows the jurisdictional pattern for all other crimes.

When the Crime Committed Is a "Major" Crime

Persons Involved	Jurisdiction
Indian accused, Indian victim	Federal government (Major Crimes Act) and tribal government (inherent sovereignty)
Indian accused, non-Indian victim	Federal government (Major Crimes Act) and tribal government (inherent sovereignty)
Non-Indian accused, Indian victim	Federal government only (Indian Country Crimes Act)
Non-Indian accused, non-Indian victim	State government only

When the Crime Committed Is Not a "Major" Crime

Persons Involved	Jurisdiction
Indian accused, Indian victim	Tribal government only (inherent sovereignty)
Indian accused, non-Indian victim	Federal government (Indian Country Crimes Act) and tribal government (inherent sovereignty)
Non-Indian accused, Indian victim	Federal government only (Indian Country Crimes Act)

| Non-Indian accused, non-Indian victim | State government only |

Are nonmember Indians considered to be Indians for purposes of criminal jurisdiction?

Indian tribes, as noted earlier, may prosecute tribal members, but not non-Indians, who violate tribal law. But there are thousands of nonmember Indians who visit or live on someone else's reservation. May the tribe prosecute them as well?

In 1990, the Supreme Court held in *Duro v. Reina*[13] that Indian tribes could not prosecute nonmember Indians without express authorization from Congress. Congress then passed a law affirming the inherent right of Indian tribes to prosecute nonmember Indians to the same extent as tribal members.[14]

Why is the crime rate in Indian country so high?

According to recent studies, including a report issued by the U.S. Justice Department in 1999, violent crime occurs more than twice as frequently per capita on Indian reservations as elsewhere, with sexual abuse against women occurring three times as frequently; and violent crime in Indian country is increasing, while it is decreasing nationally. Since 1992, the homicide rate on Indian reservations has risen by 87 percent, while it has fallen nationally by 22 percent. Reports of child abuse and child neglect among Indians jumped 18 percent between 1992 and 1995, while it decreased in the rest of the country by 8 percent. Nearly a third of all Indians between the ages of eighteen and twenty-four are victims of violence.[15]

There are complex reasons for the high crime rate in Indian country. One reason is alcoholism, which is a severe problem on many reservations. "By some law enforcement estimates, alcohol abuse is related to at least 75 percent of all violent crime on reservations."[16] Another cause of reservation crime is impoverished living conditions, along with feelings of depression and despair caused by unemployment, substandard housing, and poor health care.

Indian tribes have the primary responsibility of ensuring the safety of reservation residents. Their ability to do so, however, has been limited by the fact that (1) the Supreme Court ruled in *Oliphant* that Indian tribes lack criminal jurisdiction over non-Indians; (2) in 1968, Congress reduced the punishments that tribal courts can impose to one year in jail and to a fine of $5,000, even for serious crimes; and (3) many tribes lack the financial resources necessary to maintain an adequate police force and criminal court system.

In addition to these factors, it is also evident that federal officials have done a poor job enforcing federal criminal laws in Indian country. Assistant Secretary of Indian Affairs Kevin Gover admitted in 1998 that federal law enforcement on Indian reservations has been woefully inadequate for many years.[17] Congress has given federal officials substantial responsibilities to enforce the law on Indian reservations but has not committed the human and financial resources to accomplish the task, and when federal agencies must decide where their law enforcement dollars should be spent, Indian reservations are often shortchanged.

Since 1999, the U.S. Justice Department has awarded more than $125 million in grants to Indian communities in twenty-seven states to hire, train, and equip police officers and to build new jails and detention facilities. This will help, but a great deal more is needed, and it does not address one of the major shortcomings: the inadequate number of federal law enforcement officers assigned to investigate and prosecute reservation crime, especially in the rural communities that comprise much of Indian country.[18] For example, the Navajo reservation and the state of West Virginia are similar in size, but whereas West Virginia employs five thousand police officers to patrol its territory, the Navajos employ only two hundred.

The causes of reservation crime are complex, and so are the cures. But it is clear that greater efforts must be made by tribes and the federal government to reduce the needless suffering that is occurring on Indian reservations due to the high crime rate.

A. Crimes by Indians Against Indians in Non–P.L. 280 States

What jurisdiction does the tribe have over a reservation crime committed by one Indian against another?

Indian tribes have the inherent right to enforce their criminal laws against tribal members, regardless of the race of the victim.[19] In fact, the tribe has exclusive jurisdiction over these crimes unless Congress has authorized the state or the federal government to also prosecute them, as the

Supreme Court recognized in the *Worcester* and *Ex parte Crow Dog* cases cited earlier.[20]

What jurisdiction does the state have over these crimes?

None, unless the state has been given this jurisdiction by Congress. As explained in chapter 7, state laws can apply in Indian country without congressional consent but only if the enforcement of those laws would not significantly infringe on tribal self-government. Tribal self-government would be seriously undermined by state prosecution of reservation Indians. As a result, only those states authorized by Congress to prosecute reservation crimes committed by Indians may do so, such as the P.L. 280 states, regardless of the race of the victim.[21]

What jurisdiction does the federal government have over these crimes?

The Supreme Court held in *Ex parte Crow Dog* that the federal government lacks jurisdiction to prosecute Indians for crimes committed against other Indians in Indian country unless Congress has *expressly* conferred that power. Congress has passed only one law, the Major Crimes Act of 1885,[22] that confers jurisdiction on federal officials over intratribal crimes, and only a handful of offenses are covered by the MCA.

It would seem, then, that the federal government may not prosecute Indians for crimes committed against other Indians except for the several crimes listed in the MCA. However, some federal courts have extended the federal government's jurisdiction to two other categories of crimes, although the Supreme Court has yet to approve either extension. The first category consists of the "wherever committed" crimes: those crimes that Congress intended (or so these courts have held) to be prosecuted by the federal government wherever they are committed, such as the crimes of counterfeiting, tampering with the U.S. mail, and assaulting a federal officer. Courts have held that tribal members may be prosecuted for these crimes even though Congress has not expressly authorized federal officials to enforce them on reservation Indians.[23]

Second, courts have held that Indians may be prosecuted for a non-MCA offense when they are already being prosecuted for an "underlying" MCA offense. For example, an Indian who kills another Indian with a firearm may be prosecuted for the MCA offense of murder and also for the non-MCA offense of using a firearm in relation to a crime of violence, and may be convicted of both crimes.[24]

May Indian tribes still exercise jurisdiction over the "major" crimes?

The MCA authorizes the federal government to prosecute more than a dozen crimes when committed by an Indian in Indian country. Neither the MCA nor any other law removes the tribe's inherent right to prosecute those same crimes. It is a well-established rule of Indian law that tribal powers remain intact unless Congress has clearly abrogated them.[25] Accordingly, it should be presumed that Indian tribes have the right to prosecute tribal members for the crimes listed in the MCA.[26]

Many tribes, though, have stopped prosecuting Indians for the crimes listed in the MCA, such as murder and rape, partly because the federal government prosecutes them and partly because Congress has limited the punishments that tribal courts may impose: one year in jail and a $5,000 fine.[27] Some tribes continue to prosecute these crimes and often choose to exercise that authority when the federal government has declined to prosecute an Indian who the tribe believes should be prosecuted.[28]

If a tribe prosecutes an Indian, may the federal government later prosecute that person for the same offense?

There are two provisions of law that would seem to bar the federal government from prosecuting an Indian who has already been prosecuted for the same crime in tribal court. The first is the Double Jeopardy Clause of the Fifth Amendment to the U.S. Constitution, which guarantees that no person shall be "subject for the same offense to be twice put in jeopardy of life or limb." (The term *same offense* as used in the Double Jeopardy Clause applies to "lesser included" offenses.[29] A lesser included offense is a crime necessarily committed whenever a greater offense occurs. For example, the crime of assault is always committed when a murder is committed; therefore, a person convicted of assault cannot later be prosecuted for murder arising out of the same incident against the same victim, and likewise, a conviction or acquittal for murder precludes a later prosecution for assault.)

The Supreme Court has held, however, that the Double Jeopardy Clause applies only to successive prosecutions by the same government and not to successive prosecutions by different governments.[30] Thus, if a person's conduct simultaneously violates both state and federal law, both the state and federal government may prosecute that person. (To illustrate, if a person robs a bank in Phoenix protected by the Federal Deposit Insurance Corporation, that person could be prosecuted by Arizona authorities for robbing a bank in Arizona and prosecuted by federal authorities for robbing a bank protected by the FDIC, a federal crime.)

In *United States v. Wheeler,*[31] the Court was asked to decide whether the federal government could prosecute an Indian for statutory rape after a tribal court had convicted him of contributing to the delinquency of a minor, a lesser included offense. The defendant argued that tribal governments are merely arms of the federal government and, therefore, a second prosecution would constitute double jeopardy because the same government would be prosecuting twice. The Supreme Court disagreed. In a decision of far-reaching significance, the Court recognized that although Congress can abolish tribal powers, it is not the source of them: Indian tribes exercise original, *inherent* powers, and their courts are not arms of the federal government. Consequently, the Double Jeopardy Clause was inapplicable, the Court held, and the defendant could be prosecuted in federal court under the MCA after being prosecuted in tribal court for the same (or a lesser included) offense.[32]

A Double Jeopardy issue does exist, though, regarding second prosecutions of nonmember Indians. It was just explained that the Supreme Court held in *Duro v. Reina* in 1990 that Indian tribes lack the inherent authority to prosecute nonmember Indians, but that in response to *Duro,* Congress passed a law stating that tribes have the "inherent power" to prosecute these offenses. Without question, Congress can *delegate* to Indian tribes the power to prosecute nonmember Indians. However, this law "recognizes" that tribes inherently have this power, despite the fact that the Supreme Court held just the opposite in *Duro.* If the law must be viewed as a delegation of federal power (because Congress cannot recognize an inherent tribal power that the Supreme Court held does not exist), then when tribal and federal courts both prosecute a nonmember Indian for the same offense, the second prosecution would violate the Double Jeopardy Clause. On the other hand, if Congress is permitted to "recognize" an inherent power, then double prosecutions are permitted in this context just as they are permitted in the context addressed in *Wheeler.* Ultimately, the Supreme Court will determine whether Congress may overrule *Duro* in this manner, without violating the Double Jeopardy Clause.[33]

The other provision of law that seems to bar a second prosecution for the same crime is the Indian County Crimes Act. As noted earlier, the ICCA prohibits the federal government from prosecuting an Indian "who has been punished by the local law of the tribe." This clause clearly seems to prohibit a double prosecution whenever the tribe has prosecuted first. Federal courts, though, have held that this clause applies only "to federal laws where the situs [location] of the crime is an element of the offense."[34] Given that few federal crimes make location an element of the offense (in other words, a murder is a murder regardless of where it is committed), the potential reach of this clause has been narrowed substantially.

The MCA uses the term *Indian* without defining it. Is this constitutional? If so, who is an *Indian* for purposes of the act?

The MCA applies only to crimes committed by an "Indian." The federal government therefore must prove in all MCA prosecutions that the defendant is an Indian. Yet the MCA does not define the term *Indian,* leading some people to argue that the act is unconstitutionally vague. The courts have rejected this argument, ruling that although the MCA does not define the term, the word *Indian* is adequately defined in other statutes and in court cases.[35] The Supreme Court has noted the issue but has not resolved it,[36] although it has upheld convictions under the act.[37]

The lack of a definition of *Indian* causes difficulties. Some courts have held that anyone who has Indian blood is an Indian for purposes of the MCA, while other courts have held that MCA jurisdiction is lacking unless the defendant is a member of a federally recognized tribe[38] or is a descendent of a tribal member and is considered to be an Indian by the Indian community.[39]

Is the MCA unconstitutional because it results in Indians being treated differently than non-Indians in some situations?

An Indian who murders someone on the reservation can be punished by the federal government under the MCA, whereas a non-Indian who murders another non-Indian on the reservation can only be punished under state law.[40] If the MCA happens to punish murder more severely than the state does (for example, the federal government may have capital punishment and the state may not), an Indian who commits the same offense as a non-Indian could receive a harsher sentence.

In *United States v. Antelope,*[41] the Supreme Court held that the MCA is not unconstitutional even though it may subject an Indian to a harsher penalty than a non-Indian who commits the same crime. Congress has the right to treat Indians as a separate group because they have a unique status under the Constitution. Therefore, any benefits or detriments the MCA imposes on Indians are within the power of Congress to impose.

In a jury trial under the MCA, is the Indian defendant entitled to a "lesser included offense" instruction?

A defendant in a criminal prosecution often will request the judge to give the jury a "lesser included offense" instruction. This instructs the jury that they may find the defendant guilty of a less severe but included offense if they believe that the facts do not warrant conviction of the offense charged. This instruction often works to the advantage of the accused because, without it, the jury might find the defendant guilty of the more serious offense rather than acquit. In a prosecution for murder, for example, the defendant will often request an instruction on manslaughter whenever the facts could lead a jury to believe that although a homicide occurred, it was done unintentionally rather than intentionally.

Until 1973, federal courts did not give lesser included offense instructions in prosecutions under the MCA unless the lesser offense was one of the crimes listed in the MCA. The courts reasoned that they could not permit a jury to convict a defendant of a crime that the federal government was prohibited from prosecuting originally.

In *Keeble v. United States* (1973),[42] the Supreme Court held that the Constitution requires courts to offer a lesser included offense instruction in an MCA case just as in other cases. This means, of course, that the jury then has the power to convict the defendant of the lesser offense instead of the MCA offense.[43] Courts in MCA cases have also held that the government may request a lesser included offense instruction even if the defendant refuses to ask for one, which is the rule in non-MCA prosecutions as well.[44]

B. Crimes by Indians Against Non-Indians in Non–P.L. 280 States

Jurisdiction over crimes committed by Indians against non-Indians in Indian country follows the same pattern as the Indian-against-Indian crimes, with one significant difference. For reasons explained below, the federal government has greater jurisdiction over these offenses.

What jurisdiction does the tribe have over crimes committed by an Indian against a non-Indian in Indian country?

Indian tribes have the inherent right to enforce their criminal laws on Indians who commit crimes on the reservation.[45] The tribe may exercise this power regardless of the race of the victim.

What jurisdiction does the state have over these crimes?

None, unless Congress has expressly authorized the state to prosecute Indians who commit these offenses.[46] Several states have been given this authority, and the extent of their criminal jurisdiction is discussed later in this chapter.

What jurisdiction does the federal government have over these crimes?

As a result of three laws passed by Congress (and court decisions interpreting them), virtually every federal crime can be prosecuted by the federal government when committed by an Indian against a non-Indian in Indian country. The most far-reaching law is the Indian Country Crimes Act (also known as the General Crimes Act and the Federal Enclaves Crimes Act).[47] This law authorizes the federal government to prosecute any Indian who violates a federal "enclave law" against a non-Indian within the reservation. Enclave laws were enacted by Congress to govern activities on federal enclaves, such as national parks, post offices, military installations, and Indian reservations. These laws are quite comprehensive and create an extensive criminal code.

The second law is the Assimilative Crimes Act (ACA).[48] The ACA makes it a federal crime to engage in any conduct on a federal enclave that is a crime in the state where the enclave is located unless the activity is already a crime under an enclave law. In other words, the ACA transforms all state crimes into federal crimes if they are not federal crimes already.[49] The combined effect of the ICCA and the ACA is to make Indians subject to all federal enclave crimes *and* all state crimes (that are not already federal crimes) whenever the victim is a non-Indian.

The third basis for federal jurisdiction is the Major Crimes Act.[50] The

MCA authorizes the federal government to prosecute more than a dozen major crimes in Indian country when committed by an Indian, regardless of the race of the victim.

Most if not all MCA crimes are also crimes under federal enclave law. Therefore, when an Indian commits any of these crimes against a non-Indian, a prosecution can be commenced under both the MCA and the ICCA. Courts have held, though, that because the MCA is more specific than the ICCA regarding the major crimes, Indians must be prosecuted under the MCA whenever the two overlap.[51] These laws overlap only when an Indian commits a crime against a non-Indian that is both a major crime and a federal enclave crime. The laws do not overlap when the crime is not a major crime or when the victim is an Indian; only the ICCA applies in the first situation and only the MCA applies in the second.

C. Crimes by Non-Indians Against Indians in Non–P.L. 280 States

The jurisdictional pattern governing crimes by non-Indians against Indians in Indian country (in non–P.L. 280 states) is simple: only the federal government has jurisdiction. The tribe has no jurisdiction over these offenses. In *Oliphant v. Suquamish Indian Tribe* (1978),[52] the Supreme Court held that Indian tribes may not prosecute non-Indians without the express consent of Congress. Congress has not consented to this type of tribal jurisdiction, and thus no tribe may prosecute non-Indians.

The federal government, on the other hand, does have this authority. As just discussed, the ICCA authorizes the federal government to prosecute non-Indians who commit crimes against Indians in violation of a federal enclave law, and the ACA makes all state criminal laws applicable to Indian country that are not already federal crimes. The combination of these two laws gives the federal government full criminal jurisdiction over crimes committed by a non-Indian against an Indian in Indian country.[53]

As for state jurisdiction, it has long been presumed that the ICCA abrogated the state's power to prosecute non-Indians for crimes committed against Indians in Indian country, although the act itself is silent on this subject. The Supreme Court has not squarely addressed this issue, but some of its decisions suggest that the federal government has exclusive jurisdiction to prosecute these crimes.[54] As one state court recently noted: "The prevailing rule has always been that federal courts have exclusive jurisdiction over an offense committed in Indian country by an non-Indian against the person or property of an Indian."[55]

D. Crimes by Non-Indians Against Non-Indians in Indian Country

In the 1832 case of *Worcester v. Georgia*,[56] the Supreme Court held that a state has no criminal jurisdiction in Indian country without congressional consent, even to prosecute crimes committed by non-Indians. The Court modified this rule in *United States v. McBratney* (1881),[57] allowing the state in that case to prosecute a non-Indian who murdered another non-Indian in Indian country. It is now well settled that states may prosecute non-Indians for crimes committed against other non-Indians in Indian country.[58]

The tribe has no jurisdiction over these crimes for reasons discussed earlier: the Supreme Court ruled in *Oliphant* in 1978 that Indian tribes lack criminal jurisdiction over non-Indians. The federal government does not have jurisdiction, either, unless the crime is one of the "wherever committed" crimes discussed earlier (which are federal crimes wherever they are committed), such as the crime of assaulting a federal officer. (To illustrate, if a non-Indian assaulted another non-Indian, the state would normally have jurisdiction, but if the victim was an FBI agent or federal postal worker assaulted on the job, the federal government would have jurisdiction.)

Although it is the state and not the tribe that is responsible for prosecuting crimes committed by one non-Indian against another on the reservation, courts have held that tribal police—exercising the tribe's inherent sovereign powers—may arrest non-Indian lawbreakers and deliver them to state police.[59] The Supreme Court has indicated that tribes may exercise that authority.[60] (Courts have also held that state police on Indian reservations may perform a similar function, arresting Indians who they observe violating the law and then transferring them to tribal or federal officers for prosecution.)[61]

E. Criminal Jurisdiction in P.L. 280 States

State criminal laws, for reasons already explained, do not apply in Indian country unless Congress has given its express consent, with the sole exception (the "*McBratney* exception") being that a state may prosecute non-Indians who commit crimes against other non-Indians. In 1953, Congress enacted Public Law 83-280,[62] which for the first time consented to substantial state criminal jurisdiction in Indian country.

What is the effect of P.L. 280?

The scope of P.L. 280 is discussed earlier in this chapter. To summarize, P.L. 280 required the six mandatory states (Alaska, California, Minnesota, Nebraska, Oregon, and Wisconsin) to enforce their criminal laws in Indian country to the same extent they enforce them elsewhere in the state. P.L. 280 gave the forty-four option states the choice of assuming the same criminal jurisdiction the mandatory states had received, and several of them passed laws accepting some amount of criminal jurisdiction in Indian country, as illustrated in the lists in chapter 7. To the extent a state acquired P.L. 280 jurisdiction, reservation Indians can be arrested by state law enforcement officials and tried in state courts in the same manner as other citizens of the state.

Several of the option states assumed only partial criminal jurisdiction in Indian country. As a result, some crimes committed by Indians are prosecuted by the state (under P.L. 280) and other crimes by the federal government (under the federal laws discussed earlier in this chapter). Occasionally, a single activity can give rise to both a federal and a state prosecution.[63] In addition, as discussed below, the tribe retains the inherent authority to prosecute Indians who commit crimes in Indian country, regardless of whether the state or federal government has been authorized by Congress to prosecute them.

Are there any limits to the state's criminal jurisdiction under P.L. 280?

Yes. P.L. 280 contains a "savings" clause that expressly exempts three subject areas from state jurisdiction. First, the state may not tax, encumber, or alienate Indian trust property. Second, it may not regulate the use of Indian trust property in any manner that conflicts with federal law. Third, the state may not deprive an Indian or tribe of federally guaranteed hunting, fishing, or trapping rights and the right to license, control, and regulate the same.[64]

These limitations are very important. Reservation Indians, even in the six mandatory states, need not comply with state laws on zoning, hunting, fishing, or trapping, nor pay property taxes on their trust lands, and the state may not impose criminal penalties for their failure to do so.[65]

As explained in chapter 7, Congress conferred broad criminal jurisdiction on the mandatory states but very little civil jurisdiction; the only civil jurisdiction the states acquired is the ability to resolve disputes in state courts that arise in Indian country. Accordingly, when a state prosecutes an Indian in Indian country under P.L. 280, it is necessary to determine whether the state is exercising its criminal or civil powers—given that some prosecutions are *civil* in nature—because if the prosecution is civil, it exceeds the authority conferred by P.L. 280. The Supreme Court applied this principle in *California v. Cabazon Band of Mission Indians* (1987),[66] drawing a line for P.L. 280 purposes between those activities prohibited by the state and those allowed but regulated, the so-called criminal/prohibitory versus the civil/regulatory distinction. In *Cabazon Band,* the Court held that California, although a mandatory P.L. 280 state, could not prosecute Indians who engaged in high stakes bingo within the reservation, even though their conduct violated state law. In reaching this decision, the Court carefully examined California's gambling laws and found that various types of gambling (such as lotteries and bingo for charity organizations) were legal under state law. Consequently, the Court said, California's ban on high-stakes bingo was civil/regulatory, not criminal/prohibitory, and thus beyond the state's authority under P.L. 280.

In similar fashion, the Supreme Court of Minnesota held in 1999 that P.L. 280 did not confer on Minnesota (another mandatory state) jurisdiction to enforce on reservation Indians various traffic laws, including prohibitions on speeding and driving without a license, because these were civil/regulatory and not criminal/prohibitory.[67] On the other hand, when a P.L. 280 state prohibits all sales of fireworks except by licensed and trained persons, it may prosecute reservation Indians who violate that prohibition, a federal court has held.[68] Similarly, when a state completely bans the consumption of liquor by persons under the age of twenty-one, it may prosecute reservation Indians for underage drinking.[69] In those situations, the state is applying its criminal rather than its civil jurisdiction.

Did P.L. 280 abrogate the tribe's criminal jurisdiction?

Courts have held that P.L. 280 did not limit the tribe's criminal jurisdiction. As one court recently noted, "[N]othing in the language or history of Public Law 280 indicates an intent by Congress to diminish tribal authority."[70] In P.L. 280 states, an Indian can be tried twice for the same offense, once by the tribe and once by the state. As noted earlier, it does not violate the Double Jeopardy Clause when two separate governments both prosecute a person for the same criminal activity.[71]

Did P.L. 280 abrogate the federal government's criminal jurisdiction in the P.L. 280 states?

To a large extent, it did. Indeed, a primary motive for enacting P.L. 280 was to shift to the states the financial and administrative burden of reservation law enforcement, as explained in chapter 7. The federal government retains criminal jurisdiction only over the "wherever committed" federal crimes: those offenses that Congress intended to be prosecuted by the federal government wherever they are committed, such as counterfeiting or assaulting a federal officer.[72]

Have any other states received criminal jurisdiction in Indian country, besides the P.L. 280 states?

Yes, at least nine states have. Specific acts of Congress have given Colorado, Connecticut, Iowa, Kansas, Maine, New York, North Dakota, Oklahoma, and Rhode Island some criminal jurisdiction in Indian country.[73] The jurisdiction received by Connecticut, New York, and Oklahoma is discussed in chapter 15.

In addition, a federal law, Title 18, U.S. Code, Sec. 1161 authorizes all states to regulate liquor transactions within Indian country.[74] This law permits all states to prosecute persons—Indians and non-Indians alike—who violate the state's liquor laws on the reservation.[75]

F. Jurisdiction over Victimless Crimes in Indian Country

What is a victimless crime?

Certain activities have been made crimes even though they cause no identifiable physical harm to anyone or anything and are called victimless crimes. These activities are banned because society believes the activities are harmful to the individual or to the community in general. Adultery, prostitution, gambling, and possession of marijuana are examples of victimless crimes. Most traffic offenses, such as driving with a faulty taillight or speeding, are also victimless crimes unless they happen to result in a traffic accident.

When an Indian commits a victimless crime in Indian country, which government has jurisdiction to prosecute it: the tribe, the state, or the federal government?

Victimless crimes committed on the reservation by Indians are always subject to the tribe's criminal jurisdiction, given that an Indian tribe, as already explained, has the inherent right to impose its criminal laws on Indians. The state, on the other hand, never has jurisdiction without express congressional consent, such as that found in P.L. 280.

A more difficult problem is how to determine the extent to which the federal government may have jurisdiction over these crimes. Victimless crimes are considered to be crimes against the community at large. The Major Crimes Act authorizes the federal government to prosecute certain major crimes, none of them victimless. Therefore, if the federal government has any authority over victimless crimes, it can be found only in the Indian Country Crimes Act. Yet the ICCA contains an express exception, discussed earlier, that withholds jurisdiction from the federal government over any crime committed by one Indian against another. This exception would seem to preclude federal jurisdiction over victimless crimes, which have to be viewed (as just noted) as a crime against the Indian community at large.

Courts have rendered conflicting decisions on this matter, however. In 1916, the Supreme Court held in *United States v. Quiver*[76] that the federal government could not prosecute an Indian for committing adultery with another Indian on the reservation because of the exception contained in the ICCA. In recent years, however, at least three federal courts have allowed the federal government to prosecute reservation Indians for gambling, distributing marijuana, and selling fireworks, all of which are victimless crimes, contrary to the rationale of *Quiver*.[77] Two of these decisions did not even mention *Quiver* and the third opined that *Quiver* exempts only the federal prosecution of a crime related to "internal and social" tribal matters, such as adultery.[78] It would be helpful if the Supreme Court addressed this issue once again.

Which government has jurisdiction when a non-Indian commits a victimless crime in Indian country?

Both the state and federal governments may have the authority to prosecute a non-Indian who commits a victimless crime in Indian country, but one thing is clear: the tribe does not. As already explained, the Supreme Court held in *Oliphant* that Indian tribes may not exercise criminal jurisdiction over non-Indians.

The U.S. Justice Department has taken the position that the state, not the federal government, has jurisdiction over victimless crimes committed by non-Indians, unless their behavior directly threatens the interests of the tribe or its members.[79] Several courts have agreed with this view,[80] even though it conflicts with the notion that a victimless crime is an offense against the community. (If the crime is viewed as an offense against the community, then the state could not prosecute these "non-Indian vs. Indian" crimes without the express consent of Congress, for reasons explained earlier.)

G. PROBLEMS RELATING TO EXTRADITION

It often happens that a person will commit a crime in one state and flee to another state to escape prosecution. Extradition provides the means by which the "fleeing" state can obtain custody of this person from the "asylum" state. The U.S. Constitution provides that if one state is asked by the governor of another state to "deliver up" a person accused of crime, it must comply with that request.[81]

Tribal governments can become involved with extradition issues in three situations: when an Indian commits a crime on the reservation and flees elsewhere; when an Indian commits a crime off the reservation and flees to the reservation; and when a non-Indian commits a crime off the reservation and flees to the reservation. Indian tribes, then, sometimes seek extradition and sometimes are asked to extradite.

Does the Constitution's Extradition Clause apply to tribal governments?

No. More than a century ago, the Supreme Court held that the provisions contained in the U.S. Constitution do not apply to tribal governments unless Congress expressly makes them applicable.[82] Congress has not made the Extradition Clause applicable to Indian tribes; accordingly, courts have held that it is inapplicable.[83] Tribal and state officials have no duty to honor each other's extradition requests, although nothing prevents them from doing so, either.[84] In order to avoid the appearance of harboring criminals and to assist each other in prosecuting lawbreakers, many tribes and their surrounding states have entered into extradition agreements.

Are state officers allowed to enter the reservation and arrest an Indian who has committed a crime in state territory?

Until recently, the prevailing view was that unless Congress had expressly authorized the state to exercise criminal jurisdiction on the reservation, state officials had no right to enter the reservation to arrest an Indian, even for a crime committed off the reservation in state territory. Instead, the state had to file a petition in tribal court and ask that the suspect be extradited.[85] However, in *Nevada v. Hicks* (2001),[86] the Supreme Court held that as a general rule, all forms of state judicial process, including arrest and search warrants, may be served by state law enforcement officers on Indians within the reservation for their off-reservation activities. In that case, the Court upheld the right of state game wardens to carry out a state search warrant directed at the home of a reservation Indian who was accused of poaching bighorn sheep outside the reservation. As a result of *Hicks,* it is now clear that state law enforcement officers may enter a reservation "to investigate or prosecute violations of state law occurring off the reservation."[87]

Which government has jurisdiction over off-reservation crimes committed by Indians?

It is "well established," the Supreme Court said in *Hicks* (2001), "that States have criminal jurisdiction over reservation Indians for crimes committed . . . off the reservation."[88] Indeed, as just mentioned, state law enforcement officers are permitted to enter the reservation to investigate or prosecute crimes that they believe were committed by an Indian off the reservation, and they do not need to obtain permission from tribal officials to do so. An Indian who engages in an activity outside the reservation that is a crime under state law can be punished in the same fashion as a non-Indian who commits that crime.[89]

Of course, Indians who possess a federal right to engage in an activity that is banned by the state may not be prosecuted by the state when they exercise their federal rights.[90] Many tribal members, for example, have a right under federal law to hunt or fish off the reservation in a manner that would otherwise violate state law, and they may not be prosecuted by the state for exercising those rights. Chapters 4 and 11 discuss this subject in further detail.

NOTES

1. *Duro v. Reina,* 495 U.S. 676, 680 n.1 (1990).

2. As explained in ch. 5, sec. A, Congress has plenary power over Indian affairs, and it can limit or expand tribal, state, and federal powers in Indian country.

3. *U.S. v. Wheeler,* 435 U.S. 313, 328 (1978). *See also Oliphant v. Suquamish Indian Tribe,* 435 U.S. 191 (1978). This subject is discussed in ch. 6, sec. B(6).

4. 435 U.S. 191 (1978).

5. 31 U.S. 515 (1832).

6. 109 U.S. 556 (1883).

7. 104 U.S. 621 (1881).

8. 18 U.S.C. Sec. 1162, 28 U.S.C. Sec. 1360.

9. 18 U.S.C. Sec. 1152.

10. 18 U.S.C. Sec. 1153.

11. *See Wheeler,* note 3 above, 435 U.S. at 322–26.

12. 109 U.S. 556 (1883).

13. 495 U.S. 676 (1990).

14. Pub. L. No. 101-511, Sec. 8077, 104 Stat. 1856, 1892–93 (1990) and Pub L. No. 102-137, Sec. 1, 105 Stat. 646 (1991), codified at 25 U.S.C. Sec. 1301(2), (4).

15. *See* U.S. Dept. of Justice, "American Indians and Crime," (Feb. 1999). These statistics and the report are discussed in "Indians More Vulnerable to Violent Crime," *Rocky Mountain News* (Feb. 15, 1999) at 46A; "Feds Talk Crime," *Indian Country Today* (Sept. 27, 1997) at A1; and in "Violent Crimes Against Indians Exceed National Average," *Indian Country Today* (Mar. 1, 1999) at A1.

16. Kevin Johnson, "Tribal Police Isolated in Darkness, Distance," *USA Today* (Mar. 22, 2000) at 19A.

17. Statement of Kevin Gover quoted in "Funding Increases Will Take 'Hard Work,'" *Indian Country Today* (Oct. 12, 1998) at A2.

18. *See* "FBI Focuses on Reservation Crime," *Indian Country Today* (Dec. 1, 1997) at A2.

19. *Wheeler,* note 3 above, 435 U.S. at 326. *See also Washington v. Yakima Indian Nation,* 439 U.S. 463 (1979); *Confederated Tribes of Colville Reservation v. Washington,* 938 F.2d 146, 149 (9th Cir. 1991), *cert. denied,* 503 U.S. 997 (1992).

20. *U.S. v. Antelope,* 430 U.S. 641, 643 n.2 (1977); *U.S. v. Jackson,* 600 F.2d 1283 (9th Cir. 1979); *U.S. v. Barquin,* 799 F.2d 619 (10th Cir. 1986).

21. *Yakima Indian Nation,* note 19 above, 439 U.S. at 470–71; *U.S. v. John,* 437 U.S. 634 (1978); *Worcester v. Georgia,* 31 U.S. 515 (1832).

22. 18 U.S.C. Sec. 1153. The MCA is reproduced in appendix D. A year after the

act was passed, the Supreme Court upheld its constitutionality in *U.S. v. Kagama*, 118 U.S. 375 (1886).

23. *See U.S. v. Brisk*, 171 F.3d 514, 520–22 (7th Cir. 2001); *U.S. v. Wadena*, 152 F.3d 831, 841 (8th Cir. 1998), *cert. denied*, 526 U.S. 1050 (1999); *U.S. v. Begay*, 42 F.3d 486 500 (9th Cir. 1994), *cert. denied*, 516 U.S. 826 (1995). *See also Wheeler*, note 3 above, 435 U.S. at 330 n.30. *Contra: U.S. v. Welch*, 822 F.2d 460, 464 (4th Cir. 1987). *See also U.S. v. Markiewicz*, 978 F.2d 786 (2d Cir. 1992), *cert. denied*, 506 U.S. 1086 (1993).

24. *U.S. v. Laughing*, 855 F.2d 659 (9th Cir. 1988); *U.S. v. Goodface*, 835 F.2d 1233 (8th Cir. 1987).

25. This subject is discussed in ch. 4, notes 42–47 and accompanying text.

26. *See Wetsit v. Stafne*, 44 F.3d 823, 825 (9th Cir. 1995).

27. *See* 25 U.S.C. Sec. 1302(7).

28. *See Wetsit v. Stafne*, 44 F.3d 823, 825 (9th Cir. 1995) (noting that many major crimes on a reservation "would still go unpunished" if tribes did not prosecute them).

29. *Brown v. Ohio*, 432 U.S. 161 (1977).

30. *Heath v. Alabama*, 474 U.S. 82, 88 (1985); *Bartkus v. Illinois*, 359 U.S. 121 (1959).

31. 435 U.S. 313 (1978).

32. *See also Wetsit v. Stafne*, 44 F.3d 823, 826 (9th Cir. 1995) (holding that an Indian may be prosecuted in tribal court after being acquitted in federal court on similar charges); *U.S. v. Pluff*, 253 F.3d 490 (9th Cir. 2001) (holding that federal and not state law determines the resolution of MCA double jeopardy issues).

33. *See U.S. v. Weaselhead*, 36 F. Supp. 908 (D. Neb. 1997), *aff'd by equally divided vote*, 165 F.3d 1209 (8th Cir. 1998) *(en banc)*, *cert. denied*, 528 U.S. 829 (1999) (holding that these second prosecutions do not constitute double jeopardy); *U.S. v. Enas*, 255 F.3d 662 (9th Cir. 2001) *(en banc)* (same).

34. *U.S. v. Yannott*, 42 F.3d 999, 1003–4 (6th Cir. 1994), *cert. denied*, 513 U.S. 1182 (1995). *U.S. v. La Plant*, 156 F. Supp. 660 (D. Mont. 1957), might be the only reported decision that dismissed federal charges against an Indian convicted of the same offense in tribal court.

35. *U.S. v. Broncheau*, 597 F.2d 1260 (9th Cir. 1979); *U.S. v. Heath*, 509 F.2d 16 (9th Cir. 1974). *See also U.S. v. Mazurie*, 419 U.S. 544, 553 (1975).

36. *Antelope*, note 20 above, 430 U.S. at 646 n.7.

37. *See, e.g., Keeble v. U.S.*, 412 U.S. 205 (1973); *Wheeler*, note 3 above; *Kagama*, note 22 above.

38. In *Ex parte Pero*, 99 F.2d 28 (7th Cir. 1938), *cert. denied*, 306 U.S. 643 (1939), the court allowed someone with Indian blood to be prosecuted under the MCA even though he was not enrolled in a federally recognized tribe. Recent cases disagree with that holding. *See LaPier v. McCormick*, 986 F.2d 303 (9th Cir. 1993); *Heath*, note 35 above; *St. Cloud v. U.S.*, 702 F. Supp. 1456 (D.S.D. 1988).

39. *See LaPier*, note 38 above; *U.S. v. Dodge*, 538 F.2d 770 (8th Cir. 1976), *cert. denied*, 429 U.S. 1099 (1977); *U.S. v. Lossiah*, 537 F.2d 1250 (4th Cir. 1976).

40. *U.S. v. McBratney*, 104 U.S. 621 (1882).

41. 430 U.S. 641 (1977). *See also U.S. v. Keys*, 103 F.3d 758 (9th Cir. 1996); *Broncheau*, note 35 above.

42. 412 U.S. 205 (1973).

43. *See U.S. v. Walkingeagle*, 974 F.2d 551 (4th Cir. 1992), *cert. denied*, 507 U.S. 1019 (1993); *Felicia v. U.S.*, 495 F.2d 353 (8th Cir.), *cert. denied*, 419 U.S. 849 (1974); *U.S. v. Bowman*, 679 F.2d 798 (9th Cir. 1982).

44. *U.S. v. Thompson*, 492 F.2d 359, 362 (8th Cir. 1974). For criticism of this holding, *see* T. Vollman, "Criminal Jurisdiction in Indian Country," 22 *U. Kan. L. Rev.* 387 (1974). In *Keeble v. U.S.*, 412 U.S. 205, 214 n.4 (1973), the Court questions whether the government should be able to request a lesser included offense instruction.

45. *See* cases cited in note 3 above and accompanying text.

46. *See* cases cited in note 21 above and accompanying text. *See also Williams v. U.S.*, 327 U.S. 711 (1946); *State v. Greenwalt*, 663 P.2d 1178 (Mont. 1983).

47. 18 U.S.C. Sec. 1152. The Indian Country Crimes Act is reproduced in appendix C.

48. 18 U.S.C. Sec. 13. The Supreme Court has upheld the validity of this law as applied to reservation Indians. *See Williams*, note 46 above.

49. *U.S. v. Sharpnack*, 355 U.S. 286 (1958). Examples of ACA prosecutions against Indians include *U.S. v. Thunder Hawk*, 127 F.3d 705 (8th Cir. 1997); *U.S. v. Johnson*, 967 F.2d 1431 (10th Cir. 1992), *cert. denied*, 506 U.S. 1082 (1993); *U.S. v. Marcyes*, 557 F.2d 1361 (9th Cir. 1977).

50. 18 U.S.C. Sec. 1153. The MCA was discussed earlier in this chapter.

51. *See U.S. v. John*, 587 F.2d 683 (5th Cir.), *cert. denied*, 441 U.S. 925 (1979).

52. 435 U.S. 191 (1978).

53. *Donnelly v. U.S.*, 228 U.S. 243 (1939); *U.S. v. Chavez*, 290 U.S. 357 (1933). The burden is on the federal government to prove that the defendant is one race and the victim is another, in order to establish criminal jurisdiction under the ICCA. *See U.S. v. Lawrence*, 51 F.3d 150 (9th Cir. 1995). Normally, the indictment must specify the races of the victim and the defendant. *See U.S. v. Prentiss*, 256 F.3d 971 (10th Cir. 2001) *(en banc), on remand*, 273 F.3d 1277 (10th Cir. 2001).

54. *Williams*, note 46 above, 327 U.S. at 714; *Williams v. Lee*, 358 U.S. 217, 220 (1958). *See also U.S. v. Big Crow*, 523 F.2d 955 (8th Cir. 1975), *cert. denied*, 424 U.S. 920 (1976).

55. *South Dakota v. Larson*, 455 N.W.2d 600 (S.D. 1990). *See also State v. Flint*, 756 P.2d 324 (Ariz. App. 1988), *cert. denied*, 492 U.S. 911 (1989); *Greenwalt*, note 46 above; *St. Cloud v. U.S.*, 702 F. Supp. 1456, 1458 (D.S.D. 1988).

56. 31 U.S. 515 (1832).

57. 104 U.S. 621 (1881).

58. *Wheeler*, note 3 above, 435 U.S. at 324 n.21; *Antelope*, note 20 above, 430 U.S. at 643 n.2. *See also Ryder v. State*, 648 P.2d 774 (N.M. 1982), *aff'd on other grounds*, 648 P.2d 774 (N.M. 1982).

59. *State v. Horseman*, 866 P.2d 1110 (Mont. 1993); *Washington v. Schmuck*, 850 P.2d 1332 (Wash. 1993), *cert. denied*, 510 U.S. 931 (1993); *Ryder*, note 58 above. *See also Ortiz-Barraza v. U.S.*, 512 F.2d 1176, 1179 (9th Cir. 1975).

60. *See Duro v. Reina*, 495 U.S. 676, 697 (1990) (recognizing that "tribal officers may exercise their power to detain the [nonmember] offender and transport him to the proper authorities.")

61. *See U.S. v. Patch*, 114 F.3d 131 (9th Cir.), *cert. denied*, 552 U.S. 983 (1997).

62. 18 U.S.C. Sec. 1162, 28 U.S.C. Sec. 1360, as amended by 25 U.S.C. Secs. 1321–26.

63. *See Idaho v. Marek*, 736 P.2d 1314 (Idaho 1987); *Idaho v. Major*, 725 P.2d 115 (Idaho 1986).

64. 18 U.S.C. Sec. 1162(b) (mandatory states); 25 U.S.C. Sec. 1321(b) (option states).

65. This rule is discussed in chs. 7 and 9. The one exception to this rule is that Indians and tribes are required to comply with certain state conservation laws. This exception is explained in ch. 11.

66. 480 U.S. 202 (1987).

67. *State v. Johnson*, 598 N.W.2d 680 (Minn. 1999). *See also State v. Stone*, 572 N.W.2d 725 (Minn. 1997); *State v. R.M.H.*, 617 N.W.2d 55 (Minn. 2000).

68. *Quechan Indian Tribe v. McMullen*, 984 F.2d 304 (9th Cir. 1993).

69. *State v. Robinson*, 572 N.W.2d 720 (Minn. 1997).

70. *Native Village of Venetie I.R.A. Council v. Alaska*, 944 F.2d 548, 560 (9th Cir. 1991), *rev'd on other grounds*, 522 U.S. 520 (1998); *Schmuck*, note 59 above, 850 P.2d at 1344. *See also Walker v. Rushing*, 898 F.2d 672 (8th Cir. 1990).

71. *See* notes 31–32 above and accompanying text. *See also Maine v. Mitchell*, 712 A.2d 1033 (Maine 1998) (holding that a state could prosecute an Indian after he was prosecuted in tribal court for the same offense). *But see Booth v. State*, 903 P.2d 1079 (Alaska App. 1995) (holding that state law prohibits a second prosecution, even though federal law does not).

72. *See Wadena*, note 23 above, 152 F.3d at 842. *See also Negonsett v. Samuels*, 507 U.S. 99, 105 (1993) (holding that the federal law conferring criminal jurisdiction on Kansas, cited in note 73 below, expressly reserved to the federal government jurisdiction to enforce crimes covered by the ICCA).

73. *See* Public Law 98-290, Sec. 5, 98 Stat. 201 (1984) (Colorado) (giving Colorado criminal and civil jurisdiction in Ignacio, Colorado, and any other municipality incorporated under Colorado law within the Southern Ute Indian reservation), *see U.S. v. Burch*, 169 F.3d 666 (10th Cir. 1999); Act of June 30, 1948, ch. 759, 62 Stat. 1161 (Iowa), *see Youngbear v. Brewer*, 415 F. Supp. 807 (N.D. Iowa 1976), *aff'd*, 549 F.2d 74 (8th Cir. 1977); 18 U.S.C. Sec. 3243 (Kansas); Act of May 31, 1946, ch. 279, 60 Stat. 229 (North Dakota), *see Negonsett v. Samuels*, 507 U.S. 99, 103–4 (1993) (holding that the Kansas statute conferred criminal jurisdiction on that state and also noting that the Iowa and North Dakota laws are similarly worded, and thus they likely confer similar jurisdiction on those states); 25 U.S.C. Secs. 1721–35 (Maine), *see Maine v. Mitchell*, 712 A.2d 1033 (Maine 1998); 25 U.S.C. sec. 1708 (conferring jurisdiction on Rhode Island over the Narragansett reservation).

74. *Rice v. Rehner*, 463 U.S. 713 (1983).

75. *Fort Belknap Indian Community v. Mazurek*, 43 F.3d 428 (9th Cir. 1994), *cert. denied*, 516 U.S. 806 (1995).

76. 241 U.S. 602 (1916). *See also In re Mayfield*, 141 U.S. 107 (1891) (the ICCA does not authorize the prosecution of an Indian for adultery with a non-Indian).

77. *U.S. v. Sosseur*, 181 F.2d 873 (7th Cir. 1950); *U.S. v. Blue*, 722 F.2d 383 (8th Cir.

1983); and *U.S. v. Marcyes*, 557 F.2d 1361 (9th Cir. 1977), respectively. *See also U.S. v. Thunder Hawk*, 127 F.3d 705 (8th Cir. 1997) (allowing federal prosecution of the victimless crime of driving under the influence).

78. *Blue*, note 77 above, 722 F.2d at 386.

79. U.S. Dept. of Justice, Office of Legal Counsel, "Memorandum to Benjamin R. Civiletti: Jurisdiction over Victimless Crimes Committed by Non-Indians in Indian Country," *reprinted in* 6 Indian L. Rep. K-I (Aug. 1979).

80. *Montana ex rel. Poll, Lindlief, and Juneau v. Montana Ninth Judicial Dist. Ct.*, 851 P.2d 405 (Mont. 1993); *State v. Thomas*, 760 P.2d 96 (Mont. 1988); *State v. Burrola*, 669 P.2d 614 (Ariz. App. 1983); *State v. Warner*, 379 P.2d 66 (N.M. 1963).

81. U.S. Const., art. IV, sec. 2. The process of extradition is explained in *Pacileo v. Walker*, 449 U.S. 86 (1980).

82. *Talton v. Mayes*, 163 U.S. 379 (1896).

83. *See, e.g., State of Arizona ex rel. Merrill v. Turtle*, 413 F.2d 683 (9th Cir. 1969); *Schauer v. Burleigh County*, 17 Indian L. Rep. 3132, 3136 (D.N.D. 1987). *See also Northern Cheyenne Tribe v. Crow Tribe*, 11 Indian L. Rep. 6006 (Crow Ct. App. 1983) (lack of extradition agreement between two tribes precludes one tribe from honoring extradition request from other tribe).

84. *Schauer*, note 83 above.

85. *City of Farmington v. Bennally*, 892 P.2d 629 (N.M. Ct. App.), *cert. denied*, 890 P.2d 1321 (N.M. 1995); *Bennally v. Marcum*, 553 P.2d 1270 (N.M. 1976); *Turtle*, note 83 above; *State v. Spotted Horse*, 462 N.W.2d 463 (S.D. 1990).

86. 121 S.Ct. 2304 (2001).

87. *Nevada v. Hicks*, 121 S.Ct. 2304, 2313 (2001).

88. *Id.* at 2312.

89. *Id.* at 2312–13. *See also Ward v. Race Horse*, 163 U.S. 504 (1896), *overruled on other grounds, Minnesota v. Mille Lacs Band of Chippewa Indians*, 526 U.S. 172 (1999); *DeCoteau v. District County Court*, 420 U.S. 425, 427 n.2 (1975). *See also State v. Clark*, 3 P.3d 689 (N.M. App. 2000) (state has jurisdiction to prosecute Indian who initiated criminal activity on the reservation, by stealing horses, and engaged in continuing criminal activity off the reservation, by trying to sell them).

90. *See Mattz v. Arnett*, 412 U.S. 481, 505 (1973); *U.S. v. Azure*, 801 F.2d 336 (8th Cir. 1986); *U.S. v. Sohappy*, 770 F.2d 816 (9th Cir. 1985), *cert. denied*, 477 U.S. 906 (1986); *U.S. v. Burnett*, 777 F.2d 593 (10th Cir. 1985), *cert. denied*, 476 U.S. 1106 (1986).

IX

Civil Jurisdiction in Indian Country

What is civil jurisdiction?

E very government has two broad powers: criminal jurisdiction and civil jurisdiction. Criminal jurisdiction maintains law and order. Civil jurisdiction maintains everything else, particularly a society's culture and values. Most family matters, such as marriage, divorce, child custody, and adoptions, and most property matters, such as taxation, land use (zoning), inheritance, and the sale of goods and services, are regulated through the government's civil jurisdiction. A government that loses its right to regulate civil matters eventually loses its identity.

A. TRIBAL JURISDICTION

Does an Indian tribe have the right to exercise civil jurisdiction within the entire reservation?

Exercising civil jurisdiction is vital to the success of Indian tribes. No one questions the fact that an Indian tribe, unless limited by Congress, may exercise the full range of its civil jurisdiction over tribal members within the reservation. Tribal members who wish to marry, divorce, adopt children, develop their land, or engage in a commercial enterprise on the reservation may do so only if they comply with tribal law.[1]

With regard to non-Indians, the answer is more complex. It was presumed until recently that Indian tribes had the inherent right to exercise broad civil jurisdiction over non-Indians on the reservation. As early as 1904, the Supreme Court held that an Indian tribe could require non-Indians to pay a personal property tax on the value of their cattle grazing (pursuant to leases with the tribe and tribal members) on Indian trust land

167

within the reservation.[2] The Court rested its decision on the principle that Indian tribes, like other governments, have the inherent right to exclude nonmembers from their territory; therefore, they have the lesser right to set the conditions on which nonmembers may enter and remain in that territory. In 1956, a federal appellate court relied on that rationale to uphold the right of a tribe to tax non-Indians on the value of their leasehold interests in trust land.[3]

Similarly, in 1982 in *Merrion v. Jicarilla Apache Tribe,*[4] the Supreme Court, using sweeping language, upheld the right of an Indian tribe to tax a non-Indian oil company's operations on tribal trust land, explaining that Indian tribes have the inherent right "to tribal self-government and territorial management," a power the Court said "derives from the tribe's general authority, as sovereign, to control economic activity within its jurisdiction."[5] The following year, in a case upholding the right of Indian tribes to regulate hunting and fishing by non-Indians on tribal lands, the Court once again used broad language, stating that Indian tribes have the inherent right "to exclude nonmembers entirely or to condition their presence on the reservation."[6] As recently as 1987, the Supreme Court stated: "Tribal authority over the activities of non-Indians on reservation lands is an important part of tribal sovereignty."[7]

Consistent with those cases, other courts affirmed the right of Indian tribes to tax non-Indians on the value of minerals they extracted from a tribal member's trust land;[8] to require that non-Indians obtain a tribal business license in order to engage in commerce with the tribe or tribal members on the reservation;[9] and to require that non-Indians pay a tribal sales tax on goods purchased on the reservation from an Indian tribe.[10] It was also recognized that tribal courts, as part of a divorce decree, may award child support against the non-Indian parent of a reservation Indian child.[11]

1. Tribal Authority over Non-Indians on Land Owned by Non-Indians

All of the cases discussed above involved a tribe's ability to regulate the activities of non-Indians on *Indian trust* land. It was not until 1981 that the Supreme Court decided a case involving tribal jurisdiction over non-Indians on land within the reservation owned by *non-Indians.* (As explained in chapter 1, the General Allotment Act of 1887 (GAA) opened most Indian reservations to settlement by non-Indians, and today millions of acres of reservation land are owned by non-Indians.) In *Montana v. United States* (1981),[12] the Court held that an Indian tribe could not regulate hunting and fishing by non-Indians on land they owned within the reservation unless the tribe could show either (1) that these non-Indians have entered into "consensual relationships with the tribe or its members, through commercial dealing, contracts, leases, or other arrangements," or (2) that the activity of these non-Indians "threatens or has some direct effect on the political integrity, the economic security, or the health and welfare of the tribe."[13] (These have become known as the two "*Montana* exceptions.")

The Court based its decision in *Montana* on the fact that the non-Indian in that case had acquired his land as a result of the GAA. The Court held that when Congress allows non-Indians to purchase land on an Indian reservation, the tribe loses its exclusive control over that land. A tribe may not exclude someone from the reservation who has a federal right to be there. The Court then said that having lost the greater power to exclude, the tribe necessarily lost the lesser power to regulate hunting and fishing on that land by the owner. Eight years later, the Court applied this principle in *Brendale v. Confederated Tribes and Bands of Yakima Indian Nation* (1989)[14] and held that the Yakima Indian Nation lacked the authority to zone non-Indian land in an area of the reservation in which half the land in the vicinity was owned by non-Indians, unless the tribe could prove the existence of one of the two "*Montana* exceptions": either that the landowner had a consensual business arrangement or relationship with the tribe, or that the landowner's conduct threatened a substantial tribal interest.

The Supreme Court further diluted tribal civil jurisdiction in *South Dakota v. Bourland* (1993).[15] Both *Montana* and *Brendale* had involved privately *owned* land. In *Bourland,* the Court considered whether an Indian tribe could regulate the activities of non-Indians who had a federal right to *use* (but not own) reservation land. In that case, a portion of an Indian reservation had been set aside by Congress for the construction of a dam. The dam provided flood control and created a lake that was opened by Congress to use by the general public for boating and other recreational purposes. The entire area, though, remained tribal trust land. The tribe therefore argued that it could regulate non-Indian activities within that territory. The Court held, however, that when Congress gives nonmembers a right to use reservation land, this "implies the loss" of the tribe's right to exclude those persons from it and that once the tribe loses the right to exclude, it no longer may regulate the activities of nonmembers on that land unless the tribe can prove that a "*Montana* exception" exists.[16]

In *Strate v. A-1 Contractors* (1997),[17] the Supreme Court took this principle one step further and held that a tribal court could not hear a civil dispute arising out of a traffic accident between two non-Indians that occurred on a state highway within the reservation, in which the driver of a truck severely injured the driver of a car. The Court held that the right-of-way given by Congress to North Dakota to construct the highway removed the tribe's right to exclude non-Indians from that land—even though the land remained in trust status—and having lost the right to exclude, the tribe necessarily lost the power to regulate the activities of non-Indians occurring on that property. This overall loss of jurisdiction, the Court said, extends to a tribe's adjudicatory (judicial) powers, stripping tribal courts of the authority they would otherwise have to resolve disputes arising on the reservation.

At first glance, it might seem that the second "*Montana* exception" permits broad tribal jurisdiction over non-Indians. This exception allows tribes to regulate all activities by nonmembers on the reservation that have a "direct effect" on the political integrity, economic security, or health and welfare of the tribe. The Supreme Court stated in *Brendale*, however, that the tribal interest at stake must be "demonstrably serious" and that the non-Indian's activity must "imperil" that interest, not just affect it in some fashion.[18] This has proven to be a difficult test to meet. In *Strate,* for instance, the Court refused to find that the tribe had a sufficiently serious interest at stake to justify the exercise of the tribe's judicial powers, even though the truck driver at fault in that case could just as easily have hit a car driven by a tribal member, and despite the tribe's obvious interest in ensuring safe driving on reservation roads. Moreover, the person injured in the car, although a non-Indian, was married to a tribal member and her children were enrolled members of the tribe, but even this was insufficient to confer jurisdiction on tribal courts.

The Supreme Court struck another blow to tribal sovereignty in *Atkinson Trading Co., Inc. v. Shirley* (2001).[19] The issue in that case was whether the Navajo Nation could assess a hotel occupancy tax on guests who rented rooms at a hotel owned by a non-Indian and located on land within the reservation also owned by a non-Indian. The tribe defended its tax on the grounds, among others, that many of these guests came to the hotel because of its location on the reservation and took advantage of what the reservation had to offer; also, the tribe was providing police, emergency medical, and fire protection to the hotel and its guests.

The Supreme Court, however, broadly applied its *Montana* line of cases and invalidated the tribal tax. The Court's earlier cases stand for the general principle, the Court said, that due to their "incorporation" into the United States and their "dependent" status, Indian tribes have necessarily lost many of their original powers.[20] One power they have lost is the authority to regulate the activities of non-Indians on non-Indian land, except to the extent permitted by the two *Montana* exceptions.[21] The first exception, which allows tribes to regulate nonmember activity when a "consensual relationship" exists, was not present in the *Atkinson* case, the Court said, because the hotel guests had not entered into a sufficiently close relationship with the tribe to satisfy this exception merely by having entered the reservation. The Court found that the second *Montana* exception—which permits a tribe to regulate non-Indian activity that imperils a substantial tribal interest—was not present, either, because nothing indicated that by staying at the hotel, these nonmembers imperiled a substantial tribal interest.

In short, beginning with *Montana* in 1981, the Supreme Court has created the principle that "the civil authority of Indian tribes and their courts with respect to non-Indian fee lands generally does not extend to the activities of nonmembers of the tribe," unless Congress has expressly conferred that power upon the tribe, or the tribe can show the existence of a *Montana* exception.[22] Citing these recent Supreme Court cases, the U.S. Court of Appeals for the Ninth Circuit has held that a tribal court lacks jurisdiction to resolve a dispute between a tribal member and a county regarding the legality of a county tax on that member's privately owned land on the reservation;[23] that a tribal court lacks jurisdiction to hear a case filed by a member against a nonmember arising out of an accident on a state highway running through the reservation;[24] that a tribal court has no jurisdiction over a suit filed by a tribal member against state police officers alleging false arrest, because the arrest occurred on fee land and the tribe had consented to allow the state to exercise criminal jurisdiction on that land;[25] that an Indian tribe lacked authority to compel the state to abide by tribal employment laws in constructing a highway on a state-owned right-of-way;[26] that a tribal court may not hear a suit filed against a railroad by the estates of two tribal members who were killed when a train collided with their car on a congressionally granted right-of-way within the reservation;[27] and that a tribe lacks the power to tax the value of an easement given by Congress to a utility company on reservation trust land.[28]

On several occasions, Indian tribes have successfully proven the existence of a *Montana* exception and have thus been allowed to regulate non-Indian conduct on non-Indian land. One tribe satisfied the first exception (the *consensual relationship* exception) by showing that a non-Indian company had entered into leases with the tribe and tribal members for mining minerals from their trust lands and that the company had agreed to comply with tribal regulations regarding the hiring of tribal members.[29] In another case, a tribe met the second *Montana* exception (the *substantial tribal interest* exception) when it showed that pollution spewing from land on the reservation owned by non-Indians threatened the tribe's water supply.[30] Tribes also may enforce their health and building requirements[31] and their clean air regulations[32] on reservation non-Indians when necessary to protect substantial tribal interests. Thus, tribal authority over non-Indians on non-Indian land has been greatly reduced but is not foreclosed.

2. Tribal Authority over Non-Indians on Indian Trust Land

All of the cases just discussed dealt with tribal authority to regulate the activities of non-Indians on *non-Indian* land within the reservation. Each new case further diluted tribal authority. Still, though, it was presumed that these cases had little, if any, relevance to the ability of tribes to regulate the activities of non-Indians on *Indian trust* land. Indeed, the Supreme Court in *Montana* expressly confirmed the prevailing notion that "tribes retain considerable control over nonmember conduct on tribal land."[33]

Twenty years after giving tribes that reassurance in *Montana*, the Supreme Court rescinded it in *Nevada v. Hicks* (2001).[34] As discussed more fully in chapter 6 (in subsections 7 and 9), the Court held in *Hicks* that land ownership is just one of many factors to consider in determining whether an Indian tribe may regulate non-Indian conduct within the reservation, and that the general rule is "that the inherent sovereign powers of an Indian tribe do not extend to the activities of nonmembers of the tribe."[35] In *Hicks,* the Court prohibited a tribal court from hearing a case filed by a tribal member against state game wardens who had committed what the member claimed was an illegal search of his home on the reservation.

In recent years, then, the Supreme Court has radically changed the general principles regarding tribal jurisdiction over nonmembers on the reservation.[36] Today, the general rule is that Indian tribes lack jurisdiction over non-Indians on the reservation—with respect to their activities on privately owned *and* on Indian trust land—unless the tribe can show that one of the two *Montana* exceptions justifies the application of tribal authority.

Can non-Indians be sued in tribal court?

In some situations they can, but in others, they cannot. The Supreme Court held in *Montana, Brendale, Bourland,* and *Atkinson* that there are situations in which tribes have lost their ability to regulate the conduct of non-Indians. In *Strate* and *Hicks,* the Court extended that rule to tribal court jurisdiction, holding that a tribe's *adjudicatory* jurisdiction (the authority of its courts to resolve disputes) is no broader than its *regulatory* jurisdiction (the power of its legislature to regulate conduct).

Those cases also confirm, though, that there are certain instances in which Indian tribes *are* permitted to exercise regulatory and adjudicatory authority over non-Indians: the instances covered by the two *Montana* exceptions. The general rule is that when a tribe has the right to regulate the activity of a non-Indian, the non-Indian can be sued in tribal court to resolve disputes concerning that activity.[37] Conversely, no suit can be heard in tribal court unless the tribe has the power to regulate that conduct in the first place.[38] Of course, a tribal court may hear the case only if it has been authorized by tribal law to do so, but many tribal courts have been authorized to hear cases arising on the reservation involving non-Indians.[39]

In some instances, a tribal court is the *only* court that may hear the case. The Supreme Court's 1959 decision in *Williams v. Lee*[40] illustrates this principle. The Court held in *Williams v. Lee* that a suit by a non-Indian against an Indian for breach of contract arising out of a reservation transaction could only be heard in tribal court because intervention by a state court into contracts arising on the reservation involving a tribal member would substantially interfere with tribal sovereignty. Thus, although recent federal court decisions have reduced the range of non-Indian activities that Indian tribes may regulate, tribal courts continue to play an indispensable role in resolving disputes emanating from those activities that the tribes *can* regulate.[41]

What procedure must a non-Indian follow in order to challenge a tribe's jurisdiction?

As just explained, a tribe may lawfully exercise its civil jurisdiction over non-Indians in certain situations but not in others. Non-Indians who are being subjected to tribal authority—for example, non-Indians who are being taxed by a tribe—may therefore wish to challenge the tribe's authority, claiming that this is one of the situations in which the tribe lacks jurisdiction.

In *National Farmers Union Insurance Co. v. Crow Tribe of Indians* (1985),[42] the Supreme Court held that the question of whether a tribe has exceeded its lawful jurisdiction is a "federal question" that federal courts are authorized to decide. However, the Court also held that non-Indians who wish to challenge the tribe's jurisdiction must first raise the issue in a tribal court before seeking a ruling from a federal court.[43] Federal courts have the final word regarding the scope of a tribe's jurisdiction over a non-Indian, but federal courts normally should not address this question until the tribe's own courts have done so. An exhaustion requirement of this nature, the Court held, performs three functions: it furthers the current congressional policy of supporting tribal self-government; it promotes the administration of justice; and it obtains the benefit of tribal expertise on issues of tribal jurisdiction.[44] If the tribe has an appellate court, non-Indians must exhaust that avenue, too, before submitting the jurisdictional question to a federal court.[45]

Non-Indians do not have to exhaust tribal remedies, the Court held in *National Farmers,* if the tribe does not have a court system or if exhausting tribal remedies would be futile or unreasonably slow.[46] But exhaustion normally is required,[47] even if it is alleged that the tribal court is biased or incompetent.[48] Allowing non-Indians to bypass tribal courts would ignore "the important congressional interest advanced by the tribal exhaustion rule."[49] Tribal courts are sophisticated courts capable of fairly deciding complex legal and factual issues, including challenges to their own jurisdiction.[50] Even the federal government is required to exhaust tribal remedies when commencing an action against a tribal member over which a tribal court would have jurisdiction.[51]

Here again, though, recent Supreme Court decisions have diluted tribal protections. In its 1997 decision in *Strate* and even more pointedly in its 2001 decision in *Hicks,* the Supreme Court relaxed the principle announced in *National Farmers*. The Court added what it acknowledged was "a broader exception" to the exhaustion requirement by allowing non-Indians to bypass tribal courts and immediately file their claim in a federal court whenever "it is plain" that the tribe lacks jurisdiction over the non-Indian activity in question.[52] This new exception would seem to be at odds with all three of the reasons (listed above) given by the Court in *National Farmers* for having created the exhaustion requirement in the first place.

In those instances in which a case proceeds in tribal court and is then appealed to a federal court, all findings of fact made by the tribal court must be accepted as conclusive by the federal court unless it finds them clearly erroneous; thus, a person normally may not relitigate factual issues in federal court that were lost in tribal court.[53] In addition, a tribal court's interpretation of tribal law is binding on federal courts.[54] These rules apply regardless of whether a non-Indian is suing an Indian or an Indian is suing a non-Indian.[55]

What civil jurisdiction has Congress authorized Indian tribes to exercise?

Congress has the power to authorize Indian tribes to exercise civil jurisdiction, and it has exercised that power on a few occasions.[56] Congress has authorized tribes to regulate the distribution of alcoholic beverages on the reservation.[57] Congress has also authorized federally recognized Indian tribes to administer and apply various environmental laws on the reservation, including the Clean Water Act, the Clean Air Act, and the Safe Drinking Water Act.[58] Tribes likely had the inherent authority to regulate the activities covered by these laws anyway, but courts need not decide the question because of Congress's authorization.[59]

Does Public Law 83–280 limit tribal civil jurisdiction?

No. Public Law 83–280, discussed in chapter 7, gives to certain states the power to exercise some amount of criminal and civil jurisdiction in Indian country. Nothing in that law removes the power of Indian tribes to exercise their inherent authority over the same subjects.[60] In those situations in which Congress has authorized the state to act, the state and tribe would have concurrent jurisdiction.

B. State Jurisdiction

Does the state have the right to exercise civil jurisdiction in Indian country?

Immediately after the United States became a nation, state govern-ments tried to extend their laws into Indian territory in a deliberate effort to control Indian life and culture. They would have succeeded far more than they did had it not been for the U.S. Supreme Court. Recent deci-sions of the Court, especially the ones just discussed, have substantially reduced *tribal* jurisdiction over *non-Indians.* For the most part, however, the Court has not significantly expanded *state* jurisdiction over *Indians,* although here, too, recent Supreme Court decisions have diluted some tribal protections created in the Court's earlier cases.

In 1832 in *Worcester v. Georgia,*[61] the Supreme Court established the rule that state officials may not exercise any authority in Indian country without the express authorization of Congress. Indian tribes have the in-herent right to regulate their internal affairs, the Court said, and state officials may intervene in these affairs only with congressional consent.

Even today, civil jurisdiction over Indians in Indian country remains almost entirely a tribal matter. This is because (1) Congress has authorized relatively few extensions of state law into Indian country, and (2) the Su-preme Court has defended the right of Indian tribes and their members to remain free of state jurisdiction in the absence of this authorization.

The Supreme Court, however, has since modified the *Worcester* "abso-lute" rule, and state governments may now exercise certain powers in In-dian country without Congress's consent. As explained in chapter 7, sec-tion C, the Supreme Court has replaced the *Worcester* rule with two tests: the *infringement* and the *federal preemption* tests. Unless Congress has given its express consent, a state law may be enforced in Indian country only if it passes both tests.

These tests are virtually impossible to pass when the law or regulation at issue primarily impacts the tribe or its members for their on-reservation activities. As the Court confirmed in *Hicks,* "When on-reservation con-duct involving only Indians is at issue, state law is generally inapplicable."[62] To illustrate, the Supreme Court has held that a state, unless authorized by Congress, may not tax the income that Indians who live on the reser-vation earn from reservation employment,[63] the personal property Indians own on the reservation,[64] the sale of goods to Indians within the reservation,[65] motor fuels purchased by Indians or by the tribe for travel within the reservation,[66] profits made by a non-Indian company from the sale of equipment to a tribal business,[67] the fuel used by a non-Indian company hauling tribal timber on tribal roads,[68] profits made by a non-Indian construction company when it builds a school on the reservation for an Indian tribe,[69] or the income that a tribe receives when it leases land for mineral development.[70] In nontax cases, the Supreme Court has held that in the absence of congressional consent, a state may not require non-Indians who hunt on tribal lands to comply with state game laws,[71] and it may not regulate tribal gambling operations within the reservation.[72] Based on these decisions, lower federal courts have held that states lack the authority to regulate the placement of billboards,[73] the disposal of hazardous waste,[74] and the harvesting of tribal timber[75] on the reservation. Additionally, states are not allowed to enforce their child support laws on reservation Indians[76] or their rent control laws on reservation trust land.[77]

The only significant effect that the Supreme Court's modern analysis has had on state jurisdiction over reservation Indians involves activities that these Indians engaged in outside the reservation. The Supreme Court has held that although the state normally may not exercise its jurisdiction over reservation Indians, it *may* serve search and arrest warrants and other forms of judicial process on reservation Indians for conduct they engaged in off the reservation.[78]

Switching from the absolute barrier in *Worcester* to the infringement and preemption tests used today, however, has had an enormous effect on state jurisdiction over reservation *non-Indians*. As explained in chapter 7, a presumption exists due to recent Supreme Court decisions that non-Indians on the reservation must comply with all state laws unless they enjoy an express immunity under federal law. With respect to state taxation, for instance, courts have held that reservation non-Indians must pay almost all the taxes they would pay off the reservation, and the only taxes they are immune from paying are those in which the burden of the tax falls on the tribe or its members. (For instance, non-Indians cannot be required to collect state sales taxes on sales they make on the reservation to the tribe or a tribal member.)

The Supreme Court has held that state civil jurisdiction over non-Indians is so broad that Indian tribes and their members can be required to collect state sales taxes on their sales of goods to non-Indians, despite the administrative and financial burdens of doing so, and even though this may discourage non-Indians from purchasing goods on the reservation.[79] Indian merchants can also be required to keep detailed records of their sales to non-Indians so that state tax officials can ensure that the state's taxes are being collected.[80] If tribal vendors refuse to collect these taxes, state officials may enforce their rights, the Supreme Court has held, by seizing off the reservation the goods being shipped to the tribe for sale to non-Indians.[81]

What jurisdiction do the state courts have to decide disputes within Indian country?

A state's adjudicatory (judicial) authority in Indian country is no greater than its regulatory (legislative) authority. This was made clear by the Supreme Court in *Williams v. Lee* (1959),[82] mentioned earlier. The issue in that case was whether a non-Indian store owner could sue a Navajo Indian in state court regarding a contract dispute that arose on the Navajo Reservation. The Supreme Court ruled that the state court could not exercise jurisdiction over the dispute because to do so "would undermine the authority of tribal courts over Reservation affairs and hence would infringe on the right of the Indians to govern themselves,"[83] given that the Navajos had established tribal courts to hear such cases.

Similarly, courts have held that unless Congress has given its express consent, a state court may not decide adoption cases arising on the reservation in which all parties to the proceeding are tribal members;[84] may not issue an eviction order against an Indian tenant who rents property on the reservation;[85] may not hear negligence claims between Indians and non-Indians, such as lawsuits stemming from car accidents, that arise on Indian trust land;[86] may not garnish the wages of an Indian employed on the reservation[87] or attach Indian property located there;[88] may not resolve reservation commercial disputes even if one of the parties is a non-Indian[89] or disputes involving interests in Indian land;[90] may not enter divorce decrees involving reservation Indians, even if one spouse is a non-Indian;[91] and may not involuntarily commit a reservation Indian to a state mental hospital.[92] Federal courts can issue an injunction against any state court that begins to hear an Indian case over which it clearly lacks jurisdiction.[93] In most of the cases just discussed, the courts acknowledged that the state had an interest at stake. But the state's interest was deemed insignificant when compared with the federal and tribal interests in promoting tribal self-government, and therefore the state's conduct failed either the infringement or the preemption test or both.

What civil jurisdiction has Congress expressly authorized the states to apply in Indian country?

States can acquire civil jurisdiction in Indian country by congressional consent, and Congress has passed several laws consenting to certain types of jurisdiction. Some laws confer jurisdiction over particular tribes, while others confer jurisdiction over particular subject areas, such as allowing states to regulate the sale of alcoholic beverages in Indian country. These laws are discussed in chapter 7, section B.

For jurisdictional purposes, is a state-chartered corporation owned by Indians considered Indian or non-Indian?

Corporations that are licensed under state law usually are considered non-Indian for jurisdictional purposes even if they are Indian-owned. Therefore, a lawsuit brought by a non-Indian against a state-chartered Indian corporation must be filed in state court rather than in tribal court.[94]

On the other hand, an Indian-owned corporation that is licensed under tribal or federal law rather than state law is considered Indian for jurisdictional purposes. In that situation, the corporation could not be sued in state court regarding a reservation contract dispute.[95]

Can a situation arise in which no court has jurisdiction over a reservation dispute?

Yes. As with the federal and state governments, tribal governments are not required to authorize their courts to hear every type of controversy. Consequently, an aggrieved party may have no court capable of hearing his or her case regarding a reservation dispute if only a tribal court has the right to hear the case but the tribal council has not authorized it to resolve that type of dispute.[96]

A similar predicament occurs when the government—whether tribal, state, or federal—has violated someone's rights, but the aggrieved party is unable to sue due to the government's sovereign immunity. As explained in chapter 18, governments enjoy an immunity from most lawsuits unless they have consented to be sued. As a result, no court may be authorized to hear cases alleging a violation of rights by the tribal, state, or federal governments.

May a state serve process on an Indian within the reservation for an activity that occurred off the reservation?

Indians who leave the reservation are subject to state jurisdiction, unless they are engaged in an activity protected by federal law.[97] A reservation Indian, for example, who causes an car accident while off the reservation may be sued for damages in state court. No lawsuit can begin, though, until the plaintiff files with the court a summons and complaint and the defendant is served with a copy of them. This procedure is called *service of process.*

In *Hicks* in 2001, the Supreme Court stated that state officials have the authority to serve process on Indians on the reservation for activities they engaged in off the reservation.[98] Prior to that decision, most courts that considered the question had held that Indians may be served with process on the reservation for their off-reservation activities,[99] but some courts had held that a tribal officer or Indian process server, rather than a state officer, had to serve the papers.[100] No such requirement was suggested in *Hicks*. With respect to suits against non-Indians brought by other non-Indians, courts have held that process may be served within the reservation and that state officers have the authority to serve the papers.[101]

May a state court enforce a judgment against an Indian by seizing reservation property owned by that person?

When a person is sued for money damages and loses the case, the court issues a judgment and orders that person (the *judgment debtor*) to pay the amount awarded. If the money is not paid, the court can order court officials to seize and sell property belonging to the judgment debtor so as to pay (satisfy) the judgment.

As a general rule, a court may not seize property located outside its territorial jurisdiction.[102] Applying that principle in this context, a state court would not be able to seize Indian property within an Indian reservation. The few courts that have addressed this question have reached inconsistent decisions, some holding that state courts have the power to seize property on the reservation, and some holding that no such power exists.[103] A noted authority has criticized state court seizures of reservation

Indian property as violative of tribal sovereignty unless state officials first obtain a tribal court order permitting enforcement of the state decree.[104]

Must state and tribal governments give "full faith and credit" to each other's laws and court decrees?

The U.S. Constitution expressly requires each state to give "full faith and credit" to the laws and court decisions of another state.[105] Chaos would likely result if no such requirement existed, given that one state could refuse to recognize even a marriage, divorce, or adoption performed in another state.

There is nothing in the Constitution that requires a state and a tribe to give full faith and credit to each other's laws and court decisions. But to avoid a similar chaos and to promote mutual respect, courts have recognized that states and tribes must extend full faith and credit (or comity) to one another and recognize the validity of each other's laws and court decrees,[106] except when doing so would violate public policy or where, in the case of a court decision, the court lacked jurisdiction to decide the case.[107] Some states and tribes have passed laws that require their courts to give full faith and credit to the laws and court decrees of other jurisdictions.[108]

If states and tribes do not extend comity to one another, this can cause bitterness and tremendous personal loss. Marriages and divorces will have uncertain validity in other jurisdictions, and reservation Indians will have difficulty purchasing goods on credit or borrowing money outside the reservation if businesses and lenders believe they may have difficulty enforcing their contracts or state court judgments in tribal court.

Federal courts, as well, normally should extend comity to tribal court orders.[109] As one federal court recently noted, "[A]s a general principle, federal courts should recognize and enforce tribal judgments."[110]

C. FEDERAL JURISDICTION

Which civil laws have the federal government been authorized to apply in Indian country?

Federal civil laws, as with state civil laws, may not be applied in Indian county without the approval of Congress.[111] Congress has given such authorization in quite a few subject areas. As explained in chapter 5, federal officials have authority to regulate reservation trade with Indians; control the sale, use, and inheritance of Indian trust land; control the sale and use of reservation trust resources, such as timber, oil, gas, and other minerals; and regulate the quality of air and water on Indian reservations. The tribe is permitted to regulate in these areas as well, provided that its laws do not conflict with federal laws.[112]

NOTES

1. *See, e.g., Fisher v. District Court*, 424 U.S. 382 (1976); *Santa Clara Pueblo v. Martinez*, 436 U.S. 49 (1978); *Akins v. Penobscot Nation*, 130 F.3d 482 (1st Cir. 1997).

2. *Morris v. Hitchcock*, 194 U.S. 384 (1904).

3. *Iron Crow v. Oglala Sioux Tribe*, 231 F.2d 89 (8th Cir. 1956).

4. 455 U.S. 130 (1982).

5. *Merrion v. Jicarilla Tribe*, 455 U.S. 130, 137 (1982).

6. *New Mexico v. Mescalero Apache Tribe*, 462 U.S. 324, 333 (1983). *See also Merrion*, note 5 above, 455 U.S. at 144–45; *Hardin v. White Mountain Apache Tribe*, 779 F.2d 476 (9th Cir. 1985).

7. *Iowa Mutual Ins. Co. v. LaPlante*, 480 U.S. 9, 18 (1987).

8. *Mustang Production Co. v. Harrison*, 94 F.3d 1382 (10th Cir. 1996), *cert. denied*, 520 U.S. 1139 (1997).

9. *Ashcroft v. U.S.*, 679 F.2d 196 (9th Cir.), *cert. denied*, 459 U.S. 1201 (1983).

10. *Washington v. Confederated Tribes of the Colville Indian Reservation*, 447 U.S. 134 (1980).

11. *Sanders v. Robinson*, 864 F.2d 630 (9th Cir. 1988), *cert. denied*, 490 U.S. 943 (1989).

12. 450 U.S. 544 (1981).

13. *Montana v. U.S.*, 450 U.S. 544, 565–66 (1981).

14. 492 U.S. 408 (1989).

15. 508 U.S. 679 (1993).

16. *South Dakota v. Bourland*, 508 U.S. 679, 689 (1993).

17. 520 U.S. 438 (1997).

18. *Brendale v. Confederated Tribes and Bands of Yakima Indian Nation*, 492 U.S. 408, 431 (1989).

19. 121 S.Ct. 1825 (2001).

20. *Atkinson Trading Co., Inc. v. Shirley*, 121 S.Ct. 1825, 1830 (2001).

21. *Id.*

22. *Strate v. A-1 Contractors*, 520 U.S. 438, 453 (1997) (internal quotation omitted). On occasion, Congress has delegated to tribes the authority to regulate non-Indian activities on lands on the reservation. *See* notes 58–59 below and accompanying text.

23. *Yellowstone County v. Pease*, 96 F.3d 1169 (9th Cir. 1996).

24. *Wilson v. Marchington*, 127 F.3d 805 (9th Cir. 1997), *cert. denied*, 523 U.S. 1074 (1998).

25. *County of Lewis v. Allen*, 163 F.3d 509 (9th Cir. 1998) *(en banc)*.

26. *Montana Dept. of Transportation v. King*, 191 F.3d 1108 (9th Cir. 1999).

27. *Burlington Northern R.R. Co. v. Red Wolf*, 196 F.3d 1059 (9th Cir. 1999), *cert. denied*, 120 S.Ct. 1964 (2000).

28. *Big Horn County Electric Cooperative, Inc. v. Adams*, 219 F.3d 944 (9th Cir. 2000).

29. *FMC v. Shoshone-Bannock Tribes*, 905 F.2d 1311 (9th Cir. 1990), *cert. denied*, 499 U.S. 943 (1991).

30. See *State of Montana v. U.S. Environmental Protection Agency*, 137 F.3d 1135 (9th Cir. 1998). *See also City of Albuquerque v. Browner*, 97 F.3d 415 (10th Cir. 1996) (water quality regulation); *Stock West Corp. v. Taylor*, 964 F.2d 912 (9th Cir. 1992) *(en banc)* (holding that tribal court could have jurisdiction even when both parties to suit are non-Indian when substantial tribal interests are at stake).

31. *Cardin v. De La Cruz*, 671 F.2d 363 (9th Cir.), *cert. denied*, 459 U.S. 967 (1982).

32. *Nance v. E.P.A.*, 645 F.2d 701 (9th Cir. 1981).

33. *Montana v. U.S.*, note 13 above, 450 U.S. at 557. *See also Strate*, note 22 above, 520 U.S. at 454.

34. 121 S.Ct. 2304 (2001).

35. *Nevada v. Hicks*, 121 S.Ct. 2304, 2313 (2001) (quoting *Montana v. U.S.*, note 13 above, 450 U.S. at 565).

36. For an excellent, comprehensive discussion of how the Supreme Court has radically altered federal Indian law in recent years, see David Getches, "Beyond Indian Law: The Rehnquist Court's Pursuit of States' Rights, Color-Blind Justice and Mainstream Values," 86 *Minn. L. Rev.* 267 (2001).

37. *See Iowa Mutual*, note 7 above, 480 U.S. at 18.

38. *See Pease*, note 23 above, 96 F.3d at 1175.

39. *See, e.g., Rosebud Housing Auth. v. La Creek Elec. Coop.*, 13 Indian L. Rep. 6030 (Rbd. Sx. Tr. Ct. 1986); *Ft. Peck Housing Auth. v. Home Savings & Loan Ass'n*, 16 Indian L. Rep. 6083 (Ft. Peck Tr. Ct. 1989); *McDonald v. Harlan Racine and Guar. Nat. Ins. Co.*, 15 Indian L. Rep. 6003 (C.S. and K. Tr. Ct. 1988).

40. 358 U.S. 217 (1959).

41. *See Wellman v. Chevron U.S.A., Inc.*, 815 F.2d 577 (9th Cir. 1987); *Risse v. Meeks*, 585 N.W.2d 875 (S.D. 1998).

42. 471 U.S. 845 (1985).

43. *National Farmers Union Ins. Co. v. Crow Tribe of Indians*, 471 U.S. 845 (1985). *See also Native Village of Tyonek v. Puckett*, 890 F.2d 1054 (9th Cir. 1989), *cert. denied*, 494 U.S. 1081 (1990).

44. *National Farmers Union*, note 43 above, 471 U.S. at 856–57. *See also Texaco, Inc. v. Hale*, 81 F.3d 934 (10th Cir. 1996); *Pittsburgh & Midway Coal Mining Co. v. Watchman*, 52 F.3d 1531 (10th Cir. 1995); *Stock West Corp. v. Taylor*, note 30 above, 964 F.2d at 920; *Duncan Energy Co. v. Three Affiliated Tribes*, 27 F.3d 1294, 1300 (8th Cir. 1994), *cert. denied*, 513 U.S. 1103 (1995).

45. *Iowa Mutual,* note 7 above.

46. *National Farmers Union,* note 43 above, 471 U.S. at 856 n.21. *See Krempel v. The Prairie Island Indian Community,* 125 F.3d 621 (8th Cir. 1997) (lack of a tribal court obviates need to exhaust tribal remedies); *Basil Cook Enterprises, Inc. v. St. Regis Mohawk Tribe,* 117 F.3d 61, 67 (2d Cir. 1997); *State of Montana Dept. of Transportation v. King,* note 26 above, 191 F.3d at 1115; *Blue Legs v. U.S. Bureau of Indian Affairs,* 867 F.2d 1094, 1097–98 (8th Cir. 1989).

47. *See Ninigret Development Corp. v. Narragansett Indian Wetuomuck Housing Authority,* 207 F.3d 21 (1st Cir. 2000); *Pittsburgh & Midway Coal,* note 44 above; *Allstate Indemnity Co. v. Stump,* 191 F.3d 1097 (9th Cir. 1999), as amended by, 197 F.3d 1031 (9th Cir. 1999); *Johnson v. Gila River Indian Community,* 174 F.3d 1032 (9th Cir. 1999), *cert. denied,* 528 U.S. 875 (1999) (even a two-year delay in deciding an appeal is not necessarily grounds to avoid exhausting tribal remedies).

48. *Iowa Mutual,* note 7 above.

49. *Kerr-McGee Corp. v. Farley,* 115 F.3d 1498, 1507 (10th Cir. 1997).

50. *Id. See also Davis v. Mile Lack Band of Chippewa Indians,* 193 F.3d 990 (8th Cir. 1999).

51. *U.S. v. Tsosie,* 92 F.3d 1037, 1044 (9th Cir. 1996).

52. *Hicks,* note 35 above, 121 S.Ct. at 2315, citing *Strate,* note 22 above, 520 U.S. at 459–60. *See also Boxx v. Long Warrior,* 265 F.3d 771, 778 (9th Cir. 2001), *cert. denied,* 122 S.Ct. 1790 (2002).

53. *Iowa Mutual,* note 7 above, 480 U.S. at 18–19. *See also FMC,* note 29 above, 905 F.2d at 1313; *Mustang Production Co.,* note 8 above, 94 F.3d at 1384.

54. *Basil Cook Enterprises,* note 46 above, 117 F.3d at 66; *Sanders,* note 11 above.

55. *See, e.g., National Farmers Union,* note 43 above, and *Stock West, Inc. v. Confederated Tribes of the Colville Reservation,* 873 F.2d 1221 (9th Cir. 1989) (suit by Indian against non-Indian initiated in tribal court); *Wellman,* note 41 above (suit by Indian against non-Indian initiated in federal court); *Brown Constr. Co. v. Washoe Housing Auth.,* 835 F.2d 1327 (10th Cir. 1988) and *Weeks Constr. Inc. v. Oglala Sioux Housing Auth.,* 797 F.2d 668 (8th Cir. 1986) (suit by non-Indian against Indian initiated in federal court).

56. "There are few examples of congressional delegation of authority to tribes." Felix Cohen, *Handbook of Federal Indian Law* (Charlottesville: Michie Co., 1982) at 253.

57. 18 U.S.C. Sec. 1161. *See U.S. v. Mazurie,* 419 U.S. 544 (1975). The subject is discussed in more detail in ch. 6, sec. B(8). *See also Bugenig v. Hoopa Valley Tribe,* 266 F.3d 1201 (9th Cir. 2001) *(en banc), cert. denied,* 122 S.Ct. 1296 (2002) (express statutory authority to regulate non-Indian property on the reservation).

58. *See* D. F. Coursen, "Tribes as States: Indian Tribal Authority to Regulate and Enforce Federal Environmental Laws and Regulations," 23 *Environmental Law Reporter* 10579 (1993). *See State of Montana v. U.S. Environmental Protection Agency,* note 30 above (Clean Water Act); *Administrator, State of Arizona v. U.S. Environmental Protection Agency,* 151 F.3d 1205 (9th Cir. 1998), *amended,* 170 F.3d 870 (9th Cir. 1999) (Clean Air Act).

59. *National Farmers Union,* note 43 above. *See also Native Village of Tyonek v. Puckett,* note 43 above.

60. *Walker v. Rushing,* 898 F.2d 672, 675 (8th Cir. 1990).

61. 31 U.S. 515 (1832).

62. *Hicks,* note 35 above, 121 S.Ct. at 2311 (internal quotation omitted).

63. *McClanahan v. Arizona Tax Commission,* 411 U.S. 164 (1973).

64. *Bryan v. Itasca County,* 426 U.S. 373 (1976).

65. *Moe v. Confederated Salish and Kootenai Tribes,* 425 U.S. 463 (1976).

66. *Oklahoma Tax Commission v. Chickasaw Nation,* 515 U.S. 450 (1995).

67. *Central Machinery Co. v. Arizona Tax Commission,* 448 U.S. 160 (1980).

68. *White Mountain Apache Tribe v. Bracker,* 448 U.S. 136 (1980).

69. *Ramah Navajo School Board, Inc. v. Bureau of Revenue,* 458 U.S. 832 (1982).

70. *Montana v. Blackfeet Tribe,* 471 U.S. 759 (1985).

71. *Mescalero Apache Tribe,* note 6 above.

72. *California v. Cabazon Band of Mission Indians,* 480 U.S. 202 (1987); *Tamiami Partners v. Miccosukee Tribe of Indians,* 63 F.3d 1030, 1033 (11th Cir. 1995); *Cabazon Band of Mission Indians v. Wilson,* 124 F.3d 1050 (9th Cir. 1994).

73. *California v. Naegle Outdoor Adv. Co.,* 698 P.2d 150 (Cal. 1985), *cert. denied,* 475 U.S. 1045 (1986).

74. *Washington Dept. of Ecology v. EPA,* 752 F.2d 1465 (9th Cir. 1985).

75. *In re Blue Lake Forest Products, Inc.,* 30 F.3d 1138 (9th Cir.), *cert. denied,* 513 U.S. 1059 (1994).

76. *Flammond v. Flammond,* 621 P.2d 471 (Mont. 1980); *Jackson County v. Swayney,* 352 S.E.2d 413 (N.C. App. 1987), *cert. denied,* 484 U.S. 826 (1987). *But see State ex rel. Dept. of Human Services v. Jojola,* 660 P.2d 590 (N.M. 1983), *cert. denied,* 464 U.S. 803 (1983).

77. *Segundo v. City of Rancho Mirage,* 813 F.2d 1387 (9th Cir. 1987).

78. *Hicks,* note 35 above.

79. *Moe,* note 65 above; *Oklahoma Tax Comm'n v. Citizen Band Potawatomi Indian Tribe,* 498 U.S. 505 (1991). *See also Fort Mojave Tribe v. County of San Bernardino,* 543 F.2d 1253 (9th Cir. 1976), *cert. denied,* 430 U.S. 983 (1977).

80. *Washington v. Confederated Tribes of the Colville Reservation,* note 10 above.

81. *Potawatomi Tribe,* note 79 above, 498 U.S. at 514; *Dept. of Taxation and Finance of New York v. Milhelm Attea & Bros., Inc.,* 512 U.S. 61 (1994).

82. 358 U.S. 217 (1959).

83. *Williams v. Lee,* 358 U.S. 217, 223 (1959).

84. *Fisher,* note 1 above. The subject of child custody is discussed at length in ch. 17. *See also McKenzie County Social Service Board v. C.G.,* 633 N.W.2d 157 (N.D. 2001) (state court may not determine paternity of an Indian child when all parties reside on the reservation).

85. *Chino v. Chino,* 561 P.2d 476 (N.M. 1977).

86. *Milbank Mut. Ins. Co. v. Eagleman,* 705 P.2d 1117 (Mont. 1985); *Wyoming ex rel. Peterson v. District Court,* 617 P.2d 1056 (Wyo. 1980); *Enriquez v. Superior Court,* 565 P.2d 522 (Ariz. App. 1977). *But see Red Wolf,* note 27 above (holding that tribal court lacked jurisdiction to resolve a dispute stemming from an accident on a railroad's right-of-way located on the reservation).

87. *Joe v. Marcum,* 621 F.2d 358 (10th Cir. 1980); *Begay v. Roberts,* 807 P.2d 1111 (Ariz. App. 1991). *Contra, Little Horn State Bank v. Stops,* 555 P.2d 211 (Mont. 1976), *cert. denied,* 431 U.S. 924 (1977).

88. *Annis v. Dewey County Bank,* 335 F. Supp. 133 (D.S.D. 1971).

89. *General Constructors, Inc. v. Chewculator, Inc.,* 21 P.3d 604 (Mont. 2001); *Tohono O'odham Nation v. Schwartz,* 837 F. Supp. 1024 (D. Ariz. 1993); *Great Western Casinos Inc. v. Morongo Band of Mission Indians,* 88 Cal. Rptr.2d 828 (Cal. App. 1999).

90. *McKay v. Kalyton* 204 U.S. 458 (1907); *Krause v. Newman,* 943 P.2d 1328 (Mont. 1997); *Matter of Guardianship of Sasse,* 363 N.W.2d 209 (S.D. 1985); *Conroy v. Conroy,* 575 F.2d 175 (8th Cir. 1978). *But see Lonewolf v. Lonewolf,* 657 P.2d 627 (N.M. 1982); *Smith Plumbing Co., Inc. v. Aetna Cas. & Surety Co.,* 720 P.2d 499 (Ariz. 1984), *cert. denied,* 479 U.S. 987 (1986).

91. *In re Marriage of Limpy,* 636 P.2d 266 (Mont. 1981).

92. *White v. Califano,* 437 F. Supp. 543 (D.S.D. 1977), *aff'd,* 581 F.2d 697 (8th Cir. 1978).

93. *White Mountain Apache Tribe v. Smith Plumbing Co.,* 856 F.2d 1301, 1304–6 (9th Cir. 1988); *Tohono O'odham Nation,* note 89 above, 837 F. Supp. at 1029; *Seneca-Cayuga Tribe of Oklahoma v. Oklahoma,* 874 F.2d 709 (10th Cir. 1989).

94. *Airvator, Inc. v. Turtle Mountain Mfg. Co.,* 329 N.W.2d 596 (N.D. 1983).

95. *Seneca-Cayuga Tribe,* note 93 above.

96. *See Schantz v. White Lightning,* 231 N.W.2d 812 (N.D. 1975); *Schantz v. White Lightning,* 502 F.2d 67 (8th Cir. 1974).

97. This principle is discussed in ch. 7, sec. D.

98. *Hicks,* note 35 above, 121 S.Ct. at 2313.

99. *See, e.g., State Securities, Inc. v. Anderson,* 506 P.2d 786 (N.M. 1973); *Little Horn State Bank,* note 87 above. *See also Puyallup Tribe, Inc. v. Dept. of Game,* 433 U.S. 165 (1977) (allowing a case to proceed in which Indian defendants had been served by state officers on the reservation in suit challenging off-reservation fishing rights).

100. *Bradley v. Deloria,* 587 N.W.2d 591 (S.D. 1998); *Wells v. Wells,* 451 N.W.2d 402 (S.D. 1990); *Dixon v. Picopa Constr. Co.,* 772 P.2d 1104 (Ariz. 1989); *Martin v. Denver Juvenile Court,* 493 P.2d 1093 (Colo. 1972).

101. *See State v. Zaman,* 984 P.2d 528 (Ariz. 1999), and cases cited therein.

102. *See* 30 *Am. Jur.2d, "Executions and Enforcement of Judgments," Sec.* 213; 6 *Am. Jur.2d,* "Attachments and Garnishments," Sec. 25.

103. *See* cases cited in note 87 above and accompanying text.

104. Cohen, note 56 above, at 359.

105. U.S. Const., art. IV, sec. 1.

106. *Tom v. Sutton,* 533 F.2d 1101 (9th Cir. 1976); *Fredericks v. Eide-Kirschmann Ford,* 462 N.W.2d 164 (N.D. 1990); *Mexican v. Circle Bear,* 370 N.W.2d 737 (S.D. 1985); *Sheppard v. Sheppard,* 655 P.2d 895 (Idaho 1985); *Wippert v. Blackfeet Tribe,* 654 P.2d 512 (Mont. 1982); *Brown v. Babbitt Ford,* 571 P.2d 689 (Ariz. App. 1977); *In re Matter of the Marriage of Red Fox,* 542 P.2d 918 (Ore. App. 1975).

107. *See Marchington,* note 24 above, 127 F.3d at 807–12. *But see Bird v. Glacier Electric Corp, Inc.,* 255 F.3d 1136 (9th Cir. 2001) (rejecting comity where tribe violated due process).

108. *See, e.g.,* S.D.C.L. Sec. 1–1–25(2)(b) (permitting South Dakota courts to recognize a tribal judgment if the courts of that tribe recognize the orders and judgments of the

South Dakota courts); Okla. Stat. tit. 12, Sec. 728(b) (similar Oklahoma law); Wis. Stat. Sec. 806.245(1)(e) (similar Wisconsin statute discussed in *Teague v. Bad River Band of Lake Superior Chippewa Indians*, 612 N.W.2d 709, 720 (Wis. 2000), and *Airvator, Inc.*, note 94 above; Wyo. Stat. Ann. Sec. 5–1–111(a)(iv) (similar Wyoming statute). *See also* S. Feldman and D. Withey, "Resolving State-Tribal Jurisdictional Dilemmas," 70 *Judicature* 154, 155 (1995).

109. *Smith v. Confederated Tribes of the Warm Springs Reservation*, 783 F.2d 1409, 1411 (9th Cir.), *cert. denied*, 479 U.S. 964 (1986); *Santa Clara Pueblo*, note 1 above, 436 U.S. at 66 n.21; *Sanders*, note 11 above.

110. *Marchington*, note 24 above, 127 F.3d at 810.

111. *Northwest South Dakota Prod. Credit Ass'n v. Smith*, 784 F.2d 323, 326–27 (8th Cir. 1986); *U.S. v. Winnebago Tribe of Nebraska*, 542 F.2d 1002 (8th Cir. 1976); *U.S. v. Morris*, 754 F. Supp. 185 (D.N.M. 1991); *Administrative Appeal of the Morongo Band of Mission Indians*, IBIA 79–18-A (1980), *reprinted in* 7 Indian L. Rep. 5002

112. *See, e.g., U.S. v. Wheeler*, 435 U.S. 313 (1978); 55 Interior Dec. 14 (1934) ("Powers of Indian Tribes"); *Reich v. Mashantucket Sand and Gravel*, 95 F.3d 174 (2d Cir. 1996) (holding that federal laws regarding occupational safety apply to tribal corporations).

Taxation

Operating a government and providing services to the public cost money. Taxation is a principal means—and for many governments, the primary means—of raising this money.

As a general rule, a government can tax all persons and property within its borders. People on Indian reservations may therefore find themselves being taxed by three governments: federal, state, and tribal. Below is an explanation of which taxes they are obligated to pay.

This chapter uses some terms that need to be defined at the outset. These include *trust land, allotted and unallotted trust land,* and *fee land.*

Trust land is land owned by the federal government that has been set aside for the exclusive use of an Indian or tribe. The Indian or tribe assigned this land is called the "beneficial owner."

Allotted trust land is trust land that the federal government has assigned to an Indian, and the assigned parcel is called an "allotment." *Unallotted trust land* is trust land that has been assigned by the government to a tribe. Indian trust land, in other words, is either allotted or unallotted, depending on whether the beneficial owner is an Indian or a tribe.

Fee land is land that is privately owned. It is also called deeded or fee-patented land because someone holds a deed (fee-patent) to it. Indians and tribes can obtain fee land by purchasing it, inheriting it, or receiving it as a gift, just as everyone else can.

Most of these terms originated with the General Allotment Act of 1887 (GAA), also known as the Dawes Act.[1] Under the GAA, unallotted tribal trust land was divided into allotments by the federal government and then assigned (allotted) to tribal members. (Why Congress did this, and the harm it caused to Indian tribes, is discussed elsewhere in this book.)[2] In 1934, Congress ended both practices required by the GAA: the practice of removing land from the tribe and allotting it to tribal members and the practice of forcing Indians to accept deeds to their allotments.[3] However, by the time the GAA was repealed in 1934, millions of acres of land had been removed from tribes and allotted to tribal members, and deeds to many of these allotments had been forced upon the Indian allottees. These events had enormous tax consequences for all three governments: federal, state, and tribal, as discussed in this chapter.

A. FEDERAL TAXATION

Do reservation Indians pay federal taxes?

Yes. In *Squire v. Capoeman* (1956),[4] the Supreme Court held that Indians are obligated to pay the same federal income taxes applicable to everyone else unless Congress has conferred an express immunity through a treaty or statute. The Court said: "We agree with the Government that Indians are citizens and that in ordinary affairs of life, not governed by treaty or remedial legislation, they are subject to the payment of income taxes as are other citizens."[5]

The principle that Indians must pay the same federal taxes other citizens pay unless a federal statute or treaty provides an express exemption is contrary to the principle that governs most other areas of federal Indian law. Generally, a federal law does not apply to reservation Indians unless Congress expressly makes it applicable.[6] A federal tax law, in contrast, applies to reservation Indians unless Congress expressly makes it inapplicable. Even treaties that guarantee to tribal members "peaceful possession" and "free use and enjoyment" of their lands are insufficient to confer an immunity from federal taxation; the exemption must be express.[7] As the Supreme Court recently stated, Indians are not entitled to exemptions from federal taxes "unless those exemptions are clearly expressed."[8]

The tax code of the United States subjects "every individual" to taxation on all income from "whatever source obtained,"[9] unless an express immunity has been conferred by Congress. As a result, reservation Indians must pay federal income taxes on the money they earn from employment[10] (even if they are tribal officials and their salary is paid from tribal funds)[11] and on any money distributed to them from tribal sources, such as proceeds from the rental of tribal lands[12] or from the sale of tribal minerals.[13] They also are subject to all other types of federal taxes, such as the federal excise tax on diesel fuel,[14] unless an express immunity applies. A number of tribes have profitable casinos and distribute to tribal members a share of the proceeds; leaving nothing to chance, Congress passed a law expressly subjecting that money to federal income taxation.[15]

What about the provision in the U.S. Constitution that refers to "Indians not taxed"? Doesn't that provide a general exemption from federal taxation?

No. The clause "Indians not taxed" appears in the section of the Constitution that describes the number of representatives a state is entitled to seat in the U.S. House of Representatives.[16] The Constitution requires each state to exclude "Indians not taxed" in counting its population for purposes of congressional apportionment. At the time the Constitution was written, Indians were not U.S. citizens, and they were not taxed. Today, Indians are citizens, they are taxed, and they are counted for apportionment purposes. The clause "Indians not taxed" no longer has any practical relevance. In any event, it does not provide an exemption from federal taxation because that was not its intent.[17]

Has Congress given Indians any express exemptions from federal taxes?

Congress has given Indians a few exemptions. For instance, Congress has expressly exempted from federal taxation the "judgment funds" (sometimes also called "judgment proceeds") paid to Indians for the loss of their property.[18]

The Just Compensation Clause of the Fifth Amendment requires that the federal government pay adequate compensation whenever it takes private property from someone. The Supreme Court has held that land reserved to an Indian tribe by a treaty or statute is private property protected by the Just Compensation Clause.[19] In those instances in which Congress has paid compensation to a tribe for taking its land and the tribe then distributed the proceeds to tribal members, those members need not report that money as taxable income.

In 1988, Congress passed a law conferring a tax immunity on income earned by a tribal member exercising a federally guaranteed right to fish. As a result, income earned by Indians exercising federal fishing rights is tax exempt.[20]

Indians have also been given an express tax immunity on the value of trust land and trust money they inherit.[21] Even if an Indian inherits trust land that contains valuable minerals, he or she pays no tax on that inheritance.

Additionally, Congress has exempted from federal taxation all income earned directly from an Indian's *trust allotment*. The General Allotment Act of 1887[22] confers that immunity, the Supreme Court held in *Squire*.[23]

As already noted, the Court held in *Squire* that Indians must pay federal income taxes unless they have an express exemption. After stating that general rule, the Court then held in *Squire* that the GAA conferred an express immunity. The issue in that case was whether an Indian who sold timber from trust land allotted to him under the GAA was obligated to pay federal taxes on the income. In ruling in favor of the Indian, the Court relied on both the overall purpose of the GAA and some express language contained within it. The overall purpose of the GAA was to enable Indians to become economically self-sufficient by using the allotments of trust land that the federal government had allocated to them. This purpose would be frustrated, the Court said, if the federal government could tax the income earned from the allotment. Moreover, the GAA expressly provides that if the Indian allottee receives a deed to the allotment, this removes "all restrictions as to . . . taxation."[24] This clause, the Court said, indicates that Congress did not want the land or income earned from selling the land's timber and other natural resources to be taxed while it remained in trust status.[25]

Under the *Squire* rule, Indians who farm or ranch on their trust allotments;[26] sell timber, oil, or minerals from them;[27] or lease their lands to others for those purposes[28] do not pay federal taxes on the income they earn. They also are exempt from taxation on income earned from an allotment they received as a gift or by exchanging other land for it.[29]

Does *Squire* exempt from federal taxation all income earned from the use of trust land?

Squire can be interpreted broadly or narrowly. Broadly, it exempts Indians from paying taxes on all income earned from the use of allotted trust land. The Internal Revenue Service (IRS) has given *Squire* a narrow interpretation,[30] however, and federal courts have generally upheld that narrow construction. First, courts have held that *Squire* only exempts income earned from trust allotments belonging to the taxpayer. Income earned from the use of someone else's allotment or from the tribe's unallotted trust land is subject to federal taxation because, the courts have held, the purpose of the GAA was to provide Indians with an allotment from which they could earn a living and not to make other land available for that purpose.[31] Thus, an Indian who raises cattle on his or her own trust allotment and on land leased from the tribe must pay taxes on the portion of the operation occurring on tribal land.

Second, the *Squire* exemption does not apply to income earned from investing allotment proceeds, that is, to "reinvestment" income.[32] To illustrate, if the taxpayer in *Squire* took the income he earned from selling his timber and deposited it into a bank account, the interest he earned on the account would be taxable as reinvestment income.

Third, courts have held that *Squire* only exempts income earned *directly* from the taxpayer's allotment and not indirectly as a result of improvements made to the land. Allottees, as previously explained, may farm, log, or mine their allotments tax free, but if they build a store[33] or motel[34] on that allotment, the income earned is taxable. The Supreme Court has not yet addressed this issue, but lower federal courts have drawn a distinction between income earned when the value of the allotment is diminished through the sale of its resources on the one hand and income earned from improvements made to the property on the other hand and have allowed the government to tax income made from improvements.[35] These court decisions, though, would seem to strip *Squire* of much of its meaning and undermine the purpose of the GAA, which was to encourage Indians to use their property in order to become economically self-sufficient.

To summarize, Indians normally pay the same federal taxes everyone else pays. Due to express immunities, Indians are not taxed on their judgment proceeds, on income earned directly from their own trust allotments, on the value of trust land they inherit, or on income earned from exercising federal fishing rights.

To what extent are Indian tribes taxed by the federal government?

Congress has passed laws that provide to the states and to their political subdivisions an immunity from most federal taxes.[36] Although Indian tribes are not mentioned in these laws, it was assumed until 1982 that they enjoyed the same immunity, and the IRS had ruled that tribes were exempt from federal income taxes.[37]

In 1982, a federal appellate court ruled that Indian tribes were not exempt from federal taxation, because no such immunity had been expressly conferred by Congress.[38] In response to this decision, Congress enacted the Indian Tribal Governmental Tax Status Act of 1982.[39] This law expressly exempts tribes from having to pay certain federal taxes, such as most fuel taxes and manufacturer excise taxes, provided that the services or products for which the tax exemption is claimed will be used for an essential government function.[40] Several taxes that state governments are exempt from paying are not listed in the 1982 act. These include unemployment taxes (FUTA)[41] and insurance contribution taxes (social security, or FICA),[42] and the IRS takes the position that Indian tribes, unlike state governments, must withhold these taxes from payments made to their employees, just as private employers must do.[43] In most other situations, the IRS views Indian tribes as nontaxable entities and has allowed them to claim the same immunities from federal taxation that state governments have been given through federal statutes, even though no federal law expressly confers those immunities.[44] As a result, Indian tribes may operate their own businesses (incorporated under tribal law or under a federal charter) exempt from federal income taxation, even if the income is earned off the reservation, although tribal businesses are not exempt from federal taxes if incorporated under *state* law.[45] (As explained later in this chapter, there are some advantages to being incorporated under state law, but along with those advantages comes a tax liability.)

May Congress abolish an Indian tax exemption?

Yes. Congress may abolish a tax immunity previously given to Indians, even one conferred by a treaty,[46] but the extinguishment of a tax immunity is a "taking" of property under the Just Compensation Clause for which compensation must be paid.[47] Given its importance, the Supreme Court has held that a tax immunity will remain in effect until Congress expresses a clear intention to abolish it.[48]

B. STATE TAXATION

State governments have an obvious interest in seeking to tax tribes, Indians, and non-Indians in Indian country, as a means of raising revenue. For the reasons that follow, Indians and tribes have an immunity from almost all state taxes while on the reservation, whereas reservation non-Indians normally must pay state taxes.

As explained in chapter 7, unless Congress has given its express consent, a state may not regulate any activity in Indian country where doing so would violate a federal law or treaty (the *preemption* test) or infringe on the right of the tribe to be self-governing (the *infringement* test). As a result of this principle, Indians and tribes remain free of most state taxes in Indian country.

The Supreme Court has decided nearly a dozen cases involving state taxation without congressional consent of reservation Indians or tribes.[49] In every situation but one, the Court invalidated the tax. (The one exception, discussed later, allows states to tax the sale of goods by an Indian or tribe to *nonmembers*.) The Court has repeatedly held that "Indian tribes and individuals generally are exempt from state taxation within their own territory"[50] in the absence of "unmistakably clear" congressional consent to the imposition of the tax.[51]

States have urged the Supreme Court to use a "balancing" test in reviewing the legality of state taxation of Indians and tribes, in which the state's interests in imposing the tax and raising revenue are balanced against the Indian's or tribe's interests in avoiding the tax. The Court has declined to do so, explaining that "when a State attempts to levy a tax directly on an Indian tribe or its members inside Indian country, rather than on non-Indians, we have employed, instead of a balancing inquiry, a more categorical approach," which holds that the tax is preempted unless Congress has given its express consent.[52]

1. State Taxation of Individual Indians in Indian Country

Do reservation Indians have to pay state income taxes?

No. The Supreme Court ruled in 1973 that Indians who live and work on the reservation may not be assessed state income taxes.[53]

Do reservation Indians have to pay state personal property taxes?

No. The Supreme Court ruled in 1976 that personal property on the reservation owned by a tribal member is exempt from state taxation.[54] This exemption applies even if the state has acquired jurisdiction under Public Law 83–280 (P.L. 280)[55] because, as explained in chapter 7, this law did not consent to state taxation in Indian country.

Consequently, states may not require Indians to pay personal property taxes on such things as automobiles, mobile homes, furnishings, or equipment located within the reservation. Reservation Indians who register their automobiles or mobile homes with the state can only be charged a registration fee and need not pay any portion of the license fee that is actually a personal property tax.[56] Also, if an Indian marries a non-Indian, the personal property they own on the reservation is not taxable by the state even though part of it may be said to belong to the non-Indian spouse.[57]

Do reservation Indians have to pay state sales taxes on purchases made within the reservation?

No. Indians who purchase goods or services on their reservation cannot be charged a state sales tax. This is true regardless of whether the seller is an Indian,[58] a non-Indian,[59] or the tribe,[60] and even if the item is to be used off the reservation.[61]

May a state tax the value of Indian or tribal trust land?

No. Trust land is owned by the federal government, and federal land cannot be taxed by the state without congressional consent. Congress has not consented to state taxation of trust land. Therefore, trust land is immune from state taxation, whether the beneficial owner is an Indian or a tribe,[62] and even if the land is located off the reservation.[63]

Permanent attachments to land, such as a house, a fence, or a well, are considered to be part of the land. Therefore, these improvements cannot be taxed when they are attached to trust land.[64]

May a state impose an inheritance tax on the estate of a reservation Indian?

In the absence of express consent, courts have prohibited states from taxing the estates of reservation Indians, regardless of whether the property being inherited is in trust status or in fee.[65]

Which other state taxes have been invalidated as applied to reservation Indians?

In addition to the taxes already mentioned, a state may not impose a vendor's license fee on a reservation Indian business,[66] a tax on cigarettes sold to reservation Indians,[67] or a tax on motor fuel purchased on the reservation by an Indian,[68] unless Congress has consented. Such consent cannot be inferred, and if a federal statute is unclear as to whether consent has been given, the ambiguity must be resolved in favor of the Indians.[69]

To illustrate, a law passed by Congress in 1940 authorizes states to impose income, sales, and use taxes in any "Federal area,"[70] which arguably could include Indian reservations. In 1965, the Supreme Court held that this statute failed to provide clear consent, and the Court prohibited a state from relying on it as a basis to tax reservation Indians.[71] Another federal law authorizes states to tax the sale of gasoline sold "on United States military or other reservations."[72] The Supreme Court has held that this law fails to provide the express consent necessary to confer state taxing authority in Indian country.[73] Similarly, a law passed in 1938 authorizes states to tax the production of oil and gas on federal lands.[74] The Supreme Court held that this law, too, failed to give express consent to state taxation of oil and gas production by Indian tribes on the reservation.[75]

Which taxes has Congress authorized the states to impose?

Congress has passed only a couple of laws expressly consenting to state taxation of reservation Indians and tribes. For instance, Congress has authorized states to tax on-reservation sales of liquor to Indians.[76] Congress has also authorized the states, as part of the authority they obtained under the General Allotment Act of 1887 (GAA),[77] to tax the value of land that Indians and tribes own privately ("nontrust" or "fee" land).[78]

States initially argued that P.L. 280, passed by Congress in 1953, gave broad consent to state taxation in Indian country. As mentioned earlier, the Supreme Court held that no portion of P.L. 280 consents to the taxation of Indians or tribes.[79]

May a state refuse to provide services to reservation Indians on the grounds that they are exempt from state taxation?

No. Reservation Indians may not be denied the full rights and benefits of state citizenship even though they are exempt from most state taxes.[80] For example, a state may not condition the right to vote in state elections on the payment of property taxes, thereby discriminating against Indians who pay no taxes on their trust allotments.[81]

Indians acquired their tax immunities as part of the compensation they received for the vast amounts of land that tribes relinquished to the federal government. Indians, in other words, paid in advance for the tax immunities they now enjoy.

Non-Indians often claim that a state suffers financially from having an Indian reservation within its borders due to these tax immunities and that tribes receive more money from states and local communities than they contribute to them. Those claims are not supported by the facts. A study conducted in 1993 by the Arizona Commission of Indian Affairs found that for every $1 that Arizona spent on a tribe, it received back nearly $42 by taxing the businesses operating on the reservation, by taxing the sale of goods that Indians and tribes bought off the reservation and by taxing the income of the non-Indian businesses and persons who sold them those goods.[82] A report issued in 1999 by Gov. Gary Locke of Washington found that Washington's Indian tribes contributed more than $1 billion to the state's economy, far exceeding the cost of providing programs and services to them.[83]

Many Indian tribes anchor the economies of surrounding communities through their successful business ventures. A 1999 study found that the Nez Perce Tribe in Idaho contributed more than $46 million a year to the local economy, and its economic development was responsible for creating almost three thousand jobs in the region.[84] The Mashantucket Pequot Tribe of Connecticut, which operates a huge casino that draws forty-one thousand people a day, shares 25 percent of its earnings from slot machines with the state, an amount that exceeded $1 billion in the years 1993–2000. Also, the thousands of jobs and enormous business generated locally by this casino and the one operated a few miles away by the Mohegan Tribe have helped save the economy of southeastern Connecticut from financial ruin caused by deteriorating manufacturing and defense industries.[85] The Oneida Tribe in New York, which operates a successful casino, is the largest employer in a two-county area. Of the thirty-two hundred jobs created by the tribe, 85 percent are held by non-Indians, and the tribe's payroll exceeds $64 million.[86] Even in those states in which Indian reservations are poor, tribal members eventually spend off the reservation the money they earn from reservation employment or receive from federal and state programs. This spending stimulates the state and local economy and raises revenue for the state through its sales, business, and income taxes. Thus, few states (if any) suffer financially, and most prosper considerably, by the presence of Indian reservations within their borders.

Are nonmember Indians entitled to the same tax immunities that tribal members enjoy?

Indians located on a reservation other than their own (nonmember Indians) are not entitled to the tax immunities enjoyed by tribal members. This rule was announced by the Supreme Court in a 1980 case, which held that although tribal members are exempt from paying state sales taxes on goods purchased on the reservation, nonmember Indians "stand on the same footing as non-Indians" and must pay those taxes.[87]

2. State Taxation of Indian Tribes in Indian Country

As noted above, the Supreme Court has developed a "categorical" test to determine the validity of a state tax on Indian tribes and their members in Indian country: if Congress has expressly authorized the tax, it is valid, and without that consent, it is not. Thus, a state may not tax income earned by a tribe on the reservation,[88] including income received from the lease of tribal land to non-Indians for oil and gas production[89] or other mineral development,[90] because Congress has not given its consent.

Every tax that a state has attempted to impose on an Indian tribe regarding a reservation activity has been invalidated by the courts unless Congress had consented to the tax, with one exception. Courts have allowed states to assess a certain type of *pass-through* tax. A pass-through tax is one that is paid by the buyer but is collected by the seller, who then sends it to the government. A sales tax is a pass-through tax. The Supreme Court held in 1976 that a tribe, when it sells cigarettes to *non-Indians,* may be required to collect the state's cigarette and sales taxes and pass them along to the state, even though Congress had not given its consent to this extension of state jurisdiction in Indian country.[91] In 1980, the Court held that a state also may require the tribe to keep detailed records of its sales to non-Indians so that state tax officials can determine whether the tribe is paying the correct amount of taxes.[92] The Court admitted these collection and record-keeping requirements imposed a burden on the tribe, but such "minimal" burdens are permitted when the state has a right to assess the tax in the first place, which the Court held was the case here.[93] The Court also admitted that allowing the state to tax these sales could have a harmful effect on tribal income. After all, if a tribal business does not have to charge the state's sales tax, its prices will be lower than off-reservation businesses, attracting customers to the reservation. The Court held that Indians are not entitled to such an "artificial" advantage when they sell products imported from outside the reservation to non-Indians.[94]

In 1995, in *Oklahoma Tax Commission v. Chickasaw Nation,*[95] the Supreme Court held that a state may create a pass-through tax simply by choosing the right language in the tax statute. The issue in *Chickasaw Nation* was whether an Oklahoma Indian tribe that operated a gasoline service station on its reservation had to pay Oklahoma's motor fuels tax when it purchased motor fuels for resale. The Court closely examined the Oklahoma law in question and found that by the way it was worded, the tax was imposed on the retailer (which in this instance was the tribe) rather than on the person who purchased the fuel at the pump. The Court therefore applied the "categorical" test and invalidated the tax because Congress had not consented to it. Had the Oklahoma law declared that the tax must be paid by the customer at the pump, the Court said, a valid "pass-through" tax would have been created regarding tribal sales to non-Indian customers.[96] Citing *Chickasaw Nation,* a federal appellate court recently allowed a state to tax the motor fuels sold by a non-Indian wholesale distributor to an Indian tribe. The court acknowledged that the wholesaler would "simply pass on the cost of the tax to the Tribe in the wholesale price" (and thus the tribe would ultimately pay the tax), but the court held that the tax was valid because it was being assessed against the wholesaler, a non-Indian entity subject to state taxation.[97]

Not all pass-through taxes are valid, however. The preemption test prohibits states from significantly interfering with federal programs and laws regulating Indians and tribes. In one case, a state pass-through tax on motor fuels, similar to the kind the Court in *Chickasaw Nation* indicated would be acceptable, was invalidated because the court found that it would interfere with the operation of a federal Indian program.[98] In another case, a state tax on off-track betting—a tax normally paid by the customer when the bet is made (and, thus, a pass-through tax because the bettor, not the facility, is actually paying the tax)—could not be imposed on a tribal wagering facility because the tax significantly interfered with federal policies set forth in the Indian Gaming Regulatory Act of 1988.[99] (The Gaming Act is discussed in chapter 16.)

In determining whether a state tax on Indian tribes fails the preemption test, several factors must be considered (as discussed in chapter 7). One factor is whether the tribe has added anything of value to the goods the state is trying to tax. In the cigarette ("smoke shop") cases mentioned earlier, one reason why the Supreme Court required tribes to collect state taxes on their sales of cigarettes to non-Indians is that the tribe had added nothing of value to the cigarettes but had simply purchased them off the reservation for resale. In contrast, when tribes have added value to the product, the state's pass-through sales taxes have been invalidated by the courts. States have been prevented from taxing the sale of tribal timber to non-Indians[100] and the value of leases of tribal land for mineral production[101] because the state was providing no services in exchange for the money it was seeking to collect from the tribe, and the entire value of the product being taxed was generated by the tribe on the reservation. Given these cases, if tribes wish to sell cigarettes tax free to non-Indians, they can grow the tobacco on the reservation or purchase the tobacco in bulk and manufacture the cigarettes on the reservation, and by adding something of value to the product, it would likely be exempt from state taxation.[102]

May Indian tribes and tribal members immediately file suit in federal court to challenge the validity of a state tax?

Tribes may, but their members may not. A federal law known as the Tax Injunction Act[103] prohibits all persons from challenging a state tax in federal court "where a plain, speedy and efficient remedy may be had in the courts of such state." Every state allows for tax challenges to be filed in state court, and individual Indians must exhaust their state remedies before seeking review in a federal court.

Indian tribes are exempt from this exhaustion requirement. A federal statute[104] allows tribes to file suit in federal court to challenge the constitutionality of a state tax law without first exhausting state remedies.[105]

If tribes fail to pay state taxes lawfully owed, what can the state do about it?

As just discussed, a state may tax Indian tribes in certain circumstances. But what if the tribe refuses to pay: what can the state do about it? That was the question presented to the Supreme Court in *Oklahoma Tax Commission v. Citizen Band Potawatomi Indian Tribe of Oklahoma* (1991).[106] In that case, Oklahoma sued the Potawatomi Tribe seeking to collect $2.7 million in taxes the tribe allegedly owed from sales of cigarettes to non-Indians during a six-year period. (This large figure indicates that the tribe was selling cigarettes by the truckload to people seeking to avoid paying state taxes.) The Court dismissed the lawsuit on the grounds of tribal sovereign immunity, which (as explained in chapter 18) protects Indian tribes from being sued unless Congress or the tribe has consented to the suit. In doing so, however, the Court warned Indian tribes that unless they pay state taxes they legally owe, (1) the Court might allow states to collect these taxes directly out of the pockets of tribal officials;

(2) the Court would allow states to seize cigarettes being shipped to the reservation and confiscate them until the taxes were paid; or (3) Congress might be pressured by states into passing a law consenting to these types of suits against Indian tribes.[107]

In a 1994 case, the Supreme Court made good on one of these threats and upheld the right of New York to confiscate cigarettes shipped from an off-reservation wholesaler to tribal vendors who were refusing to pay the state's cigarette taxes.[108] Also, federal prosecutors have begun arresting Indians under federal laws that make it a crime to traffic in contraband cigarettes, when these Indians have attempted to sell to non-Indians un-stamped cigarettes (that is, cigarettes that do not carry the state's tax stamp).[109]

In recent years, bills have been introduced in Congress that would require the federal government to withhold federal funds from those tribes that refuse to pay state taxes they lawfully owed. While these bills were defeated, similar efforts can be expected in the future if tribes refuse to pay taxes that the courts have permitted states to assess. A number of tribes have entered into agreements with states regarding their tax liabili-ties. In the state of Washington, for instance, an agreement was reached in 2001 between state officials and officials from fourteen Washington tribes, under which the tribes will collect the state's cigarette tax on sales of cigarettes to non-Indians but, as a result of a sharing formula, will be able to sell the cigarettes at a slightly lower price and to use the resulting revenue to provide tribal services and improve governmental infrastruc-ture.[110]

3. State Taxation of Off-Reservation Indians

In *Mescalero Apache Tribe v. Jones* (1973),[111] the Supreme Court held that a state could tax the income earned by a tribally owned ski resort located on federal land outside of Indian country. Indians and tribes going beyond reservation boundaries, the Court said, are subject to the same state laws otherwise applicable to everyone else unless they have an express immu-nity under federal law.

Applying that principle, the Supreme Court held in 1995 that Indians who live outside of Indian country are obligated to pay state income taxes—even if they work on the reservation for the tribe.[112] Likewise, In-dians who leave the reservation even briefly must pay state sales taxes on any goods they purchase off the reservation,[113] and they can be assessed state taxes on any real estate and personal property located outside the reservation.[114]

4. State Taxation of Indian and Tribal Corporations

Under what circumstances can an Indian or tribal corporation be taxed by the state?

Indian tribes can create corporations under tribal law, under state law, and for those tribes organized under the Indian Reorganization Act, as explained in chapter 5, under a federal charter. Each alternative has advantages and disadvantages. Corporations organized under tribal or federal law are exempt from state taxation.[115] But some tribes have chosen to incorporate a business under state law in order to gain the protection from personal liability for their managers that such laws often provide. Although the Supreme Court suggested in a 1973 case that immunity from state taxation should not "turn on the particular form in which the Tribe chooses to conduct its business,"[116] the prevailing view is that an Indian or tribal business incorporated under state law is subject to state taxation.[117] The IRS has issued a formal rule to that effect.[118]

5. State Taxation of Reservation Non-Indians

Do non-Indians on the reservation have to pay state taxes?

Non-Indians must pay most state taxes. As explained earlier, a state may not extend its jurisdiction into Indian country if doing so would violate a federal law or treaty (the preemption test) or infringe on the right of the tribe to make its own laws and be ruled by them (the infringement test). Most state taxes imposed solely on reservation non-Indians will pass both tests. Of course, the enforcement of any state law on the reservation infringes to some extent on tribal self-government, but the Supreme Court has held that certain "minimal" infringements are permitted.[119] Taxes that apply exclusively to non-Indians—including income, personal property, real estate, gasoline, and cigarette taxes—have been upheld by the courts under that principle.[120]

Just because the taxpayer is non-Indian does not mean that the tax is valid. This is especially true regarding pass-through taxes, which as explained earlier, are taxes that the seller collects and sends to the state but are really paid by the buyer of the goods. If an Indian tribe were to purchase farm equipment on the reservation from a non-Indian dealer, the state could not require the dealer to collect the state's sales tax. In that situation, although it would be the dealer remitting the tax to the state, the tax would actually be paid by the tribe, and tribes are immune from such taxation.[121]

A state's attempt to tax a reservation non-Indian therefore requires a "particularized examination," the Supreme Court has held, in which a number of factors must be considered. These factors (and court cases employing them) are discussed in chapter 7. Among the factors to consider are whether the activity being taxed by the state is already regulated by the federal government, whether the state is providing any services in return for the money it seeks to collect, and whether the burden of the tax would fall on the tribe or on a non-Indian. In one case, for example, the Supreme Court held that a state could not tax the profits made by a non-Indian construction company that built a school on the reservation for the tribe;[122] in another case, the Court invalidated a state motor carrier registration tax and a fuel tax imposed on a non-Indian company that hauled on tribal roads the timber it had cut from tribal lands;[123] and in a third case, the Court invalidated a state gross proceeds tax imposed on a reservation store owned by a non-Indian because the vast majority of the store's customers were Navajo Indians.[124] In each case, the state provided no services in return for the taxes it sought to collect, and the burden of paying those taxes would ultimately fall on the tribes or their members. Similarly, in 1991 the New Mexico Supreme Court declared invalid a state tax imposed on the income earned by a non-Indian company when it provided consulting services to an Indian tribe, given that the state contributed no services in return for the money it was trying to collect, and the tribe would ultimately pay the tax because the company would raise its prices— as every company normally does—by the same amount of state taxes it had to pay.[125]

A slight shift in one or more of these factors can lead to a different result, as evidenced by *Cotton Petroleum Corp. v. New Mexico*, a case decided by the Supreme Court in 1989.[126] In *Cotton Petroleum*, discussed further in chapter 7, the Court held that New Mexico could tax a non-Indian company on the value of oil and gas it produced from tribal lands despite the fact that New Mexico would net millions of dollars more in taxes than it would spend on services to the producer and to the tribe. The

Court upheld the tax on the grounds that the state was providing some amount of services to the company, and the company and tribal members received an "intangible benefit" from the state, the Court said, when they left the reservation and used state services off the reservation.[127]

Consistent with *Cotton Petroleum,* courts have permitted states to tax a railroad on the value of its right-of-way across tribal land;[128] to tax a non-Indian rancher on the value of livestock grazing on tribal land;[129] to tax tribal sales of cigarettes to non-Indians;[130] to tax a non-Indian's lease-hold interest in tribal lands;[131] to tax a non-Indian who leased a hotel owned by an Indian tribe on the money he made from renting rooms and selling food to non-Indian guests;[132] to tax ticket sales to non-Indians for events held on the reservation in a facility leased by a non-Indian from the tribe;[133] and to tax the sale of goods by a non-Indian storeowner to non-Indian customers at a shopping center located on land leased from an Indian tribe.[134] In each case, the court acknowledged that the tribe might suffer some financial loss if these non-Indian lessors or customers decided against using tribal services but that the state was providing some services of its own in return for the tax money it was collecting, and most if not all of the tax burden fell on the non-Indian customer, not the tribe.

C. Tribal Taxation

A few Indian tribes own lucrative businesses from which they raise all the revenue they need, but for most tribes, exercising the power to tax is a critical necessity. Indian tribes possess the inherent right to tax, as the Supreme Court stated in *Merrion v. Jicarilla Apache Tribe* (1982):[135]

The power to tax is an essential attribute of Indian sovereignty because it is a necessary instrument of self-government and territorial management. This power enables a tribal government to raise revenues for its essential services. . . . [I]t derives from the tribe's general authority, as sovereign, to control economic activity within its jurisdiction, and to defray the cost of providing governmental services by requiring contributions from persons or enterprises engaged in economic activities within that jurisdiction.[136]

May an Indian tribe tax its members on the reservation?

Yes. An Indian tribe's power to tax is an essential attribute of its sovereignty. A tribe surely may exercise that power over its own members on the reservation.

May an Indian tribe tax nonmembers on the reservation?

Cases involving tribal taxation of reservation nonmembers fall into two broad categories: taxation of activities occurring on *Indian* land and taxation of activities occurring on *non-Indian* land. Until recently, all of the "taxation of nonmember" cases involved activities on Indian land, and the tribes always won. For instance, the Supreme Court held in 1904 that Indian tribes could assess a personal property tax on the value of cattle owned by a non-Indian and grazing on Indian land,[137] and in 1980 the Court held that non-Indians may be required to pay a tribal sales tax when they buy goods from Indian vendors on the reservation.[138] In 1982, the Court was asked to decide in *Merrion* whether an Indian tribe could tax the value of oil and gas extracted by a non-Indian company from wells located on tribal land. The oil company challenged the tax on the grounds that the company and the tribe had entered into a contract in which the tribe received royalties on the oil and gas produced; the company contended that the tribe had waived its right to tax by agreeing to receive the royalties. The Supreme Court disagreed, holding that Indian tribes retain the inherent right to tax the production of minerals from tribal lands unless that right has been expressly waived, and the Court found no such waiver in the tribe's contract with the oil company.[139]

The tax at issue in *Merrion* had been approved by the Secretary of the Interior, but as the Supreme Court held three years later in *Kerr-McGee Corp. v. Navajo Tribe* (1985),[140] a tribe need not obtain the federal government's consent before it taxes non-Indians on Indian land. In *Kerr-McGee*, the Court held that an Indian tribe had the inherent right to tax non-Indians on the value of their leasehold interests in tribal trust land and therefore did not need secretarial approval to impose the tax.[141]

Tribal taxation of non-Indians on *non-Indian* land within the reservation raises a more complex set of issues. (As explained earlier in this chapter, millions of acres of reservation land is now owned by non-Indians as a result of the GAA, and thus the issue of whether Indian tribes may tax activities occurring on this land has enormous implications.) The Supreme Court held in *Montana v. United States* (1981)[142] that Indian tribes may not regulate hunting and fishing by non-Indians on non-Indian land within the reservation except in two limited circumstances: when the tribe can prove that (1) the non-Indian owner has entered into a "consensual relationship" with the tribe or a tribal member, such as a business contract or lease, or (2) when the conduct of the non-Indian "threatens or has some direct effect on the political integrity, the economic security, or the health or welfare of the tribe."[143] As discussed in chapter 9, the Supreme Court has since applied the *Montana* rule in other situations in which tribes have attempted to regulate the conduct of non-Indians on non-Indian land. In each instance, the tribe failed to prove that either of the two "*Montana* exceptions" existed, and was therefore prevented from regulating the non-Indian's conduct.[144]

In 2001, the Supreme Court applied the *Montana* rule in a tax case, *Atkinson Trading Co., Inc. v. Shirley*.[145] In *Atkinson* (discussed in more detail in chapter 9), the Court held that an Indian tribe could not require a non-Indian hotel owner, whose hotel was located on non-Indian land within the reservation, to collect from the hotel's guests a tribal occupancy tax. The Court held that due to their "incorporation" into the United States and their resulting "dependent" status, Indian tribes have lost many of their powers.[146] In particular, tribal authority over non-Indians on non-Indian land is "sharply circumscribed."[147] The Court confined its 1982 decision in *Merrion*—and the broad language in that case regarding a tribe's right to territorial management—"to transactions occurring on *trust lands* and significantly involving a tribe or its members."[148] Tribal authority on non-Indian land, on the other hand, is governed by the general rule set forth in *Montana,* which is "that Indian tribes lack civil authority over nonmembers on non-Indian fee land."[149] Although an Indian tribe, the Court said, may charge a non-Indian landowner "an appropriate fee" for any municipal service it actually provides (such as fire or police protection), the amount of the assessment must be tailored to the exact service rendered, and the tribe may not impose an overall tax.[150]

As a result of *Atkinson,* which is the first case decided by the Supreme Court involving tribal taxation of non-Indians on non-Indian land, a tribe may impose such a tax only if it can prove the existence of one of the two "*Montana* exceptions." For instance, non-Indians who enter into consensual business relationships with the tribe may be taxed on their reservation business activities[151] and may be required to purchase a tribal license.[152] Unless the tribal tax can be justified under the *Montana* exceptions, however, it cannot validly be imposed.

Does tribal taxation of non-Indians constitute taxation without representation?

Non-Indians taxed by Indian tribes sometimes have argued that this constitutes "taxation without representation" because they cannot vote in tribal elections. It is a common misconception, however, that a tax is illegal unless the taxpayer can vote in that jurisdiction. The federal and state governments tax people, including aliens, who cannot vote in federal and state elections. Residents of one state who purchase goods in another state pay that state's sales taxes yet cannot vote in its elections. Likewise, the fact that non-Indians cannot become members of a tribe or vote in tribal elections does not deprive the tribe of the right to tax them.[153] Non-Indians have the right to challenge the legality of any tribal tax imposed on them,[154] although courts have held that such challenges normally must first be brought in tribal court before a federal court may consider whether the tax violates federal law.[155]

NOTES

1. 25 U.S.C. Secs. 331–58.

2. *See* ch. 1, sec. D; ch. 5, sec. B; and ch. 7, sec. B.

3. The General Allotment Act was repealed by the Indian Reorganization Act, 25 U.S.C. Secs. 461 *et seq.*

4. 351 U.S. 1 (1956).

5. *Squire v. Capoeman,* 351 U.S. 1, 5–6 (1956).

6. *See Elk v. Wilkins,* 112 U.S. 95 (1884); *Carpenter v. Shaw,* 280 U.S. 363 (1930); *U.S. v. Winnebago Tribe of Nebraska,* 542 F.2d 1003 (8th Cir. 1976). *But see FPC v. Tuscarora Indian Nation,* 362 U.S. 99, 120 (1960).

7. *Chickasaw Nation v. U.S.,* 122 S.Ct. 528, 535 (2001); *Cook v. U.S.,* 86 F.3d 1095 (Fed. Cir.), *cert. denied,* 519 U.S. 932 (1996); *Lazore v. Commissioner,* 11 F.3d 1180, 1187 (3d Cir. 1993).

8. *Chickasaw Nation v. U.S.,* note 7 above, 122 S.Ct. at 535.

9. 26 U.S.C. Sec. 61.

10. *Jourdain v. Commissioner,* 617 F.2d 507 (8th Cir. 1980). *See also Lazore,* note 7 above.

11. *Hoptowit v. Commissioner,* 709 F.2d 564 (9th Cir. 1983).

12. *Anderson v. U.S.,* 845 F.2d 206 (9th Cir.), *cert. denied,* 488 U.S. 966 (1988).

13. *Choteau v. Burnet,* 283 U.S. 691 (1931).

14. *Cook,* note 7 above.

15. 25 U.S.C. Sec. 2710(b)(3)(D)(1994).

16. U.S. Const., art. I, sec. 2, cl. 3.

17. *Lazore,* note 7 above, 11 F.3d at 1187; *U.S. v. Willie,* 941 F.2d 1384, 1400 (10th Cir. 1991), *cert. denied,* 502 U.S. 1106 (1992).

18. 25 U.S.C. Sec. 1407.

19. *See* ch. 5, notes 21–24, and accompanying text.

20. 26 U.S.C. Sec. 7873. *See Hall v. Commissioner,* T.C.Memo. 1998–336, 25 Indian L. Rep. 7067 (1998).

21. Rev. Rul. 69–164. *See Asenap v. U.S.,* 283 F. Supp. 566 (W.D. Okla. 1968); *Landman v. U.S.,* 71 F. Supp. 640 (Ct. Cl.), *cert. denied,* 332 U.S. 815 (1947).

22. 25 U.S.C. Secs. 331–58.

23. 351 U.S. 1 (1956).

24. 25 U.S.C. Sec. 349.

25. *Squire,* note 5 above, 351 U.S. at 10.

26. *Stevens v. Commissioner,* 452 F.2d 741 (9th Cir. 1971).

27. *Squire,* note 5 above (timber); *Kirschling v. U.S.,* 746 F.2d 512 (9th Cir. 1984) (timber); *U.S. v. Daney,* 370 F.2d 791 (10th Cir. 1966) (oil); *Hayes Big Eagle v. U.S.,* 300 F.2d 765 (Ct. Cl. 1962) (minerals).

28. *U.S. v. Hallam,* 304 F.2d 620 (10th Cir. 1962).

29. *Stevens,* note 26 above. *See also Kirkwood v. Arenas,* 243 F.2d 863 (9th Cir. 1957); *Kirschling,* note 27 above. With respect to exchanges of land, *see* 25 U.S.C. Sec. 463(e).

30. *See* Rev. Rul. 67–284 (1967).

31. *Holt v. Commissioner,* 364 F.2d 38 (8th Cir. 1966), *cert. denied,* 386 U.S. 931 (1967); *U.S. v. Anderson,* 625 F.2d 910 (9th Cir. 1980).

32. *Superintendent of Five Civilized Tribes v. Commissioner,* 295 U.S. 418 (1935).

33. *Dillon v. U.S.,* 792 F.2d 849 (9th Cir. 1986), *cert. denied sub nom. Cross v. U.S.,* 480 U.S. 930 (1987).

34. *Critzer v. U.S.,* 597 F.2d 708 (Ct. Cl. 1979) *(en banc), cert. denied,* 444 U.S. 92 (1979); *Hale v. U.S.,* 579 F. Supp. 646 (E.D. Wash. 1984); *Saunooke v. U.S.,* 9 Cl. Ct. 537 (1986). *See also Beck v. Commissioner,* T.C.Memo. 1994–122, 21 Indian L. Rep. 7055 (1994), *affirmed,* 64 F.3d 655 (4th Cir. 1995) (unpublished) (income derived from the rental of apartments on trust land is taxable).

35. In addition to the cases cited in notes 33 and 34, *see Arviso v. Comm'r of Internal Revenue,* T.C. Memo 1992–685 (Nov. 30, 1992); *Cabazon Indian Casino v. IRS,* 57 B.R. 398, 402 (9th Cir. Bankr. App. 1986).

36. *See, e.g.,* 26 U.S.C. Secs. 3121(b)(7) and 3306(c)(7), exempting states and their political subdivisions from paying taxes under the Federal Insurance Contribution Act and the Federal Unemployment Tax Act.

37. *See* Rev. Rul. 67–284 and Rev. Rul. 81–291.

38. *Confederated Tribes v. Kurtz,* 691 F.2d 878 (9th Cir. 1982), *cert. denied,* 460 U.S. 1040 (1983).

39. 26 U.S.C. Sec. 7871.

40. *See, e.g.,* 26 U.S.C. Sec. 7871(b).

41. 26 U.S.C. Secs. 3301–11.

42. 26 U.S.C. Secs. 3101–26.

43. *See* Rev. Rul. 59–354; *Cabazon Indian Casino v. IRS,* note 35 above. *See also* Rev. Rul. 58–610, 1958–2 C.B. 815 (ruling that the sale of an automobile to an Indian tribe for government purposes was subject to federal excise taxes); Rev. Rul. 94–81, 1994–2 C.B. 412 (ruling that tribes must pay wagering excise taxes and occupational taxes).

44. *See* Rev. Rul. 67–284, 1967–2 C.B. 55; Rev. Rul. 81–295, 1981–2 C.B. 15; Rev. Rul. 94–16, 1994–1 C.B. 19.

45. Rev. Rul. 94–16.

46. *Lone Wolf v. Hitchcock,* 187 U.S. 553 (1903).

47. *Choate v. Trapp,* 224 U.S. 665 (1912).

48. *Board of County Commissioners v. Seber,* 318 U.S. 705 (1943).

49. *McClanahan v. Arizona Tax Commission,* 411 U.S. 164 (1973); *Moe v. Confederated Salish and Kootenai Tribes,* 425 U.S. 463 (1976); *Bryan v. Itasca County, Minnesota,* 426 U.S. 373 (1976); *Washington v. Confederated Tribes of Colville Indian Reservation,* 447 U.S. 134, 163 (1980); *Montana v. Blackfeet Tribe,* 471 U.S. 759 (1985); *California State Board of Equalization v. Chemehuevi Indian Tribe,* 474 U.S. 9 (1985); *Crow Tribe of Indians v. Montana,* 819 F.2d 895 (9th Cir. 1987), *aff'd,* 484 U.S. 997 (1988); *County of Yakima v. Confederated Tribes and Bands of the Yakima Indian Nation,* 502 U.S. 251, 258 (1992); *Oklahoma Tax Comm'n v. Sac and Fox Nation,* 508 U.S. 114 (1993); *Oklahoma Tax Comm'n v. Chickasaw Nation,* 515 U.S. 450 (1995); *Cass County, Minnesota v. Leech Lake Band of Chippewa Indians,* 524 U.S. 103 (1998).

50. *Blackfeet Tribe,* note 49 above, 471 U.S. at 764.

51. *County of Yakima,* note 49 above, 502 U.S. at 258, quoting *Blackfeet Tribe,* note 49 above, 471 U.S. at 765.

52. *Oklahoma Tax Comm'n v. Chickasaw Nation,* note 49 above, 515 U.S. at 458. *See also McClanahan,* note 49 above, 411 U.S. at 171; *California v. Cabazon Band of Mission Indians,* 480 U.S. 202, 215 n.17 (1987).

53. *McClanahan,* note 49 above. *See also Eastern Band of Cherokee Indians v. Lynch,* 632 F.2d 373 (4th Cir. 1980). *But see Maryboy v. Utah State Tax Comm'n,* 904 P.2d 662 (Utah 1995), *cert. denied,* 517 U.S. 1220 (1996) (holding that Utah could lawfully tax the salary paid by a county to an elected county commissioner who was an Indian living on the reservation).

54. *Moe,* note 49 above.

55. *Bryan,* note 49 above.

56. *Oklahoma Tax Comm'n v. Sac and Fox Nation,* note 49 above, 508 U.S. at 127–28; *Washington v. Confederated Tribes of Colville,* note 49 above, 447 U.S. at 163; *U.S. on behalf of the Cheyenne River Sioux Tribe v. State of South Dakota,* 105 F.3d 1552 (8th Cir.), *cert. denied,* 522 U.S. 981 (1997).

57. *Makah Indian Tribe v. Callam County,* 440 P.2d 442 (Wash. 1968).

58. *Moe,* note 49 above.

59. *Washington State Dept. of Revenue v. Wofford,* 622 P.2d 1278 (Wash. Ct. App.), *cert. denied,* 454 U.S. 965 (1981).

60. *Washington v. Confederated Tribes of Colville,* note 49 above.

61. *Wofford,* note 59 above. *But see Washington v. Confederated Tribes of Colville,* note 49 above (state may be able to impose a motor vehicle tax proportionate to the amount of the vehicle's off-reservation use).

62. *The Kansas Indians,* 72 U.S. 737 (1867); *McCurdy v. U.S.,* 264 U.S. 484 (1924); *Brooks v. Nez Perce Co., Idaho,* 670 F.2d 835 (9th Cir. 1982); *Houlton Band of Maliseet Indians v. Town of Houlton,* 950 F. Supp. 408 (D. Me. 1996).

63. *Mescalero Apache Tribe v. Jones,* 411 U.S. 145 (1973).

64. *U.S. v. Rickert,* 188 U.S. 432 (1903).

65. *See Oklahoma Tax Comm'n v. U.S.,* 319 U.S. 598 (1942); *West v. Oklahoma Tax*

Comm'n, 334 U.S. 717 (1947); *Estate of Johnson,* 125 Cal. App.3d 1044 (Ct. App.1st 1982).

66. *Moe,* note 49 above.

67. *Id.*

68. *Marty Indian School Board, Inc. v. South Dakota,* 824 F.2d 684 (8th Cir. 1987).

69. *See Bryan,* note 49 above, 426 U.S. at 392 and cases cited therein; *Blackfeet Tribe,* note 49 above, 471 U.S. at 764.

70. 4 U.S.C. Secs. 105–10.

71. *Warren Trading Post v. Arizona Tax Comm'n,* 380 U.S. 685, 691 n.18 (1965).

72. 4 U.S.C. Sec. 104.

73. *White Mountain Apache Tribe v. Bracker,* 448 U.S. 136 (1980).

74. 28 U.S.C. Secs. 396a, 398.

75. *Blackfeet Tribe,* note 49 above.

76. 18 U.S.C. Sec. 1161. *See Rice v. Rehner,* 463 U.S. 713 (1983).

77. 25 U.S.C. Sec. 331 *et seq.*

78. *See County of Yakima,* note 49 above (individually owned land); *Leech Lake Band,* note 49 above (tribally owned land).

79. *See Bryan,* note 49 above.

80. This subject is discussed in ch. 13, sec. B.

81. *Prince v. Board of Education,* 543 P.2d 1176 (N.M. 1975); *Goodluck v. Apache County,* 417 F. Supp. 13 (D. Ariz. 1975), *aff'd sub nom. Apache County v. U.S.,* 429 U.S. 876 (1976).

82. *See* "Tribes Represent Multi-Million-Dollar Asset for Arizona," *Indian Country Today* (Feb. 4, 1993) at A6.

83. *See* "Washington Tribes Boost State Economy by $1 Billion," *Indian Country Today* (Feb. 8, 1999) at A6.

84. *See* "Nez Perce: 3,000 Jobs, $46.6 Million to Idaho Economy," *Indian Country Today* (Feb. 22, 1999) at B7.

85. *See* report issued by the University of Connecticut Center for Economic Analysis, Nov. 28, 2000, reported in "Computer Study Says Pequot Casino Saved the Connecticut Economy," *Indian Country Today* (Dec. 6, 2000) at A6. *See also* "Mohegans Up the Ante," *Hartford Courant* (June 10, 2001) at A1, A3.

86. *See* "Oneida Indian Nation Lifts Central New York Economy," *Indian Country Today* (Apr. 11, 2001) at C3.

87. *Washington v. Confederated Tribes of Colville,* note 49 above, 447 U.S. at 154–59. *See also Duro v. Reina,* 495 U.S. 676, 687 (1990); *La Rock v. Wisconsin Dept. of Rev.,* 621 N.W.2d 907 (Wis. 2001). A couple of states, though, have passed laws granting an exemption from state income taxation to all Indians in Indian country within the state. *See* Or. Rev. Stat. Sec. 316.777 (1999); Idaho Code Sec. 63–3026A(4)(b)(iv) (2000).

88. *Indian Country, U.S.A., Inc. v. Oklahoma,* 829 F.2d 967 (10th Cir. 1987), *cert. denied,* 487 U.S. 1218 (1988). *Cf. Rice v. Rehner,* 463 U.S. 713 (1983) (state can tax tribal liquor sales because Congress has given its express consent).

89. *Blackfeet Tribe,* note 49 above.

90. *Crow Tribe of Indians,* note 49 above.

91. *Moe,* note 49 above.

92. *Washington v. Confederated Tribes of Colville,* note 49 above. *See also Chemehuevi,* note 49 above; *Oklahoma Tax Comm'n v. Citizen Band Potawatomi Indian Tribe,* 498 U.S. 505 (1991).

93. *Moe,* note 49 above, 425 U.S. at 483.

94. *Washington v. Confederated Tribes of Colville,* note 49 above, 447 U.S. at 151 n.27.

95. 515 U.S. 450 (1995).

96. *Oklahoma Tax Comm'n v. Chickasaw Nation,* note 49 above, 515 U.S. at 460. Thus, if the tax burden falls on the tribe, the state tax is invalid absent express congressional consent. *See Goodman Oil Co. v. Idaho State Tax Comm'n,* 28 P.3d 996 (Idaho 2001), *cert. denied,* 122 S.Ct. 1068 (2002).

97. *Sac and Fox Nation of Missouri v. Pierce,* 213 F.3d 566, 579 (10th Cir. 2000), *cert. denied,* 121 S.Ct. 1078 (2001).

98. *Ramah Navajo School Board, Inc. v. New Mexico Taxation and Revenue Department,* 977 P.2d 1021 (N.M. App.), *cert. denied,* 528 U.S. 928 (1999).

99. *Cabazon Band of Mission Indians v. Wilson,* 124 F.3d 1050 (9th Cir. 1994).

100. *Hoopa Valley Tribe v. Nevins,* 881 F.2d 657 (9th Cir. 1989), *cert. denied,* 495 U.S. 1055 (1990).

101. *Blackfeet Tribe,* note 49 above.

102. *Compare Gila River Indian Community v. Waddell,* 967 F.2d 1404, 1407 (9th Cir. 1992) (invalidating a state tax because the tribe had added something of value to the product being taxed) and *Salt River Pima–Maricopa Indian Community v. Arizona,* 50 F.3d 734, 738 (9th Cir. 1995), *cert. denied,* 516 U.S. 868 (1995) (upholding a state tax because the tribe was seeking to market a tax immunity and had not added anything of value to the product). *See also Agua Caliente Band of Cahuilla Indians v. Hardin,* 223 F.3d 1041 (9th Cir. 2000) (noting that a tribe that purchases food products off the reservation and then prepares and cooks the food in its casino restaurant may be exempt from state taxation on food sales even to non-Indians).

103. 28 U.S.C. Sec. 1341.

104. 28 U.S.C. Sec. 1362.

105. *Blatchford v. Native Village of Noatak,* 501 U.S. 775 (1991); *Moe,* note 49 above, 425 U.S. at 474–75; *Tunica-Biloxi Tribe v. Louisiana,* 964 F.2d 1536, 1538 n.5 (5th Cir. 1992). *See also Osceola v. Florida Dept. of Revenue,* 893 F.2d 1231 (11th Cir. 1990), *cert. denied,* 498 U.S. 1025 (1991) (individual Indians must exhaust state remedies). This subject is discussed in more detail in ch. 18.

106. 498 U.S. 505 (1991).

107. *Potawatomi Indian Tribe,* note 92 above, 498 U.S. at 514 (internal citations omitted).

108. *See Yakama Indian Nation v. State of Washington, Department of Revenue,* 176 F.3d 1241 (9th Cir. 1999), *cert. denied,* 528 U.S. 1116 (2000).

109. *See U.S. v. Baker,* 63 F.3d 1478 (9th Cir. 1995), *cert. denied,* 516 U.S. 1097 (1996).

110. *See* "Gov. Locke Signs Cigarette Tax Measure," *Indian Country Today* (May 23, 2001) at A2. The state of New York, tired of the often violent resistance from Indians from

whom the state sought to collect its cigarette taxes, has ceased trying to collect them, to the dismay of off-reservation cigarette vendors whose prices are thus higher. *See N.Y. Ass'n of Convenience Stores v. Urbach*, 712 N.Y.S.2d 220 (App.Div. 2001), *cert. denied*, 122 S.Ct. 647 (2001).

111. 422 U.S. 145 (1973).

112. *Oklahoma Tax Comm'n v. Chickasaw Nation*, note 49 above. *See also Jefferson v. Commissioner of Revenue*, 631 N.W.2d 391 (Minn. 2001), *cert. denied*, 122 S.Ct. 1304 (2002).

113. *Tunica-Biloxi Tribe*, note 105 above.

114. *Salt River Pima–Maricopa Indian Community v. Yavapi County*, 50 F.3d 739 (9th Cir. 1995).

115. *Cohen v. Little Six, Inc.*, 543 N.W.2d 376, 379 (Minn. App. 1996); *Dixon v. Picopa Constr. Co.*, 772 P.2d 1104, 1109–10 (Ariz. 1989).

116. *Mescalero Apache Tribe*, note 63, 411 U.S. at 157 n.13.

117. *Baraga Products, Inc. v. Comm'r of Revenue*, 971 F. Supp. 294 (W.D. Mich. 1997), *aff'd without published opinion*, 156 F.3d 1228 (6th Cir. 1998).

118. Rev. Rul. 94–16, 1994–1 C.B. 19 (1994).

119. *Moe*, note 49 above; *Washington v. Confederated Tribes of Colville*, note 49 above.

120. *See, e.g., Thomas v. Gay*, 169 U.S. 264 (1898) (personal property tax); *Utah & No. Ry. v. Fisher*, 116 U.S. 28 (1885) (real estate); *Loveness v. Arizona Dept. of Revenue*, 963 P.2d 303 (Ariz. App. 1998), *cert. denied*, 525 U.S. 1178 (1999) (income). *See also* 25 U.S.C. Sec. 379.

121. *Washington v. Confederated Tribes of Colville*, note 49 above.

122. *Ramah Navajo School Board, Inc. v. Bureau of Revenue*, 458 U.S. 832 (1982).

123. *Bracker*, note 73 above.

124. *Warren Trading Post*, note 71 above.

125. *New Mexico Taxation and Revenue Dept. v. Laguna Industries, Inc.*, 855 P.2d 127 (N.M. 1993).

126. 490 U.S. 163 (1989). *See also Northern Border Pipeline Co. v. Montana*, 772 P.2d 829 (Mont. 1989).

127. *Cotton Petroleum Corp. v. New Mexico*, 490 U.S. 163, 189 (1989).

128. *Maricopa and P.R.R. v. Arizona Territory*, 156 U.S. 347 (1895).

129. *Montana Catholic Missions v. Missoula County*, 200 U.S. 118 (1906).

130. *Chemehuevi* and *Moe*, note 49 above. *See also State ex rel. Arizona Dept. of Revenue v. Dillon*, 826 P.2d 1186 (Ariz. App. 1991).

131. *Fort Mojave Tribe v. County of San Bernadino*, 543 F.2d 1253 (9th Cir. 1976), *cert. denied*, 430 U.S. 983 (1977); *Pimalco, Inc. v. Maricopa County*, 937 P.2d 1198 (Ariz. App. 1997).

132. *Yavapai-Prescott Indian Tribe v. Scott*, 117 F.3d 1107 (9th Cir. 1997), *cert. denied*, 522 U.S. 1076 (1998).

133. *Gila River Indian Community v. Waddell*, 91 F.3d 1232 (9th Cir. 1996).

134. *Salt River Pima–Maricopa Indian Community v. Arizona*, note 102 above.

135. 455 U.S. 130 (1982).

136. *Merrion v. Jicarilla Apache Tribe*, 455 U.S. 130, 137 (1982).

137. *Morris v. Hitchcock,* 194 U.S. 384 (1904).

138. *Washington v. Confederated Tribes of Colville,* note 49 above, 447 U.S. at 152–53.

139. *Merrion,* note 136 above. *See also Mustang Production Co. v. Harrison,* 94 F.3d 1382 (10th Cir. 1996), *cert. denied,* 520 U.S. 1139 (1997) (holding that a tribe may tax the value of oil and gas produced on individual Indian trust allotments).

140. 471 U.S. 195 (1985).

141. *Kerr-McGee Corp. v. Navajo Tribe,* 471 U.S. 195 (1985).

142. 450 U.S. 544 (1981).

143. *Montana v. U.S.,* 450 U.S. 544, 565–66 (1981).

144. *See, e.g., Strate v. A-1 Contractors,* 520 U.S. 438, 446 (1997); *Brendale v. Confederated Tribes and Bands of the Yakima Indian Nation,* 492 U.S. 408 (1989).

145. 121 S.Ct. 1825 (2001).

146. *Atkinson Trading Co., Inc. v. Shirley,* 121 S.Ct. 1830 (2001).

147. *Id.*

148. *Id.* at 1831 (emphasis in original).

149. *Id.* at 1832.

150. *Id.* at 1833. *See also Big Horn County Electric Cooperative v. Adams,* 219 F.3d 944 (9th Cir. 2000) (holding that an Indian tribe could not tax the value of a utility company's leasehold interest in trust land acquired by a congressionally granted right-of-way).

151. *Washington v. Confederated Tribes of Colville,* note 49 above; *FMC v. Shoshone-Bannock Tribes,* 905 F.2d 1311 (9th Cir. 1990); *Snow v. Quinault Indian Nation,* 709 F.2d 1319 (9th Cir. 1983), *cert. denied,* 467 U.S. 1214 (1984).

152. *Buster v. Wright,* 135 F. 947 (8th Cir. 1905), *appeal dismissed,* 203 U.S. 599 (1906).

153. *See U.S. v. Mazurie,* 419 U.S. 544, 558 (1975); *Bugenig v. Hoopa Valley Tribe,* 266 F.3d 1201, 1233 (9th Cir. 2001) *(en banc), cert. denied,* 122 S.Ct. 1296 (2002).

154. *See, e.g., Big Horn County Electric,* note 150 above.

155. *Duncan Energy Co. v. Three Affiliated Tribes of Ft. Berthold Reservation,* 27 F.3d 1294 (8th Cir. 1994), *cert. denied,* 513 U.S. 1103 (1995); *Texaco, Inc. v. Hale,* 81 F.3d 934 (10th Cir. 1975).

XI

Indian Hunting and Fishing Rights

Hunting and fishing have always been of vital importance to Indians. Traditionally, access to wildlife was "not much less necessary to the existence of the Indians than the atmosphere they breathed,"[1] and this is still true on many reservations. As a member of the Gwich'in Indians of northeastern Alaska recently stated while explaining the tribe's strong opposition to expanded oil exploration in Alaska that would threaten caribou habitats: "It is our belief that the future of the Gwich'in and the future of the caribou are the same."[2]

Until the reservation system was created in the nineteenth century, many western tribes were nomadic, pursuing the seasonal migrations of deer, elk, bison, and anadromous fish. (Anadromous fish, including many kinds of salmon, are born in fresh water, migrate to the ocean until they are adults, and return to the place where they were born to spawn.) As the Supreme Court explained in *Washington v. Washington State Commercial Passenger Fishing Vessel Ass'n* (1979),[3] regarding the extent to which fishing was essential to the survival of the Indians of the Northwest:

One hundred and twenty-five years ago . . . anadromous fish were even more important to most of the population of western Washington than they are today. At that time, about three-fourths of the approximately 10,000 inhabitants of the area were Indians. Although in some respects the cultures of the different tribes varied, . . . all of them shared a vital and unifying dependence on anadromous fish.

Religious rites were intended to insure the continual return of the salmon and the trout; the seasonal and geographic variations in the runs of the different species determined the movements of the largely nomadic tribes. Fish constituted a major part of the Indian diet, was used for commercial purposes, and indeed was traded in substantial volume. The Indians developed food-preservation techniques

214

that enabled them to store fish throughout the year and to transport it over great distances. They used a wide variety of methods to catch fish including the precursors of all modern netting techniques. Their usual and accustomed fishing places were numerous and were scattered throughout the area, and included marine as well as fresh-water areas.[4]

As a result of treaties and statutes more than a century old, Indians have a right to take a considerable amount of wildlife. However, millions of non-Indians now vie for the same resources, both for sport and commercial purposes. Today, the demand for wildlife has greatly outstripped its supply, and many non-Indians deeply resent Indian hunting and fishing rights. Few areas of Indian law have created such bitter—and sometimes violent—rivalry and jealousy. Non-Indians fishers in Wisconsin have fired shotguns at Indian treaty fishers, thrown rocks at their children, and chanted "Spear an Indian, save a walleye. Drown 'em, drown 'em," as Indians entered their boats.[5] Indian fishers in Alaska have also been fired upon, and a court recently found that an administrator in the Alaska Department of Fish and Game used racial slurs in referring to Indians and had illegally discriminated against them.[6] In Washington, laws were passed prohibiting state officials from enforcing Indian treaty fishing rights until federal courts intervened and ordered state officials to obey those treaties.[7] In January 2001, vandals cut more that a half-mile of gill nets that tribal fishers had dropped through the ice into Munising Bay in Michigan, and a local newspaper reported that the conflict between Indian and non-Indian fishers was "heating up."[8]

Many species of wildlife on which tribes once subsisted have become scarce or extinct due to the large number of non-Indians who now live in the region and the degree to which these non-Indians have changed and degraded the natural environment. Dams constructed on the Columbia River in the Northwest have destroyed more than 90 percent of the 16 million salmon that once swam in the river, on which many Indian tribes had depended.[9] On the nearby Snake River, less than 2,000 salmon migrated upstream to Idaho in 1993, one-tenth the number just four years earlier.[10] The twenty tribes that comprise the Northwest Indian Fisheries Commission, including the Lummi, Muckleshoot, Nisqually, and Tulalip, harvested 5.3 million salmon in 1985; by 2000, the number had plummeted to 500,000.[11] These tribes, whose members once earned a decent living from catching and selling salmon, now face unemployment rates more than ten times the national average.[12] For obvious reasons, Indians are extremely concerned about protecting the future of these resources.

Treaties and statutes that guarantee hunting and fishing rights have been interpreted by the courts to include gathering and trapping rights for those tribes that obtained their food by those methods.[13] Throughout this chapter, references to hunting and fishing rights encompass gathering and trapping rights unless the contrary is indicated.

Which tribes still have hunting and fishing rights?

Every Indian tribe has the inherent right to be self-governing, and this encompasses the right to regulate wildlife found within its territory.[14] A tribe's inherent powers can be limited by Congress, as explained in chapter 6, but unless that has occurred, each tribe retains its original right to hunt and fish on tribal lands. "The right to hunt and fish on reservation land is a long-established tribal right."[15]

The right to hunt and fish was expressly guaranteed to many tribes in their treaties with the United States, but this right is presumed to exist even if the treaty does not mention it. As the Supreme Court explained in 1905, a treaty should not be viewed as a grant of rights to the Indians but as a taking of rights from them; thus, if a treaty is silent on the subject of Indian hunting and fishing rights, those rights were not limited by the treaty and are presumed to still exist in full force.[16] Each tribe is presumed to retain its traditional right to hunt and fish, regardless of whether its reservation was created by a treaty, statute, or an executive order,[17] and regardless of whether the reservation includes any of the tribe's original homelands.[18] (As explained in chapter 4, the United States ended treaty making with Indian tribes in 1871, but until then treaties were a common method of negotiation between the United States and tribes. Prior to 1871, reservations often were created by a treaty, whereas after 1871 they were created by statute or executive order.)

Congress has the power to extinguish (abrogate) Indian hunting and fishing rights, but a court will not recognize an abrogation of these vital rights unless Congress has clearly expressed its intention to eliminate them.[19] Abrogation of Indian rights may not be inferred, and any ambiguous language in a treaty or statute must be interpreted in favor of the Indians.[20] These are among the "canons of treaty and statutory construction" discussed in chapter 4. Applying these canons, the Supreme Court recently held that Indians whose treaty guaranteed them the right to fish at a certain location off the reservation in Minnesota "until required to remove by the President" may continue to fish at that location until the President has a *legitimate* reason to remove them—that is, until they misbehaved in some fashion—because this is how the Indians would likely have interpreted the treaty at the time they signed it.[21] Based on the same canons, the Court also held in that case that the tribe's treaty rights were not abrogated by the federal law that admitted Minnesota into the Union, given the lack of express language in that law abrogating the treaty.[22]

In other cases applying these canons, the Supreme Court has held that federal conservation laws prohibiting the taking of certain plants or animals will not be construed to have abrogated Indian treaty rights unless there is "clear evidence" that Congress actually considered whether to protect the treaty or protect the environment "and chose to resolve that conflict by abrogating the treaty."[23] Similarly, in *Menominee Tribe v. United States* (1968),[24] the Supreme Court held that the Menominee Tribe retained its hunting and fishing rights even though Congress had terminated[25] its reservation. The termination statute did not expressly abrogate those rights; therefore, the Court said, the Menominees could continue to hunt and fish within the terminated area. (The Menominee Tribe, terminated in the 1950s, was restored to federal status in 1973 and once again has a reservation in Wisconsin.)[26]

Do Indian tribes still possess their aboriginal hunting and fishing rights?

Indian tribes are recognized as possessing an "aboriginal right" to occupy and use forever their original (aboriginal) territory,[27] including the right to harvest the wildlife found on that territory.[28] However, aboriginal rights are lost whenever Congress removes the land from the tribe's control and assigns it to a purpose inconsistent with tribal ownership.[29]

Nearly all of the land in the United States has been assigned to a use inconsistent with the assertion of aboriginal rights: the land has either been sold to private parties or set aside for public use, such as a national park. Consequently, few *off-reservation* aboriginal rights remain, and any rights that Indians have to hunt or fish outside the reservation usually are derived from the types of treaties and statutes just discussed.[30] Tribes continue to possess *on-reservation* aboriginal rights, but in that situation, they would likely possess federally guaranteed rights to hunt and fish by virtue of the treaty, statute, or executive order that created the reservation, and they would not need to also claim aboriginal rights.

When a navigable waterway is included within the boundaries of an Indian reservation, who owns the land underneath it?

Valuable plants and animals live in the land underneath navigable waterways; perhaps the clearest example are clams and oysters found in off-shore tidelands. Although the general rule is that a tribe may hunt, fish, gather, and trap all wildlife within its territory even if the treaty that created the reservation is silent as to these rights, an exception exists for the beds of navigable water. The Supreme Court has held that there is "a strong presumption against conveyance" of this land to an Indian tribe,[31] and tribes may not take plants and animals found in submerged lands of navigable waterways unless Congress clearly conferred that right.[32] As discussed later in this chapter, a number of treaties did expressly confer on certain tribes the right to take shellfish in navigable waterways.

Is a tribe entitled to compensation when Congress abrogates its hunting and fishing rights?

Yes. The Fifth Amendment to the Constitution requires the federal government to pay compensation whenever it takes private property. The Supreme Court has held that Indian hunting and fishing rights are a form of property protected by the Fifth Amendment; thus, any loss of them is a "taking" that entitles the tribe to fair compensation.[33] These rights, however, must first have been formally recognized by the federal government in some treaty, statute, or executive order; the government does not have to compensate a tribe for the loss of property interests not formally recognized, including aboriginal rights.[34]

Does it violate the Constitution to give Indians special hunting and fishing rights?

As the native inhabitants of this continent, Indians constitute a unique political group. Indians have always been the subject of "special" federal treatment, sometimes to their benefit and often to their detriment. Non-Indians have challenged some of the benefits Indians have received, alleging they constitute impermissible race discrimination. For reasons explained in chapter 5, section A, courts generally reject these challenges on the grounds that Congress has broad authority to regulate Indian affairs.

Those who criticize the benefits Indians possess under federal law often overlook the fact that Indians, by having relinquished to the United States most of their ancestral lands, paid a heavy price to obtain them.[35]

Do hunting and fishing rights belong to the tribe or to the tribe's members as individuals?

In most situations, it makes no difference whether the right to hunt and fish is classified as a tribal right or as an individual right. If a state law, for instance, interferes with a tribe's treaty rights, both the tribe and its members can file suit to challenge it.[36]

Indian hunting and fishing rights ultimately belong to the tribe, however, and thus the tribe has the power to regulate the hunting and fishing activities of tribal members.[37] Likewise, if Congress takes away these rights and must then pay compensation for the value of the loss, the money is paid to the tribe, which decides how it should be distributed.[38]

Are treaties between the United States and other countries regulating wildlife automatically applicable to Indian activities?

No. As explained earlier, while Congress has the power to abrogate Indian hunting and fishing rights, it must do so explicitly. Therefore, an international treaty does not *automatically* limit Indian hunting and fishing rights. Indian tribes in the Northwest, for instance, whose fishing rights are protected by a treaty with the United States may continue to use certain nets in exercising those rights, even though the United States subsequently signed a treaty with Canada prohibiting the use of this gear, given that there is nothing in that treaty expressly abrogating Indian fishing rights.[39]

May Indian tribes use hunting and fishing methods that did not exist when their treaties were signed?

Yes. The right to hunt and fish carries with it the right to use modern techniques for obtaining wildlife.[40] A tribe that fished from the shore when its treaty was signed may today use motorized boats to assist them in catching fish.[41]

The right to hunt and fish also includes the right to take wildlife that was not readily available when the reservation was created. A tribe that once hunted bison (with a bow and arrow) is today entitled to hunt deer (with a rifle) in exercising its treaty rights.[42] Moreover, when a state creates a fish hatchery program to replace the natural fish taken by non-Indians, the tribe has a right to catch these replacement fish as part of its treaty share.[43] As a general rule, if an Indian tribe has a right to take wildlife in an area, it may continue to do so regardless of changes to that area caused by human habitation or deliberate intervention (such as the construction of a dam) and may modify its practices of catching fish and game to account for these changed circumstances.[44]

In exercising its hunting and fishing rights, a tribe is limited by only two restrictions, other than those it imposes upon itself. First, it may not take so much wildlife that it endangers continuation (propagation) of the species in violation of state or federal conservation laws. Second, it may not take any wildlife that Congress has expressly prohibited it from taking. These restrictions are discussed later in this chapter.

A. On-Reservation Hunting and Fishing

Many Indian reservations are located in unpopulated areas of the United States where fish and game are plentiful. This wildlife provides food for tribal members and also offers an opportunity for commercial and sport activity.

Most tribes that have harvestable wildlife on their reservations have created licensing and conservation programs and closely manage their resources, and some sell licenses to non-Indians as a means of raising revenue. The Mescalero Apache Tribe in New Mexico, for instance, developed a fish hatchery program and sells fishing licenses; the tribe also raised a sizable herd of elk and sells hunting licenses. To accommodate the resulting tourism, the tribe constructed a motel and restaurant.[45]

There are three groups of people who may want to hunt or fish on an Indian reservation: tribal members, nonmembers who live on the reservation, and nonmembers who live off the reservation. There also are three governments that conceivably could regulate the taking of wildlife on an Indian reservation: the tribe, the state, and the United States. The jurisdiction that each government has over these three groups is discussed below.

May the tribe regulate on-reservation hunting and fishing?

Indian tribes have the inherent right "to manage the use of their territory and resources," and this includes the right to regulate hunting and fishing by members[46] and nonmembers[47] on tribal lands and to prohibit all such activity if the tribe so decides. Congress may restrict these tribal powers, but it has done so only in narrow circumstances.[48]

Hunting and fishing is taken very seriously on most reservations because it is directly related to the cultural and religious heritage of the tribe and because many tribal members depend on wildlife for food. Most tribes strictly regulate the time, place, and manner of hunting and fishing on the reservation and enforce these rules on tribal members through the tribal courts.[49] Congress has made it a federal crime to hunt or fish on tribal land without the tribe's permission,[50] and thus the federal government assists tribes in enforcing their conservation laws on nonmembers.

In *Montana v. United States* (1981),[51] the Supreme Court created a significant exception to the rule that Indian tribes may regulate all hunting and fishing within the reservation. Tribes have limited powers, the Court held in *Montana,* to regulate non-Indian hunting and fishing on *non-Indian* land within the reservation, and a tribe may impose its laws only when (1) the activity of the non-Indian owner significantly threatens the tribe's political integrity, economic security, or health and welfare, or (2) the owner has entered into a consensual relationship, such as a contract or lease, with the tribe. (As explained in chapter 1, in 1887 Congress passed the General Allotment Act, which opened most Indian reservations to settlement by non-Indians, and millions of acres of reservation land is now owned by non-Indians.) Thus, if a non-Indian owner's fishing imperils the availability of subsistence food for tribal members, the tribe could regulate that activity,[52] but when neither of these "*Montana* exceptions" is present, state law rather than tribal law governs non-Indian hunting and fishing on non-Indian land.[53]

May the state regulate on-reservation hunting and fishing?

As explained in chapter 7, unless Congress has given its express consent, a state may not enforce a law on an Indian reservation when doing so would infringe on the tribe's right of self-government (the *infringement* test) or would violate federal law (the *preemption* test). Congress has not consented to the enforcement of state conservation laws on Indian reservations. Even Public Law 83-280, in which Congress consented to state jurisdiction over certain crimes committed in Indian country, expressly withholds consent to state regulation of Indian hunting and fishing rights.[54]

Given the absence of congressional consent, courts have uniformly struck down under the infringement or preemption test efforts by states to regulate the taking of wildlife on *tribal* land by tribal members[55] or by non-members.[56] The only exception to this rule, and it is a narrow one, was created in *Puyallup Tribe, Inc. v. Department of Game* (1968).[57] The Supreme Court held in *Puyallup* that a state may regulate hunting and fishing on tribal lands when necessary to ensure propagation of the species. The measures that a state may and may not take in this situation are discussed later in this chapter.

In short, the state's authority with respect to on-reservation hunting and fishing is limited to the circumstances addressed in *Montana* and *Puyallup*. Under *Montana*, the state may regulate non-Indians who hunt and fish on non-Indian-owned land. Under *Puyallup*, the state may regulate hunting and fishing on tribal land when absolutely essential for conservation purposes. The state has no other jurisdiction over reservation hunting and fishing.

May the federal government regulate on-reservation hunting and fishing?

Congress may regulate every aspect of on-reservation hunting and fishing, and may even abrogate the right of Indians to engage in that activity and eliminate the reservation.[58] But unless Congress has expressly conferred such a power, federal officials may not regulate hunting and fishing on an Indian reservation.[59]

Most of the powers that Congress has conferred on federal officials to regulate the taking of wildlife on Indian reservations assists—rather than limits—the enforcement of tribal law. First, Congress has made it a *federal* crime to hunt or fish within an Indian reservation in a manner contrary to *tribal* law;[60] it also has made it a federal crime to "transport, sell, receive, acquire or purchase any fish or wildlife" in violation of tribal or federal law.[61] These criminal laws help compensate for the fact that the Supreme Court ruled in 1978 that Indian tribes may not prosecute non-Indians.[62] With the passage of these laws, all persons—including non-Indians, tribal members,[63] and nonmember Indians[64]—who violate tribal game laws are subject to federal prosecution.

Moreover, Congress has directed federal officials to adopt conservation measures to protect certain animals, many of which are vital to Indian tribes. The Endangered Species Act (ESA)[65] requires federal agencies to insure that all actions funded, authorized, or carried out by a federal agency will not jeopardize an endangered species. Acting pursuant to the ESA, federal agencies have prohibited non-Indians from overharvesting certain endangered wildlife so as to protect the right of tribes to harvest a sufficient number of those animals for food.[66] Similarly, the Magnuson Fishery Conservation and Management Act (the Magnuson Act)[67] requires the Secretary of Commerce to regulate the taking of certain fish within two hundred miles of the shore, and the act expressly requires that the Secretary enforce this law consistent with Indian treaty rights.[68] Under the Magnuson Act, the Secretary must curtail ocean fishing by non-Indians so as to ensure that a sufficient supply of fish will be available to fulfill the federal government's treaty and trust obligations to Indian tribes.[69]

Laws passed in 1976[70] and 1980[71] obligate the federal agencies that oversee the operation of hydroelectric dams on rivers in the Northwest to protect and enhance the fish and wildlife affected by the dams. As one court has noted, these laws require that the preservation fish and animals be placed "on a par with [developing] energy" in determining the construction and operation of these dams.[72]

The National Environmental Policy Act (NEPA)[73] requires that an environmental impact statement (EIS) be prepared whenever any major federal action could significantly affect the quality of the environment.[74] The act also requires the agency to study and describe alternative measures whenever a proposed action would have a significant environmental impact.[75] A tribe thus has a right under NEPA to discover *beforehand* how an agency's proposed action could affect its hunting and fishing rights, and the tribe can file suit to halt implementation of the planned project if it appears its rights will be jeopardized by the project.[76]

The Bald and Golden Eagle Protection Act[77] is another measure that requires federal officials to consider Indian interests in the administration of federal conservation laws. The act prohibits the taking, possession, sale, export, and import of bald and golden eagles and their parts (such as feathers and talons). This law, the Supreme Court held in *United States v. Dion* (1986),[78] abrogated Indian treaty rights to hunt eagles in any manner inconsistent with the act's prohibitions protecting these birds. However, the act expressly authorizes the Secretary of the Interior to issue permits allowing the taking, possession, and transportation of eagles and eagle parts "for the religious purposes of Indian tribes."[79] Obviously, then, Congress wished to accommodate the spiritual needs of Indians while also protecting eagles.[80] Pursuant to this authorization, the Secretary has issued a set of regulations under which members of federally recognized Indian tribes can obtain permits to possess and use eagles and eagle parts.[81]

B. Off-Reservation Hunting and Fishing

What kinds of off-reservation hunting and fishing rights do Indians have?

Many Indians have a federally protected right to hunt and fish outside the reservation, although the exact scope of these rights varies. Indians have acquired these rights through one of two methods. First, Congress has reduced the size of or eliminated an Indian reservation without abrogating the tribe's hunting and fishing rights on the land being removed.[82] Few tribes, though, acquired off-reservation rights in this manner because Congress almost always abrogated a tribe's hunting and fishing rights when it diminished or terminated a reservation.[83]

The second method was used more frequently: Congress expressly conferred upon the tribe through a treaty or statute a right to hunt or fish outside the reservation. Some tribes have a treaty right to hunt on "unoccupied and unclaimed" lands outside the reservation, or words to that effect.[84] This gives tribal members a right to hunt on unsettled public lands, such as uninhabited portions of national forests and state parks, even if hunting at those locations is otherwise restricted or prohibited.[85]

Various bands of Chippewa signed a treaty in 1854 in which they relinquished a sizeable portion of land (the "ceded territory") in what is now Minnesota. The treaty expressly guaranteed that the Chippewa "shall have the right to hunt and fish" in any area within the ceded territory that remained unsettled, and tribal members exercise those rights today on thousands of acres of land. Similar treaties were signed with other bands of Chippewa in the Great Lakes region, and these off-reservation rights also cover thousands of acres. The signatory tribes have created their own agency to regulate the use of these rights.[86]

Several tribes in the Northwest have treaties that guarantee them the right to harvest shellfish (such as mussels, clams, and oysters) outside the reservation.[87] In addition, many tribes in the Northwest were guaranteed in their treaties a right to fish "at all usual and accustomed grounds and stations," both on and off the reservation.[88] None of these "grounds and stations" were identified in the treaties, causing bitter disputes decades later as non-Indians began settling in areas claimed as traditional fishing sites by these treaty tribes. In *United States v. Washington*,[89] a federal court of appeals defined "usual and accustomed grounds and stations" as being all sites where tribal members customarily fished at or before the time the treaty was signed, however distant from the tribe's usual home and regardless of whether other tribes also fished in the same waters.[90] Although this required tribes to prove where their members had fished generations ago, a difficult task given the absence of written records,[91] many sites have now been identified. Given that these tribes pursued anadromous salmon—which spend their adult life in the ocean and return to rivers and streams to spawn—some of the grounds and stations in which these fish were caught are located out in the ocean, while others are located on the shore lines and river banks that provided access to these fish during their spawning migrations.[92]

Once a court recognizes the existence of a traditional fishing site, members of the tribe have a right to reach that location and to fish there. If the site is a shore line or river bank now owned by non-Indians, tribal members have a right to fish there regardless of whether the private owner consents,[93] and if private land surrounds the site, Indians have a right to cross that land in order to reach their fishing grounds.[94]

The exercise of off-reservation tribal fishing rights has caused tremendous friction. First, as just mentioned, tribes are permitted to travel across land privately owned by non-Indians in order to reach and use their traditional grounds and stations, a right that these private owners often resent. Second, fishing is taken very seriously by non-Indians for sport and commercial purposes, especially in the Northwest and on the Great Lakes where it is a multimillion-dollar business, and Indian treaty fishing competes with these interests.

Tribes, however, have every reason to assert their treaty rights, having relinquished vast landholdings in exchange for them. Maintaining these off-reservation sites was of primary concern to the treaty tribes. As the Supreme Court has stated regarding the Northwest Indian treaties:

All of the treaties were negotiated by Isaac Stevens, the first Governor and first Superintendent of Indian Affairs of the Washington Territory, and a small group of advisors. Contemporaneous documents make it clear that these people recognized the vital importance of the fisheries to the Indians and wanted to protect them from the risk that non-Indian settlers might seek to monopolize their fisheries. There is no evidence of the precise understanding the Indians had of any of the specific English terms and phrases in the treaty. It is perfectly clear, however, that the Indians were vitally interested in protecting their right to take fish at usual and accustomed places, whether on or off the reservations, and that they were invited by the white negotiators to rely and in fact did rely heavily on the good faith of the United States to protect that right.[95]

As the Court indicated, the government agents who wrote these treaties wished to protect Indian fisheries. However, their promise to do so was easy to make at the time because few non-Indians lived in that area of the country, and the fish supply seemed inexhaustible.[96] Today, the demand for fish far exceeds the supply, and many non-Indians resent and oppose these Indian treaty rights. Indians in numerous states, including Washington, Oregon, Idaho, Michigan, and Wisconsin, frequently have had to rely on federal courts to protect their rights.[97] Yet state officials, pressured by their non-Indian constituents, have ignored even some of these federal court decisions. The Washington legislature, for example, went so far as to pass a law prohibiting state officials from enforcing Indian treaty fishing rights, but in *Washington v. Washington State Commercial Passenger Fishing Vessel Ass'n* (1979),[98] the Supreme Court declared that law unconstitutional. The Court warned state officials in that case that it was "prepared to uphold the use of stern measures to require respect for federal court orders."[99]

May the tribe regulate Indian hunting and fishing outside the reservation?

As explained in chapter 7, section D, Indian tribes normally may not enforce their laws or regulate activities outside the reservation unless Congress has expressly conferred that right upon the tribe. This includes the regulation of off-reservation hunting and fishing; state law governs that activity in the absence of some federal law to the contrary. As just indicated, Congress has conferred off-reservation hunting and fishing rights upon a number of tribes. Those tribes that possess off-reservation rights may regulate the exercise of those rights by tribal members and may prosecute tribal members in tribal court for any violations.[100] Indian tribes may not prosecute non-Indians,[101] but tribes may sue them in federal court for violating the tribe's off-reservation rights, and the court can order them to halt their activities.[102]

May the state regulate Indian hunting and fishing outside the reservation?

States have the inherent right to regulate hunting and fishing within their borders.[103] Indians who hunt or fish outside the reservation must comply with the same state laws applicable to everyone else unless they possess an express immunity under federal law.

Many Indians do have off-reservation hunting and fishing rights, as just explained. By virtue of the Supremacy Clause in the U.S. Constitution, a federal right is superior to a state right when the two conflict.[104] Therefore, a state may not interfere with the exercise of a federal right, such as an Indian treaty right.[105]

Yet even in this situation, the state has some authority. The Supreme Court has created two exceptions to the rule that a state may not regulate off-reservation Indian treaty rights. The first of these exceptions applies to all Indian hunting and fishing, both within the reservation and outside of it. The second exception applies only to those tribes that happen to have a particular clause—the "in common with" clause—in their treaties conferring off-reservation rights.

1. The "Conservation Necessity" Exception

The first exception to the rule that a state may not interfere with Indian treaty rights to hunt and fish is the *Puyallup* "conservation necessity" exception, mentioned earlier. The Supreme Court held in 1968 in *Puyallup* that a state may limit Indian treaty rights "in the interest of conservation,"[106] both on and off the reservation, and prohibit tribes from engaging in any activity that would endanger continuation of the species. The Court has given no solid justification for allowing the state to regulate a tribal and federal right—a power the state normally does not have unless Congress expressly confers it—and numerous commentators have criticized this holding.[107] As one federal court stated, "[T]he basis for [this] state regulation has never been explained satisfactorily."[108] According to the Supreme Court, the conservation necessity exception "accommodates both the State's interest in management of its natural resources and the [tribe's] federally guaranteed treaty rights,"[109] but the Court has not explained how the state acquired the authority to impose its jurisdiction on these federal rights in the first place.

This exception, though, is a narrow one and may be used only as a last resort. In order to be valid, the Supreme Court has held, a state conservation regulation must pass three tests. First, the state must show that its regulation is reasonable and necessary to perpetuate the species and, second, that the regulation is the least restrictive means of achieving this goal. If alternative methods of conservation are available that are less injurious to the tribe's treaty rights, they must be utilized.[110] Third, the regulation must not discriminate against Indians, either by placing greater burdens on them than on non-Indians or by imposing restrictions that have the effect of preventing Indians from taking their treaty share of the resource.[111] It is only when no other alternative exists that a state may prohibit Indians from taking a species of fish near extinction, provided that the ban is equally applicable to non-Indians.[112] Whenever a state seeks to restrict Indian treaty rights under the conservation exception, a court must hold a hearing and carefully consider whether the state's restriction passes all three tests, unless the state is requiring nothing more than what the tribe enacted as its own conservation measures.[113]

A state may require tribal members to carry identification cards so that state game wardens can identify them as possessing treaty rights.[114] A state may allow non-Indians to fish at a protected Indian site provided that tribal members are not prevented from catching their treaty share of fish at that location.[115]

On the other hand, restrictions that are unreasonable, unnecessary, or discriminatory are invalid. A state may not prevent the tribe from taking its fair share of treaty wildlife unless absolutely necessary. The facts of *Puyallup* and the specific holding in that case illustrate this principle. At issue in that case was a regulation by the state of Washington that prohibited the use of nets to catch certain fish. The ban applied to everyone equally, Indian and non-Indian, and the state argued it was therefore reasonable and nondiscriminatory. But the Supreme Court invalidated the ban because Indians, who represent about 5 percent of Washington's population, cannot possibly catch their full treaty entitlement of fish unless they use nets. Thus, the state's conservation measure impermissably discriminated against Indians in violation of the treaty because an alternative method of protecting the fish was available: the state could have limited the number of fish that *non-Indians* could take so as to allow Indians to capture their full treaty share without endangering the species.[116]

As *Puyallup* demonstrates, Indians exercising federal treaty rights are not required to obey "neutral" state restrictions that have the effect of unnecessarily limiting their rights.[117] State officials who violate clearly established Indian hunting or fishing rights may be sued for damages to compensate for any injury their illegal actions cause,[118] and courts may also issue injunctions designed to halt future violations.[119]

2. The "In Common With" Exception

As just indicated, one exception to the rule that Indian hunting and fishing rights may not be regulated by the state is "conservation necessity." A second exception exists in certain states, including most states in the Northwest, as a result of particular treaty language.

The same sentence appears in virtually all the treaties with Northwest tribes: the tribes are guaranteed "the right of taking fish at all usual and accustomed grounds and stations . . . in common with all citizens of the Territory." The first clause in that sentence—the "grounds and stations" clause discussed earlier—guarantees the *tribes* that they may fish at all of their traditional sites, free from unnecessary state interference. This clause does not confer any powers on the state. However, the second clause in that sentence—the "in common with" clause—gives the *states* considerable power: the right to regulate the *amount* of fish that tribes can catch at these sites.

The treaties do not explain the meaning of the "in common with" clause. Decades after the signing of these treaties, when the supply of fish could no longer satisfy the demand of a vastly increased population of non-Indians, state and tribal officials attempted to agree on an interpretation, but they failed. State officials contended that the clause assured the tribes nothing more than an equal opportunity to catch fish, whereas the tribes (and the United States on their behalf) argued that it reserved to the Indians a set amount of the available catch. (In determining the "available" catch, one must subtract from the total fish population the number of "escapement" fish that must be allowed to avoid capture so as to spawn and propagate the species.) In *Washington v. Washington State Commercial Passenger Fishing Vessel Ass'n* (1979),[120] the Supreme Court interpreted the "in common with" clause to mean that Indians have a right to take a certain percentage of the available catch—up to 50 percent—and not just an opportunity to cast a fishing line along with the tens of thousands of non-Indians who now fish in the area. As a result, the state must prevent non-Indians from taking more than their share.[121]

The Supreme Court also held, though, that the "in common with" language not only gives Indians a right to a certain amount of fish, it also

gives non-Indians a right to the remainder. "Both sides have a right, secured by treaty, to take a fair share of the available fish. That, we think, is
what the parties to the treaties intended when they secured to the Indians
the right of taking fish in common with other citizens."[122] Moreover, the
Court held, the "in common with" clause *prohibits* tribes from taking their
full 50 percent share whenever a lesser amount would provide tribal members with "a moderate living." The Court explained:

It bears repeating, however, that the 50% figure imposes a maximum but not a
minimum allocation. . . . If, for example, a tribe should dwindle to just a few
members, or if it should find other sources of support that lead it to abandon its
fisheries, a 45% or 50% allocation of an entire run that passes through its cus-
tomary fishing grounds would be manifestly inappropriate because the livelihood
of the tribe under those circumstances could not reasonably require an allotment
of a large number of fish.[123]

Using the Court's "moderate living" standard, four situations can occur, and three have occurred already. The first possibility is that the state
must prevent *the tribe* from capturing its entire 50 percent share because
otherwise tribal income from selling the fish would exceed a moderate
living. There are no reported court cases indicating that this situation has
occurred, but as tribes improve their technological capability of catching
fish (such as by purchasing the large fishing vessels that non-Indian fishers
use to catch salmon in the ocean), this could happen.

In a recent decision, a federal court slightly modified the "moderate
living" standard in a unique case involving the treaty harvesting of shellfish. The court held that in an area where a private company had enhanced
certain tidelands, which had the effect of increasing the supply of shellfish
to a number greater than had existed at the time of the treaty signing, the
tribe was not entitled to take its 50 percent share even though the tribe
was relatively poor; rather, the tribe could take only 50 percent of the
amount of shellfish that had grown there naturally at the time the treaty
was signed. The court emphasized that this restriction applied only to enhanced beds of shellfish; at all other protected treaty sites, the tribe was
entitled to its full 50 percent share of the resource, even if the site is now
privately owned by non-Indians.[124]

The second possibility is that the state must prevent *non-Indians* from taking more than their 50 percent share. This situation occurs all the time.[125] The third possibility is that even when the tribe takes its 50 percent share, tribal members still cannot earn a moderate living. This is the situation in northern Wisconsin,[126] and likely other areas as well, where the available catch is insufficient to produce considerable income. Thus far, the federal courts have not permitted treaty tribes to take more than 50 percent of the resource even in that situation.[127]

The fourth possibility, which also has occurred, is that one group fails to take its full share of the wildlife. In that event, the other group is permitted to take more than its entitlement rather than waste the available catch.[128]

Not all treaties that guarantee off-reservation hunting and fishing rights contain an "in common with" clause. Tribes that are not restricted in that respect need not share the resource, and the state may only regulate the tribe's activities under the *Puyallup* "conservation necessity" standard.[129]

May the federal government regulate off-reservation Indian hunting and fishing?

Congress has the power to regulate every aspect of Indian hunting and fishing and may even abrogate Indian treaty rights to hunt and fish, provided that it pays just compensation to the tribe for the value of the loss.[130] Congress, though, has rarely limited tribal hunting and fishing rights. On the contrary, as stated earlier, Congress has passed several laws designed to protect the plants and animals important to Indian tribes, such as the Environmental Protection Act, the Magnuson Act, and the National Environmental Protection Act. In implementing these laws, federal agencies, consistent with their trust responsibilities to Indians, may curtail access to wildlife by non-Indians when necessary to protect tribal rights.[131] Federal officials also have been authorized by Congress to file suit on behalf of Indian tribes to protect their hunting and fishing rights, and quite a few of these lawsuits have been filed.[132]

To assist treaty tribes in exercising their off-reservation hunting and fishing rights, the Secretary of the Interior has enacted regulations under which identification cards will be issued by the Bureau of Indian Affairs (or by the tribe, if it decides to undertake this task) to tribal members eligible to exercise the tribe's treaty rights.[133] These cards serve as proof to tribal, state, and federal law enforcement officers that the authorized holder is entitled to exercise the fishing rights secured by the treaty identified on the card.

Notes

1. *U.S. v. Winans,* 198 U.S. 371, 381 (1905).

2. "Former Colorado AG Nominated for Interior," *Indian Country Today* (Jan. 10, 2000) at A1, A3.

3. 443 U.S. 658 (1979).

4. *Washington v. Washington State Commercial Passenger Fishing Vessel Ass'n,* 443 U.S. 658, 664–66 (1979) (citations omitted).

5. *Lac Du Flambeau Band of Lake Superior Chippewa Indians v. Stop Treaty Abuse–Wisconsin,* 843 F. Supp. 1284 (W.D. Wis. 1994), *aff'd,* 41 F.3d 1190 (7th Cir. 1994), *cert. denied,* 514 U.S. 1096 (1995).

6. *Johnson v. Alaska State Dept. of Fish and Game,* 836 P.2d 896 (Alas. 1991).

7. *See Passenger Fishing Vessel,* note 4 above.

8. "Tribal Gill Nets Damaged in Disputed Waters," *Indian Country Today* (Jan. 24, 2001) at B2.

9. *See Northwest Resource Information Center, Inc. v. Northwest Power Planning Council,* 35 F.3d 1371, 1377 n.8 (9th Cir. 1994), *cert. denied,* 516 U.S. 806 (1995).

10. "Pacific Salmon in Crisis," *Denver Rocky Mountain News* (July 18, 1994) at 27A.

11. "The Salmon People: Tribes in Crisis," *American Indian Report* (July 2000) at 13.

12. *Id.* at 16.

13. *See U.S. v. Aanerud,* 893 F.2d 956 (8th Cir.), *cert. denied,* 498 U.S. 822 (1990); *People v. LeBlanc,* 248 N.W.2d 199 (Mich. 1976); *State v. Tinno,* 497 P.2d 1386 (Idaho 1972).

14. *New Mexico v. Mescalero Apache Tribe,* 462 U.S. 324 (1983).

15. *U.S. v. Felter,* 752 F.2d 1505, 1509 (10th Cir. 1985).

16. *Winans,* note 1 above, 198 U.S. at 381; *Menominee Tribe v. U.S.,* 391 U.S. 404 (1968); *State v. Coffee,* 556 P.2d 1185, 1189 (Idaho 1976).

17. *U.S. v. Dion,* 476 U.S. 734, 745 n.8 (1986); *Parravano v. Babbitt,* 70 F.3d 539, 545 (9th Cir. 1995), *cert. denied,* 518 U.S. 1016 (1996). *But see Confederated Tribes of Chehalis Indian Reservation v. Washington,* 96 F.3d 334, 343 (9th Cir. 1996), *cert. denied,* 520 U.S. 1168 (1997) (holding that the executive order reservation at issue in that case did not confer hunting and fishing rights on the tribe).

18. *Alaska Pacific Fisheries v. U.S.,* 248 U.S. 78 (1918).

19. *Minnesota v. Mille Lacs Band of Chippewa Indians,* 526 U.S. 172, 202–3 (1999).

20. *See, e.g., Menominee Tribe,* note 16 above; *U.S. v. Felter,* note 15 above. *But see Oregon Dept. of Fish and Wildlife v. Klamath Indian Tribe,* 473 U.S. 753 (1985). For a full discussion of treaty interpretation, *see* ch. 4.

21. *Lac Courte Oreilles Band of Lake Superior Chippewa Indians v. Voight,* 700 F.2d 341 (7th Cir.), *cert. denied,* 464 U.S. 805 (1983). *See also Minnesota v. Mille Lacs Band of Chippewa Indians,* note 19 above.

22. *Minnesota v. Mille Lacs Band of Chippewa Indians,* note 19 above. In so holding, the Supreme Court overruled a line of cases, including *Ward v. Race Horse,* 163 U.S. 504 (1996), which suggested that Indian treaty rights were impliedly abrogated when a state was admitted into the Union.

23. *Minnesota v. Mille Lacs Band of Chippewa Indians,* note 19 above, 526 U.S. at 202–3; *Dion,* note 17 above, 476 U.S. at 740; *U.S. v. Bresette,* 761 F. Supp. 658, 662–63 (D. Minn. 1991). *See also U.S. v. Peterson,* 121 F.Supp.2d 1309 (D. Mont. 2000) (holding that when Congress created Glacier National Park and expressly prohibited all hunting in the park, this abrogated a tribe's treaty right to hunt on that off-reservation land).

24. 391 U.S. 404 (1968). However, statutory language which removes "all right, title and interest" of a tribe in certain land has been held to extinguish the tribe's hunting and fishing rights on the land. *Red Lake Band of Chippewa Indians v. Minnesota,* 614 F.2d 1161 (8th Cir.), *cert. denied,* 449 U.S. 905 (1980). *See also Oregon Dept.,* note 20 above.

25. The subject of termination is discussed in ch. 1 and in ch. 5, sec. B.

26. *See* discussion in ch. 1, note 69, and accompanying text.

27. *Tee-Hit-Ton Indians v. U.S.,* 348 U.S. 272, 279 (1955).

28. *Oregon Dept.,* note 20 above; *Western Shoshone National Council v. Molini,* 951 F.2d 200, 203 (9th Cir. 1991), *cert. denied,* 506 U.S. 822 (1992).

29. *U.S. v. Santa Fe Pacific R.R. Co.,* 314 U.S. 339, 347 (1941); *Confederated Tribes of Chehalis,* note 17 above, 96 F.3d at 341.

30. *Confederated Tribes of Chehalis,* note 17 above, 96 F.3d at 341; *Molini,* note 28 above, 951 F.2d at 202–3; *Whiterock v. Nebraska,* 918 P.2d 1309 (Nev. 1996). In *Commonwealth v. Maxim,* 708 N.E.2d 636 (Mass. 1999), the court recognized the continued existence of aboriginal rights to take shellfish for tribal subsistence needs.

31. *Montana v. U.S.,* 450 U.S. 544, 552 (1981).

32. *See U.S. v. Aam,* 887 F.2d 190 (9th Cir. 1989), and cases cited therein.

33. *Menominee Tribe,* note 16 above, 391 U.S. at 413; *Hynes v. Grimes Packing Co.,* 337 U.S. 86, 105 (1949). This subject is discussed in ch. 4, note 24, and accompanying text.

34. *See, e.g., Tee-Hit-Ton,* note 27 above; *Inupiat Community of the Arctic Slope v. U.S.,* 680 F.2d 122 (Ct. Cl.), *cert. denied,* 459 U.S. 969 (1982). This subject is discussed in ch. 2, sec. D.

35. *See generally U.S. v. Washington,* 157 F.3d 630, 651 (9th Cir.), *cert. denied,* 526 U.S. 1060 (1999); *Mille Lacs Band of Chippewa Indians v. Minnesota,* 124 F.3d 904, 934 (8th Cir. 1997), *aff'd,* 527 U.S. 122 (1999); *U.S. v. Michigan,* 653 F.2d 277 (6th Cir. 1981).

36. *Puyallup Tribe, Inc. v. Dept. of Game,* 433 U.S. 165 (1977) (suit by tribe); *Sohappy v. Smith,* 302 F. Supp. 899 (D. Or. 1969) (suit by tribal members).

37. *U.S. v. Washington,* 384 F. Supp. 312 (W.D. Wash. 1974), *aff'd,* 520 F.2d 676 (9th Cir. 1975), *cert. denied,* 423 U.S. 1086 (1976).

38. *Whitefoot v. U.S.,* 293 F.2d 658 (Ct. Cl. 1961), *cert. denied,* 369 U.S. 818 (1962).

39. *U.S. v. Washington,* note 37 above, 520 F.2d at 689–90. *See also U.S. v. Cutler,* 37 F. Supp. 724 (D. Idaho 1941).

40. *See Grand Traverse Band of Ottawa and Chippewa Indians v. Director, Michigan Dept. of Nat. Res.,* 141 F.3d 635, 639 (6th Cir.), *cert. denied,* 525 U.S. 1040 (1998); *Lac Courte Oreilles Band of Lake Superior Chippewa Indians v. Wisconsin,* 653 F. Supp. 1420, 1430 (W.D. Wis. 1987).

41. *Grand Traverse Band of Ohawa and Chippewa Indians v. Director, Michigan Dept. of Nat. Res.,* 971 F. Supp 282, 289 (W.D. Mich. 1995), *aff'd,* 141 F.3d 635 (6th Cir.), *cert. denied,* 525 U.S. 1040 (1998); *U.S. v. Washington,* note 37 above, 384 F. Supp. at 402. *See also Peterson v. Christensen,* 455 F. Supp. 1095, 1099 (E.D. Wis. 1978). *But see U.S. v. Gotchnik,* 222 F.3d 506 (8th Cir. 2000) (holding that a treaty right to fish does not permit tribal members to use motorized boats to reach a protected site, in an area where motorized boats are prohibited by federal law).

42. *U.S. v. Finch,* 548 F.2d 822, 832 (9th Cir. 1976), *vacated on other grounds,* 433 U.S. 676 (1977). *See also U.S. v. Washington,* note 35 above, 157 F.3d at 643; *Aanerud,* note 13 above; *Lac Courte Oreilles Band of Lake Superior Chippewa Indians v. Wisconsin,* note 40 above, 653 F. Supp. at 1426–28.

43. *U.S. v. Washington,* 759 F.2d 1353, 1358–60 (9th Cir. 1985) *(en banc), cert. denied,* 474 U.S. 994 (1985); *Mattz v. Superior Court,* 46 Cal.3d 355 (Cal. 1988), *cert. denied,* 489 U.S. 1078 (1989). *See also U.S. Washington,* note 35 above, 157 F.3d at 651–52 (same rule applies to replenishment shellfish).

44. *U.S. v. Washington,* note 35 above, 157 F.3d at 651–52; *Kittitas Reclamation District v. Sunnyside Valley Irrigation District,* 763 F.2d 1032 (9th Cir.) *cert. denied,* 474 U.S. 1032 (1985).

45. *See New Mexico v. Mescalero Apache Tribe,* note 14 above.

46. *Id.,* 462 U.S. at 335. *See also Puyallup Tribe, Inc. v. Dept. of Game,* note 36 above; *U.S. v. Williams,* 898 F.2d 727 (9th Cir. 1990).

47. *See New Mexico v. Mescalero Apache Tribe,* note 14 above. *See also Montana,* note 31 above, 450 U.S. at 558; *Quechan Tribe v. Rowe,* 531 F.2d 408 (9th Cir. 1976). Although tribes lack the authority to prosecute nonmembers, *see Oliphant v. Suquamish Indian Tribe,* 435 U.S. 191 (1978), in certain circumstances they may expel them from the reservation. *See Merrion v. Jicarilla Apache Tribe,* 455 U.S. 130 (1982).

48. For instance, Congress has prohibited all persons, including Indians, from killing bald and golden eagles, although Indians can obtain an exemption in certain circumstances. *See* notes 79–81 below and accompanying text.

49. *See Nelson v. Yurok Tribe,* 27 Indian L. Rep. 6234 (Northw. Regional Tr. Ct. App. 1999); *Confederated Tribes of the Umatilla Indian Reservation v. Bronson,* 19 Indian L. Rep. 6075 (Umat. Tr ct. 1992); *Lower Elwha Klallam Indian Tribe v. Bolstrom,* 19 Indian L. Rep. 6026 (L. Elwha Ct. App. 1997); *Muckleshoot Indian Tribe v. Moses,* 16 Indian L. Rep. 6073 (Muckleshoot Tr. Ct. App. 1989).

50. 18 U.S.C. Sec. 1165. *See Quechan Tribe,* note 47 above.

51. 450 U.S. 544 (1981).

52. *See Lower Brule Tribe v. South Dakota,* 104 F.3d 1017 (8th Cir.), *cert. denied,* 522 U.S. 816 (1997); *South Dakota v. Bourland,* 39 F.3d 868 (8th Cir. 1994).

53. *See Montana,* note 31 above. *See also South Dakota v. Bourland,* 508 U.S. 679

(1993) (holding that the *Montana* rule of limited tribal jurisdiction applies to trust land located within a reservation that has been opened by Congress for public use).

54. 18 U.S.C. Sec. 1162(b). *See Quechan Tribe,* note 47 above.

55. *See* cases cited in notes 1, 14, and 16 above. *See also Tulee v. Washington,* 315 U.S. 681 (1942); *Confederated Salish and Kootenai Tribes v. State of Montana,* 750 F. Supp. 446 (D. Mont. 1990).

56. *New Mexico v. Mescalero Apache Tribe,* note 14 above.

57. 391 U.S. 392 (1968).

58. *Menominee Tribe,* note 16 above.

59. *See Sohappy, Sr. v. Hodel,* 911 F.2d 1312 (9th Cir. 1990); *Northern Arapaho Tribe v. Hodel,* 808 F.2d 741, 748 (10th Cir. 1987); *Confederated Tribes of the Umatilla Indian Reservation v. Alexander,* 440 F. Supp. 553 (D. Ore. 1977).

60. 18 U.S.C. Sec. 1165. *See U.S. v. Von Murdock,* 132 F.3d 534 (10th Cir. 1997), *cert. denied,* 525 U.S. 810 (1998). *But see Cassidy v. U.S.,* 875 F. Supp. 1438 (E.D. Wash. 1994) (holding that Sec. 1165 may not be applied unless the tribe has exclusive jurisdiction to hunt and fish at the site). One court has held that Sec. 1165 may not be applied to tribal members at all. *See U.S. v. Jackson,* 600 F.2d 1283 (9th Cir. 1979).

61. 16 U.S.C. Sec. 3371 *et seq.* This law is known as the Lacey Act. *See U.S. v. Eberhardt,* 789 F.2d 1354 (9th Cir. 1986).

62. *Oliphant,* note 47 above.

63. *U.S. v. Sandia,* 188 F.3d 1215 (10th Cir. 1999); *U.S. v. Sohappy,* 770 F.2d 816, 819 (9th Cir. 1985), *cert. denied,* 477 U.S. 906 (1986).

64. *See Von Murdock,* note 60 above; *U.S. v. Big Eagle,* 881 F.2d 539 (8th Cir. 1989), *cert. denied,* 493 U.S. 1084 (1990).

65. 16 U.S.C. Secs. 1531 *et seq.*

66. *See Washington v. Daley,* 173 F.3d 1158 (9th Cir. 1999). The ESA has also been held to authorize federal officials to halt the taking of endangered species by Indians. *See U.S. v. Billie,* 667 F. Supp. 1485 (S.D. Fla. 1985). *See also Metcalf v. Daley,* 214 F.3d 1135 (9th Cir. 2000) (holding that federal officials must consider whether the taking of gray whales by the Makah Tribe violates the ESA). For a discussion of the ESA and its impact on Indian tribes, *see* J. M. Regis-Civetta, "The Effect of the Endangered Species Act on Tribal Economic Development in Indian Country," *50 Wash. U. J. and Contemp. Law* 303 (1996).

67. 16 U.S.C. Secs. 1801 *et seq.*

68. *Id.* Sec. 1854(b). *See also U.S. v. Sohappy,* note 63 above.

69. *See Washington v. Daley,* note 66 above, 173 F.3d at 1168; *Parravano,* note 17 above, 70 F.3d at 546. *See also Northwest Sea Farms, Inc. v. U.S. Army Corps of Engineers,* 931 F. Supp. 1515 (W.D. Wash. 1996) (finding a similar duty under the Rivers and Harbors Act, 33 U.S.C. Sec. 403); *Eberhardt,* note 61 above (finding a general trust duty to protect Indian fisheries).

70. Fish and Wildlife Coordination Act of 1976, 16 U.S.C. Secs. 661 *et seq.*

71. Northwest Power Act, 16 U.S.C. Secs. 839 *et seq.*

72. *Northwest Resource Information,* note 9 above, 35 F.3d at 1388.

73. 42 U.S.C. Secs. 4321–35.

74. 42 U.S.C. Sec. 4322(2)(c).

75. 42 U.S.C. Sec. 4332(2)(e). *See Metcalf v. Daley,* note 66 above; *Sangre De Cristo Development Co. v. U.S.,* 932 F.2d 891 (10th Cir. 1991), *cert. denied,* 503 U.S. 1004 (1992); *Muckleshoot Indian Tribe v. U.S. Forest Service,* 177 F.3d 800 (9th Cir. 1999).

76. *See Save the Yaak Committee v. Block,* 840 F.2d 714 (9th Cir. 1988).

77. 16 U.S. Sec. 668(a).

78. 476 U.S. 734 (1986).

79. 16 U.S.C. Sec 668(a).

80. *See* H.R. Rep. No. 1450, 87th Cong., 2d Sess. (1962); S. Rep. No. 1986, 87th Cong., 2d Sess. at 3–7 (1962); *Dion,* note 17 above, 476 U.S. at 740–44.

81. 50 C.F.R. Sec. 22.22. The Secretary of Interior has ruled that only members of federally recognized Indian tribes may qualify for a permit, and the courts have thus far upheld that limitation, even though no such limit is expressly mandated by the Eagle Protection Act. *See Gibson v. Babbitt,* 223 F.3d 1256 (11th Cir. 2000). *See also U.S. v. Hugs,* 109 F.3d 1375 (9th Cir. 1997) (generally upholding the Secretary's permit system); *U.S. v. Gonzales,* 957 F. Supp. 1225 (D.N.M. 1997) (holding that an Indian need not explain the precise religious purpose for which the eagle parts will be used in order to qualify for a permit).

82. *See Menominee Tribe,* note 16 above; *Kimball v. Callahan,* 590 F.2d 768 (9th Cir.), *cert. denied,* 444 U.S. 826 (1979); *Lac Courte Oreilles Band of Lake Superior Chippewa Indians v. Voight,* note 21 above, 700 F.2d at 364.

83. *See Confederated Tribes of Chehalis,* note 17 above; *White Earth Band Chippewa v. Alexander,* 683 F.2d 1129, 1135 (8th Cir. 1982); *State v. Butcher,* 563 N.W.2d 776, 783 (Minn. App. 1997).

84. *See Antoine v. Washington,* 420 U.S. 194 (1975) ("open and unclaimed land"); *Washington v. Buchanan,* 978 P.2d 1070 (Wash. 1999) (same); *Tinno,* note 13 above ("the unoccupied lands of the United States"). *See also Holcomb v. Confederated Tribes of the Umatilla Indian Reservation,* 382 F.2d 1013 (9th Cir. 1967).

85. *Antoine, Buchanan, Holcomb,* note 84 above. *See also State v. Stasso,* 563 P.2d 562 (Mont. 1977); *State v. Arthur,* 261 P.2d 135 (Idaho 1953). In *State v. Cutler,* 708 P.2d 853 (Idaho 1985), the court held that a treaty right to hunt on the unclaimed lands "of the United States" did not entitle tribal members to hunt on unclaimed lands now owned by the state.

86. *See Lac Courte Oreilles Band of Lake Superior Chippewa Indians v. Voight,* note 21 above, 700 F.2d at 362–35.

87. *U.S. v. Washington,* note 35 above, 157 F.3d at 646–47.

88. *See Winans,* note 1 above; *U.S. v. Washington,* note 35 above; *Lac Courte Oreilles Band of Lake Superior Chippewa Indians v. Voight,* note 21 above.

89. 384 F. Supp. 312 (W.D. Wash. 1974), *aff'd*, 520 F.2d 676 (9th Cir. 1975), *cert. denied,* 423 U.S. 1086 (1976).

90. *Id.,* 384 F. Supp. at 332. *See also U.S. v. Washington,* 730 F.2d 1314, 1318 (9th Cir. 1984); *Midwater Trawlers Corp. v. U.S. Dept. of Commerce,* 139 F. Supp.2d 1136, 1142–43 (W.D. Wash. 2000).

91. These difficulties are illustrated in *State v. Petit,* 558 P.2d 796 (Wash. 1977), and *U.S. v. Lummi Indian Tribe,* 841 F.2d 317 (9th Cir. 1988). The location of these protected

sites is still being litigated. *See U.S. v. Muckleshoot Indian Tribe*, 235 F.3d 429 (9th Cir. 2000), *cert. denied*, 122 S.Ct. 344 (2001).

92. *See U.S. v. Washington*, note 37 above.

93. *Winans*, note 1 above.

94. *Winans*, note 1 above; *Seufort Bros. v. U.S.*, 249 U.S. 194 (1919); *U.S. v. Washington*, note 35 above, 157 F.3d at 654.

95. *Passenger Fishing Vessel*, note 4 above, 443 U.S. at 666–67.

96. *See id.* at 666.

97. *See* cases cited in notes 4, 35, and 37 above. *See also Confederated Tribes and Bands of the Yakama Indian Nation v. Baldridge*, 898 F. Supp. 1477 (W.D. Wash. 1995), *aff'd without opinion*, 91 F.3d 1366 (9th Cir. 1996).

98. 443 U.S. 685 (1979).

99. *Id.* at 696.

100. *Settler v. Lameer*, 507 F.2d 231 (9th Cir. 1974); *U.S. v. Washington*, note 37 above, 384 F. Supp. at 340–42.

101. *Oliphant*, note 47 above.

102. *See Passenger Fishing Vessel*, note 4 above, and accompanying text.

103. *Geer v. Connecticut*, 161 U.S. 519 (1896).

104. U.S. Const., art. VI, sec. 2. *See Missouri v. Holland*, 252 U.S. 416 (1920); *Douglas v. Seacoast Products, Inc.*, 431 U.S. 265 (1977).

105. *Minnesota v. Mille Lacs Band of Chippewa Indians*, note 19 above, 526 U.S. at 204; *Mescalero Apache Tribe v. Jones*, 411 U.S. 145, 148 (1973); *Tulee*, note 55 above.

106. *Puyallup Tribe v. Dept. of Game*, 391 U.S. 392, 398 (1968). *See also Minnesota v. Mille Lacs Band of Chippewa Indians*, note 19 above, 526 U.S. at 205.

107. *See* Ralph Johnson, "The State Versus Indian Off-Reservation Fishing: United States Supreme Court Error," 47 *Wash. L. Rev.* 207 (1972); *Note* "State Regulation of Lake Superior Chippewa Off-Reservation Usufructuary Rights," 11 *Hamline L. Rev.* 153 (1988).

108. *Lac Courte Oreilles Band of Lake Superior Chippewa Indians v. Voight*, note 21 above, 740 F. Supp. at 1421.

109. *Minnesota v. Mille Lacs Band of Chippewa Indians*, note 19 above, 527 U.S. at 205.

110. *Puyallup Tribe, Inc. v. Dept. of Game*, note 36 above. *See also U.S. v. Michigan*, note 35 above; *U.S. v. Oregon*, 769 F.2d 1410, 1416 (9th Cir. 1985).

111. *See* cases cited in note 106 above. *See also U.S. v. Washington*, note 37 above, 384 F. Supp. at 342, 402–4; *U.S. v. Washington*, 143 F. Supp.2d 218 (W.D. Wash. 2001).

112. *U.S. v. Oregon*, 657 F.2d 1009 (9th Cir. 1981).

113. *Passenger Fishing Vessel*, note 4 above, 443 U.S. at 679; *Washington State Charterboat Ass'n v. Baldridge*, 702 F.2d 820 (9th Cir. 1983), *cert. denied*, 464 U.S. 1053 (1984).

114. *Puyallup Tribe, Inc. v. Dept. of Game*, note 36 above; *Puyallup Tribe v. Dept. of Game*, note 106 above; *Dept. of Game of Washington v. Puyallup Tribe*, 414 U.S. 44 (1973); *Sohappy v. Smith*, note 36 above, 302 F. Supp. at 907–8. *But see U.S. v. Oregon*, 718 F.2d 299 (9th Cir. 1983).

115. *Puyallup Tribe, Inc. v. Dept. of Game*, note 36 above.

116. *Dept. of Game v. Puyallup Tribe,* note 114 above, 414 U.S. at 48.

117. *Puyallup Tribe, Inc. v. Dept. of Game,* note 36; *Dept. of Game v. Puyallup Tribe,* note 114 above; *Tulee,* note 55 above. *See also Shoshone-Bannock Tribes v. Fish and Game Commission of Idaho,* 42 F.3d 1278, 1283 (9th Cir. 1994) (holding that, in order to regulate a tribe's treaty rights, "the state must demonstrate that the tribe's own conservation measures are insufficient to meet the needs of conservation.")

118. *Shoshone-Bannock,* note 117 above, 42 F.3d at 1295–96.

119. *See* cases cited in notes 4–7 and accompanying text.

120. 443 U.S. 685 (1979).

121. *See* cases cited in notes 4 and 37 above.

122. *Passenger Fishing Vessel,* note 4 above, 443 U.S. at 684–85. *See also Puyallup Tribe, Inc. v. Dept. of Game,* note 36 above, and cases cited in note 111 above.

123. *Passenger Fishing Vessel,* note 4 above, 443 U.S. at 686–87. *See also Lac Courte Oreilles Band of Lake Superior Chippewa Indians v. Wisconsin,* note 40 above, 653 F. Supp. at 1434, 1435.

124. *U.S. v. Washington,* note 35 above, 157 F.3d at 640–53.

125. *See* note 98 above and accompanying text. *See also U.S. v. Washington,* note 111 above.

126. *Lac Courte Oreilles Band of Lake Superior Chippewa Indians v. Wisconsin,* 686 F. Supp. 226 (W.D. Wis. 1988).

127. *See Lac Courte Oreilles Band of Lake Superior Chippewa Indians v. Wisconsin,* 740 F. Supp. 1400 (W.D. Wis. 1990).

128. *U.S. v. Washington,* 761 F.2d 1404 (9th Cir. 1985).

129. *See Mille Lacs Band of Chippewa Indians v. Minnesota,* note 35 above, 124 F.3d at 929–32; *Lac Courte Oreilles Band of Lake Superior Chippewa Indians v. Wisconsin,* note 40 above, 653 F. Supp. at 1434.

130. *See* notes 33 and 34 above and accompanying text.

131. *See, e.g., Washington v. Daley,* note 66 above, and *Parravano v. Babbitt,* note 17 above.

132. *See, e.g., U.S. v. Washington,* note 35 above; *U.S. v. Michigan,* note 35 above.

133. C.F.R. Part 249. *See Sault Ste. Marie Tribe of Chippewa Indians v. Minneapolis Area Director, BIA,* IBIA 95-150-A (24 Indian L. Rep. 1997).

XII

Indian Water Rights

The western portion of the United States is arid or semiarid, and the supply of water is far from sufficient to meet demand. With populations soaring and commerce increasing, the need for water is becoming ever more critical. The most pressing resource concern in virtually every western state is that of obtaining more water. Water in the West is synonymous with progress, and municipal governments, agriculture, business, mineral development, and wildlife management compete for this scarce resource.[1]

The Supreme Court has recognized—in what has become known as the *Winters* doctrine—that Indian tribes have rights to a vast amount of water. Given the scarcity of water, tribes have become very concerned about preserving these rights and have been (or currently are) involved in lawsuits or negotiations in most western states seeking to defend them.

What is the *Winters* doctrine?

The most important case in Indian water law is *Winters v. United States*,[2] decided by the Supreme Court in 1908. The issue in *Winters* was whether a landowner could dam a stream on his property in order to irrigate his own land, thereby preventing an adequate amount of water from reaching a downstream Indian reservation. The reservation had been created by Congress eight years before the landowner bought his land, but the statute that created the reservation made no mention of water rights. The landowner therefore argued that the tribe was not entitled to any particular amount of water, and he was free to divert the stream to his own use.

The Supreme Court ruled in favor of the tribe. The reservation was arid and of little value without irrigation. Congress must have intended, the Court said, to reserve to the Indians enough water to irrigate their lands and make the reservation viable and productive. The Court ruled that Congress has the power to reserve water for federal lands, and by implication it exercises this power every time it creates an Indian reservation. Therefore, a sufficient amount of water had to reach the reservation to enable the tribe to fulfill the purpose for which it was created. The Court ordered the landowner to dismantle the dam.

The *Winters* doctrine, also known as the *implied reservation* or *reserved water rights* doctrine, has been consistently upheld by the Supreme Court. In *Arizona v. California* (1963),[3] the Supreme Court had to decide whether an Indian tribe was entitled to enough water to irrigate its entire reservation, even though a large part of the reservation had never been irrigated. The executive order that created the reservation was silent on the subject of water rights. Citing *Winters,* the Court said that whenever an Indian reservation is created by the federal government, there is an "implied reservation of water rights . . . necessary to make the reservation livable."[4] The tribe was entitled to an amount of water, the Court held, that would "satisfy the future as well as the present needs of the Indian reservation," that is, the amount necessary "to irrigate all the practicably irrigable acreage on the reservation."[5]

The *Winters* doctrine applies to all federal land areas, not just Indian reservations. In *Cappaert v. United States* (1976),[6] discussed later in this chapter, the Supreme Court applied the *Winters* doctrine to Death Valley National Monument and held that whenever the federal government sets aside land for a particular purpose, sufficient water rights are reserved by implication to accomplish that purpose.

The four basic principles of the *Winters* doctrine are as follows: (1) Congress has the right to reserve water for federal lands, including Indian reservations;[7] (2) When Congress sets aside land for a specific purpose, it reserves by implication a sufficient quantity of water to fulfill that purpose;[8] (3) Indian reservations are created by Congress with the intention of making them habitable and productive, and whatever water is necessary to meet this goal is reserved by implication for the tribe's use;[9] (4) All Indian reservations are entitled to *Winters* rights, whether the reservation was created by a federal statute or treaty or by the President through an executive order.[10] Thus, even if the statute, treaty, or executive order creating the reservation says nothing about water rights, the tribe is presumed to have a right to enough water to satisfy the reservation's purpose, that is, enough water to meet the tribe's present and future needs.[11]

What gives Congress the power to reserve water for Indians?

Article I, section 8, clause 3 of the Constitution (the Commerce Clause) gives Congress the power to regulate commerce with the Indian tribes. This gives Congress complete authority over Indian affairs,[12] including the power to grant water rights to Indians.[13]

What is the doctrine of prior appropriation and how does it differ from the Winters doctrine?

As non-Indian settlers moved westward during the nineteenth century, they quickly developed rules to govern the allocation of water. Without these rules they would have engaged in endless warfare over this scarce resource. The rules they developed have been codified into law in every western state and are known as the *doctrine of prior appropriation*. This doctrine has four basic principles. First, the earliest appropriator of water (the person with the earliest "priority date") has a continuing right to use the same amount of water from the same source as was initially diverted from that source whenever the water is available, and subsequent appropriators *(junior interests)* may only use whatever remains. Each junior interest—based on its priority date—may then in turn take its full water entitlement. This is the "first in time, first in right" principle. Second, these water rights are property rights that exist separately from any rights in the land; thus, they do not "run" with the land but can be retained, sold, or leased independently from any sale or lease of the land. Third, in times of scarcity the person with the earliest priority date may appropriate his or her entire water entitlement even if no water remains for junior interests. Finally, appropriative rights are forfeited if unused for a significant period of time.[14]

To illustrate these principles, assume that Mr. A and Ms. B live along the same stream, and Ms. C lives behind Mr. A. In 1860, Mr. A begins diverting five hundred acre-feet of water a year from the stream, and he registers his claim under applicable state law. The next year, Ms. B does the same thing. By making the first diversion, Mr. A has a "priority date" superior to that of Ms. B. In times of drought, he may use his entire entitlement even if nothing remains for Ms. B. Ten years later, if Mr. A sells his water rights to Ms. C, she acquires Mr. A's priority date (even if her property does not touch the stream), superior to Ms. B's rights. Ms. C may later sell those water rights to anyone she chooses unless she has forfeited them due to nonuse.

Indian water rights (*Winters* rights) are created and governed by federal law, while appropriative rights are created and governed by state law.[15] *Winters* rights differ from rights under the doctrine of prior appropriation in two significant respects. First, Indian water rights are *reserved*. Therefore, (1) a tribe cannot lose its *Winters* rights through nonuse, and (2) the amount of water a tribe is entitled to use is not determined by and limited to the tribe's initial use. On the contrary, a tribe with *Winters* rights is entitled to take all the water it needs to fulfill the purpose for which its reservation was created, provided that at the time the reservation was created this amount of water had not been appropriated by a landowner with a superior priority date.[16] Most Indian reservations in the West were created before non-Indians acquired much or any land in the region. As a result, Indian water rights usually have the earliest priority date, and thus they are *very* valuable.

The priority of Indian water rights is never later than the date on which the reservation was created, even if many years pass before the tribe begins using this water, and even if the tribe has yet to use all of its entitlement.[17] In certain situations, a tribe's priority date is earlier than when the reservation was created. For example, if a tribe has always caught fish from a particular lake, and a treaty recognizes the tribe's continuing right to do so, then the priority date for this use of water is "time immemorial."[18] In these situations, the tribe obviously has the senior water interest. When water is reserved for a use that did not exist prior to the creation of the reservation, the priority date is the date the reservation was created. On some reservations, then, a tribe has two priority dates, one for a new use of water (the date the reservation was created) and one for a historical use (time immemorial).[19]

Indians enjoy the best of both worlds when it comes to water rights. The appropriation doctrine protects Indians even though they are not bound by its limitations. It protects them by making sure junior interests take none of the water Indians are entitled to use under the *Winters* doctrine. Yet Indians are exempt from the rule that current (and future) water use is limited to initial water use and that water rights can be forfeited by nonuse. By virtue of the *Winters* reserved rights doctrine, Indians may use whatever water is necessary to accomplish the reservation's purpose and may increase their usage if their need for water increases at a later date.

An Indian tribe, consistent with the doctrine of prior appropriation, has no obligation to share its *Winters* rights with any junior interest.[20] However, if the tribe and another water user have the same priority date (a situation that can occur, as explained below, when a non-Indian buys reservation land) and there is an insufficient water supply, the water must then be shared equally between them.[21]

Which water laws govern the use of water in the eastern states?

Water use in the eastern states is governed by a different set of rules, known as the *riparian* doctrine. This doctrine is more egalitarian than the appropriation doctrine, reflecting the fact that water is usually plentiful in the East. Under the riparian doctrine, water rights run with the land (as opposed to being separate from it, as under the appropriation doctrine), and prior use does not create a vested right to continued use. In time of scarcity, the available water supply is distributed proportionally among all users. In states governed by the riparian doctrine, Indian reservations presumably have the same *Winters* rights as they do in the West, but this issue has never been litigated because eastern reservations usually have an adequate water supply.

May a tribe exercising its Winters rights use subsurface as well as surface water?

Underground and surface water in a region is often hydrologically interrelated. Thus, for example, extracting water from an underground well can cause the water level in a nearby lake to drop. That was the situation, in fact, in the *Cappaert* case cited earlier. In *Cappaert,* the Supreme Court ordered junior interests one hundred miles from a lake located on a national monument to curtail their use of well water after receiving proof that the lake and the wells were hydrologically interrelated, such that taking water from the wells depleted the water in the lake to dangerously low levels.[22] Given the interrelationship between surface and underground water, a tribe ought to be able to use either one in satisfying its *Winters* rights.[23]

How much water is an Indian reservation entitled to use?

The short answer to this question is that a tribe is entitled to use as much water as is necessary to fulfill the purpose of the reservation once senior claims, if any, have taken their entitlement. But in order to actually quantify the tribe's entitlement in terms of gallons or acre-feet of water, one must engage in two complicated inquiries: (1) what is the purpose of the reservation, and (2) precisely what quantity of water is needed to fulfill that purpose?

1. *Purpose:* One purpose for which all Indian reservations were created is to serve as a permanent and economically viable home for the Indians who live there. Thus, every reservation is entitled to enough water to at least satisfy its subsistence needs and, as the Supreme Court held in *Arizona v. California,* "to make the reservation livable."[24]

Creating a viable home is the ultimate purpose of every Indian reservation. However, many reservations were created with other specific purposes in mind. Some tribes were expected to engage in fishing, hunting, farming, ranching, or some other means of attaining a livelihood on their reservation. One court has stated that in order to determine congressional intent regarding any particular reservation, at least three factors must be considered: the history of the tribe for which the reservation was created (including the tribe's historical use of water); the stated and implied intentions of those who created the reservation; and the tribe's need to maintain itself under changed circumstances.[25] In that case, *Colville Confederated Tribes v. Walton,*[26] a confederation of six Indian tribes called the Colvilles filed suit against a non-Indian named Walton who owned land on their reservation. The Colvilles had two traditional sources of food: crops and fish caught from the Columbia River. After the Columbia River was dammed by the federal government, the Colvilles constructed a lake on their reservation, supplied it with trout, and began relying on the trout for some of their food. The Colvilles claimed Walton was using so much water to irrigate his land that the tribes lacked enough water to irrigate their crops, and also that Walton's use of water was causing the water level of their lake to drop, endangering their fish supply.

Using the three factors listed above, the court ruled in favor of the Colvilles and restricted Walton's use of water. The reservation was created, as all reservations presumptively are, in order to give the Colvilles a viable home. Accordingly, when Congress created the Colville reservation, it reserved by implication to the Colvilles enough water to continue their traditional fishing and agricultural activities. Due to changed circumstances, the Colvilles now needed enough water to maintain their lake. Walton's claim to water was not senior in time to the tribe's claim. Therefore, the court held, Walton was not permitted to interfere with the tribe's ability to irrigate its lands and maintain its fishery.

Other courts have reached similar conclusions in analogous situations. For example, courts presume that when Congress creates a reservation for a tribe that traditionally depended on hunting and fishing for food, Congress intended to reserve to the tribe enough water to keep its forests, streams, and lakes capable of supporting the game and fish it needs to prosper.[27] Indians who traditionally were agrarian or were intended by Congress to become agrarian are entitled to enough water to irrigate all tribal lands reasonably capable of producing crops.[28]

But what if the purpose of a reservation should change: can Indian water usage change with it? The Supreme Court has yet to decide this question, but the answer should be "yes." After all, the purpose of every Indian reservation, as explained earlier, is to provide the tribe with a permanent home and a livable environment. People's needs change over time. Two hundred years ago, most people in the United States worked on farms, whereas today less than 5 percent do. That change in lifestyle also produced a change in water use.

Similarly, if reservations are to serve as permanent homes, then Indians must be allowed to shift their water use as their needs change and as technology develops. Water that Congress might have intended for agricultural use a century ago should be available for industrial development today.[29] As the court stated in *Walton*, "[P]ermitting Indians to determine how to use reserved water is consistent with the general purpose for the creation of an Indian reservation—providing a homeland for the survival and growth of the Indians and their way of life."[30] Similarly, a tribe may use technological advances that were not foreseen at the time the reservation was created, such as electric pumps to irrigate their lands, provided that the tribe uses no more water than its legal entitlement.[31] In short, in determining the purpose of an Indian reservation, one must always factor in the federal goal of Indian self-sufficiency. Thus, tribes exercising their *Winters* rights should be permitted to use water for any lawful purpose, even if that specific use was not originally contemplated by Congress.[32]

2. *Quantity:* Under the *Winters* doctrine, Indian tribes are reserved a sufficient quantity of water to fulfill the purpose of the reservation. But as the Montana Supreme Court recently noted, "reserved water rights are difficult to quantify."[33] One must first determine the congressional purpose of the reservation, which could be to develop agriculture, to promote industry, to preserve hunting and fishing habitats, or even all of those purposes. One must then determine how much water is needed to accomplish those goals and from what sources the tribe can acquire that water.

The Supreme Court has held that an agrarian tribe is entitled to enough water to irrigate all the "practicably irrigable acreage" (PIA) on the reservation.[34] PIA has two components: the land must be of sufficient quality to sustain a crop, and the cost of supplying water to that crop must not be unreasonable. (In other words, a tribe normally would not be allowed to irrigate a desert.) Thus, determining the amount of water agrarian tribes are entitled to use involves consideration of climate, soil types, topography, transportation of water, evaporation during transportation, and marketability of crops.[35] Likewise, quantifying the water rights of tribes dependent on hunting requires a careful examination of weather and seasonal fluctuations, availability of forage, natural predators of available game, and changes in surrounding land usage that might affect the availability of game, especially migrating game.[36] Scientific and technical evidence is always necessary to determine the exact amount of water a tribe needs to satisfy its various goals.

Whether there is an economic "cap" on the amount of water an Indian tribe may receive has yet to be determined by the courts. In the 1976 *Cappaert* case, the Supreme Court stated that the *Winters* doctrine "reserves only that amount of water necessary to fulfill the purpose of the reservation, no more."[37] Moreover, in an Indian fishing rights case (discussed in chapter 11), the Supreme Court held that "Indian treaty rights to a natural resource . . . secures so much as, but not more than, is necessary to provide the Indians with a livelihood—that is to say, a moderate living."[38] Assuming that the Court would apply the "moderate living" standard to this context,[39] the *Winters* doctrine reserves to the tribe and its members enough water to make them economically self-sufficient but not enough to make them rich. However, this "moderate living" standard was announced in a case interpreting a treaty that required the tribe to share wildlife with the rest of the citizenry; neither *Winters* water rights nor water rights under the doctrine of prior appropriation historically encompass that same duty.

Is water reserved for the tribe's recreational and environmental needs?

Yes. Under the *Winters* doctrine, *every* reserve of federal land, including an Indian reservation, is entitled to enough water to fulfill the purpose for which it was created. The purpose of every Indian reservation is to serve as a permanent and viable home for the Indians who live there. This purpose cannot be fulfilled unless the reservation offers recreational opportunities and a decent, hospitable environment. In *Winters,* the Court expressly noted that the tribe had a reserved right to water not only for agricultural purposes but for "acts of civilization."[40] If a tribe wishes to build a community swimming pool or if tribal members want to water their lawns, they have a right under the *Winters* doctrine to use water for these purposes.

In *United States v. New Mexico* (1978),[41] the Supreme Court was asked to determine whether Congress, when it created the Rio Mimbres National Forest in New Mexico, reserved by implication enough water to promote recreational opportunities in addition to the obvious purpose of preserving the forest. The Court reviewed the legislative history of this federal reserve and found no such congressional intent. Therefore, the Court said, water needed for recreational purposes was not reserved under the *Winters* doctrine and had to be obtained under state law as any other user would obtain it, that is, under the doctrine of prior appropriation.

Nothing in *United States v. New Mexico* suggests that an Indian reservation is not entitled to use water for environmental and recreational needs. The overall federal purpose of providing a tribe with a permanent, self-sufficient home, as one court recently stated in this context, "is a broad one and must be liberally construed."[42] Therefore, water for a broad range of human activity should be included in the *Winters* doctrine, although not every court has agreed with this principle.[43]

Are Indian tribes using the full amount of their Winters rights? If not, who is using the remainder?

There may not be a single tribe currently using its entire *Winters* entitlement of water. Lack of funds is the main reason. Few tribes have the financial ability, for instance, to irrigate all practicably irrigable acreage or to develop all the minerals on their reservation. "Most reservations have used only a fraction of their reserved water."[44]

In the West, when a tribe does not use its entire entitlement to water, someone else surely is using the rest. A controversial issue today is whether tribes are permitted to sell or lease to outsiders the water they are not using on the reservation, as a number of tribes have begun doing. At least one commentator has criticized that effort, arguing that Congress did not intend for tribes to profit in this fashion,[45] but other commentators take a contrary view.[46] At least one court has indicated that Indian tribes have the right to sell or lease to the highest bidder their unused *Winters* rights.[47]

Some tribes could become enormously wealthy by selling or leasing *Winters* rights that they are not now using, although the tribe, of course, must first have those rights quantified. In the *Arizona v. California* case discussed earlier, five Indian tribes were declared entitled to nearly one million acre-feet of water from the Colorado River,[48] roughly 6 percent of its flow. Some fifteen million people in seven states are dependent upon water from the Colorado River,[49] and these five tribes could cause a severe crisis if they began appropriating their full *Winters* rights. Likewise, if the Navajo Nation, which has a reservation the size of West Virginia, sought to enforce its entire *Winters* claim, it "could dry up most of the west."[50] In a case decided in 2000, the Supreme Court held that the Quechan Tribe on the Fort Yuma Indian Reservation in Arizona may be entitled to take seventy-eight thousand acre-feet of water a year from the lower Colorado River basin, nearly 1 percent of the water flow and an amount that would supply seventy-eight thousand families with water for a year, worth millions of dollars.[51]

From the tribe's perspective, there are advantages and disadvantages to quantifying its water rights. The main advantages are that once its rights are quantified, the tribe can begin using the water for its own needs or sell or lease it to other water users at market price. Also, it is more difficult for the federal government to overlook a tribe's quantified rights when considering the creation of new federal projects.[52] However, as explained earlier, tribes are permitted to increase their water usage if a change in circumstances requires it. Therefore, the disadvantage of quantification is that the tribe will be locked into a fixed entitlement that later may be inadequate. Moreover, quantification is very expensive, and few tribes can afford it.

Likewise, quantification of *Winters* rights presents advantages and disadvantages for junior interests. The main advantage is that quantification removes uncertainty regarding the extent of the tribe's claim, allowing junior interests to plan for the future. As one court stated in 1981, tribal "open-ended water rights are a growing source of conflict and uncertainty in the West. Until their extent is determined, state-created water rights cannot be relied upon by property owners."[53] Tribal quantification, however, presents a significant risk for junior interests: the tribe may discover that its entitlement is so large, it can now charge junior interests for water. Some farmers and ranchers will be unable to meet the cost.

Most observers, including the National Water Commission, recommend that tribes quantify their water rights so as to eliminate the uncertainty that now clouds western development and that the federal government assist them in quantifying their rights.[54] Currently, lawsuits are pending covering most major water systems in the western region of the United States except for those in which settlements have already been reached. These cases are enormous in scope. A case pending in Arizona to apportion water flowing in the Gila and Little Colorado Rivers involves more than seventy-seven thousand claims and twenty-seven thousand parties. Litigating the case is a nightmare; the case is entering its eighth decade of litigation, and each side has spent millions of dollars in litigation costs.[55]

Although non-Indian water users may have to begin paying an Indian tribe for water they have thus far been using for free, most are now pressing for quantification of Indian water rights. By far the best solution is for Indians and their non-Indian neighbors, with the assistance of federal and state officials, to negotiate a fair resolution of competing water claims to avoid the cost of litigation as well as the bitterness that lawsuits usually produce. Tribes and water users in Arizona, Montana, and Oklahoma have been successful in this process.[56]

Under what circumstances may a tribe regulate the use of water by a non-Indian, both on and off the reservation?

In the *Winters* case, a tribe was allowed to limit a non-Indian's water usage outside the reservation. In *Walton,* a tribe was allowed to limit a non-Indian's water usage on the reservation. As these cases illustrate, non-Indians both on and off the reservation may not interfere with a tribe's senior right to reserved water. Tribes, however, may not regulate the use of "excess" (or "surplus") water—that is, water not needed to satisfy the tribe's *Winters* rights—by non-Indians even on land they own within the reservation.[57]

In addition to limiting the *amount* of water that non-Indians may use, tribes may also prevent non-Indians from degrading the *quality* of the tribe's water. In one case, farmers whose properties were located upstream from an Indian reservation were ordered to stop using pollutants that made the tribe's water saline.[58] Recent court decisions, including *City of Albuquerque v. Browner*[59] and *Montana v. U.S. Environmental Protection Agency,*[60] demonstrate that the Clean Water Act of 1972 (CWA)[61] vests Indian tribes with considerable authority to protect the quality of their water supply.[62] The CWA was amended in 1987 to confer on Indian tribes the same power that states have under the act to prohibit certain pollutants from being emitted into the water supply. In *City of Albuquerque,* the court held that an Indian tribe was authorized by the CWA to establish more stringent water quality standards than those issued by the federal government, and the tribe could compel an upstream municipality, the city of Albuquerque, to stop polluting river water used downstream by the tribe. The court found that enforcing these water quality standards were "in accord with powers inherent in Indian tribal sovereignty."[63] The court in the *Montana* case ruled similarly, holding that the CWA authorized an Indian tribe to regulate the discharge of pollutants by non-Indians on land they owned within the reservation that degraded the tribe's water.

Under what circumstances may state courts resolve Indian water rights disputes?

Water reserved under the *Winters* doctrine is governed exclusively by federal law because *Winters* rights are federal rights.[64] Unless Congress gives its consent, disputes concerning these federal rights may not be heard and decided (adjudicated) in a state court because the United States— which owns all federal water rights—may not be sued in state courts without congressional consent.

This consent was given in 1952 when Congress passed a law called the McCarran Amendment,[65] which authorizes state courts to adjudicate all federally secured rights to water, including Indian *Winters* rights, in a river or other water source that traverses the state. Suits filed under the McCarran Amendment must be "comprehensive" in scope, the Supreme Court has said, so as to avoid piecemeal litigation,[66] but they need not seek to adjudicate every hydrologically related water source included in a tribe's *Winter* rights. For example, the lawsuit can seek to determine a tribe's right to surface water without also seeking a determination on its right to underground water.[67]

When a state court adjudicates federal water rights under the McCarran Amendment, it must apply federal and not state law. That is, the court must apply the *Winters* doctrine. The McCarran Amendment did nothing to change the nature of federal water rights; it only authorized state courts to resolve disputes regarding them.[68] Nor did the amendment remove the right of federal courts to hear these same claims.[69] The tribe may appeal any state court determination of its *Winters* rights to the U.S. Supreme Court.[70]

In general, federal courts have been more protective of Indian water rights than have state courts. Indians and non-Indians both know this. For this reason, Indians usually file their water claims in federal court, while non-Indians usually file theirs in state court. A water rights claim filed in state court may be removed to a federal court in certain situations,[71] but these cases tend to be so enormous in scope that federal courts try to avoid them. Even when Indians win the race to the courthouse and file in federal court, the case is likely to be dismissed if non-Indians soon thereafter file a similar suit in state court, provided that the state court has the ability to determine rights to this water regarding all the parties in the federal lawsuit.[72] The fact that state officials have openly opposed a tribe's claim to water, moreover, may not be used as an argument against having a state court adjudicate that claim, unless the court itself has shown that it is biased.[73]

Is a state allowed to regulate the use of water within an Indian reservation?

States are allowed to regulate water usage on a reservation only to a limited extent, if at all. As explained in chapter 7, state laws normally may not be enforced in Indian country without the express consent of Congress. Based on that principle, a strong argument can be made that states have no power to regulate water usage on an Indian reservation. (As just explained, a federal law known as the McCarran Amendment consents to having federal water claims *adjudicated* in a state court; it does not consent, however, to state *regulation* of federal water rights.) One court has held that a state may regulate the water nonmembers of the tribe are entitled to use on land they own within the reservation.[74] Given the general legal principles just described, state jurisdiction should not extend further than this, absent congressional consent.[75]

Those states that received jurisdiction in Indian country under Public Law 83–280 (discussed in chapter 7) have no better claim to regulate reservation water usage than the rest of the states. Public Law 83–280 contains a provision expressly excluding state authority over tribal water.[76]

Are Indian water rights protected by the Just Compensation Clause?

The Just Compensation Clause of the Fifth Amendment to the Constitution, as discussed in chapter 5, entitles Indians and tribes to receive fair compensation whenever the federal government eliminates or diminishes their vested property rights. This rule applies to Indian *Winters* rights, which are vested rights.[77]

May Indians transfer their Winters rights to non-Indians when they sell their reservation land?

In 1887, Congress passed the General Allotment Act,[78] under which many Indians (after a period of years) received a deed from the federal government to a parcel (an "allotment") of reservation land. Upon receipt of the deed, the allottee became the owner of the allotment and could sell it at anytime to anyone. Since 1887, many allottees have sold their deeded allotments to non-Indians. In a recent case[79] one of these non-Indian owners claimed to have *Winters* rights. The tribe argued, on the other hand, that *Winters* rights are automatically lost whenever Indian land is acquired by a non-Indian.

The U.S. Court of Appeals for the Ninth Circuit, which decided the case on appeal, ruled in favor of the non-Indian. The court relied on a 1939 decision of the Supreme Court, which held that each Indian who obtains a deed to reservation land acquires a share of the reservation's *Winters* rights.[80] Based on that ruling, the Ninth Circuit decided that Indian allottees must have the right to sell their water rights to any subsequent purchaser so that these allottees can profit from their allotment—after all, an allotment is worth more with water rights than without them.[81] The court went on to hold, however, that the purchaser does not acquire the allottee's full *Winters* rights. Under the *Winters* doctrine, water is reserved to meet present and future needs. A purchaser, on the other hand, is entitled only to the water *then* being used by the allottee, plus any additional water that the purchaser puts to use "with reasonable diligence after the passage of title."[82] For the purchaser, it is "use it or lose it."[83] As for all subsequent purchasers or heirs of the first purchaser, they are limited to the amount of water appropriated and continuously used by the initial purchaser.[84] The U.S. Supreme Court has not addressed the issue of transferability of *Winters* rights but probably will eventually, as this issue affects a large number of people and millions of dollars in water rights.[85]

Does the federal government have an obligation to protect Indian water rights?

Yes. As explained in chapter 3, the federal government has a trust responsibility to enhance tribal autonomy and self-government and protect

Indian property, a duty arising out of its nearly four hundred treaties with Indian tribes in which tribes exchanged land for these types of assurances. Water is essential to tribal self-government and economic independence, as the *Winters* doctrine indicates. Therefore, the federal government has an affirmative duty to protect tribal water rights, to assure adequate supplies of water to Indian reservations, and to manage tribal water in the best interests of the tribe.[86] Courts have recognized that federal agencies may be sued for ignoring or violating these trust duties, and examples of such lawsuits are discussed in chapter 3.[87]

The federal government, rather than the tribe, holds legal title to a tribe's *Winters* rights. For this reason, a tribe cannot prevent the federal government from representing the tribe's interests in court, even if the tribe distrusts the government's motives or abilities.[88] Similarly, an Indian tribe cannot compel the United States to file suit on behalf of the tribe seeking to protect its water rights unless a treaty or statute, directly or by implication, imposes that duty.[89]

Thus, tribes do not own the water reserved to them under the *Winters* doctrine—the federal government does. However, they do have the right to use that water, and they are entitled to file suit to protect that right.[90]

What efforts has the federal government made to protect Indian water rights?

Only occasionally has the federal government made a determined, good faith effort to protect Indian water rights. As the National Water Commission stated in its 1973 report to Congress:[91]

During most of this 50-year period [following the Supreme Court's 1908 decision in the *Winters* case], the United States was pursuing the policy of encouraging the settlement of the West and the creation of family-sized farms on its arid lands. In retrospect, it can be seen that this policy was pursued with little or no regard for Indian water rights and the *Winters* doctrine. With the encouragement, or at least the cooperation, of the Secretary of the Interior—the very office entrusted with protection of all Indian rights—many large irrigation projects were constructed on streams that flowed through or bordered Indian reservations, sometimes above and more often below the reservations. With few exceptions, the projects were planned and built by the federal government without any attempt to define, let alone protect, prior rights that Indian tribes might have had in the waters used for the projects. . . . In the history of the United States Government's treatment of

Indian tribes, its failure to protect Indian water rights for use on the reservations it set aside for them is one of the sorrier chapters.

The federal government often has conflicts of interests when it comes to water rights. It is obligated on one hand to protect tribal rights, yet it also has a continuing obligation to maintain national parks and national forests, to promote land development, and to undertake reclamation projects, all of which require water. Frequently, government agencies, when faced with scarce water resources, ignore Indian water rights in favor of other interests. As President Nixon admitted in 1970, "[T]here is considerable evidence that the Indians are the losers when such situations arise."[92]

The Supreme Court has held that tribal water rights are not violated simply because the federal government may have conflicting responsibilities in a given situation. In *Nevada v. United States* (1983),[93] the Court held that the government's obligation to protect Indian water rights is equal to its obligation to protect various other federal water interests, and tribes cannot expect in those situations to receive sole or even paramount consideration.[94] When these conflicts do arise, it is in the tribe's best interests to hire its own attorney and intervene in any pending lawsuit, given that a judgment against the United States (as the owner of the tribe's water rights) is binding on the tribe as well.[95] Indeed, the court's decision is binding on the tribe even if the tribe later proves that the federal government inadequately represented the tribe's interests in the lawsuit.[96]

Indians and tribes are not without some protection. Chapter 18 describes the types of lawsuits that can be brought to enforce Indian rights, including Indian water rights. If federal officials ignore their responsibilities, Indians can file suit against the federal government for money damages to compensate for past injuries[97] and seek court orders preventing further violations of their water rights.[98]

NOTES

1. For a further discussion of the water shortage in the West, *see* National Water Comm'n, *Water Policies for the Future—Final Report to the President and to the Congress of the United States* (Washington, D.C.: Government Printing Office, 1973) at 8–9; David H. Getches, *Water Law in a Nutshell* (St. Paul: West Group, 1997); A. Dan Tarlock, *Law of Water Rights and Resources* (New York: C. Boardman, 1988).

2. 207 U.S. 564 (1908).

3. 373 U.S. 546 (1963).

4. *Arizona v. California*, 373 U.S. 546, 600 (1963).

5. *Id.*

6. 426 U.S. 128 (1976).

7. *Winters v. U.S.*, 207 U.S. 564 (1908); *U.S. v. New Mexico*, 438 U.S. 696, 698 (1978).

8. *New Mexico*, note 7 above, 438 U.S. at 700; *Cappaert v. U.S.*, 426 U.S. 128, 139 (1976).

9. *Winters*, note 7 above; *Arizona v. California*, note 4 above, 373 U.S. at 600. *See also* cases cited in note 8 above.

10. *Arizona v. California*, note 4 above, 373 U.S. at 598.

11. *Id. See also Arizona v. California*, 530 U.S. 392 (2000); *Alaska Pacific Fisheries v. U.S.*, 248 U.S. 78 (1918); *U.S. v. Winans*, 198 U.S. 371, 381 (1905). For a further discussion of the *Winters* doctrine, *see* the authorities cited in note 1 above.

12. This subject is discussed in ch. 5, sec. A.

13. *Winters*, note 7 above, 207 U.S. at 577; *Cappaert*, note 8 above, 426 U.S. at 138.

14. For additional information on the doctrine of prior appropriation, *see* the authorities cited in note 1 above. *See also U.S. v. Oregon*, 44 F.3d 758, 763–64 (9th Cir. 1994), *cert. denied*, 516 U.S. 943 (1995); *In Re General Adjudication of All Rights to the Water in the Gila River System and Source*, 35 P.3d 68, 71–72 (Ariz. 2001).

15. *Cappaert*, note 8 above, 426 U.S. at 145. *See also Colorado River Water Conservation Dist. v. U.S.*, 424 U.S. 800 (1976).

16. *Cappaert*, note 8 above, 426 U.S. at 139; *Winters*, note 7 above. For a comparison of the two doctrines, *see General Adjudication of Gila River*, note 14 above, 35 P.3d at 71–73.

17. *Arizona v. California*, note 4 above, 373 U.S. at 600; *Cappaert*, note 8 above.

18. *See U.S. v. Adair*, 723 F.2d 1394, 1412–15 (9th Cir. 1983), *cert. denied*, 467 U.S. 1252 (1984). *See also Klamath Water Users Protective Ass'n v. Patterson*, 204 F.3d 1206, 1214 (9th Cir. 1999), *cert. denied*, 121 S.Ct. 44 (2000).

19. *See Arizona v. California*, note 4 above, 373 U.S. at 600; *Adair*, note 18 above, 723 F.2d at 1412–15. *See also* R. Collins, "Indian Allotment Water Rights," 20 *Land and Water L. Rev.* 421, 426 n.20 (1985).

20. *Cappaert*, note 8 above, 426 U.S. at 138–39; *Arizona v. California*, note 4 above, 373 U.S. at 597; *Joint Board of Control of the Flathead, Mission and Jocko Irrigation Dist. v. U.S.*, 832 F.2d 1127, 1132 (9th Cir. 1987), *cert. denied*, 486 U.S. 1007 (1988); *Kittitas Reclamation Dist. v. Sunnyside Valley Irrigation Dist.*, 763 F.2d 1032 (9th Cir.), *cert. denied*, 474 U.S. 1032 (1985).

21. *Colville Confederated Tribes v. Walton*, 752 F.2d 397, 405 (9th Cir. 1985), *cert. denied*, 475 U.S. 1010 (1986).

22. *Cappaert*, note 8 above, 426 U.S. at 142–43; *New Mexico v. Aamodt*, 618 F. Supp. 993, 1010 (D.N.M. 1985). *But see In re General Adjudication of All Rights to the Use of Water in the Big Horn River System*, 753 P.2d 76 (Wyo. 1988), *aff'd by equally divided court*, 492 U.S. 406 (1989) (where ground and surface water are not interrelated, *Winters* rights do not extend to ground water).

23. For further discussion of this topic, *see* R. N. Morrison, "State and Federal Law in Conflict over Indian and Other Federal Reserved Water Rights," 2 *Drake J. Agric. L.* 1, 10 (1997).

24. *Arizona v. California*, note 4 above, 373 U.S. at 599. *See also The Kansas Indians*, 72 U.S. 737, 752–54 (1867); *Winans*, note 11 above, 198 U.S. at 381; *General Adjudication of Gila River*, note 14 above, 35 P.3d at 74–76.

25. *Colville Confederated Tribes v. Walton*, 647 F.2d 42 (9th Cir. 1981), *cert. denied*, 454 U.S. 1092 (1981).

26. 647 F.2d 42 (9th Cir. 1981), *cert. denied*, 454 U.S. 1092 (1981).

27. *Carson-Truckee Conservancy Dist. v. Clark*, 741 F.2d 257 (9th Cir. 1984); *Adair*, note 18 above; *Pyramid Lake Paiute Tribe v. Morton*, 354 F. Supp. 252 (D.D.C. 1972).

28. *Arizona v. California*, note 4 above; *U.S. v. Anderson*, 736 F.2d 1358 (9th Cir. 1984). *But see General Adjudication of Big Horn River*, note 22 above (when tribe historically is agrarian, reservation water was not reserved for nonagrarian purposes).

29. *Winans*, note 11 above, 198 U.S. at 381; *Alaska Pacific Fisheries*, note 11 above. *Cf. Federal Power Comm'n v. Oregon*, 349 U.S. 435, 444 (1960); *Arizona v. California*, 439 U.S. 419, 422 (1979) (supplemental decree).

30. *Walton*, note 25 above, 647 F.2d at 49. *See also Walton*, note 21 above, 752 F.2d at 405.

31. *Arizona v. California*, note 4 above, 373 U.S. at 600–601. This is generally true under both the *Winters* doctrine and the doctrine of prior appropriation. *See Farmers Highline Canal and Reservoir Co. v. City of Golden*, 272 P.2d 629 (Colo. 1954); *Walton*, note 21 above.

32. *General Adjudication of Gila River*, note 14 above, 35 P.3d at 74 (citation omitted). *See also U.S. v. Anderson*, note 28 above, 736 F.2d at 1365. *But see General Adjudication of Big Horn River*, note 22 above (holding that a tribe could not divert water that Congress intended for agriculture in order to improve tribal fisheries).

33. *In the Matter of the Application for Beneficial Water Use Permit*, 923 P.2d 1073, 1079 (Mont. 1996).

34. *See* note 5 above and accompanying text.

35. *See, e.g., General Adjudication of Gila River*, note 14 above, 35 P.3d at 77–81; *Walton*, note 21 above.

36. *Adair*, note 18 above, 723 F.2d 1411. *See also Joint Bd. of Control*, note 20 above, 832 F.2d at 1131–32 (water for tribal fisheries); *Arizona v. California*, note 4 above, 373 U.S. at 599–600 (water for agricultural purposes).

37. *Cappaert*, note 8 above, 426 U.S. at 141.

38. *Washington v. Washington State Commercial Passenger Fishing Vessel Ass'n*, 443 U.S. 658, 686 (1979).

39. At least one court has indicated that this standard applies when quantifying Indian water rights. *See In the Matter of the Application for Beneficial Water Use Permit*, 923 P.2d 1073, 1077 (Mont. 1996). *See also General Adjudication of Gila River*, note 14 above, 35 P.3d at 77 (noting that the *Winters* doctrine incorporates the concept of "minimal need").

40. *Winters*, note 7 above, 207 US at 576.

41. 438 U.S. 696 (1978).

42. *Walton,* note 25 above, 647 F.2d at 47. *See also General Adjudication of Gila River,* note 14 above, 35 P.3d at 76; *Montana ex rel. Greeley v. Confederated Salish and Kootenai Tribes,* 712 P.2d 754, 767 (Mont. 1985). *See also U.S. v. Finch,* 548 F.2d 822, 832 (9th Cir. 1976), *rev'd on other grounds,* 433 U.S. 676 (1977); *Pyramid Lake,* note 27 above.

43. *See General Adjudication of Big Horn River,* note 22 above.

44. *Beneficial Water Use,* note 39 above, 923 P.2d at 1078 (internal citation omitted).

45. Jack D. Palma II, "Considerations and Conclusions Concerning the Transferability of Indian Water Rights," 20 *Nat. Resources J.* 91 (1980).

46. *See* Chris Seldin, "Interstate Marketing of Indian Water Rights," 87 *Cal. L. Rev.* 1545 (1999); David Getches, "Management and Marketing of Indian Water," 58 *U. Colo. L. Rev.* 515, 541–48 (1988).

47. *Walton,* note 21 above, 752 F.2d at 404.

48. *Arizona v. California,* note 4, 373 U.S. at 596.

49. *See* Seldin, note 46 above, at 1550–51.

50. Karen Crass, "Eroding the *Winters* Right: Non-Indian Water Users' Attempt to Limit the Scope of the Indian Superior Entitlement to Western Water to Prevent Tribes from Water Brokering," *U. Den. Water L. Rev.* 109, 119 (Fall 1997).

51. *Arizona v. California,* 530 U.S. 392 (2000). *See* "Quechan Win Supreme Court Victory over Colorado River Water Rights," *Indian Country Today* (July 5, 2000) at A2.

52. *See* Crass, note 50 above, at 118.

53. *Walton,* note 25 above, 647 F.2d at 48. *See also Confederated Salish and Kootenai Tribes v. Clinch,* 992 P.2d 244 (Mont. 1999) (non-Indians who own land within an Indian reservation may not be granted permits to use more water until the tribe's *Winters* rights have been quantified).

54. For a further discussion of this subject *see* David Getches et al., *Federal Indian Law.* 4th ed. (St. Paul, West Group, 1998) at 816–54.

55. *See San Carlos Apache Tribe v. Bolton,* 977 P.2d 790 (Ariz. 1999); *U.S. v. Gila Valley Irrigation Dist.,* 920 F. Supp. 1444 (D. Ariz. 1996), *aff'd,* 117 F.3d 425 (9th Cir. 1997).

56. *See, e.g.,* "Chippewa-Cree Tribe, State of Montana sign Historic Compact," *Native American Rights Fund Legal Review* (Summer/Fall 1997) at 1–8; "Choctaw and Chickasaw Nations Sign Water Compact with Oklahoma," *Indian Country Today* (Oct. 25, 2000) at A3 (seeking a settlement to water supplies serving nearly half of Oklahoma City and surrounding areas); "Gila River Water Claim Settlement Expected in About a Month," *Indian Country Today* (Dec. 27, 2000) at A8.

57. *U.S. v. Anderson,* note 28 above, 736 F.2d at 1365. *Cf., Montana v. U.S.,* 450 U.S. 544 (1981).

58. *U.S. v. Gila Valley Irrigation Dist.,* 920 F. Supp. 1444 (D. Ariz. 1996), *aff'd,* 117 F.3d 425 (9th Cir. 1997).

59. 97 F.3d 415 (10th Cir. 1996), *cert. denied.,* 522 U.S. 965 (1997).

60. 137 F.3d 1135 (9th Cir. 1998), *cert. denied,* 525 U.S. 921 (1998). *See also Wisconsin v. Environmental Protection Agency,* 266 F.3d 741 (7th Cir. 2001).

61. 33 U.S.C. Secs. 1251–1387.

62. 33 U.S.C. Sec. 1377(e).
63. *City of Albuquerque v. Browner,* 97 F.3d 415, 423 (10th Cir. 1996).
64. *Colorado River,* note 15 above, 424 U.S. at 813.
65. 43 U.S.C. Sec. 666(a).
66. *U.S. v. District Court for Eagle County,* 401 U.S. 520, 523 (1971).
67. *U.S. v. Oregon,* note 14 above, 44 F.3d at 768–69.
68. *Arizona v. San Carlos Apache Tribe,* 463 U.S. 543, 571 (1983); *Colorado River,* note 15 above, 424 U.S. at 820. *See also Beneficial Water Use,* note 39 above, 923 P.2d at 1078; *U.S. v. Oregon,* note 14 above (holding that McCarran Amendment cases may be initiated in state administrative agencies before being reviewed by a state court).
69. 28 U.S.C. Secs. 1345, 1361. *See Cappaert,* note 8 above, 426 U.S. at 145.
70. *San Carlos,* note 68 above, at 463 U.S. at 551, 571.
71. The removal of cases from state court to federal court is governed by 28 U.S.C. Sec. 1441(a). For a discussion of how this statute applies to water claims, *see Colorado River,* note 15 above, and *San Carlos,* note 68 above.
72. *See* cases cited in note 71 above and *U.S. v. Bluewater-Toltec Irrigation Dist.,* 580 F. Supp. 1434 (D.N.M. 1984).
73. *U.S. v. Oregon,* note 14 above, 44 F.3d at 772.
74. *U.S. v. Anderson,* note 28 above. *See also Holly v. Confederated Tribes and Bands of Yakima Indian Nation,* 655 F. Supp. 557 (E.D. Wash. 1985), *aff'd,* 812 F.2d 714 (9th Cir.), *cert. denied,* 484 U.S. 8233 (1987).
75. *But see General Adjudication of Big Horn River,* note 22 above (holding that state law governs a tribe's water rights when the tribe seeks to change the use of water from agricultural purposes, protected by the tribe's *Winters* rights, to supply an instream fishery, a use not protected by the tribe's *Winters* rights).
76. 28 U.S.C. Sec. 1360(b).
77. *See* ch. 5, notes 23–26 and accompanying text, and *Gila River Pima–Maricopa Indian Community v. U.S.,* 684 F.2d 852 (Ct. Cl. 1982).
78. 25 U.S.C. Secs. 331 *et seq.* The General Allotment Act is discussed in ch. 1, and ch. 7, sec. B.
79. *Walton,* note 21 above. *See also Skeem v. U.S.,* 273 F.2d 93 (9th Cir. 1921) (holding that *Winters* rights can be leased).
80. *U.S. v. Powers,* 305 U.S. 527 (1939).
81. At least one other court has ruled similarly. *See General Adjudication of Big Horn River,* note 22 above (Indian allottees who obtain deeds to their allotment acquire *Winters* rights along with them).
82. *Walton,* note 25 above, 647 F.2d at 51.
83. *U.S. v. Anderson,* note 28 above, 736 F.2d at 1362.
84. *Walton,* note 25 above, 647 F.2d at 51; *Walton,* note 21 above, 752 F.2d at 422.
85. For a discussion of these various arguments, *see* Getches et al., at 814–16.
86. *Lane v. Pueblo of Santa Rosa,* 249 U.S. 110 (1919); *Klamath Water Users Protective Ass'n,* note 18 above; *White Mountain Apache Tribe v. Hodel,* 784 F.2d 921 (9th Cir. 1986), *cert. denied,* 479 U.S. 1006 (1987); *Adair,* note 18 above; *Pyramid Lake,* note 27 above.
87. *See, e.g., Pyramid Lake,* note 27 above; *Gila Valley,* note 58 above; *White Mountain Apache Tribe v. U.S.,* 11 Cl. Ct. 614 (1987).

88. *See, e.g., White Mountain Apache Tribe v. U.S.,* note 87 above.

89. *Shoshone-Bannock Tribes v. Reno,* 56 F.3d 1476 (9th Cir. 1995).

90. *See Walton,* note 21 above; *Pyramid Lake,* note 27 above; *San Carlos,* note 68 above.

91. National Water Comm'n, note 1 above, at 474–75.

92. H.R. Doc. No. 363, 91st Cong., 2d Sess., 10, *reprinted in* 116 Cong. Rec. 23258, 23261 (1970).

93. 463 U.S. 110 (1983).

94. *Nevada v. U.S.,* 463 U.S. 128 (1983). *See also Arizona v. California,* 460 U.S. 605, 627–28 (1983).

95. *San Carlos,* note 68 above, 463 U.S. at 566 n.17; *White Mountain Apache Tribe v. Hodel,* note 86 above, 784 F.2d at 925.

96. *Nevada v. U.S.,* note 94 above, 463 U.S. at 110. *See also Arizona v. California,* note 94 above, 460 U.S. at 620; *U.S. v. Alpine Land and Reservoir Co.,* 887 F.2d 207 (9th Cir. 1989); *Pyramid Lake,* note 27 above.

97. *See* cases cited in note 87 above and *Northern Paiute Nation v. U.S.,* 9 Cl. Ct. 639 (1986). *See generally U.S. v. Mitchell,* 463 U.S. 206 (1983).

98. *See* cases cited in note 96 above and *U.S. v. Winnebago Tribe,* 542 F.2d 1002 (8th Cir. 1976).

XIII

Civil Rights of Indians

What is a civil right?

A civil right is a standard of liberty or justice that is designed to protect a person from government abuse.

Do Indians have the same civil rights as other citizens?

Yes. Indians born in this country are citizens of the United States[1] and of the state in which they live.[2] Indians have the same civil rights with respect to the federal and state governments as all other citizens.[3] The most important rights that all citizens share are those enumerated in the Bill of Rights (the first ten amendments to the U.S. Constitution), including the freedoms of speech, press, and religion; protection against cruel and unusual punishment; the right to bail; the right to a trial by jury; protection against self-incrimination; the right to due process of law; and protection against unreasonable search and seizure. In addition to the civil rights set forth in the Constitution, Congress has passed numerous laws that confer civil rights in various situations, such as laws prohibiting discrimination in employment and in housing.

It would take many pages to discuss all the civil rights that Indians and other citizens have. Instead, this chapter focuses on those rights that are particularly important to Indians in their dealings with the state and federal governments. (Chapter 14 discusses the rights of Indians in their dealings with tribal governments.)

A. FREEDOM OF RELIGION

Which provisions of the Constitution guarantee freedom of religion?

The U.S. Constitution contains two "religion" clauses, both of which are found in the First Amendment: the Establishment Clause and the Free Exercise Clause. They read as follows: "Congress shall make no law respecting an establishment of religion or prohibiting the free exercise thereof." These clauses, originally directed only at Congress, were made applicable to state governments with the passage of the Fourteenth Amendment, which was added to the Constitution in 1868 following the Civil War.[4]

What rights are conferred by the Establishment and Free Exercise Clauses?

Many Europeans who first settled in what is now the United States were driven from their homelands because of their religious beliefs and came here to find freedom of worship. The Establishment and Free Exercise Clauses were included in the Constitution in order to help make their dream a reality.[5]

The Establishment Clause guarantees the separation of church and state. The federal and state governments must remain entirely neutral in religious matters. This protects the *government* from becoming enmeshed in religious strife, while at the same time it safeguards *religion* from government interference. Government agencies may not promote or sponsor religious exercises, and religious adherents may not use the government to advance their faith or inhibit the faith of others.[6]

The Free Exercise Clause guarantees freedom of worship. People in this country remain free to believe in any religion of their choosing, or no religion at all, and to follow their own conscience in matters of religion.[7] Taken together, the Free Exercise and Establishment Clauses ensure that religion in this country will be left to individual and family choice and that the government will not seek to meddle in religious affairs, prefer one religion over another, or favor religion over nonreligion.

How do these clauses protect Indians?

Religion has special significance to Indians. In the traditional Indian perspective, religion is not something separate from life; the spirit world is part of everything, and one's goal is to live in harmony with nature. In few other societies is the role of religion as central to its members' existence as it is in Indian societies.[8] Therefore, the Free Exercise Clause and its guarantee of religious freedom is especially important to Indians.

Until recently, courts had interpreted the Free Exercise Clause as forbidding the government from engaging in any action that interfered with someone's religious freedom unless the government could demonstrate the action was necessary, it served a compelling government interest, and no less injurious alternative was available—the *compelling interest test.* Under this test, the activity in question had to be more than just reasonable or rational; the government had to prove that in order for the government to accomplish a substantial and legitimate objective this particular encroachment on religious freedom was necessary.[9]

But in recent years, the Supreme Court has drastically narrowed the protections afforded by the Free Exercise Clause. The Court held in a series of four cases (three of which involved Indians and the fourth involved Muslims) that uniformly applied, religiously "neutral" laws need only pass the *rational basis test* and not the compelling interest test. The less-stringent rational basis test requires only that the law or activity in question have any rational basis in order to pass judicial scrutiny. To illustrate, the Supreme Court held in *Bowen v. Roy* (1986)[10] that the federal government could deny social security benefits to an Indian whose religious beliefs prevented him from being "named" by a number and who, because of those beliefs, had refused to apply for a social security card. According to the Court, the law itself was "neutral" because it required everyone to obtain a number as a condition of qualifying for benefits, and therefore the government was entitled to enforce it without granting exemptions, despite its harmful effect on certain faiths. In *Lyng v. Northwest Indian Cemetery Protective Association* (1988),[11] the Supreme Court held that the federal government may use its land in any reasonable manner even if that use "could have devastating effects on traditional Indian religious practices."[12] The Court in *Lyng* permitted the federal government to build a road through a sacred Indian site despite the fact that the road could have skirted the site, albeit at a greater cost; the Court found it "rational" to save the money and desecrate the site.

Applying the same standard, the Supreme Court held in *O'Lone v. Estate of Shabazz* (1987)[13] that uniformly applied prison regulations are valid if rational, even if they prevent religious practitioners from engaging in an activity required by their faith. In that case, the Court permitted prison officials to prevent Muslim inmates from stopping their work for several minutes during the afternoon in order to pray, upholding a "neutral" prison regulation that required inmates to work all afternoon.

In Oregon, as in most states, employees fired from their jobs for good cause do not qualify for certain unemployment compensation benefits. In

Employment Division v. Smith (1990),[14] the Supreme Court considered whether this "neutral" law could be applied so as to deny unemployment benefits to two Indians who had been fired from their jobs for having ingested peyote as a sacrament during a religious ceremony conducted during their off-duty hours. The Court upheld the application of the law to these religious adherents, reaffirming the principle that "generally applicable, religion-neutral laws" need only be reasonable to be valid even if they "have the effect of burdening a particular religious practice."[15] Using that test, the Court denied the Indians a religious exemption and upheld the loss of their unemployment benefits.

The switch from the compelling interest to the rational basis test places all religious practices in danger of being restricted by some "neutral" law, but in reality, it threatens the practices of minority religions far more than those of mainstream religions. This is because government officials are unlikely to pass a law or undertake an activity that would harm a majority practice. Imagine the uproar that would occur if the city of New York announced plans to tear down St. Patrick's Cathedral in order to build a road. Yet government officials in *Lyng* were permitted to make a similar "neutral" decision and build a road through a site no less sacred to an Indian tribe than St. Patrick's Cathedral is to Catholics. In the *O'Lone* case, prison officials enacted a "neutral" rule requiring all inmates to work in the afternoon, but it is doubtful they would have enacted a rule requiring everyone to work on Sunday mornings, even though that rule would be equally as "neutral." Therefore, these recent Supreme Court decisions, although a danger to all religious faiths, are of special concern to practitioners of minority religions whose practices can now be destroyed either intentionally or inadvertently by some "neutral" law or action. Prior to these recent cases, for instance, Indians who challenged prison rules requiring all inmates to have short hair won many of these challenges on Free Exercise grounds,[16] but they almost never win them now.[17]

What is the American Indian Religious Freedom Act of 1978 and the Religious Freedom Restoration Act of 1992?

After conducting an extensive investigation, the U.S. House of Representatives issued a report in 1978 that concluded that Indian religious practices were being severely disrupted, often inadvertently, by state and federal laws and activities.[18] The report found that Indians had been prevented from visiting their sacred sites, denied the use of religious sacra-

ments, and prevented from performing worship services in their traditional manner due to unnecessary government interference, and the report
recommended that Congress enact remedial legislation.

Congress responded by passing a joint resolution called the American
Indian Religious Freedom Act (AIRFA) in 1978.[19] As with all joint reso-
lutions, AIRFA does not have the same status as a federal law and contains
no penalty provision that can be imposed against violators. Still, AIRFA
declares a policy that Congress has pledged itself to pursue:

[H]enceforth it shall be the policy of the United States to protect and preserve
for Native Americans their inherent right of freedom of belief, expression, and
exercise of traditional religions of the American Indian . . . including but not limited to access to sites, use and possession of sacred objects, and the freedom to
worship through ceremonials and traditional rites.

AIRFA has not been very effective, however, due to the absence of a
penalty provision. In *Lyng,* discussed earlier, the Supreme Court stated
that AIRFA has "no teeth in it," and the Court essentially ignored it.[20]
Other courts have said that AIRFA only requires public officials to "consider" Indian interests and not necessarily to act in accordance with
them.[21]

Rather than amend AIRFA, in 1993 Congress sought a broader remedy
and enacted the Religious Freedom Restoration Act (RFRA), a law supported by numerous religious groups that were concerned about the Supreme Court's recent Free Exercise decisions.[22] Designed to overrule the
Bowen-Lyng-O'Lone-Smith line of cases, RFRA ordered federal courts to
use the compelling interest test rather than the rational basis test in deciding all cases in which a citizen alleged a violation of the Free Exercise
Clause.[23]

Four years later, however, in *City of Boerne v. Flores* (1997),[24] the Supreme Court held that RFRA was unconstitutional as applied to state and
municipal laws and activities. Nothing in the Constitution confers on
Congress the power, the Court held, to authorize courts to apply a judicial
standard in interpreting the Free Exercise Clause (or any other constitutional provision) other than the standard that the Supreme Court held was
mandated. As a result of *City of Boerne,* courts considering Free Exercise
challenges to state and local laws must use the rational basis test. One
federal court recently decided, though, that RFRA is valid as applied to

actions taken by *federal* officials, an issue not addressed by the Court in *City of Boerne*.[25] Congress has the constitutional authority, the decision said, to dictate the method by which *federal* actions are reviewed in the courts, and the court held that by virtue of RFRA, the compelling interest test must be used in deciding Free Exercise cases involving the federal government.

Nothing in *City of Boerne* limits the ability of Congress—or the ability of state legislatures—to *create* a new civil right by statute; it only prevents Congress from determining what standards a court will use when it *interprets* constitutional rights.[26] A far different situation would have been presented, in other words, had Congress passed a law creating a right to engage in religious practices unless the government proved a compelling need to curtail that right, as opposed to passing RFRA, which attempted to order courts to apply a particular test in deciding Free Exercise cases. Indians and other groups have therefore renewed their efforts in the federal and state legislatures, urging them to pass laws protecting their religious practices. Some of these efforts have been successful. For example, several states[27] and the federal government[28] have passed laws protecting the sacramental use of peyote. The federal law prohibits the states from making it a crime for an Indian to use, possess, or transport peyote "for *bona fide* traditional ceremonial purposes in connection with the practice of a traditional Indian religion."[29] Congress has also conferred a special exemption (discussed in chapter 11) under the Bald and Golden Eagle Protection Act,[30] by authorizing the Secretary of the Interior to permit Indians to possess eagles and eagle parts (such as feathers and talons) for use in religious ceremonies.[31]

How can Indians protect their sacred sites?

Most religions have sacred sites, and Indian religions are no exception. Indian religious sites have received little protection from state and federal agencies, as the *Lyng* case illustrates. Federal agencies have constructed dams that flooded sacred Indian lands,[32] banned Indian groups from holding religious ceremonies at sacred sites located on federal land,[33] and allowed a ski area to be built on federal land sacred to an Indian tribe.[34]

In 1996, in an effort to offer more protection to Indian sacred sites, President Clinton issued an executive order that requires federal agencies to avoid causing unnecessary harm to the physical integrity of Indian sacred sites and to accommodate access to, and use of, sacred sites by Indian religious practitioners.[35] Consistent with that order, the National Park Service issued a plan to limit access by climbers and tourists to Devil's Tower in Wyoming (which is located on federal land administered by the National Park Service) during the month of June, when Indians hold religious ceremonies there.[36]

B. INDIANS AS STATE CITIZENS

What rights do Indians have as state citizens?

Indians are entitled to the same benefits and privileges as other state citizens.[37] They are guaranteed this equality by the Equal Protection Clause of the Fourteenth Amendment, which reads: "No State shall . . . deny to any person within its jurisdiction the equal protection of the laws." This clause, among other things, prohibits state officials from discriminating against any person on account of race, color, creed, or religion unless the state has a compelling interest that necessitates this discrimination.[38]

Do state officials discriminate against Indians?

The federal district court in Colorado recently noted, "The history of discrimination against Native Americans in the United States, and Colorado in particular, goes back well over 100 years."[39] As a result of discrimination, Indians have had to go to court in numerous states to secure their equal right under the law to hold state public office,[40] to attend public schools,[41] to receive state public assistance,[42] to serve as jurors in state courts,[43] to obtain state game licenses,[44] to obtain state business licenses,[45] to appear as witnesses in state courts,[46] to receive the same municipal services that other citizens receive,[47] and to receive equal assistance from state officials in locating absent parents who owe child support.[48] Recently, when New Mexico was facing an unexpected budget shortfall, state officials chose to save money by cutting funds for health programs on the Navajo Reservation while leaving non-Indian health programs untouched, a decision a federal appellate court found to be "motivated by discriminatory intent."[49]

"English-only" laws have been enacted in a number of states, conditioning government programs on the ability of the applicant to speak or write in English. Ironically, in 2000 the federal government awarded medals to some of the Navajo "code talkers" who risked their lives during

World War II sending messages by radio on the front lines of battle in the Navajo language, a "code" that the Japanese and Germans were never able to break. Today, many native speakers are ineligible for various state-run programs due to these "English-only" laws.

State officials sometimes seek to justify their discrimination against Indians by pointing out that Indians have special rights under federal treaties and laws[50] and do not pay certain state taxes.[51] True, Indians have special rights and receive special benefits from the federal government, but so do many other groups, and yet no one denies them the full rights of citizenship. Moreover, as explained in chapter 3, Indian tribes have "pre-paid" for those rights by relinquishing vast landholdings to the federal government in exchange for them. It is particularly unfair to label Indians as being "special citizens" when on the whole they are the most impoverished and disadvantaged group in our society.[52] As one writer has stated on this subject:

Any American who has been on an Indian reservation knows very well that Indians are not "equal." The highest infant mortality rate and lowest life expectancy in the country reflect massive unmet health needs. Family income is by far the lowest in the nation. Housing and education deficits are greater than in any other sector of our society.

The fact that Indians have some special treaty rights is perfectly consistent with our form of government. The essence of American democracy is to provide "special benefits." We have special benefits for veterans, the elderly, the infirm, elementary and secondary school students, small businessmen, laborers, non-English speaking minorities and uncounted others. In our system, equality is achieved by a melding of many special programs which are directed toward special groups.

Thus Indian treaty rights, which were paid for so dearly by the tribes, cannot fairly be isolated. It is ironic, and brutally so, that there are those who would claim that the Indians are "favored" or "more than equal."[53]

To be sure, many state officials do not discriminate against Indians, and some discriminate in their favor. For instance, in Santa Fe, New Mexico, Indian merchants have been given a monopoly on selling handcrafted jewelry on the grounds of the state museum over the objections of non-Indian merchants,[54] and in 1999, the warden of the South Dakota State Penitentiary authorized Indians to smoke from ceremonial pipes in their religious ceremonies even though smoking is otherwise banned in the prison. The Minnesota legislature passed a law giving Indian teachers job protections not provided to other teachers in order to foster their hiring and retention.[55]

C. THE RIGHT TO VOTE

Is the right to vote protected by federal law?

Yes. The right to vote is the most basic civil right in a democracy because it is the means by which citizens choose their government.[56] The right to vote is protected by federal law. The Fifteenth Amendment to the Constitution guarantees that no citizen shall be denied the right to vote in a state or federal election on account of race or color. In addition, both the U.S. Constitution and the Voting Rights Act of 1965 protect all persons from having to pay a fee or pass a literacy test in order to vote.[57] The 1975 amendments to this act prohibit discrimination against persons whose primary language is other than English,[58] and Indians are expressly recognized as a language minority group under these amendments.[59] The amendments require that wherever necessary to facilitate voting rights, state election officials must distribute voter registration information in the local language and conduct bilingual elections, which include using bilingual election officials at polling places.[60]

What can Indians do if subjected to discrimination in exercising their voting rights?

Indians are often the victims of discrimination in voting. As one court noted in a 2001 decision, "There is ample evidence that American Indians have historically been the subject of discrimination in the area of voting."[61] Indians in some states were denied the right to vote based solely on the fact that they lived on an Indian reservation,[62] and in other states, they were denied the right to vote merely because they lived on federal trust land and thus paid no state property taxes.[63] As a result of court decisions, the law is now well settled that Indians have the right to cast a ballot for all elected officials who administer over them, regardless of whether the Indians live on a reservation or pay state taxes.

The right to vote includes the right to cast a *meaningful* ballot, one that gives the voter a fair and equal opportunity to elect the candidate of his or her choice (and, similarly, gives each candidate a fair and equal opportunity to get elected). Yet some state and local officials have deliberately used voting schemes that made it more difficult for Indian voters to cast a meaningful ballot and for Indian candidates to get elected. For example, in 1991 the South Dakota legislature adopted a redistricting plan for the state House of Representatives in an area of the state that has a high Indian population but in which no Indian had ever been elected, despite the fact that Indians occasionally appeared on the ballot. Under the new plan, a district was created that for the first time would contain a majority (67 percent) of Indians. However, just before the next election, the legislature abolished that district and, by reconfiguring the districts, reduced the Indian population in any district to no more than 36 percent. Indian voters filed a lawsuit challenging the new plan, citing both the Voting Rights Act and provisions of state law. The court ruled in favor of the Indian plaintiffs, requiring the state to restore the 1991 plan,[64] and in the very next election, an Indian was elected from the majority-Indian district. Similar challenges to voting schemes in Colorado[65] and Montana[66] have produced similar results, with courts finding that these schemes had been created with the deliberate intent to dilute the Indian vote.

D. Protection Against Private Discrimination

Do Indians have any protection against discrimination by private persons?

The civil rights just discussed, including all of the rights conferred by the Bill of Rights, apply only to *government* activities. They offer no protection against purely private discrimination.[67] Yet many of the basic necessities of life, including employment and housing, often involve decisions and actions taken entirely by private individuals. In order to ensure that citizens are not denied these basic necessities due to unfair *private* discrimination, Congress has passed civil rights laws that prohibit various forms of discrimination by one individual or group against another.

These federal civil rights laws protect all citizens, Indians and non-Indians alike. As a result of these laws, Indians who are discriminated against on account of race, color, creed, religion, sex, or national origin with respect to housing,[68] employment,[69] commercial transactions,[70] or access to public accommodations[71] in most instances can file suit in federal court to halt this discrimination and recover damages for any injury suffered.

While private discrimination has been reduced in certain areas, by no means has it been eliminated. In 1996, the Fair Housing Office in Billings, Montana, found that nearly two-thirds of the Indian people who had sought private housing in Billings had been discriminated against, and its study found that the level of discrimination was increasing rather than decreasing.[72] These acts of private discrimination can be redressed under the federal civil rights laws discussed above, and perpetrators can be required to pay damages, court costs, and attorney's fees. For example, a federal court recently found that a group of non-Indians in Wisconsin had made racist statements against Indians and had urged other non-Indians to use any means available, including violence, to prevent Indians from exercising their federal treaty rights to fish in Wisconsin lakes. Finding that this conduct violated a federal civil rights law that guarantees all citizens the equal right to hold and use personal property,[73] the court ordered a halt to all such activities and assessed more than $240,000 in litigation costs and attorney's fees against the group.[74]

In March 2000, the South Dakota Advisory Committee to the U.S. Commission on Civil Rights issued a report after conducting hearings regarding discrimination against Indians in South Dakota. The report referred to "ample research" demonstrating disparities between Indians and non-Indians in "income, health, education, employment, and housing." According to the report, many Indians believe "that prejudice and bigotry play out on many levels, including the workplace, schools, business, and public accommodations."[75] Given the federal civil rights laws cited above, Indians have remedies for violations of this nature.

E. PROTECTION OF BURIAL REMAINS

What is the Native American Graves Protection and Repatriation Act?

An investigation conducted during the late 1980s revealed that tens of thousands of Indian human remains and Indian religious and cultural objects were held by federal agencies and by museums that received federal funds. The Smithsonian Institute in Washington, D.C., owned by the federal government, held over seventeen thousand Indian skeletal remains, and the Denver Art Museum, also publicly funded, possessed more than eighty thousand Indian artifacts and the remains of eighty-six Indians. Until 1989, the federal government "had a firm policy which encouraged the acquisition and retention" of Indian skeletons and artifacts by federal agencies and by museums.[76]

In 1989, Congress passed the National Museum of the American Indian Act,[77] which required the Smithsonian to inventory and seek to identify the origins of its Indian collection using scientific and historical data and to notify the tribes of origin. Those tribes could then consult with the Smithsonian and arrange for the recovery of all objects that originally belonged to the tribe.

One year later in 1990, Congress passed a similar but much broader act called the Native American Graves Protection and Repatriation Act (NAGPRA).[78] This historic law had two main purposes: (1) to allow tribes to recover religious and cultural items belonging to them that were held in federally funded institutions, and (2) to protect the right of tribes to safeguard remains and artifacts that might be found or excavated in the future.

As to the first purpose, NAGPRA required all federal agencies (except the Smithsonian, which was already covered by the earlier act) and all museums receiving federal funds to inventory their collections of Indian human remains and cultural and religious objects and, through scientific and historical data, attempt to identify the tribe of origin. Each tribe of origin had to be sent an inventory by November 16, 1995, of the items that might belong to that tribe. The tribe then had the right to inspect the items and request that those belonging to the tribe be returned immediately.[79]

As a result of this process, more than four hundred Indian tribes have reclaimed in excess of three hundred thousand items. Several museums lost most of their entire collection of Indian artifacts. Many of the items being returned had been stolen from the tribes long ago.[80]

As for NAGPRA's second purpose, the act ensures that any future excavation on federal or tribal land in an area that may contain Indian artifacts or human remains will be governed by strict regulations (one of which requires tribal consent to excavate in certain circumstances) and assures that tribes will be promptly notified if any items protected by the act are discovered.[81] NAGPRA, however, does not apply to objects discovered on any other land, including land owned by state and local governments.[82]

NAGPRA contains a penalty provision that helps enforce the law. The act makes it a federal crime to knowingly sell, purchase, use for profit, or transport for sale or profit any cultural items or other artifacts or Indian human remains obtained in violation of the act. Violators face a punishment of up to five years in prison for each offense.[83] In a recent case, a person who attempted to sell Indian artifacts in violation of NAGPRA received a thirty-three-month sentence in a federal prison.[84]

F. RACIAL STEREOTYPING

Indians, among other racial minorities, are often the victims of negative racial stereotyping. Racial stereotyping can be illegal when combined with certain actions, including those discussed earlier in this chapter that deny Indians the right to vote based on race. But many forms of racial stereotyping are not illegal, despite the harm they cause. Racial slurs and the depiction of negative images of a race are examples of stereotyping that may not be illegal but that usually prevent a society from achieving social justice and internal harmony.

Those who engage in such stereotyping may be unaware of the harm they are causing. They might even believe that what they are doing is positive rather than negative stereotyping. For example, the owner of the Washington Redskins football team has defended the continued use of "Redskins" on the grounds that it glorifies the fierce and brave fighting spirit of Indians. He has refused to change the team's name despite numerous requests from Indians to do so, and even after the Metropolitan Washington Council of Governments passed a resolution finding that the name was "demeaning and dehumanizing to Native Americans" and urged him to change it.[85] As for the buck-toothed Indian used as the logo of the Cleveland Indians baseball team, it would be difficult for anyone to say it carried any positive message about Indians. According to a recent study, more than six hundred public schools voluntarily discontinued using Indian names, symbols, rituals, and mascots, but some thirty-five hundred still do.[86]

For many Indians, creating a national holiday commemorating Christopher Columbus is no more appropriate than creating a holiday commemorating Adolf Hitler. Columbus may deserve credit for discovering *for Europeans* a new continent. However, as discussed in chapter 1, he did not discover North America, in which hundreds of nations were already thriving. Moreover, Columbus's own journal and other historical accounts demonstrate that he was mainly interested in making himself and his patrons rich, and Columbus engaged in cruel and barbaric means to achieve that goal. In his journal, Columbus speaks highly of the native peoples (whom he called "Indios"), stating: "They are the best people in the world and above all the gentlest—without knowledge of what is evil—nor do they murder or steal. . . . They love their neighbors as themselves and have the sweetest talk in the world, . . . always laughing."[87] But Columbus saw these generous qualities as weaknesses, and he exploited them. He wrote in his journal: "They would make fine servants. With fifty men we could subjugate them all and make them do whatever we want."[88] He ordered the Indians to bring him gold, and he tortured, killed, or enslaved any who refused or failed. Within four years of his arrival in 1492, nearly one-third of the estimated three hundred thousand inhabitants of Hispaniola had been killed or enslaved, and according to one historian, less than five hundred remained in Hispaniola by 1548.[89]

Racial stereotyping and distortions of history along racial lines rarely can be changed or remedied through lawsuits. It is not illegal, for example, to call someone a redskin. Stereotyping is often the product of decades—if not centuries—of unsuspecting bias and misconception and is best eradicated through education. Dissemination of a highly acclaimed video, *The Drums of October: Legacy of a Pernicious Hero,*[90] for example, would do much to educate the public on why it should transform Columbus Day (and why it should change the name of the holiday to "Americas Day") so that it celebrates the positive aspects of both European and native cultures, instead of the man.[91]

NOTES

1. In 1924, Congress passed a law, 8 U.S.C. Sec. 1401(a)(2), that conferred United States citizenship on all Indians born in the United States. Some Indians had become citizens earlier in treaties with the United States or by statutes passed by Congress conferring citizenship on particular tribes or groups of Indians.

2. The Fourteenth Amendment to the Constitution provides that all persons "born or naturalized in the United States . . . are citizens of the United States and of the State wherein they reside." Indians are entitled to the full protection of the Fourteenth Amendment. *See Goodluck v. Apache County,* 417 F. Supp. 13 (D. Ariz. 1975), *aff'd sub nom. Apache County v. U.S.,* 429 U.S. 876 (1976).

3. This subject is discussed in sections B, C, and D of this chapter.

4. *Everson v. Board of Education*, 330 U.S. 1 (1947); *McCollum v. Board of Education*, 333 U.S. 203 (1948).

5. *See Engel v. Vitale*, 370 U.S. 421 (1962); *Abington School District v. Schempp*, 374 U.S. 203 (1963).

6. *See Engel* and *Abington*, note 5 above. *See also Epperson v. Arkansas*, 393 U.S. 97 (1968).

7. *Wisconsin v. Yoder*, 406 U.S. 205 (1972); *Thomas v. Review Board*, 450 U.S. 707 (1981).

8. *See* John Rhodes, "An American Tradition: The Religious Persecution of Native Americans," 52 *Mont. L. Rev.* 13 (1991); Russel L. Barsh, "The Illusion of Religious Freedom for Indigenous Americans," 65 *Or. L. Rev.* 363 (1986).

9. For a discussion of the compelling interest test, *see generally Edenfield v. Fane*, 507 U.S. 761 (1993); *City of Akron v. Akron Center for Reproductive Health*, 462 U.S. 416, 444 (1983); *Loving v. Virginia*, 388 U.S. 1 (1967).

10. 476 U.S. 693 (1986).

11. 485 U.S. 439 (1988). *See also Fools Crow v. Gullet*, 706 F.2d 856 (8th Cir.), *cert. denied*, 464 U.S. 997 (1983); *Badoni v. Higginson*, 638 F.2d 172 (10th Cir. 1980), *cert. denied*, 452 U.S. 954 (1981); *Sequoyah v. TVA*, 620 F.2d 1159 (6th Cir.), *cert. denied*, 449 U.S. 953 (1980).

12. *Lyng v. Northwest Indian Cemetery Protective Association*, 485 U.S. 439, 451 (1988).

13. 482 U.S. 342 (1987).

14. 494 U.S. 872 (1990).

15. *Employment Division v. Smith*, 494 U.S. 872, 886 n.3 (1990).

16. *See, e.g., Teterud v. Burns*, 522 F.2d 357 (8th Cir. 1975).

17. Cases upholding a prison ban on long hair despite the Free Exercise challenges of inmates include *Harris v. Chapman*, 97 F.3d 499, 503–4 (11th Cir. 1996); *Hamilton v. Schriro*, 74 F.3d 1545, 1551 (8th Cir. 1996); *Pollack v. Marshall*, 845 F.2d 656 (6th Cir.), *cert. denied*, 488 U.S. 897 (1988). *See also Allen v. Toombs*, 827 F.2d 563 (9th Cir. 1987) (ban on sweat lodge); *Standing Deer v. Carlson*, 831 F.2d 1525 (9th Cir. 1987) (ban on headgear). However, courts have required prison officials, even under the rational basis test, to show proof and not rely merely on speculation that the activity in question is a threat to prison security. *See Swift v. Lewis*, 901 F.2d 730 (9th Cir. 1990) (long hair); *Sapa Najin v. Gunter*, 857 F.2d 463 (8th Cir. 1988) (access to spiritual leaders); *Whitney v. Brown*, 882 F.2d 1068 (6th Cir. 1989) (attending religious services). *See generally Youngbear v. Thalacker*, 17 F.Supp.2d 902 (N.D. Iowa 2001).

18. H.R. Rep. No. 1308, 95th Cong., 2d Sess., *reprinted in* 1978 U.S. Code Cong. & Admin. News 1262.

19. S.J. Res. 102, Aug. 11, 1978, Pub. L. No. 95–341, 92 Stat. 469, *codified in part* 42 U.S.C. Sec. 1996.

20. *Lyng*, note 12 above, 485 U.S. at 455.

21. *See Wilson v. Block*, 708 F.2d 735, 746 (D.C. Cir.), *cert. denied*, 464 U.S. 956 (1983); *Standing Deer*, note 17 above, 831 F.2d at 1530.

22. 42 U.S.C. Sec. 2000bb *et seq.*

23. 42 U.S.C. Sec. 2000bb(b)(1).

24. 521 U.S. 507 (1997).

25. *Kikumura v. Hurley,* 242 F.3d 950 (10th Cir. 2001).

26. As the Court recognized in *Employment Division v. Smith,* 494 U.S. 872, 890 (1990), the federal and state legislatures remain free to create new rights. Many state constitutions and state laws provide greater religious protections than the Free Exercise Clause. *See, e.g., Humphrey v. Lane,* 728 N.E.2d 1039 (Ohio 2000) (holding that the Ohio constitution prohibits prison administrators from requiring Indian prison officer to cut his hair in violation of his religious beliefs).

27. *See, e.g.,* Ariz. Rev. Stat. Ann. Sec. 13–3402(b)(1)-(3) (1989); Colo. Rev. Stat. Sec. 12–22–317(3) (1985); N.M. Stat. Ann. Sec. 30–31–6(D) (Supp. 1989).

28. 42 U.S.C. Sec. 1996a; *see* 21 C.F.R. Sec. 1307.31 (1990). *See Peyote Way Church of God, Inc. v. Thornburgh,* 922 F.2d 1210 (5th Cir. 1991).

29. 42 U.S.C. Sec. 1996a(b)(1).

30. 16 U.S.C. Sec. 668(a).

31. The Secretary's regulations are contained in 50 C.F.R. Part 22.

32. *See Badoni* and *Sequoyah,* note 11 above.

33. *U.S. v. Means,* 858 F.2d 404 (8th Cir. 1988).

34. *Wilson,* note 21 above.

35. Exec. Order 13007, 61 Fed. Reg. 26771 (1996).

36. *See Bear Lodge Multiple Use Ass'n v. Babbitt,* 175 F.3d 814 (10th Cir. 1999), *cert. denied,* 529 U.S. 1037 (2000). Many Indians are urging Congress to pass legislation specially protecting Indian sacred sites. *See* Suzan Harjo, "Protecting Native Peoples' Sacred Places," *reprinted in Indian Country Today* (Apr. 3, 2002), at A5.

37. *See* note 2 above.

38. *See generally Shaw v. Reno,* 509 U.S. 630 (1993); *Plyler v. Doe,* 457 U.S. 202, 207 (1982); *Brown v. Board of Education,* 347 U.S. 483 (1954).

39. *Cuthair v. Montezuma-Cortez Colorado Sch. Dist.,* 7 F. Supp.2d 1152, 1155 (D. Colo. 1998).

40. *Shirley v. Superior Court,* 513 P.2d 939 (Ariz. 1973), *cert. denied,* 415 U.S. 917 (1974).

41. *Piper v. Big Pine School Dist.,* 226 P.2d 926 (Cal. 1924); *Dewey County v. U.S.,* 26 F.2d 434 (8th Cir. 1928).

42. *Acosta v. San Diego County,* 272 P.2d 92 (Cal. 1954); *State Bd. of Pub. Welfare v. Board of Comm'rs,* 137 S.E.2d 801 (N.C. 1964).

43. *Denison v. State,* 268 P. 617 (Ariz. 1928).

44. *Begay v. Sawtelle,* 88 P.2d 999 (Ariz. 1939).

45. *Bradley v. Arizona Corp. Comm'n,* 141 P.2d 524 (Ariz. 1943).

46. *Fernandez v. State,* 144 P. 640 (Ariz. 1914).

47. *McMasters v. Chase,* 573 F.2d 1011 (8th Cir. 1978); *U.S. v. City of Oneida, N.Y.,* Civ. No. 77-Civ.-399 (D.N.Y. 1977), *reprinted in* 4 Indian L. Rep. K-18 (1977).

48. *Howe v. Ellenbecker,* 8 F.3d 1258 (8th Cir. 1993), *cert. denied,* 511 U.S. 1005 (1994).

49. *Navajo Nation v. State of New Mexico,* 975 F.2d 741, 743 (10th Cir. 1992), *cert. denied,* 507 U.S. 986 (1993).

50. *See, e.g.,* ch. 11 (hunting and fishing rights) and ch. 12 (water rights).

51. *See, e.g., Brough v. Appawora,* 553 P.2d 934 (Utah 1976), *vacated,* 431 U.S. 901 (1977); *Acosta,* note 42 above; *State Bd. of Pub. Welfare,* note 42 above.

52. *See* the discussion of this subject in ch. 1. *See also* American Indian Policy Review Commission, *Final Report* (Washington, D.C.: Government Printing Office, 1977) at 87–94.

53. C. Wilkinson, "Several Myths Muddy Understanding of Indian Fishing Dispute," *Oregon Journal* (July 20, 1976) at 10.

54. *Livingston v. Ewing,* 601 F.2d 1110 (10th Cir.), *cert. denied,* 444 U.S. 870 (1979).

55. *See Kreuth v. Indep. Sch. Dist. No. 38,* 496 N.W.2d 829 (Minn. App.), *review denied,* 1993 Minn. Lexis 285 (Minn. 1993).

56. *Wesberry v. Sanders,* 376 U.S. 1, 17 (1964); *Harper v. Virginia Board of Elections,* 383 U.S. 663 (1966).

57. 42 U.S.C. Secs. 1973 *et seq.*

58. 42 U.S.C. Sec. 1973aa-1a.

59. *Id.,* Sec. 1973aa-1a(e).

60. *Id. See U.S. v. County of San Juan,* 7 Indian L. Rep. 3077 (D.N.M. 1980). *See also U.S. v. Metropolitan Dade County, Florida,* 815 F. Supp. 1475 (S.D. Fla. 1993).

61. *U.S. v. Blaine County,* 157 F. Supp.2d 1145, 1152 (D. Mont. 2001). *See also Little Thunder v. South Dakota,* 518 F.2d 1253 (8th Cir. 1975).

62. *Harrison v. Laveen,* 196 P.2d 456 (Ariz. 1948).

63. *See Goodluck,* note 2 above. *See also Prince v. Board of Education,* 543 P.2d 1176 (N.M. 1975).

64. *See In re Certification of Question of Law From U.S. Dist. Court, Dist. of South Dakota,* 615 N.W.2d 590 (S.D. 200); *Emery v. Hunt,* Civ. No. 00–3008 (D.S.D., order entered Aug. 10, 2000).

65. *Cuthair,* note 39 above.

66. *See Old Person v. Cooney,* 230 F.3d 1113 (9th Cir. 2000); *Windy Boy v. County of Big Horn,* 647 F. Supp. 1002 (D. Mont. 1986). *See also Buckanaga v. Sisseton Ind. Sch. Dist.,* 804 F.2d 469 (8th Cir. 1986).

67. *Civil Rights Cases,* 109 U.S. 3 (1883).

68. 42 U.S.C. Secs. 3601 *et seq.*

69. 42 U.S.C. Secs. 2000e *et seq. See Dawavendewa v. Salt River Project Agricultural Improvement and Power Dist.,* 154 F.3d 1117 (9th Cir. 1998).

70. 42 U.S.C. Secs. 1981, 1982. *See, e.g., Scott v. Eversole Mortuary,* 522 F.2d 1110 (9th Cir. 1975).

71. 42 U.S.C. Secs. 2000a *et seq.*

72. The report is cited in "Discrimination on the Rise in Montana," *Indian Country Today* (Jan. 25, 1996) at A3.

73. 42 U.S.C. Sec. 1982.

74. *Lac Du Flambeau Band of Lake Superior Chippewa Indians v. Stop Treaty Abuse–Wisconsin, Inc.,* 41 F.3d 1190 (7th Cir. 1995), *cert. denied,* 514 U.S. 1096 (1995).

75. South Dakota Advisory Committee to the U.S. Commission on Civil Rights, "Native Americans in South Dakota: An Erosion of Confidence in the Justice System" (March 2000) at 39.

76. "Repatriation Act Protects Native Burial Remains," *NARF Legal Review* (Winter 1990) at 2.

77. 20 U.S.C. Secs. 80q to 80q-15.

78. 25 U.S.C. Secs. 3001–13.

79. However, only federally recognized tribes have a right to demand that an object be returned under NAGPRA. *See* 25 U.S.C. Sec. 3001(7).

80. *See* T. A. Livesay, "The Impact of the Federal Repatriation Claims on State Operated Museums," 24 *Ariz. St. L.J.* 293 (1992).

81. *See Yankton Sioux Tribe v. U.S. Army Corps of Engineers,* 83 F. Supp.2d 1047 (D.S.D. 2000) (enjoining federal officials from raising the water level of a lake located on federal property until tribal officials were given an opportunity to remove artifacts and human remains discovered in the area to be flooded).

82. 25 U.S.C. Sec. 3002(a). *See Romero v. Becken,* 256 F.3d 349 (5th Cir. 2001).

83. 18 U.S.C. Sec. 1170. *See San Idelfonso v. Ridlon,* 103 F.3d 936 (10th Cir. 1996); *U.S. v. Carrow,* 119 F.3d 796, 799–800 (10th Cir. 1997), *cert. denied,* 522 U.S. 1133 (1998).

84. *U.S. v. Tidwell,* 191 F.3d 976 (9th Cir. 1999).

85. *See* "'Redskins' Means Indians Don't Matter," *Indian Country Today* (editorial) (Jan. 23, 2002) at A4.

86. *See* Rebecca Adamson, "Taking Tribal Sovereignty to the Market," *Indian Country Today* (Jan. 16, 2002) at A3. A list of these names is available on the American Indian Cultural Support website: <www.aics.org/mascots>.

87. Quoted in Howard Zinn, *Christopher Columbus and the Myth of Human Progress, 1492–1992* (Amsterdam: Open Magazine Pamphlet Series, 1992) at 2.

88. *Id.*

89. *Id.,* at 3.

90. The video *The Drums of October: Legacy of a Pernicious Hero* is produced by Lori Windle, Echomaker Productions, 2001. A copy can be obtained for $15 (which includes postage and handling) from All Nations Alliance, c/o Escuela Tlatelolco, 2949 No. Federal Blvd., Denver, CO 80211. The phone number is 303–964–8993.

91. Many people have long been calling for a transformation of Columbus Day. The Denver, Colorado, chapter of the American Indian Movement has helped focus national attention on this issue. One of its leaders, Glenn Morris, organized a coalition of diverse groups committed to transforming the holiday. Further information can be obtained from the Internet website: <http: www.transformcolumbusday.org>.

XIV

The Indian Civil Rights Act

Congress passed the Indian Civil Rights Act (ICRA) in 1968.[1] The ICRA is a highly controversial law because it authorizes federal courts to intervene in *intratribal* disputes and overrule decisions made by tribal officials in internal government matters. No other law confers that power.

Broadly, the ICRA does two things. First, it bestows numerous rights on all persons subject to the jurisdiction of a tribal government. Second, it authorizes federal courts to protect and enforce many of those rights. Thus, the ICRA limits the power of tribes by conferring civil rights upon all persons subject to tribal law and gives federal courts the power to enforce those rights in various contexts.

Why did Congress pass the Indian Civil Rights Act?

In 1832 in *Worcester v. Georgia,* the Supreme Court recognized that Indian tribes are "distinct, independent political communities, retaining their original natural rights" in matters of local government.[2] Congress has the power, the Court said, to limit tribal powers, but unless Congress exercises that power, each tribe retains its inherent right to be self-governing.

Consistent with that principle, the Supreme Court held in 1896 in *Talton v. Mayes*[3] that Indian tribes are not obligated to conform their governments—or their methods of governing—to the standards imposed on the state and federal governments by the U.S. Constitution. Indian tribes retain the right to govern themselves as their members see fit, unless and until Congress limits that right.

These Supreme Court decisions had the effect of leaving intratribal disputes entirely in the hands of the tribe. Indians who objected to the way they were being treated by tribal officials had to resolve their com-

278

plaints within the tribe. Federal courts could not hear claims filed against an Indian tribe involving an internal dispute, even suits alleging that tribal officials had engaged in discriminatory or abusive activity that would violate the U.S. Constitution if done by a state or federal official.[4]

In 1962, a subcommittee of the U.S. Senate began a series of hearings concerning the administration of justice by tribal governments.[5] Many tribal members testified that on some reservations tribal officials were tyrannical and biased, elections were rigged, tribal courts were corrupt and unfair, and tribal members were being denied their rights under tribal law. These witnesses asked Congress to pass legislation protecting them from further abuse.[6]

Other tribal members strongly disputed these allegations. Moreover, they said, there was no need for federal intervention in tribal affairs. If some members of the tribe had complaints about tribal government, they should work them out within the tribe, not have some outsider impose "white man's" law on the tribe. In addition, many of these witnesses opposed the very notion that individuals should be given rights by the federal government that they could then assert against the tribe, because Indian values traditionally place the rights of the community above the needs or interests of individuals.

Some members of Congress who heard this testimony were startled and distressed to learn the U.S. Constitution was inapplicable to tribal powers. This meant that thousands of U.S. citizens were living under a form of government that did not have to respect the civil rights conferred by the Bill of Rights. As one senator stated at the conclusion of the hearings:

As the hearings developed and as the evidence and testimony were taken, I believe all of us who were students of the law were jarred and shocked by the conditions as far as constitutional rights for members of the Indian tribes were concerned. There was found to be unchecked and unlimited authority over many facets of Indian rights. . . . The Constitution simply was not applicable.[7]

The end result of these hearings was the passage of the Indian Civil Rights Act. The purpose of the act was "to ensure that the American Indian is afforded the broad Constitutional rights secured to other Americans . . . [in order to] protect individual Indians from arbitrary and unjust actions of tribal governments."[8]

The Indian Civil Rights Act (25 U.S.C. §§ 1301–41) has five parts, only one of which confers civil rights (secs. 1301–3). The other parts concern such matters as how a state can acquire or relinquish jurisdiction over an Indian reservation, and these are discussed elsewhere in this book.[9] In this chapter, all references to the ICRA relate to the civil rights portion of the act.

What rights are conferred by the ICRA?

Most of the civil rights conferred by the U.S. Constitution are conferred by the ICRA. Some senators initially suggested that every civil right conferred by the Constitution be included in the ICRA. But it was pointed out that certain provisions of the Constitution would seriously undermine, if not destroy, tribal government. For instance, if tribes had to comply with the Fifteenth Amendment, they could not discriminate in voting on account of race or color.[10] This would mean that non-Indians who lived on the reservation could vote in tribal elections and hold tribal office, something that Congress was not trying to accomplish.

The Establishment Clause of the First Amendment presented another unique problem. That clause requires the federal and state governments to remain completely neutral in religious matters.[11] If this provision were enforced on Indian reservations, it would seriously disrupt those tribal governments in which religion (and religious leaders) have always played a central role in governing the tribe.

In deference to the unique needs of Indian tribes, the ICRA does not contain an Establishment Clause, and it does not prevent a tribe from discriminating in voting on account of race or color. In addition, in order to avoid imposing undue financial hardships, tribes are not required to convene a jury in civil trials or, in criminal cases, to issue grand jury indictments or appoint counsel for indigent defendants, rights that are conferred by the U.S. Constitution.[12] The rights conferred by the ICRA are listed in section 1302 of the act, which is reproduced in appendix A of this book. Among them are the right to free speech, press, and assembly; protection against unreasonable search and seizure; the right to a speedy trial; the right to hire a lawyer in a criminal case; protection against self-incrimination; protection against cruel and unusual punishment; and the right to equal protection of tribal law and to due process of law.

Does the ICRA protect non-Indians as well as Indians?

Yes. The ICRA applies to "any person" who is subject to the jurisdiction of a tribal government.[13]

Does the ICRA limit the criminal punishments that tribal courts can impose?

Yes. The ICRA limits tribal punishment in criminal cases to one year of imprisonment and a $5,000 fine or both.[14] A person who commits two crimes can receive two one-year sentences to be served consecutively.[15]

Have tribes had to alter some of their institutions and practices because of the ICRA?

Yes. In order to comply with the ICRA, tribes have had to make some changes in how they govern, including how their courts operate. Tribes have been required to advise criminal defendants of their right to a trial by jury;[16] to write their criminal laws in clear and unambiguous language;[17] to prohibit the trial judge from also acting as the prosecutor;[18] to adequately record the proceedings in the tribe's trial court so that an appellate court can determine what occurred during the trial;[19] and to ensure that arrests are made in compliance with the procedures mandated by the ICRA.[20]

The rights in the ICRA were borrowed from the U.S. Constitution. Are they being interpreted similarly?

The rights contained in the ICRA were patterned after rights contained in the Bill of Rights and the Fourteenth Amendment to the Constitution and are nearly a verbatim rendition of them. However, this does not necessarily mean that the rights in the ICRA must be interpreted the same way that federal courts interpret the rights in the Constitution. Indeed, "there is a definite trend by tribal courts" toward the view that Congress did not intend for them to follow federal court decisions "jot-for-jot" when interpreting the ICRA.[21]

The main reason Congress enacted the ICRA was to protect individuals from certain abuses, but Congress also was concerned about the unique political, cultural, religious, and financial needs of the tribe. This explains why Congress refused to include in the ICRA all of the civil rights contained in the Constitution.[22] The ICRA reflects a balance between individual liberties on the one hand and tribal needs on the other. "[The] ICRA's legislative history reflects that Congress carefully balanced the desire to protect the rights of Native Americans with the desire to avoid extensive interference with internal tribal affairs."[23] Courts have balanced both interests in interpreting and applying the act and have been particularly reluctant to apply the ICRA in a manner that would "significantly impair a tribal practice or alter a custom firmly embedded in Indian culture."[24]

If you are facing criminal charges in tribal court and cannot afford a lawyer, must the tribe hire one for you?

No. The Sixth Amendment to the U.S. Constitution requires state and federal courts to appoint counsel for indigent defendants in criminal cases.[25] During the Senate hearings on the ICRA, tribal leaders asked Congress not to impose that duty on tribal courts because of the tremendous expense.[26] This testimony persuaded Congress. The ICRA guarantees a criminal defendant the right to counsel only "at his own expense;"[27] thus, tribal courts are not required to appoint counsel in criminal cases even if the defendant cannot afford to hire one.[28]

If a tribe violates rights protected by the ICRA, what can be done about it? Can the tribe be sued?

The ICRA contains a long list of rights but just one remedy, which is set forth in section 1303. Section 1303 states in its entirety: "The privilege of the writ of habeas corpus shall be available to any person, in a court of the United States, to test the legality of his detention by order of an Indian tribe."

A writ of habeas corpus is a court decree ordering that a person being held in custody be brought before the court so the lawfulness of the detention can be assessed. The writ is served upon the person's custodian, that is, the person who is holding the petitioner.

Any person being imprisoned by an Indian tribe in violation of the ICRA may petition a federal court for a writ of habeas corpus.[29] At least one federal court has held that a writ of habeas corpus is also available under the ICRA to challenge certain child custody determinations made by tribal courts,[30] but other courts have held that such writs are not available under the ICRA.[31]

Federal courts have created the rule that a petition for writ of habeas corpus may not be sought in a federal court until the petitioner has first exhausted available tribal remedies, such as by first filing a petition for writ of habeas corpus in tribal court. As explained more fully in chapter 9, section A, the exhaustion requirement maximizes tribal independence and prevents unnecessary federal intervention in tribal affairs.[32] A failure to exhaust tribal remedies is allowed only in limited circumstances, such as when the delay caused by proceeding in tribal court would likely cause the petitioner to suffer irreparable injury.[33]

Given that the ICRA provides only one remedy—a writ of habeas corpus, which a court can issue *only* when the petitioner is being imprisoned —it is apparent that certain rights conferred by the ICRA cannot be remedied in a federal court. For instance, if a tribe violates the ICRA's Just Compensation Clause by taking property without compensation, or if the tribe violates the ICRA's Equal Protection Clause and refuses to enroll persons as members of the tribe or permit them to run for tribal office despite their eligibility, the federal courts are not allowed to intervene because no detention is involved. Those persons would have federal rights but no federal remedies.[34]

For several years after the ICRA was passed, many federal courts were accepting and deciding these types of "noncustodial" ICRA cases—cases in which the petitioner was *not* in custody. The courts held that the ICRA waived the tribe's sovereign immunity with respect to each right conferred by it, thereby authorizing federal courts to resolve all disputes arising under the ICRA.[35] (The origin and scope of tribal sovereign immunity is discussed in chapter 18.) But in 1978—ten years after the ICRA was enacted—the Supreme Court held in *Santa Clara Pueblo v. Martinez*[36] that the writ of habeas corpus is the only remedy that federal courts may grant under the ICRA. Indeed, the Court said, given that a writ of habeas corpus is directed to the individual who is actually holding the petitioner in custody and not to the government itself, by authorizing such lawsuits the ICRA did not waive tribal sovereign immunity *at all.* Tribal officials, the Court explained, were still required to obey the entire ICRA, but federal courts could enforce the act only when the petitioner was in custody. In all other cases—the "noncustodial" violations—complainants could only seek a remedy in a *tribal* forum, such as a tribal court, the tribal council, or at the ballot box by voting tribal officials out of office.

Both before *Santa Clara Pueblo* and even after it, numerous noncustodial ICRA lawsuits were filed against tribal officials in federal court raising allegations of misconduct. These suits claimed, for example, that tribal officials had illegally denied membership to the petitioner or her right to be a candidate for tribal office; that tribal elections were fraudulent; that a tribe had wrongfully confiscated private property; that tribal officials illegally removed the petitioner from the tribe's membership rolls; and that the petitioner had been fired from tribal employment in retaliation for having criticized a tribal official.[37] Prior to *Santa Clara Pueblo,* federal courts accepted these types of cases, but now they may not; even though a federal right conferred by the ICRA may have been violated, the tribe enjoys sovereign immunity from all lawsuits of that nature filed in federal court.[38] Since *Santa Clara Pueblo,* only one federal court has accepted a noncustodial case under the ICRA, a lawsuit filed by a non-Indian whose rights were allegedly violated by a tribe, and he had no recourse within the tribe to challenge what was occurring.[39] But this decision is inconsistent with *Santa Clara Pueblo,* and the same court that decided that case essentially repudiated it in subsequent cases and has not accepted any additional noncustodial ICRA lawsuits.[40] The well-established rule is that no one may pursue a lawsuit in federal court under the ICRA unless he or she is imprisoned by tribal officials, and even then, only after exhausting all available tribal remedies.

In a recent case, some tribal members filed suit in federal court under the ICRA alleging that tribal officials had banished them from their reservation for life for having committed "treason," and had stripped them of all rights of membership. In a 2 to 1 decision, a federal appellate court held that banishment under these circumstances was similar enough to a criminal prosecution that it should be viewed as a custodial case under the ICRA, and the court allowed the case to proceed.[41]

If the federal courts cannot hear the ICRA claim, do alternatives exist?

The Supreme Court held in *Santa Clara Pueblo,* as just explained, that noncustodial cases cannot be heard in a federal court under the ICRA due to the tribe's sovereign immunity from suit. The Court indicated, though, that these noncustodial cases can be heard in a tribal forum. "Tribal forums are available," the Court said in *Santa Clara Pueblo,* "to vindicate rights created by the ICRA, and section 1302 has the substantial and intended effect of changing the law which these forums are obliged to apply."[42] In a later case, the Supreme Court reiterated its understanding that the ICRA provides all persons "with various protections against unfair treatment."[43]

These statements, however, were "dicta" in those cases. ("Dicta" are statements in a court opinion that are not necessary to the decision being rendered and therefore have no binding, obligatory effect.) The Supreme Court apparently believes that noncustodial ICRA cases can be heard in a tribal forum, but no decision of the Court has imposed that duty. Many tribal courts have held that the ICRA does *not* waive tribal immunity from suit in tribal court and have refused to adjudicate ICRA claims.[44] Other tribal courts have reached the opposite conclusion, holding that the ICRA does waive the tribe's sovereign immunity from suit in tribal court for violations of that act, although a few of these courts have allowed suits to proceed that seek only injunctive relief and have not allowed suits seeking damages.[45]

Some tribes have enacted laws or adopted provisions in their constitutions expressly consenting to ICRA suits in tribal court. The Constitution of the Three Affiliated Tribes of the Ft. Berthold Reservation in North Dakota confers on its tribal courts "the authority to enforce the provisions of the Indian Civil Rights Act" and waives the tribe's immunity from ICRA lawsuits.[46] The Constitution of the Grand Traverse Band of Ottawa and Chippewa Indians in Michigan takes a compromise position. It allows ICRA suits against the tribe for declaratory or injunctive relief, but a suit seeking damages is permitted only if the tribal council has passed a law expressly permitting it.[47] The Supreme Court stated in *Santa Clara Pueblo* that Indian tribes have the option under the ICRA of designating which forum will hear disputes arising under the act,[48] and some tribes have enacted laws allowing tribal members to bring their ICRA grievances to the tribal council rather than to the tribal court.[49]

On some reservations, then, victims of noncustodial ICRA violations can seek a remedy in a tribal forum, either because the tribal court has ruled that the ICRA waives the tribe's immunity or because the tribal council has passed an ordinance expressly consenting to ICRA lawsuits. On other reservations, victims of noncustodial ICRA violations have no judicial remedy at all, federal or tribal.

Tribal courts that are permitted to hear ICRA cases have issued some strong rulings against tribal officials found to have committed ICRA violations. Tribal officials were ordered by a tribal court to repay money taken from the tribe in violation of tribal law; a tribal council was ordered to reinstate a tribal judge that the council had illegally expelled from office; tribal officials who were preventing a tribal member from living on the reservation were ordered to provide that person with a fair hearing on the issue; tribal supervisors were ordered to reinstate a non-Indian employee of the tribe's casino whom they had fired without a fair hearing; and tribal officials were ordered not to remove some Indian children from the custody of their grandmother until she was given a fair hearing regarding the need for their removal.[50]

For a few years after the Supreme Court's 1978 decision in *Santa Clara Pueblo,* it appeared that the Bureau of Indian Affairs (BIA) would take an active role in enforcing the ICRA. In 1980, the BIA warned tribes that violations of the ICRA could result in the loss of federal funds or, in those instances in which tribal election laws had been violated, a refusal by the federal government to recognize tribal officials as being legitimately seated.[51] Since then, the BIA has done very little to enforce the ICRA, and its director admitted in 1988 that the BIA had developed a hands-off policy with regard to most ICRA violations.[52]

In 1992, the Interior Board of Indian Affairs, which hears administrative appeals of decisions made by officials within the BIA, held that the BIA "has the authority and the responsibility to decline to recognize the results of a tribal election when it finds that a violation of ICRA has tainted the election results."[53] However, this power has rarely been exercised, as discussed in chapter 5, section B(2).

A federal criminal law prohibits persons from conspiring to deny another person their civil rights.[54] One federal court has ruled that tribal members who conspire to rig a tribal election, thereby denying members of their rights under the ICRA, can be prosecuted under federal conspiracy laws.[55] This provides another option in enforcing the ICRA in those instances in which tribal officials have conspired amongst themselves to deprive someone of rights protected by the ICRA.

Should the ICRA be amended so as to authorize federal suits against tribal governments?

As just indicated, many victims of ICRA violations have no judicial remedy, tribal or federal. This does not mean, however, that Congress should amend the ICRA, as many people are urging, and authorize federal courts to resolve all ICRA disputes.

In 1989 and again in 1990, a bill was introduced in Congress that if passed would have authorized federal courts to hear all types of ICRA cases. Similar to the controversy that raged when the ICRA was first proposed in the 1960s, opponents of these bills argued that their passage would dilute tribal powers, interfere with tribal autonomy, and permit outsiders to resolve tribal disputes, many of which concern tribal customs and traditions about which these outsiders know nothing.[56] Proponents of the bills, on the other hand, argued that ICRA violations are so injurious that resort to a federal court is necessary if basic civil rights are to be respected[57] and that the absence of an impartial forum to resolve these disputes is creating disrespect for tribal law and tribal officials. Without a federal court "safety net," proponents contend, reservation Indians are the only people in the United States whose fundamental civil liberties can be violated without the opportunity for court review. Lack of a federal court remedy for ICRA violations is especially troublesome in those situations in which complainants allege that they have been illegally denied membership in a tribe or illegally disenrolled from a tribe, given that these people cannot vote in tribal elections and usually lack all opportunity for redress within the tribe, both judicially and politically.[58]

In 1999, the newspaper *Indian Country Today* stated in an editorial that "strengthening the Indian Civil Rights Act must become a priority." According to the editors of the paper, "[W]e get at least one call a week detailing Indian government abuses against its own citizens. Misappropriation of money, handouts to relatives, nepotism and abuse of sovereignty are a few of the problems facing many Indian communities." Also cited was retaliation against tribal members "who attempt to expose corrupt leaders or stand up for their civil rights." The editorial recommended that the ICRA be amended to permit federal courts to hear these types of disputes.[59]

A federal court has stated that "the effect, after *Santa Clara Pueblo*, of the ICRA is to create rights while withholding any meaningful remedies to enforce them . . . but it is for Congress, not the courts, to resolve this state of affairs."[60] Whether Indians lack meaningful remedies on their reservations and, even if so, whether Congress should intervene, are questions very much in controversy.

Notes

1. 25 U.S.C. Secs. 1301 *et seq.*

2. *Worcester v. Georgia*, 31 U.S. 515, 559 (1832).

3. *Talton v. Mayes*, 163 U.S. 376 (1896). *See also U.S. v. Wheeler*, 435 U.S. 313 (1978).

4. *See Santa Clara Pueblo v. Martinez*, 436 U.S. 49 (1978); *Native American Church*

v. Navajo Tribal Council, 272 F.2d 131 (10th Cir. 1959); *Twin Cities Chippewa Tribal Council v. Minnesota Chippewa Tribe,* 370 F.2d 529 (8th Cir. 1967). *But see Colliflower v. Garland,* 342 F.2d 369 (9th Cir. 1965).

5. The legislative history of the Indian Civil Rights Act is discussed in *Santa Clara Pueblo v. Martinez,* 436 U.S. 49 (1978). *See also* Donald Burnett, "An Historical Analysis of the 1968 'Indian Civil Rights' Act," 9 *Harv. J. on Legis.* 557 (1972).

6. *See* Alvin J. Ziontz, "In Defense of Tribal Sovereignty: An Analysis of Judicial Error in Construction of the Indian Civil Rights Act," 20 *S. Dak. L. Rev.* 1–2 (1975); Joseph de Raismes, "The Indian Civil Rights Act of 1968 and the Pursuit of Responsible Tribal Self-Government," 20 *S. Dak. L. Rev.* 59, 73 (1975).

7. 113 Cong. Rec. part 26, p. 35473, 90th Cong., 1st Sess. (Dec. 7, 1967) (statement of Sen. Hruska [R. Neb.]).

8. S. Rep. No. 841, 90th Cong., 1st Sess. 6 (1967). *See Santa Clara Pueblo,* note 4 above, 436 U.S. at 61.

9. *See, e.g.,* ch. 7, sec. B, which discusses part 3 of the ICRA (assumption and retro-cession of state jurisdiction over Indian reservations).

10. The Fifteenth Amendment states in pertinent part: "The right of citizens of the United States to vote shall not be denied or abridged by the United States or by any State on account of race, color, or previous condition of servitude."

11. *See* ch. 13, note 6 and accompanying text.

12. The reason why these various protections were omitted from the ICRA is ex-plained in *Santa Clara Pueblo,* note 4 above, 436 U.S. at 66–70. *See also* Burnett, note 5 above. It should also be noted that the U.S. Constitution does not expressly require that counsel be appointed to an indigent criminal defendant, but the Supreme Court has inter-preted the Sixth Amendment's right to counsel and the Fifth and Fourteenth Amendment's right to due process of law as requiring federal and state courts to do so. *See Gideon v. Wainwright,* 372 U.S. 335 (1963).

13. 25 U.S.C. Sec. 1302.

14. 25 U.S.C. Sec. 1302(7).

15. *See Means v. Northern Cheyenne Tribal Court,* 154 F.3d 941, 942 n.1 (9th Cir. 1998); *Ramos v. Pyramid Lake Tribal Court,* 13 Indian L. Rep. 3003 (D. Nev. 1985); *Tuckta v. Cruz,* 16 Indian L. Rep. 3102 (D. Or. 1988).

16. *Red Elk v. Silk,* 10 Indian L. Rep. 3109 (D. Mont. 1983). *Cf. U.S. v. McGahuey,* 10 Indian L. Rep. 6051 (Hoopa Ct. Ind. Off. 1983) (if no imprisonment, no right to a jury trial).

17. *Big Eagle v. Andera,* 508 F.2d 1293 (8th Cir. 1975), *on remand,* 418 F. Supp. 126 (D.S.D. 1976); *Burns Paiute Indian Tribe v. Dick,* 22 Indian L. Rep. 6016 (Burns Paiute Ct. App. 1994).

18. *Wounded Knee v. Andera,* 416 F. Supp. 1236 (D.S.D. 1976).

19. *Rosebud Sioux Tribe v. White Hat,* 11 Indian L. Rep. 6033 (Intertr. Ct. App. 1983).

20. *Walker River Paiute Tribe v. Jake,* 23 Indian L. Rep. 6024 (Walk. Riv. Tr. Ct. 1996).

21. *Nevada v. Hicks,* 121 S.Ct. 2304, 2323 (2001) (Souter, J., concurring), citing Nell

Jessup Newton, "Tribal Court Praxis: One Year in the Life of Twenty Indian Tribal Courts," 22 *Am. Ind. L. Rev.* 285, 344 n.238 (1998).

22. *See Santa Clara Pueblo*, note 4 above, 436 U.S. at 66–70; *Tom v. Sutton*, 533 F.2d 1101, 1103–4 (9th Cir. 1976).

23. *U.S. v. Doherty*, 126 F.3d 769, 779 (6th Cir. 1997), *cert. denied*, 524 U.S. 917 (1998).

24. *Howlett v. Salish and Kootenai Tribes*, 529 F.2d 233, 234 (9th Cir. 1976). *See also Wounded Head v. Tribal Council*, 507 F.2d 1079 (8th Cir. 1975). Tribal practices of recent vintage, or those that significantly impinge on the freedoms protected by the ICRA, have not been accorded the same dignity. *See Selam v. Warm Springs Tribal Correctional Facility*, 134 F.3d 948 (9th Cir. 1998); *Doherty*, note 23 above, 126 F.3d at 779–81; *Wounded Knee*, note 18 above; *White Eagle v. One Feather*, 478 F.2d 1311 (8th Cir. 1973); *Randall v. Yakima Nation Tribal Court*, 841 F.2d 897 (9th Cir. 1988).

25. *See Argersinger v. Hamlin*, 407 U.S. 25 (1972).

26. *See* Burnett, note 5 above.

27. 25 U.S.C. Sec. 1302(6).

28. *See Doherty*, note 23 above; *Tom v. Sutton*, 533 F.2d 1101 (9th Cir. 1976).

29. *See* cases cited in notes 15–20 above.

30. *DeMent v. Oglala Sioux Tribal Court*, 874 F.2d 510 (8th Cir. 1989).

31. *Sandman v. Dakota*, 7 F.3d 234 (6th Cir. 1993) (unpublished decision); *Weatherwax on Behalf of Carlson v. Fairbanks*, 619 F. Supp. 294, 296 (D. Mont. 1985); *LaBeau v. Dakota*, 815 F. Supp. 1074, 1076–77 (W.D. Mich. 1993).

32. *See National Farmers Union Ins. Co. v. Crow Tribe*, 471 U.S. 845, 856 (1985); *Selam*, note 24 above; *Lyda v. Tah-Bone*, 962 F. Supp. 1434 (D. Utah 1997).

33. *See Johnson v. Gila River Indian Community*, 174 F.3d 1032, 1036 (9th Cir.), *cert. denied*, 528 U.S. 875 (1999); *St. Marks v. Chippewa-Cree Tribe*, 545 F.2d 1188, 1189–90 (9th Cir. 1976); *Wounded Knee*, note 18 above; *DeMent*, note 30 above. *See also National Farmers Union Ins. Co. v. Crow Tribe*, 471 U.S. 845, 856 n.21 (1985).

34. *See* cases cited in notes 37 and 38 below and accompanying text.

35. *See, e.g., Luxon v. Rosebud Sioux Tribe*, 455 F.2d 698 (8th Cir. 1972); *Johnson v. Lower Elwha Tribal Community*, 484 F.2d 200 (9th Cir. 1973).

36. 436 U.S. 49 (1978).

37. *See Luxon*, note 35 above (denial of candidacy); *Johnson v. Lower Elwha*, note 35 above (fraudulent election); *Ordinance 59 Ass'n v. U.S. Dept. of the Interior*, 163 F.3d 1150 (10th Cir. 1998) (denial of membership); *Olguin v. Lucero*, 87 F.3d 401 (10th Cir. 1996), *cert. denied*, 519 U.S. 982 (1997) (fired from employment); *Shenandoah v. U.S. Dept. of Interior*, 159 F.3d 708, 713–14 (2d Cir. 1996) (stricken from membership roll); *Anderson v. Las Vegas Tribe of Paiute Indians*, 103 F.3d 137 (9th Cir. 1996), *cert. denied*, 520 U.S. 1169 (1997) (same). *See also Nero v. Cherokee Nation*, 892 F.2d 1457 (10th Cir. 1989); *Shortbull v. Looking Elk*, 677 F.2d 645 (8th Cir.), *cert. denied*, 459 U.S. 907 (1982); *Wheeler v. Swimmer*, 835 F.2d 259 (10th Cir. 1987); *Crowe v. Eastern Band of Cherokee Indians*, 506 F.2d 1231 (4th Cir. 1974).

38. *See Demontiney v. U.S.*, 255 F.3d 801, 814–15 (9th Cir. 2001); *Ordinance 59*, note 37 above; *Shenandoah v. U.S. Dept. of Interior*, note 37 above; *Johnson v. Gila River*,

note 33 above; *Shannon v. Houlton Band of Maliseet Indians*, 54 F. Supp.2d 35 (D. Maine. 1999). Even if a tribal court imposes a fine—but does not impose any period of incarceration on the defendant—the defendant cannot seek review of the tribal court's order in a federal court. *See Moore v. Nelson, Jr.*, 270 F.3d 789 (9th Cir. 2001).

39. *Dry Creek Lodge, Inc. v. U.S.*, 623 F.2d 682 (10th Cir. 1980), *cert. denied*, 449 U.S. 1118 (1981).

40. *See Olguin v. Lucero*, 87 F.3d 401 (10th Cir.), *cert. denied*, 519 U.S. 982 (1996); *Bank of Oklahoma v. Muscogee (Creek) Nation*, 972 F.2d 1166, 1170 (10th Cir. 1992); *White v. Pueblo of San Juan*, 728 F.2d 1307, 1313 (10th Cir. 1984).

41. *Poodry v. Tonawanda Band of Seneca Indians*, 85 F.3d 874, 876–78 (2d Cir.), *cert. denied*, 519 U.S. 1041 (1996). This is not to say that all banishment cases can be pursued under the ICRA. *See Alire v. Jackson*, 65 F. Supp.2d 1124 (D. Ore. 1999).

42. *Santa Clara Pueblo*, note 4 above, 436 U.S. at 65.

43. *Iowa Mutual Ins. Co. v. LaPlante*, 480 U.S. 9, 19 (1987).

44. *See Shenandoah v. Halbritter*, 28 Indian L. Rep. 6036 (Oneida Nation Ct. 2001); *Smith d/b/a Frosty's v. Confederated Salish & Kootenai Tribes*, 23 Indian L. Rep. 6256 (C.S. and K.T. 1996); *Pawnee Tribe of Oklahoma v. Franseen*, 19 Indian L. Rep. 6006 (Ct. Ind. App.-Pawnee 1991); *Johnson v. Navajo Nation*, 14 Indian L. Rep. 6037, 6040 (Nav. Sup. Ct. 1987); *Satiacum v. Sterud*, 10 Indian L. Rep. 6013 (Puyallup Tr. Ct. 1983); *Garman v. Fort Belknap Community Council*, 11 Indian L. Rep. 6017 (Ft. Belknap Tr. Ct. 1984); *Stone v. Sonday*, 10 Indian L. Rep. 6039 (Colv. Tr. Ct. 1983).

45. *See Works v. Fallon Paiute–Shoshone Tribe*, 24 Indian L. Rep. 6078 (Inter-Tr. Ct. App. 1997); *Burns Paiute Indian Tribe v. Dick*, 22 Indian L. Rep. 6016 (Burns Paiute Ct. App. 1994); *Davis v. Keplin*, 18 Indian L. Rep. 6148 (Turt. Mt. Tr. Ct. 1991) *Dupree v. Cheyenne River Housing Auth.*, 16 Indian L. Rep. 6106 (Chy. R. Sx. Tr. Ct. App. 1988); *Miller v. Adams*, 10 Indian L. Rep. 6034 (Intertr. Ct. App. 1982). *See also Lawrence v. So. Puget Sound Inter-Tribal Housing Auth.*, 14 Indian L. Rep. 6011 (Suq. Tr. Ct. 1987); *Comm. for Better Tribal Government v. So. Ute Election Board*, 17 Indian L. Rep. 6145 (S. Ute. Tr. Ct. 1990). *See also Clement v. LeCompte*, 22 Indian L. Rep. 6111 (Chy. R. Sx. Ct. App. 1994) (holding that the ICRA waives immunity for certain claims against tribal officials but not against the tribe).

46. *See, e.g., Drags Wolf v. Tribal Business Council of the Three Affiliated Tribes*, 17 Indian L. Rep. 6051 (Ft. Bert. Tr. Ct. 1990); *Bordeaux v. Wilkinson*, 21 Indian L. Rep. 6131 (Ft. Bert. Tr. Ct. 1993). The Constitution of the Menominee Indian Tribe of Wisconsin, art. XVIII, contains a similar provision.

47. Constitution of the Grand Traverse Band of Ottawa and Chippewa Indians (1998), art. XIII, sec. 2.

48. *Santa Clara Pueblo*, note 4 above, 426 U.S. at 65–66 nn.21 and 22.

49. *See Brady v. Brady*, 27 Indian L. Rep. 6125 (Intertribal Ct. App. Nev. 2000) (noting that Yomba Shoshone Tribe has enacted an ordinance allowing election disputes to be resolved by the tribal council rather than the tribal court).

50. *See respectively Bordeaux*, note 46 above; *McKinney v. Business Council of the Shoshone-Paiute Tribes*, 20 Indian L. Rep. 6020 (Duck Valley Tr. Ct. 1993); *Burns Paiute Indian Tribe v. Dick*, 22 Indian L. Rep. 6016 (Burns Paiute Tr. Ct. 1994); *Grossi v. Mashan-*

tucket *Pequot Gaming Enterprise,* 26 Indian L. Rep. 6112 (Mash. Pequot Ct. App. 1998); *In re The Welfare of D.D.,* 22 Indian L. Rep. 6020 (Port Gam. S'Klallam Ct. App. 1994).

51. "Interior Department/Bureau of Indian Affairs Policy Regarding Relationship with Tribal Governments," June 12, 1980, discussed in 7 Indian L. Rep. 6021 (Aug. 1980). *See generally* Alvin Ziontz, "After Martinez: Indian Civil Rights under Tribal Government," 12 *U.C. Davis L. Rev.* 1 (1979).

52. Statement of Ross Swimmer, *Hearings on the Enforcement of the ICRA of 1968 Before the U.S. Commission on Civil Rights,* (Washington, D.C., Jan. 28, 1988) at 13.

53. *United Keetoowah Band of Cherokee Indians in Oklahoma v. Muskogee Area Director, BIA,* IBIA 91–60-A (June 24, 1992), *reprinted in* 19 Indian L. Rep. 7121 (1992).

54. 18 U.S.C. Sec. 241.

55. *U.S. v. Wadena,* 152 F.3d 831 (8th Cir. 1997), *cert. denied,* 526 U.S. 1050 (1999).

56. *See* Ziontz, note 6 above.

57. Many of these violations are recorded in *Hearings on the Enforcement of the ICRA of 1968 Before the U.S. Commission on Civil Right,* Rapid City, S.D., hearings (1986); Flagstaff, Ariz., hearings (1987); and Washington, D.C., hearings (1988).

58. Allegations of this nature were made by the complainants in the *Shenandoah* and *Anderson* cases cited in note 37 above.

59. "Civil Rights Are Basic Rights," *Indian Country Today* (editorial) (Jan. 11, 1999) at A4.

60. *Wells v. Philbrick,* 486 F. Supp. 807, 809 (D.S.D. 1980). *See also Shortbull v. Looking Elk,* 677 F.2d 645 (8th Cir.), *cert. denied,* 459 U.S. 907 (1982).

XV

The Unique Status of
Certain Indian Groups

Certain Native American groups have long had a special status under federal law or have recently been the subject of unique legislation. These groups include the tribes in Connecticut, the Pueblos of New Mexico, Alaska Natives, Oklahoma Indians, New York Indians, and the nonrecognized tribes. This chapter discusses the federal government's unique relationship with each of these groups.

A. The Connecticut Tribes

What is the unique legal status of the Connecticut tribes?

The state of Connecticut has given official recognition to five indigenous tribes: Paucatuck Eastern Pequot, Mashantucket Pequot, Schaghticoke, Golden Hill Paugussett, and Mohegan.[1] Each tribe has a reservation assigned to its use. Until 1983, there were no *federally* recognized Indian tribes in Connecticut. (The process of obtaining federal recognition is discussed later in this chapter.) Federal recognition was accorded to the Mashantucket Pequot Tribe in 1983 and to the Mohegan Nation in 1994. In June 2002, two groups claiming to be separate tribes, the Eastern Pequots and the Paucatuck Eastern Pequots, gained recognition as one tribe known as the "historic Eastern Pequot Tribe." At least eight other tribal groups from Connecticut are presently seeking federal recognition: Schaghticoke, Golden Hill Paugussett, Mohegan Tribe and Nation of Norwich, Nehantic, Southern Pequot, Pequot Mohegan, Poquonnock Pequot, and Western Pequot Tribal Nation of New Haven. In addition, two groups of Nipmuc Indians based in Massachusetts are seeking federal recognition and could try to establish a reservation in northeastern Connecticut, part of their original territory. Other tribes once occupying land that is now Connecticut include the Agawam, Unca, Quinnipiac, Podunk, Hammonasset, Niantic, and Tunxis.

Twenty years ago, the Mashantucket Pequots were an obscure and impoverished tribe. Now they own the largest gambling facility in the world, the Foxwoods Resort Casino. Foxwoods grossed $69.4 million from its slot machines during the *month* of May 2002, while at the same time the nearby Mohegan Sun Casino owned by the Mohegan Nation of Connecticut took in $62.4 million.[2] Connecticut receives one-quarter of the profits from the two tribes' slot machines, and these royalties contribute more than $300 million a year to the state treasury. In addition, Foxwoods is responsible (directly and indirectly) for creating more than forty-one thousand jobs and adding $1.2 billion to the economy, and according to an independent study issued in November 2000, the casino saved the economy of southeastern Connecticut from financial crisis caused by the downturn in the region's defense and manufacturing industries.[3]

Not everyone is pleased with these casinos, however. Many local residents deplore the traffic jams and commercial development that the casinos have brought to their once-quiet communities. Housing prices have soared in nearby towns, making it difficult for first-time buyers to purchase homes, although some homeowners on congested roads close to the casinos have watched the value of their homes plummet. Local businesses are finding it difficult to hire and retain employees because they cannot compete with the higher wages and lucrative benefit packages being offered by the tribes. In the communities where the eight tribal groups seeking federal recognition want to create new reservations, many non-Indians worry about similar changes, and the local governments are concerned about the additional municipal services that will be required if casinos are built. A few communities, though, would like to see a casino open nearby so as to improve their economies.[4] The stakes are high, economically and politically. Elected officials in Connecticut, under pressure from their constituents, are seeking ways to change the process by which tribes are officially recognized by the federal government and assigned reservations, and they want local communities to have more of a voice in how these tribes may use their land.[5]

1. The Mashantucket Pequot Tribe

In the early seventeenth century, the Pequots were the most powerful tribe in Connecticut. They permitted the English to establish some settlements within their territory but began resisting further expansions. In April 1637, a Pequot raid killed nine settlers. In retaliation for their resistance, the English assembled an army of some five hundred men led by John Mason, and warriors from the Narragansett, Mohegan, and Niantic Tribes, historic enemies of the Pequots, joined the force. The army attacked a Pequot village at nighttime, slaughtering virtually the entire village of four hundred men, women, and children. The army later attacked other Pequot villages. Within a year, nearly half of the estimated three thousand Pequots had been killed. The Pequots were forced to sign the Treaty of Hartford in 1638, under which they were forbidden to live in the territory.

Some Pequots remained in the area, however, and others later returned. During the late seventeenth century, the state assigned the Pequots a reservation in the town of Ledyard. The size of the reservation was gradually reduced over the years, and by the mid-1970s, it consisted of just 184 acres. Tribal members began investigating whether part of the reservation had been removed from the Pequots in violation of the Indian Nonintercourse Act,[6] a federal law passed in 1790 that prohibits the sale of Indian tribal land without the approval of Congress. It appeared that at least 800 acres of Pequot land had been taken by the state in 1855 in violation of the act, and the Pequots filed a lawsuit in 1976 seeking to recover possession of that land.

In 1983, Congress settled the dispute regarding the Pequots' land claims by enacting the Mashantucket Pequot Land Claims Settlement Act (also called the Connecticut Land Claims Settlement Act).[7] The act granted federal recognition to the Mashantucket Pequot Tribe and created a reservation that eventually encompassed (after the tribe purchased land with settlement funds) more than 1,000 acres. The tribe has about 250 enrolled members.

In 1986, the Pequots opened a very successful high-stakes bingo operation on the reservation. After passage of the Indian Gaming Regulatory Act (IGRA)[8] in 1988, negotiations were commenced with the state to open a gaming casino. With the assistance of a federal mediator, the state and tribe agreed upon a gambling compact, and the tribe opened its Foxwoods Resort Casino in February 1992. Foxwoods has been successful beyond imagination. By 2000, the tribe had earned $4 *billion* from its slot machines (and additional millions from its gambling tables, hotel, and restaurants), and the state received $1 billion as its one-quarter share of the profits from the slot machines. In 1997, the tribe opened a $100 million museum and Indian library, the largest of its kind.

Recently, the tribe purchased more than 4,500 acres of land outside the reservation and requested that the Secretary of the Interior convert 160 acres of that land into federal trust status and add it to the reservation. Citizens of three nearby Connecticut towns—Ledyard, Preston, and North Stonington—held rallies denouncing the tribe and its efforts to expand the reservation, and the towns petitioned the Secretary to deny the tribe's request. When the Secretary granted the tribe's application to convert the land into trust status, the towns, joined by the state, filed a lawsuit in federal court challenging the decision. In 2000, a federal court of appeals ruled in favor of the tribe,[9] upsetting many non-Indians who fear that the Pequots will now significantly increase the size of its reservation and casino through additional conversions of land into trust status. Adding to the controversy, a book published in 2000 accused the Mashantucket Pequots of fraudulently claiming to be Pequots and having deceived Congress into granting them federal recognition.[10] These charges are strenuously denied by the tribe, and factual flaws in the book have been pointed out.[11]

The 1983 Settlement Act is unclear as to whether Congress has authorized the state of Connecticut to exercise criminal and/or civil jurisdiction over tribal members on the reservation. The Connecticut Supreme Court has interpreted the act as authorizing criminal jurisdiction[12] and civil adjudicatory jurisdiction,[13] but the court has acknowledged that the language of the Settlement Act is ambiguous.[14] Further challenges (in federal court if not in state court) are likely.

2. The Mohegan Tribe

The Mohegan Indians were among the first to greet European colonists, and for the most part, they lived in harmony with them. They were assigned a reservation of 2,700 acres by the state of Connecticut, but the state partially eliminated it in 1861, and by 1872 all the land had been disbursed to tribal members. These divestitures probably violated the Indian Nonintercourse Act of 1790 because the land was taken from the tribe without the consent of the federal government. A lawsuit filed by the tribe seeking to regain possession of some 2,500 acres of land in the town of Montville was given a boost in 1981 when a federal appellate court agreed with the tribe that the Nonintercourse Act protects eastern land claims as well as western and that non–federally recognized tribes (as the Mohegans were at the time) may seek to regain land taken in violation of the act.[15]

The Mohegans applied for federal recognition in 1978. The Secretary of the Interior granted their application sixteen years later in 1994. That same year, Congress enacted the Mohegan Nation of Connecticut Land Claims Settlement Act,[16] under which the tribe's land claims were settled and a 240-acre reservation was eventually created. The tribe's casino is located there, but no one lives on the reservation. The casino has been enormously profitable, grossing more than $60 million a month, and a new hotel will soon open that will be the second tallest building in the state. The tribe recently announced plans to open a shellfish hatchery, a processing plant, and a barn to raise and process oysters and clams.[17]

The Mohegan Tribe has approximately one thousand members. Most members are cousins to each other in the fourth or fifth degree, having descended from a handful of families that remained in the area after the reservation was eliminated in 1861.

3. The Historic Eastern Pequot Tribe

A reservation was created for the Paucatuck Eastern Pequot Tribe in October 1683 by an act of the Connecticut Colonial Assembly, and the Indian title to this land has never been extinguished. (Indian title is defined in chapter 2.) The state of Connecticut created a 224-acre reservation for the tribe and recognized the tribe's autonomy.[18] The reservation is located in North Stonington, not far from the Mashantucket Pequot Reservation. The tribe applied for federal recognition in 1989 and received preliminary recognition from the Department of the Interior in the waning days of the Clinton administration in 2001. Also living on the reservation was a group of Indians called the Eastern Pequots, which sought federal recognition as a separate tribe. In June 2002, the Department ruled that the Paucatucks and Easterns should be jointly recognized as the "historic Eastern Pequot Tribe," finding that they shared a common ancestry.

The Paucatucks, prior to gaining recognition, had announced plans to open a casino if its application for recognition was granted. However, knowing that many local residents opposed the plan, the tribe sent a card to fifteen thousand residents in North Stonington in December 2000 promising that if the tribe received recognition, it would build a casino only in a community that "puts out a welcome mat."[19] Now that the tribe is federally recognized, at least one more gambling casino for Connecticut is a near certainty.

4. The Schaghticoke Tribe

The Schaghticoke's 400-acre reservation is located in Kent, bordering on New York, and the tribe has about three hundred members. The Schaghticokes applied for federal recognition in 1981. When the Department of the Interior still had not acted on the application in 2000, a federal court, criticizing the Department's delay, agreed to decide whether the tribe qualified for federal recognition,[20] and a decision is expected soon. The tribe is seeking to regain possession of lands once part of its territory, including 148 acres now owned by a utility company.[21] Local residents are so distressed about the prospect of losing land and the opening of a casino in their community that in late 2000 they approved spending $200,000 of town funds to investigate whether the Schaghticokes meet all the requirements for federal recognition as claimed in their application.[22]

5. The Paugussett Tribe

The Paugussett Tribe has two reservations, a quarter-acre lot in Trumbull known as the Golden Hill Reservation, and 106 acres in Colchester, purchased in 1981 with the help of a federal grant. The tribe applied to the Department of the Interior for federal recognition in 1982. The Department initially rejected the application; but in 1999 the Secretary of the Interior announced that the earlier decision is being reviewed, and a final decision is pending. The Paugussetts have filed lawsuits seeking to recover land allegedly taken from the tribe in violation of the Indian Nonintercourse Act, including parts of the town of Southbury and most of downtown Bridgeport.[23] Tribal members have announced plans to build a casino in Bridgeport if the tribe is granted recognition and those lands are restored,[24] and they have already found a developer to invest in the project.[25]

B. THE PUEBLOS OF NEW MEXICO

Native communities were well established in what is now New Mexico long before the Spanish conquistadors entered the region during the seventeenth century. Each community had its own government, language, and culture. Today there are nineteen Pueblos in New Mexico, each a different tribe politically and culturally.

The Spanish felt it was their duty to "civilize" the Pueblo Indians. To help accomplish this, they built a church in each Pueblo and then issued a land grant recognizing the Pueblo's ownership of all land surrounding the church for one league (2.6 miles) in every direction.[26] Spain also passed laws prohibiting non-Indians from living or trespassing on Pueblo land.

After Mexico gained its independence from Spain, the Mexican government reaffirmed these land grants and extended Mexican citizenship to the Pueblo Indians. However, the Mexican government did little to protect the Pueblos from being attacked by outsiders, and many Pueblos lost land during this period.

The United States acquired the territory of New Mexico in an 1848 treaty with Mexico, the Treaty of Guadalupe Hidalgo. In the treaty, the United States promised to preserve the land rights that Mexico had granted to the Pueblos. Congress then enacted laws acknowledging the right of the Pueblos to own their lands and conferred U.S. citizenship on the Pueblo Indians.

The federal government did little to protect the Pueblos, and once again they were attacked by non-Indians and some of their land was stolen. In 1876, some Pueblos filed suit to recover their land under the Indian Nonintercourse Act of 1790, which prohibits the taking of tribal land unless the federal government consents. The suit was dismissed, however, when the Supreme Court ruled that the Pueblos were not "Indian tribes" eligible for protection under federal law.[27]

In 1913, the Supreme Court reversed its 1876 decision and ruled that the Pueblos are in fact "Indian tribes" for purposes of federal protection.[28] Soon thereafter, Congress appropriated funds for the construction of schools, bridges, roads, and irrigation systems within the Pueblos and passed laws that protected Pueblo lands, the most notable of which was the Pueblo Lands Act of 1924.[29] The act created a special commission, the Pueblo Lands Board, to review all land claims raised by the Pueblos. If the board determined that a Pueblo lost land illegally, it was required to issue a report to that effect. This obligated the U.S. Attorney General to file suit on behalf of the Pueblo to recover the land. Another section of the law required the federal government to compensate the Pueblos for any stolen land that for one reason or another could no longer be restored to the Pueblos. As a result of the Pueblo Lands Act, Pueblos recovered some of their stolen lands and received compensation for much of the rest.

In what respects is the relationship between the federal government and the Pueblos unique?

The Pueblos have a unique relationship with the United States. No other group of Indians has been so free of federal interference as the Pueblos. Congress has rarely intruded into Pueblo life.

It is not entirely clear why Congress has treated the Pueblos differently than other tribes, but three factors probably play a role. First, the Pueblos own their land. Most other reservations contain trust lands that are owned by the United States and are therefore closely administered by federal officials.[30] Second, few tribes other than the Pueblos have obtained rights to land from foreign nations. Finally, the Pueblos have remained highly traditional and are well known for their industriousness and close church affiliation.[31] In any event, the Pueblos have been spared much of the harm that other tribes have suffered. No Pueblo was ever forced to sign a treaty with the United States, and not a single piece of Pueblo land was removed under the General Allotment Act of 1887 (GAA). (The GAA is discussed in chapter 1.)

As noted earlier, the Supreme Court denied federal protection to the Pueblos in 1876, but the Court reversed that ruling in 1913. It is now settled that the Pueblos have a trust relationship with the federal government and, thus, are entitled to the same benefits and services other federally recognized tribes receive.[32] The federal government's trust obligation is not diminished by the fact that the Pueblos own their land[33] or because the Pueblos have incorporated themselves under state law.[34] In short, the Pueblos enjoy all the benefits that other federally recognized tribes enjoy and yet have avoided some laws that have harmed other tribes.

C. Alaska Natives

The land that is now the state of Alaska has long been inhabited by American Indians, Eskimos, and Aleuts.[35] When Alaska was purchased from Russia in 1867, its Native population was scattered in some two hundred villages located principally along the southern and far northwestern coasts. Hunting and fishing were the main sources of livelihood, and they remain vitally important today.

Native peoples in Alaska have a unique historical background with the United States. For decades after the purchase of Alaska, few non-Indians ventured to the area. As a result, there were no competing land claims, no wars between Natives and settlers, and no treaties signed with any Native group in Alaska. The Native peoples were left largely undisturbed. Congress made no effort to determine the legal status of Native land claims in the Alaska territory.

When Congress enacts Indian legislation, it usually states that the law applies also to Eskimos and Aleuts, except in those rare situations in which Congress intends to exclude them. The Citizenship Act of 1924, which extended U.S. citizenship to all Indians born in the United States, expressly included the Eskimos, Aleuts, and Indians of the Alaska Territory.[36] The Indian Reorganization Act of 1934[37] (discussed in chapters 1 and 5), initially excluded Alaska Natives from coverage under the act but was amended in 1936 to include them.[38]

In 1955, the Supreme Court was asked to decide whether the Alaska Natives had *recognized title* (a term defined in chapter 2) to their aboriginal territory—thus entitling them to compensation if their land was taken from them—or whether their interest was possessory only, which would allow it to be taken by the federal government without the payment of compensation. In *Tee-Hit-Ton v. United States,*[39] the Court held that the Natives lacked recognized title. Consequently, when the federal government allowed Alaska to become a state in 1958 and lands were set aside for the state, any claim to those lands by Native peoples was extinguished without compensation. However, millions of acres of land was also set aside by the federal government for the Native population, and Alaska had to agree, as a condition of becoming a state, to disclaim all right and title to that land.[40]

In what respects do the Alaska Natives have a unique relationship with the United States?

In 1971, Congress passed a comprehensive law regarding the land rights of Alaska's eighty thousand Native inhabitants. Despite the Supreme Court's decision in *Tee-Hit-Ton,* which held that the land of the Alaska Natives could be taken without compensation, Congress agreed to compensate the Natives for taking their aboriginal land rights and also agreed to convey large tracts of land to them with full rights of ownership. This law, the Alaska Native Claims Settlement Act (ANCSA),[41] changed the nature of the government's relationship with the Alaska Natives and gave them rights and interests not enjoyed by any other indigenous group.

The ANCSA gave Alaska Natives $962.5 million in compensation for extinguishing all of their aboriginal land claims, and in addition, it gave them ownership rights to 40 million acres of land.[42] Of these 40 million acres, the surface estate in 22 million acres was divided among the two hundred Native villages according to their population, with each village selecting its homelands and incorporating itself under state law. The remaining 18 million acres and the subsurface estate of the entire 40 million acres were conveyed to thirteen Native regional corporations. (Thus, the 22 million acres patented to the villages are dually owned: the surface is owned by the village corporation, while the subsurface is owned by the regional corporation.)[43] The corporations were given fee title to these estates, thus allowing the corporate owners to sell their interests at anytime to anyone.

All persons living on December 18, 1971, and possessing one-quarter or more Native blood were automatically enrolled in a regional corporation and issued one hundred shares of its corporate stock. The ANCSA requires each regional corporation to use its land and resources for the profit of its shareholders. As originally enacted, the ANCSA prohibited shareholders from selling their shares for twenty years (until 1991), and it also exempted the land owned by Native corporations from state and local taxation during this same twenty-year period. In 1988, Congress amended the ANCSA and extended the restrictions on state taxation indefinitely, and permitted the corporations to extend indefinitely the restriction on sales of stock. But Congress also permitted each corporation to issue and sell new stock to non-Natives, and Congress rejected the Natives' request to allow the corporations to transfer their interests in land only to tribal governments.

The ANCSA was enacted by Congress with the hope that litigation could be avoided regarding Native land claims. While it has resolved some disputes, it has created others. Congress has amended the ANCSA numerous times in an effort to resolve these disputes, but litigation regarding the effect and interpretation of this law is likely to continue for many years.

One post-ANCSA issue in sharp dispute was whether the land set apart for Natives under the act is *Indian country* (a term defined in chapter 2). This issue was addressed by the Supreme Court in *Alaska v. Native Village of Venetie Tribal Government* (1998).[44] In that case, a village corporation had conveyed its land to a tribal government. The tribe then sought to tax the profits made by a construction company when it built a public school under a state contract on that land, a power the tribe could exercise only if the land was Indian country. The Supreme Court held that ANCSA land is not Indian country even when owned by a tribe, and the Court thus invalidated the tax.

Congress has enacted other laws unique to Alaska Natives. The Reindeer Industry Act[45] provides federal funds and property to the Alaska Natives for sustaining the economic use of reindeer. The Alaska National Interest Lands Conservation Act of 1980 (ANILCA)[46] gives all persons living in the rural areas of the state—95 percent of whom are Natives—a priority right to hunt and fish on public lands for their subsistence needs over all other uses of these natural resources and requires the U.S. Department of the Interior to enforce these subsistence rights if the state fails to do so.

ANILCA has generated bitter controversy between Natives and non-Natives. Many non-Natives deeply resent having to set aside a substantial portion of Alaska's fish and game to Native peoples. This resentment only deepened when the Department of the Interior announced a few years ago that state officials were doing such a poor job protecting Native subsistence rights that federal officials were stepping in to ensure their protection, and a federal appellate court upheld broad regulatory control by the Department.[47] However, in a surprising (if not shocking) reversal of positions, Alaska Governor Tony Knowles, after meeting with the lead Native plaintiff in the federal case, eighty-six-year-old Katie John, announced in August 2001 that the state was abandoning its opposition and would henceforth support and defend Native subsistence rights under ANILCA.[48]

Some federal laws governing the Alaska Natives are unique to them, but they and their tribal organizations are entitled to receive the same federal services available to Indians and tribes generally. The ANCSA did not diminish their right to participate in federal Indian programs.[49] Lingering questions regarding the federal status of the Alaska Native groups were resolved in 1993 when the Department of the Interior issued a ruling stating that the Native villages and corporations have the same status as tribes in the contiguous forty-eight states and are "entitled to the same protection, immunities, and privileges as other acknowledged tribes."[50] Currently, more than 230 tribal groups in Alaska are recognized by the federal government as having a trust relationship with the United States.

State officials in Alaska have strongly opposed the assertion of authority by Native governments and are continually attempting to erode or have Congress erode their powers. They contend that Native tribal groups lack the powers of self-government enjoyed by other Indian tribes. This contention was supported by the Alaska Supreme Court, which ruled in a 1988 case that most Native groups in Alaska are "not self-governing or in any meaningful sense sovereign."[51] The Alaska legislature appropriated $1 million of public funds to fight the tribe in the *Venetie* case. Recent developments, however, are encouraging. As just noted, the Governor of Alaska in August 2001 changed his stance regarding subsistence hunting and fishing by Natives. In an equally surprising move, the Alaska Supreme Court reversed three of its prior decisions and ruled in 2001 that "Alaska Native tribes are sovereign powers under federal law" and therefore had the right, as was the specific issue in that case, to enforce the provisions of the Indian Child Welfare Act.[52] (The Indian Child Welfare Act is discussed in chapter 17.)

The U.S. Supreme Court has not determined the full extent to which Native villages in Alaska may exercise the powers of self-government, although it decided in *Venetie* that their territory does not constitute Indian country. As a result of *Venetie,* the tribal groups that own ANCSA land may not exercise governmental powers over activities occurring on the land. *Venetie* was thus a terrible blow to tribal governments, undermining their ability to be self-governing, both politically and economically.

Many governmental powers of Indian tribes can be exercised without a land base, however. These include the power to determine tribal membership, regulate domestic relations among tribal members, punish tribal members who violate tribal law, and regulate the inheritance of tribal property. Based on the principles of Indian law discussed in chapter 6—including the principle that Indian tribes retain all of their original rights except those that Congress has expressly removed or which the tribes have lost due to their "dependent" status under federal authority—Alaska Native groups are presumed to possess these remaining governmental powers.[53] Congress has declared that federally recognized Alaska Native groups are eligible to administer federal programs under the Indian Self-Determination and Education Assistance Act of 1975[54] (a law discussed in chapter 5), thus confirming that these federally recognized groups possess some governmental powers. However, the full range of their authority over members and non-members has yet to be resolved.

D. Oklahoma Indians

The area that is now the state of Oklahoma was named "Indian Territory" by Congress during the 1830s and was set aside exclusively for Indians. Congress chose this largely barren land as a virtual dumping ground for many eastern tribes (and, later, for many western tribes as well) that were forcibly removed from lands desired by non-Indian settlers. Today, there are more than forty tribes located in Oklahoma, thirty-seven of which are federally recognized. Only a few of these tribes—including the Osage, Caddo, Wichita, Kiowa, and Comanches—are indigenous.[55] More than a quarter-million Indians now live in Oklahoma, approximately 12 percent of the state's population.[56]

The first eastern tribes to be removed to Indian Territory were the Cherokees, Choctaws, Chickasaws, Creeks, and Seminoles. These tribes—often called the Five Civilized Tribes because they had an advanced governmental structure long before the nineteenth century and operated their own schools and courts—each signed a treaty with the United States under which the tribe obtained a reservation in Indian Territory. The treaty assured the tribe it would not be further disturbed by non-Indians, it would own its land perpetually, and its reservation would never become part of a state without the tribe's consent.[57]

The Five Civilized Tribes were removed from their homelands with brute force in the 1830s, and the manner in which the army marched them literally at bayonet point more than a thousand miles to Indian Territory is one of the most shameful episodes in U.S. history. The Indians had inadequate food and winter clothing. Thousands contracted smallpox, cholera, and dysentery. The army forced the tribes to leave along the route those who became too weak to walk, including many children and tribal elders. Of the estimated sixty thousand tribal members who embarked on the *Trail of Tears,* a term first applied to the Cherokee experience, as many as fifteen thousand died.[58]

The federal government initially honored its promise to leave these tribes alone once they arrived in Indian Territory. After the Civil War, however, Congress needed to find space to relocate tribes from other lands now coveted by non-Indian settlers. Two of the Civilized Tribes, the Choctaws and Chickasaws, had owned slaves and had sided with the Confederacy during the war, and several leaders of the other tribes had been sympathetic to the South. This provided a convenient excuse for taking tribal lands. Allegedly as a penalty for sympathizing with the Confederacy, all five tribes lost the western portion of their reservations. (Congress, in contrast, took no lands away from the Confederate states themselves.) These vacated lands were then assigned by Congress to more than thirty other tribes, including the Sac and Fox from the Great Lakes region, the Cheyenne from the Northwest, and the Kickapoo and Apache from the Southwest.

The territory not taken from the tribes remained officially closed to non-Indian settlement, consistent with the earlier treaties. Eventually, as so often happened elsewhere in the country, the government broke those treaty promises. By the end of the nineteenth century, Congress had passed laws opening vast areas of Indian land to settlement, and additional treaty lands were taken by non-Indian settlers, without any opposition by the federal government. Some tribes lost their entire reservations and were left with small, isolated parcels of land.[59] By 1907, non-Indians so vastly outnumbered the Indians that the territory was admitted into the Union as the state of Oklahoma.

In what ways do the Indians living in Oklahoma have a unique relationship with the United States?

For the most part, Oklahoma tribes have the same rights and powers as tribes in the rest of the country and have the same trust relationship with the federal government. However, largely due to their unique history, Congress has created a set of laws dealing exclusively with Oklahoma tribes, especially the Five Civilized Tribes and the Osage Tribe.[60] These laws slightly limit tribal powers with regard to the control of tribal property, providing, for example, that state law (rather than tribal or federal law) will govern the alienation, partition, and heirship of Indian land. Congress also has placed most of the resources and income of the Osage Tribe under the direct control of the Secretary of the Interior.[61] In addition, the Osage appear to be the only tribe in the country whose form of government is dictated by federal statute, including the determination of who may vote in tribal elections.[62]

As explained in chapter 1, Congress enacted the General Allotment Act in 1887, which authorized the President of the United States to sell "surplus" tribal lands to non-Indians. The Five Civilized Tribes were excluded from the act because their treaties with the United States gave them complete and perpetual ownership of their land; their land had not been placed into trust status. Nevertheless, Congress wanted these tribes to sell some of their land so that non-Indians could move into those areas. When the tribes refused to sell, an angry Congress retaliated by passing the Curtis Act in 1898.[63] This act not only forced the allotment of tribal lands, but it also abolished all tribal courts and removed certain powers of self-government from the tribes, including the right to collect taxes.

In 1934, when Congress passed the Indian Reorganization Act (IRA) (discussed in chapter 1), which ended the forced sale of additional tribal lands, it excluded the Oklahoma tribes from its protections. Congress had a change of heart in 1936, and the Oklahoma Indian Welfare Act (OIWA) was passed.[64] The OIWA provides to Oklahoma tribes the same rights, protections, and benefits as the IRA. It restored to the tribes the right to establish tribal courts having both civil and criminal jurisdiction.[65] For many years after passage of the OIWA, though, federal officials often discouraged Oklahoma tribes from exercising their rights, prompting a federal court in 1976 to describe their attitude as "bureaucratic imperialism" designed to "frustrate, debilitate, and generally prevent from functioning the tribal governments."[66] Improvements have been made in recent years, and the Secretary of the Interior has even purchased lands for some Oklahoma tribes, as authorized by the OIWA. In 1959, during the termination era, Congress terminated the federal status of three Oklahoma tribes—Wyandotte, Peoria, and Ottawa—but Congress restored their federal status in 1977.[67]

As explained in chapter 3, every tribe that has a treaty with the United States has a trust relationship with the federal government unless Congress has terminated that relationship. Oklahoma tribes are no exception to this rule. Most of the Oklahoma tribes have at least one treaty with the United States. In a 1943 case, the Supreme Court confirmed that these Oklahoma treaties create trust responsibilities similar to those created by other Indian treaties.[68]

It is now well established that the federally recognized tribes in Oklahoma possess the same powers of self-government other recognized tribes possess.[69] In a 1991 case, the Supreme Court held that the Potawatomi Tribe of Oklahoma, as all other federally recognized tribes, "exercise inherent sovereign authority over their members and their territory."[70] The Court held in the 1991 case that although the Potawatomi do not have a formal reservation but have only a few isolated parcels of trust land, that land is nevertheless Indian country.[71] As a result, Oklahoma lacks general civil[72] and criminal[73] jurisdiction over Indians on that land.

Consistent with the improved relations between the federal government and the tribes in Oklahoma, the Oklahoma legislature passed a law in 1988 recognizing the unique status of its Indian tribes and their inherent right of self-government. The statute commits the state to "work in a spirit of cooperation with all federally recognized Indian Tribes."[74]

E. NEW YORK INDIANS

The Europeans who first settled in what is now New York were greeted by the Haudenosaunee (or Six Nations Iroquois Confederacy), the most powerful group of Indians north of Mexico. The confederacy, formed hundreds of years before Europeans first arrived in New York, consisted of six tribes: Seneca, Cayuga, Onondaga, Oneida, Mohawk, and Tuscarora. The territory controlled by the confederacy at one time extended from what is now New England to the Mississippi River and from upper Canada into North Carolina.

The Iroquois Confederacy played an important role in the early history of the United States. The confederacy's alliance with England during the so-called French and Indian War (also called the Seven Years War, a war between France and England that ended in 1763) helped assure a British victory over France and established England as the primary European power in the Northeast. The confederacy, however, became divided during the American Revolutionary War. Two of the six tribes—the Oneidas and the Tuscaroras—sided with the American colonists, and the others sided with England.[75]

The treaty that ended the war between the United States and Great Britain was signed in 1783. The next year, the United States signed treaties with all six nations of the Iroquois Confederacy. These treaties established boundary lines for each tribe's territory and guaranteed that the tribe would remain free from outside interference.[76] Additional treaties with tribes in New York were signed in 1796 and in 1814.[77]

By the 1820s, New York land was so coveted by non-Indians that the federal government compelled a large number of Indians to leave New York and relocate on reservations in Wisconsin and Kansas, and some were later moved further west.[78] Many Indians remained in New York, however, and today there are nine Indian reservations in the state.

Controversies currently exist in New York regarding Indian land claims, involving tens of thousands of New York residents and millions of dollars worth of land. As mentioned earlier in this chapter, Congress passed a law in 1790 called the Indian Nonintercourse Act (INA), which prohibited the sale of tribal land without the federal government's approval. Both before the INA and afterwards, the state of New York as well as individual settlers purchased tribal land without federal approval. Courts have ruled that these pre-INA purchases are valid,[79] but the post-INA purchases are not.[80] During the past thirty years, several New York tribes have filed lawsuits in federal court seeking to recover vast tracts of land, much of it privately owned, which they claim were illegally taken. They also seek to obtain nearly two hundred years' worth of back rent from the state and certain private parties for having used those lands.

For example, the Cayuga Indian Nation filed suit to recover approximately 64,027 acres of land in upstate New York (in Seneca and Cayuga Counties) and nearly $335 million in rent. In that case, a federal district court ruled that the tribe could not recover the land but was entitled to have a jury determine an adequate amount of compensation for its loss. The jury awarded the tribe $36.9 million, an amount far less than the tribe requested, and it is appealing the decision.[81] Another New York tribe, the Onondaga, is seeking to recover some 70,000 acres of land, including nearly all of the city of Syracuse. The Oneidas, who have been litigating their case for nearly thirty years, probably have the largest claim, involving nearly 250,000 acres of land in what is now Madison and Oneida Counties.[82] The Seneca Tribe has land claims as well, and one case has been pending for nearly twenty years.[83] In 1892, the federal government negotiated a lease on behalf of the Senecas of a portion of their land so the city of Salamanca could be built. The lease provided for extremely low rents to be paid to the Senecas, and when the lease expired in 1990, the tribe increased rents dramatically.

The Oneida Indian Nation is the largest employer in a two-county area, operating a casino, resort hotel, and a farm, and it owns a marina at the south end of Lake Oneida. The casino employs three thousand people and has an annual payroll of more than $64 million.[84] The tribe has become the economic anchor of the region. Most of the other New York tribes have also become economically important to their regions due to their business ventures.

In what respects is the relationship between the New York Indians and the federal government unique?

Congress has passed laws dealing exclusively with the tribes in New York. It was initially unclear whether these laws authorized New York to exercise jurisdiction on the state's Indian reservations.[85] Congress clarified the situation in 1984 by expressly conferring criminal jurisdiction on New York, much the same as Public Law 83–280 (discussed in chapter 7) confers criminal jurisdiction on some other states. This law gives jurisdiction to New York over "all offenses committed by or against Indians on Indian reservations within the State of New York,"[86] but it expressly denies New York the right to regulate any hunting or fishing rights guaranteed the Indians by federal law.

With regard to civil jurisdiction, in 1950 Congress passed a law[87] that confers authority on the courts of New York to resolve civil disputes involving reservation Indians. The law expressly denies the state the right to regulate Indian hunting and fishing activities protected by federal law, and it prohibits the state from taxing, levying upon, or selling reservation trust lands. In 1976, the U.S. Supreme Court reviewed a similar law applicable to other states and held that it did not confer general civil jurisdiction upon the state over reservation Indians but only allows state courts to resolve reservation disputes that parties might decide to file in state court.[88] It is therefore presumed that New York has no greater civil jurisdiction than this adjudicatory authority.

New York, then, may exercise its criminal jurisdiction in Indian country but has very little civil jurisdiction. It may not exceed its authority,[89] for example, by seeking to tax the sale of goods to Indians on the reservation.[90] Moreover, as courts have ruled in related contexts, Indian tribes in New York should not be viewed as having been divested of any of their inherent powers merely because the state has been authorized to exercise some of its powers in Indian country.[91]

F. Nonrecognized Tribes

Congress has created many programs for Indian tribes and their members, including housing, social services, medical programs, economic development and educational assistance. Not every tribe is eligible to participate in them, however, because Congress has limited most federal Indian programs to "acknowledged" or "recognized" tribes: those tribes whose existence has been officially and formally acknowledged by the federal government.[92] To date, more than 560 tribes and tribal groups have received formal recognition, and new tribes are added to the list almost every year. Federal law requires that the Department of the Interior publish annually a list of all federally recognized tribes.[93] The list can be obtained from the following Internet website: <http://www.doi.gov/bia/tribes/entry.html>.

How can a tribe become recognized by the federal government?

Only Congress has the authority to grant federal recognition to an Indian tribe, but Congress has delegated that power to the Secretary of the Interior. In 1978, the Secretary created an administrative process managed by the Bureau of Indian Affairs (BIA)—and issued a set of regulations to govern it—whereby Indian tribes can petition for and obtain federal acknowledgment.[94]

The Secretary's regulations impose seven criteria that Indian tribes must meet in order to become federally recognized. The petitioning group must prove: (1) that it has been from historical times until the present, on a continuous basis, identified as American Indian; (2) that a substantial portion of the group inhabits a specific area or lives in a community viewed as American Indian, distinct from other populations in the area; and (3) that the group has maintained governmental authority over its members as an autonomous entity throughout history until the present. In addition, the group must (4) submit a copy of its current governing documents including its membership criteria; (5) prove that the group's membership consists primarily of persons who are not members of any other Indian tribe; (6) submit a list of all known current members; and (7) show that the group has not been the subject of federal legislation expressly terminating its relationship with the U.S. government.[95] A sub-agency within the BIA, the Branch of Acknowledgment and Research (BAR), evaluates all petitions for tribal recognition and then issues a report and recommendation to the Secretary of the Interior for a final determination. A petitioning group has no right to a hearing[96] and is not entitled to see the materials submitted by others regarding its application. The Secretary's decision to grant or deny the group's application can be challenged in federal court.[97]

Few activities of the BIA have been as severely criticized as its handling of the recognition process. Critics accuse the BIA of applying the rules in a discriminatory fashion, delaying the process excessively and making the process too expensive for many groups to afford. Since 1978, for instance, the BIA has received nearly 250 petitions for recognition. Final decisions have been issued in fewer than thirty cases,[98] and many applicants have already spent more than $250,000 in the process.[99] The Samish Tribal Organization in Washington, after waiting more than twenty-five years for the BIA to rule on its application, filed suit against the BIA and requested that the court grant the tribe's application. After giving the BIA several opportunities to act on the tribe's application, the court granted the tribe's request for recognition. In justifying its decision to circumvent the administrative process, the court stated that the "excessive delays and government misconduct" regarding the handling of the tribe's petition for recognition were "so extreme that the court has no confidence in the agency's ability to decide the matter expeditiously or fairly."[100] Courts, though, have refused to consider a group's request for federal recognition when the group had circumvented the administrative process.[101]

The person in charge of the BIA in 2000, Assistant Secretary of Indian Affairs Kevin Gover, admitted that the BIA's recognition process was so flawed that in his opinion, Congress should create an independent commission to handle recognition decisions under criteria established by Congress.[102] Bills were introduced in Congress in recent years that would essentially have done just that but were defeated because many members of Congress believe that the recognition process should remain within the BIA and doubt that an independent commission would cure the current problems. In 2001, the U.S. General Accounting Office issued a report highly critical of the BIA recognition process, finding fault with the BIA's criteria for recognition, implementation of the criteria, and the slowness of the process.[103] The Assistant Secretary of Indian Affairs in the Bush Administration, Neal McCaleb, responded by saying that he was aware of these difficulties and was working to solve them.[104]

Many tribes are ineligible for federal recognition because of the last of the seven criteria: they were terminated by Congress between 1953 and 1968 (during the *termination era* discussed in chapter 1). Other tribes have been denied federal recognition because of difficulties in proving continuous political or geographic existence,[105] which can be a cruel basis for denying recognition given what the federal government has done to displace, disrupt, disorganize, scatter, and assimilate so many tribes.

Due to the flaws and delays in the administrative process, some tribes have asked Congress to pass a law recognizing them as tribal governments, and some of these requests have been successful.[106] Other tribes besides the

Samish have filed suit and asked the federal courts to rule on their applications for recognition, given the failure of the Secretary of the Interior to act on their applications within a reasonable time.[107]

What relationship does a nonrecognized tribe have with the United States?

A nonrecognized tribe has no relationship with the United States, according to the Department of the Interior. The Interior Department has issued a regulation stating that "acknowledgment of tribal existence by the Department is a prerequisite to the protection, services and benefits from the Federal Government available to Indian tribes."[108] Thus, the economic consequences of nonrecognition are severe. Nonrecognized tribes generally are ineligible to receive the millions of dollars in assistance most recognized Indian tribes receive yearly in various federal programs and services.

Congress, not the Interior Department, has the final word as to whether a tribe should be federally recognized or whether a nonrecognized tribe may nevertheless receive certain federal benefits, and a court may reverse any decision by the Department that is contrary to the will of Congress. A tribe first must exhaust its remedies within the Interior Department, but thereafter it may seek federal review of the Department's decision to deny eligibility for a federal benefit or program.[109] Courts have held, for example, that nonrecognized tribes and their members may enforce treaties they have with the United States[110] and are entitled to participate in federal programs that Congress has not restricted to recognized tribes.[111] In limited situations, then, even nonrecognized tribes are entitled to certain federal protections, but for the most part, the decision not to acknowledge an Indian tribe is crippling because it denies access to most federal Indian programs and the money, assistance, and opportunities that go with it.

NOTES

1. Conn. Gen. Stat. Secs. 47–63.

2. "Casino Slots Still a Jackpot for States," *Hartford Courant* (June 15, 2002) at A10. "Slot Revenue Flat at Casino," *Hartford Courant* (Aug. 17, 2001) at A4.

3. Report issued by the University of Connecticut Center for Economic Analysis, Nov. 28, 2000, reported in "Computer Study Says Pequot Casino Saved the Connecticut Economy," *Indian Country Today* (Dec. 6, 2000) at A6. *See also* "Mohegans Up the Ante," *Hartford Courant* (June 10, 2001) at A1, A3.

4. The mayor of New London, Connecticut, when presented with a plan by the Eastern Pequot Indians to open a casino in the town, hailed the project as an opportunity to revive the city's decaying economy. *See* "Tribe Pitching Urban Casino," *Hartford Courant* (Mar. 22, 2001) at A9.

5. *See* "Dodd: Suspend Tribal Recognition Process," *Hartford Courant* (Feb. 7, 2001) at A4.

6. 25 U.S.C. Sec. 177.

7. 25 U.S.C. Secs. 1751 *et seq.*

8. 25 U.S.C. Sec. 2710(d).

9. *State of Connecticut v. U.S. Dept. of the Interior,* 228 F.3d 82 (2d Cir. 2000), *cert. denied,* 121 S.Ct. 1732 (2001).

10. *See* Jeff Benedict, *Without Reservation: The Making of America's Most Powerful Indian Tribe and Foxwoods, the World's Largest Casino* (New York: HarperCollins, 2000).

11. *See, e.g.,* Joel Lang, "Reading Jeff Benedict," *Sunday Magazine of the Hartford Courant* (Dec. 3, 2000) at 4–11.

12. *See State v. Spears,* 662 A.2d 80 (Conn.), *cert. denied,* 516 U.S. 1009 (1995).

13. *See Charles v. Charles,* 701 A.2d 650 (Conn. 1997), *cert. denied,* 523 U.S. 1136 (1998) (upholding the right of state courts to issue divorce decrees involving tribal members living on the reservation).

14. *See Spears,* note 12 above, 662 A.2d at 86–87.

15. *Mohegan Tribe v. State of Connecticut,* 638 F.2d 612 (2d Cir.), *cert. denied,* 452 U.S. 968 (1981).

16. 25 U.S.C. Sec. 1775.

17. "Mohegan Tribe Enters Shellfish Business," *Indian Country Today* (Dec. 13, 2000) at B3.

18. *See* Conn. Gen. Stat. Secs. 47–59a. The tribe's legal status is discussed in *State v. Sebastian,* 701 A.2d 13 (Conn. 1997).

19. "Paucatucks Send Residents a Holiday Promise," *Indian Country Today* (Jan. 17, 2001) at C5.

20. *See U.S. v. 43.47 Acres of Land,* 2000 U.S.Dist. LEXIS 14289 (D. Conn. 2000).

21. *See* "Schaghticoke Sue Power Company over Land Claim," *Indian Country Today* (May 17, 2000) at A7.

22. *See* "Kent Residents Support Probe of Schaghticoke Tribal Claims," *Hartford Courant* (Oct. 26, 2000) at A7.

23. A suit filed in state court was dismissed because the plaintiffs had not received approval from the tribe to pursue the claim and thus lacked standing. *See Golden Hill Paugussett Tribe of Indians v. Town of Southbury,* 651 A.2d 1246 (Conn. 1995). *See also* Joel Lang, "The Sons and Daughters of Rising Star," *Sunday Magazine of the Hartford Courant* (Feb. 20, 1994). A suit filed in federal court was placed "on hold" pending a determination on the tribe's application to the Interior Department for recognition. *Golden Hill Paugussett Tribe v. Weicker,* 39 F.3d 51 (2d Cir. 1994). The tribe appears to have a substantial claim.

See "Land Claims of the Golden Hill Paugussett Tribe: Are They 'Holding Hostages' or Asserting Valid Property Rights?" 26 *William Mitchell L. Rev.* 1009 (2000).

24. "Schaghticoke Accuse Paugussetts of Stealing Ancestors," *Indian Country Today* (May 10, 2000) at B2.

25. "Golden Hill Paugussetts of Connecticut," *Indian County Today* (April 12, 2000) at B4.

26. *See Pueblo of Sandia v. Babbitt,* 231 F.3d 878, 879 n.1 (D.C. Cir. 2000).

27. *U.S. v. Joseph,* 94 U.S. 614 (1876).

28. *U.S. v. Sandoval,* 231 U.S. 28 (1913).

29. 25 U.S.C. Sec. 331. *See generally Mountain States Telephone and Telegraph Co. v. Pueblo of Santa Ana,* 472 U.S. 237 (1985); *U.S. v. Thompson,* 941 F.2d 1074 (10th Cir. 1991).

30. The degree to which the federal government regulates reservation lands is explained in ch. 5, sec. B.

31. *Joseph,* note 27 above, 99 U.S. at 616–19.

32. *See Sandoval,* note 28 above; *U.S. v. Chavez,* 290 U.S. 357 (1933).

33. *See U.S. v. Candelaria,* 271 U.S. 432 (1926); *State of New Mexico v. Aamodt,* 537 F.2d 1102 (10th Cir. 1976), *cert. denied,* 429 U.S. 1121 (1977); *Plains Electric G. and T. Co-op., Inc. v. Pueblo of Laguna,* 542 F.2d 1375 (10th Cir. 1976).

34. *See Lane v. Pueblo of Santa Rosa,* 249 U.S. 110 (1919).

35. As explained in ch. 2, sec. A, the Eskimos and Aleuts are ethnologically distinct from, but related to, the American Indian.

36. 8 U.S.C. Sec. 1401(a)(2).

37. 25 U.S.C. Secs. 461 *et seq.* For a discussion of this act, *see* ch. 1.

38. 25 U.S.C. Sec. 473a.

39. 348 U.S. 272 (1955).

40. 72 Stat. 339 (1958), the Alaska Statehood Act.

41. Pub. L. No. 92–203, 85 Stat. 688, codified as amended at 43 U.S.C. Secs. 1601–28.

42. In 1891, Congress created a reservation for the Metlakatla Indian Community on Annette Island in the Alaska Territory. This reservation was not affected by the provisions of the ANCSA. *See* 43 U.S.C. Sec. 1618(a).

43. *See Tyonek Native Corp. v. Cook Inlet Region, Inc.,* 853 F.2d 727 (9th Cir. 1988).

44. 522 U.S. 520 (1998).

45. 25 U.S.C. Sec. 500.

46. 16 U.S.C. Sec. 3120. *See Kenaitze Indian Tribe v. Alaska,* 860 F.2d 312 (9th Cir. 1988). *See also Amoco Production Co. v. Village of Gambell,* 480 U.S. 531 (1987) (holding that the ANILCA does not apply to any subsistence interest that Natives may have in the outercontinental shelf).

47. *See John v. U.S.,* 247 F.3d 1032 (9th Cir. 2001) *(en banc), reaffirming Alaska v. Babbitt,* 72 F.3d 698 (9th Cir. 1995), *cert. denied,* 516 U.S. 1036 (1996).

48. *See* "Katie John Prevails in Subsistence Fight," *NARF Legal Review* (Summer/Fall 2001) at 1–6.

49. The ANCSA expressly provides that the act is not a "substitute for any govern-

mental programs otherwise available to the native people of Alaska. . . . " 43 U.S.C. Sec. 1626(a).

50. Fed. Reg. Oct. 21, 1993, 58 Fed. Reg. 54,364–65.

51. *Native Village of Stevens v. Alaska Management and Planning,* 757 P.2d 32, 34 (Alaska 1988).

52. *In re C.R.H.,* 29 P.3d 849, 851 n.5 (Alaska 2001).

53. *See In re C.R.H.,* note 52 above. *See also U.S. v. Wheeler,* 435 U.S. 313, 322 n.18 (1978); *Duro v. Reina,* 495 U.S. 676, 677 (1990) (recognizing that tribes have a "retained sovereignty . . . to control their own internal relations, and to preserve their own unique customs and social order [and] . . . to prescribe and enforce rules of conduct for [their] own members.")

54. 25 U.S.C. Sec. 450b(e).

55. For general information about the Oklahoma tribes, *see* R. Strickland, *The Indians in Oklahoma* (Norman: Univ. of Oklahoma Press, 1980); M. Wright, *A Guide to the Indians of Oklahoma* (Norman: Univ. of Oklahoma Press, 1951); A. Debo, *A History of the Indians of the United States* (Norman: Univ. of Oklahoma Press, 1970) at 97–98, 112–13.

56. Oklahoma Indian Affairs Commission, *Oklahoma Indian Nations Information Handbook* (2000 ed.) at 9.

57. Debo, note 55 above, at 5. *See Oklahoma Tax Commission v. Chickasaw Nation,* 515 U.S. 450 (1995) (discussing the treaties with the Choctaws and Chickasaws). *See also Muscogee (Creek) Nation v. Hodel,* 851 F.2d 1439 (D.C. Cir. 1988), *cert. denied,* 488 U.S. 1010 (1989).

58. Strickland, note 55 above, at 4; G. Foreman, *Indian Removal: The Emigration of the Five Civilized Tribes of Indians* (Norman: Univ. of Oklahoma Press, 1932) at 53–98, 206–312.

59. Debo, note 55 above, at 6–13; Wright, note 55 above, at 16.

60. *See* Felix Cohen, *Federal Indian Law* (Charlottesville: Michie Co., 1982) at 770–97.

61. The Osage Act of 1906 includes several provisions limiting tribal powers. 34 Stat. 539, 543. For further information on this subject, *see* Cohen, note 60 above, at 780, 790.

62. *See* Act of June 28, 1906, Pub. L. No. 321, 34 Stat. 539, extended by Act of Oct. 21, 1978, Pub. L. No. 95–496, 92 Stat. 1660. For a discussion of these laws, *see Fletcher v. U.S.,* 116 F.3d 1315 (10th Cir. 1997).

63. Act of June 28, 1898, ch. 517, 30 Stat. 495, 504.

64. 25 U.S.C. Secs. 501–9.

65. *Hodel,* note 57 above. *See* Strickland, note 55 above, at 73.

66. *Harjo v. Kleppe,* 420 F. Supp. 1110, 1130 (D.D.C. 1976), *aff'd sub nom. Harjo v. Andrus,* 581 F.2d 949 (D.C. Cir. 1978).

67. 70 Stat. 893, 937 and 963 (1959), and 92 Stat. 246 (1977) (codified as 25 U.S.C. Secs. 861–861c, respectively).

68. *Board of Comm'rs of Creek County v. Seber,* 318 U.S. 705, 718 (1943).

69. *See Hodel,* note 57 above; *Seneca-Cayuga Tribe of Oklahoma v. State of Oklahoma,* 874 F.2d 709 (10th Cir. 1989); Cohen, note 60 above, at 782–83. *See also Oklahoma Tax Comm'n v. Citizen Band Potawatomi Indian Tribe,* 498 U.S. 505 (1991) (Oklahoma tribe enjoys same sovereign immunity from suit as other tribes).

70. *Citizen Band Potawatomi,* note 69 above, 498 U.S. at 509.

71. *Id.* at 511. Even restricted fee land owned by an Indian but subject to a federal restraint on alienation is Indian country. *See U.S. v. Sands,* 968 F.2d 1058 (10th Cir. 1992).

72. *Citizen Band Potawatomi,* note 69 above. *See also Oklahoma Tax Commission v. Sac and Fox Nation,* 508 U.S. 114 (1993); *Indian Country, U.S.A., Inc. v. Oklahoma Tax Comm'n,* 829 F.2d 967 (10th Cir. 1987), *cert. denied sub nom. Oklahoma Tax Comm'n v. Muscogee (Creek) Nation,* 487 U.S. 1218 (1988); *Seneca-Cayuga,* note 69 above (Oklahoma may not regulate tribal bingo operation on trust land).

73. *U.S. v. Burnett,* 777 F.2d 593 (10th Cir. 1985), *cert. denied,* 476 U.S. 1106 (1986); *State v. Burnett,* 671 P.2d 1165 (Okla. Crim. 1983); *State v. Klindt,* 782 P.2d 401 (Okla. Crim. 1989). *But see Eaves v. State,* 800 P.2d 251 (Okla. Crim. 1990) (Oklahoma can prosecute crime by Indian that occurred in tribal housing project).

74. 74 O.S. Sec. 1221(B) (1989).

75. *See* B. Graymont, *The Iroquois in the American Revolution* (Syracuse, N.Y.: Syracuse Univ. Press, 1972).

76. For further information on this subject, *see Federal Indian Law* (Washington, D.C.: Government Printing Office, 1958) at 967–73, and *Oneida Indian Nation of New York v. State of New York,* 860 F.2d 1145 (2d Cir. 1988), *cert. denied,* 493 U.S. 871 (1989).

77. *See* Treaty with the Seven Nations, 7 Stat. 55 (1796), and Treaty of Ghent, 8 Stat. 218 (1814). *See Canadian St. Regis Band of Mohawk Indians v. New York,* 146 F. Supp.2d 170 (N.D.N.Y. 2001).

78. *Federal Indian Law,* note 76 above, at 973–74.

79. *Oneida Indian Nation of New York v. State of New York,* note 76 above.

80. *Oneida County, New York v. Oneida Indian Nation of New York State,* 470 U.S. 226 (1985).

81. *See Cayuga Indian Nation of New York v. Pataki,* 165 F. Supp.2d 266 (N.D.N.Y. 2001).

82. *Id. See also Oneida Indian Nation of New York State v. Oneida County, New York,* 414 U.S. 661 (1974).

83. *Seneca Nation of Indians v. New York,* 178 F.3d 95 (2d Cir. 1999), *cert. denied,* 528 U.S. 1073 (2000).

84. "Oneida Indian Nation Lifts Central New York Economy," *Indian Country Today* (Apr. 11, 2001) at C3.

85. *U.S. v. Forness,* 125 F.2d 928 (2d Cir.), *cert. denied,* 316 U.S. 694 (1942).

86. 25 U.S.C. Sec. 232. *See People v. Edwards,* 432 N.Y.S.2d 567 (App. Div. 1980). A federal appellate court has ruled that the federal government may exercise concurrent criminal jurisdiction on New York reservations. *U.S. v. Cook,* 922 F.2d 1026, 1033 (2d Cir.), *cert. denied,* 500 U.S. 941 (1991).

87. 25 U.S.C. Sec. 233.

88. *Bryan v. Itasca County,* 426 U.S. 373 (1976).

89. *See John v. City of Salamanca,* 845 F.2d 37 (2d Cir. 1988), *cert. denied,* 488 U.S. 850 (1988).

90. *Herzog Bros. Trucking, Inc. v. State Tax Comm'n,* 508 N.E.2d 914 (N.Y. Ct. App.

1987), *vacated and remanded,* 487 U.S. 1212, *reinstated,* 533 N.E.2d 255 (N.Y. Ct. App. 1988).

91. As noted earlier (*see* note 86 and accompanying text) the New York statute is similar to Public Law 83–280. Courts have held that Public Law 83–280 does not divest tribes of their inherent powers; the same therefore should be true for the New York law. *See Bishop Paiute Tribe v. County of Inyo,* 291F.3d 549, 557 (9th Cir. 2002).

92. *See, e.g.,* 25 U.S.C. Secs. 450–450n.

93. The Federally Recognized Indian Tribe List Act of 1994, 25 U.S.C. Sec. 479a-1. *See also* 25 C.F.R. Sec. 83.5(a), which requires that the list be published at least once every three years.

94. 25 C.F.R. Sec. 83.

95. 25 C.F.R. Sec. 83.7.

96. The only exception to this rule occurs when the tribe is already receiving federal benefits and is subject to losing them if denied federal recognition. *See Greene v. Babbitt,* 64 F.3d 1266 (9th Cir. 1995).

97. *See Greene v. Babbitt, id.; James v. U.S. Dept. of Health and Human Services,* 824 F.2d 1132 (D.C. Cir. 1987); *Mashpee Tribe v. Watt,* 707 F.2d 23 (1st Cir.), *cert. denied,* 464 U.S. 1020 (1983); *Miami Nation of Indians of Indiana v. Babbitt,* 887 F. Supp. 1158 (N.D. Ind. 1995).

98. *See* Bureau of Indian Affairs, *Summary, Status of Acknowledgment Cases,* Internet website: <http: www.doi.gov/bia/ack_res.html>.

99. *See* John Echohawk, "The First Californians Are Still the Last," *L.A. Times* (Mar. 12, 1990) at 5.

100. *Greene v. Babbitt,* 943 F. Supp. 1278, 1281, 1288 (W.D. Wash. 1996). *See also Muwekma Tribe v. Babbitt,* 133 F. Supp.2d 42 (D.D.C. 2000).

101. *See United Tribe of Shawnee Indians v. U.S.,* 253 F.3d 543 (10th Cir. 2001); *James,* note 97 above.

102. *See* "Congress Considers New Process for Tribal Recognition," *Indian Country Today* (May 31, 2000) at A1. *See also* "Blumenthal, Gover Agree: New Tribal Recognition Process Needed," *Indian Country Today* (Nov. 28, 2001) at A3.

103. *See* "Report Finds Flaws in Tribal Recognition Process," *Indian Country Today* (Nov. 14, 2001) at A1.

104. *Id.*

105. *See, e.g., Mashpee Tribe,* note 97 above. *See also Miami Nation of Indians of Indiana v. U.S. Dept. of the Interior,* 255 F.3d 342 (7th Cir. 2001).

106. *See, e.g.,* Pub. L. 97–429, 25 U.S.C. Secs. 1300b-11 through 1300b-16 (granting recognition to the Texas Band of Kickapoo Indians); 25 U.S.C. Secs. 1751 *et seq.* (Mashantucket Pequots of Connecticut). The Narragansett Tribe of Rhode Island also obtained federal recognition by act of Congress, as discussed in *Rhode Island v. Narragansett Indian Tribe,* 19 F.3d 685 (1st Cir.), *cert. denied,* 513 U.S. 919 (1994).

107. *See Greene v. Babbitt,* note 100 above; *U.S. v. 43.47 Acres of Land,* note 20 above. *See also Muwekma Tribe,* note 100 above.

108. 25 C.F.R. Sec. 83.2 (1989).

109. *Joint Tribal Council of Passamaquoddy Tribe v. Morton,* 528 F.2d 370 (1st Cir. 1975).

110. *U.S. v. Washington,* 384 F. Supp. 312, 406 (W.D. Wash. 1974), *aff'd,* 520 F.2d 676, 692–93 (9th Cir. 1975), *cert. denied,* 423 U.S. 1086 (1976); *Greene v. Babbitt,* note 96 above, 64 F.3d at 1270.

111. *Passamaquoddy Tribe,* note 109 above; *Schmasow v. Native American Center,* 978 P.2d 304 (Mont. 1999).

XVI

Indian Gaming

In the 1970s, several Indian tribes began offering high-stakes bingo on their reservations in an effort to raise revenue for the tribe, to create jobs, and to improve the standard of living of tribal members. These bingo halls were immediately successful. Gaming suddenly emerged as an unparalleled economic opportunity for those tribes geographically situated to take advantage of it.

Two tribes in California, the Cabazon and Morongo Bands of Mission Indians, operated very profitable bingo halls on their reservations. Under California law, however, it was a misdemeanor to offer bingo except for a charity and for a maximum pot of $250, and the state attempted to enforce these restrictions on the tribes. California, as mentioned in chapter 7, is a Public Law 83–280 (P.L. 280) state, and therefore Congress has authorized California to apply its criminal laws in Indian country. California contended that its prohibitions on high-stakes bingo were criminal laws that it could apply to Indian tribes through P.L. 280.

The tribes filed suit challenging California's authority to regulate its gaming operations, and the case reached the Supreme Court in 1987. In *California v. Cabazon Band of Mission Indians,*[1] the Court distinguished between those activities *prohibited* by a state and those *allowed but regulated,* the so-called criminal/prohibitory and civil/regulatory distinction. Given that California did not prohibit all bingo gambling but only certain forms of it and, moreover, that California permitted other forms of gambling (such as lotteries and betting on horses), its restrictions on high-stakes bingo had to be viewed, the Court said, as civil/regulatory, not criminal/prohibitory. Thus, California was not authorized by P.L. 280—or by any other law or principle—to enforce its bingo regulations on the reservation.

The decision that California could not regulate reservation gaming meant essentially that no state could, because no state had more authority to regulate reservation activities than the P.L. 280 states. This was upsetting to many state officials, who wanted to control this growing industry, especially in those states that already offered gaming and were concerned about the competition. In response to the *Cabazon Band* decision, the states pressured Congress into enacting the Indian Gaming Regulatory Act (IGRA) in 1988,[2] which gives the states the power to regulate certain aspects of Indian gaming but which also allows substantial tribal autonomy.

Today, many people believe that the IGRA gives Indian tribes a power they lacked. That assumption is incorrect; in actuality, the IGRA limits tribal powers. Indian tribes had the inherent right to engage in gaming on the reservation, as the *Cabazon Band* case recognized.

The express purpose of the IGRA is to "provide a statutory basis for the operation of gaming by Indian tribes as a means of promoting tribal economic development, self-sufficiency, and strong tribal governments,"[3] while at the same time shielding tribes "from organized crime and other corrupting influences" and allowing for some state regulation of reservation gaming activities.[4] The act balances the federal government's commitment to preserving tribal self-government and promoting economic development with the need to give state governments some control over gaming enterprises conducted within their borders.

What does the IGRA require?

The IGRA is complex and detailed. The act divides Indian gaming into three classes, and each class is governed by a different set of rules. Class I gaming consists of social games played solely for prizes of minimal value, as well as traditional forms of gaming conducted during tribal ceremonies or celebrations.[5] Class I gaming may not be regulated by the state and is within the exclusive jurisdiction of the tribe.

Class II gaming consists of bingo (including electronic bingo), card games already allowed under state law, and certain forms of pull-tabs and lotto.[6] Class II gaming may be conducted by the tribe free of state regulation if (1) the state does not generally prohibit this type of gambling and (2) the tribe enacts an ordinance authorizing the gaming activity. Every state except Utah authorizes some form of gambling of this nature, and therefore every tribe except the ones in Utah may engage in Class II gaming once the tribal council authorizes it.

Class II gaming is subject to regulation by the National Indian Gaming Commission, a three-person board established by the IGRA and situated within the Department of the Interior.[7] The chair of the Commission must approve all tribal ordinances creating Class II (and Class III) gaming, under criteria set out in the act. The IGRA requires the Commission to inspect and oversee Class II gaming, unless it has granted the tribe a certificate of self-regulation. The act also regulates the manner in which tribes may spend their gaming profits and requires that the Secretary of the Interior approve the methods by which tribes distribute gaming proceeds to tribal members.[8]

Class III gaming is defined as "all forms of gaming that are not class I gaming or class II gaming"[9] and encompasses the most lucrative forms of gaming: slot machines, roulette, craps, and banked card games (which are games played against the "house" rather than against the other players), such as blackjack and baccarat. To engage in Class III gaming, the tribe must satisfy both requirements for Class II gaming, that is, it must enact an authorizing ordinance, and it must be located within a state "that permits such gaming for any purpose by any person, organization, or entity."[10] It must also meet a third requirement: the tribe must enter into a compact with the state in which the tribe receives the state's express consent to engage in the gaming activity.[11]

Some innovative games developed within the past several years have similarities to bingo (a Class II game) but also have differences, and determining whether they constitute a Class II or a Class III game can be difficult. The popular game of Keno, for example, is somewhat similar to bingo but has been held to be a Class III game due to its differences,[12] and the same is true for the game known as Pick Six, in which the player picks six numbers between one and forty-five and hopes to match two or more numbers picked at random by the computer.[13] A game called MegaMania, in which players receive "cards" displayed on a video screen of a computer terminal, is sufficiently akin to bingo to qualify as a Class II game,[14] and so is a game called Lucky Tab II, in which the player receives a tab similar in appearance to a bingo card and tries to match symbols on the card with symbols on the machine.[15]

The IGRA provides, as noted earlier, that Indian tribes may engage in Class II and Class III games that are not prohibited by the state. The state need not have authorized the *precise* game at issue as long as it has authorized the type of gambling of which the game is a part.[16] If a state should later amend its laws to prohibit a type of gaming, it is allowed to refuse to negotiate (or upon a compact's expiration, to renegotiate) a compact that would permit a tribe to engage in the forms of gambling it has prohibited.[17]

What if the state refuses to enter into a compact?

One of the most controversial and contentious features of the IGRA is the requirement that a tribe must obtain the state's written permission in a compact before engaging in Class III gaming. This gives the state considerable leverage. For one thing, the IGRA expressly permits these compacts to include provisions relating to "the application of the criminal and civil laws and regulations" of the state to the gaming activity.[18] A state can therefore demand that it be allowed to arrest Indians and non-Indians within the casino and to enforce, in the civil context, its laws regarding torts and contracts in all matters involving the gaming enterprise. The Mashantucket Pequot Tribe, for example, agreed in its compact with the state of Connecticut to allow the tribe to be sued for any injuries caused "by the negligent acts or omissions of the Gaming Enterprise" in a forum created by the tribe.[19] The compact also agrees to give the state concurrent criminal jurisdiction over crimes committed within the casino; it subjects casino employees to state licensing procedures; and it gives state gaming officials some day-to-day involvement in the operation of the casino.[20]

The IGRA does not place tribes completely at the state's mercy, however. The IGRA obligates the state to negotiate "in good faith" with the tribe in an effort to agree on a Class III compact.[21] If the state fails to negotiate in good faith, the act authorizes the tribe to file suit against the state, and if the court finds that the state failed to bargain in good faith, it can give the tribe and the state sixty days in which to agree on a compact.[22] If they still cannot agree on a compact, each side then submits its last offer to a court-appointed mediator, who selects a compact that then becomes binding on the state if the state consents.[23] If the state refuses to consent to the mediated compact, the matter is submitted to the Secretary of the Interior, who can then authorize the tribe to engage in Class III gaming in any manner consistent with the IGRA, without the state's consent.[24]

These carefully crafted procedures were undermined in 1995, however, when the Supreme Court decided *Seminole Tribe of Florida v. Florida.*[25] The Court held in *Seminole Tribe* that Congress in this situation may not strip the states of the immunity from suit they possess by virtue of the Eleventh Amendment. (As explained in chapter 18, the Eleventh Amendment confers on all states an immunity from most types of lawsuits unless the state has consented to be sued.) The Court declared unconstitutional the portion of the IGRA that sought to authorize tribes to sue a state for refusing to negotiate in good faith.[26]

What options do Indian tribes have, given *Seminole Tribe,* to obtain a Class III compact if the state refuses to negotiate in good faith?

Tribes have some alternatives if a state refuses to negotiate in good faith, although the validity of these options remains unclear. One option is for the tribe to sue the state anyway, and if the state forces the court to dismiss the case based on the Eleventh Amendment, the tribe can then proceed with the rest of the procedures set out in the IGRA, submitting its last offer to the Secretary of the Interior, who could then approve the compact after giving the state an opportunity to participate in the administrative process.[27] The Secretary has enacted regulations implementing this alternative.[28] Under these regulations, states are once again, as the IGRA intended, given an incentive to negotiate in good faith with tribes, given that their failure to participate in the process could lead to an administrative result against their interests.[29]

Still another option is for the United States to sue a state on the tribe's behalf. The Eleventh Amendment does not protect a state from lawsuits filed by the federal government.[30] The federal government's suit could then trigger the full procedural process set forth in the IGRA.

A third option—and one suggested by the Supreme Court in the *Seminole Tribe* case—is for Congress to amend the IGRA and authorize tribes to sue the state officials whose duty it is to negotiate these IGRA compacts on behalf of the state. This would avoid the barrier created by the Eleventh Amendment, which only prohibits suits against the state.[31]

A final option is for the tribe to engage in Class III gaming without a compact. A number of tribes have done so,[32] but this option is risky because the federal government may arrest and prosecute persons who engage in unauthorized gambling in Indian country,[33] and the National Indian Gaming Commission may fine a tribe or close a gaming facility if it finds that the tribe is conducting Class III gaming without a valid compact.[34] In one instance, a tribe was fined for each day it operated its casino in violation of the IGRA.[35] It is the federal government and not the state, though, that has the authority to enforce the IGRA. The IGRA preempts state law, both the state's civil injunctive powers[36] and its criminal enforcement powers,[37] unless the tribe's compact expressly confers that authority on the state.

State gaming compacts with tribes are usually mutually advantageous, and some state officials have gone to great lengths to obtain them.[38] As noted later in this chapter, tribal casinos create jobs for non-Indians, spur tourism to the state, and stimulate the surrounding economy. In addition, the state compact usually contains a profit-sharing arrangement.

What duties does the National Indian Gaming Commission have under the IGRA?

As part of the statutory plan to deal with tribal gaming, Congress created the National Indian Gaming Commission, a three-person agency within the Department of the Interior. The Commission's broad powers include approving all gaming management contracts, auditing the tribe's financial records, approving tribal-state compacts, monitoring and even shutting down games, levying fines, and issuing regulations and guidelines implementing the IGRA.[39] The Commission is funded by assessing a fee on tribal gaming revenues, up to a maximum assessment from all tribes that engage in Class III gaming of eight million dollars annually.[40]

Does the IGRA waive the tribe's sovereign immunity from suit?

Indian tribes normally may not be sued unless they have consented to be sued or Congress has passed a law expressly abrogating the tribe's immunity from suit. This principle—which applies equally to the state and federal governments—is known as the doctrine of sovereign immunity, and it is discussed at length in chapter 18.

The IGRA expressly authorizes the state and the tribe to sue one another to enforce the provisions of any tribal-state compact,[41] and this provision acts as a limited waiver of sovereign immunity for those states and tribes that have entered into compacts. These authorized suits, however, may only be filed in federal court; the IGRA preempts the operation of state law.[42]

Except for that situation, the IGRA does not waive the tribe's sovereign immunity, regardless of whether the suit seeks damages for a tort[43] or enforcement of a contract.[44] Thus, as one court held, if a chair collapses in a tribal casino while a patron is sitting in it, he or she may not file suit seeking damages for injuries unless the tribe has waived its immunity.[45] A state can attempt to compel a tribe to waive its sovereign immunity, as Connecticut successfully did in its compact with the Mashantucket Pequots (as mentioned earlier), but without such a waiver, the tribe is immune from suit except for the one situation described above that is expressly authorized by the IGRA.[46]

Has Congress prohibited any tribes from taking advantage of the IGRA?

Yes. As noted earlier, Indian tribes are prohibited by the IGRA from engaging in Class II and Class III gaming if the state prohibits all forms of gaming, a situation that exists in Utah. In addition, Congress has prohibited a few tribes from taking advantage of the IGRA, including the Passamaquoddy and Penobscot tribes in Maine, the Ysleta del Sur of Texas, the Catawbas of South Carolina, and the Narragansett of Rhode Island.[47] These tribes were the beneficiaries in recent years of federal laws that settled tribal land claims, and Congress included in those laws a provision that operated to prevent the tribe from participating in the IGRA.

May the Secretary of the Interior allow gaming to occur on newly acquired tribal lands?

The IGRA permits a federally recognized Indian tribe to establish gaming facilities on "Indian lands" within the tribe's control.[48] To qualify as "Indian lands," the tribe must have governmental authority over the territory, and the land must be in trust status.[49] Thus, a tribe cannot simply purchase land wherever it wants to and build a casino; if the land is located outside the reservation, for instance, it would first have to be converted by the Secretary of the Interior into trust status.[50]

A law passed in 1934 authorizes the Secretary of the Interior to convert into trust status any land privately owned by an Indian tribe and to purchase land with federal funds for Indian tribes that would then be placed in trust status for the tribe.[51] The IGRA, though, prohibits the Secretary from allowing gaming to occur on any land placed in trust for an Indian tribe after the date that the IGRA became effective (October 17, 1988), except in limited situations. The Secretary may approve such activities only, for example, when the tribe had no reservation on October 17, 1988; when the newly acquired lands are part of the tribe's "last recognized reservation"; or when the Secretary, after consulting with state and local officials and with officials of nearby Indian tribes, finds that a gaming facility would be in the tribe's best interests and the Governor of the state gives express consent.[52]

The ability of the Secretary to approve a new area as "Indian lands" has become a flashpoint of controversy. Many state and local officials contend that the Secretary should not approve a new casino that is opposed by the surrounding non-Indian community whose lives would be affected by it. The issue is so controversial that regulations proposed by the Clinton administration were withdrawn by the Bush administration in order to give state and local officials more time to comment on them.[53]

What has been the impact of gaming on Indian tribes?

The purpose of the IGRA was to promote "tribal economic development, self-sufficiency, and strong tribal governments."[54] The IGRA has succeeded in accomplishing those goals like no other program before it. Gaming on Indian reservations grossed $8.26 billion in 1998, up from $100 million just a decade earlier.[55] Some two hundred tribes in more than thirty states operate gaming facilities.[56]

Some tribes have refused to engage in gaming for moral and cultural reasons or to preserve their quiet communities. But most tribes that are geographically situated to support a profitable casino have one, and many of these tribes have expanded the size of their casinos in response to popular demand. In January 2001, the Santa Ana Pueblo, north of Albuquerque, New Mexico, partnered with Hyatt Hotels to open an $80 million, 350-room hotel and spa to accommodate its thriving casino, and the Isleta Pueblo south of Albuquerque recently opened a $50 million casino, creating more than five thousand jobs with a payroll exceeding $84 million.[57] These business ventures have been "a shot in the arm for the state's sagging economy."[58] In southern Arizona, the Tohono O'odham Nation is constructing a $52 million casino, while the nearby Pascua Yaqui Tribe recently opened a $65 million casino.[59] The most ambitious project is being undertaken by the Mohegan Nation of Connecticut, which is constructing an $800 million expansion to its existing, highly successful casino that will include a planetarium, the largest ballroom in the Northeast, and a 1,200-room luxury hotel.[60]

The vast majority of jobs created by Indian casinos are filled by non-Indians. More than forty thousand new jobs were created in New Mexico due to tribal gaming.[61] In the communities surrounding the casinos operated by the Coeur d'Alene Tribe in Idaho and the Umatilla Tribe in Oregon, unemployment has fallen by more than 50 percent, and millions of dollars have been added to the local economies.[62] As stated earlier, Indian tribes with the consent of the Governor of the state may obtain secretarial approval to build a casino off the reservation. One such venture is the $125 million casino built in Milwaukee by the Potawatomi Tribe, which has provided needed jobs and tax revenues to the city, so much so that officials in other Wisconsin towns are exploring similar arrangements with other tribes.[63]

Many gaming tribes make annual contributions to local schools and municipal projects. The Oneida Indian Nation in New York has contributed more than $2.2 million to seven area school districts during the past six years.[64] The Coeur d'Alene Tribe in Idaho annually distributes 5 percent of its casino profits to area schools, distributing $980,000 in cash awards in 2000.[65] The Sault Ste. Marie Tribe of Chippewa Indians of Michigan, once among the poorest communities in the state, is now the region's largest employer with a workforce of more than four thousand, and the tribe distributed $2 million to seven surrounding counties in 2000.[66]

Tribal-state compacts often provide for profit-sharing arrangements with the state government; two federally recognized tribes in Connecticut, the Mashantucket Pequots and the Mohegans, paid the state $319 million in 2000 from casino revenues under their compacts with the state.[67] A study conducted by the University of Connecticut Center for Economic Analysis found that the Pequot casino (which draws more than forty thousand visitors a day) added forty-one thousand jobs and $1.2 billion to Connecticut's economy and saved the economy of southern Connecticut from financial ruin following the downturn of the area's manufacturing and defense industries.[68]

Indian tribes with lucrative casinos now provide services to their members they were unable to previously. The Tesuque Pueblo in New Mexico built an elementary school and a Head Start center and renovated its historic plaza, a sacred place where it holds ceremonial dances.[69] The Omaha Tribe used its casino profits to upgrade its water system, to clean up twenty-two illegal dump sites on the reservation, and to purchase equipment for the repair and maintenance of tribal roads.[70] Many tribes offer full tuition scholarships to tribal members attending college and professional schools and have built or improved schools, jails, hospitals, sewer systems, and water treatment facilities with their casino profits. Tribes often use some of their gaming revenues to buy land, especially land within the reservation that had been taken from them decades ago under federal allotment policies (discussed in chapter 1). The Tulalip Tribe in Washington recently spent $7.4 million of casino profits to purchase nine hundred acres of forested land within its reservation.[71] One tribal chairperson recently stated that gaming "is restoring hope" to his tribe and is "allowing us to live out the spirit of our sovereignty" by removing tribal members from abject poverty.[72]

A handful of casinos are wildly successful. The top dozen account for nearly half of the Indian gaming revenue.[73] The Mashantucket Pequot's Foxwoods Resort Casino in Connecticut, the largest gaming establishment in the world, generates an estimated $1 billion in annual profits for the tribe.[74]

Most tribes spend their profits exclusively on community programs and services, but about fifty tribes issue per capita payments (*per caps*) to their members. Per caps range from about $50 a year per person on the Blackfeet reservation in Montana to hundreds of thousands of dollars to members of the Mashantucket Pequot Tribe in Connecticut and the Shakopee Mdewakanton Sioux Tribe in Minnesota.[75]

Gaming, though, has produced its own set of problems. As Professor Robert Porter recently noted, the "lure of making millions has . . . induced tribal governments to relinquish significant jurisdictional authority under compacts to our arch-enemies, the states," and the entire process of Indian gaming "has generated great conflict within our nations as we struggle to decide whether to pursue the gaming option, and even when we have, how we plan to spend the money."[76]

Internal conflicts generated by gaming have become bitter and divisive —and sometimes violent. Accusations have been flying on some reservations that tribal officials have stolen funds from the casino, or have refused to allow certain families to enroll their children into the tribe—or have expelled ("disenrolled") entire families from the tribe—in order to increase the size of their own per capita payments.[77] A few years ago, the Chief of the Saginaw Chippewa Tribe in Michigan, whose tribe was in a political upheaval over various gaming issues, stated: "We're used to whites being against us. Now, it's us against us. . . . It boils down to the money. . . . Sometimes, I wish we could go in a different direction [than continue to operate the casino]."[78]

Tribal gaming is heavily regulated and supervised. Many tribal-state compacts place Indian gaming facilities under the watchful eye of state regulators, and they are in any event inspected by the tribe's own regulators and by those employed by the National Indian Gaming Commission.[79] While it appears that tribal gaming has been protected from organized crime, all gaming (whether conducted on Indian reservations or in Las Vegas) can cause its own set of problems, both for individuals and for the community. For many Indian tribes and their members, however, it has meant the difference between hope and despair.

NOTES

1. 480 U.S. 202 (1987).
2. 25 U.S.C. Secs. 2710 *et seq;* 18 U.S.C. Sec. 1166.
3. *Id.,* Sec. 2702(1).
4. *Id.,* Sec. 2702(2).
5. *Id.,* Sec. 2703(6).
6. *Id.,* Sec. 2703(7). For purposes of the IGRA, *lotto* means a board game similar to bingo and not a lottery. See *Oneida Tribe of Indians v. Wisconsin,* 951 F.2d 757 (7th Cir. 1991).
7. 25 U.S.C. Secs. 2704–8.
8. *Id.,* Sec. 2710(b)(3).
9. *Id.,* Sec. 2703(8).
10. *Id.,* Sec. 2710(d)(1)(B).
11. *Id.,* Sec. 2710(d)(1)(C).
12. See *Shakopee-Mdewakanton Sioux Community v. Hope,* 16 F.3d 261 (8th Cir. 1994). *See also Cabazon Band of Mission Indians v. NIGC,* 14 F.3d 633 (D.C. Cir. 1994) (finding that the pull-tab game at issue in that case should be considered a Class III game).
13. See *Spokane Indian Tribe v. U.S.,* 972 F.2d 1090 (9th Cir. 1992).
14. *U.S. v. 103 Electronic Gambling Devices,* 223 F.3d 1091 (9th Cir. 2000); *U.S. v. 162 MegaMania Gambling Devices,* 231 F.3d 365 (10th Cir. 2000).
15. See *Diamond Game Enterprises, Inc. v. Reno,* 230 F.3d 365 (D.C. Cir. 2000).
16. See *Sycuan Band of Mission Indians v. Roache,* 54 F.3d 535, 539 (9th Cir.), *cert. denied,* 516 U.S. 912 (1995); *Mashantucket Pequot Tribe v. Connecticut,* 913 F.2d 1024 (2d Cir. 1990), *cert. denied,* 499 U.S. 975 (1991).
17. *Coeur d'Alene Tribe v. State of Idaho,* 842 F. Supp. 1268 (D. Idaho 1994), *aff'd,* 51 F.3d 876 (9th Cir.), *cert. denied,* 516 U.S. 916 (1995); *Rumsey Indian Rancheria of Wintun Indians v. Wilson,* 64 F.3d 1250 (9th Cir. 1994), *amended,* 99 F.3d 321 (1996), *cert. denied,* 521 U.S. 1118 (1997).
18. 25 U.S.C. Sec. 2710(d)(3)(B).

19. Mashantucket Pequot Tribal Laws, ch. 1, sec. 4(c). *See Schock v. Mashantucket Pequot Gaming Enterprise,* 27 Indian L. Rep. 6225, 6228 (Mash. Peq. Tr. Ct. 2000).

20. *See* "Notice of Final Mashantucket Pequot Gaming Procedures," 56 Fed. Reg. 24,996–99 (1991). *See also* Edmond Leedham, "The Indian Gaming Controversy in Connecticut: Forging A Balance Between Tribal Sovereignty and State Interests," 13 *Bridgeport L. Rev.* 649, 693 (1993).

21. 25 U.S.C. Sec. 2710(d)(3)(A).

22. *Id.,* Sec. 2710(d)(6)(B)(iii).

23. *Id.,* Sec. 2710(d)(7)(B)(iv)–(vi).

24. *Id.,* Sec. 2710(d)(7)(B)(vii).

25. 517 U.S. 44 (1996).

26. Consequently, suits against the state to enforce the "good faith" bargaining provision of the IGRA are barred in federal court unless the state has consented to suit. At least two states, California and Washington, have consented to such lawsuits. *See* Cal. Gov't Code Sec. 98005; *Hotel Employees and Restaurant Employees Int'l Union v. Davis,* 21 Cal.4th 585, 614–15, 88 Cal. Rptr.2d 56, 981 P.2d 990 (1999), and Wash. Sen. Bill 5905, Ch. 236, Laws of 2001 (effective July 22, 2001).

27. This alternative was proposed by the court of appeals that issued the decision reviewed by the Supreme Court in *Seminole Tribe. See Seminole Tribe of Florida v. Florida,* 11 F.3d 1016, 1029 (11th Cir. 1994).

28. *See* 63 Fed. Reg. 3289 (1998).

29. One commentator suggests that this coercion violates the Tenth Amendment. *See* Neil Cohen, "In What Often Appears to Be a Crapshoot Legislative Process, Congress Throws Snake Eyes When It Enacts the Indian Gaming Regulatory Act," 29 *Hofstra L. Rev.* 277, 301–6 (2000).

30. *See Arizona v. California,* 460 U.S. 605, 614 (1983).

31. *Seminole Tribe of Florida v. Florida,* 517 U.S. 44, 75 n.17 (1995). *See Pueblo v. Sandia v. Babbitt,* 47 F. Supp.2d 49, 57 (D.D.C. 1999) (recommending that Congress amend the IGRA in order "to recalibrate a balance that has tipped drastically in favor of the states" as a result of *Seminole Tribe).*

32. *See, e.g., Florida v. Seminole Tribe of Florida,* 181 F.3d 1237, 1239 (11th Cir. 1999). In *U.S. v. Spokane Tribe,* 139 F.3d 1297 (9th Cir. 1998), the court indicated that it was acceptable for tribes to engage in Class III gaming without state approval if the state ignores its duty to negotiate in good faith.

33. A law called the Johnson Act, 15 U.S.C. Secs. 1171–78 (1953), authorizes the federal government to prosecute persons who engage in unauthorized gambling in Indian country. *See Florida v. Seminole Tribe,* note 32 above, 181 F.3d at 1249; *U.S. v. Cook,* 922 F.2d 1026 (2d Cir.), *cert. denied,* 500 U.S. 941 (1991). The Johnson Act does not apply to Class II games (which are by definition authorized by state law) or to Class III games covered by a tribal-state compact. *See Cabazon Band of Mission Indians v. NIGC,* note 12, 14 F.3d at 635 n.3

34. 25 U.S.C. Sec. 2710(d)(1)(C). *See Florida v. Seminole Tribe,* note 32 above, 181 F.3d at 1244, 1248.

35. *See U.S. v. Santee Sioux Tribe,* 254 F.3d 728 (8th Cir. 2001).

36. *See Cabazon Band of Mission Indians v. Wilson,* 124 F.3d 1050, 1059–60 (9th Cir. 1997).

37. 18 U.S.C. Sec. 1166(d). *See Sycuan Band of Mission Indians,* note 16 above.

38. *See, e.g., Baird v. Norton,* 266 F.3d 408 (6th Cir. 2001); *American Greyhound Racing, Inc. v. Hull,* 146 F. Supp.2d 1012 (D. Ariz. 2001).

39. *See* 25 U.S.C. Secs. 2705–6, 2711(a)(3), 2713.

40. 25 U.S.C. Sec. 2717.

41. 25 U.S.C. Sec. 2710(d)(7)(A)(ii).

42. *Tamiami Partners v. Miccosukee Tribe of Indians,* 63 F.3d 1030, 1033 (11th Cir. 1995); *Cabazon Band of Mission Indians v. Wilson,* 37 F.3d 430, 433–35 (9th Cir. 1994).

43. *See Maxim v. Lower Sioux Indian Community,* 829 F. Supp. 277, 281–82 (D. Minn. 1993) (holding that IGRA does not waive the tribe's sovereign immunity from damages actions, although it does waive tribal immunity from suits seeking to enforce the requirements of the act); *Ross v. Flandreau Santee Sioux Tribe,* 809 F. Supp. 738, 745 (D.S.D. 1992) (same); *Cohen v. Little Six, Inc.,* 543 N.W.2d 376, 380 (Minn. 1996) (same).

44. *See Tamiami Partners, Ltd. v. Miccosukee Tribe of Indians,* note 42 above, 63 F.3d at 1049.

45. *Little Six, Inc.,* note 43 above, 543 N.W.2d at 380.

46. *See Gross v. Omaha Tribe of Nebraska,* 601 N.W.2d 82 (Iowa 1999); *Florida v. Seminole Tribe,* note 32 above, 181 F.3d at 1242.

47. *See respectively Passamaquoddy Tribe v. Maine,* 75 F.3d 784 (1st Cir. 1996); *Ysleta del Sur Pueblo v. Texas,* 36 F.3d 1325 (5th Cir. 1994), 25 U.S.C. Sec. 941*l;* and *Narragansett Indian Tribe v. National Indian Gaming Commission,* 158 F.3d 1335 (D.C. Cir. 1998). The Maine tribes are permitted by state law to engage in high-stakes bingo but they are not otherwise entitled to engage in the gaming authorized by the IGRA. *See* 17 M.R.S.A. Sec. 314-A.

48. 25 U.S.C. Secs. 2710(b)(1), (d)(1)(A)(i).

49. *Id.,* Secs. 2703(4)(B), 2710(b)(1), (d)(1)(A)(i).

50. *See Kansas v. U.S.,* 249 F.3d 1213 (10th Cir. 2001).

51. This subject is discussed in ch. 5, sec. B(5).

52. 25 U.S.C. Sec. 2719. The provision giving the Governor a power to veto the tribe's request has withstood a constitutional challenge. *See Confederated Tribes of Siletz Indian v. U.S.,* 110 F.3d 688 (9th Cir.), *cert. denied,* 522 U.S. 1027 (1997). *See also Sac and Fox Nation of Missouri v. Norton,* 240 F.3d 1250 (10th Cir. 2001) (discussing limits on Secretary's discretion to approve "Indian lands" under Sec. 2719).

53. *See* "BIA Gives States More Time to Comment on Gaming Rule," *Indian Country Today* (Jan. 9, 2002) at A1.

54. 25 U.S.C. Sec. 2702(1).

55. "Reservations with Casinos Gain Some Ground on Poverty," *Indian Country Today* (Sept. 13, 2000) at B1.

56. *See* Cohen, note 29 above, at 277–78.

57. "New Mexico Tribal Casinos Turn to Resorts," *American Indian Report* (April 2001) at 19.

58. "Isleta Casino, Where Those Hot 'Chili Peppers' Are the Drawing Card," *Indian Country Today* (Mar. 7, 2001) at C1.

59. "Pascua Yaqui to Build Largest Casino in Southern Arizona," *Indian Country Today* (Dec. 20, 2000) at B1.

60. "Mohegan Sun to Expand," *American Indian Report* (July 2000) at 23.

61. "Tribal Resorts: Latest Outgrowth of Casino Gambling in New Mexico," *Indian Country Today* (Mar. 21, 2001) at C1, C2.

62. "Indian Casinos Have Positive Area Impacts," *Indian Country Today* (Feb. 1, 1999) at A2.

63. "Wisconsin Tribes Would Move Casinos to Where the People Are," *Indian Country Today* (Mar. 21, 2001) at C1, C2.

64. "Casinos Support Local Services," *Indian Country Today* (Feb. 14, 2001) at B1.

65. "Coeur d'Alene Disburse $980,000 to Local Idaho Schools," *Indian Country Today* (Feb. 7, 2001) at C1.

66. "Sault Ste. Marie Tribe of Chippewa Indians of Michigan," *Indian Country Today* (Jan. 10, 2001) at C5.

67. *Id.* at B2.

68. "Computer Study Says Pequot Casino Saved the Connecticut Economy," *Indian Country Today* (Dec. 6, 2000) at A6.

69. "Tribal Resorts," note 61 above, at C2.

70. "Casino Omaha Profits Increase Quality of Life on Reservation," *Indian Country Today* (Aug. 17, 1994) at C2.

71. "Tulalips Buy Back 900 Former Reservation Acres," *Indian Country Today* (Feb. 28, 2001) at B5.

72. "The Gaming Industry Is Good Business," *Indian Country Today* (Aug. 17, 1998) at A8.

73. *See* "Gambling Benefits Spill from Reservations," *Indian Country Today* (Dec. 12, 2001) at D1; Jeff Hinkle, "Per Caps," *American Indian Report* (March 2001) at 12, 13; "Reservations with Casinos," note 55 above, at B1, B3.

74. Hinkle, note 73 above, at 12.

75. *Id.* at 13.

76. Robert B. Porter, "Strengthening Tribal Sovereignty Through Government Reform: What Are the Issues?" *Kan. J. L. and Pub. Policy* 72, 72–73 (Winter 1997).

77. *See Anderson v. Las Vegas Tribe of Paiute Indians*, 103 F.3d 137 (9th Cir. 1996), *cert. denied*, 520 U.S. 1169 (1997); *Ordinance 59 Ass'n v. U.S. Dept. of the Interior Secretary*, 163 F.3d 1150 (10th Cir. 1998); *Apodaca v. Silvas*, 19 F.3d 1015 (5th Cir. 1994).

78. Chief Gail Jackson, quoted in "Michigan Indians Fight over Huge Casino Profit," *Rocky Mountain News* (Dec. 17, 1994) at 34A.

79. Rick Hill, "Some Home Truths about Indian Gaming," *Indian Country Today* (Dec. 27, 2000) at A5.

XVII

The Indian Child Welfare Act

What is the Indian Child Welfare Act?

I magine the outcry if the government announced a plan to take one-fourth of all the white children in the country, separate them from their parents, and then place them in institutions or in foster or adoptive homes. Until 1978, it was as if such a plan actually existed for reservation Indian children.

An investigation conducted by Congress during the mid-1970s revealed that one-fourth of all reservation Indian children had been removed from their families by state welfare agencies and state courts and placed in foster or adoptive homes or institutions, and most had been placed in non-Indian homes located off the reservation. These forced separations had proven disastrous for many of the children involved, their parents, and their tribes.[1] The study also showed that many state social workers and judges lacked a basic knowledge of Indian culture regarding child rearing, were prejudiced in their attitudes, and removed children from their homes primarily because the family was Indian and poor. "An alarmingly high percentage" of Indian children were taken from their homes, Congress reported, because state officials "have often failed to recognize the . . . cultural and social standards prevailing in Indian communities and families."[2] In one state, the adoption rate for Indian children was eight times that of non-Indians, and in another state, Indian children were thirteen times more likely than non-Indians to be placed in foster care by state courts.[3]

The Indian Child Welfare Act (ICWA)[4] was enacted by Congress in 1978 to remedy this situation. The stated purpose of the act is "to protect the best interests of Indian children and to promote the stability and security of Indian tribes and families."[5] Congress was aware when it passed this law that nothing "is more vital to the continued existence and integrity of Indian tribes than their children."[6]

The ICWA seeks to accomplish these goals by limiting the state's ability to remove Indian children from their families and by giving tribal courts primary jurisdiction in most Indian custody cases. The ICWA places such significant restrictions on state courts in resolving Indian custody cases that many states contended it was unconstitutional, but the Supreme Court upheld the validity of the act in 1989 on the grounds that Congress has the authority to pass this type of protective legislation for Indians.[7] Since then, opponents of the ICWA—and there are many—have asked Congress to amend the act by restoring to state courts much of the authority they previously possessed to determine the custody of Indian children. Bills seeking to substantially limit the reach of the ICWA were introduced in Congress in 1996 and 1999 but failed to pass.

What does the ICWA require?

The ICWA establishes specific procedures that must be followed and rights that must be afforded to Indian children and their families by state courts in handling Indian child custody matters. To summarize, these procedures and rights—each of which is discussed in detail later—are the following:

1. If the Indian child is domiciled on an Indian reservation or has been made a ward of the tribal court, the tribal court has exclusive jurisdiction over the child in all custody matters. State courts may not adjudicate these cases.[8]

2. If the child resides off the reservation, the state and the tribal court have concurrent (shared) jurisdiction. Should a custody proceeding be initiated in state court, the court must notify the child's parents and tribe, and they each have a right to intervene in the proceeding.[9] If either the tribe or a parent requests it, the state court must transfer the case to tribal court unless one of the parents objects or "good cause" exists to deny the request.[10]

3. If the case remains in state court, the court may not terminate parental rights without proof "beyond a reasonable doubt" (or place the child in foster care without "clear and convincing evidence") that continued custody by the child's family "is likely to result in serious emotional or physical damage to the child."[11]

4. If the child's parents are indigent, they have a right to a court-appointed attorney, and separate counsel must be appointed for the child when the best interests of the child require it.[12]

5. Before a state court may place an Indian child in a non-Indian adoptive home, the court must give sequential placement preference to, first, the child's extended family, second, to other members of the child's tribe, and third, to other Indian families, unless "good cause" exists to ignore this preference hierarchy.[13] A similar hierarchy is imposed in foster-care placements.[14]

6. If a state court's placement of an Indian child violates the ICWA, it is subject to invalidation upon the petition of a parent or custodian of the child or of the child's tribe.[15]

7. Tribal court custody decisions are entitled to the same "full faith and credit" as state court custody decisions, meaning that they normally must be respected and enforced by other courts.[16]

8. The state must keep accurate records of all Indian child placements to which the ICWA applies and make them available to the federal government and to the tribe.[17] In addition, when an adopted Indian child becomes eighteen years old, the state must provide the child upon his or her request the names and tribal affiliation(s) of the child's biological parents.[18]

As these procedures and rights reflect, the ICWA creates a dual jurisdictional system that favors the tribe. When the child lives on the reservation, state courts have no jurisdiction to determine the child's custody. When the child lives off the reservation, tribes and states have concurrent jurisdiction, but jurisdiction presumptively lies in the tribe because the state court must transfer the case to tribal court upon request of the tribe or one of the child's parents, except in limited circumstances. Moreover, even when the case remains in state court, the ICWA allows tribes to intervene, reflecting Congress's conclusion that state courts are more likely to make proper placement decisions if made aware of the tribe's social and cultural values.[19] State courts are placed on notice by the ICWA, as the Montana Supreme Court recently stated, "that they are, in fact, a significant part of the problem" regarding the high number of improper Indian placements, and that "tribal courts are uniquely and inherently more qualified than state courts to determine custody in the best interests of an Indian child."[20]

When a custody proceeding involves an Indian child, what must a state court do immediately?

When a proceeding is filed in state court regarding the placement of a child who might have some Indian blood, the court must promptly undertake two inquiries. First, the court must determine whether the child is an *Indian child* as that term is defined in the ICWA. If the child is not an Indian child, the ICWA is inapplicable and the court may proceed to handle the case entirely under state law.

The ICWA defines *Indian child* as any unmarried person under eighteen years of age who is enrolled in a tribe or who is the biological child of a tribal member and is eligible for enrollment.[21] The child's tribe must be contacted to determine whether the child is enrolled or enrollable, and the state court must accept as final the tribe's decision regarding membership.[22] However, the burden of proof rests with the party claiming that the child is an Indian child—that is, it rests with the party claiming that the ICWA is applicable—and a mere claim that the child has some Indian blood is not itself sufficient to satisfy that burden without proof that the child is enrolled or enrollable in a particular tribe.[23]

Second, a state court must promptly determine whether the child is domiciled on or off the reservation. As noted above, if the child resides on the reservation (or has been made a ward of the tribal court), then only the tribal court has jurisdiction, and any proceeding commenced in state court must be dismissed. This rule was enforced by the Supreme Court in *Mississippi Band of Choctaw Indians v. Holyfield* (1989).[24] In *Holyfield*, a married Indian couple left the reservation shortly before the birth of their twins and signed papers allowing the children to be adopted by the Holyfields, a non-Indian couple who had arranged for the adoption. After the children were born, the Holyfields obtained an adoption decree from a state court based on the consent of the parents. The tribe, however, challenged the validity of the decree, arguing that the state court lacked jurisdiction over the children. The state court rejected the tribe's argument, but the Supreme Court held that even though the twins were born off the reservation, their parents—and thus the children—were *legally domiciled* on the reservation because that is where the parents actually lived and intended to live in the future. Consequently, exclusive jurisdiction rested with the tribal court, and the state court adoption decree was void. Even the children's own parents, the Court held, could not defeat the tribe's rights under the ICWA. "Congress was concerned not solely about the interests of Indian children and families, but also about the impact on the tribes themselves of the large numbers of Indian children adopted by non-Indians."[25]

As *Holyfield* makes clear, a child can be located off the reservation and yet be domiciled on the reservation for purposes of the ICWA.[26] Citing *Holyfield*, the South Dakota Supreme Court ruled in a 1997 case that an Indian mother who had lived off the reservation for several years was still legally domiciled on the reservation because she moved back there after her child was born and testified that she intended to remain there indefinitely; thus, the tribal court had exclusive jurisdiction regarding the child's placement.[27]

Does the ICWA impose restrictions on state courts in *voluntary* placement proceedings?

Removal of a child from the home can be voluntary or involuntary, depending on whether the parents or legal custodians consent to the removal. The ICWA applies in both situations, but state courts have more authority when removal is voluntary. (Of course, as *Holyfield* illustrates, if the removal is voluntary but the child is domiciled on the reservation, state courts have no jurisdiction at all.)

When removal from the home is voluntary (and the child resides off the reservation), the state is not required to notify the tribe, and the tribe cannot insist on having the case transferred to tribal court.[28] The ICWA does have some application, though, because if the court grants the petition to remove the child, the court must follow the sequential placement hierarchy set out in the act, thus preferring an Indian home to a non-Indian home for the placement.[29]

Does the ICWA impose restrictions on state courts in *involuntary* placement proceedings?

In every involuntary foster care or adoption proceeding in state court involving an Indian child, the party seeking the child's removal "shall notify the parent or Indian custodian and the Indian child's tribe, by registered mail with return receipt requested, of the pending proceedings and of their right of intervention."[30] The parent, custodian, and tribe then have the right to intervene "at any point in the proceeding."[31]

Providing notice is mandatory. The rights of the tribe and parents/custodians are meaningless unless they are notified of the proceeding;

therefore, if notice is not given, any subsequent court decision is void.[32] Notice must be sent even if the court is uncertain whether the child is Indian but it appears that he or she might be, and it must be sent regardless of how late in the proceedings a child's possible Indian heritage is discovered.[33]

Notice must be adequate and reasonable under the circumstances. Thus, a state welfare agency's decision to place notice of the court hearing in a newspaper violates the ICWA when the agency knows where a parent lives and fails to notify the parent more directly.[34] When the identity of a parent or the tribe cannot be determined by the court, the ICWA requires that notice of the proceeding be given to the Secretary of the Interior, who then has fifteen days to try and discover the identities of the parents and relevant tribe(s) and notify them of the proceeding.[35]

May a state court deny a request to transfer the proceeding to tribal court?

As just explained, the ICWA allows both the tribe and the parents/custodians to intervene in the state court case at any time. In addition, they are entitled to request that the case be transferred to the tribal court,[36] where the child's custody will then be determined according to tribal law.[37]

Once a state court receives a petition from a parent or a tribal official to transfer the case, it must grant the request except in three situations: (1) a parent objects to the transfer;[38] (2) the tribal court declines to accept the case;[39] or (3) "good cause" exists to deny the request.[40] The *good cause* exception has engendered considerable controversy because the ICWA does not define the term. Court decisions and the official "Guidelines for State Courts" issued by the Bureau of Indian Affairs (BIA) indicate that the following situations might constitute good cause to deny a transfer request: (1) the tribe, parent, or custodian did not file the request promptly after receiving notice, and the proceeding is in an advanced stage when the request is received;[41] (2) the Indian child is over twelve years of age and objects to the transfer; (3) the evidence necessary to decide the case could not be presented adequately in the tribal court without undue hardship to the parties or to the witnesses; or (4) the child is more than five years old, the parents are not available, and the child has had little or no contact with the tribe or tribal members.[42]

The burden of proving good cause rests with the party opposing the transfer to tribal court,[43] and it is not an easy burden to meet. It is often argued that a child's lack of contact with the tribe should be good cause to deny a transfer, but most courts have recognized that adopting such a rule would only encourage the early removal of children from the reservation; moreover, it would overlook the interests of the tribe, the child's extended family, and the child's own interests to have custody determined by a tribal court even though the parents have had little contact with the tribe.[44] Likewise, geography alone should not be determinative; a request to transfer should not be denied simply because it would be inconvenient for off-reservation witnesses to testify in tribal court, given that it is just as difficult for reservation witnesses to travel to the state court.[45] State courts, however, often cite geography as one reason, sometimes as their only or their main reason, for denying a tribe's request to have a case transferred.[46]

As the Supreme Court recognized in *Holyfield*, although tribes and states have concurrent jurisdiction in certain situations involving Indian custody determinations, the ICWA creates "presumptively tribal" jurisdiction.[47] Given this congressional intent, as the Alaska Supreme Court recently noted, when a state court is faced with a transfer petition, there should be "a strong presumption in favor of transfer," and the good cause exception should not be viewed as "an invitation for our courts" to deny transferring a case to tribal court unless compelling facts warrant it.[48]

What proof must be shown in order to terminate parental rights in ICWA cases?

The ICWA provides that parental rights may not be terminated by a state court except "by evidence beyond a reasonable doubt, including testimony of qualified expert witnesses" that continued custody by the parent(s) "is likely to result in serious emotional or physical damage to the child."[49] In addition, it must be shown that "active efforts have been made to provide remedial services and rehabilitative programs" to the family and that these failed to cure the problem or deficiency in the child's present situation.[50]

Indian parents, just like non-Indian parents, are sometimes unfit to raise a child. But Indian parents must not be stripped of their parental rights simply because an adoptive family is more secure financially than they are or because the judge disapproves of a tribe's child-rearing practices and traditions. As the Supreme Court noted in *Holyfield*, the ICWA seeks to make sure "that Indian child welfare determinations are not based on a white, middle-class standard which, in many cases, forecloses placement with [an] Indian family."[51] On the other hand, substantial evidence that a parent's behavior constitutes abuse, neglect, or abandonment under tribal law or custom—especially evidence of physical abuse—is sufficient to justify the termination of parental rights provided that remedial services have been tried and failed.[52] As the BIA Guidelines explains:

> [Under the ICWA, a] child may not be removed simply because there is someone willing to raise a child who is likely to do a better job or that it would be "in the best interests of the child" for him to live with someone else. . . . It must be shown that it is dangerous for the child to remain with his or her present custodian."[53]

The ICWA does not replace state standards for determining parental termination. On the contrary, the ICWA imposes a dual burden of proof by requiring that a termination of parental rights not be declared unless both the state's standards and the ICWA standards are met.[54]

Who is an expert witness for purposes of the ICWA?

As just indicated, in order to justify permanent parental termination, testimony from "qualified expert witnesses" must be submitted on the issue of whether continued placement in the home is likely to cause serious emotional or physical injury to the child. This testimony will reduce the risk that the case will be decided based on prejudice or cultural bias and will be determined instead within the context of the tribe's culture and child-rearing customs, which could be different from white, middle-class practices and customs.[55] For example, to many Anglo-Americans, leaving a child for long periods of time with a grandparent or uncle may seem like abandonment, whereas such conduct is both encouraged and expected on many Indian reservations.

The BIA Guidelines lists three categories of persons eligible to serve as experts under the ICWA: (1) a member of the child's tribe who is knowledgeable in tribal child-rearing customs; (2) a lay expert who has substantial experience in delivering family-care services to Indians and has knowledge of the tribe's cultural standards; and (3) someone specially trained in the area in which he or she is testifying (a child-care professional).[56] The ICWA states that "expert witnesses" must be called to testify in termination proceedings, but courts have held that one expert is normally sufficient, provided that this person is qualified to testify on the issues most relevant to that particular case.[57]

Once the state court has determined that the Indian child must be removed from the home, where may the court then place the child?

Whenever a state court decides that an Indian child needs to be removed from his or her home either temporarily or permanently, the court must first consider placing the child with members of the extended family, other members of the child's tribe, or other Indian families. The state court may only place the child in some other environment, including a non-Indian home, if good cause exists.[58] These preference requirements reflect a federal presumption that placement in an Indian home is almost always in an Indian child's best interests.[59]

The ICWA does not define what constitutes "good cause" to avoid the act's preferential-placement hierarchy, and this gives state courts some discretion.[60] Given the overall congressional intent to leave Indian children in Indian homes and communities, state courts should rarely deviate from doing so, and the burden of proof must be placed on the person seeking an exception.[61] The BIA Guidelines suggests that a good cause finding must be based on one or more of the following factors: the request of the parents or of the child if the child is of sufficient age and maturity to make an informed decision; expert testimony regarding the child's particular physical or emotional needs; and the unavailability of suitable alternative placements within the Indian community.[62] In one case, an Indian mother's preference for the prospective adoptive non-Indian parents and the child's bond with them (developed during a foster-care placement), coupled with the uncertainty over the child's future if not adopted, was sufficient cause to overcome the ICWA's preferential-placement requirements.[63] In another case, a court deviated from the hierarchy because the Indian mother wished to have this particular non-Indian family adopt her child, the child related well with the family, and evidence indicated that placement with someone in the Indian community would make it easy for the abusive father to gain access to the child.[64]

The good cause exception to the placement hierarchy is not a "best interests" test, inviting state courts to speculate on whether a child would benefit from living in a non-Indian community.[65] It is true, though, that the act's remedial section (section 1914) provides a remedy for other vio-

lations of the act but not for the failure of a state court to obey the placement hierarchy, leading some courts to claim that compliance with the
hierarchy is optional.[66]

Does the ICWA place any limits on the ability of a parent to consent to the removal of an Indian child from the home?

Yes. Parents sometimes decide to voluntarily relinquish custody of their
children, and the ICWA allows Indian parents to exercise this option. But
the ICWA places limits on the type and manner of consent that is acceptable, in order to protect the interests of the child and the tribe, as well as
to protect against an Indian parent improvidently relinquishing custody.

In order for an Indian parent or custodian to give valid consent to a
foster care or adoptive placement, the consent must be in writing and must
be recorded before a judge, and the judge must certify that the terms and
consequences of the consent were explained to the parent in a language he
or she understands.[67] A parent who signs a form that does not comply with
these requirements may later withdraw his or her consent.[68] Moreover, the
consent is invalid if given prior to, or within ten days after, the child's
birth.[69] Consent to temporary foster care placement may be withdrawn by
the parent at any time, and the child must then be returned to the parent.[70]
Consent for an adoption may be withdrawn by the parent at any time
prior to the entry of a final decree,[71] but once the adoption decree is final,
it cannot be withdrawn except on proof of duress or fraud in an action
filed within two years after entry of the decree.[72]

If an Indian child has been living with an adoptive family for years, can the adoption be invalidated under the ICWA?

In some situations, an adoption can be invalidated. If a state court
placed an Indian child in an adoptive home without complying with the
ICWA but an adoption decree has not yet been issued, then the parent,
custodian, or tribe can have the placement set aside even if many years
have elapsed.[73] The proceeding would be transferred to the tribal court,
which could return the child to the same home or make some other placement.[74]

Even if an adoption decree has already been entered, it is subject to
being voided if it was procured in a manner that violated the ICWA, as
in instances in which a tribe or a parent was not notified of the proceed-

ing. In that situation, the decree terminating parental rights can be invalidated and the case would begin anew.[75] The ICWA does not set any time limits on such a challenge, and courts are split as to whether a state court may apply in ICWA cases the statutory limitations that apply in custody cases governed entirely by state law.[76] It would be helpful if Congress amended the ICWA to clarify what time limit (a "statute of limitations") applies to this type of challenge under the ICWA.

Does an unwed father have rights under the ICWA?

Under the ICWA, each parent must be given notice of a child custody proceeding; each parent may request that the proceeding be transferred to tribal court; and each parent may veto a transfer request made by the other parent or by the tribe. A *parent* for purposes of the ICWA is defined as any biological or adoptive parent of an Indian child.[77] Thus, unwed fathers have rights under the ICWA, and non-Indian fathers have the same rights in this regard as Indian fathers.

However, as defined in the act, a parent "does not include the unwed father where paternity has not been acknowledged or established."[78] Courts have held that if the child's Indian blood comes entirely from the father, and the father does not acknowledge paternity and paternity is not established, the father's tribe may not participate in any state court custody proceeding because the tribe's only link to the child is through the father.[79]

Must notice to the tribe be given in emergency custody determinations initiated in state court?

No. The ICWA provides that the notice requirements of the act may be ignored temporarily when an emergency placement is needed "to prevent imminent physical damage or harm to the child." After this initial placement, the state court must "expeditiously initiate a child custody proceeding" and satisfy the usual notice requirements.[80]

May a state court custody decision be appealed to a federal court?

Section 1914 of the ICWA provides that the parent, custodian, or tribe of an Indian child removed from the home in a state court custody case "may petition any court of competent jurisdiction to invalidate such action" if the state violated certain listed portions of the act. Federal courts are courts of "competent jurisdiction," and therefore one could argue that Congress has authorized them to review all state court ICWA decrees, but this is not how the act has been interpreted.

State courts are courts of competent jurisdiction under the ICWA, too. As is true in most other areas of the law, an ICWA case in state court may only be appealed within the state's appellate court system and from there to the U.S. Supreme Court.[81] In both ICWA and non-ICWA custody cases, a federal court is not permitted to review a state court's decree unless it is "fundamentally flawed" on constitutional grounds.[82] However, if the tribe or a parent had been excluded from the state court proceeding— and thus no opportunity existed to protect the interests of the tribe or parent—either one may challenge the state court decree in a federal court, without the need to pursue a state appeal, on the grounds that it violated the ICWA or the U.S. Constitution.[83]

Once a proceeding has been commenced in a state court, another party to the proceeding may not "forum shop" and file a similar action in federal court, asking that court to decide the case before the state court does.[84] The same general rule applies in this situation as in the one just discussed, that is, a party usually may not have a federal court intervene in or review a state court proceeding, ICWA or non-ICWA, except in very limited circumstances.

Does the ICWA apply in *all* Indian custody cases?

The ICWA does not apply in several situations in which the custody of an Indian child is being determined. The act does not apply if the Indian child is not a tribal member or eligible for membership[85] or if the child's tribe is not recognized by the federal government as an Indian tribe.[86] The ICWA also does not apply to custody disputes, including divorce or separation proceedings, in which custody of the child is to be awarded to one of the parents,[87] or to placements made in juvenile delinquency proceedings when the child has committed an act that if committed by an adult would be deemed a crime.[88]

Courts have created a few other exceptions. One court held that the ICWA did not apply when an Indian child, who had already been awarded to the custody of its non-Indian mother in a divorce proceeding and was living off the reservation, was being adopted by her new non-Indian spouse.[89] However, the majority of courts have held that the ICWA applies in such cases.[90] Another court held that the ICWA does not apply to intrafamily custody disputes, such as those in which a parent and grandparent are fighting for custody,[91] but most courts have held that any proceeding that could result in the removal of an Indian child from his or her home is covered by the act except for the express exemptions listed in the act itself.[92]

By far the most controversial and far-reaching court-created exception is known as the "existing Indian family" doctrine. Several courts have held that the ICWA does not apply to any placement proceeding—even to an adoption—in which the Indian child's parents have not maintained a significant social, cultural, and political relationship with their tribe.[93] According to these courts, the goal of the ICWA was to prevent the unwarranted removal of an Indian child from an existing Indian family unit or Indian community, that is, to prevent state courts from interfering with the raising of a child in the Indian way. When neither the parents nor the child have maintained any "Indian" ties or relationships, the ICWA does not apply because it was not intended to apply, these courts have held. In one case, the parents of twins voluntarily consented to have their children adopted by a non-Indian couple. The natural mother was non-Indian, and the father, although Indian, maintained no contacts with his tribe; in addition, the couple resided off the reservation. The father's tribe sought to intervene in the state court adoption proceeding. However, the court held that the ICWA does not apply to a voluntary termination proceeding involving an Indian child not domiciled on the reservation "unless the child's biological parent, or parents, are not only of American Indian descent, but also maintain a significant social, cultural or political relationship with their tribe."[94] This same doctrine was applied in a case in which a non-Indian mother consented the day her illegitimate child was born to have the child adopted by a non-Indian couple, despite the fact that the Indian father of the child and his tribe both sought to intervene and challenge the adoption.[95]

The majority of courts have rejected the "existing Indian family" doctrine as being inconsistent with the ICWA.[96] These courts have recognized, as did the Supreme Court in *Holyfield*, that the ICWA reflects a congressional concern not only for the interests of Indian parents but also for the harm caused to tribes when their children are adopted by non-Indians.[97] Moreover, Indian children have an interest in maintaining a relationship with the tribe even if their parents do not. Therefore, these courts have said, the ICWA should be applied even when the parents have not themselves been involved in the Indian community.[98] According to the majority view, the "existing Indian family" doctrine "allows the dominant society to judge whether the parent's cultural background meets its view of what 'Indian culture' should be [and] puts the state courts right back into the position from which Congress had removed them" when it passed the ICWA.[99]

Are tribes within Public Law 83–280 states covered by the ICWA?

Public Law 83–280 (P.L. 280), passed in 1953 (and discussed in chapter 7), gave certain states some jurisdiction in Indian country. However, nothing in P.L. 280 removes the powers and protection that Congress conferred twenty-five years later in the ICWA on all federally recognized tribes. A confusing provision in the ICWA states that before a tribe located in a P.L. 280 state may "reassume jurisdiction over Indian child custody proceedings, such tribe shall present to the Secretary [of the Interior] for approval a petition to reassume such jurisdiction which includes a suitable plan to exercise such jurisdiction."[100] However, nothing in that provision was intended by Congress to divest tribes of the powers they inherently possessed, and it merely reflects the fact that in P.L. 280 states, the state enjoys concurrent (shared) jurisdiction with the tribe over children domiciled on the reservation. Once the Secretary approves a tribe's petition, the state loses concurrent jurisdiction and the tribe has exclusive jurisdiction. But even if the Secretary denies a petition (or the tribe does not submit one), the tribe may exercise its ICWA powers.[101] For example, the tribe can request that a custody proceeding commenced in state court be transferred to tribal court, exactly as tribes in non-P.L. 280 states can do.[102]

Have state courts obeyed the ICWA?

Congress enacted the ICWA because state courts "have often failed to recognize the essential tribal relations of Indian people and the cultural and social standards prevailing in Indian communities and families."[103] Since passage of the ICWA, most state courts have acted responsibly and commendably, recognizing, as one court stated, a "duty to preserve the unique cultural heritage and integrity of the American Indians"[104] by faithfully following the procedures, and affording the rights required by, the ICWA.

The ICWA gives courts leeway in certain areas, such as in determining when good cause exists to deny transferring a case to tribal court and in determining whether good cause exists to avoid the placement hierarchy, as discussed earlier. Some states have used this discretion to reach decisions that appear inconsistent with the ICWA.[105] However, as time goes on, even greater acceptance of, and adherence to, the intent and terms of the ICWA will likely be achieved.[106]

NOTES

1. See *Mississippi Band of Choctaw Indians v. Holyfield*, 490 U.S. 30, 32 (1989). *See also* B. J. Jones, *The Indian Child Welfare Act Handbook* (Chicago: Section of Family Law, American Bar Association, 1995); Myers, Gardner, and Geary, "Adoption of Native American Children and the Indian Child Welfare Act," 18 *S. Ct. J.* 17 (1994); Comment, "The Indian Child Welfare Act of 1978," 60 *U. Colo. L. Rev.* 131 (1989); R. Tellinghuisen, "The Indian Child Welfare Act of 1978," 34 *S.D.L. Rev.* 660 (1989).

2. 25 U.S.C. Sec. 1901.

3. *See* "Indian Child Welfare Program Hearings Before the Subcomm. on Indian Affairs," U.S. Senate, 93d Cong., 2d Sess. 15 (Apr. 8, 1974), *reprinted in* 1978 U.S.C.C.A.N. 1530, 7531 (Statement of William Byler).

4. 25 U.S.C. Secs. 1901–63.

5. 25 U.S.C. Sec. 1902.

6. 25 U.S.C. Sec. 1901(3).

7. *See Holyfield*, note 1 above.

8. 25 U.S.C. Sec. 1911(a).

9. *Id.*, Secs. 1912(a) and 1911(c), respectively.

10. *Id.*, Sec. 1911(b).

11. *Id.*, Secs. 1912(f) and (e), respectively.

12. *Id.*, Sec. 1912(b). *See In re Custody of A.K.H.*, 502 N.W.2d 790 (Minn. App. 1993); *In re G.L.O.C.*, 668 P.2d 235 (Mont. 1983); *In re M.E.M.*, 635 P.2d 1313 (Mont. 1981).

13. 25 U.S.C. Sec. 1915(a). *See* discussion later in this chapter.

14. 25 U.S.C. Sec. 1915(b). *See In re Bird Head*, 331 N.W.2d 785 (Neb. 1983).

15. 25 U.S.C. Sec. 1914. The ICWA defines *Indian custodian* as any Indian person who has legal custody of an Indian child under tribal custom or under state or tribal law or who has received temporary custody from a parent of the child. *See* 25 U.S.C. Sec. 1903(6).

16. *Id.*, Sec. 1911(d).

17. *Id.*, Sec. 1915(e).

18. *Id.*, Sec. 1917.

19. *See J.W. v. R.J.*, 951 P.2d 1206, 1212 (Alaska 1998).

20. *In re Marriage of Skillen*, 956 P.2d 1, 11 (Mont. 1998).

21. 25 U.S.C. Sec. 1903(4).

22. *In the Interest of A.P.*, 961 P.2d 706 (Kan. App. 1998); *In re Adoption of Riffle*, 922 P.2d 510, 513 (Mont. 1996); *In re Junious M.*, 144 Cal. App.3d 786, 193 Cal. Rptr. 40, 43 (Cal. App. 1983). If it appears that the child could be a member of, or eligible for membership in, two tribes, the state must contact both of them. See *In re J.W.*, 498 N.W.2d 417 (Iowa App. 1993).

23. *In re A.S.*, 614 N.W.2d 385 (S.D. 2000); *Matter of Baby Boy Doe*, 849 P.2d 925, 931 (Idaho 1993), *cert. denied*, 510 U.S. 860 (1993).

24. 490 U.S. 30 (1989). See also Tellinghuisen, note 1 above, at 666.

25. *Holyfield*, note 1 above, 490 U.S. at 49.

26. In addition to *Holyfield*, note 1 above, see *In re Pima County Juvenile Action*, 635 P.2d 187 (Ariz. App. 1981), *cert. denied*, 455 U.S. 1007 (1982); and *In re Baby Child*, 700 P.2d 198 (N.M. App. 1985).

27. *In the Interest of G.R.F.*, 569 N.W.2d 29 (S.D. 1997). But see *People in re S.G.V.E.*; 634 N.W.2d 88, 92 (S.D. 2000) (holding that child, only recently removed by mother from the reservation, was domiciled off the reservation because there was no evidence that mother intended to return to the reservation).

28. See *Navajo Nation v. Superior Court of the State of Washington*, 47 F. Supp.2d 1233, 1237 (E.D. Wash. 1999). See also *Catholic Social Services, Inc. v. C.A.A.*, 783 P.2d 1159 (Alaska 1989), *cert. denied*, 495 U.S. 948 (1990).

29. 25 U.S.C. Sec. 1915. But see *Navajo Nation v. Superior Court*, note 28 above, 47 F. Supp.2d at 1242–43 (holding that even if the state court fails to comply with the ICWA's placement requirements, neither the tribe nor the family can obtain a judicial remedy).

30. 25 U.S.C. Sec. 1912.

31. *Id.*, Sec. 1911(c). See *In re Alicia S.*, 65 Cal. App.4th 79, 82, 76 Cal. Rptr.2d 121 (1998); *In the Matter of the Adoption of Riffle*, 902 P.2d 542, 545 (Mont. 1995); *Matter of Guardianship of Q.G.M.*, 808 P.2d 684, 688–89 (Okla. 1991).

32. See *In re Levi U.*, 92 Cal. Rptr.2d 648 (Cal. App. 2000); *In re N.A.H.*, 418 N.W.2d 310, 311 (S.D. 1988); *In re J.W.*, note 22 above; *In re Kahlen*, 233 Cal. App.3d 1414, 285 Cal. Rptr. 507 (1991). Some courts have held, however, that strict compliance with the ICWA's notice provisions is not required when the tribe has received actual notice. See *In re B.I.E.*, 422 N.W.2d 597, 599–600 (S.D. 1988).

33. *In re Kahlen*, note 32 above, 233 Cal. App. at 1424; *In re Pedro N*, 35 Cal. App.4th 183, 41 Cal. Rptr.2d 819, 821 (1995); *In re M.C.P.*, 571 A.2d 627 (Vt. 1989); *In Interest of H.D.*, 729 P.2d 1234 (Kan. 1986); *Junious M.*, note 22 above, 193 Cal. Rptr. at 43 n.7.

34. *Kickapoo Tribe v. Radar*, 822 F.2d 1493 (10th Cir. 1987).

35. 25 U.S.C. Sec. 1912(a).

36. *Id.*, Sec. 1911(b).

37. See *Holyfield*, note 1 above; *In the Matter of Stephanie Jean Pann*, 21 Indian L. Rep. 6141, 6142 (Sault Ste. Marie Tr. Ct. 1993). *Cf. People of the Rosebud Sioux Tribe in the Interest of J.E.*, 10 Indian L. Rep. 6114 (Rbd. Sx. Ct. App. 1992) (holding that it is "axiomatic" that the tribe should adopt as its law the notice requirements of the ICWA).

38. See *In the Interest of A.E.*, 572 N.W.2d 579 (Iowa 1997) (holding that even a non-Indian parent can veto a tribe's request to have the case transferred); *In the Matter of*

the Appeal in Maricopa County, Juvenile Action, 922 P.2d 319, 321–22 (Ariz. App. 1996) (if a parent objects, the case cannot be transferred); *People ex rel. K.D.,* 630 N.W.2d 492 (S.D. 2001) (same). Congress has allowed parents in off-reservation custody proceedings to object to tribal court jurisdiction, but as *Holyfield* illustrates, note 1 above, on-reservation parents have no similar authority. *See In re Larrisa G.,* 51 Cal. Rptr.2d 16, 22 (Cal. App. 1996).

39. *See In the Interest of C.Y.,* 925 P.2d 447 (Kan. App. 1996) (holding that even if a tribal officer declines a transfer, it is the tribal court that must decline; otherwise, the case must be transferred unless a parent vetoes the transfer or good cause exists to deny the transfer).

40. 25 U.S.C. Sec. 1911(b).

41. *See, e.g., In the Matter of A.P.,* 962 P.2d 1186 (Mont. 1998); *In the Matter of the Dependency and Neglect of A.L.,* 442 N.W.2d 233 (S.D. 1989); *Matter of Wayne R.N.,* 757 P.2d 1333 (N.M. App. 1988). *Compare People in Interest of J.L.P.,* 870 P.2d 1252 (Colo. App. 1994) (transferring case even though transfer request was made one year after tribe received notice because case was not in advanced stage), and *In re Robert T.,* 246 Cal. Rptr. 168 (1988) (holding that sixteen-month delay justified denial of transfer request when proceedings were in advanced stage).

42. *See* Bureau of Indian Affairs, "Guidelines for State Courts: Indian Child Custody Proceedings," 44 Fed. Reg. 67584, 67591 (1978).

43. 25 U.S.C. Sec. 1911(b); Bureau of Indian Affairs, note 42 above, 44 Fed. Reg. at 67591. *See J.L.P.,* note 41 above; *In Interest of Armell,* 550 N.E.2d 1060 (Ill. App. 1990); *In re M.E.M.,* note 12 above, 635 P.2d at 1317.

44. *See, e.g., Junious M.,* note 22 above; *In Interest of J.L.P.,* note 41 above; *In re Appeal in Cocomino County Juvenile Action,* 736 P.2d 829 (Ariz. 1987); *In re Adoption of Holloway,* 732 P.2d 962 (Utah 1986). *But see Robert T.,* note 41 above.

45. *See Pima County,* note 26 above. *But see In Interest of J.R.H.,* 358 N.W.2d 311 (Iowa 1984); *Chester County Dept. of Social Services v. Coleman,* 399 S.E.2d 773 (S.C. 1990), *cert. denied,* 500 U.S. 918 (1991).

46. *See In the Interest of A.P.,* note 22 above; *In the Interest of C.W.,* 479 N.W.2d 105, 113 (Neb. 1992).

47. *Holyfield,* note 1 above, 490 U.S. at 36.

48. *In the Matter of C.R.H.,* 29 P.3d 849, 853 n.16, 854 (Alaska 2001) (internal citation omitted).

49. 25 U.S.C. Sec. 1912(f). *See In the Interest of B.S.,* 566 N.W.2d 446 (S.D. 1997).

50. 25 U.S.C. Sec. 1912(d). *See A.A. v. State of Alaska Dept. of Family and Youth Services,* 982 P.2d 256, 262 n.20 (Alaska 1999); *In re Charles,* 688 P.2d 1354 (Or. App. 1984). The requirement of services applies only to proceedings in state court, not in tribal court. *Mother v. Colville Confederated Tribes,* 24 Indian L. Rep. 6026 (Colv. Ct. App. 1996).

51. *Holyfield,* note 1 above, 490 U.S. at 37.

52. *See San Diego County Dept. of Social Services v. Gina L.,* 74 Cal. Rptr.2d 642 (Cal. App. 1998); *In the Matter of Baby Boy Doe,* 902 P.2d 477 (Idaho 1995); *Matter of S.D.,* 402 N.W.2d 346 (S.D. 1987); *In the Matter of M.E.M., Jr.,* 679 P.2d 1241 (Mont. 1983).

53. Bureau of Indian Affairs, note 42 above, 44 Fed. Reg. at 67593.

54. *See J. W. v. R.J.*, note 19 above; *K.E. v. Utah*, 912 P.2d 1002 (Utah App. 1996); *In re Elliott*, 554 N.W.2d 32 (Mich. App. 1996); *In re Bluebird*, 411 S.E.2d 820, 823 (N.C. App. 1992); *In re D.S.P.*, 480 N.W.2d 234, 238–39 (S.D. 1991).

55. Bureau of Indian Affairs, note 42 above, 44 Fed. Reg. at 67593. *See K.E. v. Utah*, note 54 above.

56. Bureau of Indian Affairs, note 42 above, 44 Fed. Reg. at 67593. Some courts have held that other factors may be considered in choosing an expert, but normally ICWA experts must have expertise beyond the usual social-worker qualifications. *See K.E. v. Utah* and *In re Elliott*, note 54 above; *In re D.S.P.*, 480 N.W.2d 234, 240 (Wis. 1992).

57. *Matter of Baby Boy Doe*, note 52 above; *D.A.W. v. State*, 699 P.2d 340 (Alaska 1985). *See also In re T.O.*, 759 P.2d 1308 (Alaska 1988).

58. 25 U.S.C. Sec. 1915(a) (adoptions) and 1915(b) (foster care). *See In re Bird Head*, 331 N.W.2d 785 (Neb. 1983).

59. *Holyfield*, note 1 above, 409 U.S. at 37; *In the Matter of C.H.*, 997 P.2d 776 (Mont. 2000).

60. *Kern County Dept. of Human Services v. Mishola S.*, 76 Cal. Rptr.2d 121 (Cal. App. 1998); *Bird Head*, note 58 above.

61. *See In the Matter of the Welfare of S.N.R.*, 617 N.W.2d 77 (Minn. App. 2000); *Riffle*, note 22 above.

62. Bureau of Indian Affairs, note 42 above, 44 Fed. Reg. at 67594.

63. *Matter of Adoption of F.H.*, 851 P.2d 1361, 1363–64 (Alaska 1993). *See also Adoption of N.P.S.*, 868 P.2d 934 (Alaska 1994).

64. *Matter of Baby Boy Doe*, note 52 above, at 487.

65. *Matter of Custody of S.E.G.*, 521 N.W.2d 357, 363 (Minn. 1994), *cert. denied*, 513 U.S. 1127 (1995). *See also Riffle*, note 22 above, 922 P.2d at 514.

66. *See In the Interest of J.W.*, 528 N.W.2d 657 (Iowa App. 1995).

67. 25 U.S.C. Sec. 1913(a).

68. *E.C.D. v. D.B.*, 27 Indian L. Rep. 6001 (Chey. R. Ct. App. 1999).

69. 25 U.S.C. Sec. 1913(a).

70. *Id.*, Sec. 1913(b).

71. *Id.*, Sec. 1913(c). *See Quinn v. Walters*, 845 P.2d 206 (Or. 1993); *Harvick v. Harvick*, 828 P.2d 769 (Alaska 1992).

72. 25 U.S.C. Sec. 1913(d).

73. *See Holyfield*, note 1 above.

74. Of course, the tribal court can decline to accept the case, and a parent can prevent the transfer by objecting to it. *See* 25 U.S.C. Sec. 1911(b).

75. *In re N.A.H.*, note 32 above; *In re Custody of S.B.R.*, 719 P.2d 154 (Wash. App. 1986). *But see Matter of S.Z.*, 325 N.W.2d 53 (S.D. 1982) (court excuses the deficiencies).

76. *See* J. Trentadue and M. DeMontigny, "The Indian Child Welfare Act of 1978: A Practitioner's Perspective," 62 *N.D.L. Rev.* 487, 536 (1986). *Compare Navajo Nation v. Superior Court*, note 28 above, and *In re Adoption of T.N.F.*, 781 P.2d 973 (Alaska 1989), *cert. denied*, 494 U.S. 1030 (1990).

77. 25 U.S.C. Sec. 1903(9).

78. *Id.*

79. *See, e.g., In re Adoption of Baby Boy D,* 742 P.2d 1059 (Okla. 1985), *cert. denied,* 484 U.S. 1072 (1988); *In the Matter of Adoption of a Child of Indian Heritage,* 543 A.2d 925 (N.J. 1988).

80. 25 U.S.C. Sec. 1922. *See In re J.W.,* note 22 above; *D.E.D. v. State,* 704 P.2d 774 (Alaska 1985).

81. *Comanche Indian Tribe of Oklahoma v. Hovis,* 53 F.3d 298 (10th Cir. 1995), *cert. denied,* 516 U.S. 916 (1995); *Kiowa Tribe of Oklahoma v. Lewis,* 777 F.2d 587 (10th Cir. 1985), *cert. denied,* 479 U.S. 872 (1986).

82. *Kickapoo Tribe,* note 34 above; *Kiowa Tribe,* note 81 above.

83. *See Roman-Nose v. New Mexico Dept. of Human Services,* 967 F.2d 435, 437 (10th Cir. 1992); *Navajo Nation v. Superior Court,* note 28 above, 47 F. Supp.2d at 1240–41.

84. *Morrow v. Winslow,* 94 F.3d 1386 (10th Cir. 1996), *cert. denied,* 520 U.S. 1143 (1997).

85. 25 U.S.C. Sec. 1903(4).

86. *Id.,* Sec. 1903(8). *See In re Wanomi P.,* 264 Cal. Rptr. 623 (Cal. App. 1989). The subject of federal recognition is discussed in ch. 15, sec. F.

87. ·25 U.S.C. Sec. 1903(1). *See Application of Defender,* 435 N.W.2d 717 (S.D. 1989); *Eastern Band of Cherokee Indians v. Larch,* 872 F.2d 66 (4th Cir. 1989). The ICWA is inapplicable even if the child's parents are unmarried but custody is to be awarded to one of them. *See John v. Baker,* 982 P.2d 738, 747 (Alaska 1999). However, a custody contest between a father and a stepfather is subject to the requirements of the ICWA. *See J.W. v. R.J.,* note 19 above.

88. 25 U.S.C. Sec. 1903(1).

89. *Johnson v. Howard,* 741 P.2d 1386 (Okla. 1985). *See also Matter of Adoption of D.M.J.,* 741 P.2d 1386 (Okla. 1985).

90. *See J.R.H.,* note 45 above; *In re Custody of S.B.R.,* note 75 above.

91. *In re Bertelson,* 617 P.2d 121 (Mont. 1980).

92. *A.B.M. v. M.H.,* 651 P.2d 1170 (Alaska 1982), *cert. denied,* 461 U.S. 914 (1983); *Q.G.M.,* note 31 above.

93. *Rye v. Weasel,* 934 S.W.2d 257 (Ky. 1996); *In re Bridget R.,* 49 Cal. Rptr.2d 507 (Cal. App. 1996), *cert. denied,* 519 U.S. 1060 (1997); *In the Matter of S.C. and J.C.,* 833 P.2d 1249 (Okla. 1992); *In re D.S.,* 577 N.E.2d 572 (Ind. 1991); *Matter of Adoption of Baby Boy L.,* 643 P.2d 168 (Kan. 1982).

94. *In re Bridget R.,* note 93 above, 49 Cal. Rptr.2d at 516. This case and the "existing Indian family" exception may have been effectively overruled in California by the passage of Cal. Fam. Code sec. 7810.

95. *In re Adoption of Baby Boy D,* note 79 above.

96. *Kern County Dept.,* note 60 above; *State, In Interest of D.A.C.,* 933 P.2d 993, 999 (Utah App. 1997); *In re Elliott,* 554 N.W.2d 32, 35–36 (Mich. App. 1996); *Riffle,* note 22 above; *Baby Boy Doe,* note 23 above; *In re Adoption of Quinn,* 845 P.2d 206, 209 (Or. App. 1993). *See also Tubridy v. Iron Bear,* 657 N.E.2d 935, 946–53 (Ill. 1995) (McMorrow, J., dissenting), *cert. denied,* 517 U.S. 1104 (1996) (discussing how the doctrine is inconsistent with ICWA's legislative history).

97. *Holyfield,* note 1 above, 409 U.S. at 49.

98. *See Holyfield, id.,* at 49–50; *Alicia S.,* note 31 above; *In re Kahlen W.,* note 32 above, 233 Cal. App.3d at 1424.

99. *In re Adoption of Quinn,* note 96 above, 845 P.2d at 209, quoted in *State, In Interest of D.A.C.,* note 96 above, 933 P.22 at 999, and *Alicia S.,* note 31 above, 76 Cal. Rptr.2d at 128.

100. 25 U.S.C. Sec. 1918(a).

101. *See C.R.H.,* note 48 above, 29 P.3d at 852–53; *Native Village of Venetie I.R.A. Council v. Alaska,* 944 F.2d 548, 560–62 (9th Cir. 1991).

102. *See* cases cited in note 101 above.

103. 25 U.S.C. Sec. 1901(5).

104. *Riffle,* note 22 above, 922 P.2d at 514. *See also Matter of Custody of S.E.G.,* note 65 above.

105. *See J.R.H.* and *Coleman,* note 45 above. *See also In the Matter of T.S.,* 801 P.2d 77 (Mont. 1990), *cert. denied,* 500 U.S. 917 (1991); *People in Interest of J.J.,* 454 N.W.2d 317 (S.D. 1990); *In the Matter of Adoption of John Michael Baade,* 462 N.W.2d 485 (S.D. 1990); *In the Interest of C.W.,* note 46 above. Courts have held that the ICWA does not authorize the award of damages but only the return of the child to parents whose rights were violated under the act. *See Fletcher v. Florida,* 858 F. Supp. 169 (M.D. Fla. 1994).

106. An example of this is the evolution that appears to have occurred in the Alaska Supreme Court. *Compare Native Village of Nenana v. State Dept. of Health and Human Services,* 722 P.2d 219 (Alaska 1986) *with C.R.H.,* note 48 above (reversing *Nenana*).

XVIII

Judicial Review

This chapter is designed to help Indians and tribes obtain a remedy from a court if their rights have been violated by a government, whether tribal, state, or federal. Bear in mind that litigation is usually costly in terms of time, money, effort, and emotional stress, and in most situations it should be used only as a last resort.

Before filing suit, research is necessary to determine whether a judicial remedy exists for the injury that has occurred, especially in lawsuits in which the only, or the principle, defendant is a government. The Supreme Court has held that the tribal,[1] state,[2] and federal[3] governments enjoy "sovereign immunity" from suit, which means that these governments may not be sued unless their immunity has been waived. The doctrine of sovereign immunity was created by the Court to protect these governments from financial ruin due to the misconduct of an employee. Sovereign immunity protects the government's financial assets and political integrity, although it has the unfortunate side effect of leaving innocent victims of government negligence or abuse without a judicial remedy.

Congress has the authority to waive the federal government's sovereign immunity by passing a law consenting to a suit.[4] Congress can also waive the immunity of state[5] and tribal[6] governments, but unless it does, those governments may be sued only if *they* consent to be sued.

A. Suits Against a Tribe

The Supreme Court confirmed in 1991 that Indian tribes "exercise inherent sovereign authority over their members and their territory. Suits against Indian tribes are thus barred by sovereign immunity absent a clear waiver by the tribe or congressional abrogation."[7] An Indian tribe's immunity from suit "is a necessary corollary to Indian sovereignty and self-governance."[8] A waiver of a tribe's immunity by Congress or by the tribe must be "unequivocally expressed" and will not be inferred.[9]

The Supreme Court discussed the broad scope of tribal sovereign immunity in *Kiowa Tribe of Oklahoma v. Manufacturing Technologies, Inc.* (1998).[10] In that case, a private corporation sued an Indian tribe in state court, claiming that the tribe had defaulted on a contract with the company and owed it money. The tribe asked the court to dismiss the case due to the tribe's sovereign immunity, but the court rejected this defense on the grounds that the tribe had signed the contract off the reservation and the lawsuit involved a commercial, rather than a governmental, activity. The Supreme Court overturned the state court decision. The Court held that Indian tribes enjoy sovereign immunity for both governmental and commercial activities, whether conducted on or off the reservation, unless Congress or the tribe has consented to the suit, and the Court saw no evidence that such consent had been given here.[11]

Congress has enacted a few laws—but only a few—that waive tribal immunity in specific instances. For example, Congress has authorized the Navajo and Hopi Tribes to sue one another in federal court to resolve a property dispute between them.[12] Congress also has authorized the filing of lawsuits against the federal, state, and tribal governments concerning hazardous waste disposal.[13] The Safe Drinking Water Act has been held to waive tribal immunity for certain violations of that act.[14]

Given that Congress rarely has waived tribal sovereign immunity, Indian tribes are immune from most types of lawsuits unless they have consented to be sued. Courts have dismissed for lack of jurisdiction lawsuits that sought to challenge tribal membership requirements,[15] a tribal zoning law,[16] and a tribal hunting and fishing regulation.[17] Courts have also dismissed suits on sovereign immunity grounds that sought to recover a debt allegedly owed by a tribe;[18] to enforce a tribal lease;[19] to determine the ownership of land in which the tribe had an interest;[20] to seize tribal assets;[21] to challenge tribal election results or procedures;[22] to collect state taxes allegedly owed by a tribe;[23] to recover damages as a result of injuries suffered by patrons[24] and employees[25] of a tribal casino and by employees of a tribally owned corporation injured at work;[26] and to recover damages based on a tribe's alleged copyright infringement.[27] The Indian Self-Determination and Education Assistance Act of 1975, under which Indian tribes operate numerous programs funded by federal agencies, expressly states that nothing in the act waives tribal sovereign immunity for claims arising from those operations,[28] and thus tribes may not be sued under that law, either.

Courts have broadly applied the doctrine of tribal sovereign immunity in reaching these decisions, rejecting arguments that only federally recognized tribes are entitled to claim sovereign immunity from suit;[29] that a state government may waive a tribe's immunity;[30] that tribal officials may be sued under a federal law (42 U.S.C. § 1983) that authorizes suits against *state* officials;[31] that tribes waiving immunity from some claims thereby waive immunity from other claims;[32] that tribal immunity does not apply to lawsuits brought by nonmembers;[33] and that acceptance of federal funds by a tribe waives its immunity from any suit challenging the manner in which the tribe has spent those funds.[34]

Indian tribes may assert their sovereign immunity even though no alternative forum exists in which the claim can be adjudicated,[35] and they may raise their immunity defense at any time during the litigation.[36] If the court denies the tribe's motion to dismiss, the tribe immediately may appeal that ruling.[37]

A court cannot hear and resolve (adjudicate) a claim unless all necessary (indispensable) parties are included (joined) in the action.[38] Accordingly, many lawsuits that otherwise raised valid claims have been dismissed for failure to join an Indian tribe due to its sovereign immunity, even when other parties having an interest in the case *may* be brought before the court. Examples include lawsuits that sought to determine rights in a mineral lease in which a tribe had an interest;[39] the ownership of land in which a tribe had an interest;[40] the constitutionality of a federal law that settled a land dispute involving two Indian tribes;[41] the validity of a ruling by the U.S. Department of the Interior allocating fish resources to various Indian tribes;[42] and the validity of a contract between a tribe and another party.[43] Sometimes the plaintiffs in these types of cases are Indian tribes seeking to sue other tribes to determine rights in a shared resource[44] or tribal members suing their own tribe in federal[45] or tribal[46] court; Indian tribes enjoy sovereign immunity from those lawsuits as well.

In cases in which a tribe's interests will not be affected by the outcome, or when its interests are being adequately represented by the United States which is a party to the case, the tribe is not an indispensable party; thus, its presence in the lawsuit is not required.[47] Merely because the United States is a party, however, does not mean that it is representing, or can adequately represent, an absent tribe's interests. In some lawsuits, the United States takes a position contrary to the position taken by an affected tribe[48] or is representing multiple tribes with competing interests,[49] and in those situations each tribe would be an indispensable party.

Do tribal agencies and corporations share the tribe's immunity from suit?

Yes. Indian tribes have the same general authority as other governments to create agencies for governmental and commercial purposes, and these entities enjoy the tribe's immunity from suit unless waived by Congress or by the tribe.[50] Tribal housing authorities, for example, are governmental entities that normally enjoy the tribe's immunity from suit absent a waiver,[51] and so do tribal corporations,[52] even with respect to activities conducted off the reservation.[53] Many tribal corporations are authorized in their corporate charters, similar to most non-Indian corporate charters, to "sue and be sued" in the corporate name. These clauses do not waive the tribe's immunity by themselves.[54]

Many standard commercial contracts contain an *arbitration clause* committing the parties to use arbitration (rather than more costly and time-consuming litigation) to resolve disputes arising under the contract. The Supreme Court has held that when a tribe signs a contract containing an arbitration clause, the tribe waives its immunity from any suit that seeks to enforce the decision made by the arbiter.[55] Waiver is presumed even if the contract does not contain express language waiving the tribe's immunity; consent to suit to enforce the arbitration decision is implied by the very presence of an arbitration agreement.[56] However, a tribe does not waive its own immunity when it waives a corporation's immunity.[57]

May tribal officials be sued personally if they violate someone's rights?

Let's say that an Indian tribe has created a three-person agency to determine who qualifies for tribal membership, and the agency has just rejected Jane Doe's membership application. Ms. Doe believes that the agency should have accepted her application and that the denial was due to the three officials' prejudice against her. What judicial remedy might she have?

For reasons just explained, Ms. Doe may not file suit against the tribe or the agency due to the tribe's sovereign immunity. May she, though, sue the three officials *personally* seeking to have the court order them to accept her application?

The Supreme Court has indicated that tribal officials *may* be sued in their individual capacities. The Court stated in a 1978 case that tribal officials are "not protected by the tribe's immunity from suit."[58] But that statement was *dicta;* that is, it was not necessary to the actual holding of the case and therefore has no binding effect.

Indeed, the majority of lower federal courts that have addressed the question have held, despite the Supreme Court's dicta, that "when tribal officials act in their official capacity and within the scope of their authority they are immune [from suit], even if they act in error."[59] The majority view is that tribal officials who act within their proper and delegated authority enjoy the tribe's immunity from suit, both with respect to damages and to declaratory and injunctive relief.[60] In one case, for example, a non-Indian who was excluded from the reservation by order of a tribal council sued the tribal officials who enforced the council's order, seeking declaratory and injunctive relief (that would enable him to return to the reservation) and damages. The court dismissed the lawsuit on the grounds that "all of the individual defendants here were acting within the scope of their delegated authority" in enforcing the order and therefore were immune from suit.[61] A few courts have taken a contrary position, though, at least with respect to the award of declaratory and injunctive relief. One such court recently held in expressly rejecting the majority view, that "tribal officials are not immune from suits for declaratory and injunctive relief," and neither is the tribe itself.[62]

Even under the majority view, however, tribal officials share the tribe's sovereign immunity *only* when they are acting under their proper and delegated authority. Courts have held that tribal officials lose their immunity when (1) they have acted outside the authority vested in them under tribal law or (2) they have "acted outside the amount of authority that the sovereign is capable of bestowing," that is, beyond the authority that the tribe *could* give them.[63] In a recent case, a utility company obtained a federal court order halting the assessment of a tribal tax by suing the tribal tax officials responsible for collecting it; the court denied their defense of sovereign immunity on the grounds that "the officials acted in violation of federal law in enforcing the tax."[64]

Applying this exception to the hypothetical question asked earlier, Ms. Doe could sue the members of the agency *if* she could show that the denial of her application violated a tribal or federal law. However, she still would face another legal hurdle in bringing such a lawsuit. Courts have held that a lawsuit may not be maintained against a tribal official when the *remedy* being sought can only be provided by the *tribe*, that is, when the tribe is "the real party in interest." As one court recently stated, the law "does not permit individual officers of a sovereign [Indian tribe] to be sued when the relief requested would, in effect, require the sovereign's specific performance."[65] For example, in the tax case just discussed, the court issued an injunction prohibiting tax officials from seeking to collect the tax in the future, but the court refused to order the tribe to refund the taxes these officials had illegally collected in the past because that money was in the tribal treasury, and the tribe could not be ordered to provide any remedy.[66] Therefore, applying those principles to the hypothetical question asked earlier, Ms. Doe would likely be barred by the tribe's sovereign immunity from seeking an order requiring the members of the agency to accept her application, given that "the real party in interest" in such a case would be the tribe, and the tribe cannot be ordered to provide a remedy.[67]

In order to share in the tribe's sovereign immunity, a tribal employee must be a "tribal official," and not merely a tribal employee. Determining who is a tribal official depends on a host of factors, which include whether the person makes tribal policy or only implements it and what was the nature and source of the power being exercised at the time of the incident in question. Persons who occupy high offices in tribal government always qualify as "tribal officials" when exercising their lawful authority, but court decisions make clear that other persons can qualify, including non-Indian attorneys representing tribes.[68] One court extended the tribe's immunity to a tribal police officer who was enforcing a tribal council's direct order,[69] whereas another court denied immunity to tribal officers who supervised a tribal casino.[70]

It bears repeating that under the majority view, even in those cases in which a tribal employee lost or did not have the tribe's immunity from suit, the employee's actions did not waive the *tribe's* immunity from suit. Tribal officials can lose their own immunity, but their misconduct cannot result in the tribe losing its immunity.[71]

Does sovereign immunity protect a tribe against suits by state governments?

Yes. State governments and their officials have no more right to sue an Indian tribe than anyone else does.[72] This is true even for those states that received certain authority over reservation Indians under Public Law 83–280 (discussed in chapter 7), as nothing in that law waives tribal sovereign immunity from suit.[73]

Does sovereign immunity protect a tribe against suit by the federal government?

No. An Indian tribe may not assert a sovereign immunity defense against the United States.[74] The federal government may sue an Indian tribe whether the tribe consents or not.

Does the tribe waive its immunity by filing a lawsuit?

A tribe does not waive its immunity from suit when it files its own lawsuits, and thus a party being sued by an Indian tribe is not automatically entitled to file a counterclaim against the tribe.[75] "The perceived inequity" in this situation—allowing a tribe to raise its claims against the defendant but preventing the defendant from raising its claims against the tribe—"must be accepted in view of the overriding federal and tribal interests" in preserving the tribe's immunity, the Supreme Court has stated.[76] However, once a tribe raises a claim, *that* claim may be fully adjudicated even if it results in a damages award against the tribe.[77]

What types of lawsuits are authorized by the Indian Civil Rights Act of 1968?

This subject is discussed in detail in chapter 14. To briefly summarize, the Indian Civil Rights Act of 1968 (ICRA) confers certain civil rights upon all persons subject to the jurisdiction of an Indian tribe. However, it contains only one remedy provision, and this provision authorizes persons imprisoned by an Indian tribe, who believe their incarceration violates the ICRA, to have a federal court determine the legality of their detention.[78] The ICRA does not waive the tribe's immunity from suit in *federal* court, the Supreme Court has held;[79] it only authorizes a suit against the person holding the prisoner. (A suit of that nature is not a suit against the government but only against the person who is actually detaining the prisoner.) Accordingly, the only types of suits authorized in federal court under the ICRA are suits seeking the release of someone detained by a tribal official, and suit would be brought against that official.

However, as explained in chapter 14, some tribal courts have held that the ICRA waives tribal immunity from suit in *tribal* court for various types of ICRA violations. On those reservations, a wider variety of lawsuits under the ICRA may be brought in tribal court than may be brought in federal court.

In what circumstances have Indian tribes waived their sovereign immunity from suit, and which tribal officials may waive the tribe's immunity?

Many Indian tribes, in either their constitutions or laws, identify which officers or agencies of the tribe have the power to waive the tribe's sovereign immunity and under what circumstances that authority may be exercised. In the absence of a specific conferral of such power, it is presumed that the tribal legislative body has the authority to effect a waiver of the tribe's immunity.[80]

Indian tribes have the right to waive their sovereign immunity from suit and to make that waiver be as broad or as narrow as they choose.[81] Tribes exercise that option in a host of situations. For instance, a tribe that needs to borrow money from a bank will surely be required by the bank to waive its immunity as a condition of receiving the loan. Without such a waiver, the bank would be unable to sue the tribe in the event of a default in loan payments, and the bank would likely refuse to lend money under those conditions.[82] Tribes often agree to waive their immunity in these and other commercial settings. If the tribe wished, it could pass a law broadly waiving tribal immunity from all suits seeking to enforce a tribal contract. In the alternative, the tribe could agree to waive its immunity in the contract itself, a process that allows the tribe to choose which contracts would then be subject to judicial review.

Some tribes have consented to suit in tribal court for violations of the Indian Civil Rights Act, thus permitting their members to obtain a judicial remedy if their ICRA rights have been violated.[83] The Hopi Tribe has waived its immunity from suit in tribal court by tribal employees seeking to enforce the tribe's employment policies.[84] The Mashantucket Pequot Tribe, which owns a large gambling casino, has waived its immunity for injuries caused "by the negligent acts or omissions of the Gaming Enterprise."[85] The Navajo Nation has waived its immunity in four situations: (1) when suit against the Nation is expressly authorized by federal law; (2) when the Nation's council has expressly waived tribal immunity; (3) when suit is filed claiming a commercial liability that does not exceed the Nation's insurance coverage; and (4) when the suit alleges a violation of a federal or tribal civil right and the remedy is limited to seeking future enforcement of the right (and not damages for its past violation).[86]

The federal and state governments have waived their immunity in many more situations than have tribes. A growing number of non-Indians —and Indians—have criticized the broad scope of tribal immunity. In 1997, then-U.S. senator Slade Gorton from the state of Washington urged Congress to pass a law waiving tribal immunity from most types of lawsuits. In support of his bill, he noted that Indian tribes operating gambling casinos lure patrons to their premises but then "hide" behind sovereign immunity when patrons are injured due to the negligence of a casino employee. He wrote an editorial stating, "I feel strongly that Indian tribes' ability to avoid any lawsuit it wishes is a direct affront to the meaning of justice in today's world."[87] His bill did not pass, but similar efforts in the future can be expected. Tribes would likely defuse these criticisms by enacting limited waivers of immunity to suits filed against a tribe in tribal court. The tribe could then purchase insurance protecting itself from any unexpected depletion of the tribal treasury.

B. Suits Against a State

Indians and tribes have numerous federal rights, as explained in the earlier chapters of this book. Due to a variety of jurisdictional statutes that Congress has passed, most violations of these rights can be adjudicated (heard and decided) in a federal court. The four most important jurisdictional statutes under which Indians and tribes may file suit in federal court to vindicate their federal rights are the following: Title 28, U.S. Code, Sec. 1331; Title 28, U.S. Code, Sec. 1362; Title 28, U.S. Code, Sec. 1353; and Title 28, U.S. Code, Sec. 1343(3).

Before discussing these statutes, the scope of every state's sovereign immunity needs to be explained. The Eleventh Amendment to the U.S. Constitution provides that the "judicial power of the United States shall not be construed to extend to any suit in law or equity, commenced or prosecuted against one of the United States by citizens of another state, or by citizens or subjects of any foreign state." The Supreme Court has interpreted the Eleventh Amendment broadly, holding that unless Congress has abrogated a state's immunity or the state has chosen to waive it, "a federal court is not competent to render judgment against a nonconsenting state,"[88] even in lawsuits filed against the state by one of its own citizens.[89] In 1991, the Court held that an Indian tribe has no greater right to defeat a state's Eleventh Amendment immunity than anyone else has; thus, states are immune from unconsented lawsuits filed by Indian tribes.[90] The Eleventh Amendment immunity extends to agencies acting under the authority of the state,[91] although it does not shield the state's counties or other political subdivisions.[92] Even lawsuits alleging that a state is violating the U.S. Constitution may not be maintained against a state in federal court unless a waiver of immunity has occurred, regardless of whether the suit seeks damages from the state for past violations[93] or an injunction preventing future violations;[94] thus, a state must be dismissed from any federal lawsuit in which it is named as a defendant against its will.

This same immunity applies to suits against state officials.[95] There is, however, a significant exception to this rule. In *Ex parte Young* (1908),[96] the Supreme Court held that the Eleventh Amendment does not prevent a federal court from issuing injunctive relief against a state official to halt a continuing violation of federal law. The reason why the Eleventh Amendment does not bar such relief, the Court said, is that federal law is supreme, and no state can ever authorize its employees to violate federal law. Consequently, a lawsuit alleging that a state employee is violating federal law cannot possibly be a suit against the state, because a state could never have authorized that conduct.[97]

As a result of *Ex parte Young,* a wide range of federal violations can be remedied in federal court by suing the state officials engaging in these activities.[98] Relying on the *Young* exception to state immunity, an Indian tribe obtained an order enjoining state officials from continuing to violate the tribe's treaty fishing rights,[99] and tribes have enjoined the collection of state taxes being imposed in violation of federal law.[100]

Suits against state officials do not qualify for the *Ex parte Young* exception when "the real party in interest" is the state itself and not the officers being sued. That situation occurs, for example, when a victory for the plaintiff would result in the payment of damages from the state treasury[101] or would cause the state to lose an interest in land.[102] To illustrate, a tribe may obtain an order from a federal court enjoining state tax officials from collecting an illegal tax in the *future* but it may not obtain an order, due to the Eleventh Amendment, requiring the state to refund any money the tribe already paid into the state treasury.[103]

A state can consent to suit in federal court, but a waiver will not be deemed to have occurred unless the consent is clear and explicit.[104] A state's consent to suit in state court does not operate as a consent to suit in federal court[105] or in tribal court[106] unless the state has expressly consented to suit in those fora.

It was stated at the outset of this chapter that Congress has the power to waive state sovereign immunity. That power is limited, however. In *Seminole Tribe of Florida v. Florida* (1996),[107] the Supreme Court held that the Commerce Clause of the U.S. Constitution does not authorize Congress to waive a state's Eleventh Amendment immunity. It now appears that Congress only has the power to waive state sovereign immunity regarding those interests covered by the Fourteenth Amendment (which protects against certain types of discrimination) and the Fifteenth Amendment (which protects the right to vote).[108] With respect to most other matters, a state can be sued only if it consents to be sued.

What jurisdiction is conferred by section 1331?

Section 1331 confers jurisdiction upon the federal courts over any civil action that "arises under the Constitution, laws or treaties of the United States." This statute has broad application to Indians and tribes because they have many rights that come from the Constitution, laws, and treaties of the United States.[109] But merely because a court has been authorized to hear a case does not mean it may proceed to do so if the defendant is a nonconsenting state. On the contrary, in that situation the case would have to be dismissed because the defendant enjoys an Eleventh Amendment immunity from suit.[110]

What jurisdiction is conferred by section 1362?

Section 1362 authorizes federal courts to hear "all civil actions brought by an Indian tribe or band . . . wherein the matter in controversy arises under the Constitution, laws or treaties of the United States." This law, passed by Congress in 1966, permits Indian tribes to file suit in federal court in their own name to vindicate their federal rights.[111] Section 1362 allows a tribe, for example, to challenge a state sales tax that violates the tribe's federal rights (or the rights of tribal members as a group)[112] and to protect land given the tribe by federal treaty or statute.[113]

Federal court jurisdiction under section 1362 is available only when the tribe is seeking to protect a federal right. A lawsuit seeking to enforce rights under state law, such as a suit to enforce a private contract, may not be filed in federal court under section 1362 (or 1331).[114] Moreover, section 1362 is available to Indian tribes but not to tribal corporations, even those owned entirely by the tribe.[115]

In *Blatchford v. Native Village of Noatak* (1991),[116] the Supreme Court held that section 1362 does not waive a state's sovereign immunity from suit. Once again, the Court recognized that a court may have the power to hear a case, but the case must be dismissed if the defendant is a state asserting a valid Eleventh Amendment immunity. The Supreme Court, though, has carved out an exception to this rule that permits suits to be filed by Indian tribes under section 1362 challenging state taxation of activities occurring on Indian trust land.[117] Thus, a state generally enjoys sovereign immunity from unconsented suits by Indian tribes even under section 1362, except for suits challenging the validity of state taxation of activities on Indian land.[118]

What jurisdiction is conferred by section 1353?

Under the General Allotment Act of 1887,[119] thousands of Indians were issued allotments of trust land, with the prospect of eventually receiving deeds to these parcels. Section 1353 was enacted by Congress to help Indians protect their rights to—and in—these trust allotments.[120] For example, Indians who lease their allotments to a private party are authorized by section 1353 to file a damages action if that party violates the lease,[121] and Indians may also sue state officials pursuant section 1353 who interfere with an Indian's use or enjoyment of an allotment.[122]

What jurisdiction is conferred by section 1343(3)?

Soon after the Civil War, Congress enacted a civil rights act (42 U.S.C. Sec. 1983) that prohibits state officials from depriving a person of "any right, privilege or immunity secured by the Constitution of the United States or by any Act of Congress providing for equal rights of citizens." Its jurisdictional counterpart—the statute that authorizes federal courts to adjudicate violations of section 1983—is Title 28, U.S. Code, Sec. 1343(3).

Together, these two laws allow persons to sue state officials in federal court for violations of their federal rights.[123] Similarly, if a tribal police officer is cross-deputized and is exercising state authority at the time he or she violates a person's federal rights, this officer may be sued in federal court under section 1983.[124] If a court finds that federal rights are being violated, it may issue an injunction halting those activities in the future and, in appropriate cases, may award money damages to compensate the victim for any harm or injury the official caused in the past.[125] One court recently held that state officials may be held personally liable in money damages for violating a tribe's treaty fishing rights.[126] Municipal governments (cities and towns) may be sued under section 1983 in the same way that state officials can.[127] In *Nevada v. Hicks* (2001),[128] the Supreme Court held that tribal courts may not hear cases brought under section 1983 against state officials but that tribal members may file such cases (as everyone else can) in a state or federal court.

May the federal government sue a state on behalf of an Indian or tribe?

Yes. As explained in chapter 3, the United States is the legal trustee of many Indian and tribal interests, and it has a duty to protect those interests. As trustee, the federal government may, and it frequently does, file suit against state governments and their officials on behalf of Indians and tribes.[129] The Eleventh Amendment provides the state with no shield against lawsuits filed by the federal government, the Supreme Court has held.[130] The United States, for instance, may sue a state to recover back taxes that Indians illegally paid a state, even though the Eleventh Amendment prevents the Indians themselves from filing a similar lawsuit.[131]

Lawsuits filed by the United States do not require the consent of the Indian or tribe on whose behalf it is brought,[132] although in those situations, the Indian or tribe usually has the right to intervene as a party in the case.[133] If the Indian or tribe disagrees with the position taken by the federal government, the court must accept the government's position as controlling if the lawsuit involves trust property (property owned by the United States and held in trust for an Indian or tribe).[134] In fact, when trust property is involved, the federal government may sue a state even after the tribe has already sued that state and lost. This is because a tribe sues to protect its possessory interest in trust property, whereas the federal government can sue to protect its ownership rights, a different legal interest.[135]

A federal law appears to require the federal government to file suit on behalf of an Indian tribe whenever the tribe requests it.[136] However, the courts have rejected that interpretation and held that the United States need not file suit unless a treaty, statute, or agreement expressly imposes such a duty in that instance.[137]

Although the United States can sue on behalf of Indians and tribes, this does not prevent Indians and tribes from suing on their own behalf or a tribe from suing on behalf of its members.[138] If the tribe does sue on its own, the United States will not be bound by the court's decision regarding trust property owned by the government unless it intervenes in the case.[139] If a federal court finds that the rights of Indians or tribes have been violated, the court must issue all necessary remedies, including injunctive relief and damages.[140] Federal courts can even order state officials to undertake activities prohibited by state law when necessary to protect a tribe's or tribal member's federal rights.[141]

C. Suits Against the United States

Indians and tribes have acquired federal rights through treaties, statutes, executive orders, and agreements. Many of these rights have been violated at one time or another by Congress or by federal agencies and officials, and violations continue to occur on occasion.

As explained earlier, no one may sue the United States unless Congress has waived the government's immunity in that situation and consented to suit. Congress has consented to a wide variety of lawsuits against the United States, but unless a waiver has occurred, victims of government misconduct have no judicial remedy for the violation of their rights.[142]

Under what circumstances may the United States be sued for money damages?

Congress has consented to certain claims against the United States for money damages. The Federal Tort Claims Act (FTCA)[143] is one of the primary laws under which damages can be recovered from the federal government. The FTCA consents to suit for:

loss of property, or personal injury or death, caused by the negligent or wrongful act or omission of any employee of the Government while acting within the scope of his office or employment, under the circumstances where the United States, if a private person, would be liable to the claimant in accordance with the law of the place where the act or omission occurred.

The FTCA allows recovery of damages against the United States for most injuries caused by a wrongful or negligent act (a tort) committed by a federal official acting within the scope of his or her authority. The agency that employed the official who caused the injury pays any money judgment awarded under the FTCA. FTCA claims must first be filed with the federal agency responsible for the harm; if the agency does not pay the claim within 180 days, a lawsuit may then be filed in federal court against the United States.[144] (A claimant has two years from when the injury occurred to file a claim with the agency.)[145] FTCA suits have been filed against federal agencies by Indians and tribes for the wrongful flooding of tribal land;[146] for injuries sustained by a student at a federal boarding school due to the negligence of school employees;[147] for the wrongful removal of property by federal agents from Indian land;[148] for damage done to Indian property;[149] and for providing inadequate medical care at an Indian Health Service hospital.[150]

The Indian Self-Determination and Education Assistance Act of 1975 (ISDEA),[151] under which tribes may operate federally funded programs on the reservation pursuant to federal contracts ("638 contracts"), expressly provides that tribal employees performing services under these contracts are federal employees when acting within the scope of their employment.[152] The federal government thus may be sued under the FTCA for the actions of these employees.[153]

Many tribal police departments receive ISDEA funding from the Bureau of Indian Affairs (BIA). In addition, tribal police often are cross-deputized as BIA officers. Persons wrongly injured by these tribal officers may recover damages from the BIA under the FTCA if a court finds that at the time of the incident in question, the officer was acting within the scope of his or her *federal* (rather than tribal) employment.[154]

The FTCA contains an "exception provision," which exempts various types of injuries from coverage under the act,[155] including injuries caused by war or by a breach of contract. In addition, all "discretionary functions" are exempted, meaning that the federal government is liable only when a statute, regulation, or policy *requires* an employee to undertake a certain activity, and the employee then fails to undertake it.[156] Under this exception, the federal government is not liable when the employee is permitted by law to exercise independent judgment.[157] This exception is not easy to apply, and courts have reached inconsistent decisions in determining what actions an employee is required to perform and what actions the employee may choose not to perform.

Another statute that authorizes certain money claims against the federal government is the Tucker Act.[158] Whereas the FTCA allows recovery for torts, the Tucker Act allows recovery for a breach of contract or other express or implied obligation by the government. The Tucker Act waives the federal government's sovereign immunity with respect to any action "founded either upon the Constitution, or any Act of Congress, or any regulation of an executive department, or upon any express or implied contract with the United States."[159] An injured party may file a claim against the United States either in the Court of Federal Claims[160] (which until 1993 was named the Court of Claims) or in a federal district court, although the government's liability in cases filed in district court is limited to $10,000.[161] Appeals from the Court of Federal Claims are made to the Court of Appeals for the Federal Circuit, while appeals from a federal district court are made to the court of appeals for the circuit in which the district court is located. The Tucker Act requires that cases be filed within six years from the date the injury occurred.[162]

In *United States v. Mitchell* (1983),[163] the Supreme Court held that federal statutes and regulations that give federal agencies comprehensive supervision or control over the management of tribal resources thereby create express or implied obligations for which these agencies may be held liable for damages under the Tucker Act.[164] As explained in chapter 3, statutes and regulations that create only a "general" trust obligation do not provide a basis for a damages award,[165] but when Congress has delegated express or implied duties to an agency, the agency may be sued for damages for failing to perform them.[166] Under the Tucker Act, Indians may recover damages when federal officials mismanage Indian trust resources, such as timber, land, oil and gas, or money deposited in federal Indian accounts.[167] The Tucker Act also permits recovery of compensation when Congress takes property from a tribe under the government's power of eminent domain, a power that authorizes the taking of land for a public purpose.[168]

The Tucker Act, however, does not allow tribes to sue the government for a breach of treaty obligations.[169] In 1946, Congress filled this void by enacting the Indian Claims Commission Act (ICCA).[170] The ICCA authorized any "identifiable group" of Indians to seek compensatory damages against the United States for the value of any land or other property conferred by a treaty that was later taken by the federal government through force, fraud, or mistake. The ICCA also allowed recovery based on the federal government's failure to engage in "fair and honorable dealings," such as those situations in which the government had "purchased" the tribe's land, but the price it paid was clearly unfair.[171] Under the ICCA, tribes may obtain damages for the loss of their land and resources found on or under the land, such as timber, water, and minerals.[172]

The ICCA created the Indian Claims Commission (ICC) to resolve the tribal claims. Tribes had five years in which to file a claim, although this deadline was later extended for a few tribes. Hundreds of claims were filed, many of which are still pending; in 2000, the Supreme Court decided a claim filed with the ICC in 1951.[173] The ICC was abolished by Congress in 1978, and its pending cases were transferred to the United States Court of Claims (now, the Court of Federal Claims). Under the ICCA, after all appeals are exhausted, Congress appropriates any funds awarded to the tribe, and the Secretary of the Interior submits a plan to Congress for disbursing these "judgment proceeds" to the tribe.

May a lawsuit seeking money damages be filed directly against a federal official?

Government officials acting within the scope of their delegated and lawful authority enjoy the sovereign's immunity from suit and, like the government, may not be sued for damages without the consent of Congress.[174] The *federal government* may be sued under the FTCA or the Tucker Act based on the actions of its employees, but the employees themselves are cloaked with sovereign immunity and may not be sued personally.

When federal officials exceed their delegated authority, such as when they violate someone's constitutional rights, they are not protected by sovereign immunity. In such instances, lawsuits may be maintained against these officials in their individual capacity, and they may be held personally liable in money damages for engaging in any conduct that they knew or should have known was illegal or unauthorized.[175]

When may the federal government be sued for declaratory or injunctive relief?

The FTCA and the Tucker Act authorize the award of damages for *past* injuries. Many disputes with the federal government, however, concern activities that are ongoing or are planned for the *future,* and the relief sought is a declaration of rights and an injunction preventing the government from undertaking that activity in the future. Suppose the Army Corps of Engineers has just announced plans to construct a dam that would flood tribal land protected by a treaty. In that situation, obviously, the tribe would want to prevent the flooding, not wait until the injury has occurred and seek compensatory damages.[176]

The most useful statute to obtain this type of *nonmonetary* remedy is the Administrative Procedure Act (APA).[177] The APA waives the sovereign immunity of the United States in all actions challenging a final decision of a federal agency and seeking injunctive relief (often called *prospective* or *equitable relief)* or seeking a declaration of rights (a *declaratory judgment),* except to the extent that "(1) a statute precludes judicial review, or (2) agency action is committed to agency discretion by law."[178] Thus, the APA allows equitable suits seeking to halt ongoing or anticipated misconduct by a federal agency. APA lawsuits may be heard in federal court under jurisdictional statutes discussed earlier, Title 28, U.S. Code, Sec. 1331 and (when suit is filed by a tribe) Title 28, U.S. Code, Sec. 1362.[179]

The APA authorizes federal courts to set aside any agency action found to be "arbitrary, capricious or otherwise not in accordance with law," as well as to compel agency action unlawfully withheld or delayed.[180] Pursuant to the APA, the Secretary of the Interior has been sued for ignoring a duty to regulate the leasing of Indian land;[181] for ignoring a duty to regulate commerce on Indian reservations;[182] for failing to recognize the legal status of a tribal government in the manner required by federal law;[183] for failing to rule on a tribe's application for federal recognition;[184] for failing to distribute federal benefits to Indians as required by law;[185] for wrongly interfering in a tribal election;[186] for wrongly closing an Indian boarding school;[187] for decisions taken regarding the approval of oil and gas leases involving Indian mineral interests;[188] and for failing to properly manage Indian trust money deposited in bank accounts under the Secretary's control and supervision.[189]

A number of federal statutes provide that agency action in certain matters is "final" or "conclusive." When that occurs, courts may not review the agency's decision under the APA; judicial review is barred by the government's sovereign immunity.[190] In *Lincoln v. Vigil* (1993),[191] the Supreme Court held that when Congress allocates funds to a federal agency without directing that they be spent on a particular program, a decision by the agency to discontinue a program funded through those general funds may not be reviewed by a court under the APA; a "lump-sum" appropriation bestows final and conclusive authority on the agency in deciding how to spend that money.

Courts reviewing an agency decision under the APA may not overturn it unless the decision is arbitrary and capricious, even if some better decision could have been made.[192] The agency, though, must carefully explain the basis for its decision and show that it properly considered all relevant factors; otherwise, the decision must be returned (remanded) to the agency for the development of an adequate factual record.[193]

Before suit is filed against a federal agency, must the agency's administrative remedies be exhausted?

Federal agencies have an administrative appeals process, and in most instances all administrative appeals must be exhausted before a court will proceed with a lawsuit.[194] The Department of the Interior has several levels of appeals before an agency decision becomes final. A decision by a Department official on the reservation can be appealed to the Area Director, from there to the Assistant Secretary of the Interior, and in cases involving the interpretation of a federal law, from the Assistant Secretary to the Board of Indian Appeals.[195]

What standards must a court use in reviewing Indian cases?

The Supreme Court has recognized that the United States has "moral obligations of the highest responsibility and trust" to Indians[196] and must use "great care" in its dealings with them.[197] Consequently, as explained more fully in chapter 3, any government action harmful to Indian interests must be judged using "the most exacting fiduciary standards."[198]

NOTES

1. *Kiowa Tribe of Oklahoma v. Manufacturing Technologies, Inc.,* 523 U.S. 751 (1998); *Oklahoma Tax Comm'n v. Citizen Band Potawatomi Indian Tribe,* 498 U.S. 505 (1991); *Santa Clara Pueblo v. Martinez,* 436 U.S. 49 (1978).
2. *Edelman v. Jordan,* 415 U.S. 651 (1974).
3. *U.S. v. Sherwood,* 312 U.S. 584 (1941).

4. *U.S. v. Testan,* 424 U.S. 392, 399 (1976).

5. *Hutto v. Finney,* 437 U.S. 678 (1978).

6. *Santa Clara Pueblo,* note 1 above.

7. *Oklahoma Tax Comm'n v. Citizen Band Potawatomi Indian Tribe,* note 1 above, 498 U.S. at 509 (citation omitted). *See also Santa Clara Pueblo,* note 1 above; *Seneca-Cayuga Tribe of Oklahoma v. Oklahoma,* 874 F.2d 709, 714 (10th Cir. 1989).

8. *Three Affiliated Tribes v. Wold Engineering,* 476 U.S. 877, 890 (1985).

9. *Santa Clara Pueblo,* note 1 above, 436 U.S. at 58. *See also Florida Paraplegic Ass'n., Inc. v. Miccosukee Tribe,* 116 F.3d 1126 (11th Cir. 1999); *American Indian Agricultural Credit Consortium v. Standing Rock Sioux Tribe,* 780 F.2d 1374, 1377–81 (8th Cir. 1985).

10. 523 U.S. 751 (1998).

11. *Id.* at 758.

12. *See Sekaquaptewa v. McDonald,* 591 F.2d 1289 (9th Cir. 1979).

13. *See Public Service Co. of Colorado v. Shoshone-Bannock Tribe,* 30 F.3d 1203 (9th Cir. 1994); *Blue Legs v. BIA,* 867 F.2d 1094 (8th Cir. 1989).

14. *Osage Tribal Council v. U.S. Dept. of Labor,* 187 F.3d 1174 (10th Cir. 1999), *cert. denied,* 530 U.S. 1229 (2000).

15. *Santa Clara Pueblo,* note 1 above.

16. *Trans-Canada Enterprises, Ltd. v. Muckleshoot Indian Tribe,* 634 F.2d 474 (9th Cir. 1980).

17. *People of California ex rel. Dept. of Fish and Game v. Quechan Tribe of Indians,* 595 F.2d 1153 (9th Cir. 1979).

18. *Kiowa Tribe of Oklahoma v. Manufacturing Technologies, Inc.,* note 1 above; *Demontiney v. U.S.,* 255 F.3d 801 (9th Cir. 2001); *Ramey Constr. Co., Inc. v. Apache Tribe,* 673 F.2d 315 (10th Cir. 1982); *Bottomly v. Passamaquoddy Tribe,* 599 F.2d 1061 (1st Cir. 1979).

19. *McClendon v. U.S.,* 885 F.2d 627 (9th Cir. 1989).

20. *Pit River Home and Agricultural Cooperative Ass'n v. U.S.,* 30 F.3d 1088, 1011 (9th Cir. 1994); *Lomayaktewa v. Hathaway,* 520 F.2d 1324 (9th Cir. 1975), *cert. denied,* 425 U.S. 903 (1976).

21. *Aircraft Equipment Co. v. Kiowa Tribe of Oklahoma,* 2 P.2d 338 (Okla. 2000); *North Sea Products Ltd. v. Clipper Sea Foods Co.,* 595 P.2d 938 (Wash. 1979).

22. *Nero v. Cherokee Nation,* 892 F.2d 1457 (10th Cir. 1989); *Runs After v. U.S.,* 766 F.2d 347 (8th Cir. 1985); *Goodface v. Goodrope,* 708 F.2d 335 (8th Cir. 1983).

23. *Oklahoma Tax Comm'n v. Citizen Band Potawatomi Indian Tribe,* note 1 above.

24. *Trudgeon v. Fantasy Springs Casino,* 71 Cal.App.4th 632, 637–45, 84 Cal. Rptr.2d 65 (1999); *Cohen v. Little Six, Inc.,* 561 N.W.2d 889 (Minn. 1997), *cert denied,* 524 U.S. 903 (1998); *Romanella v. Haywood,* 933 F. Supp. 163 (D. Conn. 1996), *aff'd on other grounds,* 114 F.3d 15 (2d Cir. 1997); *Gross v. Omaha Tribe of Nebraska,* 601 N.W.2d 82 (Iowa 1999). *But see Jones v. Chitimacha Tribe of Louisiana,* 23 Indian L. Rep. 6225 (Chitimacha Ct. App. 1996) (tribe had expressly waived its immunity from such suits).

25. *Holmes v. St. Croix Casino,* 26 Indian L. Rep. 6089 (St. Croix Tr. App. 1999); *Long v. Mohegan Tribal Gaming Authority,* 25 Indian L. Rep. 6111 (Mohegan Gam. Disputes Tr. Ct. 1997).

26. *Adams v. Moapa Band of Paiute Indians,* 991 F. Supp. 1218 (D. Nev. 1997).

27. *Bassett v. Mashantucket Pequot Tribe,* 204 F.3d 343 (2d Cir. 2000).

28. 25 U.S.C. Sec. 450n(1). *See Demontiney*, note 18 above, 255 F.3d at 813–14.

29. *Bottomly*, note 18 above. The subject of federal recognition is discussed in ch. 15, sec. F.

30. *Id. See also Haile v. Saunooke*, 246 F.2d 293, 297–98 (4th Cir. 1957).

31. *E.F.W. v. St. Stephen's Mission Indian School*, 264 F.3d 1297 (10th Cir. 2001); *Williams v. Board of County Comm'rs*, 963 P.2d 522, 526 (N.M. Ct. App. 1998); *McKinney v. State of Oklahoma*, 925 F.2d 363, 365 (10th Cir. 1991); *Jicarilla Apache Tribe v. Andrus*, 687 F.2d 1324 (10th Cir. 1982).

32. *Atkinson v. Haldane*, 569 P.2d 151 (Alaska 1977). *See also Boe v. Fort Belknap Indian Community*, 455 F. Supp. 462 (D. Mont. 1978).

33. *Demontiney*, note 18 above, 255 F.3d at 814; *Lineen v. Gila River Indian Community*, 276 F.3d 489 (9th Cir. 2002). *Wilson v. Turtle Mountain Band of Chippewa Indians*, 459 F. Supp. 366 (D.N.D. 1978).

34. *Sanderline v. Seminole Tribe of Florida*, 243 F.3d 1282 (11th Cir. 2001). *See also Naff v. Colville Confederated Tribes*, 22 Indian L. Rep. 6032 (Colv. Ct. App. 1995) (a tribe does not automatically waive immunity from lawsuits seeking to vindicate rights that the tribe has conferred; waiver must be express).

35. *Pit River Home*, note 20 above, 30 F.3d at 1102.

36. *Id.*, 30 F.3d at 1100; *Hagen v. Sisseton-Wahpeton Community College*, 205 F.3d 1040 (8th Cir. 2000).

37. *Osage Tribal Council*, note 14 above; *Tamiami Partners, Ltd. v. Miccosukee Tribe of Indians of Florida*, 63 F.3d 1030, 1050 (11th Cir. 1995).

38. *See* Rule 19 Federal Rules of Civil Procedure.

39. *Lomayaktewa*, note 20 above, 520 F.2d at 1326. *See also Kescoli v. Babbitt*, 101 F.3d 1304, 1309 (9th Cir. 1996).

40. *Quileute Indian Tribe v. Babbitt*, 18 F.3d 1456, 1459 (9th Cir. 1994); *Maynard v. Narragansett Indian Tribe*, 984 F.2d 14 (1st Cir. 1993).

41. *Shermoen v. U.S.*, 982 F.2d 1312, 1317 (9th Cir. 1992), *cert. denied*, 509 U.S. 903 (1993). *See also Clinton v. Babbitt*, 180 F.3d 1081 (9th Cir. 1999).

42. *Makah Indian Tribe v. Verity*, 910 F.2d 555, 558 (9th Cir. 1990).

43. *U.S. ex rel. Hall v. Tribal Development Corp.*, 100 F.3d 476, 479 (9th Cir. 1996). *See also Fluent v. Salamanca Indian Lease Auth.*, 928 F.2d 542, 547 (2d Cir.), *cert. denied*, 502 U.S. 818 (1991); *Enterprise Mgt. Consultants v. U.S. ex rel. Hodel*, 883 F.2d 890 (10th Cir. 1989).

44. *See, e.g., Quileute Indian Tribe*, note 40 above; *Keweenau Bay Indian Community v. Michigan*, 11 F.3d 1341 (6th Cir 1993); *Wichita and Affiliated Tribes of Oklahoma v. Hodel*, 788 F.2d 765, 774–78 (D.C. Cir. 1986).

45. *Kescoli*, note 39 above; *Shermoen*, note 41 above.

46. *Brady v. Brady*, 27 Indian L. Rep. 6125 (Inter-Tribal Ct. App. Nev. 2000); *Charging Hawk v. Rosebud Housing Auth.*, 27 Indian L. Rep. 6269 (Rosebud Sx. Tr. Ct. 2000); *Teasley v. Kootenai Tribe of Idaho*, 25 Indian L. Rep 6148 (Kootenai Tr. Ct. 1998).

47. *Sac and Fox Nation of Missouri v. Norton*, 240 F.3d 1250, 1258–59 (10th Cir. 2001), *cert. denied*, 122 S.Ct. 807 (2002); *Southwest Center for Biological Diversity v. Babbitt*, 150 F.3d 1152, 1154 (9th Cir. 1998); *Cherokee Nation of Oklahoma v. Babbitt*, 117 F.3d 1489 (D.C. Cir. 1997).

48. *Makah Indian Tribe v. Verity*, note 42 above, 910 F.2d at 558.

49. *Pit River Home,* note 20 above, 30 F.3d at 1011; *Quileute Indian Tribe,* note 40 above, 18 F.3d at 1460.

50. *See Hagen,* note 36 above; *Pink v. Modoc Indian Health Project,* 157 F.3d 1185, 1188 (9th Cir. 1998), *cert. denied,* 528 U.S. 877 (1999); *Dillon v. Yankton Sioux Tribal Housing Authority,* 144 F.3d 581 (8th Cir. 1998) (governmental); *Florida Paraplegic,* note 9 above; *Calvello v. Yankton Sioux Tribe,* 899 F. Supp. 431, 438 (D.S.D. 1995) (commercial).

51. *See Dillon,* note 50 above.

52. *Namakagon Devel. Co. v. Bois Forte Res. Housing Auth.,* 517 F.2d 508 (8th Cir. 1975); *Hickey v. Crow Creek Housing Auth.,* 379 F. Supp. 1002 (D.S.D. 1974); *North Sea Products,* note 21 above.

53. *In re Greene,* 980 F.2d 590 (9th Cir. 1992), *cert. denied,* 510 U.S. 1039 (1994).

54. *Dillon,* note 50 above; *Lineen,* note 33 above; *Ransom v. St. Regis Mohawk Educ. and Community Fund, Inc.,* 658 N.E.2d 989, 994–95 (N.Y. Ct. App. 1995); *Atkinson,* note 32 above; *Sturgeon Electric Co. Inc. v. Aha Macav Power Service,* 26 Indian L. Rep., 6026 (Ft. Mojave App. 1998). *But see Rosebud Sioux Tribe v. A&P Steel, Inc.,* 874 F.2d 550 (8th Cir. 1989), and *Hagen v. Sisseton-Wahpeton Community College,* 205 F.3d 1040, 1044 (8th Cir. 2000) (noting a conflict in cases on this point).

55. *C & L Enterprises v. Citizen Band Potawatomi Indian Tribe,* 121 S.Ct. 1589 (2001).

56. *Id.,* 121 S.Ct. at 1595–96.

57. *Ute Distribution Corp. v. Ute Indian Tribe,* 149 F.3d 1260 (10th Cir. 1998); *Rosebud Sioux Tribe v. Val-U Construction Co.,* 50 F.3d 560, 563 (8th Cir 1995); *Ramey,* note 18 above.

58. *Santa Clara Pueblo,* note 1 above, 436 U.S. at 59.

59. *Thompson v. Crow Tribe of Indians,* 962 P.2d 577, 365–66 (Mont. 1998), citing *Imperial Granite Co. v. Pala Band of Mission Indians,* 940 F.2d 1269, 1271 (9th Cir. 1991), and *U.S. v. Yakima Tribal Court,* 806 F.2d 853, 859 (9th Cir. 1986), *cert. denied,* 481 U.S. 1069 (1987). *See also U.S. v. Oregon,* 657 F.2d 1009, 1012 n.8 (9th Cir. 1981); *Hardin v. White Mountain Apache Tribe,* 779 F.2d 476 (9th Cir. 1985); *Nero,* note 22 above.

60. *Dawavendewa v. Salt River Project,* 276 F.3d 1150, 1159–60 (9th Cir. 2002). *Burlington Northern R.R. Co. v. Blackfeet Tribe,* 924 F.2d 899, 901 (9th Cir. 1991), *cert. denied,* 505 U.S. 1212 (1992), *overruled on other grounds, Big Horn County Electric Cooperative, Inc. v. Adams,* 219 F.3d 944 (9th Cir. 2000); *Smith v. Babbitt,* 875 F. Supp. 1353, 1365 (D. Minn. 1995), *aff'd,* 100 F.3d 556 (8th Cir. 1996), *cert. denied,* 522 U.S. 807 (1997); *Ordinance 59 Ass'n v. U.S. Dept. of the Interior,* 163 F.3d 1150 (10th Cir. 1998) (suit under ICRA).

61. *Hardin,* note 59 above, 779 F.2d at 479. For a further discussion of this subject, *see* Timothy Joranko, "Tribal Self-Determination Unfettered: Toward A Rule of Absolute Official Immunity From Damages In Federal Court," 26 *Ariz. St. L. J.* 987 (1994); Alvin Ziontz, "After Martinez: Indian Civil Rights under Tribal Government," 12 *U.C. Davis L. Rev.* 1 (1979).

62. *Comstock Oil & Gas, Inc. v. Alabama and Coushatta Tribes of Texas,* 261 F.3d 567, 570–71 (5th Cir. 2001), *cert. denied,* 122 S.Ct. 1438 (2002).

63. *See Bassett,* note 27 above; *Arizona Public Service Co. v. Aspaas,* 77 F.3d 1128,

1133–34 (9th Cir. 1996) ("Tribal sovereign immunity, however, does not bar a suit for prospective relief against tribal officers allegedly acting in violation of federal law."); *Baker Electric Cooperative, Inc. v. Devils Lake Sioux Indian Tribe,* 28 F.3d 1466, 1471–72 (8th Cir. 1994); *Tenneco Oil Co. v. Sac and Fox Tribe of Indians,* 725 F.2d 572, 574 (10th Cir. 1974); *Imperial Granite,* note 59 above, 940 F.2d at 1274; *Kanai Oil and Gas v. Dept. of the Interior,* 671 F.2d 383 (10th Cir. 1982). *But see Romero v. Peterson,* 930 F.2d 1502, 1505 (10th Cir. 1991) (indicating that tribal officials can never be sued for damages, even for violations of federal law).

64. *Big Horn County Electric,* note 60 above, 219 F.3d at 954 (9th Cir. 2000).

65. *Tamiami Partners, Ltd. v. Miccosukee Tribe,* 177 F.3d 1212, 1225 (11th Cir. 1999).

66. *Big Horn County Electric,* note 60 above. *See also Oklahoma Tax Comm'n v. Citizen Band of Potawatomi Tribe,* note 1 above, 498 U.S. at 514 (recognizing that tribal sovereign immunity prevents a state from collecting taxes from a tribe).

67. *See generally Idaho v. Coeur d'Alene Tribe of Idaho,* 521 U.S. 261 (1997).

68. *Tamiami Partners, Ltd. v. Miccosukee Tribe,* note 65 above, 177 F.3d at 1225 n.15; *Davis v. Littell,* 398 F.2d 83, 85 (9th Cir. 1968); *Great Western Casinos, Inc. v. Morongo Band of Mission Indians,* 74 Cal. App.4th 1407, 88 Cal. Rptr.2d 828 (Cal. Ct. App. 1999), *cert. denied,* 121 S.Ct. 45 (2000).

69. *Hardin,* note 59 above, 779 F.2d at 479–80. *But see Baugus v. Brunson,* 890 F. Supp. 908 (E.D. Cal. 1995) (security officer at tribal casino is not entitled to share tribe's immunity from suit).

70. *Tamiami Partners, Ltd. v. Miccosukee Tribe of Florida,* note 37 above.

71. *See Oklahoma Tax Comm'n v. Citizen Band Potawatomi Tribe,* note 1 above; *Big Horn County Electric,* note 60 above; *Chemehuevi Indian Tribe v. California State Bd. of Equalization,* 757 F.2d 1047 (9th Cir.), *rev'd on other grounds,* 474 U.S. 9 (1985).

72. *Puyallup Tribe, Inc. v. Washington Dept. of Game,* 433 U.S. 165 (1972); *Wold Engineering,* note 8 above; *Seneca-Cayuga,* note 7 above.

73. *Bishop Paiute v. County of Inyo,* 291 F.3d 549 (9th Cir. 2002); *Houghtaling v. Seminole Tribe of Florida,* 611 So.2d 1235 (Fla. 1993); *Atkinson,* note 32 above.

74. *E.E.O.C. v. Karuk Tribe Housing Auth.,* 260 F.3d 1071, 1075 (9th Cir. 2001); *Florida Paraplegic,* note 9 above, 166 F.3d at 1135; *Reich v. Mashantucket Sand and Gravel,* 95 F.3d 174, 182 (2d. Cir. 1996); *Quileute Indian Tribe,* note 40 above, 18 F.3d at 1459–60.

75. *Oklahoma Tax Comm'n v. Citizen Band Potawatomi Indian Tribe,* note 1 above, 498 U.S. at 509. *See also Pit River Home,* note 20 above, 30 F.3d at 1100; *Wichita and Affiliated Tribes,* note 44 above.

76. *Wold Engineering,* note 8 above, 476 U.S. at 893. *See also Rupp v. Omaha Indian Tribe,* 45 F.3d 1241 (8th Cir. 1995), and *U.S. v. Oregon,* note 59 above.

77. *See Rupp* and *U.S. v. Oregon,* note 59 above, and *A&P Steel,* note 54 above.

78. *See* 25 U.S.C. secs. 1302, 1303.

79. *Santa Clara Pueblo,* note 1 above. A tribe does not waive its immunity merely by incorporating the ICRA into its constitution. *See Demontiney,* note 18 above, 255 F.3d at 814.

80. *See Aspaas,* note 63 above, 77 F.3d at 1134–35.

81. *C & L Enterprises*, note 55 above; *Missouri River Services, Inc. v. Omaha Tribe of Nebraska*, 267 F.3d 848, 852–53 (8th Cir. 2001); *Aspaas*, note 63 above, 77 F.3d at 1135; *McClenden*, note 19 above; *American Indian Agricultural Credit Consortium, Inc. v. Standing Rock Sioux Tribe*, 780 F.2d 1374 (8th Cir. 1985). A waiver, however, will not be implied. See *Maynard*, note 40 above.

82. See *Calvello*, note 50 above, 899 F. Supp. at 438.

83. This subject is discussed in ch. 14.

84. *Martin v. Hopi Tribe*, 25 Indian L. Rep. 6185 (Hopi App. 1996). *See also Loley v. Navajo Nation Dept. of Employment and Training*, 27 Indian L. Rep. 6079 (Nav. Sup. Ct. 1999).

85. IV M.P.T.L. ch. 1, sec. 4(c). See *Schock v. Mashantucket Pequot Gaming Enterprise*, 27 Indian L. Rep. 6225, 6228 (Mash. Peq. Tr. Ct. 2000).

86. See 1 Nav. T.C. Sec. 353(a) (1980), discussed in *Raymond v. Navajo Agricultural Products Industry*, 22 Indian L. Rep. 6100 (Nav. Sup. Ct. 1995). *See also Pouley v. Confederated Tribes of the Colville Reservation*, 23 Indian L. Rep. 6143, 6150 (Colv. Tr. Ct. 1996) (Colville Tribe has waived its immunity for certain damages actions up to the limit of an insurance policy), and *Hoffman v. Colville Confederated Tribes*, 24 Indian L. Rep. 6163 n.7 (Colv. Ct. App. 1997) (the tribe has consented to suit for correction of blood quantum decrees, but only for injunctive relief).

87. "Gorton Promises to Limit Tribal Sovereign Immunity," *Indian Country Today* (Nov. 11, 1997) at A5.

88. *Employees v. Missouri Public Health Dept.*, 411 U.S. 279, 284 (1973).

89. *Hans v. Louisiana*, 134 U.S. 1 (1890).

90. *Blatchford v. Native Village of Noatak*, 501 U.S. 775 (1991).

91. *Coeur d'Alene*, note 67 above; *Ford Motor Co. v. Dept. of the Treasury*, 323 U.S. 459, 464 (1945); *Miccosukee Tribe of Indians of Florida v. Florida State Athletic Commission*, 226 F.3d 1226 (11th Cir. 2000).

92. *Lake County Estates v. Tahoe Planning Agency*, 440 U.S. 391, 401 (1978).

93. *Blatchford*, note 90 above.

94. *Coeur d'Alene*, note 67 above; *Alabama v. Pugh*, 438 U.S. 781 (1978).

95. See *Coeur d'Alene*, note 67 above.

96. 209 U.S. 123 (1908).

97. *Ex parte Young*, 209 U.S. 123, 160 (1908). *See also Pennhurst State Sch. & Hosp. v. Halderman*, 465 U.S. 89, 102–3 (1984); *Agua Caliente Band of Cahuilla Indians v. Hardin*, 223 F.3d 1041, 1045 (9th Cir. 2000), *cert. denied*, 121 S.Ct. 1485 (2001); *ANR Pipeline Co. v. LaFever*, 150 F.3d 1178, 1188 (10th Cir. 1998).

98. *Coeur d'Alene*, note 67 above, 521 U.S. at 281.

99. *Washington v. Washington State Commercial Passenger Fishing Vessel Ass'n*, 443 U.S. 658, 695–96 (1979). *See also Fond Du Lac Band of Chippewa Indians v. Carlson*, 68 F.3d 253 (8th Cir. 1995).

100. *See, e.g., Agua Caliente*, note 97 above.

101. See *Edelman*, note 2 above.

102. *Coeur d'Alene*, note 67 above.

103. See *Edelman*, note 2 above. *See also Big Horn County Electric*, note 60 above, 219 F.3d at 955.

104. *Atascadero State Hosp. v. Scanlon*, 473 U.S. 234, 241 (1985); *Pennhurst*, note 97 above, 465 U.S. at 99.

105. *See* cases cited in the above note.

106. *Montana v. Gilham*, 133 F.3d 1133 (9th Cir. 1998).

107. 517 U.S. 44 (1996).

108. *See Ysleta Del Sur Pueblo v. Laney*, 199 F.3d 281 (5th Cir. 2000) (holding that tribe is barred by Eleventh Amendment from suing a state to recover lands allegedly seized in violation of the Indian Nonintercourse Act, 25 U.S.C. Sec. 177).

109. *See County of Oneida v. Oneida Indian Nation*, 470 U.S. 226 (1985); *Sycuan Band of Mission Indians v. Roache*, 54 F.3d 535, 538 (9th Cir. 1995).

110. *See* cases cited in notes 90 and 91 above.

111. *See Moe v. Confederated Salish and Kootenai Tribes*, 425 U.S. 463 (1976); *State of Idaho v. Andrus*, 720 F.2d 1461 (9th Cir. 1983), *cert. denied*, 469 U.S. 824 (1984).

112. *See Oklahoma Tax Comm'n v. Sac and Fox Nation*, 508 U.S. 114, 120 (1993); *Moe*, note 111 above; *Agua Caliente*, note 97 above, 223 F.3d at 1049 n.8; *Sac and Fox Nation of Missouri v. Pierce*, 213 F.3d 566, 572–73 (10th Cir. 2000), *cert. denied*, 531 U.S. 1144 (2001). *See also Knight v. Shoshone and Arapaho Tribes*, 670 F.2d 900 (10th Cir. 1982).

113. *Poafpybitty v. Skelly Oil Co.*, 390 U.S. 365 (1968); *Pueblo of Isleta v. Universal Constructions, Inc.*, 570 F.2d 300 (10th Cir. 1978); *Schaghticoke Tribe of Indians v. Kent School Corp.*, 423 F. Supp. 780 (D. Conn. 1976).

114. *Gila River Indian Community v. Hennington, Durham & Richardson*, 626 F.2d 708 (9th Cir. 1980), *cert. denied*, 451 U.S. 911 (1981).

115. *Navajo Tribal Utility Auth. v. Arizona Dept. of Revenue*, 608 F.2d 1228 (9th Cir. 1979).

116. 501 U.S. 775 (1991).

117. *Blatchford*, note 90 above, 501 U.S. at 784, citing *Moe*, note 111, 425 U.S. at 472–73. *See also Pierce*, note 112 above, 213 F.3d at 571–72.

118. *See Blatchford*, note 90 above, 501 U.S. at 785 n.3; *Agua Caliente*, note 97 above, 223 F.3d at 1049 n.8; *U.S. v. State of South Dakota*, 105 F.3d 1552, 1560 n.15 (8th Cir. 1997).

119. 25 U.S.C. Secs. 331 *et seq.*

120. *See U.S. v. Mottaz*, 476 U.S. 834 (1986).

121. *Poafpybitty*, note 113 above. *But see U.S. v. Turtle Mountain Housing Auth.*, 816 F.2d 1273 (8th Cir. 1987) (damages for trespass on an allotment cannot be recovered under section 1353).

122. *See Poafpybitty*, note 113 above; *Begay v. Albers*, 721 F.2d 1274 (10th Cir. 1983).

123. *See Hafer v. Melo*, 502 U.S. 21, 28 (1991); *Golden State Transit Corp. v. City of Los Angeles*, 493 U.S. 103 (1989); *Procunier v. Navarette*, 434 U.S. 555 (1978).

124. *Evans v. McKay*, 869 F.2d 1341 (9th Cir. 1989).

125. *See* cases cited in note 60 above. However, if the state official acted in "good faith," damages are not normally recoverable unless the official's acts violated clearly established federal rights "of which a reasonable person would have known." *See Procunier*, note 123 above, 434 U.S. at 562; *Mitchell v. Forsyth*, 472 U.S. 511 (1985).

126. *Shoshone-Bannock Tribes v. Fish & Game Commission, Idaho*, 42 F.3d 1278, 1285–86 (9th Cir. 1994).

127. *Monell v. N.Y. City Dept. of Social Services*, 436 U.S. 658 (1978). Municipal governments do not have the qualified immunity from a damages action that state officials normally have. See *Owen v. City of Independence*, 445 U.S. 622 (1980).

128. 121 S.Ct. 2304 (2001).

129. *Wilson v. Omaha Indian Tribe*, 442 U.S. 653 (1979); *U.S. v. Rickert*, 188 U.S. 432 (1903); *Heckman v. U.S.*, 224 U.S. 413 (1912); *Winters v. U.S.*, 207 U.S. 564 (1908); *U.S. v. City of Pawhuska*, 502 F.2d 821 (10th Cir. 1974).

130. See *Seminole Tribe of Florida v. Florida*, 517 U.S. 44, 71 n.14 (1996); *Blatchford*, note 90 above, 501 U.S. at 782–83.

131. *U.S. ex rel. Cheyenne River Sioux Tribe v. State of South Dakota*, 102 F. Supp.2d 1166, 1177 (D.S.D. 2000).

132. *Poafpybitty*, note 113 above; *Rickert*, note 129 above.

133. *Arizona v. California*, 460 U.S. 605 (1983); *State of New Mexico v. Aamodt*, 537 F.2d 1102 (10th Cir. 1976), *cert. denied*, 429 U.S. 1121 (1977).

134. *Arizona v. California*, note 133 above; *Pueblo of Picuris v. Abeyta*, 50 F.2d 12 (10th Cir. 1931).

135. *U.S. v. Candelaria*, 271 U.S. 432 (1926); *Choctaw and Chickasaw Nations v. Seitz*, 193 F.2d 456 (10th Cir. 1951).

136. 25 U.S.C. Sec. 175.

137. *Heckman*, note 129 above; *Shoshone-Bannock Tribes v. Reno*, 56 F.3d 1476, 1482 (D.C. Cir. 1995). But see *Chemehuevi Indian Tribe v. Wilson*, 987 F. Supp. 804, 809 (N.D. Cal. 1997).

138. *Puyallup Tribe*, note 72 above. See also cases cited in note 112 above.

139. See cases cited in note 135 above.

140. *Bell v. Hood*, 327 U.S. 678, 684 (1946); *Bivens v. Six Unknown Named Agents*, 403 U.S. 388, 396–97 (1971).

141. *Washington v. Washington State Commercial Passenger Fishing Vessel Ass'n*, 443 U.S. 658 (1979).

142. See, e.g., *Affiliated Ute Citizens v. U.S.*, 406 U.S. 128, 141–42 (1972); *U.S. v. White Mountain Apache Tribe*, 784 F.2d 917, 920 n.10 (9th Cir. 1986).

143. 28 U.S.C. Secs. 1346(b), 2671–80.

144. 28 U.S.C. Sec. 2675. See *McNeil v. U.S.*, 508 U.S. 106 (1993).

145. 28 U.S.C. Sec. 2401(b).

146. See *Dalehite v. U.S.*, 346 U.S. 15, 45 (1953); *Rayonier, Inc. v. U.S.*, 352 U.S. 315 (1957).

147. *Bryant v. U.S.*, 565 F.2d 650 (10th Cir. 1977).

148. *Hatahley v. U.S.*, 351, U.S. 173 (1956).

149. *Red Lake Band of Chippewa Indians v. U.S.*, 800 F.2d 1187 (D.C. Cir. 1986).

150. *Simmons v. U.S.*, 740 F.2d 1023 (9th Cir. 1986); *LaRoche v. U.S.*, 730 F.2d 538 (8th Cir. 1985); *Cheromiah v. U.S.*, 55 F. Supp.2d 1295 (D.N.M. 1999).

151. 25 U.S.C. Secs. 450 *et seq.*

152. *Id.*, Sec. 450f(d).

153. 28 U.S.C. Sec. 2680 (1990).

154. See *St. John v. U.S.*, 240 F.3d 671 (8th Cir. 2001); *Red Elk v. U.S.*, 62 F.3d 1102 (8th Cir. 1995). In addition to suing the BIA under the FTCA, a suit against the officers

in their individual capacity is also possible in certain situations. *See* note 175 below and accompanying text.

155. 28 U.S.C. Sec. 2680.

156. *Berkovitz v. U.S.*, 486 U.S. 531, 536 (1988). *See also Summers v. U.S.*, 905 F.2d 1212, 1214 (9th Cir. 1990); *Webster v. U.S.*, 823 F. Supp. 1544 (D. Mont. 1992), *aff'd*, 22 F.3d 221 (9th Cir. 1994).

157. 28 U.S.C. Sec. 2680(a). *See U.S. v. Gaubert*, 499 U.S. 315 (1991).

158. 28 U.S.C. Secs. 1346(a)(2), 1491. *See generally Testan*, note 4 above.

159. 28 U.S.C. Secs. 1346(a)(2), 1491. *See U.S. v. Mitchell*, 463 U.S. 206 (1983); *Bowen v. Public Agencies Opposed to Social Sec. Entrapment*, 477 U.S. 41, 55–56 (1986); *Nutt v. U.S.*, 12 Cl. Ct. 345, 351 (1987), *aff'd*, 847 F.2d 791 (Fed. Cir. 1988), *cert. denied*, 488 U.S. 1004 (1989).

160. 28 U.S.C. Secs. 1491 and 28 U.S.C. Sec. 1505, known as the Indian Tucker Act, which allows claims filed by Indian tribes.

161. 28 U.S.C. Sec. 1346(a)(2). *See Catawba Indian Tribe of Carolina v. U.S.*, 982 F.2d 1564 (Fed. Cir. 1993), *cert. denied*, 509 U.S. 904 (1993).

162. 28 U.S.C. Sec. 2401(a). The statute of limitations has been liberally construed so as not to bar a meritorious claim. *See Duncan v. U.S.*, 667 F.2d 36 (Ct. Cl. 1981), *cert. denied*, 463 U.S. 1228 (1983). *But see Jones v. U.S.*, 801 F.2d 1334, 1335 (Fed. Cir. 1986), *cert. denied*, 481 U.S. 1013 (1987); *Hopland Band of Pomo Indians v. U.S.*, 855 F.2d 1573 (Fed. Cir. 1988).

163. 463 U.S. 206 (1983).

164. *See also Angle v. U.S.*, 709 F.2d 570 (9th Cir. 1983).

165. *U.S. v. Mitchell*, 445 U.S. 535 (1980).

166. See ch. 3, notes 64–73, and accompanying text. *See generally Cobell v. Babbitt*, 91 F. Supp.2d 1 (D.D.C. 2000), *aff'd*, 240 F.3d 108 (D.C. Cir. 2001).

167. *U.S. v. Mitchell*, note 165 above; *Apache Tribe v. U.S.*, 43 Fed. Cl. 155 (1999); *Duncan*, note 162 above; *Manchester Band of Pomo Indians, Inc. v. U.S.*, 363 F. Supp. 1238 (N.D. Cal. 1973); *Navajo Tribe of Indians v. U.S.*, 624 F.2d 981 (Ct. Cl. 1980); *Cobell v. Babbitt*, note 166 above.

168. *See Yearsley v. Ross Construction Co.*, 309 U.S. 18, 21 (1940); *Bay View, Inc. v. Ahtna, Inc.*, 105 F.3d 1281 (9th Cir. 1997); *NRG Co. v. U.S.*, 30 Fed. Cl. 460 (1994).

169. 28 U.S.C. Sec. 1502.

170. 25 U.S.C. Secs. 70 to 70v-3. The purpose of the act is discussed in *U.S. v. Dann*, 470 U.S. 39 (1985).

171. 25 U.S.C. Sec. 70a(5). *See U.S. v. Sioux Nation of Indians*, 448 U.S. 371 (1980); *Confederated Tribes of Colville Reservation v. U.S.*, 964 F.2d 1102, 1110 (Fed. Cir. 1992); *Cherokee Nation of Oklahoma v. U.S.*, 937 F.2d 1539 (10th Cir. 1991); *Minnesota Chippewa Tribe v. U.S.*, 768 F.2d 338 (Cl. Ct. 1986); *Gila River Puma–Maricopa Indian Community v. U.S.*, 684 F.2d 852 (Cl. Ct. 1982).

172. *See, e.g.*, cases cited in note 171 above and *Northern Paiute Nation v. U.S.*, 10 Cl. Ct. 401 (1986).

173. *Arizona v. California*, 530 U.S. 392 (2000).

174. *See Florida v. U.S. Dept. of Interior*, 768 F.2d 1248 (11th Cir. 1985), *cert. denied*, 475 U.S. 1011 (1986); *U.S. v. Yakima Tribal Court*, note 59 above.

175. *See Harlow v. Fitzgerald,* 457 U.S. 800 (1982); *Bivens,* note 140 above; *Butz v. Economu,* 438 U.S. 478 (1978); *Romero,* note 63 above, 930 F.2d at 1507; *U.S. v. Yakima Tribal Court,* note 59 above, 806 F.2d at 860.

176. *See, e.g., U.S. v. Winnebago Tribe of Nebraska,* 542 F.2d 1002 (8th Cir. 1976).

177. 5 U.S.C. Secs. 701 *et seq.*

178. 5 U.S.C. Sec. 701(A). *See, e.g., U.S. v. Mitchell,* note 159, 463 U.S. at 227 n.3; *Coomes v. Adkinson,* 414 F. Supp. 975, 984–85 (D.S.D. 1976).

179. The APA is not itself a jurisdictional statute. *Califano v. Sanders,* 430 U.S. 99 (1977).

180. 5 U.S.C. Sec. 706(1), (2)(A). *See, e.g., Assiniboine and Sioux Tribes v. Board of Oil and Gas Exploration,* 792 F.2d 782 (9th Cir. 1986); *Preston v. Heckler,* 734 F.2d 1359 (9th Cir. 1984); *Muwekma Tribe v. Babbitt,* 133 F. Supp.2d 42 (D.D.C. 2001).

181. *Coomes,* note 178 above.

182. *Rockbridge v. Lincoln,* 449 F.2d 567 (9th Cir. 1971).

183. *Harjo v. Kleppe,* 420 F. Supp. 1110 (D.D.C. 1976), *aff'd sub nom. Harjo v. Andrus,* 581 F.2d 949 (D.C. Cir. 1978).

184. *See Muwekma,* note 180 above; *Hein v. Capitan Grande Band of Diegueno Mission Indians,* 201 F.3d 1256 (9th Cir. 2000).

185. *Pence v. Kleppe,* 529 F.2d 135 (9th Cir. 1976). *See also Morton v. Ruiz,* 415 U.S. 199 (1974).

186. *Thomas v. U.S.,* 141 F. Supp.2d 1185 (W.D. Wis. 2001); *Ike v. U.S. Dept. of the Interior,* 9 Indian L. Rep. 3043 (D. Nev. 1982).

187. *Cheyenne-Arapaho Tribes v. Watt,* 9 Indian L. Rep. 3053 (D.D.C. 1982); *Omaha Tribe of Nebraska v. Watt,* 9 Indian L. Rep. 3117 (D. Neb. 1982).

188. *Woods Petroleum Corp. v. Dept. of Interior,* 47 F.3d 1032 (10th Cir.) (*en banc*), *cert. denied,* 516 U.S. 805 (1995).

189. *Cobell v. Babbitt,* note 166 above.

190. *Lincoln v. Vigil,* 508 U.S. 182, 193–95 (1993); *First Moon v. White Tail,* 270 U.S. 243 (1926); *Merrill Ditch-Liners, Inc. v. Pablo,* 670 F.2d 139 (9th Cir. 1982); *Johnson v. Kleppe,* 596 F.2d 950 (10th Cir. 1979).

191. 508 U.S. 182 (1993).

192. *See Motor Vehicle Mfrs. Ass'n v. State Farm Mutual Automobile Ins. Co.,* 463 U.S. 29, 43 (1983); *Citizens to Preserve Overton Park v. Volpe,* 401 U.S. 402, 415–16 (1971); *Moapa Band of Paiute Indians v. U.S. Dept. of Interior,* 747 F.2d 563 (9th Cir. 1983).

193. *Northwest Resource Information Center, Inc. v. Puget Sound Power Planning Council,* 35 F.3d 1371 (9th Cir. 1994), *cert. denied,* 516 U.S. 806 (1995).

194. *See Faras v. Hodel,* 845 F.2d 202 (9th Cir. 1988); *White Mountain Apache Tribe v. Hodel,* 840 F.2d 675 (9th Cir. 1988).

195. 25 C.F.R. Secs. 2.1 *et seq.*

196. *Seminole Nation v. U.S.,* 316 U.S. 286, 297 (1942).

197. *U.S. v. Mason,* 412 U.S. 391, 398 (1973).

198. *Seminole Nation v. U.S.,* note 196 above, 316 U.S. at 297. *See also U.S. v. Mitchell,* note 159 above.

APPENDIX A

The Indian Civil Rights Act
(25 U.S.C. §§ 1301–3)

§ *1301. Definitions*

For purposes of this subchapter, the term— (1) "Indian tribe" means any tribe, band, or other group of Indians subject to the jurisdiction of the United States and recognized as possessing powers of self-government;

(2) "powers of self-government" means and includes all governmental powers possessed by an Indian tribe, executive, legislative, and judicial, and all offices, bodies, and tribunals by and through which they are executed, including courts of Indian offenses; and means the inherent power of Indian tribes, hereby recognized and affirmed, to exercise criminal jurisdiction over all Indians;

(3) "Indian court" means any Indian tribal court or court of Indian offense; and

(4) "Indian" means any person who would be subject to the jurisdiction of the United States as an Indian under section 1153 of Title 18 if that person were to commit an offense listed in that section in Indian country to which that section applies.

§ *1302. Constitutional rights*

No Indian tribe in exercising powers of self-government shall— (1) make or enforce any law prohibiting the free exercise of religion, or abridging the freedom of speech, or of the press, or the right of the people peaceably to assemble and to petition for a redress of grievances;

(2) violate the right of the people to be secure in their persons, houses, papers, and effects against unreasonable search and seizures, nor issue warrants, but upon probable cause, supported by oath or affirmation, and particularly describing the place to be searched and the person or thing to be seized;

(3) subject any person for the same offense to be twice put in jeopardy;

(4) compel any person in any criminal case to be a witness against himself;

(5) take any private property for a public use without just compensation;

(6) deny to any person in a criminal proceeding the right to a speedy and public trial, to be informed of the nature and cause of the accusation, to be con-

fronted with the witnesses against him, to have compulsory process for obtaining witnesses in his favor, and at his own expense to have the assistance of counsel for his defense;

(7) require excessive bail, impose excessive fines, inflict cruel and unusual punishments, and in no event impose for conviction of any one offense any penalty or punishment greater than imprisonment for a term of one year and a fine of $5,000, or both;

(8) deny to any person within its jurisdiction the equal protection of its laws or deprive any person of liberty or property without due process of law;

(9) pass any bill of attainder or ex post facto law; or

(10) deny to any person accused of an offense punishable by imprisonment the right, upon request, to a trial by jury of not less than six persons.

§ 1303. *Habeas corpus*

The privilege of the writ of habeas corpus shall be available to any person, in a court of the United States, to test the legality of his detention by order of an Indian tribe.

APPENDIX B

Public Law 83-280
(18 U.S.C. § 1162, 28 U.S.C. § 1360)

§ *1162. State jurisdiction over offenses committed by or against Indians in the Indian country*

(a) Each of the States or Territories listed in the following table shall have jurisdiction over offenses committed by or against Indians in the areas of Indian country listed opposite the name of the State or Territory to the same extent that such State or Territory has jurisdiction over offenses committed elsewhere within the State or Territory, and the criminal laws of such State or Territory shall have the same force and effect within such Indian country as they have elsewhere within the State or Territory:

State or Territory of Indian Country Affected

Alaska	All Indian country within the State, except that on Annette Islands; the Metlakatla Indian community may exercise jurisdiction over offenses committed by Indians in the same manner in which such jurisdiction may be exercised by Indian tribes in Indian country over which State jurisdiction has not been extended.
California	All Indian country within the State
Minnesota	All Indian country within the State, except the Red Lake Reservation
Nebraska	All Indian country within the State
Oregon	All Indian country within the State, except the Warm Springs Reservation
Wisconsin	All Indian country within the State

(b) Nothing in this section shall authorize the alienation, encumbrance, or taxation of any real or personal property, including water rights, belonging to any Indian or any Indian tribe, band, or community that is held in trust by the United States or is subject to a restriction against alienation imposed by the United States; or shall authorize regulation of the use of such property in a manner inconsistent with any Federal treaty, agreement, or statute or with any regulation made pursuant thereto; or shall deprive any Indian or any Indian tribe, band, or community of any right, privilege, or immunity afforded under Federal treaty, agreement, or statute with respect to hunting, trapping, or fishing or the control, licensing, or regulation thereof.

(c) The provisions of sections 1152 and 1153 of this chapter [reproduced in appendixes C and D of this book] shall not be applicable within the areas of Indian country listed in subsection (a) of this section as areas over which the several States have exclusive jurisdiction.

§ 1360. State civil jurisdiction in actions to which Indians are parties

(a) Each of the States listed in the following table shall have jurisdiction over civil causes of action between Indians or to which Indians are parties which arise in the areas of Indian country listed opposite the name of the State to the same extent that such State has jurisdiction over other civil causes of action, and those civil laws of such State that are of general application to private persons or private property shall have the same force and effect within such Indian country as they have elsewhere within the State:

State of Indian Country Affected

Alaska	All Indian country within the State
California	All Indian country within the State
Minnesota	All Indian country within the State, except the Red Lake Reservation
Nebraska	All Indian country within the State
Oregon	All Indian country within the State, except the Warm Springs Reservation
Wisconsin	All Indian country within the State

(b) Nothing in this section shall authorize the alienation, encumbrance, or taxation of any real or personal property, including water rights, belonging to any

Indian or any Indian tribe, band, or community that is held in trust by the United States or is subject to a restriction against alienation imposed by the United States; or shall authorize regulation of the use of such property in a manner inconsistent with any Federal treaty, agreement, or statute or with any regulation made pursuant thereto; or shall confer jurisdiction upon the State to adjudicate, in probate proceedings or otherwise, the ownership or right to possession of such property or any interest therein.

(c) Any tribal ordinance or custom heretofore or hereafter adopted by an Indian tribe, band, or community in the exercise of any authority which it may possess shall, if not inconsistent with any applicable civil law of the State, be given full force and effect in the determination of civil causes of action pursuant to this section.

Appendix C

The Indian Country Crimes Act
(18 U.S.C. § 1152)

§ 1152. Laws governing

Except as otherwise expressly provided by law, the general laws of the United States as to the punishment of offenses committed in any place within the sole and exclusive jurisdiction of the United States, except the District of Columbia, shall extend to the Indian country.

This section shall not extend to offenses committed by one Indian against the person or property of another Indian, nor to any Indian committing any offense in the Indian country who has been punished by the local law of the tribe, or to any case where, by treaty stipulations, the exclusive jurisdiction over such offenses is or may be secured to the Indian tribes respectively.

APPENDIX D

The Major Crimes Act
(18 U.S.C. § 1153)

§ *1153. Offenses committed within Indian country*

(a) Any Indian who commits against the person or property of another Indian or other person any of the following offenses, namely, murder, manslaughter, kidnapping, maiming, a felony under chapter 109A, incest, assault with intent to commit murder, assault with a dangerous weapon, assault resulting in serious bodily injury (as defined in section 1365 of this title), an assault against an individual who has not attained the age of 16 years, arson, burglary, robbery, and a felony under section 661 of this title [18 U.S.C. § 661, i.e., theft] within the Indian country, shall be subject to the same law and penalties as all other persons committing any of the above offenses, within the exclusive jurisdiction of the United States.

(b) Any offense referred to in subsection (a) of this section that is not defined and punished by Federal law in force within the exclusive jurisdiction of the United States shall be defined and punished in accordance with the laws of the State in which such offense was committed as are in force at the time of such offense.

APPENDIX E

"Indian Country"
(18 U.S.C. § 1151)

§ *1151. Indian country defined*

Except as otherwise provided in sections 1154 and 1156 of this title, the term "Indian country," as used in this chapter, means (a) all land within the limits of any Indian reservation under the jurisdiction of the United States Government, notwithstanding the issuance of any patent, and, including rights-of-way running through the reservation, (b) all dependent Indian communities within the borders of the United States whether within the original or subsequently acquired territory thereof, and whether within or without the limits of a state, and (c) all Indian allotments, the Indian titles to which have not been extinguished, including rights-of-way running through the same.

Appendix F

Indian Tribes in the States

The following is a state-by-state listing of Indian tribes or groups that are federally recognized and eligible for funding and services from the Bureau of Indian Affairs (BIA) because of their status as Indian tribes. In addition, the list includes Indian tribes or groups that are recognized by the states. This acknowledges their status within the state but does not guarantee funding from the state or the federal government. State-recognized Indian tribes are not federally recognized; however, federally recognized tribes also may be state-recognized.

The source for this list is the National Conference of State Legislatures, 1560 Broadway, Suite 700, Denver, CO 80202, info@ncsl.org (autoresponse directory). For a current list of federally recognized tribes produced by the Bureau of Indian Affairs in alphabetical order, *see* <www.doi.gov/bia/tribes/entry.html>.

Alabama

Federally Recognized
Poarch Band of Creeks

State-Recognized
Cherokees of N.E. Alabama
Cherokees of S.E. Alabama
Echota Cherokees
MaChis Lower Alabama Creek Tribe
Mowa Band of Choctaws
Star Clan–Muscogee Creek Tribe

Alaska

Federally Recognized
Afognak, Village of
Akhiok, Native Village of

Akiachak Native Community
Akiak Native Community
Akutan, Native Village of
Alakanuk, Village of
Alatna Village
Aleknagik, Native Village of
Algaaciq Native Village (St. Mary's)
Allakaket Village
Ambler, Native Village of
Anaktuvuk Pass, Village of
Andreafski, Yupiit of
Angoon Community Association
Aniak, Village of
Anvik Village
Arctic Village (*See* Venetie Tribal Government, Native Village of)
Asa'carsarmiut Tribe (formerly Native Village of Mountain Village)
Atka, Native Village of
Atmautluak, Village of
Atqasuk Village (Atkasook)
Barrow Inupiat Traditional Government, Native Village of (formerly Native
    Village of Barrow)
Beaver Village
Belkofski, Native Village of
Bill Moore's Slough, Village of
Birch Creek Village
Brevig Mission, Native Village of
Buckland, Native Village of
Cantwell, Native Village of
Chalkyitsik Village
Chanega, Native Village of (Chenega)
Chefornak, Village of
Chevak Native Village
Chickaloon Native Village
Chignik, Native Village of
Chignik Lagoon, Native Village of
Chignik Lake Village
Chilkat Indian Village (Kluckwan)
Chilkoot Indian Association (Haines)
Chinik Eskimo Community (Golovin)
Chistochina, Native Village of
Chitina, Native Village of

Chuathbaluk, Native Village of (Russian Mission, Kuskokwim)
Chuloonawick Native Village
Circle Native Community
Clark's Point, Village of
Council, Native Village of
Craig Community Association
Crooked Creek, Village of
Curyung Tribal Council (formerly Native Village of Dillingham)
Deering, Native Village of
Diomede, Native Village of (Inalik)
Dot Lake, Village of
Douglas Indian Association
Eagle, Native Village of
Eek, Native Village of
Egegik Village
Eklutna Native Village
Ekuk, Native Village of
Ekwok Village
Elim, Native Village of
Emmonak Village
Evansville Village (Bettles Field)
Eyak, Native Village of (Cordova)
False Pass, Native Village of
Fort Yukon, Native Village of
Gakona, Native Village of
Galena Village (Louden Village)
Gambell, Native Village of
Georgetown, Native Village of
Goodnews Bay, Native Village of
Grayling, Organized Village of (Holikachuk)
Gulkana Village
Hamilton, Native Village of
Healy Lake Village
Holy Cross Village
Hoonah Indian Association
Hooper Bay, Native Village of
Hughes Village
Huslia Village
Hydaburg Cooperative Association
Igiugig Village
Iliamna, Village of

Inupiat Community of the Arctic Slope
Iqurmuit Traditional Council (formerly Native Village of Russian Mission)
Ivanoff Bay Village
Kaguyak Village
Kake, Organized Village of
Kaktovik Village (Barter Island)
Kalskag, Village of
Kaltag, Village of
Kanatak, Native Village of
Karluk, Native Village of
Kasaan, Organized Village of
Kasigluk, Native Village of
Kenaitze Indian Tribe
Ketchikan Indian Corporation
Kiana, Native Village of
King Cove, Agdaagux Tribe of
King Island Native Community
King Salmon Tribe
Kipnuk, Native Village of
Kivalina, Native Village of
Klawock Cooperative Association
Kluti Kaah, Native Village of (Copper Center)
Knik Tribe
Kobuk, Native Village of
Kokhanok Village
Koliganek Village (*See* New Koliganek Village Council)
Kongiganak, Native Village of
Kotlik, Village of
Kotzebue, Native Village of
Koyuk, Native Village of
Koyukuk Native Village
Kwethluk, Organized Village of
Kwigillingok, Native Village of
Kwinhagak, Native Village of (Quinhagak)
Larsen Bay, Native Village of
Lesnoi Village (Woody Island)
Levelock Village
Lime Village
Lower Kalskag, Village of
Manley Hot Springs Village
Manokotak Village

Marshall, Native Village of (Fortuna Ledge)
Mary's Igloo, Native Village of
McGrath Native Village
Mekoryuk, Native Village of
Mentasta Traditional Council (formerly Mentasta Lake Village)
Metlakatla Indian Community, Annette Island Reserve
Minto, Native Village of
Naknek Native Village
Nanwalek, Native Village of (English Bay)
Napaimute, Native Village of
Napakiak, Native Village of
Napaskiak, Native Village of
Nelson Lagoon, Native Village of
Nenana Native Association
Newhalen Village
New Koliganek Village Council (formerly Koliganek Village)
New Stuyahok Village
Newtok Village
Nightmute, Native Village of
Nikolai Village
Nikolski, Native Village of
Ninilchik Village
Noatak, Native Village of
Nome Eskimo Community
Nondalton Village
Noorvik Native Community
Northway Village
Nuiqsut, Native Village of (Nooiksut)
Nulato Village
Nunapitchuk, Native Village of
Ohogamiut, Village of
Old Harbor, Village of
Orutsararmuit Native Village (Bethel)
Oscarville Traditional Village
Ouzinkie, Native Village of
Paimiut, Native Village of
Pauloff Harbor Village
Pedro Bay Village
Perryville, Native Village of
Petersburg Indian Association
Pilot Point, Native Village of

Pilot Station Traditional Village
Pitka's Point, Native Village of
Platinum Traditional Village
Point Hope, Native Village of
Point Lay, Native Village of
Portage Creek Village (Ohgsenakale)
Port Graham, Native Village of
Port Heiden, Native Village of
Port Lions, Native Village of
Pribilof Islands Aleut Communities of St. Paul and St. George Islands
Qagan Toyagungin Tribe of Sand Point Village
Rampart Village
Red Devil, Village of
Ruby, Native Village of
Salamatoff, Village of
Savoonga, Native Village of
Saxman, Organized Village of
Saint George (*See* Pribilof Islands Aleut Communities of St. Paul and St.
    George Islands)
Saint Michael, Native Village of
Saint Paul (*See* Pribilof Islands Aleut Communities of St. Paul and St. George
    Islands)
Scammon Bay, Native Village of
Selawik, Native Village of
Seldovia Village Tribe
Shageluk Native Village
Shaktoolik, Native Village of
Sheldon's Point, Native Village of
Shishmaref, Native Village of
Shoonaq' Tribe of Kodiak
Shungnak, Native Village of
Sitka Tribe of Alaska
Skagway Village
Sleetmute, Village of
Solomon, Village of
South Naknek Village
Stebbins Community Association
Stevens, Native Village of
Stony River, Village of
Takotna Village

Tanacross, Native Village of
Tanana, Native Village of
Tatitlek, Native Village of
Tazlina, Native Village of
Telida Village
Teller, Native Village of
Tetlin, Native Village of
Tlingit and Haida Indian Tribes, Central Council of the
Togiak, Traditional Village of
Toksook Bay, Native Village of
Tuluksak Native Community
Tuntutuliak, Native Village of
Tununak, Native Village of
Twin Hills Village
Tyonek, Native Village of
Ugashik Village
Umkumiute Native Village
Unalakleet, Native Village of
Unalaska, Qawalangin Tribe of
Unga, Native Village of
Venetie, Village of (*See* Venetie Tribal Government, Native Village of)
Venetie Tribal Government, Native Village of (Arctic Village and Village of
    Venetie)
Wainwright, Village of
Wales, Native Village of
White Mountain, Native Village of
Wrangell Cooperative Association
Yakutat Tlingit Tribe

ARIZONA

Federally Recognized
Ak Chin Indian Community
Cocopah Tribe
Colorado River Indian Tribes (Arizona and California)
Fort McDowell Mohave–Apache Community
Fort Mojave Indian Tribe (Arizona, California, and Nevada)
Gila River Indian Community
Havasupai Tribe

Hopi Tribe
Hualapai Indian Tribe
Kaibab Band of Paiute Indians
Navajo Nation (Arizona, New Mexico, and Utah)
Pascua Yaqui Tribe
Quechan Tribe (Arizona and California)
Salt River Pima–Maricopa Indian Community
San Carlos Apache Tribe
San Juan Southern Paiute Tribe
Tohono O'odham Nation
Tonto Apache Tribe
White Mountain Apache Tribe
Yavapai-Apache Nation
Yavapai-Prescott Tribe

CALIFORNIA

Federally Recognized
Agua Caliente Band of Cahuilla Indians
Alturas Indian Rancheria
Augustine Band of Cahuilla Mission Indians
Bear River Band of the Rohnerville Rancheria
Berry Creek Rancheria of Maidu Indians of California
Big Lagoon Rancheria
Big Pine Band of Owens Valley Paiute Shoshone Indians
Big Sandy Rancheria of Mono Indians
Big Valley Rancheria of Pomo and Pit River Indians
Blue Lake Rancheria
Bridgeport Paiute Indian Colony
Buena Vista Rancheria of Me-Wuk Indians
Cabazon Band of Cahuilla Mission Indians
Cachil DeHe Band of Wintun Indians of the Colusa Indian Community
Cahto Indian Tribe
Cahuilla Band of Mission Indians
Campo Band of Diegueño Mission Indians
Capitan Grande Band of Diegueño Mission Indians
Capitan Grande Band of Mission Indians, Barona Group of
Capitan Grande Band of Mission Indians, Viejas (Baron Long) Group of
Cedarville Rancheria

Chemehuevi Indian Tribe
Cher-Ae Heights Indian Community
Chicken Ranch Rancheria of Me-Wuk Indians
Cloverdale Rancheria of Pomo Indians
Cold Springs Rancheria of Mono Indians
Colorado River Indian Tribes (Arizona and California)
Cortina Indian Rancheria of Wintun Indians
Coyote Valley Band of Pomo Indians
Cuyapaipe Community of Diegueño Mission Indians
Death Valley Timbi-Sha Shoshone Band
Dry Creek Rancheria of Pomo Indians
Elem Indian Colony of Pomo Indians of the Sulphur Bank Rancheria
Elk Valley Rancheria
Enterprise Rancheria of Maidu Indians
Fort Bidwell Indian Community
Fort Independence Indian Community of Paiute Indians
Fort Mojave Indian Tribe (Arizona, California and Nevada)
Graton Rancheria
Greenville Rancheria of Maidu Indians
Grindstone Indian Rancheria of Wintun-Wailaki Indians
Guidiville Rancheria
Hoopa Valley Tribe
Hopland Band of Pomo Indians
Inaja Band of Diegueño Mission Indians
Ione Band of Miwok Indians
Jackson Rancheria of Me-Wuk Indians
Jamul Indian Village
Karuk Tribe
Kashia Band of Pomo Indians of the Stewart's Point Rancheria
La Jolla Band of Luiseño Mission Indians
La Posta Band of Diegueño Mission Indians
Los Coyotes Band of Cahuilla Mission Indians
Lower Lake Rancheria
Lytton Rancheria
Manchester Band of Pomo Indians
Manzanita Band of Diegueño Mission Indians
Mechoopda Indian Tribe
Mesa Grande Band of Diegueño Mission Indians
Middletown Rancheria of Pomo Indians
Mooretown Rancheria of Maidu Indians

Morongo Band of Cahuilla Mission Indians
Northfork Rancheria of Mono Indians
Paiute-Shoshone Indians of the Bishop Community
Paiute-Shoshone Indians of the Lone Pine Community
Pala Band of Luiseño Mission Indians
Paskenta Band of Nomlaki Indians
Pauma Band of Luiseño Mission Indians
Pechanga Band of Luiseño Mission Indians
Picayune Rancheria of Chukchansi Indians
Pinoleville Rancheria of Pomo Indians
Pit River Tribe (includes Big Bend, Lookout, Montgomery Creek, and Roaring
    Creek Rancherias and XL Ranch)
Potter Valley Rancheria of Pomo Indians
Quartz Valley Indian Community
Quechan Tribe (Arizona and California)
Ramona Band or Village of Cahuilla Mission Indians
Redding Rancheria
Redwood Valley Rancheria of Pomo Indians
Resighini Rancheria (formerly known as the Coast Indian Community of
    Yurok Indians of the Esighini Rancheria)
Rincon Band of Luiseño Mission Indians
Robinson Rancheria of Pomo Indians
Round Valley Indian Tribes (formerly known as the Covelo Indian Community)
Rumsey Indian Rancheria of Wintun Indians
San Manual Band of Serrano Mission Indians
San Pasqual Band of Diegueño Mission Indians
Santa Rosa Band of Cahuilla Mission Indians
Santa Rosa Indian Community
Santa Ynez Band of Chumash Mission Indians
Santa Ysabel Band of Diegueño Mission Indians
Scotts Valley Band of Pomo Indians
Sheep Ranch Rancheria of Me-Wuk Indians
Sherwood Valley Rancheria of Pomo Indians
Shingle Springs Band of Miwok Indians
Smith River Rancheria
Soboba Band of Luiseño Mission Indians
Susanville Indian Rancheria
Sycuan Band of Diegueño Mission Indians
Table Bluff Reservation–Wiyot Tribe
Table Mountain Rancheria
Torres-Martinez Band of Cahuilla Mission Indians

Tule River Indian Tribe
Tuolumne Band of Me-Wuk Indians
Twenty-Nine Palms Band of Luiseño Mission Indians
United Auburn Indian Community
Upper Lake Band of Pomo Indians
Utu Utu Gwaitu Paiute Tribe
Washoe Tribe (Carson Colony, Dresslerville Colony, Woodfords Community,
    Stewart Community, and Washoe Ranches) (California and Nevada)
Yurok Tribe

COLORADO

Federally Recognized
Southern Ute Indian Tribe
Ute Mountain Tribe (Colorado, New Mexico, and Utah)

CONNECTICUT

Federally Recognized
Mashantucket Pequot Tribe
Mohegan Indian Tribe
Eastern Pequot Tribe

State-Recognized

Golden Hill Paugussett Tribe
Paucatuck Eastern Pequot Tribe
Schaghticoke Bands

DELAWARE

State-Recognized
Nanticoke Indians

FLORIDA

Federally Recognized
Miccosukee Tribe of Indians
Seminole Tribe (Dania, Big Cypress, Brighton, Hollywood, and Tampa
    Reservations)

GEORGIA

State-Recognized
Cherokee of Georgia Tribal Council
Georgia Tribe of Eastern Cherokee
Lower Muscogee Creek Tribe

IDAHO

Federally Recognized
Coeur D'Alene Tribe
Kootenai Tribe
Nez Perce Tribe
Shoshone-Bannock Tribes

IOWA

Federally Recognized
Sac and Fox Tribe of the Mississippi

KANSAS

Federally Recognized
Iowa Tribe (Kansas and Nebraska)
Kickapoo Tribe of Indians
Prairie Band of Potawatomi Indians
Sac and Fox Nation of Missouri (Kansas and Nebraska)

LOUISIANA

Federally Recognized
Chitimacha Tribe
Coushatta Tribe
Jena Band of Choctaw Indians
Tunica-Biloxi Indian Tribe

State-Recognized
Caddo Indian Tribe
Choctaw-Apache of Ebarb
Clifton Choctaw

Louisiana Choctaw
United Houma Nation

MAINE

Federally Recognized
Aroostook Band of Micmac Indians
Houlton Band of Maliseet Indians
Passamaquoddy Tribe
Penobscot Nation

State-Recognized
Passamaquoddy Tribe
Penobscot Nation

MASSACHUSETTS

Federally Recognized
Wampanoag Tribe of Gay Head (Aquinnah)

State-Recognized
Hassanamisco

MICHIGAN

Federally Recognized
Bay Mills Indian Community of the Sault Ste. Marie Band of Chippewa
    Indians
Grand Traverse Band of Ottawa and Chippewa Indians
Hannahville Indian Community
Huron Potawatomi, Inc.
Keweenaw Bay Indian Community of L'Anse and Ontonagon Bands of
    Chippewa Indians
Lac Vieux Desert Band of Lake Superior Chippewa Indians
Little River Band of Ottawa Indians
Little Traverse Bay Bands of Odawa Indians
Match-she-be-nash-she-wish Band of Pottawatomi Indians of Michigan (Gun
    Lake Band)
Pokagon Band of Potawatomi Indians

Saginaw Chippewa Indian Tribe
Sault Ste. Marie Tribe of Chippewa Indians

State-Recognized
Burt Lake Band of Ottawa and Chippewa Indians
Grand River Band of Ottawa Indians
Gun Lake Band of Grand River Ottawa Indians
Swan Creek Black River Confederated Ojibwa Tribes

MINNESOTA

Federally Recognized
Lower Sioux Indian Community of Minnesota Mdewakanton Sioux Indians
    Minnesota Chippewa Tribe (Six component reservations: Bois Forte Band
    [Nett Lake], Fond du Lac Band, Grand Portage Band, Leech Lake Band,
    Mille Lacs Band, and White Earth Band)
Prairie Island Indian Community of Minnesota Mdewakanton Sioux Indians
Red Lake Band of Chippewa Indians Shakopee Mdewakanton Sioux Commu-
    nity (Prior Lake) Upper Sioux Indian Community

MISSISSIPPI

Federally Recognized
Mississippi Band of Choctaw Indians

MISSOURI

State-Recognized
Chickamauga Cherokee
Northern Cherokee

MONTANA

Federally Recognized
Assiniboine and Sioux Tribes
Blackfeet Tribe
Chippewa-Cree Indians
Confederated Salish and Kootenai Tribes

Crow Tribe
Fort Belknap Indian Community
Northern Cheyenne Tribe

NEBRASKA

Federally Recognized
Iowa Tribe (Kansas and Nebraska)
Omaha Tribe
Ponca Tribe
Sac and Fox Nation of Missouri (Kansas and Nebraska)
Santee Sioux Tribe
Winnebago Tribe

NEVADA

Federally Recognized
Confederated Tribes of the Goshute Reservation (Nevada and Utah)
Duckwater Shoshone Tribe
Ely Shoshone Tribe
Fort McDermitt Paiute and Shoshone Tribes (Nevada and Oregon)
Fort Mojave Indian Tribe (Arizona, California, and Nevada)
Las Vegas Tribe of Paiute Indians of the Las Vegas Indian Colony
Lovelock Paiute Tribe of the Lovelock Indian Colony
Moapa Band of Paiute Indians
Paiute-Shoshone Tribe
Pyramid Lake Paiute Tribe
Reno-Sparks Indian Colony
Shoshone-Paiute Tribes
Summit Lake Paiute Tribe
Te-Moak Tribes of Western Shoshone Indians (Four constituent bands: Battle
    Mountain, Elko, South Fork, and Wells)
Walker River Paiute Tribe
Washoe Tribe (Nevada and California) (Carson Colony, Dresslerville Colony,
    Woodfords Community, Stewart Community, and Washoe Ranches)
Winnemucca Indian Colony
Yerington Paiute Tribe
Yomba Shoshone Tribe

NEW JERSEY

State-Recognized
Rankokus

NEW MEXICO

Federally Recognized
Jicarilla Apache Tribe
Mescalero Apache Tribe
Navajo Nation (Arizona, New Mexico, and Utah)
Pueblo of Acoma
Pueblo of Cochiti
Pueblo of Isleta
Pueblo of Jemez
Pueblo of Laguna
Pueblo of Nambe
Pueblo of Picuris
Pueblo of Pojoaque
Pueblo of Sandia
Pueblo of San Felipe
Pueblo of San Ildefonso
Pueblo of San Juan
Pueblo of Santa Ana
Pueblo of Santa Clara
Pueblo of Santo Domingo
Pueblo of Taos
Pueblo of Tesuque
Pueblo of Zia
Ute Mountain Tribe (Colorado, New Mexico, and Utah)
Zuni Tribe

NEW YORK

Federally Recognized
Cayuga Nation
Oneida Nation
Onondaga Nation
Seneca Nation
St. Regis Band of Mohawk Indians

Tonawanda Band of Seneca Indians
Tuscarora Nation

State-Recognized

Poospatuck
Shinnecock

NORTH CAROLINA

Federally Recognized

Eastern Band of Cherokee Indians

State-Recognized

Coharie
Haliwa-Saponi
Lumbee
Meherrin
Waccamaw-Siouan

NORTH DAKOTA

Federally Recognized

Spirit Lake Tribe (formerly known as the Devil's Lake Sioux Tribe)
Standing Rock Sioux Tribe (North and South Dakota)
Three Affiliated Tribes of the Fort Berthold Reservation
Turtle Mountain Band of Chippewa Indians

OKLAHOMA

Federally Recognized

Absentee-Shawnee Tribe of Indians
Alabama-Quassarte Tribal Town
Apache Tribe
Caddo Indian Tribe
Cherokee Nation
Cheyenne-Arapaho Tribes
Chickasaw Nation
Choctaw Nation
Citizen Potawatomi Nation

Comanche Indian Tribe
Delaware Tribe of Indians
Delaware Tribe of Western Oklahoma
Eastern Shawnee Tribe
Fort Sill Apache Tribe
Iowa Tribe
Kaw Nation
Kialegee Tribal Town
Kickapoo Tribe
Kiowa Indian Tribe
Miami Tribe
Modoc Tribe
Muscogee (Creek) Nation
Osage Tribe
Ottawa Tribe
Otoe-Missouria Tribe
Pawnee Indian Tribe
Peoria Tribe
Ponca Tribe
Quapaw Tribe
Sac and Fox Nation
Seminole Nation
Seneca-Cayuga Tribe
Shawnee Tribe
Thlopthlocco Tribal Town
Tonkawa Tribe
United Keetoowah Band of Cherokee Indians
Wichita and Affiliated Tribes (Wichita, Keechi, Waco, and Tawakonie)
Wyandotte Tribe

OREGON

Federally Recognized
Burns Paiute Tribe
Confederated Tribes of the Coos, Lower Umpqua and Siuslaw Indians
Confederated Tribes of the Grand Ronde Community
Confederated Tribes of the Siletz Reservation
Confederated Tribes of the Umatilla Reservation
Confederated Tribes of the Warm Springs Reservation
Coquille Tribe

Cow Creek Band of Umpqua Indians
Fort McDermitt Paiute and Shoshone Tribes (Nevada and Oregon)
Klamath Indian Tribe

RHODE ISLAND

Federally Recognized
Narragansett Indian Tribe

SOUTH CAROLINA

Federally Recognized
Catawba Indian Nation (Catawba Tribe)

SOUTH DAKOTA

Federally Recognized
Cheyenne River Sioux Tribe
Crow Creek Sioux Tribe
Lower Brule Sioux Tribe
Oglala Sioux Tribe
Rosebud Sioux Tribe
Sisseton-Wahpeton Sioux Tribe
Standing Rock Sioux Tribe (North Dakota and South Dakota)
Yankton Sioux Tribe

TEXAS

Federally Recognized
Alabama-Coushatta Tribes
Kickapoo Traditional Tribe
Ysleta Del Sur Pueblo

UTAH

Federally Recognized
Confederated Tribes of the Goshute Reservation (Nevada and Utah)
Navajo Nation (Arizona, New Mexico, and Utah)
Northwestern Band of Shoshoni Nation (Washakie)

Paiute Indian Tribe
Skull Valley Band of Goshute Indians
Ute Indian Tribe of the Uintah and Ouray Reservation
Ute Mountain Tribe (Colorado, New Mexico and Utah)

VIRGINIA

State-Recognized
Chickahominy
Eastern Chickahominy
Mattaponi
Monacan
Nansemond
Pamunkey
Rappahannock
Upper Mattaponi

WASHINGTON

Federally Recognized
Confederated Tribes and Bands of the Yakama Indian Nation
Confederated Tribes of the Chehalis Reservation
Confederated Tribes of the Colville Reservation
Cowlitz Tribe
Hoh Indian Tribe
Jamestown S'Klallam Tribe
Kalispel Indian Community
Lower Elwha Tribal Community
Lummi Tribe
Makah Indian Tribe
Muckleshoot Indian Tribe
Nisqually Indian Tribe
Nooksack Indian Tribe
Port Gamble Indian Community
Puyallup Tribe
Quileute Tribe
Quinault Tribe
Samish Indian Tribe
Sauk-Suiattle Indian Tribe
Shoalwater Bay Tribe

Skokomish Indian Tribe
Snoqualmie Indian Tribe
Spokane Tribe
Squaxin Island Tribe
Stillaguamish Tribe
Suquamish Indian Tribe
Swinomish Indians
Tulalip Tribes
Upper Skagit Indian Tribe

WISCONSIN

Federally Recognized
Bad River Band of the Lake Superior Tribe of Chippewa Indians
Forest County Potawotomi Community
Ho-Chunk Nation (formerly known as the Wisconsin Winnebago Tribe)
Lac Courte Oreilles Band of Lake Superior Chippewa Indians
Lac du Flambeau Band of Lake Superior Chippewa Indians
Menominee Indian Tribe
Oneida Tribe
Red Cliff Band of Lake Superior Chippewa Indians
Sokaogon Chippewa Community of the Mole Lake Band of Chippewa Indians
St. Croix Chippewa Indians
Stockbridge-Munsee Community of Mohican Indians

WYOMING

Federally Recognized
Arapahoe Tribe
Shoshone Tribe

INDEX

Aboriginal title. *See* Indian title

ACA. *See* Assimilative Crimes Act (ACA)

acknowledgment of tribal status, federal. *See* federal recognition of tribal status

ADA. *See* Americans with Disabilities Act (ADA)

ADEA. *See* Age Discrimination in Employment Act (ADEA)

Administrative Procedure Act (APA), 370–71

adoption: BIA guidelines under ICWA for, 341; under ICWA (*see* Indian Child Welfare Act [ICWA]); invalidation of, under ICWA, 342–43; state civil jurisdiction over, 178, 334–47; tribal regulation of, 107, 178, 334–47

Age Discrimination in Employment Act (ADEA), 110

AIRFA. *See* American Indian Religious Freedom Act (AIRFA)

Alabama, recognized tribes in, 391

Alaska: criminal jurisdiction in, 123; Indian country in, 301–2; Indian title land in, 26, 300; native peoples of, 19, 299; recognized tribes in, 391–97; unique legal status of tribes in, 299–304

Alaska National Interest Lands Conservation Act (ANILCA), 302

Alaska Native Claims Settlement Act (ANCSA), 26, 300–302

Alaska v. Native Village of Venetie Tribal Government, 301–2, 303

alcoholism, 3, 146

Aleuts, 19, 299

allotments, 8–9; cessation of, 10; inheritance of, 72–73; restricted, 23; tax exemptions for, 191–92; trust status, 23, 70–71, 74–75; water rights and, 252. *See also* General Allotment Act (GAA)

American Indian Religious Freedom Act (AIRFA), 263–65

American Revolutionary War, 2, 47, 48, 57–58; role of Indians in, 5–6, 307

Americans with Disabilities Act (ADA), 110

ANCSA. *See* Alaska Native Claims Settlement Act (ANCSA)

ANILCA. *See* Alaska National Interest Lands Conservation Act (ANILCA)

Arizona, recognized tribes in, 397–98

Arizona v. California, 240, 244, 248

assets, tribal, federal regulation of, 75–76

assimilation, 8–9

Assimilative Crimes Act (ACA), 153, 154

Atkinson Trading Co., Inc. v. Shirley, 95, 101, 105, 110, 170–71, 173, 206

Bald and Golden Eagle Protection Act, 223–24

BIA. *See* Bureau of Indian Affairs (BIA)

Bill of Rights, 260, 269, 279

Black, Hugo, 49

Blatchford v. Native Village of Noatak, 364

blood quantum, required for tribal membership, 19, 93–94

Bowen v. Roy, 262, 264

Brendale v. Confederated Tribes and Bands of Yakima Indian Nation, 169, 170, 173

Bryan v. Itasca County, Minnesota, 123

Bureau of Indian Affairs (BIA), 10, 63; employment by, in fulfilling contracts, 108; employment preference in, 61; federal recognition of tribes and, 310; "Guideline for State Courts" under ICWA, 338, 340, 341; ICRA enforcement by, 286; paternalism of, 37–38, 65; regulation of Indian fishing rights and, 231

burial remains, protection of, 270–72

Bush, George W., 14, 40, 74

Buy-Indian Act, 108

Caeppert v. United States, 240, 243, 246

California: gaming in, 319; recognized tribes

413